Reading Critically, Writing Well

A READER AND GUIDE

Rise B. Axelrod
University of California, Riverside

Charles R. Cooper
University of California, San Diego

Ellen C. Carillo
University of Connecticut

bedford/st.martin's
Macmillan Learning
Boston | New York

For Bedford/St. Martin's

Vice President, Editorial, Macmillan Learning Humanities: Edwin Hill
Executive Program Director for English: Leasa Burton
Executive Program Manager: John E. Sullivan III
Executive Marketing Manager: Joy Fisher Williams
Director of Content Development, Humanities: Jane Knetzger
Senior Developmental Editor: Evelyn Denham
Editorial Assistant: Alex Markle
Content Project Manager: Pamela Lawson
Assistant Director, Process Workflow: Susan Wein
Production Supervisor: Lawrence Guerra
Advanced Media Project Manager: Rand Thomas
Executive Media Editor: Adam Whitehurst
Senior Manager of Publishing Services: Andrea Cava
Project Management: Lumina Datamatics, Inc.
Text Permissions Manager: Kalina Ingham
Text Permissions Researcher: Kristine Janssens, Lumina Datamatics, Inc.
Photo Permissions Editor: Angela Boehler
Photo Researcher: Krystyna Borgen, Lumina Datamatics, Inc.
Director of Design, Content Management: Diana Blume
Text Design: Jerilyn Bockorick/Diana Blume
Cover Design: William Boardman
Cover Image: JamesBrey/E+/Getty Images
Printing and Binding: LSC Communications

Manufactured in the United States of America.

3   4   5   6   24   23   22

For information, write: Bedford/St. Martin's, 75 Arlington Street, Boston, MA 02116

ISBN 978-1-319-19447-5 (Student Edition)
ISBN 978-1-319-29386-4 (Instructor's Edition)

Acknowledgments
Text acknowledgments and copyrights appear at the back of the book on pages 655–657, which constitute an extension of the copyright page. Art acknowledgments and copyrights appear on the same page as the art selections they cover.

Preface

Reading Critically, Writing Well is designed for today's students living in an information-saturated culture. When students are taught to read critically — to understand, assess, evaluate, and synthesize the texts they encounter — they are better prepared not only to succeed in college but to navigate and participate in the world that surrounds them. Students who know how to read critically are also better positioned to write in ways that are influenced by the rhetorical awareness that inflects their reading experiences. Teaching critical reading alongside writing, in other words, allows students to strengthen their abilities as readers and writers simultaneously. As students learn about constructing meaning through the processes of reading and writing, *Reading Critically, Writing Well* also gives students opportunities to reflect on what they are learning, enabling students to recognize the relationship between their reading and writing practices and to apply what they are learning to other academic courses, as well as to contexts outside of the classroom. No matter their major or career track, today's college students will find practice in *Reading Critically, Writing Well* for the various kinds of writing done in college:

- Analysis of content and meaning of readings
- Analysis of the rhetorical approach
- Analysis of the kind of writing (genre)
- Writing to invent, inquire, make meaning, and reflect
- Writing in different academic genres

Hands-on activities in *Reading Critically, Writing Well* give students practice in a range of reading and writing strategies — strategies that enhance comprehension, inspire thoughtful response, stimulate critical inquiry, and foster rhetorical analysis. *Reading Critically, Writing Well* features readings from established, emerging, and student writers in every chapter and covers a wide variety of topics of urgent interest to students in order to inspire engaged reading, spark curious conversations, and provoke thoughtful writing. This new edition gives students more opportunities to practice complex reading and writing strategies, with at least one longer reading in each chapter, new "Combining Reading Strategies" activities, and a new chapter on multi-genre writing.

FEATURES OF *READING CRITICALLY, WRITING WELL*

An Inspiring and Practical Introduction to Writing

Chapter 1 introduces essential Academic Habits of Mind[*] that students need to succeed in college:

1. *Curiosity* (The desire to know more about the world)
2. *Openness* (The willingness to consider new ways of being and thinking in the world)
3. *Engagement* (A sense of investment and involvement in learning)
4. *Creativity* (The ability to use novel approaches for generating, investigating, and representing ideas)
5. *Persistence* (The ability to sustain interest in and attention to short- and long-term projects)
6. *Responsibility* (The ability to take ownership of one's actions and understand the consequences of those actions for oneself and others)
7. *Flexibility* (The ability to adapt to situations, expectations, or demands)
8. *Metacognition* (The ability to reflect on one's own thinking as well as on the individual and cultural processes used to structure knowledge).

As students complete the reading and writing that this guide supports, they will use the practices of critical analysis, rhetorical sensitivity, and empathy to foster the habits of mind needed to support transfer of writing skills beyond composition courses and ensure success throughout college.

Chapter 1 introduces these practices and habits of mind through a sequence of brief reading selections on the topic of curiosity. Each reading selection is accompanied by thought-provoking reading, writing, and discussion activities that engage students in active learning from day one, while at the same time teaching them about a crucial habit of mind that will itself empower their learning throughout college and beyond.

Additionally, Chapter 1 introduces the **sentence strategies that appear in every chapter**. These strategies model effective methods for responding to the readings and for presenting ideas in writing, helping students to see how they can enter the academic conversation across disciplines by situating their own ideas within an existing discourse.

Beyond modeling effective sentence strategies, Chapter 1 shows students how to analyze what they read by focusing on identifying the genre conventions

---

[*]These Academic Habits of Mind are taken from "The Framework for Success in Postsecondary Writing" (developed jointly by CWPA, NCTE, and the National Writing Project).

of a text, the assertions a text makes, the evidence a text presents, and the assumptions a text makes. Like the rest of the textbook, Chapter 1 first models for students how to consider these elements and then through the writing activities gives students the opportunity to practice writing about these elements for themselves.

The chapter concludes with an overview of the writing process, including a helpful reference chart: generating ideas, planning, drafting, getting feedback, revising deeply, editing, and proofreading. This section now includes a **complete model student essay** that showcases the recursive nature of the writing process. Rather than a model that moves from the initial step of generating ideas to the final step of proofreading in a linear fashion, this model shows a student returning to certain steps throughout the writing process, underscoring that recursivity is an important and productive aspect of the writing process.

Accessible, Engaging Readings

Reading Critically, Writing Well includes a great variety of readings that give instructors flexibility in constructing a course to meet the needs and interests of their students. The twelfth edition continues to feature both **professional and student writing in every chapter**, but has even more readings than previous editions, including a longer reading in each chapter as well as a new chapter of multi-genre readings. A mixture of contemporary texts alongside some classic essays gives an array of readings to analyze and learn from. Classic essays by award-winning writers such as Annie Dillard, Brent Staples, David Sedaris, Stephen King, and Malcolm Gladwell are accompanied by new readings from authors such as Atul Gawande, Wesley Morris, Robin Kimmerer, and Christie Aschwanden that engage students on contemporary topics relevant to their lives, including the implications of living in a digitally mediated world, the struggle to communicate scientific knowledge, debates surrounding healthcare reform, and reflections on identity and intersectionality.

The flexibility of *Reading Critically, Writing Well* makes it easy for instructors to create a sequence of readings based on theme, discipline, rhetorical mode, or genre. Chapters 3–10 present eight different kinds of writing, including four expository genres (autobiography, observation, reflection, and explanation of concepts) and four argument genres (evaluation, position paper on a controversial issue, speculation about causes or effects, and proposal to solve a problem). Because selections are introduced and followed by close reading activities or annotated questions that stimulate discussion and writing, instructors have the flexibility to create their own reading list from the book's many resources. The new Chapter 11 opens up this organization even further with coverage of multi-genre writing. It helps students build an essay using the features of different genres in order to meet the demands of their rhetorical situation, preparing them for college writing and beyond.

The most coverage of the reading-writing connection to support all levels of students. *Reading Critically, Writing Well* teaches students how to analyze texts and to apply what they have learned to their own writing, making the textbook an important resource for students in traditional first-year writing courses, as well as those taking a co-requisite (or ALP) course alongside first-year composition. Chapter 2, "A Catalog of Reading Strategies," prepares students with the strategies they need to analyze the selections and apply the strategies to their own writing. Instructors may emphasize writing analytically about the readings or writing rhetorically in the genre they are reading, or they may have students do both kinds of writing. Students may also practice writing as they respond to questions and activities or discuss them in small groups with peers. *Reading Critically, Writing Well* provides many opportunities for a variety of writing.

- **Writing Analytically.** The Reading for Meaning activities that follow each reading offer numerous prompts for writing analytically about the readings. Students can begin by writing brief responses to these prompts and later expand some of them into more fully developed essays. For example, using the Read to Summarize activity, they might compose brief summaries or "gist" statements that they could use as they develop their own analysis of the reading. The Read to Respond and Read to Analyze Assumptions prompts can generate longer essays. Similarly, Chapter 2's "A Catalog of Reading Strategies" could be used to generate a variety of assignments: a comparison of different readings, a synthesis essay drawing on multiple selections, a reflective essay examining how a reading challenges the readers' beliefs or values, an evaluation of a reading's logic, an analysis of its use of figurative language, or a position essay refuting a reading's argument. Each chapter's Combining Reading Strategies activities provide students with further opportunities to generate writing based on careful reading.

- **Writing Rhetorically.** Students are also given many opportunities to write in the genre they have been reading. Chapters 3–11 are framed by two guides — a Guide to Reading at the beginning of the chapter and a Guide to Writing at the end — and these chapters promote genre awareness and sensitivity to different rhetorical situations, aiding the transfer of skills from one rhetorical situation to another, so that students can learn for themselves how to approach each new writing situation. Scaffolded through example and modeling, the guides teach students to employ in their own writing the genre features and rhetorical strategies they studied in their reading.

- **Longer Writing Assignments.** The Guides to Writing have been designed to provide flexibility and to support a fuller, more developed composing process. Commonsensical and easy to follow, these writing guides teach students to:

  - assess the rhetorical situation, focusing on their purpose and audience, with special attention to the genre and medium in which they are writing;
  - ask probing analytical questions;

- practice finding answers through various kinds of research, including memory search, field research, and traditional source-based research;
- assess the effectiveness of their own writing and the writing of their class-mates;
- troubleshoot ways to improve their draft;
- reflect on their writing process

In short, the Guides to Writing help students make their writing thoughtful, clear, organized, and compelling, and ultimately effective for the rhetorical situation.

Hands-On Activities for Active Learning

Throughout *Reading Critically, Writing Well*, students are invited to learn by doing. Because these activities are clear and doable, they make it possible for even the most inexperienced readers to complete them and engage in a serious program of active learning that aligns with the four categories of learning that many writing programs across the country use to assess their students' work: rhetorical knowledge; critical thinking, reading, and composing; processes; and knowledge of conventions.

Activities include the following:

- *Before* and *As You Read* Questions. Pre-reading questions excite interest and lead students to adopt a questioning attitude as they prepare to read each selection. The questions also keep students engaged while reading as they develop rhetorical knowledge and think critically about texts.

- *Reading for Meaning* Prompts. Following each reading, these prompts provide students with three different kinds of activities to help in understanding and interpreting what they are reading:

  1. **Read to Summarize** activities enhance comprehension, giving students confidence that they can get the main idea of even hard-to-understand texts.

  2. **Read to Respond** activities inspire active engagement, leading students to explore the cultural contexts of the readings as well as their own responses to the readings.

  3. **Read to Analyze Assumptions** activities lead students to think more critically about the beliefs and values implicit in the text's word choices, examples, and assertions and also to examine the bases for their own assumptions as readers.

- *Reading Like a Writer* Activities. Following each reading, these activities show how texts work rhetorically in different writing situations to achieve the writer's purpose by addressing audience expectations and by recognizing the conventions, constraints, and possibilities of the genre and medium. Annotated and highlighted example passages analyze and explain specific features of each genre, and sentence templates show students how to generate their own sentences using the patterns they have analyzed in the readings.

- *Combining Reading Strategies* **Boxes.** These boxes help students see how combining reading strategies can deepen their understanding of a reading and provide direction for writing. They also provide models that help students practice employing multiple strategies more naturally. These critical reading strategies range from annotating, synthesizing, and comparing and contrasting to evaluating the logic of an argument and judging the writer's credibility. These strategies are also explained and illustrated in Chapter 2, using an excerpt from Martin Luther King Jr.'s "Letter from Birmingham Jail," and marginal notes throughout the book remind students to reference this catalog of reading strategies for additional guidance as they read and compose.

NEW TO THIS EDITION

New Coauthor Ellen C. Carillo

To this edition, Ellen C. Carillo (University of Connecticut) brings her expertise in the teaching of critical reading alongside writing in the composition classroom. Her research and scholarship explore the most effective ways of incorporating attention to reading in writing classrooms and underscore the importance of teaching within a metacognitive framework wherein students consistently reflect on what they are learning so they are positioned to transfer this learning to other courses, as well as to contexts beyond the classroom.

More Activities to Encourage Inquiry and Reflection

The twelfth edition helps students understand reading and writing as inquiry-driven practices propelled by curiosity. Chapter 1 introduces curiosity, among other habits of mind, showing how these habits are crucial for success in college. This inquiry-based mindset is reinforced by an inquiry-based annotated reading in each chapter, which provides **models for using annotations to pose questions while reading** — questions that may in turn spark ideas for writing as well. A **new sample student essay in Chapter 1** also models how inquiry and reflection impact the writing process by demonstrating the recursive nature of writing, including the need to return to early stages of the process, such as generating ideas and planning.

Because research has shown that when students reflect on their learning, they clarify their understanding and remember what they have learned longer, this edition emphasizes the importance of metacognition. Chapter 3, Autobiography, now features coverage of literacy narratives, including a new student literacy narrative, helping students to become more aware of their own journeys from the outset. *Reading Critically, Writing Well* also provides three opportunities in each chapter for students to reflect on their learning and also to discuss what they have learned with others: Thinking about [the Genre], Writing to Learn [the Genre], and Reflecting on [the Genre] activities. These activities are placed at important transitions in each chapter, at points when looking back at what they have learned will help students move forward more productively.

Compelling New Readings — Combined with Scaffolded Support

The more than twenty new selections in the twelfth edition of *Reading Critically, Writing Well* include writers ranging from local activists to Pulitzer Prize winners, giving students both local and global models to refer to. In "The Heroin and Opioid Crisis Is Real," local journalist Isaih Holmes makes the case for greater action to combat the opioid epidemic in his hometown of Milwaukee, while in "The Last Straw," disability activist Alice Wong argues for the importance of considering special needs in the debate on single-use plastics. Essays by well-known writers like Atul Gawande and Wesley Morris offer students thoughtful writing models that ask questions of the world around them: Why is our healthcare system the way it is? Who decides what works are canonical? And new student essays on topics from empathy to literacy to honeybees model college writing in action.

At least one new longer reading per chapter offers instructors additional options and challenges students to apply the reading strategies and analytical skills they're learning. For example, Jeff Howe's "The Rise of Crowdsourcing" encourages students to consider the recent shift from outsourcing to what Howe calls crowdsourcing, wherein companies, websites, television shows, and organizations worldwide are choosing to employ ordinary people rather than formally trained experts. The exercises that accompany this longer reading ask students to draw on what they already know about crowdsourcing — even if they don't know it by that name — and expand that knowledge by analyzing what this shift means for how we understand the concept of expertise. Similarly, as students read "I Wonder: Imagining a Black Wonder Woman" by Maya Rupert, they are asked to consider their own assumptions about race and strength while also tracking the relationship Rupert imagines among race, identity, and feminism. Throughout these and other exercises that accompany the readings, students are supported by references to specific reading strategies and the full catalog of reading strategies in Chapter 2.

Two New Chapters—Multi-Genre Writing and Strategies for Research

A new Chapter 11, "Multi-Genre Writing: Pulling It All Together," contains more complex readings than are usually present in earlier chapters, offering students opportunities to explore how authors combine genres to meet the needs of specific rhetorical situations. Students, too, are taught how they can combine different genres to most effectively respond to writing scenarios they will encounter throughout their academic careers and beyond. This chapter supports students in a range of ways as they engage in this more complex work. The main genres of each selection are listed as tags in the headnote, and the "Reading Like a Writer" exercises explore an effective genre feature of the selection as well as the elements of the writer's rhetorical position that led them to select the genres they did. In addition, the chapter contains a student selection that combines the genres of position argument, concept evaluation, and cause-and-effect arguments in order to evaluate the concepts of altruism and empathy. Finally, as students write their own multi-genre essays, they are directed to a comprehensive checklist that reviews the key considerations relevant to composing a multi-genre essay, including how to choose the appropriate genres based on the rhetorical situation and how to most effectively combine the features of multiple genres in a single essay.

A robust new Chapter 12 on the research process features strategies for research and documentation to provide students with clear, helpful guidelines for researching and evaluating sources, integrating them into their writing, and citing them correctly in MLA or APA style. With eight different genres, students have an opportunity to practice the full range of research strategies, from identifying a research question to the field research methods of observation and interview to different kinds of research. New coverage of evaluating online sources informed by online-based research practices is incorporated throughout.

Flexibility for Instructors

The new features of the twelfth edition mean that it offers more flexibility for instructors than previous editions. The individual readings chapters can each be used in any order, supported by the instruction and strategies included in Chapters 1 and 2. Instructors who want to build on the focus of a chapter can either move to the tagged multi-genre material in Chapter 11 or teach Chapter 11 as a culminating chapter. No matter the instructor's route through the textbook, students are prepared to undertake this work because they have seen it modeled for them and have had many opportunities to reflect on what they are learning along the way.

With more readings to choose from, instructors have a better variety of topics, disciplines, and styles to choose from to engage students and model writing in each genre. Analyze & Write activities, Writing Assignments, and activities in the Guides to Writing provide instructors with a range of prompts for homework, classwork, small group or class discussion, and writing assignments. This edition of *Reading Critically, Writing Well* also features **alternative tables of contents**, listing readings by theme and discipline to allow instructors the flexibility to chart a path through the readings to meet their course goals. **Sentence strategies in every chapter**, with a convenient reference index in the Instructor's Manual (downloadable from the Macmillan website), support students as they become more comfortable with academic writing.

ALIGNS WITH WPA OUTCOMES

DESIRED OUTCOMES	RELEVANT FEATURES OF *READING CRITICALLY, WRITING WELL,* TWELFTH EDITION
Rhetorical Knowledge	
Learn and use key rhetorical concepts through analyzing and composing a variety of texts.	• Chapter 1 provides students with a clear, workable definition of the rhetorical situation and asks students to apply that knowledge as they read four passages on curiosity. • Chapters 3–11 ask students to read, analyze, and compose a variety of texts. • Reading Like a Writer activities in Chapter 11 ask students to analyze how the combination of genres in the multi-genre readings work together to meet the needs of each author's rhetorical situation.
Gain experience reading and composing in several genres to understand how genre conventions shape and are shaped by readers' and writers' practices and purposes.	• Chapter 2 provides a catalog of reading strategies that help students recognize genre conventions. • Chapters 3–11 emphasize the connection between reading and composing: Analyze & Write activities ask students to read like a writer, identifying the key features of the genre. • The Guides to Writing in Chapters 3–11 lead students through the process of composing their own text in that genre.

DESIRED OUTCOMES	RELEVANT FEATURES OF *READING CRITICALLY, WRITING WELL,* TWELFTH EDITION
Develop facility in responding to a variety of situations and contexts, calling for purposeful shifts in voice, tone, level of formality, design, medium, and/or structure.	• In Chapters 3–11, students practice responding to a variety of rhetorical situations and contexts. The Guides to Writing in each of these chapters help students develop their own processes and structures. • **Read to Respond** activities in Chapters 3–11 inspire active engagement, leading students to explore the cultural contexts of the readings as well as their own responses to the readings. • Sentence strategies in each chapter help students deal with issues of voice, tone, and formality.
Understand and use a variety of technologies to address a range of audiences.	• One of the book's assumptions is that most students compose in digital spaces for varied audiences and use different media for doing so. This idea is woven throughout, especially in Chapters 3–11. • Online tutorials in Achieve for Readers and Writers include how-tos for using technology; topics include digital writing for specific audiences and purpose, creating presentations, integrating photos, and appealing to a prospective employer. Achieve for Readers and Writers also includes a robust digital writing space informed by pedagogical best practices for writing and revising.
Match the capacities of different environments (e.g., print and electronic) to varying rhetorical situations.	• Chapters 3–11 emphasize the importance of the rhetorical situation to composing. • Throughout the book students are prompted to consider how changes to the rhetorical situation, especially genre and medium, shape decisions about tone, level of formality, design, medium, and structure.

DESIRED OUTCOMES	RELEVANT FEATURES OF *READING CRITICALLY, WRITING WELL,* TWELFTH EDITION
Critical Thinking, Reading, and Composing	
Use composing and reading for inquiry, learning, thinking, and communicating in various rhetorical contexts.	• Chapter 1 defines reading and writing as forms of inquiry, underscores the importance of curiosity to success in college, and includes a sample student essay that models the role of curiosity in the writing process. • Chapter 3 on autobiography, which now includes literacy narratives, asks students to reflect on their own literacy experiences and to extrapolate from the literacy narratives they are reading. • Read to Analyze Assumptions activities in Chapters 3–11 lead students to think more critically about the beliefs and values implicit in the text's word choices, examples, and assertions and also to examine the bases of their own assumptions as readers.
Read a diverse range of texts, attending especially to relationships between assertion and evidence, patterns of organization, the interplay between verbal and nonverbal elements, and how these features function for different audiences and situations.	• Chapter 1 teaches students that critical analysis involves paying attention to how ideas are supported by evidence. • Chapters 3–11 include a range of professional selections and student essays for students to critically analyze through reading and writing. • The Guides to Writing in Chapters 3–11 offer advice on framing topics to appeal to the audience. • Sentence strategies throughout these chapters model techniques for responding to alternative views readers may hold. • Chapter 12 emphasizes the importance of using evidence in research-driven projects to effectively support one's view.

DESIRED OUTCOMES	RELEVANT FEATURES OF *READING CRITICALLY, WRITING WELL*, TWELFTH EDITION
Locate and evaluate primary and secondary research materials, including journal articles, essays, books, databases, and informal Internet sources.	• Chapter 1 includes activities that encourage students to use their curiosity to inspire research. • Chapter 12 offers extensive coverage of finding, evaluating, and using print and electronic sources, with guidance on responsibly using online sources, including interactive sources (e.g., blogs, wikis). • The "Conducting Field Research" section in Chapter 12 provides a comprehensive overview of and strategies for conducting observational studies and surveys in order to use these as primary sources.
Use strategies—such as interpretation, synthesis, response, critique, and design / redesign—to compose texts that integrate the writer's ideas with those from appropriate sources.	• Chapters 3–10 regularly ask students to anticipate and respond to opposing positions and alternative perspectives in their writing. • Sentence strategies throughout Chapters 3–11 model for students how to situate their own ideas in relation to other sources. • Chapter 12 offers detailed strategies for integrating research into an academic project. Specifically, this chapter provides advice on how to integrate and introduce quotations, how to cite paraphrases and summaries so as to distinguish them from the student's own ideas, and how to avoid plagiarism.
Processes	
Develop a writing project through multiple drafts.	• Chapter 1 includes a model student essay that shows the recursive nature of the writing process. • In Chapters 3–11, Guides to Writing prompt students to compose and revise. These chapters include activities for inventing, planning, composing, evaluating, and revising over the course of multiple drafts.

DESIRED OUTCOMES	RELEVANT FEATURES OF *READING CRITICALLY, WRITING WELL*, TWELFTH EDITION
Develop flexible strategies for reading, drafting, reviewing, collaborating, revising, rewriting, rereading, and editing.	• The student essay in Chapter 1 models the importance of flexibility to the writing process. • The Guides to Writing in Chapters 3–11 offer extensive advice on reading, drafting, rethinking, and revising at multiple stages. • Troubleshooting charts in Chapters 3–11 encourage students to discover, review, and revise, urging students to start from their strengths. • Chapter 2 provides a variety of strategies for reading analytically and critically.
Use composing processes and tools as a means to discover and reconsider ideas.	• Chapter 1 introduces the idea of using reading and writing to discover ideas and models this work in the sample student essay, which shows the student returning to the generating ideas and planning stages. • Strategies for evaluating, revising, and editing in the Guides to Writing in Chapters 3–11 help students reconsider their ideas over the course of multiple drafts.
Experience the collaborative and social aspects of writing processes.	• The Guides to Writing in Chapters 3–11 ask students to practice each genre, while making students aware that these genre definitions are useful because they are built on shared expectations and enable more effective written collaboration and communication. • Peer Review Guides in Chapters 3–11 provide opportunities to work collaboratively. • Read to Analyze Assumptions prompts throughout Chapters 3–11 often ask students to engage with classmates about the sources of their assumptions. • Students are introduced to the concept of empathy in Chapter 1 and are expected to be empathetic readers and writers willing to identify with other readers and writers, including those with different perspectives, ideas, values, or worldviews.

DESIRED OUTCOMES	RELEVANT FEATURES OF *READING CRITICALLY, WRITING WELL,* TWELFTH EDITION
Learn to give and act on productive feedback to works in progress.	• The Peer Review Guide in the Guides to Writing in Chapters 3–11 offers students specific advice on constructively critiquing the work of their classmates. • The troubleshooting chart in the Guides to Writing in Chapters 3–11 supports students as they critique their own writing and gives students detailed strategies for strengthening their essays based on their own critiques and the feedback from their peers.
Adapt composing processes for a variety of technologies and modalities.	• One of the book's assumptions is that most students compose in digital spaces for varied audiences and use different media for doing so. This idea is woven throughout, especially in Chapters 3–11. • Achieve for Readers and Writers, which can be packaged to accompany *Reading Critically, Writing Well*, offers a digital course space and writing space informed by best practices for peer review and revision. It also offers integrated digital tutorials, such as how-tos for using technology; topics include digital writing for specific audiences and purpose, creating presentations, integrating photos, and appealing to a prospective employer.
Reflect on the development of composing practices and how those practices influence their work.	• Students are introduced to the importance of metacognition, as a habit of mind, in Chapter 1. • The reflection prompts at the end of Chapters 3–11 encourage self-awareness and invite students to develop an understanding of their own experiences as readers and writers. • Sample annotated essays in Chapters 3–10 demonstrate how annotations can support reflective reading.

DESIRED OUTCOMES	RELEVANT FEATURES OF *READING CRITICALLY, WRITING WELL*, TWELFTH EDITION
Knowledge of Conventions	
Develop knowledge of linguistic structures—including grammar, punctuation, and spelling—through practice in composing and revising.	• Editing and proofreading advice appears at the end of Chapters 3–11, prompting students to check for errors in usage, punctuation, and mechanics. • Sentence strategies throughout Chapters 3–11 model for students common linguistic structures.
Understand why genre conventions for structure, paragraphing, tone, and mechanics vary.	• Chapter 1 prompts students to consider which passages on curiosity are intended for an academic audience and which are intended for a popular audience. • Chapters 3–11 emphasize the importance of the rhetorical situation and how changes to the rhetorical situation, including in genre, shape decisions about tone, level of formality, design, and structure.
Gain experience negotiating variations in genre conventions.	• Students read, analyze, and compose a variety of texts in Chapters 3–11. The Guides to Reading ask students to analyze texts in terms of the basic features of the genre and the Guides to Writing prompt students to apply these genre conventions. • Chapter 11 provides a checklist of genre features so that students can experiment with combining different genres. • Chapter 12 allows students to gain experience as they compose an academic research project.
Learn common formats and/or design features for different kinds of texts.	• Students are asked to analyze and consider the role of any visuals that accompany the readings throughout Chapters 3–11. • Questions following the sample student essay in Chapter 11 encourage students to consider alternative formats and design features for that essay.
Explore the concepts of intellectual property (such as fair use and copyright) that motivate documentation conventions.	• Chapter 12 offers detailed coverage of how to use sources fairly, and features sections dedicated to acknowledging sources and avoiding plagiarism. • Chapter 12 teaches strategies for integrating, citing, and paraphrasing sources.

DESIRED OUTCOMES	RELEVANT FEATURES OF *READING CRITICALLY, WRITING WELL*, TWELFTH EDITION
Practice applying citation conventions systematically in their own work.	• A number of the professional reading selections in Chapters 3–11 model citation conventions. • Student essays in Chapters 3–11 offer models for documenting sources. • Chapter 12 includes detailed advice for integrating and introducing quotations, citing paraphrases and summaries so as to distinguish them from the student's own ideas, and avoiding plagiarism. • Chapter 12 provides an overview of MLA and APA style requirements and a directory of common documentation models.

ACKNOWLEDGMENTS

We first want to thank our students and colleagues at the University of Connecticut, the University of California, Riverside, and the University of California, San Diego; California State University, East Bay, and California State University, San Bernardino; and the University of Nevada, Reno, who have taught us so much about reading, writing, and teaching.

We also owe a debt of gratitude to the many reviewers who made suggestions for this revision. They include Kenet Adamson, Asheville-Buncombe Tech Community College; Michael Boling, Oakland City University; Jacqueline Brady, Arizona State University; Julie Phillips Brown, Virginia Military Institute; Anthony Cavaluzzi, SUNY Adirondack; Lynn Clarkson, North Shore Community College; Abby Crew, Ph.D., Colorado Mountain College; Brian Hiatt, Frederick Community College; Spring Hyde, Lincoln College; Dr. Lisa Jennings, Valparaiso University; Sharon Johnson, Columbus State University; Steven Keeton, Baton Rough Community College; Peggy J. Lindsey, Georgia Southern University; Dr. Beatrice McKinsey, Grambling State University; Amelia Ostrowski, Walsh University; Matt Sautman, Southern Illinois University — Edwardsville; Anita Slusser, Snow College; Michael Trovato, The Ohio State University — Newark; Deron Walker, Ph.D., California Baptist University; and Marilyn Yamin, Pellissippi State Community College.

We want especially to thank our editors, who offered constructive criticism with cheerfulness and good humor, helping us meet impossible deadlines. For this new edition of *Reading Critically, Writing Well*, we are grateful to developmental editor, Evelyn Denham, who offered invaluable guidance and expertise during the course of the revision. We also owe a debt of gratitude to Alex Markle, Editorial Assistant, who supported this edition in various ways and was a pleasure to work with on the Instructor's Manual. We also want to thank Edwin Hill, Leasa Burton, and John Sullivan for their leadership and support. We are grateful for Pamela Lawson's seamless coordination of the production process, Bridget Leahy's skillful copy editing, Ron D'Souza's project management at Lumina Datamatics, Inc., Kristine Janssen's, Mark Schaefer's, and Krystyna Borgen's work on permissions and art research, and Joy Fisher Williams's help in marketing.

Rise dedicates this book to Sophie and Amalia, whose writing she very much looks forward to reading. She also thanks her husband, Steven, for his continued support and encouragement.

Ellen dedicates this book to Avi and Harris, who are becoming great readers and writers, as well as Dave who is showing them the way. She also thanks her parents, Bev and Joe Gerber, and her sister, Betsy, for their unwavering support over the years.

Rise B. Axelrod
Charles R. Cooper
Ellen C. Carillo

BEDFORD/ST. MARTIN'S PUTS YOU FIRST

From day one, our goal has been simple: to provide inspiring resources that are grounded in best practices for teaching reading and writing. For more than 35 years, Bedford/St. Martin's has partnered with the field, listening to teachers, scholars, and students about the support writers need. We are committed to helping every writing instructor make the most of our resources.

How Can We Help *You*?

- Our editors can align our resources to your outcomes through correlation and transition guides for your syllabus. Just ask us.
- Our sales representatives specialize in helping you find the right materials to support your course goals.
- Our *Bits* blog on the Bedford/St. Martin's English Community (**community .macmillan.com**) publishes fresh teaching ideas weekly. You'll also find easily downloadable professional resources and links to author webinars on our community site.

Visit **macmillanlearning.com** or contact your Bedford/St. Martin's sales representative to learn more.

Print and Digital Options for *Reading Critically, Writing Well,* Twelfth Edition

Choose the format that works best for your course, and ask about our packaging options that offer savings for students.

Print

- *Paperback.* To order the student edition, use ISBN 978-1-319-19447-5.
- *Paperback Instructor's Edition.* To order the instructor's edition, use ISBN 978-1-319-29386-4.

Digital

- *Innovative digital learning space.* Bedford/St. Martin's suite of digital tools makes it easy to get everyone on the same page by putting student writers at the center. For details, visit **macmillanlearning.com/englishdigital**.
- *Popular e-book formats.* For more details about our e-book partners, visit **macmillanlearning.com/ebooks**.
- *Inclusive Access.* Enable every student to receive their course materials through your LMS on the first day of class. Macmillan Learning's Inclusive Access program is the easiest, most affordable way to ensure all students have access to quality educational resources. Find out more at **macmillanlearning.com/inclusiveaccess**.

Your Course, Your Way

No two writing programs or classrooms are exactly alike. Our Curriculum Solutions team works with you to design custom options that provide the resources your students need. (Options below require enrollment minimums.)

- *ForeWords for English.* Customize any print resource to fit the focus of your course or program by choosing from a range of prepared topics, such as Sentence Guides for Academic Writers.
- *Macmillan Author Program (MAP).* Add excerpts or package acclaimed works from Macmillan's trade imprints to connect students with prominent authors and public conversations. A list of popular examples or academic themes is available upon request.
- *Bedford Select.* Build your own print handbook or anthology from a database of more than 800 selections, and add your own materials to create your ideal text. Package with any Bedford/St. Martin's text for additional savings. Visit **macmillanlearning.com/bedfordselect**.

Instructor Resources

You have a lot to do in your course. We want to make it easy for you to find the support you need — and to get it quickly.

The *Instructor's Manual for Reading Critically, Writing Well,* Twelfth Edition, is available in the Instructor's Edition version of the print textbook as well as in a downloadable PDF from **macmillanlearning.com**. In addition to chapter overviews and teaching tips, the instructor's manual includes sample syllabi, correlations comparing the coverage in *Reading Critically, Writing Well* to the Council of Writing Program Administrators' Outcomes Statement, classroom activities, detailed plans for every chapter of the book, and discussion of every reading. To help students get started writing, there is also a new section containing all of the sentence strategy templates in the textbook.

Brief Contents

Contents

1 ACADEMIC HABITS OF MIND: FROM READING CRITICALLY TO WRITING WELL   1

2 A CATALOG OF READING STRATEGIES   34

3 AUTOBIOGRAPHY AND LITERACY NARRATIVES   70

4 OBSERVATION   122

5 REFLECTION   177

Contents by Theme

Contents by Theme

DEFINING MEMORIES AND PERSONAL HEROES

EDUCATION AND INTELLIGENCE

Contents by Discipline

ECONOMICS

JOURNALISM

LAW AND POLITICAL SCIENCE

NEUROSCIENCE

PSYCHOLOGY

SCIENCES

SOCIOLOGY AND CULTURAL ANTHROPOLOGY

Academic Habits of Mind: From Reading Critically to Writing Well

Imagine yourself on a journey to a part of your country where you have never been. You already know the language and have some background in common with the people, but some of the traditions, customs, and laws are different from what you're accustomed to. When you arrive, you are immersed in a new job with people you haven't met before, but you are expected to know the lay of the land and the rules, including how to communicate, how to produce the products the job involves, and how to deal with difficulties.

This new place is college. Sure, you've been through high school, and you've been accepted into college, so you have what it takes to do well in your courses. But the world of college has its own special requirements and demands, and knowing what they are and how to respond to them will help you succeed. Whether you graduated from high school recently or decades ago, college is an altogether different place with different expectations.

Your professors will assume you already understand what college requires. In fact, a recent survey of college professors revealed that they expect students already to have what are often called **academic habits of mind** — ways of thinking and inquiring that people in college (and often in the world of work) use every day. As the word *habit* suggests, these skills can be acquired through practice. So what are these habits of mind?[1]

Here's a list of what we think are the most crucial habits:

- *Curiosity:* The desire to know more about the world. Curious students ask provocative questions, generate hypotheses, respond to others' ideas, and do research to learn more information. Academic questions — those raised in college — are in the context of disciplines (such as business, psychology, chemistry, history, or communications), and are part of an ongoing conversation among the disciplines' practitioners. Often the research of college professors is

---

[1] These definitions of habits of mind have been adapted from the document "The Framework for Success in Postsecondary Writing," developed jointly by CWPA, NCTE, and the National Writing Project.

based on their curiosity about these questions and their desire to find answers. Academics enjoy the free interplay of ideas; they seek out knowledge through reading and hearing about others' opinions, reasons, and evidence.

- *Openness:* The willingness to consider new ways of being and thinking in the world. Strong academic readers and writers demonstrate their openness in many ways. Their minds are open to points of view different from their own, they are open to changing their minds based on new ideas and evidence they find in what they read and write, and they are open to feedback from others about their reading and writing.

- *Engagement:* A sense of investment and involvement in learning. Students who are engaged are committed to learning. They also actively participate and take pleasure in that learning. Engaged students often perform better in their academic work because this habit of mind predisposes them to understanding material and supports their ability to apply material.

- *Creativity:* The ability to use novel approaches for generating, investigating, and representing ideas. Students who exhibit creativity may do so by developing innovative ways of viewing course materials, responding to assignments, and contributing to class discussions. They may reject more conventional perspectives and practices even in the face of resistance.

- *Persistence:* The ability to sustain interest in and attention to short- and long-term projects. Students who are persistent remain committed to projects even when faced with challenges and obstacles. Persistent students show consistent effort in their academic work. Invested in seeing projects to their conclusions, persistent students do not give up if they don't immediately succeed.

- *Responsibility:* The ability to take ownership of one's actions and understand the consequences of those actions for oneself and others. Responsible students are willing to be held accountable for their ideas as they express them through various academic activities, including reading and writing. They recognize that their ideas and any actions they take in the classroom and similar academic settings have the potential to affect others, as well as the learning environment.

- *Flexibility:* The ability to adapt to situations, expectations, or demands. Flexible readers, writers, and thinkers are able to adjust their approaches, ideas, and responses. As opposed to remaining rigid, being flexible in academic settings is marked by students' willingness to change their minds, revisit their practices, and revise their processes.

- *Metacognition:* The ability to reflect on one's own thinking as well as on the individual and cultural processes used to structure knowledge. Students who think about their own thinking are able to articulate the choices they make as they read and write, and they recognize how these choices are impacted by the world around them. Engaging in metacognitive work helps students apply what they learn in one course or context to others.

As you complete the reading and writing that this text supports, you will foster the habits of mind discussed above through the practices of critical analysis, rhetorical sensitivity, and empathy:

- *Critical analysis:* Reading and writing with an eye toward figuring out what is true, what makes sense, and how the ideas are supported by evidence — facts, events, other texts — even when that evidence challenges your own beliefs. The *values* and *beliefs* of both writer and reader (and often their communities) play a significant part in analyzing texts. We call these values and beliefs **assumptions.** Critical analysis also involves questioning your own unexamined beliefs as well as the received wisdom of others.

- *Rhetorical sensitivity:* The understanding of the purposes motivating writers and readers, the expectations of the audience, and the constraints of the **genre** and **medium,** including the ability to recognize different genres, or types, of writing (such as laboratory reports and movie reviews) and media (print or digital, visual or audio) and knowing when to use them, as well as recognizing and using vocabulary, grammar, punctuation, and spelling that is appropriate to the purpose, audience, genre, and medium in which you are writing. Rhetorical sensitivity also embraces **civility,** the ability to treat the ideas of others fairly and respectfully, even when they challenge your own beliefs and values.

- *Empathy:* A kind of emotion of identification that is experienced in relation to something or someone else. Being an empathetic reader and writer involves a willingness to identify with other readers and writers (and with their writing) who do not share your perspective, ideas, values, or worldview. Empathy is related to **civility** in that it asks you to treat the ideas of others fairly, but being empathetic depends on your openness to identifying with an idea or a person with whom or which you may not agree.

JOINING THE ACADEMIC CONVERSATION

The academic habits of mind we have been discussing are essential to success in all academic areas and disciplines (and most career paths), but these alone are not enough. You may also need to develop skills that will allow you to join the *academic conversation* on topics important to individual disciplines such as economics or biology. In your first year or two of college, you will enter a variety of academic conversations by reading textbooks and academic articles in different disciplines and by participating in discussions in class, online, and with your instructor. You might join the conversation in some disciplines for a term or a year; you might join the conversation in your major permanently. As you read this text, you will find references to these conversations and your role in them. The habits of mind we discussed above — curiosity, openness, engagement, creativity, persistence, responsibility, flexibility, and metacognition — will allow you to develop the skills you need to join these conversations.

ACTIVITY 1

Writing to Learn: Exploring Your Habits of Mind

What habits of mind do you already possess as you approach this course? To determine this, think about your past study habits or how you mastered a subject, hobby, or technology inside or outside of school. Then write down your answers to the following questions:

- What sparked your interest in the first place?

- What questions did you initially have?

- How did your questions evolve as you learned more?

- How did you go about finding out answers to your questions?

- How did the answers you found lead to further questions or additional research?

Having looked back on your experience, which habits of mind did you form as you satisfied your curiosity and followed through on your interest? As you read on, you may see that you have a head start on the habits expected of college students.

Developing Curiosity through Reading and Writing

Asking questions as you read and write is integral to developing your curiosity because this practice allows you to delve deeper into what you are reading. Additionally, engaging what you are reading by asking questions about it will help you recognize what interests you about that subject and what else you want to know about it. This active approach to reading helps you develop your critical thinking abilities. When you ask these questions and write notes in the margins of what you read, you are engaging in a process called **annotating.** Reading closely and carefully to figure out the authors' *assumptions* (beliefs and values) about an idea will help you understand their position on a topic and where it comes from. Asking and answering questions like those that follow in this section will help you figure out the authors' *perspectives*, as well as what the authors state in an explicit (or direct) way, and what they leave implicit (implied). Questions like these, in sections called Reading for Meaning, follow each reading throughout this book. We have also annotated the first reading in each chapter, adding questions and notes in the margins that demonstrate the wide range of ways to practice curiosity as you are reading. We have left space throughout for you to add your own annotations to the reading.

Read the following two passages on curiosity.[2] Each passage explains the concept of curiosity (readings in Chapter 6 also explain concepts) but does so from a different perspective.

As you read the excerpts, ask yourself these questions and write down the answers:

- What do you think are the guiding questions the writers asked themselves as they researched and wrote these texts? What in the text specifically leads you to identify these guiding questions?

- What questions do you need to ask as a reader to clarify the meaning of each of these passages?

You may want to reread the selections, noting the following:

- The *genre* (or kind) of text the authors have written

- The *assertions* (or claims) they make

- The *evidence* they supply to support their assertions/claims

- The *assumptions* they make

Ben Greenman

"The Online Curiosity Killer"

My older son, at 9, has spent 3.2 percent of his life on the Internet. I made that statistic up, though it sounds plausible. What's certain is that he has spent at least three hours on the Internet, because I saw it with my own eyes, last spring, when third grade culminated with an assignment to research rain-forest animals. His animal was the anaconda, and the Internet assisted him in writing a highly factual report that touched on the snake's habitat (semiaquatic), prey (occasional goats and ponies) and size (freaking huge).   1

He was proud of the report and brought it to me to read afterward. "There are three different kinds of anaconda" he said. "Green, yellow and dark-spotted. They're not venomous. They're constrictors. And it's the largest snake in the world."   2

"What's the second-largest?" I said.   3

He looked at me. He frowned slightly. He turned and walked away. I heard tapping in the other room, and then he came back and told me the answer.   4

---

[2] A listing of the sources of texts cited can be found at the end of the chapter.

About a month later, we took a family trip down to Miami to see my wife's parents,   5
and my wife and I slept in the room where she grew up. Among the other keepsakes
and collectibles (Pee-Wee Herman dolls, old Rolling Stone magazines), there was
an encyclopedia. I had owned the same encyclopedia, and I paged through it with a
mix of nostalgia and boredom.

I looked up anacondas and then slid out the S volume to read a bit more about   6
snakes. Did you know that most snakes only have one functional lung? I did not. Did
you know that snakes are reptiles? Yeah, I did know that. What was most interesting
about the research is what it did not tell me: the second-largest snake. I read fairly
closely, but there was no search function, and I couldn't just flip through the S volume to
get to the entry for "Second-Largest." What my son was able to do in 10 seconds, I was
unable to do in 10 minutes.

When I was a kid, I did the same reports as my son. (I mean the same kinds   7
of reports, of course — my body of work in elementary school included coruscat-
ing monographs on raccoons and airplanes and George Washington Carver.) If I had
done an anaconda report, and my teacher had asked after the second-largest snake,
I would not have simply turned, walked, typed and learned. I would have returned
to the encyclopedia, and if the answer wasn't there, I would have ended my investigation abruptly. Or maybe, if I was especially motivated, I would have gone to the
library and checked out a book about snakes, but even that would not have been a
guarantee. And so I would have most likely gone on with my life in third grade, and
then fourth, faintly feeling the burr of the question in my brain, continually assessing
how important it was to scratch that itch.

By supplying answers to questions with such ruthless efficiency, the Internet cuts   8
off the supply of an even more valuable commodity: productive frustration. Education, at least as I remember it, isn't only, or even primarily, about creating children
who are proficient with information. It's about filling them with questions that ripen,
via deferral, into genuine interests. Each of my sons passes through phases quickly:
one month they're obsessed with marine life, the next with world flags. This is not so
different from how I was (the '70s was all about robots), but what is different is how
much information they can collect, and how quickly they come to feel that they have
satisfied their hunger.

Until recently, I have been entirely complicit in the Second-Largest Snake Problem.   9
(By the way, the answer is the reticulated python.) When either of my kids has asked
me a question, I have tried to answer or, if I could not, just looked it up. Google and
I, as it turns out, know everything. But in recent weeks, I have begun playing dumb,
saying that I don't know and not offering to find out. Sometimes they'll drop the
question immediately, but sometimes they'll persist, and I'm learning not to give in to
the persistence but rather to ensure that the questions stay with them until they arrive
at a point when they know nothing for certain except that they have questions they
cannot answer so easily.

A few nights ago, my son asked me what the most-common cause of death in the   10
world is. I shrugged.

"Not sure," I said. I expected him to get up and go to the computer, but he stayed 11
at the table, and we speculated wildly for a few minutes.

"Heart attacks?" he said. "Car crashes? Old age?" He went to bed still musing. 12

Note how Greenman connects the habits of mind of curiosity and persistence by refusing to answer his sons' questions. He tries to teach them the importance of curiosity and how curiosity requires persistence, especially when search engines are available to answer all questions. Below are some questions that guide Greenman's writing and his own curiosity about his children's approaches to conducting research:

What are the drawbacks associated with having such easy and constant access to answers?

What my son was able to do in 10 seconds, I was unable to do in 10 minutes. . . . By supplying answers to questions with such ruthless efficiency, the Internet cuts off the supply of an even more valuable commodity: productive frustration. . . .

How can I help my sons become curious and persistent so that they develop genuine interests?

But in recent weeks, I have begun playing dumb, saying that I don't know and not offering to find out. Sometimes they'll drop the question immediately, but sometimes they'll persist, and I'm learning not to give in to the persistence but rather to ensure that the questions stay with them until they arrive at a point

How can I support real learning rather than just searching?

when they know nothing for certain except that they have questions they cannot answer so easily.

Consider, too, how Greenman's use of statistics helps his readers understand what genre (or kind) of text they are reading: "My older son, at 9, has spent 3.2 percent of his life on the Internet. I made that statistic up, though it sounds plausible." Making up statistics would not be acceptable in many genres, including in scientific discourse. This suggests that Greenman has not written within a genre that depends upon accurate statistical data for evidence.

Arjun Shankar and Mariam Durrani

"Curiosity and Education: A White Paper"

Many have seen curiosity as directly linked to creativity and, in some cases, have 1
argued that creativity and curiosity are synonymous (Voss and Keller, 1983). While curiosity and creativity are indeed corollary concepts, curiosity plays a far more important role in educational space precisely because it is not so directly linked with singular purposes such as profit-making. As discussed earlier, curiosity can take on both a diversive and specific form, meaning that curious individuals are not only

inclined to seek solutions to problems with particular results in mind, but can also ask questions, seek knowledge, and find answers without intending any end goal. This is not to say that curiosity will not result in new innovations. It will; and it does. In fact, the ability to seek knowledge in seemingly divergent fields has been thought of as the first step towards creativity and subsequently innovation.

Note how Shankar and Durrani rely on experts, Voss and Keller (the names that appear in the parenthetical citation at the end of the first sentence), for evidence to support their assertions. There are many additional strategies writers use to add support, such as the following:

For more information on writers' strategies for providing evidence, see Chapter 2.

- Narrating a story
- Providing facts and statistics
- Describing
- Illustrating (providing examples)
- Classifying
- Comparing and contrasting
- Reporting causes or effects
- Summarizing or paraphrasing

Now take a look at some of the readers' questions prompted by this passage:

Is there more recent research on the relationship between creativity and curiosity?

Who are Voss and Keller? Is this source credible?

Why look outside your own field? Why is innovation the end goal here?

Many have seen curiosity as directly linked to creativity and, in some cases, have argued that creativity and curiosity are synonymous (Voss and Keller, 1983). . . . The ability to seek knowledge in seemingly divergent fields has been thought of as the first step towards creativity and subsequently innovation.

For more on research, see Chapter 12: Strategies for Research and Documentation.

The *source* Shankar and Durrani cite — Voss and Keller — is one you could look up and assess for yourself.[3]

You may have to search for the underlying assumptions by analyzing the *tone* or *connotation* of the words the writer chooses or by thinking critically about the examples the writer uses. Ask yourself whose assumption the writer is giving voice to — her or his own, the wider community's, or a source's. You can see that Shankar and Durrani maintain an objective tone with few or no words that carry emotion, and that they rely primarily on an outside source to make their argument here.

[3] Hans-Georg Voss and Heidi Keller, *Curiosity and Exploration: Theories and Results* (New York: Academic Press, 2013).

One of Shankar and Durrani's assumptions is that curiosity is connected to creativity. This belief is probably true of them and true of their colleagues, who are anthropologists and educators concerned with the relationship between curiosity and creativity. If it is also true of you, the reader, then they will be successful in their argument. If, however, a reader believes that curiosity is unrelated to creativity, then Shankar and Durrani will have to provide more and different kinds of evidence to be fully persuasive.

Here are some additional questions you can ask to bring a writer's assumptions to the surface:

- What are the effects of the assumption, in the context of the essay specifically or in society more generally? See Analyzing Assumptions in Chapter 2.

- What do I think about the assumption, and is there anything in the essay that raises doubts about it?

- How does the assumption reinforce or critique commonly held views, and are there any *alternative ideas*, *beliefs*, or *values* that would challenge this assumption?

You can see that even though the authors of the excerpts above did not directly ask questions in their texts, each of them was curious about curiosity. The questions you asked as you read allowed you to engage with and think critically about the reading selections, necessary steps to take before you can write productively about a reading selection.

Analyzing Ideas

In college, you will deepen and extend your critical reading and thinking skills by reading a variety of texts that may expose you to wholly new ideas, make you question your own value system, and help you see different points of view. You will also often have opportunities to discuss what you read with your professors and classmates, and doing so will introduce you to additional critical reading strategies that can enhance your existing habits of mind. In order to get the most from texts and discussions, participants in the academic conversation examine all the ideas — their own and others' — critically but also with civility, whether they agree with them or not.

To see this process in action, read the two excerpts below, which discuss curiosity. The first is an excerpt from a popular book on curiosity, and the second is from an academic journal on education. As you read, make notes about the following:

- Any ideas that are new to you, especially those that challenge what you currently think about curiosity

- Any references to assumptions that are contrary to the writers' beliefs — look especially for values that may be currently accepted but are open to questioning

- How the writers handle assumptions that are contrary to their own

Mario Livio

"Curious," from *Why: What Makes Us Curious?*

Before seriously delving into the scientific research on curiosity, I decided (out of my   1
own personal curiosity) to take a brief detour to closely examine two individuals who, in
my view, represent two of the most curious minds to have ever existed. I believe that few
would disagree with this characterization of Leonardo da Vinci and the physicist Richard
Feynman. Leonardo's boundless interests spanned such broad swaths of art, science, and
technology that he remains to this day the quintessential Renaissance man. Art historian
Kenneth Clark appropriately called him "the most relentlessly curious man in history."
Feynman's genius and achievements in numerous branches of physics are legendary,
but he also pursued fascinations with biology, painting, safecracking, bongo playing,
attractive women, and studying Mayan hieroglyphs. . . . When asked to identify what
he thought was the key motivator for scientific discovery, Feynman replied, "It has to do
with curiosity. It has to do with wondering what makes something do something." . . .

I don't expect that even a careful inspection of the personalities of Leonardo and   2
Feynman will necessarily reveal any deep insights into the nature of curiosity. Numerous previous attempts to uncover common features in many historical figures of genius,
for instance, have exposed only a perplexing diversity with respect to the backgrounds
and psychological characteristics of these individuals. . . . This is not to say that *all*
efforts to identify a few shared characteristics are doomed to fail. . . . University of
Chicago psychologist Mihaly Csikszentmihalyi has been able to unearth a few tendencies that appear to be associated with most unusually creative persons. . . . I therefore
thought it a worthwhile exercise at least to explore whether there was anything in the
fascinating personalities of Leonardo and Feynman that could provide a clue about the
source of their truly insatiable curiosity.

Susan Engel

"The Case for Curiosity"

I think many adults implicitly believe that children naturally get less curious over   1
time. This belief isn't totally unreasonable. Data do suggest that curiosity becomes
less robust over time (Coie, 1974). And if curiosity is, as psychologists say, the urge
to explain the unexpected, then as more of everyday life becomes familiar, a child
might encounter fewer unexpected objects and events. Perhaps the reduced curiosity
of the 7-year old is simply a by-product of that child's increased knowledge.

However, adult influence may also be a factor. When researchers invite children   2
into a room containing a novel object, they find that children are very attuned to the

feedback of adults. When the experimenter makes encouraging faces or comments, children are more likely to explore the interesting object. Experiments I've done show that children show much more interest in materials when an adult visibly shows how curious he or she is about the materials.

Considering the ideas that are new to you, think about what you expect from the authors after they have raised these ideas: Do you want more information about the *concept* of curiosity? Do you need more *examples* of curiosity? Do you need more evidence of the *relevance* of curiosity to your own education and life before you can be convinced of its importance?

Reread these two excerpts to consider where and how the author responds to the statements and assumptions of people with whom they disagree. For example, note that Livio *acknowledges* the idea that he doesn't "expect that even a careful inspection of the personalities of Leonardo and Feynman will necessarily reveal any deep insights into the nature of curiosity" since "numerous previous attempts to uncover common features in many historical figures of genius, for instance, have exposed only a perplexing diversity." Then notice how he introduces this *concession* and then *refutes* it.

See Looking for Patterns of Opposition in Chapter 2.

Cue / Concession	This is not to say that all efforts to identify a few shared charac-teristics are doomed to fail. . . . University of Chicago psychologist
Refutation	Mihaly Csikszentmihalyi has been able to unearth a few tendencies that appear to be associated with most unusually creative persons. . . . I therefore thought it a worthwhile exercise at least to explore whether there was anything in the fascinating personalities of Leonardo and Feynman that could provide a clue about the source of their truly insatiable curiosity.

The author introduces the concession with a transition indicating contrast ("this is not to say") to indicate that an exception, refinement, or contradiction is coming.

Review the excerpt from Engel and notice a similar concession-cue structure, but in this case what follows is the introduction of a refinement rather than a refutation.

Cue / Concession	I think many adults implicitly believe that children naturally get less curious over time. This belief isn't totally unreasonable. Data
Refinement	do suggest that curiosity becomes less robust over time (Coie, 1974). . . . However, adult influence may also be a factor.

The author introduces the refinement with a transition indicating contrast (*however*) to indicate that an exception, refinement, or contradiction is coming.

In both cases, the authors use a similar structure that looks something like this:

Look for more
examples
and sentence
strategies in
Reading Like a
Writer sections
following the
readings in
Chapters 3–10.

▶ While .... may be true, ... is more likely to contribute to ....

▶ Although .... , I think ....

▶ .... is true, however .... also plays an important role.

▶ Researchers X and Y provide some evidence that .... occurs in some settings; however, they don't offer sufficient evidence that it occurs in all settings.

Now consider the tone that Engel uses as she acknowledges these opposing viewpoints. Notice that Engel's sentences reflect careful word choices that will not offend others, including her audience, who might disagree with her views on the causes of children's reduced curiosity. She hedges her statement with a *qualifying term*, "*may* also be," to avoid making a stronger claim than she can prove given the evidence. A stronger claim might put off her readers. Hedging also demonstrates the writer's willingness to engage in conversation about this subject.

In addition to helping to foster a courteous relationship with readers, hedging allows writers to practice at least two habits of mind: *openness* and *engagement*. As a writer, you must be willing to consider ways of thinking that are different from your own. Hedging shows that openness by creating a space for those who may not agree with you. By hedging, you are also practicing academic habits of mind, indicating a high degree of engagement or investment in learning because you are willing to participate in a conversation, including with those who might disagree with your ideas.

ACTIVITY 2

Talking to Learn: Honing Ideas through Discussion

Once you have analyzed the ways that Livio and Engel respond to others, try discussing curiosity with your classmates, friends, or family to develop your own ideas about curiosity. By discussing your reading and speculating about other ways of looking at curiosity, you practice *openness*. As you generate and test your own ideas, improving them as you refine them, you practice *metacognition*, the ability to reflect on your own thinking. You also demonstrate your ability to *analyze critically*, and you practice presenting your ideas to others with *rhetorical sensitivity*, showing *civility* while responding *empathetically* to others.

Developing Rhetorical Sensitivity

Rhetoric means the ways writers make their ideas understandable and seek to influence their readers. When you develop rhetorical sensitivity, you understand the writer's purpose, audience, context, and genre, and you recognize that the decisions the writer makes — including the types of evidence the writer includes, the kinds of vocabulary he or she chooses, and the *writing strategies* he or she uses — grow out of the *rhetorical situation*.

You probably already have a fairly sophisticated understanding of rhetorical situations: You wouldn't write a thank-you note to your great-aunt using the same tone or vocabulary that you would use when posting a social media update about a concert you attended, because you know your purpose, audience, context, and genre are very different in these two situations. Your ability to analyze the **rhetorical situation** — to identify the writer's purpose, audience, context, and genre — and to adapt your writing to your rhetorical situation is central to your success in college and beyond. Your teachers will expect you to analyze the rhetorical situation in each discipline, and by doing so, you will cultivate the skills necessary to join their academic conversation.

Asking and answering the following questions when reading *and* when writing will help you develop rhetorical sensitivity by exploring the rhetorical situation:

- What is the author's purpose?
- Who is the audience?
- What is the author's stance — perspective and attitude toward the material?
- What is the genre?
- What is the best medium or design for this text?

Asking these questions while reading will help you develop a writer's eye and will help you notice the strategies that writers use to communicate their ideas.

You may have noticed that the four passages above on curiosity were written in different styles. The texts that were written for an academic audience assumed their readers were familiar with the terminology (vocabulary) and concepts characteristic of the discipline — what we call the discipline's **discourse** — as well as its **genre conventions** (typical ways of organizing material and using sources). For example, readers familiar with scientific discourse (biology, for example) would expect a scientific report to include technical descriptions of the methods used and the results obtained and to be organized with separate sections for methods, results, discussion, and references. If the same experiment were discussed in an article for a general audience, however, readers would expect little, if any, technical detail.

Authors of academic discourse try to keep their *tone* objective and courteous, so they will be taken seriously and not provoke an emotional (and perhaps unreasonable) reaction in the reader. Less formal authors may allow passion into their writing, or they may write in a chatty tone, with informal language and direct addresses to the reader.

ACTIVITY 3

Writing to Learn: Developing Your Rhetorical Sensitivity

To develop your rhetorical sensitivity for academic writing, look again at the four passages on curiosity above to identify one that you think was written for a general audience and one written for an academic audience. What characteristics can you identify for the two types of writing? List the characteristics of the two excerpts in facing columns:

Excerpt for more general audience	Excerpt for academic audience

Now write a paragraph or two explaining the specific features that led you to identify the different audiences for these two excerpts.

ACTIVITY 4

Writing to Learn: Pulling It All Together

Look back at what you wrote for Activity 1, where you speculated about the academic habits of mind you already practice. Think now about what you have learned about the habits of mind that lead to successful thinking, reading, and writing in college and beyond. To solidify your understanding, write a note to a person — a friend, a colleague, a sibling, your own child — who is preparing for college. In a page or two, describe the habits of mind you think this person should start (or continue) practicing to ensure his or her success in college and career. Feel free to use examples from this chapter, but try as well to draw on your own experience to support your assertions.

FROM READING CRITICALLY TO WRITING WELL

As the successful novelist Stephen King says: "If you want to be a writer, you must do two things above all others: read a lot and write a lot. There's no way around these two things that I'm aware of, no shortcut." All college students have experience with reading and writing for school, and many of you have extensive experience with informal writing as well, especially on technology-based platforms such as blogs, Twitter, or messaging apps. This kind of online writing can make you more comfortable with the written word and help you become more aware of who your audience is, because your writing is directed to a variety of people other than your teachers. But for academic writing to be effective, it must grow out of the habits of mind discussed so far in this chapter: curiosity, openness, engagement, creativity, persistence, responsibility, flexibility, and metacognition.

THE WRITING PROCESS

To develop these habits of mind typical of successful college students — curiosity, openness, engagement, creativity, persistence, responsibility, flexibility, and metacognition — academic writers can take advantage of the *writing process,* which allows them to shape and hone their writing until it expresses their ideas clearly and effectively, and satisfies (and perhaps even surpasses) the expectations of their audience. By enacting these habits of mind through the practices of critical analysis, rhetorical sensitivity, civility, and empathy, you can simultaneously become a stronger reader and writer. In fact, the curiosity that drives your reading process — represented by the questions, comments, and other annotations you make while you read — should also characterize your writing process. Both reading and writing, in other words, offer opportunities to practice curiosity.

The kind of academic writing you will do in college requires curiosity, the desire to know more. This emphasis on curiosity as a defining feature of both reading and writing may seem a bit odd in a world where a quick Google search can provide answers to all of your questions in seconds. Curiosity, though, when practiced through academic reading and writing, does not involve asking questions to which there are single and immediate answers. Instead, practicing curiosity means asking and pursuing questions for which there are more than one answer. In fact, this kind of curiosity often produces more questions than answers as you linger on the complexities that your process of inquiry exposes.

We can look back at how Livio's curiosity comes through in the passage earlier in this chapter. Although Livio doesn't "expect that even a careful inspection of the personalities of Leonardo and Feynman will necessarily reveal any deep insights into the nature of curiosity," he still believes that it is a "worthwhile exercise at least to explore whether there was anything in the fascinating personalities of Leonardo and Feynman that could provide a clue about the source of their truly insatiable curiosity." Notice that Livio isn't looking for a single answer, but rather is content to *explore* whether he can find a clue about the source of Leonardo and Feynman's curiosity. His research and writing are propelled by his own curiosity, his own commitment to inquiring into the personalities of these figures even if the payoff is simply a clue. Livio is invested not just in the clue — if he finds one — but in the exploration itself. Both reading and writing are ways of exploring, of practicing curiosity, that can help you understand and think more deeply. The concepts of curiosity, inquiry, and exploration should inform your reading and writing in this course and as you make your way through the reading selections in this book, as well as the questions and assignments that follow the selections.

In Chapters 3 through 10 of *Reading Critically, Writing Well*, questions following the reading selections help you move from analyzing the selection to writing about it. Each chapter also includes a Guide to Writing to help you write in the genre of the chapter — such as autobiography, concept explanation, or position argument. You can explore and develop these ideas in drafts and then revise those drafts deeply in response to feedback from other readers. Each chapter includes the kinds of writing done in college:

- Analysis of content and meaning of the readings

- Analysis of the rhetorical approach

- Analysis of the kind of writing (genre)

- Writing in different academic genres

In college, much of the writing you submit will be formal, academic discourse in specific genres (such as research reports and essay exams). The activities in the Guides to Writing will help you develop the ideas and language that you will use in those formal writing assignments, and they include example paragraphs and sentence strategies demonstrating effective methods for presenting your ideas and responding to evidence. As writers, we rarely if ever begin with a complete understanding of our subject or a clear, detailed plan for writing about it. Instead, we write to learn, using the questions that arise while writing to inspire more writing and, nearly always, generate further ideas and deeper insights as we pursue our curiosity.

As you write, remember that the writing process is *recursive*: it does not proceed smoothly in a straight line from beginning to end, but rather may be chaotic or repetitive. The steps in the process may include the following:

- Generating questions and research ideas

- Drafting your essay

- Getting feedback from others

- Revising deeply

- Editing and proofreading

You may find yourself rethinking, rearranging, and rewriting much of your original text, so you may revisit one or more of these stages several times for one essay. The chart below illustrates some of the options you have when writing an essay.

Generating Ideas	There are many different ways to generate questions and research ideas. For example, you can • List your ideas in the form of questions to begin recognizing what makes you curious. • Brainstorm on paper or with a friend or group to get a firmer grasp of your ideas and where they might lead you. • Research to figure out what others have said and gather material for your writing so you can support and develop your ideas. • Determine which genre would be best for presenting your ideas. • Explore what you know about your audience so you can tailor your writing to their needs. • Gather material for your writing so you can support your claim when you figure out what it is.
Planning a Draft	Writers have many different ways of getting started on a draft: • They may just need a first line. • They may make an outline. • They might try an idea map or a scratch copy of the points they want to make.
Writing a Draft	Develop your draft by drawing on the questions and ideas you generated and researched earlier. You should have • A clear sense of *who* your readers are and what they need to know to be persuaded by your observations. • Some grasp of their values and beliefs, so you can anticipate the *assumptions* they will make and appeal to common ground between them and you. • A main idea, sound reasons to support it, and several kinds of evidence. You can always return to idea-generating activities as you determine what else you might need.
Getting Feedback from Others	Writers need feedback from others to determine the strengths and weaknesses of their early draft(s). Pose questions like those below to a friend, classmate, tutor, or instructor so you get the constructive criticism you need: • Is my main idea/thesis/research question clear? • What evidence is most persuasive? Least? • Are there places where you can't follow my reasoning, and can you explain why? • Do I show evidence of having practiced the habits of mind expected of college students: curiosity, openness, engagement, creativity, persistence, responsibility, flexibility, and metacognition, as expressed through critical analysis, rhetorical sensitivity, civility, and empathy? Please point out examples or where I could improve.

Revising Deeply	Many writers spend more time revising than writing their original draft, another indication that writing generates ideas. You may find that you have to • Revise your whole thesis or come up with a new research question in light of the feedback you receive from reviewers. • Expand on your ideas, sharpen your reasons, or augment your evidence. • Answer possible objections or questions. • Reorganize in light of readers' confusion. • Rework your ideas into a more reader-friendly form; trim bloated parts. It's important to allow enough time in your schedule for deep revision, since writing is generative, and you may find you have as much work to do mid-essay as you did when you were working on the original writing project.
Editing and Proofreading	To edit and proofread effectively, you need to read your essay through the eyes of your reader. This care and attention to detail yield writing that deserves the careful consideration of those reading it—whether they be specialists, colleagues, members of the general public, or, in the case of student writing, professors. Rigorously check sentences and paragraphs to make sure your writing includes the following: • A clear thesis or research question in a prominent place • Transitions between sentences and between paragraphs to help your reader follow your line of thinking • An appropriate tone given your approach to your subject and your audience • Sentence construction that helps your reader understand your points • Correct grammar and punctuation so you can communicate effectively and not confuse or annoy your reader • Correct spelling so your reader knows exactly what word you mean • Vocabulary appropriate to the subject and audience's needs

ONE STUDENT'S WRITING PROCESS

The following sample shows how a student moves through the writing process using the stages detailed in the chart above. The student is responding to an assignment asking her to research a subject that has a personal impact on her life. In order to generate ideas about her chosen topic — college affordability — the student combines a few of the options for generating ideas, including brainstorming, formulating questions, doing some initial research to see what experts say about the topic, and considering her audience. From there, the student uses an outline to plan her draft on the topic. She then writes the draft and gets feedback from others. After receiving the feedback from a peer and her instructor, she does not immediately move toward deeply revising her draft, the next step in the chart above. Capitalizing on the recursive nature of the writing process, she instead returns to the ideas she had generated and rewrites her outline, revisiting the *generating ideas* and *planning a draft* stages of the chart above. Only then does she revise deeply and conclude the process by editing and proofreading. This is, of course, one student's approach to writing and your own need not mirror it. What will likely connect your writing process and this student's process, though, is its recursivity, or the moves back to earlier stages before moving forward. Like this student, writers rarely move from idea to finished text without returning to earlier stages to revise, edit, rearrange, and rethink.

Generating Ideas

This is usually the first stage in the writing process and can take many forms. This student brainstorms ideas she has about the writing prompt, her experiences, and reading she has done. She uses an inquiry-based mindset and lists questions she has about her topic. In addition, she gathers together citations from research she has read, and makes some notes about her potential audience.

BRAINSTORMING

If I think about an issue that has had an impact on me it would be the cost of college. I never worried much about how much college would cost. My parents seemed to always be on top of things and they told me they were saving enough money and I would have choices when it came to college. Then my mom lost her job and my dad had to go on unpaid medical leave. They had to stop saving for my education. Because of the financial strain my family felt I started thinking about whether college is all that valuable. Turns out this wasn't just an issue for me. When I arrived at college, I became friendly with an older student. Even though he was returning to college after working for like twenty years he had some of the same concerns I did, although they were sort of flipped. He was the parent in the household and was concerned that if he spent all of this money earning his degree that it would put a strain on his family and interrupt his saving up for his kids' college costs. That made me realize that this is an issue that affects all kinds of people and is probably worth writing about.

- **Questions**

  Here are some of the questions I have:

  Is it worth going to college if it is a financial burden to my family?

  Do a lot of students deal with college debt?

  Are degrees from some colleges more valuable than others?

  How big of a problem is student debt?

- **Research**

  Here is what some experts say:

  "The cost of a higher education has more than doubled, when adjusted for inflation, since 1986—faster than the cost of health care, and well ahead of the median family income"

  Skibell, Arianna. "Rising Costs Brings New Focus on How Exactly Colleges Set Their Prices." *The Hechinger Report*, 1 Feb. 2016. https://hechingerreport.org/rising-costs-brings-new-focus-on-how-exactly-colleges-set-their-prices/

  "Decades ago, the small share of students lucky enough to go to college largely paid their tuition out of pocket. But today, more and more students are pursuing higher education, and they increasingly rely on debt to do so. Price alone—and whether students have the cash on hand to pay it—is no longer an adequate measure of affordability."

  Akers, Beth, et al. "The Affordability Conundrum: Value, Price, and Choice in Higher Education." *The Manhattan Institute*, April 2017. https://www.manhattan-institute.org/html/affordability-conundrum-value-price-and-choice-higher-education-10185.html

- **Audience:**

  Who is my audience? Am I writing just to my professor or to the other students in my class? How much does the audience know about this issue?

Planning a Draft

At this stage of the writing process, the student works to organize her ideas. Included here are examples of outlining and idea mapping, but other strategies can be used as well. Creating an outline allows writers to separate out the main ideas from the details that belong to each main idea. The outline then guides writers in the composition of the essay. Creating an idea map — also called a concept map or mind map — allows writers to visualize the connections among their ideas. An idea map does not depend on such a linear and rigid structure as does an outline, but it still provides a guide for composing an essay.

OUTLINING

I. College Is the New High School
    A. Almost everyone goes to college now
    B. To get even some of the most basic jobs people need a college degree
    C. It's like you don't have a choice—you have to go to college

II. College Is Very Expensive
    A. Increase in cost over the years
    B. Increase surpasses inflation
    C. Costs being paid for by grants, federal aid packages, college aid programs
    D. Students are questioning the costs
    E. Student debt crisis has reached 1.6 trillion dollars

III. The Costs of Education Affect All Kinds of Students
    A. Stories of both traditional and nontraditional students
    B. High earners like doctors and lawyers are affected
    C. All students need to think hard about the value of education since the costs are so high

IDEA MAPPING

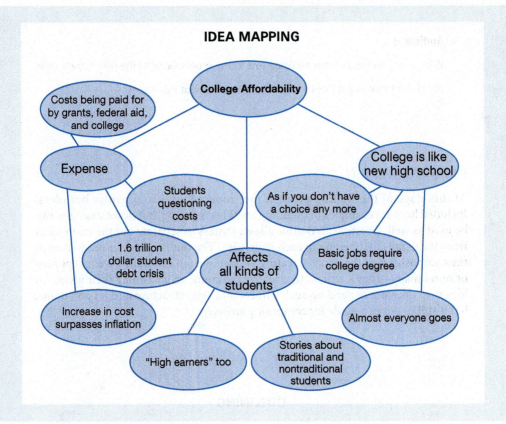

Writing a Draft

Essays can go through many drafts. Here, the student writes a first draft on her chosen subject — the cost of college.

THE HIGH COST OF COLLEGE

For many decades attending college was once of many paths someone could take on their way to a career. Now a college degree seems to be as necessary as a high school degree was decades ago. But, the value that one gets from that degree is debatable. Even with a college degree not everyone gets a job, and tuition is so expensive that many students find themselves in a lot of debt after graduation. In this essay, I will consider the problem of college affordability by exploring the viewpoints of several experts on the subject.

In their article "An Overview of American Higher Education," Sandy Baum, Charles Kurose, and Michael McPherson explain how more people are attending college now than in previous eras: "A half-century ago, college was not seen as the natural next step for most American young people who finished high school. American factories were thriving, unions were strong, and a high school graduate could reasonably expect to move right into a stable job that would support a family and allow the purchase of a car and a house. But the idea of postsecondary education was starting to catch on, and by 1960, about 45 percent of recent high school graduates began college somewhere" (19). "By 2009," they explain, "seventy-percent of high school graduates enrolled in some form of postsecondary program shortly after completing high school, and the range of options available to them had become much broader (19).

The drastic increase of students attending college drew attention to the cost of college, which, as Baum, Kurose, and McPherson show, increased dramatically even when inflation is taken into consideration: "The average price of a year at an in-state public four-year college rose to $8,244 in 2011–12 from $2,242 (in 2011 dollars) thirty years earlier—an annual growth rate of 4.4 percent beyond inflation" (26). These increases in prices are upsetting to college students, but what is interesting is that students themselves generally don't pay for college directly. Baum, Kurose, and McPherson write, "The majority of students do not actually pay the sticker prices (27). Pell and other grants through the federal government, as well as student aid money directly from the colleges, are often responsible for footing the bill. The issue is that students have to pay back these loans and that's what raises the question whether college is worth it. Personal Finance Writer Jessica Dickler reports that "many graduates [in a study of 500 college graduates ages 18 to 35 conducted by Citizens Bank] expressed buyer's remorse regarding their education. . . . Fifty-seven percent said they regret taking out as many loans as they did, and 36 percent said they would not have gone to college if they fully understood the associated costs." This shows that students leave college still unsure that all the debt they accrued was worth it.

Stacey Patton, Staff Reporter at the *Chronicle of Higher Education*, has written an article that shares the stories of many older students who make up a large percentage of students who are in debt. Patton writes, "Student-loan debt is growing fastest among adults ages 60 and older, with more than two million people in that age group now owing an average of $19,000." Her article includes story after story about people who will not only never be able to retire because they will be paying off their debt, but people who recognize that they will likely die with their debt. This subset of students with debt doesn't come to mind right away, but the number of them is really astounding. Patton explains, "Many of these older borrowers thought they could increase their marketability by earning an advanced degree later in life but are struggling to make ends meet instead. The number of people over age 50 enrolling in graduate schools more than doubled over the two decades between 1987 and 2007. . . . The total amount of outstanding student-loan debt among this age group reached $155-billion in 2012." Although an advanced degree that expanded their skill set could help older people find new jobs where they may make more money, the debt they are saddled with undermines the benefits of that newfound marketability.

The debt crisis has only gotten worse. By May 2018, student debt surpassed 1.5 trillion dollars, according to the Board of Governors of the Federal Reserve System. That number seems outrageous in and of itself, but what is interesting about it is that many of the students who are in debt are, in fact, what are considered high earners. Michael Durkheimer, a reporter for *Forbes Magazine*, points out that "contrary to what you might believe, most student debt is not held by the poor or by college dropouts. . . . If you pursue/purchase an advanced degree, you are going to have to borrow much more than you otherwise would for a bachelor's degree. And, those who attain an advanced degree often can command a higher salary." Even for these high earning graduates, they continue to ask themselves whether it was all worth it, and some don't think so: "Among those with over $100,000 in law school debt, a staggering less than 1-in-4 strongly agree that their degree was worth the cost" (Durkheimer). Of course, doctors and lawyers have to go to graduate school, and their debt is from graduate school and not just college. Still, if even those in high earning positions like lawyers and doctors have concerns about how valuable these degrees are then it shows how many different kinds of people are affected by this issue. After all, those degrees are very valuable to doctors and lawyers because those are what allow them to make so much money. This raises the issue of how one can calculate value when it comes to an education—whether that education consists of a college degree or a graduate degree. How can you measure the value of those degrees?

In conclusion, the issue of college affordability is complicated. It affects all kinds of people from undergraduates who have to pay off loans to doctors and lawyers who are saddled with debt from college *and* graduate school. In the end, each student has to decide if college is really worth the debt that will follow them into adulthood and affect the rest of their lives.

Works Cited

Baum, Sandy, et al. "An Overview of American Higher Education." *Future of Children*, vol. 23, no. 1, 2013, pp. 17–39.

Board of Governors of the Federal Reserve System. "Consumer Credit Outstanding (Levels)." 9 July 2018, https://www.federalreserve.gov/releases/g19/HIST/cc_hist_memo_levels .html

Dickler, Jennifer. "College Buyers Remorse Is Real." *CNBC*, 7 April 2016, https://www.cnbc .com/2016/04/07/college-buyers-remorse-is-real.html

Durkheimer, Michael. "Should We Care About Those with the Most Student Debt?" *Forbes*, 30 Jan. 2018, https://www.forbes.com/sites/michaeldurkheimer/2018/01/30 /should-we-care-about-those-with-the-most-student-debt/#8ee913f90d8b

Patton, Stacey. "I Fully Expect to Die with This Debt." *Chronicle of Higher Education*, vol. 59, no. 32, 19 April 2013.

Getting Feedback from Others

The following are peer responses to the questions in the "Getting Feedback from Others" section in the chart on page 17.

PEER REVIEW FEEDBACK

1. Is my main idea/thesis/research question clear?

I think your focus is on what experts say on the subject of college affordability. I'm not sure what your main idea or thesis is. I can't really find a place that shows what your main idea is. You only mention the ideas of the sources.

2. What evidence is most persuasive? Least?

You use good sources that connect to the subject of the essay. The most persuasive evidence is from Durkheimer about the older students and the debt they carry. I had never thought of that, and that source provides a lot of relevant information. The least persuasive evidence is from Baum, Kurose, and McPherson since it is pretty old. I was wondering if there is any more recent evidence.

3. Are there places where you can't follow my reasoning, and can you explain why?

It's hard to know why you are going from one source to the next in this order instead of another order since your thesis is unclear. The sources are good, but you need to have a main idea that helps me and other readers know why you are bringing in each source at each moment.

4. Do I show evidence of having practiced the habits of mind expected of college students: curiosity, openness, engagement, creativity, persistence, responsibility, flexibility, and metacognition through critical analysis, rhetorical sensitivity, civility, and empathy? Please point it out.

You seem curious about the subject of college affordability and even include a question toward the end of the essay. You are open to many different perspectives on the issue and you represent these in your essay. For example, you include sources about how older students and higher earners are part of the student debt crisis. You also seem open to feedback since you are asking me these questions and will use my answers to revise your essay. You are practicing critical analysis by considering the evidence provided by sources, although you could analyze it more closely. You are also being rhetorically sensitive as you respond to the sources and summarize them for your reader. You are courteous in how you represent the sources and how you interact with your reader who may or may not agree with you.

INSTRUCTOR FEEDBACK

In this essay you tackle a complicated subject, and so I'm very interested to see what *you* think, and what specific question or main idea you would like to pursue related to college affordability. Currently, you have included a lot of information in this essay, but it's all just dumped into the essay without any real focus. In other words, it reads like an overview or summary of different perspectives on college affordability without a specific idea, thesis, or question of your own that guides the essay. To critically analyze an issue like college affordability, you need to do more than summarize several sources on the subject. You need to develop a focus and then use your sources to help you expand your ideas. As you revise deeply, develop a thesis or question so your specific line of inquiry is clear. What is it that interests you about this subject? What are you curious about? Look back at your initial writing when you were generating ideas. Are there ideas, questions, or sources there that might help you articulate your specific interest in this subject? Another place to go is to the question you pose toward the end of the essay: "How can you measure the value of these degrees?" Maybe you can explore some version of this question in your essay. If you do so, your essay will become a more specific exploration rather than a general overview of the subject. No matter how you revise, you will likely need different evidence and sources. You may even need to delete a lot of what you have written so you can move away from a general summary and toward a specific critical analysis. Remember, too, that your conclusion should be specific to your main idea or research question. Currently, you end with a general concession that says something like "everyone has to make the decision for themselves about whether college is worth it." That sentiment could relate to all issues. Everyone has to make their own decisions about everything. What specific comments or ideas can you leave your reader with as you conclude the essay that relate directly to what you have discovered about the subject through the writing process?

Preparing to Revise

With the feedback from her classmate and her instructor in mind, the student returns to her outline and rewrites it as she prepares to deeply revise the essay. She also returns to the generating ideas stage where she notices she has a useful quote she can include in her revised outline and the essay.

REVISED OUTLINE

I. The College Degree
   A. Almost everyone goes to college now
   B. A college degree is like the new high school degree
   C. The value of a college degree is debatable
   D. We need to think about more than just the cost of college when determining the value of a college degree (my thesis)

II. College Is Very Expensive
   A. Increase in cost over the years
   B. Increase surpasses inflation
      From my initial research notes: "The cost of a higher education has more than doubled, when adjusted for inflation, since 1986 — faster than the cost of health care, and well ahead of the median family income," Arianna Skibell
   C. Recent student debt figures
   D. All kinds of people question whether the cost of college is worth it

III. Expanding the Conversation
   A. Cost is just one part of how you can judge the value of a college degree
   B. There are different values associated with different kinds of education
      1. Liberal arts education
         a. teaches you to become a lifelong learner
         b. teaches critical thinking
         c. teaches problem-solving
      2. Professionally focused education
         a. provides hands-on experience
         b. helps you make professional connections in your chosen industry
         c. allows you to focus only on the skills you need for your job

IV. Concluding Thoughts
   A. College is expensive but there are other ways to measure value
   B. Finish with a question that keeps my audience thinking about the complexity of the issue

Revising Deeply

The following revised essay shows what it looks like to really re-vise or re-see an essay in order to strengthen it. The essay also shows the *proofreading and editing* that the student completed during the final stages revision process.

Selena Jiménez
Professor Carillo
Writing 100
December 6, 2018

MEASURING THE VALUE OF COLLEGE

For many decades attending college was one of many paths someone could take on their way to a career. Now a college degree seems to be as necessary as a high school degree was decades ago. But, the value that one gets from that degree is debatable. Even with a college degree not everyone gets a job. Additionally, tuition is so expensive that many students find themselves in a lot of debt after graduation and wondering whether college was worth the cost. Although college is very expensive, measuring the value of college by focusing only on tuition and related costs oversimplifies this complicated issue.

It is very expensive to go to college. The tuition is the most expensive part of college, but there are also other costs like room and board, as well as the cost of textbooks. All of this adds up very quickly. Journalist Arianna Skibell explains just how expensive college has become: "The cost of a higher education has more than doubled, when adjusted for inflation, since 1986—faster than the cost of health care, and well ahead of the median family income." Because of these costs, the majority of students who graduate from college are faced with having to pay off huge amounts of debt. News Associate at CNBC Abigail Hess explains the situation: "Today, 70 percent of college students graduate with a significant amount of loans. Over 44 million Americans collectively hold nearly $1.5 trillion in student debt. That means that roughly one in four American adults are paying off student loans. When they graduate, the average

Jiménez 2

student loan borrower has $37,172 in student loans, a $20,000 increase from 13 years

ago." These numbers are﹎ because they provide insight into how widespread student
important

debt is, how deep the debt is, and how fast the amount of debt is growing.

　　The debt that graduates are in have caused them to think about whether their col-
has

lege educations were really worth it. Even those who have not attended college are

less convinced now they were years ago that getting a college degree is worth it. Josh
than

Mitchell and Douglas Belkin, writers for The Wall Street Journal report that Americans
Wall Street Journal should be in italics.

"are losing faith in the value of a college degree, with majorities of young adults, men

and rural residents saying college isn't worth the cost." The people who participated in

the survey conducted by the *Wall Street Journal* were divided when it came to the value

of a college degree. Forty-nine percent of those surveyed agreed with the statement that

a four-year degree "is worth the cost because people have a better chance to get a good

job and earn more money over their lifetime." Forty-seven percent said that a degree is

not worth its cost "because people often graduate without specific job skills and with

a large amount of debt to pay off." Even though the statements show that people are

almost split down the middle on whether a college degree is worth it, both groups focus

on the same aspect of the discussion: cost. The 49 percent that agreed that a four-year

degree "is worth the cost" said so because it allowed people to "earn more money" and

the forty seven percent that said the degree isn't worth it focused on the "large amount

of debt" graduates must pay off. Although the two groups disagree, they both narrowly

focus on the cost rather than considering other ways that college may be valued.

　　While the cost of college is an important part of the discussion about the value of a

college degree, it is just one part. It is necessary to look beyond cost and consider how

the value of college comes through in other ways. The value you can get from college

depends on the kind of college and the path each student chooses. Some colleges focus

on the liberal arts and offer students the opportunity to develop a broad knowledge base

and expose students to a wide range of disciplines. A liberal arts education does not neces-

sarily lead to a specific job, but it is said to lay the foundation for the kind of critical think-

ing, analytical, and problem-solving skills that students will need across careers (Anders).

Harvard Business Review should be in italics.

Journalist JM Olejarz of the Harvard Business Review reports that venture capitalist Scott Hartley values the liberal arts and "believes that this STEM-only mindset is all wrong. The main problem is that it encourages students to approach their education vocationally—to think just in terms of the jobs they're preparing for. But the barriers to entry for technical roles are dropping. Many tasks that once required specialized training can now be done with simple tools and the internet. . . . If we want to prepare students to solve large-scale human problems, Hartley argues, we must push them to widen, not narrow, their education and interests." Although Hartley admits that technical experts are needed, he maintains that "we also need people who grasp the whys and hows of human behavior." The value of a liberal arts degree, then, might be thought of in terms of its capacity to prepare students to "solve large-scale human problems" and to "grasp the whys and hows of human behavior," which are valuable skills across all careers and in life, more generally.

Hartley points out the benefits of a liberal arts education within the context of getting a job, but the value of this work goes beyond the job market. Former president of Oberlin College and current president of Pace University Marvin Krislov explains that a liberal arts education teaches students "to become lifelong learners who are their own best teachers. It enables them to take intellectual risks and to think laterally—to understand how the humanities, the arts and the sciences inform, enrich and affect one another. By connecting diverse ideas and themes across the academic disciplines, liberal arts students learn to better reason and analyze, and express their creativity and their ideas." Krislov even goes as far as describing a liberal arts degree as having "life-shaping power." This perspective shifts attention away from the cost of college and to how a particular kind of education can have lasting effects on students' lives.

The experiences that students have at more professionally-oriented colleges are meaningful, too. These students begin their studies in their chosen discipline and often have opportunities to get some hands-on experience through internship or cooperative (co-op) programs. At Drexel University, one of the nation's first cooperative education programs, "students can participate in up to three different co-ops, which equals 18 months of professional work." Drexel's website goes on to explain that "A Drexel Co-op

Jiménez 4

experience connects them with industry leaders and brings their cooperative education experiences back into the classroom. Because of this, Drexel students graduate having already built a professional network." The value of this kind of education comes from the experience that students can gain while they are in college. Students have the opportunity to work at different companies and organizations while going to school, allowing them to make connections in the professional world, which can lead to a job when they finish college. Students are also being directly educated in a specialized way that prepares them to immediately enter their chosen field, allowing them to focus all of *their* time and energy on developing the specific skill set they need.

While there are debates over whether a more "practical" education that leads directly to a specific job is more valuable than a liberal arts education, even just entertaining the differences between these kinds of educations show the different ways that a college degree can be valued. The issue of the value of a college degree is much more complicated than simply considering its cost. The discussion doesn't always have to revolve around the cost of tuition, and when it does it obscures the many other ways of valuing college and makes the issue seem simpler than it is. There is no denying that college is expensive, but with that expense come benefits like learning how to take intellectual risks and having the space to do so, learning how to become a more flexible and innovative thinker, as well as opportunities to make lasting professional connections in your chosen field. *Replace period with question mark.* How can you put a price tag on that.

Works Cited

Anders, George. *You Can Do Anything: The Surprising Power of a Useless Liberal Arts Education.* Little Brown & Co, 2017.

Drexel University. "Cooperative Education." http://drexel.edu/difference/co-op/. Accessed 8 May 2019.

Hess, Abigail. "Here's How Much the Average Student Loan Borrower Owes When They Graduate." *CNBC*, 15 Feb. 2018, https://www.cnbc.com/2018/02/15/heres-how-much-the-average-student-loan-borrower-owes-when-they-graduate.html.

Krislov, Marvin. "The Life-Shaping Power of a Liberal Arts Education." *Inside Higher Ed*, 6 Oct. 2017, https://www.insidehighered.com/views/2017/10/06/importance-liberal-arts-transforming-lives-essay.

Jiménez 5

Mitchell, Josh and Douglas Belkin. "Americans Losing Faith in College Degrees, Poll
    Finds." *Wall Street Journal*, 7 September 2017, https://www.wsj.com/articles
    /americans-losing-faith-in-college-degrees-poll-finds-1504776601.

Olejarz, J. M. "Liberal Arts in the Data Age." *Harvard Business Review*, July/Aug. 2017,
    https://hbr.org/2017/07/liberal-arts-in-the-data-age.

Skibell, Arianna. "Rising Costs Brings New Focus on How Exactly Colleges Set
    Their Prices." *The Hechinger Report*, 1 Feb. 2016, https://hechingerreport.org
    /rising-costs-brings-new-focus-on-how-exactly-colleges-set-their-prices/.

The recursivity of the writing process, as shown in this model student essay, exemplifies the habits of persistence and flexibility. As you move toward the final stages of the writing process, you may find, as did this student, that the best way to deeply revise is to revise an essay almost in its entirety. This will extend the time you will need to spend on your writing, and you'll need persistence to remain interested in and committed to your project. That persistence should be characterized by flexibility since the writing process requires a willingness to adapt your writing and thinking to reflect the feedback you have been given by your instructor and classmates, as evidenced by the model above.

ANALYZE & WRITE

1. In the model essay, where do you see the student practicing some of the habits of mind described in this chapter?

2. Find examples in the model essay where the student is practicing critical analysis and rhetorical sensitivity.

3. Compose a short response to this piece in which you practice empathy toward the student's perspective even if you disagree with it.

Having read this chapter, you are now ready to give your attention to all the strategies available to you to become a critical thinker, reader, and writer.

Sources for Texts on pp.5–11

Engel, Susan. "The Case for Curiosity." *Educational Leadership*, vol. 70, no. 5, Feb. 2013,
    pp. 36–40.

Greenman, Ben. "Online Curiosity Killer." *New York Times Magazine*, 16 Sept. 2010,
    https://www.nytimes.com/2010/09/19/magazine/19lives-t.html.

Livio, Mario. "Curious." *What Makes Us Curious?*, Simon and Schuster, 2017.

Shankar, Arjun, and Mariam Durrani. "Curiosity and Education: A White Paper."
    Center for Curiosity, http://centerforcuriosity.com/wp-content/uploads/bsk
    -pdf-manager/WhitePaper-CuriosityandEducation__2.pdf.

A Catalog of Reading Strategies

This chapter presents twenty strategies for reading critically that you can apply to the selections in this book as well as to your other college reading. Mastering these strategies will make reading much more satisfying and productive for you and help you handle difficult material with confidence.

As you read in depth about these strategies, pay attention to the purposes each strategy serves. Some strategies will help you understand the content of what you have read; others will help you understand how a text is organized; still others will help you place a text in its historical and cultural context. The reading strategies you choose should be connected to your purpose for reading. You will likely always need to understand what you have read, and many of these strategies will help you reach that goal. In particular, annotating, taking inventory, outlining, summarizing, and paraphrasing will support your comprehension. In addition to understanding what you have read, though, you may be expected to respond to it. To do so you might find that reflecting on how the text challenges your beliefs and values or recognizing how the text emotionally manipulates you are productive reading strategies that will allow you to compose that response. Alternatively, you may be asked to write an essay in which you compare and contrast two different texts. In that case, reading each text with the other text in mind — comparing and contrasting related readings — will be a productive route. In other instances, content may not matter as much as the writing techniques a writer uses. If your instructor expects you to imitate a writer's techniques or consider if you might use them in your own writing, then the "reading like a writer" strategy will be helpful.

- *Annotating:* Recording your reactions to, interpretations of, and questions about a text as you read it

- *Taking inventory:* Listing and grouping your annotations and other notes to find meaningful patterns

- *Outlining:* Listing the text's main ideas to reveal how it is organized

- *Mapping:* Visually representing specific aspects of a text in order to reveal connections among its ideas
- *Summarizing:* Distilling the main ideas or gist of a text
- *Paraphrasing:* Restating what you have read to clarify or refer to it
- *Skimming:* Quickly reading only certain portions of a text
- *Synthesizing:* Integrating into your own writing ideas and information gleaned from different sources
- *Analyzing assumptions:* Examining the values and beliefs that underlie the text, either stated directly or implied in the text's word choices
- *Contextualizing:* Placing a text in its historical and cultural context
- *Exploring the significance of figurative language:* Examining how metaphors, similes, and symbols are used in a text to convey meaning and evoke feelings
- *Analyzing visuals:* Thinking about how visual images add meaning to a text
- *Looking for patterns of opposition:* Inferring the values and assumptions embodied in the language of a text
- *Reflecting on challenges to your beliefs and values:* Examining the bases of your personal responses to a text
- *Comparing and contrasting related readings:* Exploring likenesses and differences between texts to understand them better
- *Evaluating the logic of an argument:* Determining whether an argument is well reasoned and adequately supported
- *Recognizing logical fallacies:* Looking for errors in reasoning
- *Recognizing emotional manipulation:* Identifying texts that unfairly and inappropriately use emotional appeals based on false or exaggerated claims
- *Judging the writer's credibility:* Considering whether writers represent different points of view fairly and know what they are writing about
- *Reading like a writer:* Noticing the different writing techniques an author uses in order to possibly incorporate these techniques into your own writing

ANNOTATING

Annotations are the marks — underlines, highlights, and comments — you make directly on the page as you read. Annotating can be used to record immediate reactions and questions, outline and summarize main points, and evaluate and relate the reading to other ideas and points of view.

Your annotations can take many forms, such as the following:

- Writing comments, questions, or definitions in the margins; or using comment balloons in a digital space

- Underlining, highlighting, or circling important or questionable words, phrases, or sentences

- Connecting similar or opposing ideas with lines or arrows

- Numbering related points

- Bracketing sections of the text

- Noting anything that strikes you as interesting, important, or questionable

Depending on their purpose for reading, most readers annotate in layers, adding annotations as they think about the ideas and reread key passages.

The following selection, excerpted from Martin Luther King Jr.'s "Letter from Birmingham Jail," illustrates some of the ways you can annotate as you read. Add your own annotations, if you like.

Martin Luther King Jr.

An Annotated Sample from "Letter from Birmingham Jail"

Martin Luther King Jr. (1929–1968) first came to national notice in 1955, when he led a successful boycott against the policy of restricting African American passengers to rear seats on city buses in Montgomery, Alabama, where he was minister of a Baptist church. He subsequently formed the Southern Christian Leadership Conference, which brought people of all races from all over the country to the South to fight nonviolently for racial integration. In 1963, King led demonstrations in Birmingham, Alabama, that were met with violence; a bomb was detonated in an African American church, killing four young girls. King was arrested for his role in organizing the protests, and while in prison, he wrote his "Letter from Birmingham Jail" to justify his strategy of civil disobedience, which he called "nonviolent direct action."

King begins his letter by discussing his disappointment with the lack of support he has received from white moderates, such as the group of clergy who published criticism of his organization in the local newspaper.

- **As you read,** try to infer what the clergy's specific criticisms might have been.

- Notice the tone King uses. Would you characterize the writing as apologetic, conciliatory, accusatory, or something else?

1 I must confess that over the past few years I have been gravely disappointed with the white moderate. I have almost reached the regrettable conclusion that the Negro's [great stumbling block in his stride toward freedom] is not the White Citizen's Counciler or the Ku Klux Klanner, but the white moderate, who is more devoted to "order" than to justice; who prefers a negative peace which is the absence of tension to a positive peace which is the presence of justice; who constantly says: "I agree with you in the goal you seek, but I cannot agree with your methods of direct action"; who paternalistically believes he can set the timetable for another man's freedom; who lives by a mythical concept of time and who constantly advises the Negro to wait for a "more convenient season." Shallow understanding from people of good will is more frustrating than absolute misunderstanding from people of ill will. Lukewarm acceptance is much more bewildering than outright rejection.

> Main point: White moderates block progress.
>
> Contrasts: order vs. justice, negative vs. positive peace, goals vs. methods
>
> (definition: treating others like children)
>
> more contrasts

2   I had hoped that the white moderate would understand that law and order exist for the purpose of establishing justice and that when they fail in this purpose they become the [dangerously structured dams that block the flow of social progress.] I had hoped that the white moderate would understand that the present tension in the South is a necessary phase of the transition from an [obnoxious negative peace,] in which the Negro passively accepted his unjust plight, to a [substantive and positive peace,] in which all men will respect the dignity and worth of human personality. Actually, we who engage in nonviolent direct action are not the creators of tension. We merely bring to the surface the hidden tension that is already alive. We bring it out in the open, where it can be seen and dealt with. [Like a boil that can never be cured so long as it is covered up but must be opened with all its ugliness to the natural medicines of air and light, injustice must be exposed, with all the tension its exposure creates, to the light of human conscience and the air of national opinion before it can be cured.]

> Main point: What the moderates don't understand
>
> metaphor: law and order = dams (faulty?)
>
> repeats contrast (negative/positive)
>
> Tension already exists: We help dispel it. (True?)
>
> simile: hidden tension is "like a boil"

3   In your statement you assert that our actions, even though peaceful, must be condemned because they precipitate violence. But is this a logical assertion? Isn't this like condemning a robbed man because his possession of money precipitated the evil act of robbery? Isn't this like condemning Socrates because his unswerving commitment to truth and his philosophical inquiries precipitated the act by the misguided populace in which they made him drink hemlock? Isn't this like condemning Jesus because his unique God-consciousness and never-ceasing devotion to God's will precipitated the evil act of crucifixion? We must come to see that, as the federal courts have consistently affirmed, it is wrong to urge an individual to cease his efforts to gain his basic constitutional rights because the question may precipitate violence. [Society must protect the robbed and punish the robber.]

> Main point: Questions clergymen's logic: condemning his actions = condemning robbery victim, Socrates, Jesus.
>
> repetition ("Isn't this like . . .")
>
> (Yes!)

4   I had also hoped that the white moderate would reject the myth concerning time in relation to the struggle for freedom. I have just received

example of a white moderate's view

a letter from a white brother in Texas. He writes: "All Christians know that the colored people will receive equal rights eventually, but it is possible that you are in too great a religious hurry. It has taken Christianity almost two thousand years to accomplish what it has. The teachings of Christ take time to come to earth." Such an attitude stems from a tragic misconception of time, from the strangely irrational notion that there is something in

Main point: Time must be used to do right.

the very flow of time that will inevitably cure all ills. Actually, time itself is neutral; it can be used either destructively or constructively. More and more I feel that the people of ill will have used time much more effectively than have the people of good will. We will have to repent in this gener-

Silence/passivity is as bad as hateful words and actions.

ation not merely for the [hateful words and actions of the bad people] but for the [appalling silence of the good people.] Human progress never rolls in on [wheels of inevitability;] it comes through the tireless efforts of men willing to be co-workers with God, and without this hard work, time

metaphor (mechanical?)

(stop developing)

itself becomes an ally of the forces of social stagnation. [We must use time creatively,] in the knowledge that the time is always ripe to do right.]

metaphors (song, natural world)

Now is the time to make real the promise of democracy and transform our pending [national elegy] into a creative [psalm of brotherhood.] Now is the time to lift our national policy from the [quicksand of racial injustice] to the [solid rock of human dignity.]

King accused of being an extremist.

You speak of our activity in Birmingham as extreme. At first I was rather 5 disappointed that fellow clergymen would see my nonviolent efforts as those of an extremist. I began thinking about the fact that I stand in the

Main point: Puts self in middle of two extremes: complacency and bitterness.

middle of two opposing forces in the Negro community. One is a [force of complacency,] made up in part of Negroes who, as a result of long years of oppression, are so drained of self-respect and a sense of "somebodiness" that they have adjusted to segregation; and in part of a few middle-class Negroes, who because of a degree of academic and economic security and because in some ways they profit by segregation, have become insensitive to the problems of the masses. The other [force is one of bitterness and hatred,] and it comes perilously close to advocating violence. It is expressed in the various black nationalist [groups that are springing up] across the nation, the largest and best-known being Elijah Muhammad's

Malcolm X?

Muslim movement. Nourished by the Negro's frustration over the continued existence of racial discrimination, this movement is made up of people who have lost faith in America, who have absolutely repudiated Christianity, and who have concluded that the white man is an incorrigible "devil."

Main point: Offers better choice: nonviolent protest.

I have tried to stand between these two forces, saying that we need 6 emulate neither the "do-nothingism" of the complacent nor the hatred and despair of the black nationalist. For there is the more excellent way of love

(How did nonviolence become part of King's movement?)

and nonviolent protest. I am grateful to God that, through the influence of the Negro church, the way of nonviolence became an integral part of our struggle.

7   If this philosophy had not emerged, by now many streets of the South would, I am convinced, be flowing with blood. And I am further convinced that if our white brothers dismiss as "rabble-rousers" and "outside agitators" those of us who employ nonviolent direct action, and if they refuse to support our nonviolent efforts, millions of Negroes will, out of frustration and despair, seek solace and security in black-nationalist ideologies—a development that would inevitably lead to a frightening racial nightmare.

Main point: Says movement prevents racial violence. (Threat?)

(comfort)

8   Oppressed people cannot remain oppressed forever. The yearning for freedom eventually manifests itself, and that is what has happened to the American Negro. Something within has reminded him of his birthright of freedom, and something without has reminded him that it can be gained. Consciously or unconsciously, he has been caught up by the Zeitgeist, and with his black brothers of Africa and his brown and yellow brothers of Asia, South America and the Caribbean, the United States Negro is moving with a sense of great urgency toward the [promised land of racial justice.] If one recognizes this [vital urge that has engulfed the Negro community,] one should readily understand why public demonstrations are taking place. The Negro has many [pent-up resentments] and latent frustrations, and he must release them. So let him march; let him make prayer pilgrimages to the city hall; let him go on freedom rides—and try to understand why he must do so. If his repressed emotions are not released in nonviolent ways, they will seek expression through violence; this is not a threat but a fact of history. So I have not said to my people: "Get rid of your discontent." Rather, I have tried to say that this normal and healthy discontent can be [channeled into the creative outlet of nonviolent direct action.] And now this approach is being termed extremist.

(spirit of the times)

Not a threat

Main point: Discontent is normal, healthy, and historically inevitable, but it must be channeled.

9   But though I was initially disappointed at being categorized as an extremist, as I continued to think about the matter I gradually gained a measure of satisfaction from the label. Was not Jesus an extremist for love: "Love your enemies, bless them that curse you, do good to them that hate you, and pray for them which despitefully use you, and persecute you." Was not Amos an extremist for justice: "Let justice roll down like waters and righteousness like an ever-flowing stream." Was not Paul an extremist for the Christian gospel: "I bear in my body the marks of the Lord Jesus." Was not Martin Luther an extremist: "Here I stand; I cannot do otherwise, so help me God." And John Bunyan: "I will stay in jail to the end of my days before I make a butchery of my conscience." And Abraham Lincoln: "This nation cannot survive half slave and half free." And Thomas Jefferson: "We hold these truths to be self-evident, that all men are created equal. . . ." So the question is not whether we will be extremists, but what kind of extremists we will be. Will we be extremists for hate or for love? Will we be extremists for the preservation of injustice or for the extension of justice? In that dramatic scene on Calvary's hill three men were crucified.

Main point: Redefines "extremism," embraces "extremist" label.

(Hebrew prophet)
(Christian apostle)
(founder of Protestantism)

(English preacher)

Compares self to great "extremists" — including Jesus.

We must never forget that all three were crucified for the same crime—the crime of extremism. Two were extremists for immorality, and thus fell below their environment. The other, Jesus Christ, was an extremist for love, truth and goodness, and thereby rose above his environment. Perhaps the South, the nation and the world are in dire need of creative extremists.

I had hoped that the white moderate would see this need. Perhaps I 10 was too optimistic; perhaps I expected too much. I suppose I should have realized that few members of the oppressor race can understand the deep groans and passionate yearnings of the oppressed race, and still fewer have the vision to see that [injustice must be rooted out] by strong, persistent and determined action. I am thankful, however, that some of our white brothers in the South have grasped the meaning of this social revolution and committed themselves to it. They are still all too few in quantity, but they are big in quality. Some—such as Ralph McGill, Lillian Smith, Harry Golden, James McBride Dabbs, Ann Braden and Sarah Patton Boyle—have written about our struggle in eloquent and prophetic terms. Others have marched with us down nameless streets of the South. They have languished in filthy, roach-infested jails, suffering the abuse and brutality of policemen who view them as "dirty nigger-lovers." Unlike so many of their moderate brothers and sisters, they have recognized the urgency of the moment and sensed the need for [powerful "action" antidotes] to combat the [disease of segregation.]

Margin notes:
Disappointed in the white moderate

Main point: Praises whites who have supported movement.

(Who are they?)

(been left unaided)

Metaphor: segregation is a disease.

CHECKLIST: Annotating

1. Mark the text—for example, circling words to be defined in the margin, underlining key words and phrases, or using arrows to connect related ideas.

2. Write marginal comments—for example, numbering and labeling main ideas, defining unfamiliar words, and noting your responses and questions.

3. Layer additional markings in the text and comments and questions in the margins as you reread.

TAKING INVENTORY

Taking inventory helps you analyze your annotations for different purposes. When you take inventory, you make various kinds of lists to explore patterns of meaning you find in the text. For instance, in reading the annotated passage by Martin Luther King Jr., you might have noticed that certain similes and metaphors are used or that many famous people are named. By listing the names (Socrates, Jesus, Luther, Lincoln, and so on) and then grouping them into categories (people who died for their beliefs, leaders, teachers, and religious figures), you could better understand why the writer refers to these particular people. Taking inventory of your annotations can be helpful if you plan to write about a text you are reading.

CHECKLIST: Taking Inventory

1. Examine the annotations you made for patterns, such as recurring images, repeated words and phrases, related examples or illustrations, and reliance on particular writing strategies.

2. List the items that make up a pattern.

3. Decide what the pattern might reveal about the reading.

OUTLINING

Outlining, which identifies a text's main ideas, is an especially helpful reading strategy for understanding the content and structure of a reading. The key to outlining is distinguishing between the main ideas and the supporting materials, such as reasons, examples, and quotations. You may make either an informal scratch outline or a more formal, multilevel outline. You can easily make a scratch outline summarizing the main idea of each paragraph (as in the marginal annotations on the King excerpt on pp. 36–40 that are collected in the scratch outline example below). Or, if you need to analyze a section of a text to write about it, you can take the time to make a formal outline (like the one below, which outlines part of King's essay).

Scratch outline of "Letter from Birmingham Jail"

Paragraph   1. White moderates block progress

Paragraph   2. What the moderates don't understand

Paragraph   3. Questions clergymen's logic

Paragraph   4. Time must be used to do right

Paragraph   5. Puts self in middle of two extremes: complacency and bitterness

Paragraph   6. Offers better choice: nonviolent protest

Paragraph   7. Says movement prevents racial violence

Paragraph   8. Discontent is normal, healthy, and historically inevitable, but it must be channeled

Paragraph   9. Redefines "extremism," embraces "extremist" label

Paragraph 10. Praises whites who have supported movement

Formal outline of "Letter from Birmingham Jail" (pars. 5–9)

I. Contrary to white moderates' claims, King's civil rights movement is not "extremist" in the usual sense.
   A. It stands between the extremes of passivity and radicalism in the African American community (pars. 5–6).
      1. Passivity illustrated by the oppressed and the self-interested middle class
      2. Violent radicalism illustrated in Elijah Muhammad's followers
   B. In its advocacy of love and nonviolent protest, the movement has forestalled bloodshed and kept more African Americans from joining radicals (pars. 5–7).
   C. The movement helps African Americans channel the urge for freedom that's part of the historical trend and the prevailing *Zeitgeist* (par. 8).
II. The movement can be defined as extremist if the term is redefined: "Creative extremism" is extremism in the service of love, truth, and goodness.
   A. Biblical examples including Amos, Paul, and Jesus (par. 9)
   B. Historical examples including Luther, Bunyan, Lincoln, and Jefferson (par. 9)

CHECKLIST: Outlining

To make a scratch outline of a text:

1. Reread each paragraph, summarizing the main idea or topic of the paragraph. Do not include examples, quotations, or other supporting material.

2. Your scratch outline can be part of your annotations on the text itself or collected on a separate piece of paper or in a file for later reference.

To make a formal outline of a text:

1. Decide what portion of the text you want to analyze closely.

2. Use capital Roman numerals (I, II, III) to identify the main ideas or topics.

3. Use letters (A, B, C) and Arabic numerals (1, 2, 3) to indicate the supporting ideas, examples, comparisons, and such.

MAPPING

See Chapter 1, "Idea Mapping," pp. 22–25.

Creating a map allows readers to see more clearly the connections among the ideas in a text. You may recall that in Chapter 1 the sample student essay was preceded by a map that the student developed to help organize her essay. Whether used as a writing or reading strategy, maps serve largely the same purpose — they reveal in a visual format the organization of the text, which allows you to see how ideas are related. You can draw a map by hand or use the mapping features in word-processing programs or apps. Maps can be drawn in various ways depending on your text, what you would like to represent, and your needs as a reader. A map may have one central idea with threads containing supporting ideas radiating from that central idea, or a map may be composed of different clusters, as in the example below, in order to reveal the range of relationships among the ideas, details, examples, and facts in a text.

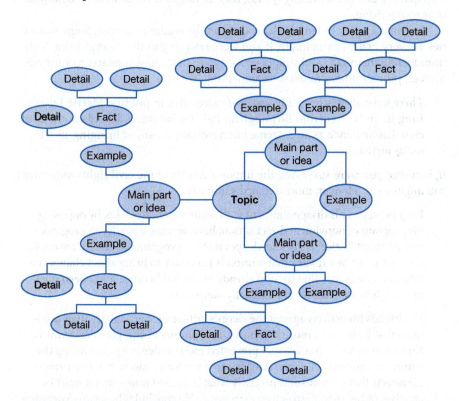

CHECKLIST: Mapping

1. Write the subject of the reading in the center of a piece of paper. Circle it.

2. Write down the main parts or ideas of the subject. Circle these, and connect them with lines to the subject in the center.

3. Write down facts, details, and examples related to these main parts or ideas. Circle these, and connect them with lines to the relevant main parts or ideas.

4. Don't be afraid to draft several maps before finding one that fits your needs as a reader. You may need to discard some maps along the way, too.

SUMMARIZING

For more
information
on integrating
sources
responsibly,
see Chapter 12,
pp. 615–626.

A **summary** is a relatively brief restatement, primarily in the reader's own words, of the reading's main ideas. Summarizing helps you understand and remember what is most significant in a reading, and it is one of the main strategies, along with quoting and paraphrasing (p. 45), used to integrate other writers' ideas into your own writing.

Summaries vary in length, depending on the reader's purpose. Some summaries are very brief. For example, if you were referring to the excerpt from "Letter from Birmingham Jail" and simply needed to indicate how it relates to your other sources, your summary might look something like this:

> There have always been advocates of extremism in politics. Martin Luther King Jr., in "Letter from Birmingham Jail," for instance, defends nonviolent civil disobedience as an extreme but necessary means of bringing about racial justice.

If, however, you were surveying the important texts of the civil rights movement, you might write a longer, more detailed summary:

> King expresses his disappointment with white moderates who, by opposing his program of nonviolent direct action, have become a barrier to progress toward racial justice. He acknowledges that his program has raised tension in the South, but he explains that tension is necessary to bring about change. Furthermore, he argues that tension already exists, but because it has been unexpressed, it is unhealthy and potentially dangerous.
>
> He defends his actions against the clergy's criticisms, particularly their argument that he is in too much of a hurry. Responding to charges of extremism, King claims that he has actually prevented racial violence by channeling the natural frustrations of oppressed African Americans into nonviolent protest. He asserts that extremism is precisely what is needed now — but it must be creative, rather than destructive, extremism. He concludes by again expressing disappointment with white moderates for not joining his effort as some other whites have.

In composing an extended summary, writers usually find it useful to outline the reading as a preliminary step to writing a summary. A paragraph-by-paragraph scratch outline (like the one on p. 41) lists the reading's main ideas in the sequence in which they appear in the original. But summarizing requires more than merely stringing together the entries in an outline; it must fill in the logical connections between the author's ideas. Notice also in the preceding example that the reader repeats selected words and phrases and refers to the author by name, indicating, with verbs like *expresses, acknowledges,* and *explains,* the writer's purpose and strategy at each point in the argument.

CHECKLIST: Summarizing

1. Make a scratch outline.

2. Write a paragraph or more that presents the author's main ideas largely in your own words. Use the outline as a guide, but reread parts of the original text as necessary.

3. To make the summary coherent, fill in connections between the ideas you present.

PARAPHRASING

Paraphrasing is restating a text by using mostly your own words. It can help you clarify the meaning of an obscure or ambiguous passage. It is one of the three ways of integrating other people's ideas and information into your own writing, along with **quoting** (reproducing exactly the language of the source text) and **summarizing** (distilling the main ideas or gist of the source text). You might choose to paraphrase rather than quote when the source's language is not especially arresting or memorable. You might paraphrase short passages but summarize longer ones.

Following are two passages. The first is from paragraph 2 of the excerpt from King's "Letter." The second passage is a paraphrase of the first:

Original

I had hoped that the white moderate would understand that law and order exist for the purpose of establishing justice and that when they fail in this purpose they become the dangerously structured dams that block the flow of social progress. I had hoped that the white moderate would understand that the present tension in the South is a necessary phase of the transition from an obnoxious negative peace, in which the Negro passively accepted his unjust plight, to a substantive and positive peace, in which all men will respect the dignity and worth of human personality.

Paraphrase

King writes that he had hoped for more understanding from white moderates — specifically that they would recognize that law and order are not ends in themselves but means to the greater end of establishing justice. When law and order do not serve this greater end, they stand in the way of progress. King expected the white moderate to recognize that the current tense situation in the South is part of a transition process that is necessary for progress. The current situation is bad because although there is peace, it is an "obnoxious" and "negative" kind of peace based on African Americans passively accepting the injustice of the status quo. A better kind of peace — one that is "substantive," real and not imaginary, as well as "positive" — requires that all people, regardless of race, be valued.

When you compare the paraphrase to the original, you can see that the paraphrase contains all the important information and ideas of the original. Notice also that the paraphrase is somewhat longer than the original (which is not always the case), refers to the writer by name, and encloses King's original words in quotation marks. The paraphrase tries to be neutral, to avoid inserting the reader's opinions or distorting the original writer's ideas.

CHECKLIST: Paraphrasing

1. Reread the passage, looking up unfamiliar words.

2. Translate the passage into your own words and sentences, putting quotation marks around any words or phrases you quote from the original.

3. Revise to ensure coherence.

SKIMMING

Skimming, or skim reading, involves quickly reading only portions of a text. When you skim, you jump around and quickly read some sentences in a text, skipping many others and sometimes skipping entire sections of a text. This reading strategy should sound familiar; perhaps you skim your social media feeds, news headlines, or even this book in this way. According to researchers, skim reading has become the "new norm" because screen reading, which encourages skimming, has affected how we read everything. While skimming does not allow for deep engagement with texts and, therefore, is inappropriate for certain academic tasks, it does have its uses.

For an essay on skim reading, see Chapter 10, pp. 476–478.

As the introduction to this chapter explains, the reading strategy you choose must depend on your purpose for reading. Skimming will not help you understand a text as do some of the other strategies that encourage slower, closer, and deeper reading. But, if you are in the early stages of conducting research and looking for sources relevant to your topic, skimming potential sources will help you determine whether those sources are relevant. For example, skimming a source's abstract, table of contents, introduction, or conclusion to get the gist of what the source is about, identifying potentially relevant areas, and then jumping from one section to the next quickly to see if it is relevant to your topic will be a much better use of your time than closely reading dozens of sources just to eliminate many of them as irrelevant. For example, if you were writing about civil rights activists, and particularly how they define peace, then King's "Letter from Birmingham Jail" might be a text worth skimming. Skimming the first paragraph would show that King defines two kinds of peace — positive peace and negative peace. From there you would skim the rest of the letter to see if King develops those ideas further. If working with a searchable digital text, a word or phrase search is also effective and can save time; however, it can overlook relevant information if the precise word you search isn't used. Skimming texts in these ways provides you with an initial sense of the text, whether it is relevant to your topic, and if it is worth returning to later to reread in deeper ways. Beyond using skimming in the early stages of a research-driven project, skimming can be a productive strategy if you are not expected to engage deeply with a text, but merely need to be able to speak to the gist of it. Otherwise, skimming is best used in combination with other reading strategies.

CHECKLIST: Skimming

1. Notice the text's title and author.

2. Read any introductory material such as a table of contents, introduction, or abstract.

3. Read the first sentence, and perhaps last sentence, of each paragraph.

4. Read the final paragraph or conclusion.

5. Take note of any promising sources you come across as you skim to investigate later.

SYNTHESIZING

Synthesizing involves presenting ideas and information gleaned from different sources. It can help you see how different sources relate to one another. For example, one reading may provide information that fills out the information in another reading, or a reading could present arguments that challenge arguments in another reading.

When you synthesize material from different sources, you construct a conversation among your sources, a conversation in which you also participate. Synthesizing is especially productive when writers use sources, as it can help not only to support their ideas, but to challenge and extend them as well.

In the following example, the reader uses a variety of sources related to the King passage (pp. 36–40) and brings them together around a central idea. Notice how multiple reading strategies — quotation, paraphrase, and summary — are all used.

Synthesis

When King defends his campaign of nonviolent direct action against the clergymen's criticism that "our actions, even though peaceful, must be condemned because they precipitate violence" (King excerpt, par. 3), he is using what Vinit Haksar calls Mohandas Gandhi's "safety-valve argument" ("Civil Disobedience and Non-Cooperation" 117). According to Haksar, Gandhi gave a "non-threatening warning of worse things to come" if his demands were not met. King similarly makes clear that advocates of actions more extreme than those he advocates are waiting in the wings: "The other force is one of bitterness and hatred, and it comes perilously close to advocating violence" (King excerpt, par. 5). King identifies this force with Elijah Muhammad, and although he does not name him, King's contemporary readers would have known that he was referring also to his disciple Malcolm X, who, according to Herbert J. Storing, "urged that Negroes take seriously the idea of revolution" ("The Case against Civil Disobedience" 90). In fact, Malcolm X accused King of being a modern-day Uncle Tom, trying "to keep us under control, to keep us passive and peaceful and nonviolent" (*Malcolm X Speaks* 12).

CHECKLIST: Synthesizing

1. Find and read a variety of sources on your topic, annotating the passages that give you ideas about the topic.

2. Look for patterns among your sources, possibly supporting or challenging your ideas or those of other sources.

3. Write a paragraph or more synthesizing your sources, using quotation, paraphrase, and summary to present what they say on the topic.

ANALYZING ASSUMPTIONS

Analyzing assumptions involves examining a reading closely to uncover the ideas, beliefs, and values that are taken for granted and assumed to be commonly accepted truths. The assumptions in a text usually reflect the writer's own attitudes or cultural traditions, but they may also represent the views of the writer's sources. Neither good nor bad in themselves, assumptions are often used to make claims and arguments that seem logical, even factual, but may actually be problematic and need to be looked at with a critical eye. Reading to analyze assumptions asks you to uncover these perspectives as well as to probe your own. Sometimes assumptions in a text are stated explicitly, but often they are only implied or hinted at through the writer's choice of words or examples.

For example, Martin Luther King Jr., in paragraph 4 of the excerpt from "Letter from Birmingham Jail" (pp. 36–40), analyzes an assumption in a letter he received. The letter writer criticizes King's civil rights movement for being impatient. According to King, the writer's idea that "the very flow of time . . . will inevitably cure all ills" represents an "attitude" and "irrational notion" that "stems from a tragic misconception of time."

King counters this assumption about time's curative power with his own assumptions about time and progress:

- "Actually, time itself is neutral."

- What counts is whether time is "used . . . destructively or constructively."

- "Human progress never rolls in on wheels of inevitability; it comes through the tireless efforts of men."

- "Now is the time."

Instead of the progress narrative believed by people with good intentions, like the letter writer, King posits an alternative worldview that requires people of goodwill to act as "co-workers with God," and not to wait and expect time to solve problems. King's assumptions lead him to the logical conclusion that failing to act or speak out against injustice is a sin of omission as surely as the sin of commission made by those who use "hateful words and actions" to disrupt progress.

Identifying assumptions in a reading can be challenging. Here are some suggestions that may help:

- Look for questionable assertions of fact, such as claims without proper support.

- Think about the key terms and their assumed definitions or connotations, the cultural assumptions underlying the way things are defined and categorized.

- Examine examples to see what values and beliefs they assume.

- Distinguish what is considered *normal* as opposed to abnormal, unconventional, strange, or deviant.

- Recognize stereotypes, prejudices, preconceptions, preferences, and speculations.

- Be alert to the writer's tone to identify the attitude (for example, dismissive, admiring, pedantic, flippant) toward the subject, sources, and audience.

Then, choose an assumption (or set of assumptions) you think plays an important role in the reading, and use these questions to think about its **rhetoric** — how it tries to achieve its purpose with the audience:

1. What is the effect of the assumption and whose interests does the assumption serve?

2. How does the assumption reinforce or critique commonly held views?

3. What alternative ideas, beliefs, or values could be used to challenge this assumption?

CHECKLIST: Analyzing Assumptions

1. Identify any assumptions — ideas, beliefs, or values — in the reading that seem problematic.

2. Choose one assumption (or set of assumptions) that plays an important role in the reading to analyze in depth.

3. Analyze how the assumption (or set of assumptions) works both in the context of the reading and in society more generally.

CONTEXTUALIZING

Contextualizing is a critical reading strategy that enables you to make inferences about a reading's historical and cultural context and to examine the differences between its context and your own.

The excerpt from King's "Letter from Birmingham Jail" is a good example of a text that benefits from being read contextually. If you knew little about the history of slavery and segregation in the United States, it would be difficult to understand the passion expressed in this passage. To understand the historical and cultural context in which King wrote his "Letter from Birmingham Jail," you could do some research on the subject. Comparing the situation at the time to situations with which you are familiar would help you understand some of your own attitudes toward King and the civil rights movement.

Notes from a contextualized reading

1. I have seen documentaries showing civil rights demonstrators being attacked by dogs, doused by fire hoses, beaten and dragged by helmeted police. Such images give me a sense of the violence, fear, and hatred that King was responding to.

   The creative tension King refers to comes across in his writing. He uses his anger and frustration to inspire his critics. He also threatens them, although he denies it. I saw a film on Malcolm X, so I could see that King was giving white people a choice between his own nonviolent way and Malcolm's more confrontational way.

2. Things have certainly changed since the 1960s. When I read King's "Letter" today, I feel like I'm reading history. But too frequently today, there are reports of police brutality and hate crimes.

> ## CHECKLIST: Contextualizing
>
> 1. Describe the historical and cultural situation as it is represented in the reading and in other sources with which you are familiar. Your knowledge may come from other reading, television or film, school, or research.
>
> 2. Compare the historical and cultural situation in which the text was written with your own historical and cultural situation. Consider how your understanding and judgment of the reading are affected by your own context.

EXPLORING THE SIGNIFICANCE OF FIGURATIVE LANGUAGE

Figurative language — metaphor, simile, and symbolism — enhances literal meaning by implying abstract ideas through vivid images and by evoking feelings and associations.

Metaphor implicitly compares two different things by identifying them with each other. For instance, when King calls the white moderate "the Negro's great stumbling block in his stride toward freedom" (par. 1), he does not mean that the white moderate literally trips the Negro who is attempting to walk toward freedom. The sentence makes sense only if understood figuratively: The white moderate trips up the Negro by frustrating every effort to achieve justice.

Simile, a more explicit form of comparison, uses the word *like* or *as* to signal the relationship of two seemingly unrelated things. King uses simile when he says that injustice is "[l]ike a boil that can never be cured so long as it is covered up" (par. 2). This simile suggests that injustice is a disease of society as a boil is a disease of the skin, and that injustice, like a boil, must be exposed or it will fester and infect the entire body.

Symbolism compares two things by making one stand for the other. King uses the white moderate as a symbol for supposed liberals and would-be supporters of civil rights who are actually frustrating the cause.

How these figures of speech are used in a text reveals something of the writer's feelings about the subject. Exploring possible meanings in a text's figurative language involves (1) annotating (as on the King essay on pp. 36–40) some of the metaphors, similes, and symbols you find in a reading; (2) grouping and labeling the figures of speech that appear to express related feelings or attitudes; and (3) writing to explore the meaning of the patterns you have found.

Grouping and labeling figures of speech

Sickness: "like a boil" (par. 2); "the disease of segregation" (par. 10)

Underground: "hidden tension" (par. 2); "injustice must be exposed" (par. 2); "injustice must be rooted out" (par. 10)

Blockage: "dams," "block the flow" (par. 2); "Human progress never rolls in on wheels of inevitability" (par. 4); "pent-up resentments," "repressed emotions" (par. 8)

Writing to explore meaning

The patterns labeled *underground* and *blockage* suggest a feeling of frustration. Inertia is a problem; movement forward toward progress or upward toward the promised land is stalled.

The simile of injustice being "like a boil" links the two patterns of underground and sickness, suggesting that a "disease" is inside the people or the society. The cure is to root out the blocked hatred and injustice as well as to release the tension or emotion that has long been repressed.

CHECKLIST: Exploring the Significance of Figurative Language

1. Annotate the figures of speech you find worth examining.

2. Group the figures of speech that appear to express related feelings and attitudes, and label each group.

3. Write one or two paragraphs exploring the meaning of the patterns you have found.

ANALYZING VISUALS

Visuals invite analysis both of their key components and their *rhetorical context*. As we "read" a visual, therefore, we should ask ourselves a series of questions: What image does the visual portray? Who created it? What *audience* is it addressing? What is it trying to get this audience to think and feel about the subject? How does it attempt to achieve this *purpose?*

Look, for example, at the visual to the right: a public service announcement (PSA) from the World Wildlife Fund (WWF). The central image in this PSA is a photo of an attractive, smiling young couple. Most of us will immediately recognize the dress, posture, and facial expressions of the young man and woman as those of a newly married couple. However, we are immediately struck by the feeling that something is wrong with the picture: a hurricane rages in the background, blowing hair and clothing, and threatening to rip the bouquet from the bride's hand.

So what do we make of the disruption of the convention (the traditional wedding photo) on which the PSA image is based? The text below the image delivers the message: "Ignoring global warming won't make it go away." The disjunction between the couple's blissful expression and the storm raging around them turns out to be the point of the PSA: Like the young couple in the picture, the PSA implies, we are all blithely ignoring the impending disaster that global warming represents. The reputable, nonprofit

FIGURE 2.1 "Wedding," from the WWF's "Beautiful Day U.S." Series

WWF's logo and URL, which constitute its "signature," are meant to be an assurance that this threat is real, and not just an idea a profit-seeking ad agency dreamt up to manipulate us.

Criteria for Analyzing Visuals

Key Components

Composition

- Of what elements is the visual composed?

- What is the focal point — that is, the place your eyes are drawn to?

- From what perspective do you view the focal point? Are you looking straight ahead at it, down at it, or up at it? If the visual is a photograph, what angle was the image shot from — straight ahead, looking down or up?

- What colors are used? Are there obvious special effects employed? Is there a frame, or are there any additional graphical elements? If so, what do these elements contribute to your "reading" of the visual?

(continued)

People/Other Main Figures

- If people are depicted, how would you describe their age, gender, subculture, ethnicity, profession, and socioeconomic class? How stereotypical or surprising are the people?

- Who is looking at whom? Do the people represented seem conscious of the viewer's gaze?

- What do the facial expressions and body language tell you about power relationships (equal, subordinate, in charge) and attitudes (self-confident, vulnerable, anxious, subservient, angry, aggressive, sad)?

Scene

- If a recognizable scene is depicted, what is its setting? What is in the background and the foreground?

- What has happened just before the image was "shot"? What will happen in the next scene?

- What, if anything, is happening just outside the visual frame?

Words

- If text is combined with the visual, what role does the text play? Is it a slogan? A famous quote? Lyrics from a well-known song?

- If the text helps you interpret the visual's overall meaning, what interpretive clues does it provide?

Tone

- What tone, or mood, does the visual convey? Is it lighthearted, somber, frightening, shocking, joyful? What elements in the visual (color, composition, words, people, setting) convey this tone?

- What is the tone of the text? Humorous? Serious? Ironic?

Context(s)

Rhetorical Context

- **What is the visual's main purpose?** Are we being asked to buy a product? Form an opinion or judgment about something? Support a political party's candidate? Take some other kind of action?

- **Who is its target audience?** Children? Men? Women? Some sub- or super-set of these groups (e.g., African American men, "tweens," seniors)?

- **Who is the author?** Who sponsored its publication? What background/ associations do the author and the sponsoring publication have? What other works have they produced?

- **Where was it published, and in what form?** Online? On television? In print? In a commercial publication (a sales brochure, billboard, ad) or an informational one (newspaper, magazine)?

- **If the visual is embedded within a document that is primarily written text, how do the written text and the visual relate to each other?** Do they convey the same message, or are they at odds in any way? What does the image contribute to the written text? Is it essential or just eye candy?

- *Social Context.* **What is the immediate social and cultural context within which the visual is operating?** If we are being asked to support a certain candidate, for example, how does the visual reinforce or counter what we already know about this candidate? What other social/ cultural knowledge does the visual assume its audience already has?

- *Historical Context.* **What historical knowledge does it assume the audience already possesses?** Does the visual refer to other historical images, figures, events, or stories that the audience would recognize? How do these historical references relate to the visual's audience and purpose?

- *Intertextuality.* **How does the visual connect, relate to, or contrast with any other significant texts, visual or otherwise, that you are aware of?** How do such considerations inform your ideas about this particular visual?

LOOKING FOR PATTERNS OF OPPOSITION

Looking for **patterns of opposition** can help the reader understand the dialogue of opposing voices and values represented in the text. All texts carry within themselves voices of opposition. These voices may echo the views and values of sources to which the writer is responding or those of potential readers the writer anticipates; they may even reflect the writer's own conflicting values. The excerpt from King's "Letter from Birmingham Jail" (pp. 36–40) is rich in oppositions: *moderate* versus *extremist, order* versus *justice.* These oppositions are not accidental; they form a significant pattern that gives a reader important information about King's argument.

A careful reading will show that King always values one of the two terms in an opposition over the other. For example, *extremist* (par. 9) is valued over *moderate* (par. 10). This preference for extremism is surprising. If King is trying to convince his readers to accept his point of view, why would he represent himself as an extremist? Studying the patterns of opposition in the text enables you to answer this question. You will see that King sets up this opposition to force his readers to examine their own values. Instead of working toward justice, he says, those who support law and order maintain the unjust status quo.

Looking for patterns of opposition involves annotating words or phrases in the reading that indicate oppositions, listing the opposing terms in pairs, deciding which term in each pair is preferred by the writer, and reflecting on the meaning of the patterns. Here is a partial list of oppositions from the King excerpt:

Listing Patterns of Opposition	
Unfavored term	**Preferred term**
moderate	extremist
order	justice
negative peace	positive peace
absence of justice	presence of justice
goals	methods
passive acceptance	direct action
hidden tension	exposed tension

CHECKLIST: Looking for Patterns of Opposition

1. Annotate the selection to identify words or phrases indicating oppositions.

2. List the pairs of oppositions. (You may have to paraphrase or even supply the opposite word or phrase if it is not stated directly in the text.)

3. For each pair of oppositions, put an asterisk next to the term that the writer seems to value or prefer over the other.

4. Write to analyze and evaluate the opposing points of view, or, in a reading that does not take a position, the alternative systems of value.

REFLECTING ON CHALLENGES TO YOUR BELIEFS AND VALUES

Reflecting on, or thinking critically about, **your own fundamental beliefs or values** may not be your first reaction when you encounter challenges in a text, such as criticism or misrepresentation. But to read thoughtfully, you need to scrutinize your own assumptions and attitudes as well as those expressed in the text you are reading. If you are like most readers, however, you will find that your assumptions and attitudes are so ingrained that you are not always fully aware of them. A good strategy for getting at these underlying beliefs and values is to identify and reflect on the ways the text challenges you and how it makes you feel — disturbed, threatened, ashamed, combative, pleased, exuberant, or some other way.

For example, here is what one student wrote about the King passage:

Reflections

In paragraph 1, Dr. King criticizes people who are "more devoted to 'order' than to justice." This criticism upsets me because today I think I would choose order over justice. When I reflect on my feelings and try to figure out where they come from, I realize that what I feel most is fear. I am terrified by the violence in society today. I'm afraid of sociopaths who don't respect the rule of law, much less the value of human life.

CHECKLIST: Reflecting on Challenges to Your Beliefs and Values

1. Identify challenges by marking where in the text you feel your beliefs and values are being opposed, criticized, or unfairly characterized.

2. Write a paragraph or two reflecting on the differences between the beliefs and values you and others hold.

COMPARING AND CONTRASTING RELATED READINGS

When you **compare** two reading selections, you look for similarities. When you **contrast** them, you look for differences. As critical reading strategies, comparing and contrasting enable you to see both texts more clearly.

Both strategies depend on how imaginative you are in preparing the grounds or basis for comparison. We often hear that it is fruitless, so to speak, to compare apples and oranges. It is true that you cannot add or multiply them, but you can put one against the other and come up with some interesting similarities and differences. For example, comparing apples and oranges in terms of their roles as symbols in Western culture could be quite productive. The grounds or basis for comparison, like a camera lens, brings some things into focus while blurring others.

To demonstrate how this strategy works, we compare and contrast the excerpt from "Letter from Birmingham Jail" (pp. 36–40) with the following selection by Lewis H. Van Dusen Jr.

Lewis H. Van Dusen Jr.

Legitimate Pressures and Illegitimate Results

A respected attorney and legal scholar, Lewis H. Van Dusen Jr. (1901–2004) served as chair of the American Bar Association Committee on Ethics and Professional Responsibility. This selection comes from the essay "Civil Disobedience: Destroyer of Democracy," which first appeared in the *American Bar Association Journal* in 1969.

- **As you read,** notice the annotations comparing this essay with the one by King.

There are many civil rights leaders who show impatience with the process of democracy. They rely on the sit-in, boycott, or mass picketing to gain speedier solutions to the problems that face every citizen. But we must realize that the legitimate pressures that [won concessions in the past] can easily escalate into the illegitimate power plays that might [extort] demands in the future.] The victories of these civil rights leaders must not shake our confidence in the democratic procedures, as the pressures of demonstration are desirable only if they take place within the limits allowed by law. Civil rights gains should continue to be won by the persuasion of Congress and other legislative bodies and by the decision of courts. Any illegal entreaty for the [rights of some] can be an injury to the [rights of others,] for mass demonstrations often trigger violence.

Those who advocate [taking the law into their own hands] should reflect that when they are disobeying what they consider to be an immoral law, they are deciding on a possibly immoral course. Their answer is that the process for democratic relief is too slow, that only mass confrontation can bring immediate action, and that any injuries

Annotations in left margin:

(to get something by force or intimidation)

King's concern with time

Paragraph numbers: 1   2

are the inevitable cost of the pursuit of justice. Their answer is, simply put, that the end justifies the means. It is this justification of any form of demonstration as a form of dissent that threatens to destroy a society built on the rule of law.

Ends vs. means debate

Any form?

The annotations in the Van Dusen selection above were made in comparison to the annotated King excerpt (pp. 36–40) and focus on contrasts between the two writers' different views on nonviolent direct action. The annotations on the Van Dusen excerpt highlight aspects of his argument against the use of nonviolent direct action. These annotations led directly to the paragraph of contrast below, which summarizes Van Dusen's argument. The second paragraph of the contrast presents King's defense, as well as some of the writer's own ideas on how King could have responded to Van Dusen.

> King and Van Dusen present radically different views of legal, nonviolent direct action, such as parades, demonstrations, boycotts, sit-ins, or pickets. Although Van Dusen acknowledges that direct action is legal, he nevertheless fears it; and he challenges it energetically in these paragraphs. He seems most concerned about the ways direct action disturbs the peace, infringes on others' rights, and threatens violence. He worries that, even though some groups make gains through direct action, the end result is that everyone else begins to doubt the validity of the usual democratic procedures of relying on legislation and the courts. He condemns advocates of direct action like King for believing that the end (in this case, racial justice) justifies the means (direct action). Van Dusen argues that demonstrations often end violently and that an organized movement like King's can in the beginning win concessions through direct action but then end up extorting demands through threats and illegal uses of power.

> In contrast, King argues that nonviolent direct action preserves the peace by bringing hidden tensions and prejudices to the surface where they can be acknowledged and addressed. Direct action enhances democracy by changing its unjust laws and thereby strengthening it. Since direct action is entirely legal, to forgo it as a strategy for change would be to turn one's back on a basic democratic principle. Although it may inconvenience people, its end (a more just social order) is entirely justified by its means (direct action). King would no doubt insist that the occasional violence that follows direct action results always from aggressive, unlawful interference with demonstrations — interference sometimes led by police officers. He might also argue that neither anarchy nor extortion followed from his group's actions.

Notice that these paragraphs address each writer's argument separately. An alternative plan would have been to compare and contrast the two writers' arguments point by point.

EVALUATING THE LOGIC OF AN ARGUMENT

An argument includes a thesis backed by reasons and support. The thesis asserts a position on a controversial issue or a solution to a problem that the writer wants readers to accept. The reasons tell readers why they should accept the thesis, and the support (such as examples, statistics, authorities, analogies, and textual evidence) gives readers grounds for accepting it. For an argument to be considered logically acceptable, it must meet the three conditions of what we call the ABC test:

A. The reasons and support must be *appropriate* to the thesis.

B. The reasons and support must be *believable*.

C. The reasons and support must be *consistent* with one another as well as complete.

Testing for Appropriateness

To evaluate the logic of an argument, you first decide whether the argument's reasons and support are appropriate. To test for appropriateness, ask these questions: How does each reason or piece of support relate to the thesis? Is the connection between reasons and support and the thesis clear and compelling?

Readers most often question the appropriateness of reasons and support when the writer argues by analogy or by invoking authority. For example, King uses both analogy and authority in paragraph 3: "Isn't this like condemning Socrates because his unswerving commitment to truth and his philosophical inquiries precipitated the act by the misguided populace in which they made him drink hemlock?" Not only must you judge the appropriateness of the analogy comparing the Greeks' condemnation of Socrates to the white moderates' condemnation of King, but you must also judge whether it is appropriate to accept Socrates as an authority. Since Socrates is generally respected for his teachings on justice, his words and actions are likely to be considered appropriate to King's situation in Birmingham.

Testing for Believability

Believability is a measure of your willingness to accept as true the reasons and support the writer gives in defense of a thesis. To test for believability, ask: On what basis am I being asked to believe this reason or support is true? If it cannot be proved true or false, how much weight does it carry?

For instance, **facts** are statements that can be proved objectively to be true. The believability of facts depends on their *accuracy* (they should not distort or misrepresent reality), their *completeness* (they should not omit important details), and the *trustworthiness* of their sources (sources should be credible).

Examples and **anecdotes** are particular instances used to support a generalization. The believability of examples depends on their *representativeness* (whether they are truly typical and thus generalizable) and their *specificity* (whether particular details make them seem true to life). Even if a vivid example or gripping anecdote does not convince readers, it usually strengthens argumentative writing by clarifying the meaning and dramatizing the point.

Statistics are numerical data. The believability of statistics depends on the *comparability* of the data, the *precision* of the methods employed to gather and analyze data, and the *trustworthiness* of the sources.

Authorities are people to whom the writer attributes expertise on a given subject. Not only must such authorities be appropriate, as mentioned earlier, but they must be *credible* as well — that is, the reader must accept them as experts on the topic at hand. King cites authorities repeatedly throughout his essay — religious leaders as well as American political figures.

Testing for Consistency and Completeness

In looking for consistency, you should be concerned that all the parts of the argument work together and that they are sufficient to convince readers to accept the thesis or at least take it seriously. To test for consistency and completeness, ask: Are any of the reasons and support contradictory? Do they provide sufficient grounds for accepting the thesis? Does the writer fail to acknowledge, concede, or refute any opposing arguments or important objections?

A thoughtful reader might regard as contradictory King's characterizing himself first as a moderate and later as an extremist opposed to the forces of violence. (King attempts to reconcile this apparent contradiction by explicitly redefining extremism in par. 9.) Similarly, the fact that King fails to examine and refute every legal recourse available to his cause might allow a critical reader to question the sufficiency of his argument.

CHECKLIST: Evaluating the Logic of an Argument

Use the ABC test to determine whether an argument makes sense:

A. *Test for appropriateness* by checking that the reasons and support are clearly and directly related to the thesis.

B. *Test for believability* by deciding whether you can accept the reasons and support as likely to be true.

C. *Test for consistency and completeness* by deciding whether the argument has any contradictions and whether any important objections or opposing views have been ignored.

RECOGNIZING LOGICAL FALLACIES

Fallacies are errors in reasoning that seem plausible and often have great persuasive power. Fallacies are not necessarily deliberate efforts to deceive readers. Writers may introduce a fallacy accidentally by not examining their own reasons or underlying assumptions, by failing to establish solid support, or by using unclear or ambiguous words. Here are some of the most common logical fallacies.

Slippery Slope

A **slippery-slope fallacy** occurs when someone asserts that if one thing happens, then a series of bad related consequences will *necessarily* follow. The name comes from the idea that if a person takes one step down a slippery slope, he or she cannot help sliding all the way to the bottom.

EXAMPLE   Marijuana should be banned because it inevitably leads to the use of other illegal drugs.

This is a fallacy because it assumes inevitability.

Post Hoc, Ergo Propter Hoc

The Latin name *post hoc, ergo propter hoc* means "after this, therefore because of this." A **post hoc fallacy** wrongly assumes that an event that occurs *after* another event is *caused* by the first event. This fallacy in causal reasoning often occurs when writers try to attribute to one cause something that has several or many causes. When complex issues are made to seem simple, look for this fallacy.

EXAMPLE   Playing first-person shooter games makes kids violent.

To avoid the *post hoc* fallacy, someone making this argument would have to prove that playing shooter games could actually cause kids to become violent. The person would also need to consider other possible causes, such as membership in gangs, alienation at school, parental abuse, and so on.

False Dilemma (Either/Or Reasoning)

The **false dilemma fallacy,** or either/or reasoning, puts readers in the position of having to choose one of two options as if there were no other choices. Here's an example: Martin Luther King Jr., in paragraph 5 of the excerpt from "Letter from Birmingham Jail" (pp. 36–40), refutes an either/or argument made by others. Arguing that the choice between a "force of complacency" or a force "of bitterness and hatred" is a false dilemma, King points out that there are other alternatives, among them the option of nonviolent protest that he represents.

Hasty Generalization

When someone makes a **hasty generalization,** he or she leaps to a conclusion without providing enough evidence to support the leap.

EXAMPLE   Crime in this city is getting worse and worse. Just yesterday, two people were held up at ATMs downtown.

Two crimes, no matter how serious, do not indicate that the overall *rate* of crime is rising. This may indeed be the case, but proving it would require statistics, not just a couple of examples.

Ad Hominem (or *Ad Personam*) Attack

An ***ad hominem*** (meaning "to the man") or ***ad personam*** ("to the person") attack occurs when writers attack the person who propounds the ideas with which they disagree, rather than attacking the ideas themselves.

EXAMPLE   My opponent, one of the richest men in the state, wants to cut taxes for himself and his rich friends.

Certainly the character and credibility (and wealth) of the writer making the argument affect how persuasive a reader finds it, but they do not affect the underlying soundness of the argument.

Straw Man

In a **straw man fallacy,** the writer oversimplifies an opponent's position in order to knock it down, like a straw scarecrow.

EXAMPLE   Climate change is nothing to worry about because the weather changes all the time.

This example uses the straw man fallacy because it pretends as though worrying about the climate is as pointless as worrying about whether it will rain tomorrow. Equating climate change to the weather makes it seem like people who sound alarms about climate change are just complainers.

Circular Reasoning (Begging the Question)

A **circular reasoning fallacy** merely restates the main claim, often by definition, without actually offering evidence to support the claim.

EXAMPLE   Same-sex marriage is wrong because marriage is between a man and a woman.

This example relies on a definition that, if accepted, would end the discussion. But it is the definition of marriage which is at issue in the argument. To support the claim, opponents of same-sex marriage would have to convince readers that their view of marriage is the only correct view.

Red Herring

The **red herring fallacy** distracts readers with irrelevant arguments. Just think of a dead fish (red herring) being dragged across a trail to distract dogs from pursuing the scent of their real target. In this case, writers use irrelevant arguments to distract readers from the real issue, perhaps because their own argument is weak and they don't want the reader to notice.

EXAMPLE   My opponent tries to blame my administration for the high price of prescription drugs, but he supports a government takeover of health care.

That the opponent supports a government takeover of health care (whether true or false) has nothing to do with whether the policies of the speaker's administration are responsible for the high price of prescription drugs.

CHECKLIST: Recognizing Logical Fallacies

1. Annotate places in the text where you stop to think "wait a minute — that doesn't make sense" or where you think the writer has "gone too far."

2. Analyze these places to see if they represent any of the fallacies discussed in this section.

3. Write a few sentences exploring what you discover.

RECOGNIZING EMOTIONAL MANIPULATION

Writers often try to arouse emotions in readers to excite their interest, make them care, or move them to take action. There is nothing wrong with appealing to readers' emotions; what is wrong is manipulating readers with false or exaggerated appeals. Therefore, you should be suspicious of writing that is overly sentimental, that cites alarming statistics and frightening anecdotes, that demonizes others and identifies itself with revered authorities, or that uses potent symbols (for example, the American flag) or emotionally loaded words (such as *racist*).

King, for example, uses the emotionally loaded word *paternalistically* to refer to the white moderate's belief that "he can set the timetable for another man's freedom" (par. 1). In the same paragraph, King uses symbolism to get an emotional reaction from readers when he compares the white moderate to the "Ku Klux Klanner." To get readers to accept his ideas, he also relies on authorities whose names evoke the greatest respect, such as Jesus and Lincoln. But some readers might object that comparing his own crusade to that of Jesus is pretentious and manipulative. A critical reader might also consider King's discussion of African American extremists in paragraph 7 to be a veiled threat designed to frighten readers into agreement.

While it's not always easy to recognize when you are being emotionally manipulated by a writer, there are some signs that you can pay attention to as you use this reading strategy. If you feel a strong emotion such as anger, fear, happiness, shame, or indignation as you are reading, then the writer has been successful in appealing to your emotions. If you feel the immediate need to either challenge or confirm what the writer says, you may be experiencing an emotional response. Finally, if you feel like you must share what you have just read with others — because of either your positive or negative response — you may be doing so because the writer has tapped into your emotions. Recognizing emotional manipulation as you read helps you gauge why you are responding to the text in the ways you are and gives you the opportunity to evaluate whether the writer is using emotional manipulation to obscure a lack of evidence or credibility.

CHECKLIST: Recognizing Emotional Manipulation

1. Annotate places in the text where you sense emotional appeals are being used.

2. Analyze the emotional appeals, explaining why you think they are or are not manipulative.

JUDGING THE WRITER'S CREDIBILITY

Writers try to persuade readers by presenting an image of themselves in their writing that will gain their readers' confidence. This image must be created indirectly, through the arguments, language, and system of values and beliefs expressed or implied in the writing. Writers establish credibility in their writing in at least three ways:

- By showing their *knowledge* of the subject
- By building *common ground* with readers
- By responding *fairly* to objections and opposing arguments

Testing for Knowledge

Writers demonstrate their knowledge through the facts and statistics they marshal, the sources they rely on for information, and the scope and depth of their understanding. As a reader, you may not be an expert on the subject yourself or know whether the facts are accurate, the sources are reliable, and the understanding is sufficient. You may need to do some research to see what others say about the subject. You can also check **credentials** — the writer's educational and professional qualifications, the respectability of the publication in which the selection first appeared, and reviews of the writer's work — to determine whether the writer is a respected authority in the field. For example, King brings with him the authority that comes from being a member of the clergy and a respected leader of the Southern Christian Leadership Conference.

Testing for Common Ground

One way writers can establish **common ground** with their readers is by basing their reasoning on shared values, beliefs, and attitudes. They use language that includes their readers (*we*) and qualify their assertions to keep them from being too extreme. Above all, they acknowledge differences of opinion. You want to notice such appeals.

King creates common ground with readers by using the inclusive pronoun *we*, suggesting shared concerns between himself and his audience. Notice, however, his use of masculine pronouns and other references ("the Negro . . . he," "our brothers"). Although King addressed his letter to male clergy, he intended it to be published in the local newspaper, where it would be read by an audience of both men and women. By using language that excludes women — a common practice at the time the selection was written — King may have missed the opportunity to build common ground with more than half of his readers.

Testing for Fairness and Understanding Bias

As you likely know, a bias is a prejudice in favor of or against a thing, person, or group, usually in a way that is considered to be unfair. Everyone has biases, whether we acknowledge them or not. Despite biases, a writer must make an effort to be fair to other points of view because doing so increases a writer's credibility. For example, Martin Luther King Jr. has many biases, and those biases should inform your evaluation of King's credibility. These biases reveal themselves through the writer's tone and word choice, and how the writer handles opposing arguments and objections to their own argument. Does King incorporate and treat other points of view fairly?

In addition to considering how an author incorporates and treats other points of view, identifying the tone of the argument — which conveys the writer's attitude toward the subject and toward the reader — can also help you gauge the author's credibility. Is the text angry? Sarcastic? Evenhanded? Shrill? Condescending? Bullying? Do you feel as if the writer is treating the subject — and you, as a reader — with fairness? King's tone might be characterized in different passages as patient (he doesn't lose his temper), respectful (he refers to white moderates as "people of good will"), or pompous (comparing himself to Jesus and Socrates).

Considered within their context, a writer's word choices can reveal both her biases and also the efforts she makes to be fair to her subject. Emotionally charged words can be an indicator of bias. For example, consider the issue of child labor. There are certain laws in the United States that make it illegal to require children to work more than a certain number of hours daily, whether in a factory or another setting. Consider the difference between describing a company as *exploiting* child workers (by forcing them to work longer hours than the law allows) and describing the company as giving child workers *an opportunity* to work off their boundless energy in the safe, monitored setting of a factory. The writer that chooses to use the word "exploit" — the more emotionally charged word — might be revealing a bias in favor of children and against the company that has employed them. As the reader, you should pay attention to the context in which emotionally charged words are used. Ultimately, emotionally charged words can signal bias, but as the reader you must consider them within their context in order to evaluate a writer's credibility. Not all words have to be emotionally charged to reveal bias, though. For example, words like "always," "never," "all," and "none" can indicate bias as well, because they usually lead to overstatements and generalizations and do not allow for other perspectives on the subject.

As a critical reader, paying particular attention to how writers treat possible differences of opinion also allows you to judge whether an author is treating the subject fairly. Be suspicious of those who ignore differences and pretend that everyone agrees with their viewpoints. When objections or opposing views are represented, consider whether they have been distorted in any way; if they are refuted, be sure they are challenged fairly — with sound reasoning and solid support.

CHECKLIST: Judging the Writer's Credibility

1. As you read and annotate, consider the writer's knowledge of the subject, how well common ground is established, and whether the writer deals fairly with objections and opposing arguments.

2. Note where you recognize bias and how it reveals itself.

3. Decide what in the essay you find credible and what you question.

READING LIKE A WRITER

Reading like a writer involves paying attention to the different writing techniques an author uses so you can decide whether you want to use those techniques in your own writing. For example, some authors incorporate many questions into their writing. Some open their writing with a personal story. Many authors incorporate outside sources into their writing. Paying attention to how they use these techniques will help you incorporate these elements into your own writing. Whereas other reading strategies help you understand the content of what you are reading, the "reading like a writer" strategy teaches you about the range of writing techniques at your disposal.

Reading like a writer is also a productive reading strategy if your instructor has asked you to compose a piece of writing along the lines of those you have read in class. If you read a published autobiography or literacy narrative, for example, and are expected to write your own, then reading like a writer can help you recognize writing techniques common in these kinds of texts.

Throughout *Reading Critically, Writing Well* you will find exercises related to this reading strategy. These exercises direct your attention to a specific feature of an author's writing and ask you to analyze it. You should then consider whether this feature is one that you are interested in trying out in your own writing.

For example, notice how Martin Luther King Jr. uses a series of rhetorical questions — questions used to make a point rather than elicit an answer — to highlight his argument that the clergymen's condemnation was not logical:

> In your statement you assert that our actions, even though peaceful, must be condemned because they precipitate violence. But is this a logical assertion? Isn't this like condemning a robbed man because his possession of money precipitated the evil act of robbery? Isn't this like condemning Socrates because his unswerving commitment to truth and his philosophical inquiries precipitated the act by the misguided populace in which they made him drink hemlock? Isn't this like condemning Jesus because his unique God-consciousness and never-ceasing devotion to God's will precipitated the evil act of crucifixion?

Notice how King's use of rhetorical questions — especially one right after another — draws the reader in and lends some dramatic effect to his argument. In this example, when you use the "reading like a writer" strategy, you think less about what King is saying and more about the effect of his use of rhetorical questions, the writing technique he is using in this section. Then you consider whether using rhetorical questions in your own writing would be effective.

CHECKLIST: Reading Like a Writer

1. Keep track of the different writing techniques a writer uses. You can do so by annotating the text or by listing the techniques on a separate page. Don't worry about using the formal or technical names for these techniques.

2. Consider the effects of these techniques and decide which you might want to try in your own writing.

3. Try out these techniques in your own writing and evaluate their effectiveness.

CHAPTER 3

Autobiography and Literacy Narratives

Writing and reading about memorable events and people can be exhilarating, leading us to think deeply about why certain experiences have meaning for us. It can also help us understand the cultural influences that helped shape who we are and what we value. Whether you are reading or writing, however, it is important to remember that autobiography is public, not private like a diary. Although it involves self-presentation and contributes to self-knowledge, this kind of writing does not require unwanted self-disclosure but does require an awareness of the rhetorical situation. For example, writing about yourself for a college admissions essay, you undoubtedly want to impress readers with such qualities as your thoughtfulness, diligence, social responsibility, and ambition. Writing for friends and family about a dodgy experience, you may want to share your anxieties but also show how you handled the situation. Writing a literacy narrative for your instructor, you may want to describe the role that reading and/or writing has played in your life, inside or outside of school.

RHETORICAL SITUATIONS FOR AUTOBIOGRAPHIES AND LITERACY NARRATIVES

You may think that only politicians and celebrities write autobiographies, but autobiographical writing is much more common, as the following examples suggest:

- As part of her college application, a high-school senior writes an autobiographical essay that shows what inspired her to want to become a biomedical researcher. She tells what happened when she did her first science experiment on the nutritional effects of different breakfast cereals.

Because the mice eating Count Chocula and Froot Loops, and not eating anything else, were dying, she convinced her teacher to let her stop the experiment early. She wants her audience of college admissions officers to appreciate her sense of responsibility and her understanding of the ethics of scientific research.

- Asked to post online a few paragraphs reflecting on a significant early child-hood memory, a student in a psychology class writes about a fishing trip he took as a six-year-old. The trip was the first time he spent alone with his father, and he recalls that although he tried hard to win his father's approval, his father criticized everything he did. Looking back on that painful event — now that he knows what a bad relationship his dad had had with his own father — the student reflects on the importance of role models in teaching people how to be good parents. He also refers to an article that helped him understand the impact of toxic parenting.

- Assigned a specific kind of autobiographical essay called a literacy narrative, a student in a writing class reflects on how early reading and writing experiences in her life influence her current interests. Looking back on the many history books that filled her childhood home, she explores how that environment led to her becoming a history major who continues to seek opportunities to travel throughout the world to learn about early civilizations.

Understanding the Relationship between Autobiography and Literacy Narratives

As you read in the introduction to this chapter, autobiographical writing allows us to think deeply about why certain experiences have meaning for us. Literacy narratives are a kind of autobiography that tell a story about a meaningful encounter with reading, writing, or language. Like the more general category of autobiographies, literacy narratives can help us understand the cultural influences that have shaped who we are and what we value. In the case of literacy narratives, those influences may come through our acts of reading, writing, and speaking. Literacy narratives, like autobiographies, often tell personal and reflective stories about the impact of reading and/or writing on a person's life. More generally, though, literacy narratives should convey a significance beyond the personal meaning they hold for the writer. Literacy narratives might inspire others to reflect on their own experiences with reading, writing, and language or might convey ideas about the very concept of literacy. Because literacy narratives are meant for an audience, readers expect writers to compose literacy narratives with rhetorical sensitivity.

Thinking about Autobiography and Literacy Narratives

Write a paragraph or two about an occasion when you told, read, heard, or saw an autobiography or literacy narrative in school, at work, or in another context.

- Who was the *audience*? Consider how communicating to the particular audience (such as a teacher rather than a friend, a college admissions committee rather than a favorite aunt) affected the tone (for example, playful, informal, satiric), details, even the choice of event or person to focus on.

- What was the main *purpose*? For example, was the goal to illustrate an idea, create a favorable impression, understand why something happened, or arouse sympathy?

- How would you rate the *rhetorical sensitivity* with which the story was presented? What made it appropriate or inappropriate for its particular audience or purpose?

A GUIDE TO READING AUTOBIOGRAPHY AND LITERACY NARRATIVES

This guide introduces you to autobiography by inviting you to analyze a brief but powerful autobiographical selection by Annie Dillard:

- *Annotations* on this first reading will help you see how to practice academic **habits of mind** such as **curiosity, openness,** and **persistence** to help you engage with and understand what you are reading. Notice how many questions the reader has as she reads. There is plenty of space for you to add your own questions and thoughts, as well, to this reading and any other in the textbook.

- *Reading for meaning* will help you grasp the event's **significance** for Dillard — what the incident meant to her both at the time she experienced it and years later when she wrote about it. It may also help you explore broader cultural meanings in Dillard's story — for example, ideas about heroism and gender.

- *Reading like a writer* will help you learn how Dillard makes her story exciting and suspenseful, as well as meaningful, by examining how she employs some basic features and strategies typical of autobiographical writing, such as:

  1. Narrating a story dramatically

  2. Presenting people and places vividly

  3. Conveying the significance powerfully

Annie Dillard

An American Childhood

Annie Dillard (b. 1945) is a prolific writer whose first book, *Pilgrim at Tinker Creek* (1974), won the Pulitzer Prize for nonfiction writing. Since then, she has written eleven other books in a variety of genres. They include *Teaching a Stone to Talk* (1982), *The Writing Life* (1989), *Mornings Like This* (1995), and *The Maytrees* (2007). Dillard has also written an autobiography of her early years, *An American Childhood* (1987), from which the following selection comes.

- **Before you read,** notice that Dillard tells us in the opening paragraph why she liked learning to play football. Think about what you liked to play as a child and why.

- **As you read,** consider why Dillard sets the scene in paragraphs 3–8 with so much specificity.

1   Some boys taught me to play football. This was fine sport. You thought up a new strategy for every play and whispered it to the others. You went out for a pass, fooling everyone. Best, you got to throw yourself mightily at someone's running legs. Either you brought him down or you hit the ground flat out on your chin, with your arms empty before you. It was all or nothing. If you hesitated in fear, you would miss and get hurt: you would take a hard fall while the kid got away, or you would get kicked in the face while the kid got away. But if you flung yourself wholeheartedly at the back of his knees — if you gathered and joined body and soul and pointed them diving fearlessly — then you likely wouldn't get hurt, and you'd stop the ball. Your fate, and your team's score, depended on your concentration and courage. Nothing girls did could compare with it.

> The author prefers how boys play to how girls play. Aren't these gender stereotypes, though?

2   Boys welcomed me at baseball, too, for I had, through enthusiastic practice, what was weirdly known as a boy's arm. In winter, in the snow, there was neither baseball nor football, so the boys and I threw snowballs at passing cars. I got in trouble throwing snowballs, and have seldom been happier since.

> Getting in trouble makes the author happy. Why?

3   On one weekday morning after Christmas, six inches of new snow had just fallen. We were standing up to our boot tops in snow on a front yard on trafficked Reynolds Street, waiting for cars. The cars traveled Reynolds Street slowly and evenly; they were targets all but wrapped in red ribbons, cream puffs. We couldn't miss.

> Cream puffs! Love this description!

4   I was seven; the boys were eight, nine, and ten. The oldest two Fahey boys were there — Mikey and Peter — polite blond boys who lived near me on Lloyd Street, and who already had four brothers and sisters. My parents

I wonder if action means trouble. Are they looking for trouble?

What does crenellated mean?

The author assumes that children are naturally solitary. Why?

approved Mikey and Peter Fahey. Chickie McBride was there, a tough kid, and Billy Paul and Mackie Kean too, from across Reynolds, where the boys grew up dark and furious, grew up skinny, knowing, and skilled. We had all drifted from our houses that morning looking for action, and had found it here on Reynolds Street.

It was cloudy but cold. The cars' tires laid behind them on the snowy 5 street a complex trail of beige chunks like crenellated castle walls.

I had stepped on some earlier; they squeaked. We could not have 6 wished for more traffic. When a car came, we all popped it one. In the intervals between cars we reverted to the natural solitude of children.

I started making an iceball—a perfect iceball, from perfectly white 7 snow, perfectly spherical, and squeezed perfectly translucent so no snow remained all the way through. (The Fahey boys and I considered it unfair actually to throw an iceball at somebody, but it had been known to happen.)

I had just embarked on the iceball project when we heard tire chains 8 come clanking from afar. A black Buick was moving toward us down the street. We all spread out, banged together some regular snowballs, took aim, and, when the Buick drew nigh, fired.

A soft snowball hit the driver's windshield right before the driver's face. 9 It made a smashed star with a hump in the middle.

Often, of course, we hit our target, but this time, the only time in all of 10 life, the car pulled over and stopped. Its wide black door opened; a man got out of it, running. He didn't even close the car door.

He ran after us, and we ran away from him, up the snowy Reynolds 11 sidewalk. At the corner, I looked back; incredibly, he was still after us. He was in city clothes: a suit and tie, street shoes. Any normal adult would have quit, having sprung us into flight and made his point. This man was gaining on us. He was a thin man, all action. All of a sudden, we were running for our lives.

Wordless, we split up. We were on our turf; we could lose ourselves in 12 the neighborhood backyards, everyone for himself. I paused and considered. Everyone had vanished except Mikey Fahey, who was just rounding the corner of a yellow brick house. Poor Mikey, I trailed him. The driver of the Buick sensibly picked the two of us to follow. The man apparently had all day.

He chased Mikey and me around the yellow house and up a backyard 13 path we knew by heart: under a low tree, up a bank, through a hedge, down some snowy steps, and across the grocery store's delivery driveway. We smashed through a gap in another hedge, entered a scruffy backyard and ran around its back porch and tight between houses to Edgerton Avenue; we ran across Edgerton to an alley and up our own sliding woodpile to the Halls' front yard; he kept coming. We ran up Lloyd Street and wound through mazy backyards toward the steep hilltop at Willard and Lang.

14   He chased us silently, block after block. He chased us silently over picket fences, through thorny hedges, between houses, around garbage cans, and across streets.

Author repeats the phrase "he chased us silently." Why?

15   Every time I glanced back, choking for breath, I expected he would have quit. He must have been as breathless as we were. His jacket strained over his body. It was an immense discovery, pounding into my hot head with every sliding, joyous step, that this ordinary adult evidently knew what I thought only children who trained at football knew: that you have to fling yourself at what you're doing, you have to point yourself, forget yourself, aim, dive.

16   Mikey and I had nowhere to go, in our own neighborhood or out of it, but away from this man who was chasing us. He impelled us forward; we compelled him to follow our route. The air was cold; every breath tore my throat. We kept running, block after block; we kept improvising, backyard after backyard, running a frantic course and choosing it simultaneously, failing always to find small places or hard places to slow him down, and discovering always, exhilarated, dismayed, that only bare speed could save us—for he would never give up, this man—and we were losing speed.

17   He chased us through the backyard labyrinths of ten blocks before he caught us by our jackets. He caught us and we all stopped.

18   We three stood staggering, half blinded, coughing, in an obscure hilltop backyard: a man in his twenties, a boy, a girl. He had released our jackets, our pursuer, our captor, our hero: he knew we weren't going anywhere. We all played by the rules. Mikey and I unzipped our jackets. I pulled off my sopping mittens. Our tracks multiplied in the backyard's new snow. We had been breaking new snow all morning. We didn't look at each other. I was cherishing my excitement. The man's lower pants legs were wet; his cuffs were full of snow, and there was a prow of snow beneath them on his shoes and socks. Some trees bordered the little flat backyard, some messy winter trees. There was no one around: a clearing in a grove, and we the only players.

Does the author mean sports players? Actors?

19   It was a long time before he could speak. I had some difficulty at first recalling why we were there. My lips felt swollen; I couldn't see out of the sides of my eyes; I kept coughing.

20   "You stupid kids," he began perfunctorily.

21   We listened perfunctorily indeed, if we listened at all, for the chewing out was redundant, a mere formality, and beside the point. The point was that he had chased us passionately without giving up, and so he had caught us. Now he came down to earth. I wanted the glory to last forever.

What he says to them doesn't matter.

22   But how could the glory have lasted forever? We could have run through every backyard in North America until we got to Panama. But when he trapped us at the lip of the Panama Canal, what precisely could

Story takes a dark turn.

he have done to prolong the drama of the chase and cap its glory? I brooded about this for the next few years. He could only have fried Mikey Fahey and me in boiling oil, say, or dismembered us piecemeal, or staked us to anthills.

None of which I really wanted, and none of which any adult was likely   23
to do, even in the spirit of fun. He could only chew us out there in the Panamanian jungle, after months or years of exalting pursuit. He could only begin, "You stupid kids," and continue in his ordinary Pittsburgh accent with his normal righteous anger and the usual common sense.

If in that snowy backyard the driver of the black Buick had cut off   24
our heads, Mikey's and mine, I would have died happy, for nothing has required so much of me since as being chased all over Pittsburgh in the middle of winter—running terrified, exhausted—by this sainted, skinny, furious redheaded man who wished to have a word with us. I don't know how he found his way back to his car.

READING FOR MEANING

For help with reading strategies like summarizing and analyzing assumptions, see Chapter 2.

1. **Read to Summarize.** Write a sentence or two explaining what happened and why.

2. **Read to Respond.** Write a paragraph analyzing your initial reactions to Dillard's story, focusing on anything that seems surprising, such as the iceball scene (pars. 6–7) or the apparent contradiction between Dillard's description of the man who chased her as a "hero" (par. 16) and her dismissal of what he said (par. 19).

3. **Read to Analyze Assumptions.** Write a paragraph or two analyzing an assumption you find intriguing in Dillard's story. Here are some ideas:

Assumptions about the value of rules and fair play. Dillard uses words like *rules* (par. 16) and *unfair* (par. 6) to suggest there are commonly accepted principles of conduct or ethics for childhood games that determine what is considered fair or right. To think critically about the assumptions in this essay related to rules and fairness, consider questions like these:

You may also try looking for patterns of opposition; see Chapter 2, pp. 55–56.

- What unwritten rule do you think the man assumes the kids have broken? Who would agree (or disagree) that what the kids did was wrong? Why?

- Even though the young Dillard admires his persistence, why might some readers question the man's decision to chase and reprimand the kids? Do you think he was right? Why or why not?

Assumptions about the superiority of boys' play. Dillard describes the way the neighborhood boys taught her to play football, claiming that "[n]othing girls did could compare with it" (par. 1).

- What does Dillard seem to be saying about social expectations regarding gender at the time (1950s) and place (Pittsburgh) that she is describing? To what extent do you share these expectations? Why?

- How have assumptions about the kinds of games considered appropriate for girls and boys changed in American culture today, if at all?

READING LIKE A WRITER

Narrating the Story

Stories of all kinds, including autobiographical stories, try to arouse the reader's curiosity, often by structuring the story around a *conflict* that grows increasingly intense until it reaches a high point or **climax.** The structural elements can be visualized in the form of a *dramatic arc* (see Figure 3.1, p. 77) and can help us analyze narratives like the chase Dillard remembers from her childhood.

To intensify the rising action of the chase, Dillard constructs a dramatic *action sequence* by using *action verbs* (instead of static verbs like *is* and *was*). In passages, like the one below, the frantic activity signaled by the verbs is amplified by a series of *prepositional phrases* that show movement through space.

Action verbs   He chased Mikey and me around the yellow house and
Prepositional   up a backyard path . . . under a low tree, up a bank, through a hedge.
phrases   [. . .] We smashed . . . entered . . . and ran. . . . (par. 12)

Other intensifying strategies include the repetition of key words and sentence patterns:

Repetition   He chased us silently, block after block. He chased us silently. . . . (par. 13)

He impelled us forward; we compelled him to follow our route. (par. 14)

Whereas the exact repetitions in the first example suggest the experience of being chased relentlessly, the sentence pattern repetition in the second example (*He impelled us . . . we compelled him*) emphasizes the connection between the man (*He*) and the children (*we*).

Climax

Rising Action   **Falling Action**

**Exposition/
Inciting Incident**   **Resolution/
Reflection**

Exposition/Inciting Incident: Background information, scene setting, *or* an introduction to the characters *or* an initial conflict or problem that sets off the action, arousing curiosity and suspense

Rising Action: The developing crisis, possibly leading to other conflicts and complications

Climax: The emotional high point, often a turning point marking a change for good or ill

Falling Action: Resolution of tension and unraveling of conflicts; may include a final surprise

Resolution/Reflection: Conflicts come to an end but may not be fully resolved, and writer reflects on the event's meaning and importance—its significance

FIGURE 3.1 DRAMATIC ARC   The shape of the arc varies. Not all stories devote the same amount of space to each element, and some may omit elements.

To keep readers oriented, writers often provide pointers such as *transitional words and phrases, verb tense*, and *adverbs and prepositions marking location in time and space*:

Time and date	On one weekday morning after Christmas . . . (par. 3)
Adverbs/Prepositions of time	
	I had just embarked on the iceball project when we heard . . .
Verb tenses showing simultaneous action	(par. 7)

ANALYZE & WRITE

Write a paragraph analyzing Dillard's construction of an action sequence.

1. Skim paragraphs 11–13, circling the action verbs, underlining adverbs and prepositions indicating movement in time and space, and highlighting any other words or phrases that contribute to the action and help orient readers. Note the verb tenses and use arrows to identify repetitions.

2. Read some of these sentences aloud to consider the effect these patterns have on the rhythm of Dillard's sentences. Also consider whether they help you visualize the action, as if it were a film.

3. Consider also how Dillard uses her point of view (*I* and *we*) in the middle of the action to dramatize the narrative. For example, think about how Dillard's story would be different if we saw the chase from an outsider's point of view watching from a distance.

Describing Places

Whether autobiography centers on an event or a person, it may also include some *description* of places. Because Dillard is describing a chase through her neighborhood, she uses a series of prepositional phrases that indicate direction or location in space. To provide specific information about the places and help readers visualize the scene, autobiographers rely on the describing strategies of *naming* objects and *detailing* their colors, shapes, and textures:

Prepositional phrase	. . . around the yellow house and up a backyard path we knew by heart;
Naming	under a low tree, up a bank, through a hedge, down some snowy
Detailing	steps, and across the grocery store's delivery driveway. (par. 12)

In addition to using these sensory images, writers may characterize and evaluate features of the scene ("perfect iceball" and "scruffy backyard" [pars. 6, 12]). Occasionally, they also use *comparisons* in the form of a *simile* or *metaphor* to add suggestive images that contribute to the overall or *dominant impression*:

Metaphor	The cars traveled Reynolds Street slowly and evenly; they were targets all but wrapped in red ribbons, cream puffs. (par. 3)

Simile   The cars' tires laid behind them on the snowy street a complex trail of
            beige chunks like crenellated castle walls. (par. 5)

ANALYZE & WRITE

Write a paragraph analyzing and evaluating Dillard's use of the describing strategies of
naming, detailing, and comparing to make the scene come to life for you.

1. Find an example where Dillard uses naming and detailing to make her
   description especially vivid and informative. Consider whether the names she
   gives to the objects in the example you chose are *concrete* or *abstract* and
   what attributes or sense impressions the details convey. What is the dominant
   impression you get from this description of the scene?

2. Choose a simile or metaphor that stands out for you. How does it help
   you imagine what the place looked and felt like to Dillard? How does the
   comparison reinforce, extend, or complicate the dominant impression?

Presenting People

The describing strategies of naming and detailing are often also used to describe
people, as in these brief descriptions of some of Dillard's playmates:

Naming   The oldest two Fahey boys were there — Mikey and Peter — polite blond
Detailing   boys . . . (par. 4)

Writers not only depict what people look like, but they sometimes also characterize or evaluate their behavior and personality. Often, just a few well-chosen details
about the way a person looks, dresses, talks, or acts will be sufficient to give readers
a vivid impression of the person:

> . . . Billy Paul and Mackie Kean too, from across Reynolds, where
> the boys grew up dark and furious, grew up skinny, knowing, and
> skilled. (par. 4)

In this example, the word *dark* may be a literal description as well as a metaphori-
cal marker of ethnicity or race. It may also describe the boys' attitude, making their
snowball throwing seem less innocuous than Dillard's.

ANALYZE & WRITE

Write a paragraph exploring the dominant impression you get of the man who chased
Dillard and Mikey.

1. Underline the words in paragraphs 10, 16, and 21 that describe the man
   physically, and circle those that characterize or evaluate him.

2. Skim paragraph 18 and the last sentence of paragraph 20, where Dillard presents the man through dialogue. Underline the details Dillard uses to describe how the man looks and sounds. What does Dillard's choice of words like "perfunctorily" (par. 18) and "normal" (par. 20) suggest about her evaluation of him? How does this evaluation affect the impression you get of the man?

Conveying the Autobiographical Significance

Autobiographers convey the significance of an event or a person in two ways: by *showing* or *telling*. Through your analysis of how Dillard narrates the story, presents people, and describes places, you have looked at some of the ways she *shows* the event's significance and creates a dominant impression. Now consider what Dillard *tells* readers. For example, when Dillard writes in the opening paragraphs about boys teaching her to play football and baseball, she is telling why these experiences were memorable and important.

Autobiographers usually tell both what they remember thinking and feeling *at the time* and what they think and feel now *as they write about the past*. Readers must infer from the ideas and the writer's choice of words whether the words convey the writer's *past* or *present perspective* — remembered feelings and thoughts or current ones. For example, consider whether you agree with this analysis, and why or why not.

Remembered feelings and thoughts	Some boys taught me to play football. This was fine sport. You thought up a new strategy for every play and whispered it to the others. (par. 1)
Present perspective	I got in trouble throwing snowballs, and have seldom been happier since. (par. 2)

ANALYZE & WRITE

Write a paragraph or two analyzing Dillard's use of showing and telling to create autobiographical significance.

1. Reread paragraphs 19–21. Choose one or two examples that convey Dillard's present perspective as she looks back and reflects on her childhood experience. Also choose one or two examples that seem to be Dillard's remembered feelings and thoughts, how she felt at the time the event occurred. How can you tell the difference?

2. Compare Dillard's remembered and present perspectives. Has her thinking changed over time? If so, how? If you detect a note of self-irony in her tone, a suggestion that she is making fun of her younger self, where do you see it and what does it tell you about Dillard's adult perspective on her younger self?

READINGS

David Sedaris

Me Talk Pretty One Day

David Sedaris (b. 1956), a humorist and social critic, is a prolific essayist, short story writer, and dramatist (in collaboration with his sister, Amy Sedaris), whose radio pieces have been featured on the popular podcast *This American Life*. Recipient of the Thurber Prize for American Humor, his writing appears regularly in the *New Yorker* magazine, and he has published more than a dozen best-selling book collections including *Me Talk Pretty One Day* (2000), from which this selection about his French language class is excerpted.

- **Before you read,** think about whether you have ever been in a "sink or swim" situation, as Sedaris is in this class. If you were in a similar situation, how did you feel at the time?

- **As you read,** notice any places where Sedaris uses humor. How does his use of humor affect your attitude toward Sedaris and the story he tells?

I've moved to Paris with hopes of learning the language. My school is an easy ten-minute walk from my apartment, and on the first day of class I arrived early, watching as the returning students greeted one another in the school lobby. Vacations were recounted, and questions were raised concerning mutual friends with names like Kang and Vlatnya. Regardless of their nationalities, everyone spoke in what sounded to me like excellent French. Some accents were better than others, but the students exhibited an ease and confidence I found intimidating. As an added discomfort, they were all young, attractive, and well dressed, causing me to feel not unlike Pa Kettle trapped backstage after a fashion show. 1

The first day of class was nerve-racking because I knew I'd be expected to perform. That's the way they do it here — it's everybody into the language pool, sink or swim. The teacher marched in, deeply tanned from a recent vacation, and proceeded to rattle off a series of administrative announcements. I've spent quite a few summers in Normandy, and I took a month-long French class before leaving New York. I'm not completely in the dark, yet I understood only half of what this woman was saying. 2

"If you have not *meimslsxp* or *lgpdmurct* by this time, then you should not be in this room. Has everyone *apzkiubjxow*? Everyone? Good, we shall begin." She spread out her lesson plan and sighed, saying, "All right, then, who knows the alphabet?" 3

It was startling because (a) I hadn't been asked that question in a while and (b) I realized, while laughing, that I myself did *not* know the alphabet. They're the same letters, but in France they're pronounced differently. I know the shape of the alphabet but had no idea what it actually sounded like. 4

"Ahh." The teacher went to the board and sketched the letter *a*. "Do we have any- 5
one in the room whose first name commences with an *ahh*?"

Two Polish Annas raised their hands, and the teacher instructed them to present 6
themselves by stating their names, nationalities, occupations, and a brief list of things
they liked and disliked in this world. The first Anna hailed from an industrial town
outside of Warsaw and had front teeth the size of tombstones. She worked as a seamstress, enjoyed quiet times with friends, and hated the mosquito.

"Oh, really," the teacher said. "How very interesting. I thought that everyone loved 7
the mosquito, but here, in front of all the world, you claim to detest him. How is it that
we've been blessed with someone as unique and original as you? Tell us, please."

The seamstress did not understand what was being said but knew that this was 8
an occasion for shame. Her rabbity mouth huffed for breath, and she stared down at
her lap as though the appropriate comeback were stitched somewhere alongside the
zipper of her slacks.

The second Anna learned from the first and claimed to love sunshine and detest 9
lies. It sounded like a translation of one of those Playmate of the Month data sheets,
the answers always written in the same loopy handwriting. "Turn-ons: Mom's famous
five-alarm chili! Turnoffs: insecurity and guys who come on too strong!!!!"

The two Polish Annas surely had clear notions of what they loved and hated, but 10
like the rest of us, they were limited in terms of vocabulary, and this made them
appear less than sophisticated. The teacher forged on, and we learned that Carlos,
the Argentine bandonion player, loved wine, music, and, in his words, "making sex
with the womens of the world." Next came a beautiful young Yugoslav who identified
herself as an optimist, saying that she loved everything that life had to offer.

The teacher licked her lips, revealing a hint of the saucebox we would later come 11
to know. She crouched low for her attack, placed her hands on the young woman's
desk, and leaned close, saying, "Oh yeah? And do you love your little war?"

While the optimist struggled to defend herself, I scrambled to think of an answer 12
to what had obviously become a trick question. How often is one asked what he
loves in this world? More to the point, how often is one asked and then publicly ridi-
culed for his answer? I recalled my mother, flushed with wine, pounding the tabletop
late one night, saying, "Love? I love a good steak cooked rare. I love my cat, and I
love . . ." My sisters and I leaned forward, waiting to hear our names.

"Tums," our mother said. "I love Tums." 13

The teacher killed some time accusing the Yugoslavian girl of masterminding a 14
program of genocide, and I jotted frantic notes in the margins of my pad. While I can
honestly say that I love leafing through medical textbooks devoted to severe derma-
tological conditions, the hobby is beyond the reach of my French vocabulary, and
acting it out would only have invited controversy.

When called upon, I delivered an effortless list of things that I detest: blood sau- 15
sage, intestinal pâtés, brain pudding. I'd learned these words the hard way. Having given it some thought, I then declared my love for IBM typewriters, the French
word for *bruise*, and my electric floor waxer. It was a short list, but still I managed
to mispronounce *IBM* and assign the wrong gender to both the floor waxer and the

typewriter. The teacher's reaction led me to believe that these mistakes were capital crimes in the country of France.

"Were you always this *palicmkrexis*?" she asked. "Even a *fiuscrzsa ticiwelmun* 16 knows that a typewriter is feminine."

I absorbed as much of her abuse as I could understand, thinking—but not say- 17 ing—that I find it ridiculous to assign a gender to an inanimate object incapable of disrobing and making an occasional fool of itself. Why refer to Lady Crack Pipe or Good Sir Dishrag when these things could never live up to all that their sex implied?

The teacher proceeded to belittle everyone from German Eva, who hated laziness, 18 to Japanese Yukari, who loved paintbrushes and soap. Italian, Thai, Dutch, Korean, and Chinese—we all left class foolishly believing that the worst was over. She'd shaken us up a little, but surely that was just an act designed to weed out the dead-weight. We didn't know it then, but the coming months would teach us what it was like to spend time in the presence of a wild animal, something completely unpredict-able. Her temperament was not based on a series of good and bad days but, rather, good and bad moments. We soon learned to dodge chalk and protect our heads and stomachs whenever she approached us with a question. She hadn't yet punched any-one, but it seemed wise to protect ourselves against the inevitable.

Though we were forbidden to speak anything but French, the teacher would occa- 19 sionally use us to practice any of her five fluent languages.

"I hate you," she said to me one afternoon. Her English was flawless. "I really, 20 really hate you." Call me sensitive, but I couldn't help but take it personally.

After being singled out as a lazy *kfdtinvfm*, I took to spending four hours a night 21 on my homework, putting in even more time whenever we were assigned an essay. I suppose I could have gotten by with less, but I was determined to create some sort of identity for myself: David the hard worker, David the cut-up. We'd have one of those "complete this sentence" exercises, and I'd fool with the thing for hours, invariably set-tling on something like "A quick run around the lake? I'd love to! Just give me a moment while I strap on my wooden leg." The teacher, through word and action, conveyed the message that if this was my idea of an identity, she wanted nothing to do with it.

My fear and discomfort crept beyond the borders of the classroom and accom- 22 panied me out onto the wide boulevards. Stopping for a coffee, asking directions, depositing money in my bank account: these things were out of the question, as they involved having to speak. Before beginning school, there'd been no shutting me up, but now I was convinced that everything I said was wrong. When the phone rang, I ignored it. If someone asked me a question, I pretended to be deaf. I knew my fear was getting the best of me when I started wondering why they don't sell cuts of meat in vending machines.

My only comfort was the knowledge that I was not alone. Huddled in the hall- 23 ways and making the most of our pathetic French, my fellow students and I engaged in the sort of conversation commonly overheard in refugee camps.

"Sometime me cry alone at night."   24

"That be common for I, also, but be more strong, you. Much work and someday 25 you talk pretty. People start love you soon. Maybe tomorrow, okay."

Unlike the French class I had taken in New York, here there was no sense of competition. When the teacher poked a shy Korean in the eyelid with a freshly sharpened pencil, we took no comfort in the fact that, unlike Hyeyoon Cho, we all knew the irregular past tense of the verb *to defeat*. In all fairness, the teacher hadn't meant to stab the girl, but neither did she spend much time apologizing, saying only, "Well, you should have been *vkkdyo* more *kdeynfulh*." 26

Over time it became impossible to believe that any of us would ever improve. Fall arrived and it rained every day, meaning we would now be scolded for the water dripping from our coats and umbrellas. It was mid-October when the teacher singled me out, saying, "Every day spent with you is like having a cesarean section." 27

And it struck me that, for the first time since arriving in France, I could understand every word that someone was saying. 28

Understanding doesn't mean that you can suddenly speak the language. Far from it. It's a small step, nothing more, yet its rewards are intoxicating and deceptive. The teacher continued her diatribe and I settled back, bathing in the subtle beauty of each new curse and insult. 29

"You exhaust me with your foolishness and reward my efforts with nothing but pain, do you understand me?" 30

The world opened up, and it was with great joy that I responded, "I know the thing that you speak exact now. Talk me more, you, plus, please, plus." 31

READING FOR MEANING

For help with reading strategies like summarizing and analyzing assumptions, see Chapter 2.

1. **Read to Summarize.** Write a sentence or two explaining what happened at the school Sedaris describes and what it reveals about Sedaris.

2. **Read to Respond.** Write a paragraph exploring your reactions to the dialogue Sedaris includes, especially his representation of what his teacher says. The first bit of dialogue reads as follows: "If you have not *meimslsxp* or *lgpdmurct* by this time, then you should not be in this room. Has everyone *apzkiubjxow*?" (par. 3).

3. **Read to Analyze Assumptions.** Write a paragraph or two analyzing an assumption you find intriguing in Sedaris's essay. For example:

   Assumptions about wanting to impress others. At the beginning of the essay Sedaris admits, "The first day of class was nerve-racking because I knew I'd be expected to perform" (par. 2). Toward the end of the essay he further explains, "After being singled out as a lazy *kfdinvfm*. . . . I was determined to create some sort of identity for myself: David the hard worker, David the cut-up" (par. 20). To think critically about these assumptions, consider questions like these:

   • Why do you think Sedaris is so concerned about how he appears to his teacher, especially in light of her attitude toward him and the other students?

- How does what the teacher thinks of Sedaris affect him outside of the class-room, and why is that significant?

Assumptions about community. Sedaris explains that despite his "fear and discomfort" (par. 21), "[my] only comfort was the knowledge that I was not alone. Huddled in the hallways and making the most of our pathetic French, my fellow students and I engaged in the sort of conversation commonly overheard in refugee camps" (par. 22). To think critically about assumptions about community consider questions like these:

- How do Sedaris's descriptions of his fellow classmates, as well as his use of direct quotations to show how they speak French, provide insight into his attitudes toward them?
- Why does this sense of community become so important to Sedaris? What do you think helped to create this community among the students?

READING LIKE A WRITER

Conveying the Autobiographical Significance

To convey the significance of the experience they are describing, autobiographers share with readers both what they were thinking at the time they are describing and how they feel now as they reflect on that past experience. Remembered thoughts and feelings — as well as current ones — are usually complex and ambivalent rather than predictable or simplistic, which is often why these experiences have lasting significance for the writer.

ANALYZE & WRITE

Write a paragraph or two analyzing the significance of Sedaris's experience at the school in Paris:

1. Reread the essay, noting passages where Sedaris is describing his remembered thoughts and feelings, as well as his current thoughts and feelings as he writes about his past. Which words or phrasing in these passages allow you to differentiate between Sedaris's past and present feelings?
2. Skim the many instances of dialogue in the piece. How does the inclusion of so much dialogue help convey the significance of the experience for Sedaris?

Molly Montgomery

Literacy Narrative: In Search of Dumplings and Dead Poets

Molly Montgomery received a B.A. in English and French from UCLA and recently earned a Master's Degree in Creative Writing from UC Davis. A writer of both fiction and nonfiction, she often writes about her identity, as well as her experiences traveling around the world. Her work has been published in *Entropy* and the *Blue Lake Review*. She is also a contributor to the *MFA Years*. "In Search of Dumplings and Dead Poets" first appeared in *Entropy*.

- **Before you read,** think about places you have chosen to visit and why. These need not be far away or exotic places.

- **As you read,** consider how Montgomery describes her various family members, as well as herself in relation to them. How does this help you understand her family dynamic?

Shakespeare's Globe Theatre in London rises from the ground 750 feet from the original site of the theater, the one built by the Chamberlain's Men. Its white timbered exterior glows like the page of a glossy picture book. It looks like it belongs in Disneyland, not Elizabethan England. The original site of the Globe was not discovered until 1989, underneath a parking lot. It's a common happenstance in Europe. Dig up a parking lot almost anywhere and you'll find a lost monument underneath. It's amazing how books and plays and culture survive, but we can misplace entire buildings. 1

I visit the theater with my mother on a whirlwind three-day trip in London. An English major in my junior year of college, I am in the middle of my semester abroad in France. During my fall break, I travel to the UK to pay tribute to my favorite dead poets. 2

It's the off season, so instead of seeing a play we take a tour. The guide takes us into the yard, where the common people watched plays for just a penny. I imagine it would have been not so different from a mosh pit at a popular concert, except there were no microphones or speakers. I gaze up at the stage, which is bare, and from this vantage point, it does not look much different from any other stage where people might perform Shakespeare. If I were actually standing in the crowd, watching a play, I would be too short to see anything. When I consider this, I think of all the other limiting factors I would have faced if I had lived in the seventeenth century. I wouldn't have been able to see: I am nearsighted and back then I would not have access to proper eyeglasses. I would have probably caught the plague anyway. 3

Then there's the undeniable fact that a person like me, with mixed race ancestry, would be unlikely to exist in Elizabethan England. As of yet, I've never heard of a 4 half-Asian woman living in Britain during Shakespeare's time. If there had been one, she probably would have been displayed as a curiosity, like Pocahontas.

Yet if I could take a time machine back, I doubt anyone would give me a second 5 glance. With my pale skin and European features, I look as white as any other Anglo-Saxon. On the other hand, my darker-skinned Chinese-American mother would not blend in at all. If we were not traveling together, I wonder if people would be able to tell we are related.

Shakespeare's Globe is the first stop on our literary pilgrimage. Next up, we visit 6 Westminster Abbey, home to graves and memorials of dozens of prominent British writers. Inside the abbey, tourists shuffle down the nave and from one tomb to another, listening intently to their free audio guides. The dead kings and queens, the coronation throne, all the relics of the British Empire pique my interest, but I am not satisfied until at last we arrive in Poets' Corner. I'm overwhelmed by all the familiar names, carved into stone: Chaucer, Longfellow, Marlowe, Dickens, Shakespeare, Keats, Shelley. Almost all men, save for a few notable exceptions—the Brontë sisters and Jane Austen. These are the literary greats that I've idolized since I was a teenager. They all write in English, my only native language, and the language of my father's side of the family. I don't know of any writers who write in the language of my mother's family, Cantonese.

After our tour, my mother and I try out the British tradition of afternoon tea in the 7 abbey's Cellarium. We eat currant scones with clotted cream. When the servers offer us milk and sugar to add to our tea, we shake our heads and laugh. We take our tea black. I have learned from my mother that this is only way to drink tea, steeping the tea leaves for so long that murky darkness overwhelms the mug. Adding something sweet to the tea would ruin its rich bitterness.

In the Heathrow airport at the end of our trip, my mother and I realize we have 8 forgotten to buy tea from the official Twinings shop when we visited. She grabs a few tins from the store in the terminal.

"If anyone asks, we didn't get these from the airport," she tells me. It will be our 9 little secret when we get back and give these tins as gifts to our friends and relatives. Does it matter where we bought the tea, when the tea leaves were probably picked by laborers in India or China? After all, tea originated in Ancient China, and only became a British staple when the British started growing it in India, which was under colonial rule. Yet when we think of tea, we often associate it with British culture, as if it arrived in Britain fully formed, divorced from the history of colonial oppression. As long as the tea has the Twinings brand stamped on it, the source of the tea is irrelevant. The tea is British.

When my mother goes to a Chinese restaurant, she asks loudly for "cha" in her 10 best Cantonese accent. It's one of the few words she knows how to say in Cantonese, and she announces this word and the handful of phrases she learned as a child like an incantation when the waiter seats us. It's not just the food she's hoping will appear, but also the recognition from the waiter that these words also belong to her.

"Saam," she says, when she, my father, and I walk into a bustling dim sum restau- 11 rant. *Three.* She gestures at the three of us, to show we are one party. The waiter answers back in Cantonese. This is beyond my mother's level of understanding, so she switches to English. Still, when we order our food, we let her speak to the waiter, as if she is our translator. She peppers Cantonese words into her order, mostly names of food dishes: *gai lan, cheung fan, ha gow, daan tat, cha siu bao*. Here, in restaurants where servers walk by with carts, trying to entice us with steamed dumplings in bamboo containers, is where I learn my mother's culture.

The first person to call me "hapa" was my grandfather, who grew up in Hawaii. 12 His family emigrated from China to Oahu two generations before he was born, when Hawaii still had a monarch. He sprinkled Hawaiian pidgin and Cantonese words into his English and told me stories about growing up on the islands, how his parents who worked at a pineapple cannery brought the sweet fruit home so often that he grew to hate its taste. "Hapa," he told me, meant half in Hawaiian. It was short for "hapa haole," or, half-white. This used to be a derogatory term for mixed-race people, but my grandpa used it as a term of endearment. Still, by calling me "hapa," he defined me not by what we shared, but by how we were different.

At school, I told people I was half-Chinese, choosing to identify as the half that 13 was different than most of my classmates, who were white. One of my friends in high school jokingly called me "Wasian"—a combination of white and Asian. She said that I fit the stereotype of a half-Asian kid well: I had high grades, but I wasn't as good at math as the full Asian kids. At the time, I laughingly accepted this moniker. But something about it didn't seem right. My mother likes to say she defied the stereotype of the smart Asian kid because she was never very good at academics. Her classmates tried to cheat by looking at her tests, and she didn't stop them. She would just tell them, "Go ahead and copy my answers, but you're probably not going to get an A."

On the other hand, I excelled at school, and I let my good grades define me. I was 14 a geek, a nerd, a bookworm. But I was also hapa, which, by the time I got to college, had become a more widespread term to refer to anyone with part-Asian heritage. I didn't know how these two parts of me fit together—being hapa and also loving books. They existed in two different realms.

I was lucky to have parents who took me on trips to places around the world. 15 Neither of them had the experience of visiting another country until they were adults. They wanted to give me the chance to see the world even as a child. So we vacationed in distant locales, usually places that my dad had already visited on business trips: Sydney, Australia, Rotterdam, the Netherlands, Vancouver, Canada. When I was fourteen, we traveled to Rome.

I told my parents that while we were in Rome, we had to visit the Shelley-Keats 16 house, a small apartment at the base of the Spanish steps where the poet Keats spent the last months of his life. At the time, I had not read much of the Romantic poets, but the little I knew about them, their tragic fates and scandalous love affairs, made me want to learn more. I wasn't clear back then how Keats and Shelley were related, although I knew plenty about Mary Shelley; I adored *Frankenstein*. The Creature was my favorite character. I mourned for the cruel way the world treated him; I understood why he lashed out against a world that was hostile to him from the moment it laid eyes on his ugliness. I was in the midst of my teenage awkward phase, with acne erupting on my face and braces on my teeth. Now the comparison seems absurd, but when I was fourteen it made sense to me. When I was twenty-two, I came back to Rome, this time on my own, and visited the Shelley-Keats house again. Pacing around the three cramped rooms of the small museum, I felt the magic that it held for me as a teenager was missing. Now I knew that Keats and Shelley had not traveled to Italy together; Shelley never even lived in the house. I pored over the letters they had on display, trying to discern the words of their loopy cursive and finding that they looked just as much like gibberish to me as the Latin inscriptions on Roman monuments. A sign in Keats' bedroom explained that none of the furniture in the room is original. When Keats died of tuberculosis, they burned all of his furniture. So the bed, the writing desk—all of these were a reconstruction, a museum set of antiques meant to stand in for objects that were much more precious.

17 This was not the bed where Keats died, I kept thinking. In this room, he took his final breath, but that dissipated long ago. There was a painting of the view from the room's window, depicting how the Piazza di Spagna would have looked to Keats. I liked that painting better than anything else in the room. It seemed to get at the heart of what I wanted to know: what was it like to be here with Keats, gazing out the window at the carriages passing by?

18 The now celebrated poet spent the last few months of his life in incredible pain, bedridden in that room. The Roman air didn't cure him, and I imagine the noises from the square below—the hoof beats from horses, the cries of the merchants, the peals of laughter, the screams of children playing in the fountain—disturbed his sleep. It isn't fair. He should have had a long life. He should have had a chance to marry and write more poetry.

19 I don't know why I care so much about a dead poet who lived two hundred years ago. Maybe it's because I've trod the same paths as him, traveling through Europe. Or maybe it's because I can step where Keats stepped, watch the view of the sunset filtering through Via Condotti from the top of the Spanish steps, and understand what his experience was like through his words. He left poetry behind and letters and journals and all sorts of tangible markers of his existence. The vast majority of dead people don't have that luxury to speak so directly to people currently living. I will never know what life was like for my great-great-grandparents who immigrated from China to Hawaii in the late 1800's, and even though my grandparents told me about their own lives, they are gone now and any untold stories have vanished with them.

20 My parents and I hit all the main sights in Rome—the Roman forum, the Colosseum, Castel Sant'Angelo, the Vatican—but we also spend an entire day searching for the one street that makes up Rome's Chinatown. I'm not sure where my mother even got the idea that there was a Chinatown in Rome, but she insists that we look for it. She is craving some authentic Chinese food, and she wants to see what Italy had to offer. We take the metro to the Esquilino district which supposedly contains Chinese shops and stores. My dad and I glance at each other and roll our eyes. We're both used to my mother fixating on something ridiculous like this, and we know from experience that it's better to just go along with it.

My mother circles the street on the map, but the map is of little use. Under the 21 heat of the June sun, my parents and I pace the cobblestones for hours, peeking into alleyways, turning down side streets, checking the map again and again. By this time, it's almost 2 PM, when many restaurants take their midday break and close. We are famished. I grow angrier with my mother by the minute. With all Rome had to offer, why are we wasting a whole day trying to find Chinese food? I don't protest out loud because I know my mother will snap right back at me, and it will lead to a fight.

Then, at last, we spot Chinese characters on a store awning. We aren't sure if it is 22 even the street we were looking for, but it is good enough for my mother. My father and I are just relieved to be able to rest our feet and eat something. We enter the dingy restaurant, whose blinds shield the light from coming in. It looks nothing like a Chinese restaurant at home. There are no circular tables, no Lazy Susans, no Chinese paintings with bold ink brushstrokes on the walls, no golden buddhas hidden in a corner. It has neat rectangular tables and checkered tablecloths, and it looks just like any other restaurant in Rome, only darker. I wonder why they let so little light seep into the restaurant. Maybe so we cannot examine the food too closely.

My mother tries to order using Cantonese, but the waitress responds in Mandarin. 23 We look over the menu, unable to read the Italian or the Chinese. We order with broken words and exaggerated gestures.

Whenever my family eats at a Chinese restaurant at home, the waiters give my 24 mother chopsticks and my father and I forks. It's one of those weird instances that reminds you that everyone around you is always assessing you and putting you into a category. My mom fits into the Chinese category, and my dad and I into the white. But here they don't even have chopsticks to give out to us. There are only forks.

At last, they bring out the noodles. From the first bite they taste strange, wrong. 25 Too firm, not slippery enough. They are not rice noodles, but pasta, and the sauce is not oyster sauce or fish sauce or even soy sauce. It's tomato-based, but it is not like the tomato chow mein I sometimes eat at home, with cooked tomatoes slices and onions. This sauce has the consistency and flavor of marinara. It has oregano, not ginger. I don't spit it out, and I don't say anything out loud, although the waiter would not understand me if I did. My mother and I look at each other, and I know we are thinking the same thing. The food tastes like disappointment.

On my various trips to Europe, I've learned to lower my expectations for Chinese 26 food because it never tastes quite right. I tried a Chinese restaurant in France when I lived there because I needed to satisfy my craving for dumplings and noodles. The restaurant was in Strasbourg, the biggest city in Alsace. My French friend recommended it, and since he had lived in the U.S. before I thought he would be a decent judge of Chinese food.

The noodles were made from rice this time, but they were served on their own 27 without any sort of meat or vegetables mixed in. They did not have enough soy sauce on them, so they tasted bland. The dumplings, which on the French menu were called "Chinese Ravioli," came out on a platter, still crackling from the pan. The first bite I took started out promising—the chewy, greasy texture felt familiar in my mouth. But the meat filling tasted nothing like pot stickers at home. There were no crunchy chives in it or ginger or even cabbage to round out the savory flavor of the meat. It was just a meatball wrapped in dough. And it was all wrong.

Then again, what made my version of Chinese food "right?" The Chinese cuisine 28 that I know and love isn't "real" Chinese food. I've never been to China, but I know that Americanized Chinese food is a breed of its own, created by the ingenuity of Chinese immigrants flocking to California in search of gold. In the mining camps, and then later, in their restaurants, they threw together whatever ingredients they had available, including vegetables that didn't even grow in China, like broccoli and tomatoes, and mixed in the spices and sauces they could import from home to con- coct something distinct. Eventually, they perfected their recipes until they were just sweet and exotic-sounding enough to pull in the American customers who wanted a taste of "the Orient." The result are the familiar dishes that my family eats at ban- quets: Broccoli and Beef, Snow Peas and Water Chestnuts, Lettuce Wraps, Kung Pao Chicken, Peking Duck.

When I was growing up, my grandparents on my mother's side attended every 29 school function that featured me, their only grandchild. In their house, they had a whole wall with pictures of me on it and cards I had given them. There was a poster made of construction paper that I had made for Grandparent's Day tacked on the wall. On Grandparent's Day, we had an assembly where we told our grandparents "I love you" in different languages and each person chose a language to write in on their poster. I wrote mine in Hawaiian: "Aloha Nui Loa" *I love you very much.* They kept that poster above all the other pictures, like it was the title of gallery exhibition.

My grandparents house was always littered with newspapers, magazines, 30 unopened letters and classified ads. My grandfather subscribed to technical maga- zines. He was a jack-of-all-trades, always fiddling with broken machines. He was the family member you called when you had a plumbing problem or needed someone to help you put up a fence. My grandmother was quiet. She didn't like to talk about her past because she grew up in an orphanage for Chinese girls in San Francisco. She liked to buy expensive make-up and she stashed cash in the nooks and crannies of the house. I don't think I ever saw either of them read a book.

The private middle school I attended in Berkeley had a tradition of putting on a 31 Shakespeare play every year. The performances were about as good as you would expect from a bunch of pre-teens, which is, to say, not very good. Still, these shows were my first exposure to Shakespeare, and I grew up adoring his plays.

As Shakespeare's shortest play, *The Tempest was* possible to perform in one sitting 32 without abridging the text. The character I played, Ariel, popped up in almost every scene, casting spells on the other characters, so I had a lot of lines to memorize. I don't think I've studied harder or practiced more for anything in my entire life than I did for that play. For months I whispered the lines to myself at home and at school. While I was waiting in line at the grocery store with my mom, I would chant my cues and response. While I ate dinner, I would recite them between bites. I wanted to get the lines exactly write, just as Shakespeare wrote them.

In my Shakespeare class in college, I learned the postcolonial critique of *The* 33 *Tempest,* how it's really about the imperial power of Prospero, the civilized white master, who controls the elements and enslaves the degenerative native Caliban. Shakespeare was writing during the age of exploration, when the British Empire colonized half of the world and claimed that it was doing the world a favor by spreading Christian civilization through violent takeover. While Caliban—ugly, brutish, and savage—fulfills the stereotype of the frightening racial other, Ariel, who is also enslaved, can be viewed as the prototype of the Uncle Tom figure, or, perhaps, as the model minority. He eagerly obeys Prospero, preferring to serve him as well as he can and wait until Prospero grants him freedom, rather than rebel. When he asks for his freedom, Prospero reminds him that he saved Ariel from a much worse fate; his last master, the horrid witch Sycorax, who imprisoned the delicate spirit inside a tree. For all of Prospero's supposed fondness for Ariel, he tells the spirit that if Ariel complains, Prospero will shut him up in the tree again, this time for good.

34   Work hard and play by rules, and someday you'll be granted freedom, the play tells us. If you don't, you deserve whatever punishment you get.

35   My mother never learned her parent's native language, and for the most part, rejected her Chinese background, preferring instead the culture of the Rolling Stones and Lucille Ball. As the first person in her family to graduate from college and as the owner of a small business, she's quite the American success story; a real "self-made" woman and the ideal assimilated minority. I sometimes joke that my mother is the whitest Chinese person I know.

36   As an adult, my mother regretted not having a stronger connection to her culture. She wanted me to learn what she had not, so she sent me every summer to Hip Wah, a Chinese summer school in Oakland. It was not an immersion program, and it didn't focus much on language. Instead, it taught a bunch of Americanized Chinese kids to appreciate our "heritage." We took brush-painting lessons, practiced Kung Fu, hung paper lanterns, colored pictures of zodiac animals, and learned the same ten words of Mandarin, which we would promptly forget as soon as the summer ended and then re-learn a year later. I was one of the only mixed race kids in the school. The only white kids in my class were two blond sisters, daughters of the former Mormon missionary who taught our Mandarin lessons.

37   My favorite part of Hip Wah was the reading contest. The school had a library of children's books by Chinese-American authors, and each class competed against the other classes to see who could read the most books by the end of the month-long program. Being the book nerd that I was, I devoured most of the books in the library. I read all of Lawrence Yep's historical novels about Chinese laborers working on the railroads or mining gold. I read books by Amy Tan and Lensey Namioka about girls who feet were bound and who came to the U.S. as picture brides, marrying strangers they had never met. At the time, I thought these books were good stories, but I didn't think they were literature, not like Keats and Shelley and Shakespeare. Literature in my mind equaled dead white men. It wasn't until I got to college that I fully appreciated Hip Wah for exposing me to the narratives of Chinese-Americans and other people of color whose stories don't get told nearly often enough. I saw my family and myself in those books, and I realized that I had stories to tell, too.

In my first writing workshop in college, I had a professor, the writer Fae Ng, who 38
encouraged me to write the stories I had inside me, my family's stories.

"But how can I write about my family when I don't even speak their language?" I 39
asked her.

"You don't have to know Cantonese to be able to write about your family," she 40
told me. "Do your research, but also write what you know. That is the best material
you have."

I know what I don't know: I had a Chinese name once, but I lost it. One time at 41
Hip Wah, we had to tell our Mandarin teacher our Chinese names because we were
going to write them out in characters on a poster. That week, I asked my Grandpa
what my Chinese name was. Meanwhile, my white Mandarin teacher assumed without asking me that I didn't have a Chinese name. She gave me one, christening me
马丽 (Mǎ lì), beautiful horse, which sounds like my name in English. I don't remember
why I didn't ask her to call me by real Chinese name. Maybe I thought it would confuse her, since it was in Cantonese. Still, I have this sticky memory of what I thought
was my Chinese name. I even remember writing it down.

A few years ago, I googled what I thought was my Chinese name, Siu Mai. Spoiler 42
alert: It's a type of dumpling. My mother used to put them in my lunches in high
school and my white friends made fun of me for eating them, telling me that they
looked like testicles. Why are you eating pigs' balls, they taunted me. At some point,
the dumplings started tasting disgusting to me because I couldn't get that image out
of my head when I saw them packed into a Tupperware. I began to throw them out
without telling my mother.

Surely that couldn't be my real Chinese name. I must be misremembering the 43
name my grandpa told me. My grandpa wasn't a malicious man, but he had a strange
sense of humor. One time at a family banquet when I was a kid, he used his chopsticks to pluck the eye from fish on the table and offered it to me.

"Ew! No!" I protested. "That's gross."   44

"The eye is the best part," he told me, and slurped it down. Then he winked.   45

I wonder if he really did tell me that Siu Mai was my Chinese name. Maybe he 46
got a kick out of it. He used to make me repeat back Cantonese phrases to him. My
favorite one was "Gōngxǐ fācái" (Happy New Year), which I would pronounce "Gong
hay fa choy." My horrible accent made him laugh.

He died when I was fourteen from lung cancer caused by asbestos festering in 47
his lungs for decades from his years working as a shipwright. With him, he took
my Chinese name. For all I know, he was calling me a dumpling, and he thought
one day I would figure it out, and we would laugh at it together, the little joke we
shared.

READING FOR MEANING

1. **Read to Summarize.** Write a sentence or two explaining the importance of
   language and culture in this literacy narrative.

For help
with reading
strategies like
summarizing
and analyzing
assumptions,
see Chapter 2.

2. **Read to Respond.** Write a paragraph exploring your reactions to this selection, which its title tells us is a literacy narrative. Referring to the section in this chapter about literacy narratives (pp. 70–72), how do you see this piece fitting into that genre?

3. **Read to Analyze Assumptions.** Write a paragraph or two analyzing an assumption you find intriguing in Montgomery's essay. For example:

Assumptions about how others view us. List the different assumptions that Montgomery makes about how others view her. To think critically about these assumptions, consider questions like these:

- What differences and similarities do you see in the assumptions made by the different kinds of people (for example, friends, family, strangers) Montgomery describes?
- How do you think these assumptions impact how Montgomery views herself in relation to her family and to Cantonese culture? How do you know?

Assumptions about literature. Throughout her essay Montgomery, discusses many different books she has read. She writes of Chinese-American writers, "At the time, I thought these books were good stories, but I didn't think they were literature, not like Keats and Shelley and Shakespeare. Literature in my mind equaled dead white men." To think critically about this assumption, consider questions like these:

- How do you think Montgomery's realization that the stories of Chinese-Americans and other people of color don't get told often enough (par. 0) informed her decision to write this literacy narrative?

READING LIKE A WRITER

Describing a Place

To describe a place, a writer may use comparisons in the form of similes and metaphors to help enrich the overall impression of the place and help readers visualize it. Montgomery opens her essay with a description of the Globe Theatre. She uses a simile to help convey her impression of the place:

Its white timbered exterior glows like the page of a glossy picture book.

ANALYZE & WRITE

Write a paragraph or two analyzing how Montgomery describes some of the other places she discusses in her essay. These places may include the various sites she visits in Europe or the Chinese restaurants she describes visiting with her mother and father.

1. Choose two places that resonate most for you as a reader and explain what it is about how Montgomery describes those places that leaves you with such a strong impression. Use specific examples from the text.

2. Also note Montgomery's use of the describing strategies of *naming*, *detailing*, and *comparing*. Pick a place or two that she describes. Which aspects of those places does she name and detail? Which sense(s) does she use to give readers an impression of these places? What is the dominant impression that you get from her description?

Saira Shah

Longing to Belong

Saira Shah (b. 1964) is a journalist and documentary filmmaker. The daughter of an Afghan father and Indian mother, she was born and educated in England. After graduating from the School of Oriental and African Studies at London University, Shah began her career as a freelance journalist and eventually became a war correspondent, receiving the Courage under Fire and Television Journalist of the Year awards for her risky reporting on conflicts in some of the world's most troubled areas. She is best known in the United States for her undercover documentary films about the Taliban rule in Afghanistan, *Beneath the Veil* (2001) and *Unholy War* (2002). "Longing to Belong," originally published in the *New York Times Magazine* in 2003, is adapted from Shah's autobiography, *The Storyteller's Daughter* (2003), which relates her search to understand her father's homeland of Afghanistan.

- **Before you read,** think about any experiences you might have had as an outsider longing to belong, such as when you moved to a new school or joined a club.

- **As you read,** think about how Shah conveys her search for her ethnic identity and the sense of cultural dislocation she experiences.

The day he disclosed his matrimonial ambitions for me, my uncle sat me at his right   1
during lunch. This was a sign of special favor, as it allowed him to feed me choice tidbits from his own plate. It was by no means an unadulterated pleasure. He would often generously withdraw a half-chewed delicacy from his mouth and lovingly cram it into mine—an Afghan habit with which I have since tried to come to terms. It was his way of telling me that I was valued, part of the family.

My brother and sister, Tahir and Safia, and my elderly aunt Amina and I were all   2
attending the wedding of my uncle's son. Although my uncle's home was closer than I'd ever been, I was not yet inside Afghanistan. This branch of my family lived in Peshawar, Pakistan. On seeing two unmarried daughters in the company of a female chaperone, my uncle obviously concluded that we had been sent to be married. I was taken aback by the visceral longing I felt to be part of this world. I had never realized that I had been starved of anything. Now, at 17, I discovered that like a princess in a fairy tale, I had been cut off from my origins. This was the point in the tale where, simply by walking through a magical door, I could recover my gardens and palaces. If I allowed my uncle to arrange a marriage for me, I would belong.

Over the next few days, the man my family wished me to marry was introduced   3
into the inner sanctum. He was a distant cousin. His luxuriant black mustache was generally considered to compensate for his lack of height. I was told breathlessly that he was a fighter pilot in the Pakistani Air Force. As an outsider, he wouldn't have

been permitted to meet an unmarried girl. But as a relative, he had free run of the house. Whenever I appeared, a female cousin would fling a child into his arms. He'd pose with it, whiskers twitching, while the women cooed their admiration.

A huge cast of relatives had assembled to see my uncle's son marry. The wedding 4 lasted nearly 14 days and ended with a reception. The bride and groom sat on an elevated stage to receive greetings. While the groom was permitted to laugh and chat, the bride was required to sit perfectly still, her eyes demurely lowered. I didn't see her move for four hours.

Watching this *tableau vivant* of a submissive Afghan bride, I knew that marriage 5 would never be my easy route to the East. I could live in my father's mythological homeland only through the eyes of the storyteller. In my desire to experience the fairy tale, I had overlooked the staggeringly obvious: the storyteller was a man. If I wanted freedom, I would have to cut my own path. I began to understand why my uncle's wife had resorted to using religion to regain some control—at least in her own home. Her piety gave her license to impose her will on others.

My putative fiancé returned to Quetta, from where he sent a constant flow of lav- 6 ish gifts. I was busy examining my hoard when my uncle's wife announced that he was on the phone. My intended was a favorite of hers; she had taken it upon herself to promote the match. As she handed me the receiver, he delivered a line culled straight from a Hindi movie: "We shall have a love-match, *ach-cha*?" Enough was enough. I slammed down the phone and went to find Aunt Amina. When she had heard me out, she said: "I'm glad that finally you've stopped this silly wild goose chase for your roots. I'll have to extricate you from this mess. Wait here while I put on something more impressive." As a piece of Islamic one-upmanship, she returned wearing not one but three head scarves of different colors.

My uncle's wife was sitting on her prayer platform in the drawing room. Amina 7 stormed in, scattering servants before her like chaff. "Your relative . . . ," was Amina's opening salvo, ". . . has been making obscene remarks to my niece." Her mouth opened, but before she could find her voice, Amina fired her heaviest guns: "Over the *telephone*!"

"How dare you!" her rival began. 8

It gave Amina exactly the opportunity she needed to move in for the kill. "What? 9 Do you support this lewd conduct? Are we living in an American movie? Since when have young people of mixed sexes been permitted to speak to each other *on the telephone*? Let alone to talk—as I regret to inform you your nephew did—of love! Since when has love had anything to do with marriage? What a dangerous and absurd concept!"

My Peshawari aunt was not only outclassed; she was out-Islamed too. "My niece 10 is a rose that hasn't been plucked," Amina said. "It is my task as her chaperone to ensure that this happy state of affairs continues. A match under such circumstances is quite out of the question. The engagement is off." My uncle's wife lost her battle for moral supremacy and, it seemed, her battle for sanity as well. In a gruff, slack-jawed way that I found unappealing, she made a sharp, inhuman sound that sounded almost like a bark.

READING FOR MEANING

For help
with reading
strategies like
summarizing
and analyzing
assumptions,
see Chapter 2.

1. **Read to Summarize**. Write a few sentences explaining what happened in this story and the roles played by Shah's two aunts.

2. **Read to Respond**. Write a paragraph about anything that seems surprising, such as Shah's uncle's assumption that she and her sister were sent to Pakistan "to be married" (par. 2) or Shah's realization that "[i]f I wanted freedom, I would have to cut my own path" (par. 5).

3. **Read to Analyze Assumptions**. Write a paragraph or two analyzing an assumption you find intriguing in Shah's essay. For example:

   Assumptions about the values underlying cultural differences. Shah begins her story by describing how her uncle feeds her (par. 1). Shah seems ambivalent about this "Afghan habit" — expressing distaste as well as gratitude.

   - What do you think are the beliefs or values underlying Shah's mixed feelings about her uncle's "Afghan habit"?
   - If you have experienced cultural difference, what was your attitude and what values affected your way of thinking?

   Assumptions about the influence of fairy tales. Shah describes herself as "a princess in a fairy tale" (par. 2) in her father's "mythological homeland" (par. 5), but romantic stories about princesses such as *Cinderella* and *The Little Mermaid* are also popular in America.

   - What are girls — and perhaps also boys — taught by the fairy tales with which you are familiar?
   - How does Shah achieve a critical perspective toward her own "desire to experience the fairy tale" (par. 5)?

READING LIKE A WRITER

Narrating the Story

Like most autobiographers, Shah employs elements of the dramatic arc to arouse readers' curiosity and build suspense, leading us to wonder what will result of her uncle and his wife's "matrimonial ambitions" for her (par. 1). The opening scene (par. 1) dramatizes the intimate parental attitude her uncle adopts toward her, initiating the matchmaking story. Paragraph 2 provides exposition, using Shah's remembered feelings and thoughts to explain her internal conflict that is ultimately acted out in the power struggle between her uncle's wife and Aunt Amina.

ANALYZE & WRITE

Write a paragraph or two analyzing how Shah constructs her narrative.

1. Look back at the dramatic arc (Figure 3.1, p. 77) and reread Shah's story, noting in the margin where you find additional *exposition*, *rising action*, *climax*, *falling action*, and *resolution* and *reflection*. (Don't be surprised if some of the elements are very brief or missing altogether.)

2. How useful is the dramatic arc as a tool for analyzing Shah's autobiographical story? How does it help you understand how different scenes relate to one another and how they dramatize the central conflict?

Combining Reading Strategies

Contextualizing in Order to Reflect on Challenges to Your Beliefs and Values

Contextualize and *reflect* on Saira Shah's autobiographical narrative "Longing to Belong," by responding to the following writing prompts:

- Describe the argument between the two aunts in paragraphs 7–10. How do they compare? What kinds of arguments do the women use? How does their argument draw on their cultural and religious context?

- Describe the historical and cultural context in "Longing to Belong." Consider how your response to the reading might differ based on your understanding of the piece's context.

- Examine the bases of your personal response to this narrative. How is your response informed by your own beliefs about arranged marriages?

- Write a paragraph reflecting on the differences and similarities between your beliefs and values and those of the author and her family members, as represented in the narrative.

For help reflecting on challenges to your beliefs and values, see Chapter 2, pp. 57.

For help contextualizing, see Chapter 2, pp. 50.

Jenée Desmond-Harris

Tupac and My Non-Thug Life

Jenée Desmond-Harris is a staff editor at *the New York Times* op-ed page. Previously she was a staff writer at *Vox.com* and at the *Root*, an online magazine dedicated to African American news and culture. She writes about the intersection of race, politics, and culture in a variety of genres. She has also contributed to *Time* magazine, MSNBC's *Powerwall,* and *xoJane* on topics ranging from her relationship with her grandmother, to the political significance of Michelle Obama's hair, to the stereotypes that hinder giving to black-teen mentoring programs. She has provided television commentary on CNN, MSNBC, and Current TV. Desmond-Harris is a graduate of Howard University and Harvard Law School, and was a recipient of a John S. Knight Journalism Fellowship at Stanford University, where she investigated "how journalists who cover stories related to the African American experience can enrich their work with essential context about race and racial inequality." The selection below was published in the *Root* in 2011. It chronicles Desmond- Harris's reaction to the murder of rap icon Tupac Shakur in a Las Vegas drive-by shooting in 1996. She mentions Tupac's mother, Afeni, as well as the "East Coast–West Coast war" — the rivalry between Tupac and the Notorious B.I.G., who was suspected of being involved in Tupac's murder.

- **Before you read,** recall a public event that affected you. Reflect on why something that didn't affect you personally nevertheless had an emotional impact on you.

- **As you read,** consider how the photograph that appeared in the *Root* article and that is reproduced here contributes to readers' understanding of the young Desmond-Harris's reaction to the news of Tupac's death. How does the photo influence your understanding of the author's persona, or self-presentation?

I learned about Tupac's death when I got home from cheerleading practice that Friday afternoon in September 1996. I was a sophomore in high school in Mill Valley, Calif. I remember trotting up my apartment building's stairs, physically tired but buzzing with the frenetic energy and possibilities for change that accompany fall and a new school year. I'd been cautiously allowing myself to think during the walk home about a topic that felt frighteningly taboo (at least in my world, where discussion of race was avoided as delicately as obesity or mental illness): what it meant to be biracial and on the school's mostly white cheerleading team instead of the mostly black dance team. I remember acknowledging, to the sound of an 8-count that still pounded in my head as I walked through the door, that I didn't really have a choice: I could memorize a series of stiff and precise motions but couldn't actually dance.

My private musings on identity and belonging—not original in the least, but novel   2
to me—were interrupted when my mom heard me slam the front door and drop my
bags: *"Your friend died!"* she called out from another room. Confused silence. *"You
know, that rapper you and Thea love so much!"*

MOURNING A DEATH IN VEGAS

The news was turned on, with coverage of the deadly Vegas shooting. Phone calls   3
were made. Ultimately my best friend, Thea, and I were left to our own 15-year-old
devices to mourn that weekend. Her mother and stepfather were out of town. Their
expansive, million-dollar home was perched on a hillside less than an hour from
Tupac's former stomping grounds in Oakland and Marin City. Of course, her home
was also worlds away from both places.

We couldn't "pour out" much alcohol undetected for a libation, so we limited   4
ourselves to doing somber shots of liqueur from a well-stocked cabinet. One each.
Tipsy, in a high-ceilinged kitchen surrounded by hardwood floors and Zen flower
arrangements, we baked cookies for his mother. We packed them up to ship to Afeni
with a handmade card. ("Did we really do that?" I asked Thea this week. I wanted to
ensure that this story, which people who know me now find hilarious, hadn't mor-
phed into some sort of personal urban legend over the past 15 years. "Yes," she said.
"We put them in a lovely tin.")

On a sound system that echoed through speakers perched discreetly throughout   5
the airy house, we played "Life Goes On" on a loop and sobbed. We analyzed lyrics
for premonitions of the tragedy. We, of course, cursed Biggie. Who knew that the East
Coast–West Coast war had two earnest soldiers in flannel pajamas, lying on a king-
size bed decorated with pink toe shoes that dangled from one of its posts? There, we
studied our pictures of Tupac and re-created his tattoos on each other's body with a
Sharpie. I got "Thug Life" on my stomach. I gave Thea "Exodus 1811" inside a giant
cross. Both are flanked by "West Side."

A snapshot taken that Monday on our high school's front lawn (seen here) shows   6
the two of us lying side by side, shirts lifted to display the tributes in black marker.
Despite our best efforts, it's the innocent, bubbly lettering of notes passed in class
and of poster boards made for social studies presentations. My hair has recently been
straightened with my first (and last) relaxer and a Gold 'N Hot flatiron on too high a
setting. Hers is slicked back with the mixture of Herbal Essences and Blue Magic that
we formulated in a bathroom laboratory.

My rainbow-striped tee and her white wifebeater capture a transition between our   7
skater-inspired Salvation Army shopping phase and the next one, during which we'd
wear the same jeans slung from our hip bones, revealing peeks of flat stomach, but
transforming ourselves from Alternative Nation to MTV Jams imitators. We would
get bubble coats in primary colors that Christmas and start using silver eyeliner,
trying—and failing—to look something like Aaliyah.

MIXED IDENTITIES: TUPAC AND ME

Did we take ourselves seriously? Did we feel a real stake in the life of this "hard- 8 core" gangsta rapper, and a real loss in his death? We did, even though we were two mixed-race girls raised by our white moms in a privileged community where we could easily rattle off the names of the small handful of other kids in town who also had one black parent: Sienna. Rashea. Brandon. Aaron. Sudan. Akio. Lauren. Alicia. Even though the most subversive thing we did was make prank calls. Even though we hadn't yet met our first boyfriends, and Shock G's proclamations about putting satin on people's panties sent us into absolute giggling fits. And even though we'd been so delicately cared for, nurtured and protected from any of life's hard edges—with special efforts made to shield us from those involving race—that we sometimes felt ready to explode with boredom. Or maybe because of all that.

I mourned Tupac's death then, and continue to mourn him now, because his 9 music represents the years when I was both forced and privileged to confront what it meant to be black. That time, like his music, was about exploring the contradictory textures of this identity: The ambience and indulgence of the fun side, as in "California Love" and "Picture Me Rollin'." But also the burdensome anxiety and outright anger—"Brenda's Got a Baby," "Changes" and "Hit 'Em Up."

For Thea and me, his songs were the musical score to our transition to high school, 10 where there emerged a vague, lunchtime geography to race: White kids perched on a sloping green lawn and the benches above it. Below, black kids sat on a wall outside

The author (left) with her friend Thea
Courtesy of Jenée Desmond-Harris

the gym. The bottom of the hill beckoned. Thea, more outgoing, with more admirers among the boys, stepped down boldly, and I followed timidly. Our formal invitations came in the form of unsolicited hall passes to go to Black Student Union meetings during free periods. We were assigned to recite Maya Angelou's "Phenomenal Woman" at the Black History Month assembly.

Tupac was the literal sound track when our school's basketball team would come 11 charging onto the court, and our ragtag group of cheerleaders kicked furiously to "Toss It Up" in a humid gymnasium. Those were the games when we might breathlessly join the dance team after our cheer during time-outs if they did the single "African step" we'd mastered for BSU performances.

EVERYTHING BLACK—AND COOL

. . . Blackness became something cool, something to which we had brand-new 12 access. We flaunted it, buying Kwanzaa candles and insisting on celebrating privately (really, just lighting the candles and excluding our friends) at a sleepover. We memorized "I Get Around" and took turns singing verses to each other as we drove through Marin County suburbs in Thea's green Toyota station wagon. Because he was with us through all of this, we were in love with Tupac and wanted to embody him. On Halloween, Thea donned a bald cap and a do-rag, penciled in her already-full eyebrows and was a dead ringer.

Tupac's music, while full of social commentary (and now even on the Vatican's 13 playlist), probably wasn't made to be a treatise on racial identity. Surely it wasn't created to accompany two girls (*little* girls, really) as they embarked on a coming-of-age journey. But it was there for us when we desperately needed it.

READING FOR MEANING

1. **Read to Summarize.** Write a sentence or two explaining the conflict that underlies Desmond-Harris's story and how she tries to resolve it.

2. **Read to Respond.** Write a paragraph exploring anything that resonates with your experience — such as Desmond-Harris's claim that Tupac's music was the "sound track" for her youth (par. 11) — or that seems surprising — such as Desmond-Harris's identification with Tupac, perhaps reflecting on why Desmond-Harris and Thea give themselves Sharpie tattoos and take a photograph showing them off (pars. 5–6).

3. **Read to Analyze Assumptions.** Write a paragraph or two analyzing an assumption you find intriguing in Desmond-Harris's essay. For example:

For help with reading strategies like summarizing and analyzing assumptions, see Chapter 2.

Assumptions about celebrity. The fifteen-year-old Desmond-Harris apparently thought of Tupac as someone she knew personally, not as some distant star but as a family "friend" (par. 2). To think critically about assumptions regarding celebrity in this essay, consider questions like these:

- How do the media contribute to the sense that we have a personal relationship with certain celebrities?

- Critics like Daniel Boorstin argue that celebrities often are admired not because of their special talents or achievements but simply because they are famous. Why do you think Desmond-Harris is so enamored of Tupac?

Assumptions about identity. Desmond-Harris tells us that as a teenager she began to explore what she calls "the contradictory textures" — "the fun side" as well as "the burdensome anxiety and outright anger" — of her biracial identity (par. 9). To think critically about assumptions regarding identity in this essay, consider questions like these:

- Desmond-Harris describes the social and racial divisions in her high school (par. 10). What kinds of divisions existed in your high school and how did they affect how you presented yourself to others?

- In the last paragraph, Desmond-Harris explains that during the period she is writing about, she and her friend had "embarked on a coming-of-age journey" (par. 13). What do you think she learned about herself from Tupac's life and from his death?

READING LIKE A WRITER

Conveying the Autobiographical Significance

Events that have lasting significance nearly always involve mixed or ambivalent feelings. Therefore, readers expect and appreciate some degree of complexity. Multiple layers of meaning make autobiographical stories more, not less, interesting. Significance that seems simplistic or predictable makes stories less successful.

ANALYZE & WRITE

Write a paragraph or two analyzing Desmond-Harris's handling of the complex personal and cultural significance of Tupac's death:

1. Skim the last two sections (pars. 8–13), noting passages where Desmond-Harris tells readers her remembered feelings and thoughts at the time and her present perspective as an adult reflecting on the experience. How does she use this dual perspective to convey complexity?

2. Look closely at paragraph 8, and highlight the following sentence strategies:

- Rhetorical questions (questions writers answer themselves)
- Repeated words and phrases
- Stylistic sentence fragments (incomplete sentences used for special effect)

What effect do these sentence strategies have on readers? How do they help convey the significance of the event for Desmond-Harris?

Combining Reading Strategies

Annotating and Taking Inventory in Order to Compare and Contrast Related Readings

Reread the autobiographical narratives "Longing to Belong" by Saira Shah (p. 96) and "Tupac and My Non-Thug Life" by Jenée Desmond-Harris (p. 100).

For help annotating and taking inventory, see Chapter 2, pp. 35–41.

- As you read, *annotate* or take notes to keep track of how the readings handle their narrator's search for identity.

- Once you're done reading, *take inventory* of what you've read. Organize your annotations or notes in order to prepare to compare and contrast the readings. What similarities and differences do you see?

Drawing on your annotations, now *compare and contrast* the autobiographical narratives by thinking about the following issues.

For help comparing and contrasting related readings, see Chapter 2, pp. 57–60.

- Both stories show teenagers in search of their cultural identity. Write a paragraph about how their searches are similar and different.

- Both authors explore what Desmond-Harris calls "the contradictory textures" of the alternative identity they are trying on (par. 9). Write a paragraph about how they resolve their contradictory feelings, if at all.

Rhea Jameson

Mrs. Maxon

Rhea Jameson was a senior in college when she wrote the following literacy narrative for an assignment in her advanced expository writing class. In this literacy narrative, Jameson focuses on her experiences learning to write throughout high school and college. She focuses, in particular, on how an early teacher affected her understanding of writing, as well as on her development as a writer.

- **Before you read,** reflect on your own experience of learning to write in school. Do you recall specific lessons your teachers taught you? Did your teachers ever disagree on what constitutes good writing or on the "rules" of writing?

- **As you read,** consider whether Jameson's ultimate attitude toward Mrs. Maxon surprises you. What does Jameson appreciate about Mrs. Maxon? Based on how Jameson opens the essay, did you expect the essay to end as it does?

Her hair always pulled back in a tight bun, her lips pursed even tighter, Mrs. Maxon's 1 eyes bore into students as a drill bores into wood. Mrs. Maxon was my sophomore year high school English teacher, and she was tyrannical in her enforcement of writing rules. She expected us to write in a specific regimented way, and if we did not, we would not pass the class. She taught us that every essay should have five paragraphs, and each paragraph should have three sentences—no more, no less. The purpose of the first sentence was to introduce the quotation that appeared in the second sentence. The second sentence was comprised of the quote you had chosen to use from whatever you had been assigned to read. The third sentence interpreted that quote. These three-sentence paragraphs had to be framed by an introduction and conclusion, structured, of course, in a particular way. The conclusion was to be arranged in the opposite order of the introduction, while making the very same points. If you deviated from this structure you lost points, in Mrs. Maxon's own words, "for each infraction." The phrase "for each infraction" echoed in my head throughout my entire sophomore year. Sometimes if I listen hard enough I can still hear Mrs. Maxon saying it.

I can also still hear Mrs. Maxon asking, "Why aren't you better at this?" 2

She meant writing. As she asked me that question just a few weeks into the school 3 year I could feel my lunch turn over in my stomach. I had told her and the rest of the class on our first day that I wanted to be a journalist. I guess I wasn't there yet.

All I could manage to say in response was "I dunno." 4

Unsatisfied with my response, she asked with disgust, "Pardon?" 5

I grumbled, "I don't know." 6

Some students would have given up at that moment—they would have believed 7 they were weren't good writers and focused their attention on something else. But I didn't. In fact, Mrs. Maxon's criticism made me want to become a better writer.

Therefore, I was pleased to find out that Mrs. Maxon didn't only tell us how many 8
paragraphs and how many sentences each paragraph of our essays should have,
but she also told us exactly how these sentences must be written. We had to start
all sentences beyond the first sentence of each paragraph with transitional phrases
like "first," "second," and "additionally." When we quoted from a reading we had to
introduce the quote with any word other than "said." Instead, Mrs. Maxon required
us to use words like "discussed," "exclaimed," and "ruminated" because these words
were "more interesting." Finally, when we analyzed the quote in each paragraph, we
needed to begin that sentence with phrases like "in sum," "therefore," and "in other
words." To further drum these rules of writing into our brains, Mrs. Maxon provided
a handout that included transition words to use as we moved from one sentence and
paragraph to the next, lists of words to use instead of "said," and phrases to signal our
interpretation of the quote.

At the time, I didn't know how I would be affected by Mrs. Maxon's approach to 9
teaching writing. She did, after all, in writing scholar Lorraine Code's words, reduce
the "available discursive possibilities" (x) to a list of arbitrary words and phrases that
she deemed appropriate for use in our essays. Instead of a creative process, writing
became more of a word search for transitions and words other than "said," and Mrs.
Maxon's handouts allowed me to simply fill in the blanks. Still, I appreciated Mrs.
Maxon's approach to teaching because it seemed as if she was teaching us exactly
how to write. She laid out the rules for us and if we wanted to write well and earn a
good grade, we followed them. And at the time, I thought that following Mrs. Maxon's rules was the key to success in my other classes, too.

As I moved through high school and then through most of college, however, I 10
struggled. While I thought that Mrs. Maxon taught me the correct way to write, I
encountered other teachers that had different ideas about writing. In fact, some of
these ideas were totally opposite from what Mrs. Maxon taught me. For example,
when I was a freshman in college, my journalism professor told me never to under-
estimate the power of the word "said," which directly opposed Mrs. Maxon's rule. In
other classes early in my college career, the conclusions of my essays, which I had
written in the "Maxon format," were marked heavily with red ink, ink that told me
that my conclusion should not simply restate my introduction. Contrary to Mrs. Maxon's instructions, I was being taught by these instructors that a conclusion should not
only restate the main idea, but that it should leave the audience with something to
think about. It turned out that the "receptive conditions" of my writing changed, and
I needed to shift away from Mrs. Maxon's rules in order to succeed (Code x).

Lorraine Code describes rhetorical spaces as "fictive but not fanciful or fixed loca- 11
tions" (ix), and my experiences as a writer certainly support that. While one teacher
controls the rhetorical space by prohibiting the repetition of the word "said" another
emphasizes the clarity of the very same word and encourages its use. What did this
mean when it came to the correct way to write? Which teacher knew better? Was
Mrs. Maxon correct? Were the other instructors correct? Whose instructions should I
follow? How do I become a good writer?

It took some time, but in my junior year of college I took a course called Intro- 12
duction to Writing Studies, and I began to understand that there is no single correct

way to write. In this course, we read essays by a variety of writing experts. While I expected to learn from these experts—once and for all—the correct way to write, I learned the exact opposite. I learned about a concept called "the rhetorical situation,"—a concept that consists of identifying a writer's purpose, audience, context, and genre—and that all writers should be able to adapt their writing to the specific rhetorical situation. I learned that the strength of a piece of writing depends on many factors, including your goals, your audience, and what genre you are writing in. Writing Professor Joe Moxley explains that students can write "more effective documents and save time by considering the audience, purpose, context, and media for a document. . . .For every writing project, you can best determine what you want to say and how you want to say it by analyzing the components of your rhetorical situation." The concept of the rhetorical situation changed everything for me as a student. While I still needed to pay attention to what each of my professors wanted, I no longer needed to seek out the correct way to write because there was no single, correct way to write. Writing was no longer a word search that called for interesting signal phrases and a bevy of transition words. Writing called for an understanding of the rhetorical situation, and in order to produce good writing, I needed to be flexible and consider each rhetorical situation I was faced with.

I now write for my college newspaper and contribute to a number of blogs online   13 as I inch ever closer to my degree in journalism. And while I know now good writing doesn't mean finding eleven different ways to say "said," I still think of Mrs. Maxon as one of my best teachers. She may have stifled my creativity and independent thought by prescribing exactly how I should write, but she also pushed me to become a better writer and gave me a solid foundation that remains important even as a senior in college.

Works Cited

Code, Lorraine. *Rhetorical Spaces: Essays on Gendered Locations*. Routledge, 1995.
Moxley, Joe. Writing Commons. "Think Rhetorically,"
    https://writingcommons.org/think-rhetorically.

READING FOR MEANING

For help
with reading
strategies like
summarizing
and analyzing
assumptions,
see Chapter 2.

1. **Read to Summarize.** Write a sentence or two describing the main idea of this literacy narrative.

2. **Read to Respond.** Write a paragraph reflecting on anything from this essay that resonates with your experience of learning how to write.

3. **Read to Analyze Assumptions.** Write a paragraph analyzing an assumption you find intriguing in this literacy narrative. For example:

    Assumptions about creativity. Near the end of the literacy narrative, Jameson comments that maybe Mrs. Maxon "stifled my creativity and independent thought by prescribing exactly how I should write, but she also pushed me to become a better writer and gave me a solid foundation that remains important even as a senior in college" (par. 13).

- What assumption is Jameson making about creativity and independent thought? How much does she value these?
- Is there something that seems more important to Jameson than creativity? Do you agree with her?

Assumptions about good teaching. Jameson describes Mrs. Maxon as one of her "best teachers" (par. 13).

- What evidence does Jameson offer to support this characterization? Are you convinced?
- Where, if anywhere, does Jameson question the value or quality of Mrs. Maxon's teaching?

READING LIKE A WRITER

Presenting People

Description and dialogue can help create a vivid portrait and provide readers with insight into the writer's attitude toward and relationship with a person. Effective descriptions name the person and include a few well-chosen details that allow readers to visualize him or her. Dialogue can make readers feel as though they were overhearing what was said and how it was said. It usually includes **speaker tags** that identify the speaker ("In Mrs. Maxon's own words" [par. 1])and may also indicate the speaker's tone or attitude ("she asked with disgust" [par. 5] and "I grumbled" [par. 6]).

> I can also still hear Mrs. Maxon asking, "Why aren't you better at this?"

She meant writing. As she asked me that question I could feel my lunch turning over in my stomach. I had told her and the rest of the class on our first day that I wanted to be a journalist. I guess I wasn't there yet.

> All I could manage to say in response was "I dunno."
> Speaker tag   Unsatisfied with my response, she asked with disgust, "Pardon?"
> I grumbled, "I don't know."

Dialogue that is quoted can be especially expressive and vivid. But when the word choice is not particularly memorable, writers usually summarize dialogue to give readers the gist and move the story along more quickly.

Summary   <u>Mrs. Maxon didn't only tell us how many paragraphs and how</u>
<u>many sentences each paragraph of our essays should have, but she</u>
<u>told us exactly how these sentences must be written.</u> (par. 8).

ANALYZE & WRITE

Write a paragraph or two analyzing Jameson's use of description and dialogue (whether quoted, paraphrased, or summarized) to portray Mrs. Maxon and to help readers understand why she was such an important figure in Jameson's education.

1. Reread the opening paragraph. Notice how Jameson opens the essay with a physical description of Mrs. Maxon. How does Jameson's description of Mrs. Maxon complement or highlight how Jameson describes Mrs. Maxon's approach to teaching writing?

2. Instead of simply explaining that Mrs. Maxon took points off for each mistake, Jameson quotes Mrs. Maxon as saying "for each infraction" (par. 1). What difference does this make? How might this approach be more effective than simply summarizing that aspect of Mrs. Maxon's way of grading?

Writing to Learn Autobiography and Literacy Narratives

Write a brief essay analyzing one of the readings in this chapter (or another selection, perhaps writing by a classmate). Explain how (and perhaps, how well) the selection works as an autobiography or literacy narrative. Consider, for example, how it uses

- the dramatic arc to make the story engaging or suspenseful;

- naming, detailing, and comparing to make people and places come alive;

- remembered feelings and thoughts, plus present perspective, to convey the personal and cultural significance.

Your essay could also reflect on how you applied one or more of the following practices as you read the selection:

- **Critical analysis** — what assumptions in the selection did you find intriguing, and why?

- **Rhetorical sensitivity** — how effective or ineffective do you think the selection is in achieving its purpose for the intended audience, given the constraints of the medium and the autobiography genre?

- **Empathy** — did you find yourself identifying with the author, and how important was this to the effectiveness of the selection?

A GUIDE TO WRITING AUTOBIOGRAPHY AND LITERACY NARRATIVES

You have probably done a good deal of analytical writing about your reading. Your instructor may also assign a capstone project to write a brief autobiography or literacy narrative of your own. This Guide to Writing offers detailed suggestions and resources to help you meet the special challenges this kind of writing presents.

THE WRITING ASSIGNMENT

Write about a significant event, including a literacy event, or person in your life.

- Choose an event or person that you feel comfortable writing about for this audience (your instructor and classmates), given your purpose (to present something meaningful).

- Consider how you can tell the story dramatically or describe the person vividly.

- Try to convey the meaning and importance in your life — what we call the autobiographical significance — of the event or person you've chosen to write about. Think about how you can lead readers to understand you better, to reflect on their own lives, to become aware of social and cultural influences, or to gain some other insights.

WRITING YOUR DRAFT

Choosing a Subject

Rather than limiting yourself to the first subject that comes to mind, take a few minutes to consider your options and list as many subjects as you can. Below are some criteria that can help you choose a promising subject, followed by suggestions for the types of events and people you might consider writing about.

The subject should

- reveal something significant, possibly by centering on a conflict (within yourself or between you and another person or institution)

- express complex or ambivalent feelings (rather than superficial or sentimental ones that oversimplify the subject or make it predictable)

- lead readers to think about their own experience and about the cultural forces that shape their lives and yours

Appropriate events might include

- a difficult situation (for example, a time you had to make a tough choice or struggled to perform a challenging task)

- an incident or encounter with another person that shaped you in a particular way or revealed a personality trait (independence, insecurity, ambition, jealousy, or heroism) that you had not recognized before

- an occasion when something did not turn out as you thought it would (for example, when you expected to be criticized but were praised or ignored instead, or when you were convinced you would succeed but failed)

- an encounter with a book (for example, a book that completely changed your perspective on a subject)

- an important moment in your development as a reader and/or writer (for example, when you struggled to read a book that all of your peers read with ease)

- an incident that affected how you communicate electronically (for example, when by accident you sent an email intended for your best friend to your professor)

An appropriate person might be

- someone who made you feel you had something worthwhile to contribute, or someone who made you feel like an outsider

- someone who helped you develop a previously unknown or undeveloped side of yourself or who led you to question assumptions or stereotypes you had about other people

- someone who surprised, pleased, or disappointed you (for example, someone you admired who let you down, or someone you did not appreciate who turned out to be admirable)

- someone who taught you how to read or write, or someone that stood in your way of developing these abilities

Shaping Your Story

Use the elements of the dramatic arc in Figure 3.1 (p. 77) to organize the story:

Sketching Out the Exposition, or Backstory. Your readers will need to understand what happened. Using the sentence strategies below as a starting point, sketch out the backstory of your event:

▶ In .... [year], while I was .... ing in ....
[location], ...

▶ [Person's name] knew all about .... because s/he was a/an .... ,
an expert on ....

▶ In past years, I had previously .... Now I was starting ....

Drafting the "Inciting Incident."   Sketch out the conflict that triggers the story. To dramatize it, try creating action sequences, using action verbs and prepositional phrases and dialogue, including speaker tags and quotation marks:

Action verb	A black Buick was moving toward us down the street. We all
Prepositional phrase	spread out, banged together some regular snowballs, took aim, and, when the Buick drew nigh, fired. (Dillard, par. 7)

Dramatizing the Rising Action and Climax.   The moment of surprise, confrontation, crisis, or discovery — the climax of your story — can be dramatized by using action sequences and by repeating key words. Some writers also include dialogue to dramatize the climax:

Action words	Amina stormed in, scattering servants before her like chaff. "Your
Dialogue	relative . . ." was Amina's opening salvo, ". . . has been making obscene remarks to my niece." Her mouth opened, but before she could find her voice, Amina fired her heaviest guns: "Over the *telephone!*" (Shah, para. 7)

Experimenting with Endings.   Try out a variety of endings. For example, refer in the ending to something from the beginning — repetition with a difference.

Winter/snow setting	In winter, in the snow, there was neither baseball nor football, so the boys and I threw snowballs at passing cars. I got in trouble throwing
Car	snowballs, and have seldom been happier since. (Dillard, par. 2)
Emotional state of happiness	If in that snowy backyard the driver of the black Buick had cut off our heads, Mikey's and mine, I would have died happy, for nothing has required so much of me since as being chased all over Pittsburgh in the middle of winter — running terrified, exhausted — by this sainted, skinny, furious redheaded man who wished to have a word with us. I don't know how he found his way back to his car. (Dillard, par. 21)

Working with Sources

Incorporating Outside Sources to Help Shape Your Story. Consider what an outside source or two might add to your autobiography or literacy narrative. Are there outside sources that would help you explain some aspect of your story?

For more on citation in MLA and APA, see Chapter 12.

Would an outside source help you develop the point you are making or help your audience understand this point? For example, consider how Jameson uses an outside source to describe the effects of Mrs. Maxon's teaching approach.

> She did, after all, in writing scholar Lorraine Code's words, reduce the "available discursive possibilities" (x) to a list of arbitrary words and phrases that she deemed appropriate for use in our essays. (Jameson, par. 9)

Using the sentence strategies below as a **starting point**, consider how you could incorporate sources into your essay:

> X characterizes the problem this way: "..."
>
> According to X, _____ is defined as "..."
>
> "...," explains X.
>
> X argues strongly in favor of the policy, pointing out that "..."

You can use these strategies to advance an **argument of your own**, or to represent an opposing view:

> I learned that the strength of a piece of writing depends on many factors, including your goals, your audience, and what genre you are writing in. Writing Professor Joe Moxley explains that students can write "more effective documents and save time by considering the audience, purpose, context, and media for a document. . . .For every writing project, you can best determine what you want to say and how you want to say it by analyzing the components of your rhetorical situation." (Jameson, par. 12)

Presenting Important People and Places

Using Naming, Detailing, and Comparing. Describe the way important people look, dress, walk, or gesture; their tones of voice and mannerisms — anything that would help readers see the person as you remember her or him.

Naming	Her hair always pulled back in a tight bun, her lips pursed
Detailing	even tighter, Mrs. Maxon's eyes bore into students as a drill
Comparing (metaphor, simile)	bores into wood. Mrs. Maxon was my sophomore year high school English teacher, and she was tyrannical in her enforcement of writing rules.

Using Dialogue. Reconstruct dialogue, using speaker tags to identify the speaker and possibly indicate the speaker's tone or attitude. Dialogue may be quoted to emphasize certain words or give readers a sense of the speaker's personality. It may also be summarized when the gist of what was said is most important.

Summarized dialogue	When called upon, I delivered an effortless list of things that I detest: blood sausage, intestinal pâtés, brain pudding. [. . .] The
Speaker tag	teacher's reaction led me to believe that these mistakes were capital crimes in the country of France.
Quoted dialogue	"Were you always this *palicmkrexis*?" she asked. "Even a *fiuscrzsa ticiwelmun* knows that a typewriter is feminine." (Sedaris, pars. 14–15)

Detailing Important Places.   Incorporate descriptions of important places, identifying where the event happened or a place you associate with the person and including specific sensory details — size, shape, color, condition, and texture of the scene or memorable objects in it — that contribute to the dominant impression you want to create. Imagine the place from the front and from the side, from a distance and from up close. Try to keep a consistent point of view, describing the place as if you were walking through the scene or moving from right to left, or front to back.

Descriptive naming & detailing	. . . Ultimately my best friend, Thea, and I were left to our own 15-year-old devices to mourn that weekend. Her mother and
Comparing	stepfather were out of town. Their expansive, million-dollar home was perched on a hillside less than an hour from Tupac's
Location information	former stomping grounds in Oakland and Marin City. Of course, her home was also worlds away from both places. (Desmond-Harris, par. 3)

Including Visuals.   Including visuals — photographs, postcards, ticket stubs — may strengthen your presentation of the event or person. If you submit your essay electronically or post it on a website, consider including snippets of video with sound as well as photographs or other memorabilia that might give readers a more vivid sense of the time, place, and people about which you are writing. If you want to use any photographs or recordings, though, be sure to request the permission of those depicted.

For more on using and analyzing visuals, see Chapter 2, pp. 52–55.

Reflecting on Your Subject

The following activities will help you think about the significance of your subject and formulate a tentative thesis statement, though the thesis in autobiography tends to be implied rather than stated explicitly.

Reviewing the Dominant Impression Your Description and Narration Create.   Write for a few minutes about the kind of impression your writing now conveys and what you would like it to convey.

- Begin by rereading. Look back at the words you chose to describe places and people, as well as the way you dramatized the story.

- Consider the tone and connotations of your word choices. What meanings or feelings do they evoke?

- Note any contradictions or changes in tone or mood that could lead you to a deeper understanding.

Exploring How You Felt at the Time.   Write for a few minutes, trying to recall your thoughts and feelings when the event was occurring or when you knew the person:

- What did you feel — in control or powerless, proud or embarrassed, vulnerable, detached, judgmental — and how did you show or express your feelings?

- What were the immediate consequences for you personally?

These sentence strategies may help you put your feelings into words:

▶ As the event started [or during or right after the event], I felt .... and ....

▶ I hoped others would think of me as ....

Exploring Your Present Perspective.   Write for a few minutes, trying to express your present thoughts and feelings as you look back on the event or person:

- How have your feelings changed, and what insights do you now have?

- Try looking at the event or person in broad cultural or social terms. For example, consider whether you or anyone else upset gender expectations or felt out of place in some way.

These sentence strategies may help you put your feelings into words:

▶ My feelings since the event [have/have not] changed in the following ways: ....

▶ At the time, I had been going through ...., which may have affected my experience by ....

Considering Your Purpose and Audience.   Write for several minutes exploring what you want your readers to understand about the significance of the event or person. Use the following questions to help clarify your thoughts:

- What will writing about this event or person enable you to suggest about yourself as an individual?

- What will it let you suggest about the social and cultural forces that helped shape you — for example, how people exercise power over one another, how family and community values and attitudes affect individuals, how economic and social conditions influence our sense of self, or how our experiences with reading and writing affect us throughout our lives?

- What about your subject do you expect will seem familiar to your readers? What do you think will surprise them, perhaps getting them to think in new ways or to question some of their assumptions and stereotypes?

Formulating a Working Thesis.   Write a few sentences trying to articulate a working thesis that explains the significance that you want your writing to convey. Even though readers do not expect autobiographical writing to include an explicit thesis statement, stating a thesis now may help you explore ambivalent feelings and lead you to a deeper understanding of your subject. It also may help you as you continue working on your draft, organizing the story, selecting descriptive details, and choosing words to relate your feelings and thoughts.

Drafting Your Story

By this point, you have done a lot of writing

- to develop a plan for telling a compelling story;

- to present people and places in vivid detail;

- to show or tell the autobiographical significance of your story in a way that will be meaningful for your readers.

Now stitch that material together to create a draft. The next section of this Guide to Writing will help you evaluate and improve your draft.

REVIEWING AND IMPROVING THE DRAFT

This section includes two guides for Peer Review and Troubleshooting Your Draft. Your instructor may arrange a peer review in class or online where you can exchange drafts with a classmate. The Peer Review Guide will help you give each other constructive feedback regarding the basic features and strategies typical of autobiographical writing. (If you want to make specific suggestions for improving the draft, see Troubleshooting Your Draft on pp. 119–120.) Also, be sure to respond to any specific concerns the writer has raised about the draft. The Troubleshooting Your Draft guide that follows will help you reread your own draft with a critical eye, sort through any feedback you've received, and consider a variety of ways to improve your draft.

A PEER REVIEW GUIDE

How effectively does the writer narrate the story?

What's Working Well: Point to a passage where the storytelling is effective—for example, where the dramatic arc is used successfully to engage your interest, arouse your curiosity, or build suspense to a climax.

What Needs Improvement: Identify a passage where the storytelling could be improved—for example, where the story loses focus, gets bogged down in details, lacks drama or suspense.

How vivid are the descriptions of people and places, and how well do the descriptions work together to create a dominant impression?

What's Working Well: Highlight an especially vivid bit of description—for example, where sensory details (sights, sounds, smells, textures) help you imagine the scene or where a photograph gives you a striking impression of a person.

What Needs Improvement: Tell the writer where description could be added, made more vivid, or changed so that it reinforces the dominant impression—for example, where you'd like to know what people look and sound like or where sensory details would help you visualize a place.

How effectively is the autobiographical significance of the event or the person conveyed?

What's Working Well: Mark a passage where the significance is clear and compelling—for example, where remembered thoughts are expressed poignantly, where the present perspective seems insightful, where dialogue helps you understand the underlying conflict, or where the strong dominant impression clarifies the significance.

What Needs Improvement: Note any passages where the significance could be clearer or more fully developed—for example, where the central conflict seems too easily resolved, where a moral seems tacked on at the end, or where more interesting insights could be drawn from the writer's interactions with and feelings about the person.

How clear and easy to follow is the organization?

What's Working Well: Point to any aspect of the organization that seems notably effective—for example, one or more transitions that clearly show how the event unfolded over time or in space.

What Needs Improvement: Let the writer know where the organization can be clearer—for example, where a transition between elements of the dramatic arc is needed or where topic sentences or headings could help orient readers.

Revising Your Draft

Revising means reenvisioning your draft, seeing it in a fresh way, given your purpose, audience, and the review from your peers. Don't hesitate to cut unconvincing or tangential material, add new material, or move passages around. The following chart may help you strengthen your essay.

TROUBLESHOOTING YOUR DRAFT

To Make the Narrative More Dramatic	
If the inciting incident does not arouse curiosity or suspense,	• Tighten the inciting incident by moving background exposition. • Show how the inciting incident stems from an underlying conflict. • Reveal the writer's anxious, fearful, or other intense feelings.
If the dramatic arc flattens and the tension slackens,	• Intensify the rising action by interspersing remembered feelings with action verbs. • Dramatize the climax with quoted dialogue and speaker tags that show strong reactions. • Propel the action through time and space with active verbs, transitions, and prepositional phrases.
If exposition or descriptive detail interrupts the drama,	• Reduce exposition by injecting small bits of background information and detail into the action, or cut it altogether. • Summarize instead of quoting lengthy dialogue, and only quote especially expressive language.
To Present People and Places Vividly	
If the description of people is vague,	• Add sensory details showing what people look and sound like. • Use speaker tags to reveal the people's attitudes and personality. • Add a comparison to help readers understand the person or relationship.
If it's hard to visualize the place,	• Add more specific nouns to name objects in the scene. • Add more sensory detail to evoke the sense of sight, touch, smell, taste, or hearing. • Use comparison to enrich the description.

If the dominant impression is weak or undercut by contradictory details,	• Add a suggestive comparison to strengthen the dominant impression. • Consider how contradictory details might show complexity in people or their relationships.
If the point of view is confusing,	• Clarify the vantage point from which the scene is described. • Make sure the point of view is consistent.
To Convey the Autobiographical Significance	
If the significance is not clear and compelling,	• Sharpen the dominant impression to *show* the significance. • Expand or add passages where you use *telling* to convey the significance directly. • Add remembered thoughts and feelings. • Articulate your present perspective on the event or person.
If the central conflict seems too easily resolved or simplistic,	• Use present perspective to explain why the conflict is so memorable and continues to be important. • Express strong feelings that were—and may still be—complicated and not fully understood. • Explain the conflict in terms of its social, cultural, or historical context.
To Make the Organization More Effective	
If there's confusion about what happened when,	• Add or clarify transitions and other time markers. • Review verb tenses to make them consistent.
If too many details seem overwhelming and it's hard to follow,	• Add or revise topic sentences. • Use present perspective to orient readers. • Consider whether headings would help.

Editing and Proofreading Your Draft

Check for errors in usage, punctuation, and mechanics, and consider matters of style. If you keep a list of errors you typically make, begin by checking your draft against this list.

Research on student writing shows that autobiographical writing often has sentence fragments, run-on sentences, and verb tense errors. Check a writer's handbook for help with these potential problems.

Reflecting on Autobiography

In this chapter, you have read literacy narratives and pieces of autobiography. You have also written one of your own. To better remember what you have learned, pause now to reflect on the reading and writing activities you completed in this chapter.

1. Write a page or so reflecting on what you have learned. Begin by describing what you are most pleased with in your essay. Then explain what you think contributed to your achievement. Be specific about this contribution.

   - If it was something you learned from the readings, indicate which readings and specifically what you learned from them.

   - If it came from the writing you did in response to prompts in this chapter, point out the section or sections that helped you most.

2. Reflect more generally on how you tend to interpret autobiographical writing, your own as well as other writers'. Consider some of the following questions:

   - In reading for meaning, do you tend to find yourself interpreting the significance of the event or person in terms of the writer's personal feelings, sense of self-esteem, or psychological well-being? Or do you more often think of significance in terms of larger social or economic influences — for example, in terms of the writer's gender, class, or ethnicity?

   - Where do you think you learned to interpret the significance of people's stories about themselves and their relationships — from your family, friends, television, school?

3. By reflecting on what you have learned about autobiography and literacy narratives, you have been practicing **metacognition,** one of the academic habits of mind.

   - Were you aware of any other habits of mind you practiced as you read and responded to the material in this chapter? If so, which habits did you find useful?

   - If not, think back now on your reading and writing processes. Can you identify any habits you practiced?

Observation

Observational writing comprises analytical, informative, and **thought-provoking** portraits, or *profiles*, of a person or a place. These profiles **may be** cultural ethnographies, ranging from "a day-in-the-life" to an extended immersion study of a community or people at work or at play. They are intensively researched, centering on the field-research techniques of detailed observations and edifying interviews. As a result, observational profiles are generally entertaining to read, sometimes amusing, and often surprising and captivating. Whether written in a college course, for the broader community, or about the workplace, observational writing mobilizes the academic habits of mind, appealing to our curiosity about the world we live in and stimulating critical analysis.

RHETORICAL SITUATIONS FOR OBSERVATIONS

Many people — including bloggers, journalists, psychologists, and cultural anthropologists — write essays based on observations and interviews, as the following examples suggest:

- For an art history course, a student writes a paper about a local artist recently commissioned to paint an outdoor mural for the city. The student visits the artist's studio and talks with him about the process of painting murals. The artist invites the student to spend the following day as a part of a team of local art students and neighborhood volunteers working on the mural under the artist's direction. This firsthand experience helps the student profile the artist, present some of the students on his team, and give readers an intimate understanding of the process and collaboration involved in mural painting.

- For a political science course, a student writes about a controversial urban renewal project to replace decaying houses with a library and park. To learn about the history of the project, she reads newspaper reports and interviews people who helped plan the project as well as some neighborhood residents and activists who oppose it. She also tours the site with the project manager to see what is actually being done.

Thinking about Observation

Recall one occasion when you reported your observations or heard or read the observations of others.

- Who was the *audience*? How did reporting observations to this audience affect the way the writer conveyed his or her perspective? For example, if the audience was already familiar with the subject, did the report arouse curiosity by taking a provocative approach, by going behind the scenes, or in some other way?

- What was the main *purpose*? What did the writer want the audience to learn? For example, was the report primarily intended to teach them something, to show them what the writer had learned, to entertain them, or for some other reason?

- How would you rate the *rhetorical sensitivity* with which the observations were presented? What made the essay appropriate or inappropriate for its particular audience or purpose?

A GUIDE TO READING OBSERVATIONS

This guide introduces you to the strategies typical of observational writing by inviting you to analyze a brief but intriguing profile of Albert Yeganeh and his unique restaurant, Soup Kitchen International:

- *Annotations* on this first reading will help you see how to practice academic **habits of mind** such as **curiosity, openness,** and **persistence** to help you engage with and understand what you are reading. Notice how many questions the reader has as she reads. There is plenty of space for you to add your own questions and thoughts, as well, to this reading and any other in the textbook.

- *Reading for meaning* will help you understand what we call the writer's **perspective** — the main idea or cultural significance that the writer wants readers to take away from reading the observational profile.

- *Reading like a writer* will help you learn how the writer makes the essay interesting and informative, by examining how he or she uses some of the *basic features* and strategies typical of observational writing:

  1. Deciding whether to take the role of a spectator or a participant

  2. Determining what information to include and how to present it

  3. Organizing the information in a way that will be entertaining to readers

  4. Conveying a perspective on the subject

The *New Yorker*

Soup

"Soup" (1989) was published anonymously in the *New Yorker*, a magazine known for its observational profiles of fascinating people and places. The subject of the article is Albert Yeganeh, the creative and demanding owner/chef of a small take-out restaurant (originally called Soup Kitchen International, now called Soup Man). Yeganeh's restaurant inspired an episode of the then-popular television sitcom *Seinfeld* called "The Soup Nazi." Apparently Yeganeh was so angry that when Jerry Seinfeld went to the restaurant after the episode aired, the chef demanded an apology and told Seinfeld to leave.

- **Before you read,** note the quotations that open the essay: "Soup is my lifeblood" and "I am extremely hard to please." The first quote clearly refers to the kind of food served at the restaurant, but the second quote seems to have a different purpose. What does it lead you to expect from the essay?

- **As you read,** think about how the writer represented Yeganeh to the original *New Yorker* readers. If you have seen the "Soup Nazi" episode, you might compare the way Yeganeh is portrayed in the sitcom to the way he is portrayed in the article. Consider also how Yeganeh is portrayed on his franchise website, *The Original Soup Man*.

When Albert Yeganeh says "Soup is my lifeblood," he means it. And   1
when he says "I am extremely hard to please," he means that, too. Working like a demon alchemist in a tiny storefront kitchen at 259-A West Fifty-fifth Street, Mr. Yeganeh creates anywhere from eight to seventeen soups every weekday. His concoctions are so popular that a wait of half an hour at the lunchtime peak is not uncommon, although there are strict rules for conduct in line. But more on that later.

> *What kind of rules could he have created for customers?*

"I am psychologically kind of a health freak," Mr. Yeganeh said the other   2
day, in a lisping staccato of Armenian origin. "And I know that soup is the greatest meal in the world. It's very good for your digestive system. And I use only the best, the freshest ingredients. I am a perfectionist. When I make a clam soup, I use three different kinds of clams. Every other place uses canned clams. I'm called crazy. I am not crazy. People don't realize why I get so upset. It's because if the soup is not perfect and I'm still selling it, it's a torture. It's *my* soup, and that's why I'm so upset. First you clean and then you cook. I don't believe that ninety-nine per cent of the restaurants in New York know how to clean a tomato. I tell my crew to wash the parsley *eight* times. If they wash it five or six times, I scare them. I tell them they'll go to jail if there is sand in the parsley. One time, I found a mushroom on the floor, and I fired that guy who left it there." He spread his arms and

> *Wow, this is a long quotation!*

added, "This place is the only one like it in . . . in . . . the whole earth! One day, I hope to learn something from the other places, but so far I haven't. For example, the other day I went to a very fancy restaurant and had borscht. I had to send it back. It was *junk*. I could see all the chemicals in it. I never use chemicals. Last weekend, I had lobster bisque in Brooklyn, a very well-known place. It was *junk*. When I make a lobster bisque, I use a whole lobster. You know, I never advertise. I don't have to. All the big-shot chefs and the kings of the hotels come here to see what *I'm* doing."

Is he arrogant?

3   As you approach Mr. Yeganeh's Soup Kitchen International from a distance, the first thing you notice about it is the awning, which proclaims "Homemade Hot, Cold, Diet Soups." The second thing you notice is an aroma so delicious that it makes you want to take a bite out of the air. The third thing you notice, in front of the kitchen, is an electric signboard that flashes, saying, "Today's Soups . . . Chicken Vegetable . . . Mexican Beef Chili . . . Cream of Watercress . . . Italian Sausage . . . Clam Bisque . . . Beef Barley . . . Due to Cold Weather . . . For Most Efficient and Fastest Service the Line Must . . . Be Kept Moving . . . Please . . . Have Your Money . . . Ready . . . Pick the Soup of Your Choice . . . Move to Your Extreme . . . Left After Ordering."

4   "I am not prejudiced against color or religion," Mr. Yeganeh told us, and he jabbed an index finger at the flashing sign. "Whoever follows that I treat very well. My regular customers don't say anything. They are very intelligent and well educated. They know I'm just trying to move the line. The New York cop is very smart—he sees everything but says nothing. But the young girl who wants to stop and tell you how nice you look and hold everyone up—*yah*!" He made a guillotining motion with his hand. "I tell you, I hate to work with the public. They treat me like a slave. My philosophy is: The customer is always wrong and I'm always right. I raised my prices to try to get rid of some of these people, but it didn't work."

Why is his philosophy the opposite of that of other business owners?

5   The other day, Mr. Yeganeh was dressed in chef's whites with orange smears across his chest, which may have been some of the carrot soup cooking in a huge pot on a little stove in one corner. A three-foot-long handheld mixer from France sat on the sink, looking like an overgrown gardening tool. Mr. Yeganeh spoke to two young helpers in a twisted Armenian-Spanish barrage, then said to us, "I have no overhead, no trained waitresses, and I have the cashier here." He pointed to himself theatrically. Beside the doorway, a glass case with fresh green celery, red and yellow peppers, and purple eggplant was topped by five big gray soup urns. According to a piece of cardboard taped to the door, you can buy Mr. Yeganeh's soups in three sizes, costing from four to fifteen dollars. The order of any well-behaved customer is accompanied by little waxpaper packets of bread, fresh vegetables (such as scallions and radishes), fresh fruit (such as cherries or an orange), a chocolate mint, and a plastic spoon. No coffee, tea, or other drinks are served.

Is cabbage really a cancer fighter?

Who knew Swiss chocolate was a soup? Note to self: look up all these soups online!

Can he really punish customers for talking too much especially when all of the dialogue included suggests that he talks a lot?

Why would people still come to his restaurant if he's abusive? Does good soup really make up for that?

"I get my recipes from books and theories and my own taste," Mr.   6
Yeganeh said. "At home, I have several hundreds of books. When I do research, I find that I don't know anything. Like cabbage is a cancer fighter, and some fish is good for your heart but some is bad. Every day, I should have one sweet, one spicy, one cream, one vegetable soup—and they *must* change, they should always taste a little different." He added that he wasn't sure how extensive his repertoire was, but that it probably includes at least eighty soups, among them African peanut butter, Greek moussaka, hamburger, Reuben, B.L.T., asparagus and caviar, Japanese shrimp miso, chicken chili, Irish corned beef and cabbage, Swiss chocolate, French calf's brain, Korean beef ball, Italian shrimp and eggplant Parmesan, buffalo, ham and egg, short rib, Russian beef Stroganoff, turkey cacciatore, and Indian mulligatawny. "The chicken and the seafood are an addiction, and when I have French garlic soup I let people have only one small container each," he said. "The doctors and nurses love that one."

A lunch line of thirty people stretched down the block from Mr.   7
Yeganeh's doorway. Behind a construction worker was a man in expensive leather, who was in front of a woman in a fur hat.

Few people spoke. Most had their money out and their orders ready.   8

At the front of the line, a woman in a brown coat couldn't decide which   9
soup to get and started to complain about the prices.

"You talk too much, dear," Mr. Yeganeh said, and motioned her to move   10
to the left. "Next!"

"Just don't talk. Do what he says," a man huddled in a blue parka   11
warned.

"He's downright rude," said a blond woman in a blue coat. "Even   12
abusive. But you can't deny it, his soup is the best."

READING FOR MEANING

For help with reading strategies like summarizing and analyzing assumptions, see Chapter 2.

1. **Read to Summarize.** Write a sentence or two briefly describing Yeganeh and his views about running a restaurant.

2. **Read to Respond.** Write a paragraph exploring your initial reactions, for example, to Yeganeh's work ethic or his ideas about food quality and health, perhaps in comparison to the quality at fast-food restaurants with which you are familiar.

3. **Read to Analyze Assumptions.** Write a paragraph or two analyzing an assumption in this essay. For example:

   Assumptions about authority. Yeganeh brags about scaring his employees and defends his right to deny service to anyone who does not follow his rules.

- When Yeganeh talks about scaring and firing his employees (par. 2), does he seem to be holding them to an appropriately high standard or is he just being a bully? In telling the story, is he showing off for the writer, making a serious point, or both?

- When Yeganeh tells a customer she talks too much and then refuses to serve her (par. 9), is he being a tyrant or is he right to use his power in this way?

Assumptions about customer service. When Yeganeh says, "The customer is always wrong and I'm always right" (par. 4), he is reversing the popular saying that the customer is always right.

- What seem to be the assumptions of the writer and of Yeganeh's customers about service?

- What influences our assumptions about service — for example, the type of restaurant (take-out or sit-down, family style or formal), how much it costs, and our attitudes toward service work and workers?

You may also try reflecting on challenges to your beliefs and values; see Chapter 2, p. 57.

READING LIKE A WRITER

Presenting Information about the Subject

Observational writing, like autobiography (Chapter 3), succeeds in large part by describing people and places vividly. The describing strategies of *naming* objects together with *detailing* their color, shape, size, texture, and other qualities enable readers to imagine what the people and places look, sound, feel, and smell like. Writers also may use *comparing* in the form of simile or metaphor to add a playful or suggestive image to the description:

Naming Detailing	The other day, Mr. Yeganeh was dressed in chef's whites with orange smears across his chest, which may have been some of the carrot soup cooking in a huge pot on a little stove in one corner.
Comparing (simile)	A three-foot-long handheld mixer from France sat on the sink, looking like an overgrown gardening tool. (par. 5)

Writers often use *speaker tags* along with dialogue to characterize people as they talk and interact with others. For example:

Speaker tag	"I am psychologically kind of a health freak," *Mr. Yeganeh said the other day, in a lisping staccato of Armenian origin.* (par. 2)

The author of "Soup" uses dialogue extensively to give readers a vivid impression of the man, his business, and his ideas. Indeed, most of the information in this selection comes from long chunks of an extended interview with Yeganeh, and the profile concludes with a brief overheard exchange between Yeganeh and two people in line.

ANALYZE & WRITE

Write a paragraph analyzing the use of naming, detailing, and comparing to present Albert Yeganeh:

1. Find a few examples in paragraphs 1–6 where you think the naming and detailing give an especially vivid description of Yeganeh. What is the dominant impression you get from this description?

2. Also find an example of comparing, either a *simile* (a comparison using *like* or *as*) or a *metaphor* (a comparison that does not use this kind of signaling word). What ideas and associations does this comparison contribute to the impression you got from the other describing strategies? How does it reinforce, extend, change, or complicate the dominant impression?

3. Reflect on what, if anything, you learn from Yeganeh about making soup or operating a restaurant.

Organizing the Information

Writers of observational essays typically rely on three basic organizational plans: *topical*, *narrative*, and *spatial*. As the following examples show, an essay may use all of these ways of arranging information. Note also the kinds of organizational cues — such as transitional words and phrases, calendar and clock time, and prepositional phrases indicating time or location — writers use for each kind of organization.

Topic Organizational cue	"I am psychologically kind of a health freak." . . . "And I know that soup is . . . very good for your digestive system. And I use only the best, the freshest ingredients. I am a perfectionist." (par. 2)
Narrative cue	The other day . . . Mr. Yeganeh spoke to two young helpers in a twisted Armenian-Spanish barrage, then said to us . . . (par. 5)
Spatial cue	*As you approach* Mr. Yeganeh's Soup Kitchen International *from a distance*, the *first thing you notice* about it is . . . *The second thing you notice* is . . . *The third thing you notice, in front of* the kitchen, is . . . (par. 3)

ANALYZE & WRITE

Write a paragraph analyzing the use of topical, narrative, and spatial organizing strategies in "Soup":

1. First, make a scratch outline of paragraphs 4, 5, and 6 of "Soup," listing the topics or kinds of information presented. (Some paragraphs include more than one topic. You do not have to list every topic, but try to identify the most important ones.)

2. Then reread paragraphs 7–11, where the writer presents a brief narrative. What, if anything, do you learn from the narrative that illuminates or adds to what you learned from the earlier paragraphs?

3. Finally, scan the essay looking for any other parts that, in addition to the passage quoted above from paragraph 3, organize the information spatially. What cues help you recognize the spatial arrangement?

Adopting an Authorial Role

In making observations and writing them up, writers have a choice of roles to perform: as a *detached spectator* or as a *participant observer*. In the **spectator** role, the writer acts as an independent reporter, watching and listening but remaining outside of the activity. In contrast, the **participant observer** becomes an insider, at least for a short time, joining in the activity with the people being interviewed and observed. We can see examples of both roles in this excerpt from the reading selection by John T. Edge (pp. 131–134):

Participant role   It's just past 4:00 on a Thursday afternoon in June at Jesse's Place . . . I sit alone at the bar, one empty bottle of Bud in front of me, a second in my hand. I drain the beer, order a third, and stare down at the pink juice spreading outward from a crumpled foil pouch and onto the bar.

> *I'm not leaving until I eat this thing,* I tell myself.

Spectator role   Half a mile down the road, behind a fence coiled with razor wire, Lionel Dufour, proprietor of Farm Fresh Food Supplier, is loading up the last truck of the day, wheeling case after case of pickled pork offal out of his cinder-block processing plant and into a semitrailer bound for Hattiesburg, Mississippi. (pars. 1–3)

ANALYZE & WRITE

Write a paragraph discussing the role the writer of "Soup" chose to adopt:

1. Find one or two signs indicating the role the writer has taken, such as the use of the first- or third-person perspective or places where the writer included insider knowledge derived from taking the role of participant observer.

2. What advantages or disadvantages do you see in the role the writer chose to take? What would have been gained (or lost) had the writer chosen a different role?

Conveying a Perspective on the Subject

Writers of observational essays, like autobiographers, convey their perspective on what is significant or intriguing about the subject in two ways: by showing and telling.

One way writers show their perspective is through the dominant impression they create. (See Presenting Information about the Subject, p. 127.) Another way writers use showing is by selecting choice quotes that give readers insight into the speaker, as in this example of Yeganeh's comments about what makes his cooking special:

Does he really want to learn from others? Do chefs really respect him or does he have delusions of grandeur?	"One day, I hope to learn something from the other places, but so far I haven't. For example, the other day I went to a very fancy restaurant and had borscht. I had to send it back. It was *junk*. . . . All the big-shot chefs and the kings of the hotels come here to see what *I'm* doing." (par. 2)

Observational writers occasionally also use telling to say explicitly what they think of the subject. More often, they imply their judgment of or attitude toward the subject through their word choices. For example, consider whether the writer is praising or criticizing Yeganeh in these opening sentences. Is the tone sarcastic, flattering, or something else?

Telling	When Albert Yeganeh says "Soup is my lifeblood," **he means it.** And when he says "I am extremely hard to please," **he means that, too.** (par. 1)

ANALYZE & WRITE

Write a paragraph examining how the writer uses showing and/or telling to convey a perspective on Yeganeh and his Soup Kitchen International:

1. Skim paragraphs 3–11, looking for examples of showing in the descriptions and in the choice of quotations. Choose one or two examples and explain what they suggest about the writer's perspective on Yeganeh as a human being, cook, and businessman.

2. Look also for one or two examples of telling. What do they add to your understanding of the writer's perspective?

READINGS

John T. Edge

I'm Not Leaving Until I Eat This Thing

John T. Edge (b. 1962) earned an MFA in creative nonfiction from Goucher College as well as an MA in southern studies from the University of Mississippi, where he currently directs the Southern Foodways Alliance at the Center for the Study of Southern Culture. A food writer for outlets such as *Oxford American*, the *New York Times*, and *Garden & Gun*, Edge has also been published in many anthologies. He has coedited several cookbooks and travel guides, and he has written several books, including *The Potlikker Papers* (2017), *Truck Food Cookbook* (2012), a study of American street food; *Southern Belly* (2007), a portrait of southern food told through profiles of people and places; and a series on iconic American foods, including *Hamburgers and Fries: An American Story* (2005) and *Donuts: An American Passion* (2006). This reading first appeared in 1999 in *Oxford American* magazine and was reprinted in the *Utne Reader*.

- **Before you read,** look at the photo on p. 133. Why do you think Edge includes a picture of a live pig in an essay about making and eating pickled pig lips? What other photos could he have used?

For more on analyzing visuals, see Chapter 2, pp. 52–55.

- **As you read,** you will see that Edge moves between two different scenes — notice that whereas Edge uses a chronological narrative to relate what happened at Jesse's Place, he uses a topical organization to present the information he learned from his observations and interview at Farm Fresh Food Supplier processing plant. Why do you think he uses different methods for presenting these two scenes?

It's just past 4:00 on a Thursday afternoon in June at Jesse's Place, a country juke 17 miles south of the Mississippi line and three miles west of Amite, Louisiana. The air conditioner hacks and spits forth torrents of Arctic air, but the heat of summer can't be kept at bay. It seeps around the splintered doorjambs and settles in, transforming the squat particleboard-plastered roadhouse into a sauna. Slowly, the dank barroom fills with grease-smeared mechanics from the truck stop up the road and farmers straight from the fields, the soles of their brogans thick with dirt clods. A few weary souls make their way over from the nearby sawmill. I sit alone at the bar, one empty bottle of Bud in front of me, a second in my hand. I drain the beer, order a third, and stare down at the pink juice spreading outward from a crumpled foil pouch and onto the bar. 1

I'm not leaving until I eat this thing, I tell myself. 2

Half a mile down the road, behind a fence coiled with razor wire, Lionel Dufour, 3
proprietor of Farm Fresh Food Supplier, is loading up the last truck of the day, wheeling case after case of pickled pork offal out of his cinder-block processing plant and
into a semitrailer bound for Hattiesburg, Mississippi.

His crew packed lips today. Yesterday, it was pickled sausage; the day before that, 4
pig feet. Tomorrow, it's pickled pig lips again. Lionel has been on the job since 2:45
in the morning, when he came in to light the boilers. Damon Landry, chief cook
and maintenance man, came in at 4:30. By 7:30, the production line was at full tilt:
six women in white smocks and blue bouffant caps, slicing ragged white fat from
the lips, tossing the good parts in glass jars, the bad parts in barrels bound for the
rendering plant. Across the aisle, filled jars clatter by on a conveyor belt as a worker
tops them off with a Kool-Aid-red slurry of hot sauce, vinegar, salt, and food coloring.
Around the corner, the jars are capped, affixed with a label, and stored in pasteboard
boxes to await shipping.

Unlike most offal—euphemistically called "variety meats"—lips belie their prov- 5
enance. Brains, milky white and globular, look like brains. Feet, the ghosts of their
cloven hoofs protruding, look like feet. Testicles look like, well, testicles. But lips are
different. Loosed from the snout, trimmed of their fat, and dyed a preternatural pink,
they look more like candy than like carrion.

At Farm Fresh, no swine root in an adjacent feedlot. No viscera-strewn killing floor 6
lurks just out of sight, down a darkened hallway. These pigs died long ago at some
Midwestern abattoir. By the time the lips arrive in Amite, they are, in essence, pig
Popsicles, 50-pound blocks of offal and ice.

"Lips are all meat," Lionel told me earlier in the day. "No gristle, no bone, no 7
nothing. They're bar food, hot and vinegary, great with a beer. Used to be the lips
ended up in sausages, headcheese, those sorts of things. A lot of them still do."

Lionel, a 50-year-old father of three with quick, intelligent eyes set deep in a 8
face the color of cordovan, is a veteran of nearly 40 years in the pickled pig lips
business. "I started out with my daddy when I wasn't much more than 10," Lionel
told me, his shy smile framed by a coarse black mustache flecked with whispers
of gray. "The meatpacking business he owned had gone broke back when I was
6, and he was peddling out of the back of his car, selling dried shrimp, napkins,
straws, tubes of plastic cups, pig feet, pig lips, whatever the bar owners needed.
He sold to black bars, white bars, sweet shops, snowball stands, you name it. We
made the rounds together after I got out of school, sometimes staying out till two or
three in the morning. I remember bringing my toy cars to this one joint and racing
them around the floor with the bar owner's son while my daddy and his father did
business."

For years after the demise of that first meatpacking company, the Dufour family 9
sold someone else's product. "We used to buy lips from Dennis Di Salvo's company
down in Belle Chasse," recalled Lionel. "As far as I can tell, his mother was the one
who came up with the idea to pickle and pack lips back in the '50s, back when she
was working for a company called Three Little Pigs over in Houma. But pretty soon,
we were selling so many lips that we had to almost beg Di Salvo's for product. That's

Shannon Brinkman Photo

when we started cooking up our own," he told me, gesturing toward the cast-iron kettle that hangs from the rafters by the front door of the plant. "My daddy started cooking lips in that very pot."

Lionel now cooks lips in 11 retrofitted milk tanks, dull stainless-steel cauldrons 10 shaped like oversized cradles. But little else has changed. Though Lionel's father has passed away, Farm Fresh remains a family-focused company. His wife, Kathy, keeps the books. His daughter, Dana, a button-cute college student who has won numerous beauty titles, takes to the road in the summer, selling lips to convenience stores and wholesalers. Soon, after he graduates from business school, Lionel's younger son, Matt, will take over operations at the plant. And his older son, a veterinarian, lent his name to one of Farm Fresh's top sellers, Jason's Pickled Pig Lips.

"We do our best to corner the market on lips," Lionel told me, his voice tinged with 11 bravado. "Sometimes they're hard to get from the packing houses. You gotta kill a lot of pigs to get enough lips to keep us going. I've got new customers calling every day; it's all I can do to keep up with demand, but I bust my ass to keep up. I do what I can for my family—and for my customers."

"When my customers tell me something," he continued, "just like when my daddy 12 told me something, I listen. If my customers wanted me to dye the lips green, I'd ask, 'What shade?' As it is, every few years we'll do some red and some blue for the Fourth of July. This year we did jars full of Mardi Gras lips—half purple, half gold," Lionel recalled with a chuckle. "I guess we'd had a few beers when we came up with that one."

Meanwhile, back at Jesse's Place, I finish my third Bud, order my fourth. *Now,* I   13
tell myself, my courage bolstered by booze, *I'm ready to eat a lip.*

They may have looked like candy in the plant, but in the barroom they're carrion   14
once again. I poke and prod the six-inch arc of pink flesh, peering up from my reverie
just in time to catch the barkeep's wife, Audrey, staring straight at me. She fixes me
with a look just this side of pity and asks, "You gonna eat that thing or make love to
it?"

Her nephew, Jerry, sidles up to a bar stool on my left. "A lot of people like   15
'em with chips," he says with a nod toward the pink juice pooling on the bar in
front of me. I offer to buy him a lip, and Audrey fishes one from a jar behind the
counter, wraps it in tinfoil, and places the whole affair on a paper towel in front
of him.

I take stock of my own cowardice, and, following Jerry's lead, reach for a bag of   16
potato chips, tear open the top with my teeth, and toss the quivering hunk of hog
flesh into the shiny interior of the bag, slick with grease and dusted with salt. Vinegar
vapors tickle my nostrils. I stifle a gag that rolls from the back of my throat, swallow
hard, and pray that the urge to vomit passes.

With a smash of my hand, the potato chips are reduced to a pulp, and I feel the   17
cold lump of the lip beneath my fist. I clasp the bag shut and shake it hard in an
effort to ensure chip coverage in all the nooks and crannies of the lip. The technique
that Jerry uses — and I mimic — is not unlike that employed by home cooks mixing
up a mess of Shake 'n Bake chicken.

I pull from the bag a coral crescent of meat now crusted with blond bits of   18
potato chips. When I chomp down, the soft flesh dissolves between my teeth. It
tastes like a flaccid cracklin', unmistakably porcine, and not altogether bad. The
chips help, providing texture where there was none. Slowly, my brow unfurrows,
my stomach ceases its fluttering.

Sensing my relief, Jerry leans over and peers into my bag. "Kind of look like   19
Frosted Flakes, don't they?" he says, by way of describing the chips rapidly turning to
mush in the pickling juice. I offer the bag to Jerry, order yet another beer, and turn to
eye the pig feet floating in a murky jar by the cash register, their blunt tips bobbing
up through a pasty white film.

READING FOR MEANING

For help
with reading
strategies like
summarizing
and analyzing
assumptions,
see Chapter 2.

1. **Read to Summarize.** Write a sentence or two explaining the main idea
   Edge wants his readers to understand about pickled pig lips and the Dufour
   family business.

2. **Read to Respond.** Write a paragraph exploring your initial thoughts about
   anything that resonates with your experience, such as Lionel Dufour's story
   about how he "made the rounds" with his father after school (par. 8) or
   Edge's attempt to eat the pig lip.

3. **Read to Analyze Assumptions.** Write a paragraph or two analyzing an assumption you find intriguing in Edge's essay. For example:

Assumptions about culture and food. For many people, foods that they did not eat as children seem strange and sometimes even repulsive. Even though he is a southerner, Edge is squeamish about eating a popular southern delicacy, pickled pig lips. To think critically about assumptions regarding culture and food, ask yourself questions like these:

- Why do you suppose Edge uses the words *courage* (par. 13) and *cowardice* (par. 16) to describe his reluctance to try pickled pig lips?
- What do you think causes food anxieties, your own as well as Edge's aversion to pickled pig lips?

Assumptions about entrepreneurship. In interviewing Lionel Dufour and observing the Farm Fresh Food Supplier factory, Edge gives readers information about one small business and its hands-on proprietor.

- Among the first things Edge tells readers about Farm Fresh is that Lionel is the "proprietor" (par. 3) but that he loads trucks and "has been on the job since 2:45 in the morning" (par. 4). What does Edge think his readers are likely to assume about the kinds of work small-business owners like Lionel do?
- Although Americans usually celebrate a strong work ethic, we also tend to value entrepreneurship over manual labor. In what ways, if any, do you see these values reflected in this essay?

READING LIKE A WRITER

Presenting Information about the Subject

Like "Soup," much of the information in this profile comes from an extended interview. Edge uses three strategies for presenting what he learned from this interview:

Quotation	"Lips are all meat," Lionel told me earlier in the day. "No gristle, no bone, no nothing." (par. 7)
Paraphrase	By the time the lips arrive in Amite, they are, in essence, pig Popsicles, 50-pound blocks of offal and ice. (par. 6)
Summary	For years after the demise of that first meatpacking company, the Dufour family sold someone else's product. (par. 9)

Writers typically choose to **quote** language that is especially vivid or memorable, giving an impression of the speaker as well as providing important information. **Paraphrase** tends to be used when the writer needs to go into detail but can put the information in a more striking form than the speaker originally used. **Summary** is often used to condense lengthy information.

From his interview with Lionel, Edge gathered a lot of information about the Dufour family history and business as well as about the various products Farm Fresh sells and their production process. In addition, Edge presents information he derived from observations, particularly in paragraphs 3 through 6. Notice how he alternates information from the interview with descriptive details from his firsthand observations. Edge even tells us what he does *not* see — blood and guts on a slaughterhouse floor (par. 6). Letting readers know what he had expected, perhaps feared, appeals to readers who may share his anxieties. Moreover, it encourages readers to embrace Edge's point of view, a process of identification that begins in the opening scene in Jesse's Place and continues through the closing paragraphs.

ANALYZE & WRITE

Write a paragraph analyzing and evaluating Edge's use of quoting, paraphrasing, and summarizing information from an interview.

1. Find at least one other example of each of these strategies in paragraphs 3–12.

2. How effective are these ways of presenting information? For example, is there any quotation that could have been better presented as paraphrase or even as summary? What would have been gained or lost?

3. Locate a passage in paragraphs 3–12 where Edge presents his observations. How do you recognize this part as coming from firsthand observations? How does the alternation of information from interviews and observations contribute to your engagement as a reader?

Combining Reading Strategies

Contextualizing in Order to Compare and Contrast Related Readings

For help comparing and contrasting related readings, see Chapter 2, pp. 57–60.

For help contextualizing, see Chapter 2, pp. 50–51.

Contextualizing is a reading strategy that involves placing a text in its historical and cultural context to understand its relevance and significance. *Comparing and contrasting related readings* is a reading strategy that is useful both in reading for meaning and in reading like a writer. This strategy is particularly applicable when writers present similar subjects, as is the case in the observational essays in this chapter by the *New Yorker* writer (p. 124) and John T. Edge (p. 131). Both Edge and the writer of "Soup" describe a business they observed and report on their interview with the business owner. Compare and contrast these related readings with a specific focus on their context by responding to the following prompts.

- What are the cultural contexts of these two businesses (and the periodicals in which these articles appeared)? What seems most significant about the two business philosophies represented in these essays?

- Compare the historical and cultural situation in which these texts were written with your own historical and cultural situation. Consider how your understanding and judgment of the reading are affected by your context.

Gabriel Thompson

A Gringo in the Lettuce Fields

Gabriel Thompson has worked as a community organizer and has written extensively about the lives of undocumented immigrants to the United States. He has published numerous articles in periodicals such as *New York* magazine, the *New York Times*, and the *Nation*. His books include *There's No José Here: Following the Hidden Lives of Mexican Immigrants* (2006), *Calling All Radicals: How Grassroots Organizers Can Help Save Our Democracy* (2007), *America's Social Arsonist: Fred Ross and Grass-roots Organizing in the Twentieth Century* (2016), *Chasing the Harvest (2017)*, and *Working in the Shadows: A Year of Doing the Jobs (Most) Americans Won't Do* (2010), from which the selection below is taken. Note the photograph on p. 140 showing lettuce cutters at work, which we added from Thompson's blog, and consider what, if anything, it adds to the essay.

- **Before you read,** consider Thompson's choice of titles: *Working in the Shadows: A Year of Doing the Jobs (Most) Americans Won't Do* and "A Gringo in the Lettuce Fields." What do these titles lead you to expect will be the subject of the observations and the writer's perspective on the subject?

- **As you read,** notice how Thompson as an outsider uses participant observation to get an insider's view of the daily experience of farm workers. What does his outsider status enable him to understand — or prevent him from understanding — about the community he has entered?

I wake up staring into the bluest blue I've ever seen. I must have fallen into a deep 1 sleep because I need several seconds to realize that I'm looking at the Arizona sky, that the pillow beneath my head is a large clump of dirt, and that a near-stranger named Manuel is standing over me, smiling. I pull myself to a sitting position. To my left, in the distance, a Border Patrol helicopter is hovering. To my right is Mexico, separated by only a few fields of lettuce. "*Buenos días,*" Manuel says.

I stand up gingerly. It's only my third day in the fields, but already my 30-year-old 2 body is failing me. I feel like someone has dropped a log on my back. And then piled that log onto a truck with many other logs, and driven that truck over my thighs. "Let's go," I say, trying to sound energetic as I fall in line behind Manuel, stumbling across rows of lettuce and thinking about "the five-day rule." The five-day rule, according to Manuel, is simple: Survive the first five days and you'll be fine. He's been a farm-worker for almost two decades, so he should know. I'm on day three of five — the goal is within sight. Of course, another way to look at my situation is that I'm on day three of what I promised myself would be a two-month immersion in the work life of the people who do a job that most Americans won't do. But thinking about the next seven weeks doesn't benefit anyone. *Day three of five.*

"Manuel! Gabriel! Let's go! ¡*Vámonos!*" yells Pedro, our foreman. Our short break 3 is over. Two dozen crew members standing near the lettuce machine are already putting on gloves and sharpening knives. Manuel and I hustle toward the machine, grab our own knives from a box of chlorinated water, and set up in neighboring rows, just as the machine starts moving slowly down another endless field.

Since the early 1980s, Yuma, Ariz., has been the "winter lettuce capital" of 4 America. Each winter, when the weather turns cold in Salinas, California—the heart of the nation's lettuce industry—temperatures in sunny Yuma are still in the 70s and 80s. At the height of Yuma's growing season, the fields surrounding the city produce virtually all of the iceberg lettuce and 90 percent of the leafy green vegetables consumed in the United States and Canada.

America's lettuce industry actually needs people like me. Before applying for field- 5 work at the local Dole headquarters, I came across several articles describing the causes of a farmworker shortage. The stories cited an aging workforce, immigration crackdowns, and long delays at the border that discourage workers with green cards who would otherwise commute to the fields from their Mexican homes.[1] Wages have been rising somewhat in response to the demand for laborers (one prominent member of the local growers association tells me average pay is now between $10 and $12 an hour), but it's widely assumed that most U.S. citizens wouldn't do the work at any price. Arizona's own Senator John McCain created a stir in 2006 when he issued a challenge to a group of union members in Washington, D.C. "I'll offer anybody here $50 an hour if you'll go pick lettuce in Yuma this season, and pick for the whole season," he said. Amid jeers, he didn't back down, telling the audience, "You can't do it, my friends."

On my first day I discover that even putting on a lettuce cutter's uniform is chal- 6 lenging (no fieldworkers, I learn, "pick" lettuce). First, I'm handed a pair of black galoshes to go over my shoes. Next comes the *gancho*, an S-shaped hook that slips over my belt to hold packets of plastic bags. A white glove goes on my right hand, a gray glove, supposedly designed to offer protection from cuts, goes on my left. Over the cloth gloves I pull on a pair of latex gloves. I put on a black hairnet, my baseball cap, and a pair of protective sunglasses. Adding to my belt a long leather sheath, I'm good to go. I feel ridiculous.

The crew is already working in the field when Pedro walks me out to them and 7 introduces me to Manuel. Manuel is holding an 18-inch knife in his hand. "Manuel has been cutting for many years, so watch him to see how it's done," Pedro says. Then he walks away. Manuel resumes cutting, following a machine that rolls along just ahead of the crew. Every several seconds Manuel bends down, grabs a head of iceberg lettuce with his left hand, and makes a quick cut with the knife in his right hand, separating the lettuce from its roots. Next, he lifts the lettuce to his stomach

---

[1] A green card is an immigration document that allows noncitizens to work legally in the United States, whether they live here or commute across the border. [Editor's note]

Courtesy of Gabriel Thompson

and makes a second cut, trimming the trunk. He shakes the lettuce, letting the outer leaves fall to the ground. With the blade still in his hand, he then brings the lettuce toward the *gancho* at his waist, and with a flick of the wrist the head is bagged and dropped onto one of the machine's extensions. Manuel does this over and over again, explaining each movement. "It's not so hard," he says. Five minutes later, Pedro reappears and tells me to grab a knife. Manuel points to a head of lettuce. "Try this one," he says.

I bend over, noticing that most of the crew has turned to watch. I take my knife   8 and make a tentative sawing motion where I assume the trunk to be, though I'm really just guessing. Grabbing the head with my left hand, I straighten up, doing my best to imitate Manuel. Only my lettuce head doesn't move; it's still securely connected to the soil. Pedro steps in. "When you make the first cut, it is like you are stabbing the lettuce." He makes a quick jabbing action. "You want to aim for the center of the lettuce, where the trunk is," he says.

Ten minutes later, after a couple of other discouraging moments, I've cut maybe   9 20 heads of lettuce and am already feeling pretty accomplished. I'm not perfect: If I don't stoop far enough, my stab—instead of landing an inch above the ground—goes right through the head of lettuce, ruining it entirely. The greatest difficulty, though, is in the trimming. I had no idea that a head of lettuce was so humongous. In order to get it into a shape that can be bagged, I trim and trim and trim, but it's taking me upward of a minute to do what Manuel does in several seconds.

Pedro offers me a suggestion. "Act like the lettuce is a bomb," he says. "Imagine 10 you've only got five seconds to get rid of it."

Surprisingly, that thought seems to work, and I'm able to greatly increase my 11 speed. For a minute or two I feel euphoric. "Look at me!" I want to shout at Pedro; I'm in the zone. But the woman who is packing the lettuce into boxes soon swivels around to face me. "Look, this lettuce is no good." She's right: I've cut the trunk too high, breaking off dozens of good leaves, which will quickly turn brown because they're attached to nothing. With her left hand she holds the bag up, and with her right she smashes it violently, making a loud pop. She turns the bag over and the massacred lettuce falls to the ground. She does the same for the three other bags I've placed on the extension. "It's okay," Manuel tells me. "You shouldn't try to go too fast when you're beginning." Pedro seconds him. "That's right. Make sure the cuts are precise and that you don't rush."

So I am to be very careful and precise, while also treating the lettuce like a bomb 12 that must be tossed aside after five seconds.

That first week on the job was one thing. By midway into week two, it isn't clear 13 to me what more I can do to keep up with the rest of the crew. I know the techniques by this time and am moving as fast as my body will permit. Yet I need to somehow *double* my current output to hold my own. I'm able to cut only one row at a time while Manuel is cutting two. Our fastest cutter, Julio, meanwhile can handle three. But how someone could cut two rows for an hour—much less an entire day—is beyond me. "Oh, you will get it," Pedro tells me one day. "You will most definitely get it." Maybe he's trying to be hopeful or inspiring, but it comes across as a threat.

That feeling aside, what strikes me about our 31-member crew is how quickly they 14 have welcomed me as one of their own. I encountered some suspicion at first, but it didn't last. Simply showing up on the second day seemed to be proof enough that I was there to work. When I faltered in the field and fell behind, hands would come across from adjacent rows to grab a head or two of my lettuce so I could catch up. People whose names I didn't yet know would ask me how I was holding up, reminding me that it would get easier as time went by. If I took a seat alone during a break, someone would call me into their group and offer a homemade taco or two.

Two months in, I make the mistake of calling in sick one Thursday. The day before, 15 I put my left hand too low on a head of lettuce. When I punched my blade through the stem, the knife struck my middle finger. Thanks to the gloves, my skin wasn't even broken, but the finger instantly turned purple. I took two painkillers to get through the afternoon, but when I wake the next morning it is still throbbing. With one call to an answering machine that morning, and another the next day, I create my own four-day weekend.

The surprise is that when I return on Monday, feeling recuperated, I wind up 16 having the hardest day of my brief career in lettuce. Within hours, my hands feel weaker than ever. By quitting time—some 10 hours after our day started—I feel like I'm going to vomit from exhaustion. A theory forms in my mind. Early in the season—say, after the first week—a farmworker's body gets thoroughly broken down. Back, legs, and arms grow sore, hands and feet swell up. A tolerance for the pain is developed, though, and two-day weekends provide just enough time for the body to recover from the trauma. My four-day break had been too long; my body actually began to recuperate, and it wanted more time to continue. Instead, it was thrown right back into the mix and rebelled. Only on my second day back did my body recover that middle ground. "I don't think the soreness goes away," I say to Manuel and two other co-workers one day. "You just forget what it's like not to be sore." Manuel, who's 37, considers this. "That's true, that's true," he says. "It always takes a few weeks at the end of the year to get back to normal, to recover."

An older co-worker, Mateo, is the one who eventually guesses that I have joined the crew because I want to write about it. "That is good," he says over coffee at his home one Sunday. "Americans should know the hard work that Mexicans do in this country." 17

Mateo is an unusual case. There aren't many other farmworkers who are still in the fields when they reach their 50s. It's simply not possible to do this work for decades and not suffer a permanently hunched back, or crooked fingers, or hands so swollen that they look as if someone has attached a valve to a finger and pumped vigorously. The punishing nature of the work helps explain why farmworkers don't live very long; the National Migrant Resources Program puts their life expectancy at 49 years. 18

"Are you cutting two rows yet?" Mateo asks me. "Yes, more or less," I say. "I thought I'd be better by now." Mateo shakes his head. "It takes a long time to learn how to really cut lettuce. It's not something that you learn after only one season. Three, maybe four seasons—then you start understanding how to really work with lettuce." 19

READING FOR MEANING

For help
with reading
strategies like
summarizing
and analyzing
assumptions,
see Chapter 2.

1. **Read to Summarize.** Write a sentence or two explaining the main idea Thompson wants his readers to understand about his observations.

2. **Read to Respond.** Write a paragraph examining anything that seems surprising, such as Thompson's amazement that the other members of the crew "welcomed [him] as one of their own" (par. 14) or his "theory" that farmworkers develop a "tolerance for the pain" (par. 16).

3. **Read to Analyze Assumptions.** Write a paragraph or two analyzing an assumption you find intriguing in Thompson's essay. For example:

   Assumptions about the ethics of undercover observation. Participant observation does not necessarily involve secrecy, but Thompson chose to keep secret his intention to write about his experience as a lettuce cutter.

   • How valuable are immersion experiences like Thompson's to the individual observing, to the group being observed, and to readers in general?

   • What ethical challenges, if any, do you see with this kind of observational writing?

   Assumptions about the kinds of work done by guest or immigrant workers. As the subtitle of his book indicates, Thompson assumes that cutting lettuce falls into the category of *Jobs (Most) Americans Won't Do.* Many of the people who traditionally do these jobs are itinerant farm workers traveling seasonally from field to field (par. 5).

- Given that wages for farmworkers are "between $10 and $12 an hour," why do you think it is "widely assumed that most U.S. citizens wouldn't do the work at any price" (par. 5)?

- Thompson seems to be surprised not only by the physical demands of the work but by the high level of skill required to do it well. What do you think most Americans assume about skilled labor versus the "unskilled" manual labor performed by guest and immigrant workers?

READING LIKE A WRITER

Adopting an Authorial Role

Thompson takes on the role of participant observer: He does not watch lettuce cutters from the sidelines but rather works among them for two months. His informal interviews take place during work or on breaks or at the homes of his coworkers during the weekend. Nevertheless, there is a significant difference between a two-month experiment and a personal account written by a lettuce cutter like Mateo after a lifetime at the job. An observational writer may participate but is always to some extent an outsider looking in.

ANALYZE & WRITE

Write a paragraph or two analyzing Thompson's use of the participant-observer role:

1. Skim the text, highlighting each time Thompson
   - reminds readers of his status as an outsider—for example, when he refers to a coworker as a "near-stranger" (par. 1)
   - tells readers about something he thinks will be unfamiliar to them—for example, when he explains people do not "'pick' lettuce" (par. 6)
   - calls attention to his own incompetence or failings—for example, when he describes his first attempt to cut lettuce (par. 8)
2. Why do you think Thompson tells us about his errors and reminds us that he is an outsider? What effect are these moves likely to have on his target audience? What are the advantages, if any, of adopting the participant-observer role (as Thompson does) instead of the spectator role (as the author of "Soup" does, for example)?

Amanda Coyne

The Long Good-Bye: Mother's Day in Federal Prison

Amanda Coyne earned a master of fine arts degree in creative writing at the University of Iowa, where she was the recipient of an Iowa Arts Fellowship. She was the cofounder of and a writer for *Alaska Dispatch News*, an award-winning online news site. Her work has appeared in such publications as *Harper's*, the *New York Times Magazine*, *Bust*, *Newsweek*, and the *Guardian*. Coyne coauthored a book about oil and politics in Alaska entitled *Crude Awakening: Money, Mavericks, and Mayhem in Alaska* (2011). In 2013, she started an influential blog about Alaska politics, and in 2015, she joined the staff of the new Alaska senator, Dan Sullivan, as a senior adviser and speechwriter. "The Long Good-Bye," her first piece of published writing, originally appeared in *Harper's*. Coyne uses direct observation and interview to study the behavior of a particular community. In this profile, Coyne examines women who have been incarcerated and separated from their children to see how the mothers and children negotiate their difficult relationships.

- **Before you read,** notice how Coyne describes the convict-moms in the opening two paragraphs. What is the dominant impression you get from that description?

- **As you read,** think about the way Coyne compares and contrasts two convict-moms and their sons — Jennifer and Toby, and Stephanie and Ellie. What insights do you get from juxtaposing these two families?

You can spot the convict-moms here in the visiting room by the way they hold and   1
touch their children and by the single flower that is perched in front of them — a rose, a tulip, a daffodil. Many of these mothers have untied the bow that attaches the flower to its silver-and-red cellophane wrapper and are using one of the many empty soda cans at hand as a vase. They sit proudly before their flower-in-a-Coke-can, amid Hershey bar wrappers, half-eaten Ding Dongs, and empty paper coffee cups. Occasionally, a mother will pick up her present and bring it to her nose when one of the bearers of the single flower — her child — asks if she likes it. And the mother will respond the way that mothers always have and always will respond when presented with a gift on this day. "Oh, I just love it. It's perfect. I'll put it in the middle of my Bible." Or, "I'll put it on my desk, right next to your school picture." And always: "It's the best one here."

But most of what is being smelled today is the children themselves. While the   2
other adults are plunking coins into the vending machines, the mothers take deep whiffs from the backs of their children's necks, or kiss and smell the backs of their knees, or take off their shoes and tickle their feet and then pull them close to their

noses. They hold them tight and take in their own second scent—the scent assuring them that these are still their children and that they still belong to them.

The visitors are allowed to bring in pockets full of coins, and today that Mother's 3 Day flower, and I know from previous visits to my older sister here at the Federal Prison Camp for women in Pekin, Illinois, that there is always an aberrant urge to gather immediately around the vending machines. The sandwiches are stale, the coffee weak, the candy bars the ones we always pass up in a convenience store. But after we hand the children over to their mothers, we gravitate toward those machines. Like milling in the kitchen at a party. We all do it, and nobody knows why. Polite conversation ensues around the microwave while the popcorn is popping and the processed-chicken sandwiches are being heated. We ask one another where we are from, how long a drive we had. An occasional whistle through the teeth, a shake of the head. "My, my, long way from home, huh?" "Staying at the Super 8 right up the road. Not a bad place." "Stayed at the Econo Lodge last time. Wasn't a good place at all." Never asking the questions we really want to ask: "What's she in for?" "How much time's she got left?" You never ask in the waiting room of a doctor's office either. Eventually, all of us—fathers, mothers, sisters, brothers, a few boyfriends, and very few husbands—return to the queen of the day, sitting at a fold-out table loaded with snacks, prepared for five or so hours of attempted normal conversation.

Most of the inmates are elaborately dressed, many in prison-crafted dresses and 4 sweaters in bright blues and pinks. They wear meticulously applied makeup in corresponding hues, and their hair is replete with loops and curls—hair that only women with the time have the time for. Some of the better seamstresses have crocheted vests and purses to match their outfits. Although the world outside would never accuse these women of making haute-couture fashion statements, the fathers and the sons and the boyfriends and the very few husbands think they look beautiful, and they tell them so repeatedly. And I can imagine the hours spent preparing for this visit—hours of needles and hooks clicking over brightly colored yards of yarn. The hours of discussing, dissecting, and bragging about these visitors—especially the men. Hours spent in the other world behind the door where we're not allowed, sharing lipsticks and mascaras, and unraveling the occasional hair-tangled hot roller, and the brushing out and lifting and teasing . . . and the giggles that abruptly change into tears without warning—things that define any female-only world. Even, or especially, if that world is a female federal prison camp.

While my sister Jennifer is with her son in the playroom, an inmate's mother 5 comes over to introduce herself to my younger sister, Charity, my brother, John, and me. She tells us about visiting her daughter in a higher-security prison before she was transferred here. The woman looks old and tired, and her shoulders sag under the weight of her recently acquired bitterness.

"Pit of fire," she says, shaking her head. "Like a pit of fire straight from hell. Never 6 seen anything like it. Like something out of an old movie about prisons." Her voice is getting louder and she looks at each of us with pleading eyes. "My *daughter* was there. Don't even get me started on that place. Women die there."

John and Charity and I silently exchange glances.   7

"My daughter would come to the visiting room with a black eye and I'd think, 'All she did was sit in the car while her boyfriend ran into the house.' She didn't even touch the stuff. Never even handled it."

She continues to stare at us, each in turn. "Ten years. That boyfriend talked and he   8 got three years. She didn't know anything. Had nothing to tell them. They gave her ten years. They called it conspiracy. Conspiracy? Aren't there real criminals out there?" She asks this with hands outstretched, waiting for an answer that none of us can give her.

The woman's daughter, the conspirator, is chasing her son through the maze of   9 chairs and tables and through the other children. She's a twenty-four-year-old blonde, whom I'll call Stephanie, with Dorothy Hamill hair and matching dimples. She looks like any girl you might see in any shopping mall in middle America. She catches her chocolate-brown son and tickles him, and they laugh and trip and fall together onto the floor and laugh harder.

Had it not been for that wait in the car, this scene would be taking place at   10 home, in a duplex Stephanie would rent while trying to finish her two-year degree in dental hygiene or respiratory therapy at the local community college. The duplex would be spotless, with a blown-up picture of her and her son over the couch and ceramic unicorns and horses occupying the shelves of the entertainment center. She would make sure that her son went to school every day with stylishly floppy pants, scrubbed teeth, and a good breakfast in his belly. Because of their difference in skin color, there would be occasional tension—caused by the strange looks from strangers, teachers, other mothers, and the bullies on the playground, who would chant after they knocked him down, "Your Momma's white, your Momma's white." But if she were home, their weekends and evenings would be spent together tran-scending those looks and healing those bruises. Now, however, their time is spent eating visiting-room junk food and his school days are spent fighting the boys in the playground who chant, "Your Momma's in prison, your Momma's in prison."

He will be ten when his mother is released, the same age my nephew will be   11 when his mother is let out. But Jennifer, my sister, was able to spend the first five years of Toby's life with him. Stephanie had Ellie after she was incarcerated. They let her hold him for eighteen hours, then sent her back to prison. She has done the "tour," and her son is a well-traveled six-year-old. He has spent weekends visiting his mother in prisons in Kentucky, Texas, Connecticut (the Pit of Fire), and now at last here, the camp—minimum security, Pekin, Illinois.

Ellie looks older than his age. But his shoulders do not droop like his grand-   12 mother's. On the contrary, his bitterness lifts them and his chin higher than a child's should be, and the childlike, wide-eyed curiosity has been replaced by defiance. You can see his emerging hostility as he and his mother play together. She tells him to pick up the toy that he threw, say, or to put the deck of cards away. His face turns sul-len, but she persists. She takes him by the shoulders and looks him in the eye, and he uses one of his hands to swat at her. She grabs the hand and he swats with the other. Eventually, she pulls him toward her and smells the top of his head, and she picks up the cards or the toy herself. After all, it is Mother's Day and she sees him so rarely.

But her acquiescence makes him angrier, and he stalks out of the playroom with his shoulders thrown back.

Toby, my brother and sister and I assure one another, will not have these resent- 14 ments. He is better taken care of than most. He is living with relatives in Wisconsin. Good, solid, middle-class, churchgoing relatives. And when he visits us, his aunts and his uncle, we take him out for adventures where we walk down the alley of a city and pretend that we are being chased by the "bad guys." We buy him fast food, and his uncle, John, keeps him up well past his bedtime enthralling him with stories of the monkeys he met in India. A perfect mix, we try to convince one another. Until we take him to see his mother and on the drive back he asks the question that most confuses him, and no doubt all the other children who spend much of their lives in prison visiting rooms: "Is my Mommy a bad guy?" It is the question that most seriously disorders his five-year-old need to clearly separate right from wrong. And because our own need is perhaps just as great, it is the question that haunts us as well.

Now, however, the answer is relatively simple. In a few years, it won't be. 15 In a few years we will have to explain mandatory minimums, and the war on drugs, and the murky conspiracy laws, and the enormous amount of money and time that federal agents pump into imprisoning low-level drug dealers and those who happen to be their friends and their lovers. In a few years he might have the reasoning skills to ask why so many armed robbers and rapists and child-molesters and, indeed, murderers are punished less severely than his mother. When he is older, we will somehow have to explain to him the difference between federal crimes, which don't allow for parole, and state crimes, which do. We will have to explain that his mother was taken from him for five years not because she was a drug dealer but because she made four phone calls for someone she loved.

But we also know it is vitally important that we explain all this without betraying 16 our bitterness. We understand the danger of abstract anger, of being disillusioned with your country, and, most of all, we do not want him to inherit that legacy. We would still like him to be raised as we were, with the idea that we live in the best country in the world with the best legal system in the world—a legal system carefully designed to be immune to political mood swings and public hysteria; a system that promises to fit the punishment to the crime. We want him to be a good citizen. We want him to have absolute faith that he lives in a fair country, a country that watches over and protects its most vulnerable citizens: its women and children.

So for now we simply say, "Toby, your mother isn't bad, she just did a bad thing. 17 Like when you put rocks in the lawn mower's gas tank. You weren't bad then, you just did a bad thing."

Once, after being given this weak explanation, he said, "I wish I could have done 18 something really bad, like my Mommy. So I could go to prison too and be with her."

It's now 3:00. Visiting ends at 3:30. The kids are getting cranky, and the adults are 19 both exhausted and wired from too many hours of conversation, too much coffee and candy. The fathers, mothers, sisters, brothers, and the few boyfriends, and the very few husbands are beginning to show signs of gathering the trash. The mothers of the infants are giving their heads one last whiff before tucking them and their paraphernalia into their respective carrying cases. The visitors meander toward the door, leaving the older children with their mothers for one last word. But the mothers never say what they want to say to their children. They say things like, "Do well in school," "Be nice to your sister," "Be good for Aunt Berry, or Grandma." They don't say, "I'm sorry I'm sorry I'm sorry. I love you more than anything else in the world and I think about you every minute and I worry about you with a pain that shoots straight to my heart, a pain so great I think I will just burst when I think of you alone, without me. I'm sorry."

We are standing in front of the double glass doors that lead to the outside world. 20 My older sister holds her son, rocking him gently. They are both crying. We give her a look and she puts him down. Charity and I grasp each of his small hands, and the four of us walk through the doors. As we're walking out, my brother sings one of his banana songs to Toby.

"Take me out to the—" and Toby yells out, "Banana store!"   21

"Buy me some—"   22

"Bananas!!"   23

"I don't care if I ever come back. For it's root, root, root for the—"   24

"Monkey team!"   25

I turn back and see a line of women standing behind the glass wall. Some of them 26 are crying, but many simply stare with dazed eyes. Stephanie is holding both of her son's hands in hers and speaking urgently to him. He is struggling, and his head is twisting violently back and forth. He frees one of his hands from her grasp, balls up his fist, and punches her in the face. Then he walks with purpose through the glass doors and out the exit. I look back at her. She is still in a crouched position. She stares, unblinking, through those doors. Her hands have left her face and are hanging on either side of her. I look away, but before I do, I see drops of blood drip from her nose, down her chin, and onto the shiny marble floor.

READING FOR MEANING

For help with reading strategies like summarizing and analyzing assumptions, see Chapter 2.

1. **Read to Summarize.** Write a sentence or two explaining the essence of what Coyne observes when she visits her sister in prison.

2. **Read to Respond.** Write a paragraph exploring your reactions to anything touching or disturbing, such as the mothers smelling their children (par. 2) or their attempts to make themselves beautiful for the visit (par. 4).

3. **Read to Analyze Assumptions.** Write a paragraph or two analyzing an assumption that interests you in Coyne's observational essay. For example:

   Assumptions about fairness and the legal system. Near the end of the essay, Coyne reveals that she wishes her nephew Toby would grow up to "have absolute faith that he lives in a fair country" (par. 16).

- Why do you think Coyne believes her sister's punishment is unfair? Why does Stephanie's mother think Stephanie's punishment is unfair? Do you agree or disagree?

- What does Coyne assume about American culture when she refers to "political mood swings and public hysteria" and when she uses the slogan "make the punishment fit the crime" (par. 16)?

Assumptions about children's rebelliousness. Coyne seems to assume that Ellie's rebellious behavior toward Stephanie is his way of responding to the enforced separation from his mother (par. 13).

- What do you think leads Coyne to make this assumption? How convincing do you think it is to assume that Ellie's behavior is caused by his separation from his mother?

- What other assumptions might one have about the causes of Ellie's behavior? For example, how do you think his grandmother's anger is likely to affect him?

READING LIKE A WRITER

Conveying a Perspective on the Subject

Unlike arguments supporting positions or justifying evaluations, which tell readers directly what the writer thinks and why, observational writing often uses comparison/contrast to lead readers to draw their own conclusion. Writers often use transitional words and phrases to make explicit the relationship between the two items being compared or contrasted. For example:

For more on comparing and contrasting, see Chapter 2.

Transition cues contrast

> **Although** the world outside would never accuse these women of making haute-couture fashion statements, the fathers and the sons and the boyfriends and the very few husbands think they look beautiful. . . . (par. 4)

Sometimes writers leave out the transition and simply juxtapose the things that are being compared or contrasted by placing them side by side.

Comma cues juxtaposition

Word choice cues comparison

> He will be ten when his mother is released, the same age my nephew will be when his mother is let out. (par. 12)

In this example, the word *same* lets readers know Coyne is pointing out a similarity between the two families. Note that she follows this sentence with an explicit transition to stress that although the two mother-son relationships are comparable, there are significant differences between them:

Transition cues   But Jennifer, my sister, was able to spend the first five years of
contrast   Toby's life with him. Stephanie had Ellie after she was incarcerated.
                   They let her hold him for eighteen hours, then sent her back to
                   prison. (par. 12)

ANALYZE & WRITE

Write a paragraph or two analyzing how Coyne uses comparison/contrast cues and juxtapositions to convey her perspective on the plight of convict-moms and their relationships with their kids.

1. Note in the margin which paragraphs focus on Coyne's sister Jennifer and her son Toby and which focus on Stephanie and her son Ellie. Mark where Coyne juxtaposes the two families and where she uses transitions to highlight the comparisons and contrasts. What differences between the two families does Coyne emphasize? What do you think she wants readers to understand about the dilemma of convict-moms and their relationship with their children?

2. Also consider how Coyne sets up a contrast in paragraphs 10–11 between what is and what could have been. What cues does she use to signal this contrast? How does this contrast help convey Coyne's perspective on the plight of women like her sister and children like her nephew?

Robin Wall Kimmerer

Asters and Goldenrods

Robin Wall Kimmerer is SUNY Distinguished Teaching Professor at the SUNY College of Environmental Science and Forestry in Syracuse, New York. She serves as the founding Director of the Center for Native Peoples and the Environment, and she is also the cofounder and past president of the Traditional Ecological Knowledge section of the Ecological Society of America and serves as a Senior Fellow for the Center for Nature and Humans. She has been a writer in residence at the Andrews Experimental Forest, the Blue Mountain Center, the Sitka Center, and the Mesa Refuge. Of European and Anishinaabe ancestry, Kimmerer is an enrolled member of the Citizen Potawatomi Nation. *Braiding Sweetgrass: Indigenous Wisdom, Scientific Knowledge and the Teachings of Plants* (2013), from which the selection below is taken, was awarded the Sigurd Olson Nature Writing Award. Her interests as both a scientist and writer revolve around humans' relationships to the land. The essay below considers how humans interact with the natural world, as well as the role of science and poetry in those interactions.

- **Before you read,** consider the title of the piece. Do you know what goldenrod and asters are? Do you expect that the essay will explain this?

- **As you read,** think about the kind of audience Kimmerer expects to be reading her piece. How much scientific background does she expect? How do her expectations affect your engagement with the piece?

1   The girl in the picture holds a slate with her name and "class of' 75" chalked in, a girl the color of deerskin with long dark hair and inky unreadable eyes that meet yours and won't look away. I remember that day. I was wearing the new plaid shirt that my parents had given me, an outfit I thought to be the hallmark of all foresters. When I looked back at the photo later in life, it was a puzzle to me. I recall being elated to be going to college, but there is no trace of that in the girl's face.

2   Even before I arrived at school, I had all of my answers prepared for the freshman intake interview. I wanted to make a good first impression. There were hardly any women at the forestry school in those days and certainly none who looked like me. The adviser peered at me over his glasses and said, "So, why do you want to major in botany?" His pencil was poised over the registrar's form.

3   How could I answer, how could I tell him that I was born a botanist, that I had shoeboxes of seeds and piles of pressed leaves under my bed, that I'd stop my bike along the road to identify a new species, that plants colored my dreams, that the plants had chosen me? So I told him the truth. I was proud of my well-planned answer, its freshman sophistication apparent to anyone, the way it showed that I already knew some plants and their habitats, that I had thought deeply about their nature and was clearly well prepared for college work. I told him that I chose botany

because I wanted to learn about why asters and goldenrod looked so beautiful together. I'm sure I was smiling then, in my red plaid shirt.

But he was not. He laid down his pencil as if there was no need to record what I had said. "Miss Wall", he said, fixing me with a disappointed smile, "I must tell you that *that* is not science. That is not at all the sort of thing with which botanists concern themselves." But he promised to put me right. "I'll enroll you in General Botany so you can learn what it is." And so it began.

I like to imagine that they were the first flowers I saw, over my mother's shoulder, as the pink blanket slipped away from my face and their colors flooded my consciousness. I've heard that early experience can attune the brain to certain stimuli, so that they are processed with greater speed and certainty, so that they can be used again and again, so that we remember. Love at first sight. Through cloudy newborn eyes their radiance formed the first botanical synapses in my wide-awake, new-born brain, which until then had encountered only the blurry gentleness of pink faces. I'm guessing all eyes were on me, a little round baby all swaddled in bunting, but mine were on Goldenrod and Asters. I was born to these flowers and they came back for my birthday every year, weaving me into our mutual celebration.

People flock to our hills for the fiery suite of October but they often miss the sublime prelude of September fields. As if harvest time were not enough—peaches, grapes, sweet corn, squash—the fields are also embroidered with drifts of golden yellow and pools of deepest purple, a masterpiece.

If a fountain could jet bouquets of chrome yellow in dazzling arches of chrysanthemum fireworks, that would be Canada Goldenrod. Each three-foot stem is a geyser of tiny gold daisies, ladylike in miniature, exuberant en masse. Where the soil is damp enough, they stand side by side with their perfect counterpart, New England Asters. Not the pale domesticates of the perennial border, the weak sauce of lav ender or sky blue, but full-on royal purple that would make a violet shrink. The daisylike fringe of purple petals surrounds a disc as bright as the sun at high noon, a golden-orange pool, just a tantalizing shade darker than the surrounding goldenrod. Alone, each is a botanical superlative. Together, the visual effect is stunning. Purple and gold, the heraldic colors of the king and queen of the meadow, a regal procession in complementary colors. I just wanted to know why.

Why do they stand beside each other when they could grow alone ? Why this particular pair? There are plenty of pinks and whites and blues dotting the fields, so is it only happenstance that the magnificence of purple and gold end up side by side? Einstein himself said that "God doesn't play dice with the universe." What is the source of this pattern? Why is the world so beautiful? It could so easily be otherwise: flowers could be ugly to us and still fulfill their own purpose. But they're not. It seemed like a good question to me.

But my adviser said, "It's not science," not what botany was about. I wanted to know why certain stems bent easily for baskets and some would break, why the biggest berries grew in the shade and why they made us medicines, which plants are edible, why those little pink orchids only grow under pines. "Not science," he said, and he ought to know, sitting in his laboratory, a learned professor of botany. "And if you want to study beauty, you should go to art school." He reminded me of my deliberations over choosing a college, when I had vacillated between training as a botanist or as a poet. Since everyone told me I couldn't do both, I'd chosen plants. He told me that science was not about beauty, not about the embrace between plants and humans.

I had no rejoinder; I had made a mistake. There was no fight in me, only embar- 10 rassment at my error. I did not have the words for resistance. He signed me up for my classes and I was dismissed to go get my photo taken for registration. I didn't think about it at the time, but it was happening all over again, an echo of my grandfather's first day at school, when he was ordered to leave everything — language, culture, family — behind. The professor made me doubt where I came from, what I knew, and claimed that his was the *right* way to think. Only he didn't cut my hair off.

In moving from a childhood in the woods to the university I had unknowingly 11 shifted between worldviews, from natural history of experience, in which I knew plants as teachers and companions to whom I was linked with mutual responsibility, into the realm of science. The questions scientists raised were not "Who are you?" but "What is it?" No one asked plants, "What can you tell us?" The primary question was "How does it work?" The botany I was taught was reductionist, mechanistic, and strictly objective. Plants were reduced to objects; they were not subjects. The way botany was conceived and taught didn't seem to leave much room for a person who thought the way I did. The only way I could make sense of it was to conclude that the things I had always believed about plants must not be true after all.

That first plant science class was a disaster. I barely scraped by with a C and 12 could not muster much enthusiasm for memorizing the concentrations of essential plant nutrients. There were times when I wanted to quit, but the more I learned, the more fascinated I became with the intricate structures that made up a leaf and the alchemy of photosynthesis. Companionship between asters and goldenrod was never mentioned, but I memorized botanical Latin as if it was poetry, eagerly tossing aside the name "goldenrod" for *Solidago canadensis*. I was mesmerized by plant ecology, evolution, taxonomy, physiology, soils, and fungi. All around me were my good teachers, the plants I found good mentors, too, warm and kind professors who were doing heart-driven science, whether they could admit it or not. They too were my teachers. And yet there was always something tapping at my shoulder, willing me to turnaround. When I did, not know how to recognize what stood behind me.

My natural inclination was to see relationships, to seek the threads that connect 13 the world, to join instead of divide. But science is rigorous in separating the observer from the observed, and the observed, from the observer. Why two flowers are beautiful together would violate the division necessary for objectivity.

I scarcely doubted the primacy of scientific thought. Following the path of 14 science trained me to separate, to distinguish perception from physical reality, to atomize complexity into its smallest components, to honor the chain of evidence and logic, to discern one thing from another, to savor the pleasure of precision. The more I did this, the better I got at it, and I was accepted to do graduate work in one of the world's finest botany programs, no doubt on the strength of the letter of recommendation from my adviser, which read, "She's done remarkably well for an Indian girl."

A master's degree, a PhD, and a faculty position followed. I am grateful for the 15 knowledge that was shared with me and deeply privileged to carry the powerful tools of science as a way of engaging the world. It took me to other plant communities, far from the asters and goldenrod. I remember feeling, as a new faculty member, as if I finally understood plants. I too began to teach the mechanics of botany, emulating the approach that I had been taught.

It reminds me of a story told by my friend Holly Youngbear Tibbetts. A plant sci- 16 entist, armed with his notebooks and equipment, is exploring the rainforests for new botanical discoveries, and he has hired an indigenous guide to lead him. Knowing the scientist's interests, the young guide takes care to point out the interesting species. The botanist looks at him appraisingly, surprised by his capacity "Well, well, young man, you certainly know the names of a lot of these plants" The guide nods and replies with downcast eyes. "Yes, I have learned the names of all the bushes, but I have yet to learn their songs."

I was teaching the names and ignoring the songs.   17

When I was in graduate school in Wisconsin, my then husband and I had the 18 good fortune to land jobs as caretakers at the university arboretum. In return for little house at the edge of the prairie, we had only to make the nighttime rounds, checking that doors and gates were secure before we left the darkness to the crickets. There was just one time that a light was left burning, a door left ajar, in the horticulture garage. There was no mischief, but as my husband checked around, I stood and idly scanned the bulletin board. There was a news clipping there with a photo of a magnificent American elm, which had just been named the champion for its species, the largest of its kind. It had name: The Louis Vieux Elm.

My heart began to pound and I knew my world was about to change, for I'd 19 known the name Louis Vieux all my life and than was his face looking at me from a news clipping. He was our Potawatomi grandfather, one who had walked all the way from the Wisconsin forests to the Kansas prairie with my grandma Sha-note. He was a leader, one who took care of the people in their hardship. That garage door was left ajar, that light was left burning, and it shone on the path back home for me. It was the beginning of a long, slow journey back to my people, called out to me by the tree that stood above their bones.

To walk the science path I had stepped off the path of indigenous knowledge. 20 But the world has a way of guiding your steps. Seemingly out of the blue came an invitation to a small gathering of Native elders, to talk about traditional knowledge of plants. One I will never forget—a Navajo woman without a day of university botany training in her life—spoke for hours and I hung on every word. One by one, name by name, she told of the plants in her valley. Where each one ships, who ate it, who lined their nests with its fibers, what kind of medicine it offered. She also shared the stories held by those plants, their origin myths, how they got their names, and what they have to tell us. She spoke of beauty.

Her words were like smelling salts waking me to what I had known back when 21 I was picking strawberries. I realized how shallow my understanding was. Her knowledge was so much deeper and wider and engaged all the human ways of understanding. She could have explained asters and goldenrod. To a new PhD, this was humbling. It was the beginning of my reclaiming that other way of knowing that I had helplessly let science supplant. I felt like a malnourished refugee invited to a feast, the dishes scented with the herbs of home.

I circled right back to where I had begun, to the question of beauty. Back to the 22 questions that science does not ask, not because they aren't important, but because science as a way of knowing is too narrow for the task. Had my adviser been a better scholar, he would have celebrated my questions, not dismissed them. He offered me only the cliché that beauty is in the eye of the beholder, and since science separates the observer and the observed, by definition beauty could not be a valid scientific question. I should have been told that my questions were bigger than science could touch.

He *was* right about beauty being in the eye of the beholder, especially when it comes 23 to purple and yellow. Color perception in humans relies on banks of specialized receptor cells, the rods and cones in the retina. The job of the cone cells is to absorb light of different wavelengths and pass it on to the brain's visual cortex, where it can be interpreted. The visible light spectrum, the rainbow of colors, is broad, so the most effective means of discerning color is not one generalized jack-of-all-trades cone cell, but rather an array of specialists, each perfectly tuned to absorb certain wavelengths. The human eye has three kinds. One type excels at detecting red and associated wavelengths. One is tuned to blue. The other optimally perceives light of two colors: purple and yellow.

The human eye is superbly equipped to detect these colors and send a signal pulsing 24 to the brain. This doesn't explain why I perceive them as beautiful, but it does explain why that combination gets my undivided attention. I asked my artist buddies about the power of purple and gold, and they sent me right to the color wheel: these two are complementary colors, as different in nature as could be. In composing a palette, putting them together makes each more vivid; just a touch of one will bring out the other. In an 1890 treatise on color perception, Goethe, who was both a scientist and a poet, wrote that "the colors diametrically opposed to each other . . . are those which *reciprocally* evoke each other in the eye." Purple and yellow are a reciprocal pair.

Our eyes are so sensitive to these wavelengths that the cones can get oversatu- 25 rated and the stimulus pours over onto the other cells. A printmaker I know showed me that if you stare for a long time at a block of Yellow and then shift your gaze to a White sheet of paper, you will see it, for a moment, as violet. This phenomenon—the colored afterimage—occurs because there is energetic reciprocity between purple and yellow pigments, which goldenrod and asters knew well before we did.

If my adviser was correct, the visual effect that so delights a human like me may be 26 irrelevant to the flowers. The real beholder whose eye they hope to catch is a bee bent on pollination. Bees perceive many flowers differently than humans do due to their perception of additional spectra such as ultraviolet radiation. As it turns out, though, goldenrod and asters appear very similarly to bee eye and human eyes. We both think they're beautiful. Their striking contrast when they grow together makes them the most attractive target in the whole meadow, a beacon for bees. Growing together, both receive more pollinator visits tan they would if they were growing alone. It's a testable hypothesis; it's a question of science, a question of art, and question of beauty.

Why are they beautiful together? It is a phenomenon simultaneously material and 27 spiritual, for which we need all wavelengths, for which we need depth perception. When I stare too long at the world with science eyes, I see an afterimage of traditional knowledge. Might science and traditional knowledge be purple and yellow to one another, might they be goldenrod and asters? We see the world more fully when we use both.

The question of goldenrod and asters was of course just emblematic of what I 28 really wanted to know. It was an architecture of relationships, of connections that I yearned to understand. I wanted to see the shimmering threads that hold it all together. And I wanted to know why we love the world, why the most ordinary scrap of meadow can rock us back on our heels in awe.

When botanists go walking the forests and fields looking for plants, we say we are 29 going on a *foray*. When writers do the same, we should call it a *metaphoray*, and the land is rich in both. We need them both; scientist and poet Jeffrey Burton Russell writes that "as the sign of a deeper truth, metaphor was close to sacrament. Because the vastness and richness of reality cannot be expressed by the overt sense of a statement alone."

Native scholar Greg Cajete has written that in indigenous ways of knowing, we 30 understand a thing only when we understand it with all four aspects of our being: mind, body, emotion, and spirit. I came to understand quite sharply when I began my training as a scientist that science privileges only one, possibly two, of those ways of knowing: mind and body. As a young person wanting to know everything about plants, I did not question this. But it is a whole human being who finds the beautiful path.

There was a time when I teetered precariously with an awkward foot in each of 31 two worlds—the scientific and the indigenous. But then I learned to fly. Or at least try. It was the bees that showed me how to move between different flowers—to drink the nectar and gather pollen from both. It is this dance of cross-pollination that can produce a new species of knowledge, a new way of being in the world. After all, there aren't two worlds, there is just this one good green earth.

That September pairing of purple and gold is lived reciprocity; its wisdom is that 32 the beauty of one is illuminated by the radiance of the other. Science and art, matter and spirit, indigenous knowledge and Western science—can they be goldenrod and asters for each other? When I am in their presence, their beauty asks me for reciprocity, to be the complementary color, to make something beautiful in response.

READING FOR MEANING

For help with reading strategies like summarizing and analyzing assumptions, see Chapter 2.

1. **Read to Summarize.** Write a sentence or two explaining the main idea Kimmerer wants her readers to understand.

2. **Read to Respond.** Write a paragraph exploring anything that resonates with your experience, such as how the adviser responds to Kimmerer in the

interview (par. 4) or how he admonishes her for her interest in "studying beauty" (par. 9).

3. **Read to Analyze Assumptions.** Write a paragraph or two analyzing an assumption you find intriguing in Kimmerer's essay. For example:

Assumptions about science. Kimmerer describes many instances in which her adviser/professor tells her that's "not science."

- What experiences inside and outside of school have helped shape your ideas about science?

- As you compare your assumptions about science with those of other students in your class, what important differences do you see, and how do you account for these differences?

Assumptions about authority. Kimmerer's adviser/professor tells her that "science was not about beauty, not about the embrace between plants and humans" (par. 9). Kimmerer describes her reaction to this statement: "I had no rejoinder; I had made a mistake. There was no fight in me. Only embarrassment at my error. . . . The professor made me doubt what I came from, what I knew, and claimed that his was the right way to think. . . . In moving from a childhood in the woods to the university I had unknowingly shifted between worldviews . . ." (pars. 10–11).

You may also try reflecting on challenges to your beliefs and values; see Chapter 2, p. 57.

- Why do you suppose many students, including Kimmerer, assume that professors know the right way to think? In reflecting on this early college experience as she wrote this piece, do you think Kimmerer still feels this way?

- What assumptions does the essay make about the two "worldviews?" Do you share these assumptions?

READING LIKE A WRITER

Conveying a Perspective on the Subject

Authors often show their perspective on a subject through the dominant impression they create. This impression may offer insight into the author, as well as the subject. In some cases, these impressions may not be explicit and the author may use suggestion or rhetorical questions (questions that are used to make a point rather than elicit immediate answers) to convey their perspective.

ANALYZE & WRITE

Write a paragraph examining how the writer conveys her perspective on the greater significance of asters and goldenrod:

1. Reread the essay, looking for examples of rhetorical questions. Explain how Kimmerer's use of rhetorical questions suggests her perspective on "the threads that connect the world" (par. 13). What does Kimmerer's use of both rhetorical and standard questions—as opposed to statements—suggest about her perspective?

2. Review the academic habits of mind listed in Chapter 1 of this book (pp. 1–3). Which academic habits of mind do you see Kimmerer, an academic herself, practicing and describing in her essay? Where in the text do these academic habits show up, and what do they help you understand about Kimmerer's perspective?

3. Notice how Kimmerer introduces some of the sources she cites.

   "In an 1890 treatise on color perception, Goethe, who was both a scientist and a poet. . ." (par. 24)

   "Scientist and poet Jeffrey Burton Russell writes. . ." (par. 29)

   "Native scholar Greg Cajete. . ." (par. 30)

How does her choice of these sources and the way she introduces them help convey her perspective?

Linda Fine

Bringing Ingenuity Back

Linda Fine wrote the following observational essay when she was a first-year college student. This essay is based on her visit to see the recently donated hand-printing presses at her campus library. She records her own observations about these antique presses, as well as how they work. Notice that she also quotes and paraphrases extensively from Sara, the librarian who explains these old-fashioned machines to her.

- **Before you read,** consider your ideas about so-called old-fashioned technologies. Are you willing to consider their relevance in a more advanced society or are you partial to the newest technologies?

- **As you read,** notice the details that Fine provides as she discusses the challenges associated with using hand-printing presses. Do these details effectively convey these challenges?

As I made my way to a set of elevators in the rear of our sleek new campus library, I passed students and librarians working at monitors wired into the university's online system. I also passed students sitting at tables with their laptops open and books piled nearby. A few students were using the photocopiers to scan pages onto their jump drives, and two printers on a corner table spewed paper as students stood nearby, chatting. I was on my way into the past to see hand-printing presses dating from the Civil War. The antique presses were donated to the university by Dr. Edward Petko because he favored the hand-press method over modern laser printing, and he hoped that the university would help keep the traditional process alive. 1

Entering an unmarked room in the basement, I saw numerous weathered wooden cases stacked twice my height and, beyond them, old iron machines in various shapes and sizes. I stepped into the room clueless but eager to learn about this nearly forgotten printing process. Sara Stilley, a thin, dark-haired woman in her late twenties, works in this room five days a week. After welcoming me, she showed me some samples of artwork she has printed. One of her most recent works was a greeting card she made for another staff member. The finished product looked very professional, but then Sara proceeded to explain to me the frustration behind this masterpiece. 2

The preparation work takes hours, and in some cases, days. Sara's difficult task is to carefully align each individual letter by hand. The letters are made up of very thin rectangular prisms, which make them difficult to handle. Not only does Sara need manual dexterity, she also needs skilled eyes to be able to tell the letters apart. If a wrong letter, font, or size has been used, she has to go back and tediously correct the frame and setup by hand. Familiarity with what the letters will look like is essential for the setup of hand printing because the letters can be confusing. The leaded letters in the printing process work like a stamp. Instead of arranging them the way they are read, the operator must position the letters upside 3 down and backward, like a mirror image. It takes time and effort to train the eye to recognize letters this way. Letters such as *n* and *u* are easily mixed up, as are *p* and *q*, and *b* and *d*. Formatting the letters correctly is a critical step in the printing process because any careless error the setup leaves a noticeable flaw in the printed document.

4   In addition to the letter conflict, Sara said, "Many times after centering the text, I would find out that I made a mistake in the formation. Instead of making it perfectly centered, I was supposed to align it to the left." I could imagine that going back and correcting the spacing would be a wearisome task.

5   This old-fashioned printing process has other problems and difficulties too. For example, humid weather causes the ink to spread out, leaving the text appearing smudgy and smeared. There may also be too much or too little ink used in a working press. Sometimes Sara will run out of a specific letter for a page. The only solution to this problem is to break apart her work into two printing processes and print half the page at a time.

6   Sara explained that back in the 1800s, printers did not number their pages when printing a book. In order to keep the pages orderly, they had to use the same word twice. For example, if a page ended with the word "boy," then the following page would have to begin with the word "boy." Not numbering the pages can easily cause them to fall out of order.

7   At this point in the interview, I had to ask her, "If using hand-printing presses can cause so many problems, why would anyone still prefer using them over laser-printing presses?"

8   Sara answered, "I feel better with what I produce. For example, personally baking a cake for someone is better and much more appreciated than simply buying one."

9   After she said that, I got the point. If I were to send out Christ-mas cards, each individual card would mean so much more if I had personally hand-printed it myself rather than buying a box of pre-printed cards at Walmart. Craftsmanship adds value and meaning that you can't find in industrialized commodities that you just buy.

10   I walked around the room and explored the shapes and sizes of the various printing presses. I saw that each machine had its own unique maneuvers. Some levers had to be pulled clockwise and pushed down. Others simply needed to be rolled across the printing bed and back. The cases and crates stacked around the presses contained lead-filled letters and hundreds of neatly stored rectangular pieces. There were keys, metal washers, wooden blocks called "furniture" to keep the letters in place, ink, and galleys—all of which, I learned, were required for the printing process.

11   At the very end of my interview, Sara demonstrated one of the many printing presses to me, the Asbern. First she carefully arranged the lead-filled text blocks on the printing bed and used a key to tighten the furniture securing the letters. As she switched the power button on, the ink rollers began to spin. A low, soft mumbling sound stirred and filled the room. Sara slipped a piece of plain white paper into the slot and steered the machine from left to right. Steering the wheel seemed like a very tough job because she was jerking her entire body to create enough torque to rotate

the wheel. Soon she turned off the machine and took the paper out. After a careful examination, she announced that it wasn't perfect. Sara handed the page to me expecting me to see what she saw, but as I looked at it, I found nothing wrong with the printing.

Squinting, she told me, "The text is not perfectly centered on the paper. It's a bit 12 crooked because I slipped in the paper at a slight angle."

Whoever would have thought that small errors, like slipping in the paper slanted, 13 would make such a big difference? This is one of the many things that make hand printing more difficult than using a modern printing press.

Had Sara not pointed out to me the imperfection in her work, however, I never 14 would have caught it. It is amazing how she can spot a flaw in her work as quickly as a professional chess player can call a checkmate. Sara's keen expertise in the area of hand-printing presses impresses me. I never thought such an old-fashioned job would provide deep insight into the beauty and value of works made by hand.

As I left the room filled with irreplaceable treasures, I thought of the time when 15 my sister, Irene, knitted a scarf for her friend on duty in Iraq. Irene was very worried about making the scarf "perfect." She was so concerned about making a mistake—or not having enough time to finish the scarf—that I wondered why she didn't simply buy a scarf at Macy's. After interviewing Sara Stilley and learning more about the ingenuity of her work, I now understood why Irene chose to make the scarf by hand. The scarf she knitted for her friend had more meaning in it than a typical scarf purchased at a department store. She expressed her loving care and support through the gift she made because it took time and effort, and not just money. There are a few holes and gaps in that scarf, but I'm sure her friend, like me, didn't see the imperfections and thought the gift was simply perfect.

READING FOR MEANING

1. **Read to Summarize.** Write a sentence or two explaining the main idea Fine wants her readers to understand about the hand-printing presses she observes.

   For help with reading strategies like summarizing and analyzing assumptions, see Chapter 2.

2. **Read to Respond.** Write a paragraph exploring anything that resonates with your experience, such as Fine's preconceptions about the superiority of laser-printing presses over hand-printing presses (par. 7).

3. **Read to Analyze Assumptions.** Write a paragraph or two analyzing an assumption you find intriguing in Fine's essay. For example:

   Assumptions about technology . Fine begins her essay by describing all of the various forms of technology she passes in her campus's sleek new library (par. 1) as she makes her way to explore the antique hand-printing presses.

- What assumptions do you have about new technology as compared to more old-fashioned or so-called outdated technologies, and where do these assumptions come from?

- Is something that is hand-pressed or hand-made, more generally, necessarily more meaningful than something created by a newer technology? Explain your answer.

Assumptions about antiques. Compare the different ways that Fine describes the hand-printing presses. Throughout the essay she uses the terms "antique" and "old-fashioned" interchangeably to describe the presses.

- How would you describe the difference between the connotations of the two terms antique and old-fashioned? Which has a more positive connotation and why?

- What message does calling something an antique as opposed to calling it old, old-fashioned, or used send? What assumptions do you have about antiques in terms of their value, and where do these assumptions come from?

READING LIKE A WRITER

Organizing the Information

Observations may be organized **topically,** with the writer bringing up a series of topics about the subject (as in "Soup"); they may be organized **narratively,** with the writer telling a story that extends over a period of time (as Thompson does); or they may be organized **spatially,** with the writer taking readers on a tour of a place, pointing out interesting sights and bringing up various topics about the subject as they move through the scene (as Fine does):

Begins by elevators	As I made my way to a set of elevators in the rear I passed students and librarians working at monitors. . . . I also passed
verbs marks spatial movement	students sitting at tables. . . . I was on my way into the past to see hand-printing presses. . . . Entering an unmarked room in the basement. . . . I stepped into the room. . . . (pars. 1–2)

Fine acts as a tour guide, or as the camera in a documentary. She marks her movement with transitional words and phrases such as "I was on my way" (par. 1) and "I stepped into the room" (par. 2). Fine describes her movements to highlight that she is on her "way into the past to see hand-printing presses" (par 1). Describing her movements in space also allows her to separate her observations about the technologically advanced section of the library from the observations she makes about the unmarked space in the basement where the old-fashioned hand-printing presses are located.

ANALYZE & WRITE

Write a paragraph analyzing how Fine orients readers as she takes them from the sleek new part of the library to the unmarked room in the basement where the hand-printing presses are located.

1. Skim the essay and find the passages where Fine takes readers from one area to another. How does she signal to readers the transition in space?

2. Find an example that shows how these spatial transitions also introduce new topics.

3. How effective or ineffective is this tour as a way of organizing information in a place like a library?

Writing to Learn Observation

Write a brief essay analyzing one of the readings in this chapter (or another selection, perhaps one by a classmate). Explain how (and perhaps, how well) the selection works as an observation. Consider, for example, how it

- presents detailed information about the subject;

- organizes the information topically, narratively, or spatially to make it interesting and clear;

- takes a detached observer or participant-observer role, or alternates between the two;

- conveys the writer's perspective on what makes the subject intriguing and/ or culturally significant.

Your essay could also reflect on how you applied one or more of the following practices as you read the selection:

- **Critical analysis** — what assumptions in the selection did you find intriguing, and why?

- **Rhetorical sensitivity** — how effective or ineffective do you think the selection is in achieving its purpose for the intended audience?

- **Empathy** — did you find yourself identifying with the author, and how important was this to the effectiveness of the selection?

A GUIDE TO WRITING OBSERVATIONAL ESSAYS

You have probably done a good deal of analytical writing about your reading. Your instructor may also assign a capstone project to write a brief observation of your own. This Guide to Writing offers detailed suggestions and resources to help you meet the special challenges observational writing presents.

THE WRITING ASSIGNMENT

Write about an intriguing or unusual place, person, or activity.

- Choose a subject that is relatively unfamiliar to your audience or a familiar subject that you can present in a fresh and surprising way.

- Research the subject, gathering detailed information primarily from close observations and interviews, and present that information in a clear, logical way that is entertaining as well as informative.

- Analyze the information you have gathered about the subject so that you can give readers insight into the subject's cultural meaning and importance.

WRITING YOUR DRAFT

Choosing a Subject

Rather than limiting yourself to the first subject that comes to mind, take a few minutes to consider your options and list as many subjects as you can. Below are some criteria that can help you choose a promising subject, followed by suggestions for the types of places, people, and activities you might consider writing about. The subject should

- spark your — and your readers' — interest and curiosity

- be accessible, allowing you to make detailed observations and conduct in-depth interviews in the time allotted

- lead to ideas about its cultural significance and meanings

Note: Whenever you write an observational report or profile, consider carefully the ethics involved in such research. You will want to treat participants fairly and with respect in the way you both approach and depict them. You may need to obtain permission from your school's ethics review board. Discuss the ethical

implications of your research with your instructor, and think carefully about the goals of your research and the effect your research will have on others.
An appropriate person might be

- someone doing work that you might want to do — a city council member, police officer, lab technician, computer programmer, attorney, salesperson

- someone with an unusual job or hobby — a dog trainer, private detective, ham radio operator, race car driver, novelist

- someone recently recognized for academic or community service or achievement

An appropriate place might be

- a place where people come together because they are of the same age, gender, sexual orientation, or ethnic group (for example, a foreign language–speaking residence hall or LGBTQ+ club) or a place where people have formed a community around a shared interest (for example, a Sunday morning pickup basketball game in the park, political campaign, or barber shop)

- a place where people are trained for a certain kind of work (for example, a police academy, CSI program, or truck driving school)

- a place where a group of people are working together for a particular purpose (for example, a laboratory where scientists are collaborating on a research project)

An appropriate activity might be

- an unconventional sporting event — a dogs' Frisbee tournament, chess match, dog sledding, log sawing and splitting competition; an amateur wrestling or boxing meet, ice-fishing contest

- a team practicing a sport or other activity (one you can observe as a curious outsider, not as an experienced participant)

- a community improvement project — graffiti cleaning, tree planting, house repairing, road or highway litter collecting

Researching Your Subject

Conducting observations and interviews takes time, so determine whether you can get permission before committing yourself too deeply, and plan your site visits carefully. The most common error students report making on this assignment is waiting too long to make that first call. Be aware, too, that the people and places you contact may not respond immediately (or at all); be sure to follow up if you have not gotten an answer to your request within a few days.

Making a Schedule.   Set up a tentative schedule for your observations and interviews. Backward planning is one of the best strategies for scheduling your time so everything gets done by your deadline:

1. Write on a calendar the date the project is due and any other interim due dates (such as the date that your first draft is due).

2. Move backward through the calendar, writing in due dates for other tasks you need to do, such as scheduling initial and follow-up interviews and observations, as well as determining when write-ups and background research should be done.

Setting Up, Preparing for, and Conducting Interviews and Observations.   The following activities will help you plan your research:

1. **Make a list of people you would like to interview or the places you would like to observe.** Include a number of possibilities in case your first choice turns you down.

For a detailed discussion of planning and conducting interviews and observations, see Chapter 12, pp. 599–606.

2. **Write out your intentions and goals,** so you can explain them clearly to others. If you would like to take on the participant-observer role, ask permission to take part in a small way for a limited time.

3. **Call or e-mail for an appointment** with your interview subject or to make arrangements to visit the site. Explain who you are and what you are doing. Student research projects are often embraced, but be prepared for your request to be rejected.

4. **Make notes about your assumptions and expectations.** For example: Why do I assume the subject will interest me and my readers? What do I already know and what do I expect to learn about my subject?

5. **Write some interview questions** in advance, or consider how best to conduct the observation.

6. **Make an audio or video recording** — if allowed — during the interview or observation, but also take careful notes, including notes about what you see, hear, and smell, as well as notes about tone, gestures, mannerisms, or overheard conversations.

Ask for stories:

Tell me how you got into ....

What surprised/pleased/frustrated you most?

Let subjects correct misconceptions:

What preconceptions/myths would you most like to bust?

Ask about the subject's past and future:

How has .... changed over the years, and where do you think it's going?

Reflecting on What You Learned.   Immediately after your interview or observation, be sure to review your notes and write down your first impressions:

▶ My dominant impression of the subject is ....

▶ The most interesting aspect of .... is .... because ....

▶ Although my thoughts about .... were confirmed, I was surprised to learn ....

Focus on *sensory details* that could paint a vivid portrait of the person or people, place, or activity, and write down any questions or concerns you might like to consider for a follow-up interview or observation.

Working with Sources

Integrating Quotations from Interviews.   As you write up your interviews and observations and begin drafting your essay, you need to choose quotations that will present information about the subject in an interesting way. To make quotations arresting, use speaker tags (*he shouts, she blurts*). Speaker tags play an important role in observational writing because they help readers visualize the speakers and imagine what they sound like.

To integrate quotations and speaker tags smoothly into your sentences, you may rely on an all-purpose verb, such as *said* or *remarked*:

"Not science," he said. (Kimmerer, par. 9)

To depict the speaker's tone or attitude more precisely and vividly, provide some context for the quotation:

At the front of the line, a woman in a brown coat couldn't decide which soup to get and started to complain about the prices. "You talk too much, dear," Mr. Yeganeh said, and motioned her to move to the left. Next!" (*New Yorker*, par. 8)

You may also add a word or phrase to a speaker tag to reveal more about how, where, when, or why the speaker speaks:

"Pit of fire," she says, shaking her head. "Like a pit of fire straight from hell. Never seen anything like it. Like something out of an old movie about prisons." Her voice is getting louder and she looks at each of us with pleading eyes. (Coyne, par. 6)

In addition to being carefully introduced, quotations must be precisely punctuated. Fortunately, there are only two general rules:

For additional help with quoting sources, see Chapter 12, pp. 615–626.

1. Enclose all quotations in quotation marks. These always come in pairs, one at the beginning and one at the end of the quotation.

2. Separate the quotation from the speaker tag with appropriate punctuation, usually a comma. But if you have more than one sentence, be careful to punctuate the separate sentences properly.

Choosing Your Role

You can take a spectator role (like Fine), a participant-observer role (like Thompson), or alternate between being a spectator and a participant (like Coyne).

Choose the spectator role to:

- provide readers with a detailed description or guided tour of the scene.

  ▶ Inside, you could see .... The room was .... and ....

  EXAMPLE   Entering an unmarked room in the basement room, I saw numerous weathered wooden cases stacked twice my height, and, beyond them, old iron machines in various shapes and sizes. (Fine, par. 2)

- create an aura of objectivity, making it appear as though you're just reporting what you see and hear without revealing that you have actually made choices about what to include in order to create a dominant impression.

  ▶ The shiny new/rusty old tools were laid out neatly/piled helter skelter on the workbench, like ....

  EXAMPLE   The cases and crates stacked around the presses contained lead-filled letters and hundreds of neatly stored rectangular pieces. There were keys, metal washers, wooden blocks. . . . (Fine, par. 10)

Caution: The spectator role may cause readers to:

- feel detached, which can lead to a lack of interest in the subject profiled

- suspect a hidden bias behind the appearance of objectivity, undermining the writer's credibility.

Choose the participant-observer role to:

- report on physical activities through the eyes of a novice, so readers can imagine doing the activity themselves:

  ▶ I picked up the .... It felt like .... and smelled/tasted/sounded like ....

EXAMPLE   The greatest difficulty, though, is in the trimming. I had no idea
               that a head of lettuce was so humongous. (Thompson, par. 9)

- reveal how others react to you:

  ▶ X interrupted me as I .... -ed.

EXAMPLE   People whose names I didn't yet know would ask me how I was
               holding up, reminding me that it would get easier as time went by.
               (Thompson, par. 14)

Caution: The participant-observer role may cause readers to:

- wonder whether your experience was unique to you, not something they
  would have experienced

- think the person, place, group, or activity being profiled seemed secondary
  in relation to the writer's experience.

Developing Your Perspective on the Subject

Explore the cultural significance of your subject. If you are focusing on a *place*
(like a library or prison visiting room), consider what intrigues you about its culture by asking yourself questions like these:

- Who are the insiders at this place and why are they there?

- How does the place affect how insiders talk, act, think, feel?

- What function does the place serve in the wider community?

- What tensions are there between insiders and outsiders or between newcomers and veterans?

  ▶ X and Y say .... because they want to .... , but they seem to feel
  .... because of the way they do ....

EXAMPLE   And I can imagine the hours spent preparing for this visit. . . . The
               hours of discussing, dissecting, and bragging about these visitors—
               especially the men. . . . and the giggles that abruptly change into
               tears without warning—things that define any female-only world.
               Even, or especially, if that world is a female federal prison camp.
               (Coyne, par. 4)

If you are focusing on an *activity* (like trying a new food or cutting lettuce), ask
yourself questions like these:

- Who benefits from it?

- What value does it have for the insider community and for the wider
  community?

- How has the activity or process changed over time, for good or ill?

- How are outsiders initiated into the activity?

  ▶ .... [date or event] marked a turning point because ....

EXAMPLE   For years after the demise of that first meatpacking company, the
Dufour family sold someone else's product. . . . "But pretty soon,
we were selling so many lips that we had to almost beg Di Salvo's
for product. That's when we started cooking up our own," he told
me, gesturing toward the cast-iron kettle that hangs from the rafters
by the front door of the plant. "My daddy started cooking lips in
that very pot."

Lionel now cooks lips in 11 retrofitted milk tanks, dull stainless-steel
cauldrons shaped like oversized cradles. But little else has changed.
(Edge, pars. 9–10)

Define your purpose and audience. Write for five minutes exploring what you
want your readers to learn about the subject and why. Use sentence strategies like
these to help clarify your thinking:

- My readers probably think .... about my subject. I can get them to
  think about X's social and cultural significance by ....

  State your main point. Review what you have written, and summarize in a
  sentence or two the main idea you want readers to take away from your profile. Readers don't expect a profile to have an explicit thesis statement, but the
  descriptive details and other information need to work together to convey the
  main idea.

Formulating a Working Thesis Statement

Review what you have written and try out a few working thesis statements that articulate your insights into, interpretations of, or ideas about the person, place, or activity
that you want readers to take away from reading the essay. Like autobiography, observational writing tends not to include an explicit thesis statement, but does include
sentences that reinforce and extend the dominant impression you have created.

For example, "Soup" opens and ends with these quotations that capture the
writer's main ideas about the subject:

When Albert Yeganeh says "Soup is my lifeblood," he means it. And when he
says "I am extremely hard to please," he means that, too. (par. 1)

"He's downright rude," said a blond woman in a blue coat. "Even abusive. But
you can't deny it, his soup is the best." (par. 12)

Thompson uses the opening two paragraphs to introduce his ideas about the arduous labor of farmworkers, but he also intersperses his insights throughout the essay.

A theory forms in my mind. Early in the season — say, after the first week — a farmworker's body gets thoroughly broken down. Back, legs, and arms grow sore, hands and feet swell up. A tolerance for the pain is developed. . . . (par. 16)

It's simply not possible to do this work for decades. (par. 18)

Considering Adding Visuals or Other Media

Think about whether visual or audio elements — photographs, a map of the layout, illustrative materials you picked up at the place or downloaded, still or moving visuals, or audio clips — would strengthen your observational essay. For example, including a photo of a pig in an essay about the production and consumption of pickled pig lips, as Edge does (see p. 133), contributes to the vivid impact of his essay. The fact that the pig seems to be smiling adds a touch of humor. For more on analyzing visuals, see Chapter 2, pp. 52–55.

Note: Be sure to cite the source of visual or audio elements you didn't create, and get permission from the source if your essay is going to be published on a website that is not password-protected.

Organizing Your Draft

As you have seen, observational profiles often include more than one kind of organization: topical, narrative, spatial. For example, Edge begins and ends with a narrative of his effort to eat a pig lip, but he organizes the middle section of his essay — his observations at Farm Fresh — topically. Nevertheless, it is helpful to consider which plan should predominate:

- To organize topically (like "Soup"), group your observations and information by topic.

- To organize narratively (like Thompson and Coyne), make a timeline and note where the information from your observations and interviews fits.

- To organize spatially (like Fine), sketch the movement from one site to another, noting where you could integrate information from observations and interviews.

For briefer essays, a scratch outline may be sufficient; for longer, more complex essays, a formal outline may be helpful. For help with outlining, see Chapter 2, pp. 41–42.

Drafting Your Observational Essay

By this point, you have done a lot of writing

- to develop something interesting to say about a subject;

- to devise a plan for presenting that information;

- to identify a role for yourself in the essay;

- to explore your perspective on the subject.

Now stitch that material together to create a draft. The next section of this Guide to Writing will help you evaluate and improve your draft.

REVIEWING AND IMPROVING THE DRAFT

This section includes two guides for Peer Review and Troubleshooting Your Draft. Your instructor may arrange a peer review in class or online where you can exchange drafts with a classmate. The Peer Review Guide will help you give each other constructive feedback regarding the basic features and strategies typical of observational essays. (If you want to make specific suggestions for improving the draft, see Troubleshooting Your Draft on pp. 173–175.) Also, be sure to respond to any specific concerns the writer has raised about the draft. The Troubleshooting Your Draft guide that follows will help you reread your own draft with a critical eye, sort through any feedback you've received, and consider a variety of ways to improve your draft.

A PEER REVIEW GUIDE

How effective is the presentation of information?

What's Working Well: Let the writer know where information is especially well presented—for example, where the place is described vividly, a process is clearly delineated, or a quotation not only relates information but also portrays the speaker.

What Needs Improvement: Indicate one passage where the presentation of information could be improved—for example, where it's hard to visualize the place or people, a process needs clarification, or you have unanswered questions.

How appropriate is the writer's role?

What's Working Well: Point to any passage where the writer's role works especially well—for example, where the spectator's apparent objectivity adds credibility, the participant observer's insider knowledge enhances interest, or the two roles balance each other.

What Needs Improvement: Note any passage where the writer's role seems unclear or ineffective—for example, where the spectator seems too removed or judgmental, the participant observer's personal experience is distracting, or alternating the two roles gets confusing.

How clear and insightful is the writer's perspective on the subject?

What's Working Well: Indicate a passage where the writer's perspective is especially clear and compelling—for example, where showing creates a strong dominant impression, telling illuminates with a pithy comment, rhetorical question, or revealing quotation, or the tone toward the subject (respectful, sarcastic, flattering, disapproving) is appropriate and well supported.

What Needs Improvement: Tell the writer where the perspective needs clarification—for example, where showing seems muddied by contradictory details, telling relates the obvious and lacks insight, or the tone (either praising or criticizing) seems inappropriate or unjustified.

How easy to follow is the organization?

What's Working Well: Mark any parts of the essay that seem notably well-organized—for example, where a narratively arranged section orients readers with time markers, a topically arranged section uses topic sentences effectively, or a spatially arranged section employs prepositional phrases to take the reader on a tour of the place.

What Needs Improvement: Identify any aspect of the organization that needs improvement—for example, where a narratively arranged section seems to drag or ramble pointlessly, a topically arranged section seems disorganized or unbalanced, or a spatially arranged section stalls or becomes confusing.

Revising Your Draft

Revising means reenvisioning your draft, trying to see it in a new way, given your purpose and audience, in order to develop an informative and engaging observational essay. Think imaginatively and boldly about cutting unconvincing material, adding new material, and moving material around. The following chart may help you strengthen your essay.

TROUBLESHOOTING YOUR DRAFT

To Organize the Observation More Clearly and Effectively	
If a narratively arranged section drags or rambles,	• Add time markers to clarify the chronology. • Give the narrative shape—for example, by arousing curiosity, or by explaining the sequence of actions in a process narrative.
If a topically arranged section seems disorganized or unbalanced,	• Try rearranging topics to see whether another order makes more sense. • Add logical transitions. • Move, cut, or condense information to restore balance.

To Organize the Observation More Clearly and Effectively	
If a spatially arranged section is confusing,	• Add transitions to orient readers. • Use prepositional phrases to show direction or movement through space.
If the opening fails to engage readers' attention,	• Think of questions you could open with, or look for an engaging image or dialogue later in the essay to move to the beginning. • Go back to your notes for other ideas. • Recall how the writers in this chapter open their essays.

To Strengthen the Writer's Perspective on the Subject	
If the dominant impression seems vague or contradictory,	• Discuss more directly the contradictions or complexities you see in the subject. • Cut or revise the language that seems vague.
If the perspective is unclear or simplistic,	• Add language or details that strengthen, extend, or clarify the writer's perspective. • Write an explicit thesis statement—and either include it or use quotations, descriptions, and rhetorical questions to convey this idea. • Add sources to explain the social, cultural, or historical context.
If the tone seems inappropriate or unsupported,	• Think about the tone's appropriateness. • Provide support so the tone seems justified.

To Present the Information More Clearly and Vividly	
If people do not come alive,	• Add speaker tags that characterize people's tones, facial expressions, and gestures. • Quote only the language that conveys personality or essential information, and paraphrase or summarize other parts.
If the place is hard to visualize,	• Identify items in the place by name using specific nouns. • Add sensory detail—describe sights, sounds, smells, tastes, textures. • Consider adding a visual—a photograph or sketch, even a film clip if your observation will appear online.
If activities or processes are not clear,	• Make sure the tense of your verbs clearly indicates the sequence of the actions. • Clarify or add transitions showing what happened when.

To Organize the Observation More Clearly and Effectively	
If the essay could bore or overwhelm readers with too much information about the subject,	• Cut obvious or extraneous information. • Consider alternating blocks of information with descriptive or narrative materials. • Try presenting more of the information through lively dialogue from interviews.
If readers' questions have not been answered,	• Look over your research notes to see if you can answer readers' questions. • If you have time, do follow-up research to find out answers to their questions.

Editing and Proofreading Your Draft

Check for errors in usage, punctuation, and mechanics, and consider matters of style. If you keep a list of errors you typically make, begin by checking your draft against this list.

From our research on student writing, we know that observational essays tend to have errors in the use of quotation marks, when writers quote the exact words of people they have interviewed. Check a writer's handbook for help with these potential problems.

Reflecting on Observation

In this chapter, you have read several observational essays critically and have written one of your own. To better remember what you have learned, pause now to reflect on the reading and writing activities you completed in this chapter.

1. Write a page or so reflecting on what you have learned. Begin by describing what you are most pleased with in your essay. Then explain what you think contributed to your achievement.

   • If it was something you learned from the readings, indicate which readings and specifically what you learned from them.

   • If it came from your research notes and write-ups, point out the parts that helped you most.

   • If you got good advice from a critical reader, explain exactly how the person helped you — perhaps by helping you recognize a problem in your draft or by helping you add a new dimension to your writing.

(continued)

2. Reflect more generally on how you tend to interpret observational writing, your own as well as other writers'. Consider some of the following questions:

   - In reading for meaning, do you find yourself paying attention to larger cultural or social contexts — for example, thinking of the subject in terms of gender, ethnicity, or class?

   - How do you think the writer's perspective influenced how you saw the subject?

3. By reflecting on what you have learned about observation, you have been practicing **metacognition**, one of the academic habits of mind.

   - Were you aware of any other habits of mind you practiced as you read and responded to the material in this chapter? If so, which habits did you find useful?

   - If not, think back now on your reading and writing processes. Can you identify any habits you used?

CHAPTER 5

Reflection

Like autobiographical and observational writing, *reflective writing* is based on the writer's personal experience. Reflective writers present something they did, saw, heard, or read in writing so vivid that the reader can imagine what they experienced. But unlike writers of autobiography and observation, reflective writers help readers imagine the experience and explore its meanings. Reflective writers use events, people, and places as springboards for thinking about society — how people live and what people believe about social change with its many opportunities and challenges; about customs in our culturally diverse society; about traditional virtues and vices; or about common hopes and fears. They do not attempt to exhaust their subjects, nor do they set themselves up as experts. Instead, writers use their reflective essays to explore ideas informally and tentatively. Reading a reflective essay can be as stimulating as having a lively conversation, often surprising us with insights and unlikely connections and encouraging us to look in new ways at even the most familiar things.

RHETORICAL SITUATIONS FOR REFLECTIONS

Writers use a wide range of occasions to reflect on some aspect of contemporary culture, as the following examples indicate:

- A former football player writes a reflective essay for his college alumni magazine about a game in which he sustained a serious injury but continued to play because playing with pain was regarded as a sign of manliness. He reflects on learning this custom from his father and later from coaches and other players, and he wonders why boys are taught not to show pain but encouraged to show aggression and competitiveness. Taking an anthropological view, he sees contemporary sports as equivalent to the kind of training Native American boys traditionally went through to become warriors, and he questions whether playing sports prepares athletes for the kinds of roles they will play in contemporary society.

- Writing a blog post for a political science course, a student reflects on her first experience voting in a presidential election. She contrasts her decision-making process — examining the candidate's experience and voting record and reading endorsements from trusted experts — with those of her acquaintances, one of whom said she chose a candidate because he reminded her of her grandfather, and another who based his choice on his dislike of the way one candidate dressed. The writer then reflects on the implications of such voting decisions.

Thinking about Reflection

Write a paragraph about an occasion when you shared a reflection with others or others shared a reflection with you — friends, classmates, relatives, acquaintances — either orally or in writing.

- Who was the *audience*? How do you think addressing the reflections to this audience affected the way they were "hooked"?

- What was the main *purpose*? How did the writer or speaker want the audience to react? Was the goal to make the audience feel or think in a particular way, or to make an experience seem strange so that audience members could see it differently?

- How would you rate the *rhetorical sensitivity* of the reflection? Did the piece engage the reader or listener? How? Was the insight surprising or motivating?

A GUIDE TO READING REFLECTIVE ESSAYS

This guide introduces you to the basic features and strategies typical of reflective writing by inviting you to analyze a powerful reflective essay by Brent Staples:

- *Annotations* on this first reading will help you see how to practice academic **habits of mind** such as **curiosity, openness,** and **persistence** to help you engage with and understand what you are reading. Notice how many questions the reader has as she reads. There is plenty of space for you to add your own questions and thoughts, as well, to this reading and any other in the textbook.

- *Reading for meaning* will help you think about the occasions that prompted Staples's reflections — about his attitudes and assumptions regarding racial profiling, and about the broader social implications of, for example, his musical choices.

- *Reading like a writer* will help you learn how Staples employs strategies typical of reflective essays, such as

1. Presenting the occasion vividly and in a way that prepares readers for the reflections

2. Developing the reflections fully, using appropriate writing strategies

3. Maintaining coherence by providing cues for readers

4. Engaging readers' interest

Brent Staples

Black Men and Public Space

Brent Staples (b. 1951) earned his Ph.D. in psychology from the University of Chicago and went on to become a journalist, writing for several magazines and newspapers. In 1985, he became assistant metropolitan editor of the *New York Times*, where he is now a member of the editorial board. His autobiography, *Parallel Time: Growing Up in Black and White* (1994), won the Anisfield-Wolf Book Award. The following essay originally appeared in *Ms.* magazine under the title "Just Walk on By." Staples revised it slightly for publication in *Harper's* under the present title.

- **Before you read,** think about a time that you frightened others by your presence or that you have been frightened by others.

- **As you read,** think about why Staples changed the title of the essay from "Just Walk on By" to "Black Men and Public Space."

1 My first victim was a woman—white, well dressed, probably in her early twenties. I came upon her late one evening on a deserted street in Hyde Park, a relatively affluent neighborhood in an otherwise mean, impoverished section of Chicago. As I swung onto the avenue behind her, there seemed to be a discreet, uninflammatory distance between us. Not so. She cast back a worried glance. To her, the youngish black man—a broad six feet two inches with a beard and billowing hair, both hands shoved into the pockets of a bulky military jacket—seemed menacingly close. After a few more quick glimpses, she picked up her pace and was soon running in earnest. Within seconds she disappeared into a cross street.

> Did he do something to this woman?

> Black, broad, beard, billowing, bulky—purposeful alliteration?

2 That was more than a decade ago, I was twenty-two years old, a graduate student newly arrived at the University of Chicago. It was in the echo of that terrified woman's footfalls that I first began to know the unwieldy inheritance I'd come into—the ability to alter public space in ugly ways. It was clear that she thought herself the quarry of a mugger, a rapist, or worse. Suffering a bout of insomnia, however, I was stalking sleep, not defenseless wayfarers. As a softy who is scarcely able to take a knife to a raw chicken—let alone hold one to a person's throat—I was surprised,

How does the author feel about being indistinguishable from muggers?

embarrassed, and dismayed all at once. Her flight made me feel like an accomplice in tyranny. It also made it clear that I was indistinguishable from the muggers who occasionally seeped into the area from the surrounding ghetto. That first encounter, and those that followed, signified that a vast, unnerving gulf lay between nighttime pedestrians—particularly women—and me. And I soon gathered that being perceived as dangerous is a hazard in itself. I only needed to turn a corner into a dicey situation, or crowd some frightened, armed person in a foyer somewhere, or make an errant move after being pulled over by a policeman. Where fear and weapons meet—and they often do in urban America—there is always the possibility of death.

In that first year, my first away from my hometown, I was to become thoroughly familiar with the language of fear. At dark, shadowy intersections, I could cross in front of a car stopped at a traffic light and elicit the thunk, thunk, thunk of the driver—black, white, male, or female—hammering down the door locks. On less traveled streets after dark, I grew accustomed to but never comfortable with people crossing to the other side of the street rather than pass me. Then there were the standard unpleasantries with policemen, doormen, bouncers, cabdrivers, and others whose business it is to screen out troublesome individuals before there is any nastiness.

I wonder when he wrote this—It's still so relevant now.

I moved to New York nearly two years ago and I have remained an avid night walker. In central Manhattan, the near-constant crowd cover minimizes tense one-on-one street encounters. Elsewhere—in SoHo, for example, where sidewalks are narrow and tightly spaced buildings shut out the sky—things can get very taut indeed.

After dark, on the warrenlike streets of Brooklyn where I live, I often see women who fear the worst from me. They seem to have set their faces on neutral, and with their purse straps strung across their chests bandolier-style, they forge ahead as though bracing themselves against being tackled. I understand, of course, that the danger they perceive is not a hallucination. Women are particularly vulnerable to street violence, and young black males are drastically overrepresented among the perpetrators of that violence. Yet these truths are no solace against the kind of alienation that comes of being ever the suspect, a fearsome entity with whom pedestrians avoid making eye contact.

How do the author's previous experiences as "scarcely noticeable" affect his reaction to how he is perceived now that he is no longer in his childhood neighborhood?

It is not altogether clear to me how I reached the ripe old age of twenty-two without being conscious of the lethality nighttime pedestrians attributed to me. Perhaps it was because in Chester, Pennsylvania, the small, angry industrial town where I came of age in the 1960s, I was scarcely noticeable against a backdrop of gang warfare, street knifings, and murders. I grew up one of the good boys, had perhaps a half-dozen fistfights. In retrospect, my shyness of combat has clear sources.

As a boy, I saw countless tough guys locked away; I have since buried several, too. They were babies, really—a teenage cousin, a brother of twenty-two, a childhood friend in his mid-twenties—all gone down in episodes of bravado played out in the streets. I came to doubt the virtues of intimidation early on. I chose, perhaps unconsciously, to remain a shadow—timid, but a survivor.

8   The fearsomeness mistakenly attributed to me in public places often has a perilous flavor. The most frightening of these confusions occurred in the late 1970s and early 1980s, when I worked as a journalist in Chicago. One day, rushing into the office of a magazine I was writing for with a deadline story in hand, I was mistaken for a burglar. The office manager called security and, with an ad hoc posse, pursued me through the labyrinthine halls, nearly to my editor's door. I had no way of proving who I was. I could only move briskly toward the company of someone who knew me.

9   Another time I was on assignment for a local paper and killing time before an interview. I entered a jewelry store on the city's affluent Near North Side. The proprietor excused herself and returned with an enormous red Doberman pinscher straining at the end of a leash. She stood, the dog extended toward me, silent to my questions, her eyes bulging nearly out of her head. I took a cursory look around, nodded, and bade her good night.

10   Relatively speaking, however, I never fared as badly as another black male journalist. He went to nearby Waukegan, Illinois, a couple of summers ago to work on a story about a murderer who was born there. Mistaking the reporter for the killer, police officers hauled him from his car at gunpoint and but for his press credentials would probably have tried to book him. Such episodes are not uncommon. Black men trade tales like this all the time.

> Is this one story really also the story of so many other black men? Do men of other races and ethnicities also experience this?

11   Over the years, I learned to smother the rage I felt at so often being taken for a criminal. Not to do so would surely have led to madness. I now take precautions to make myself less threatening. I move about with care, particularly late in the evening. I give a wide berth to nervous people on subway platforms during the wee hours, particularly when I have exchanged business clothes for jeans. If I happen to be entering a building behind some people who appear skittish, I may walk by, letting them clear the lobby before I return, so as not to seem to be following them. I have been calm and extremely congenial on those rare occasions when I've been pulled over by the police.

> Why doesn't he spend more time talking about his anger?

12   And on late-evening constitutionals I employ what has proved to be an excellent tension-reducing measure: I whistle melodies from Beethoven and Vivaldi and the more popular classical composers.

> Why does he do this just to make other people comfortable?

13   Even steely New Yorkers hunching toward nighttime destinations seem to relax, and occasionally they even join in the tune. Virtually everybody seems to sense that a mugger wouldn't be warbling bright, sunny selections from Vivaldi's *Four Seasons*.

> What does this music sound like? Remember to look up later.

14   It is my equivalent of the cow-bell that hikers wear when they know they are in bear country.

READING FOR MEANING

For help with reading strategies like summarizing and analyzing assumptions, see Chapter 2.

1. **Read to Summarize.** Write a sentence or two briefly explaining some of the occasions that prompted Staples's reflection and how Staples explores the actions he took to address these occasions.

2. **Read to Respond.** Write a paragraph analyzing your initial reactions to Staples's essay. Consider anything that seems surprising, such as Staples's reactions to being seen as threatening; or an experience similar to one you have had in which race, gender, age, or other differences caused tension.

3. **Read to Analyze Assumptions.** Write a paragraph or two analyzing an assumption you find intriguing in Staples's essay. For example:

   Assumptions about the unfairness and danger of racial profiling. The example Staples uses to begin his reflection — the young woman who suddenly becomes frightened of him (par. 1) — illustrates how often he and other black men assume they are the object of racial profiling. He sees that this faulty perception could be a danger to him and to all black men because frightened people can behave violently.

   - How did Staples become aware of racial profiling and its consequences?
   - To what extent are pedestrians aware of the effects their behavior has on black men? Is Staples right in his assumption that he has been racially profiled? Are there any other possible explanations?

   Assumptions about how musical choices affect others. Staples concludes by writing that to reduce tension on his late-night walks, he whistles Beethoven and Vivaldi along with works of other classical composers (par. 12).

   - Why is a classical piece or a "sunny selection" more effective at reducing fear than other kinds of music such as rock, country, or rap?
   - Do you think there could be another explanation for how they react to his whistling? What associations might people have with whistling? What assumptions might they make about someone who whistles?

READING LIKE A WRITER

Presenting the Occasion

Reflective writers present an occasion — something they experienced or observed — in a vivid and suggestive way that encourages readers to want to know more about the writer's thoughts. Staples begins with an occasion when his mere presence on the street frightened a woman into running away from him. He uses this event to introduce the general subject, fear resulting from racial profiling: "It was in the echo of that terrified woman's footfalls that I first began to know the unwieldy inheritance I'd come into — the ability to alter public space in ugly ways" (par. 2). Throughout the rest of the essay, Staples reflects on this "inheritance" from various angles:

- He expresses his feelings at being misperceived as a threat.

- He gives examples of other occasions when people reacted to him with fear or hostility.

- He explains the effects of racial profiling, including the danger to himself, and the "precautions" he takes to make himself appear "less threatening" (par. 11).

ANALYZE & WRITE

Write a paragraph analyzing how Staples uses examples to illustrate and explain his reflections:

1. Reread the opening sentence of paragraph 3, where Staples introduces the idea that there is a "language of fear." Then skim the rest of paragraphs 3, 5–6, and 8–10. What examples does Staples use to help readers understand how this fear is expressed?

2. What have you learned from Staples's essay about how examples can help readers understand or accept a writer's reflections? Choose one or two examples and explain why you think they work especially well to help readers understand what Staples means.

Developing the Reflections

While Staples uses an occasion to introduce his subject, his reflections explore the subject by developing his ideas. Consider, for example, the words he uses to present his "first victim" and the location where he encounters her:

Naming Detailing	My first victim was a woman — white, well dressed, probably in her early twenties. I came upon her late one evening on a deserted street in Hyde Park, a relatively affluent neighborhood in an otherwise mean, impoverished section of Chicago. (par. 1)

Staples uses a combination of words — some neutral, some with strongly negative connotations — to create a vivid picture. He also uses the word *first* to suggest that this woman was not his only "victim."

ANALYZE & WRITE

Write a paragraph analyzing how else Staples makes this occasion vivid for his readers as well as how he prepares them for the reflections that follow.

1. Reread paragraphs 1–2. Underline the names Staples uses to identify himself, and circle the details he uses to describe himself and his actions.

2. Put brackets around words and phrases in these paragraphs that suggest the larger meanings Staples will develop in subsequent paragraphs.

3. Consider Staples's tone. How do the words Staples chooses help you identify (or hinder you from identifying) with him and his "victims"? Use concrete details from the paragraphs to support your claims.

Maintaining Coherence

Reflective essays explore ideas on a subject by examining them first from one perspective and then from another, and sometimes piling up examples to illustrate the ideas. This apparently casual organization is deceptive, however, because in fact the reflective writer has used a number of strategies to create coherence. One way of achieving coherence is to refer to the subject at various points by repeating certain key words or phrases. In the opening anecdote, Staples dramatizes the woman's fear of him. He then repeats the word "fear," or synonyms for it, throughout the essay. Reflective writers also achieve coherence through carefully placed transitions. Staples uses transitions of time and place to introduce a series of examples illustrating the fear he engenders in others simply because of his race and gender:

Transition of time/place Synonym for key term **Key term**	I only needed to turn a corner into a dicey situation, or crowd some frightened, armed person in a foyer somewhere, or make an errant move after being pulled over by a policeman. Where **fear** and weapons meet — and they often do in urban America — there is always the possibility of death.
	In that first year, my first away from my hometown, I was to become thoroughly familiar with the language of **fear**. . . . Elsewhere — in SoHo, for example, where sidewalks are narrow and tightly spaced buildings shut out the sky — things can get very taut indeed. (Pars. 2–3)

ANALYZE & WRITE

Write a paragraph or two analyzing how Staples uses these strategies of repetition and transitions to maintain coherence throughout the essay:

1. Skim paragraphs 3–12, highlighting the word *fear* each time Staples uses it and circling synonyms or near synonyms for it each time they appear.

2. Now go back through the essay underlining transitions of time and place.

3. Analyze how effectively these strategies work to maintain coherence, supporting your analysis with examples from the reading.

Engaging Readers

Readers of reflective essays expect writers to engage their interest. Readers choose to read an essay because something about it catches their eye — a familiar author's name, an intriguing title, an interesting graphic. Journalists typically begin feature articles with a "hook" designed to catch readers' attention. The occasion that opens many reflective essays often serves this purpose. Staples's opening phrase, "My first victim," certainly grabs attention.

One of the ways reflective writers *keep* readers engaged is by projecting an image of themselves — sometimes called the writer's **persona** or **voice** — that readers can identify with or be curious about. Staples, for example, uses the first-person pronouns *my* and *I* to present himself in his writing and to speak directly to readers. He describes himself as "a softy" (par. 2) and explains how he felt when he realized that the woman was so frightened by him that she ran for her life. Like most reflective writers, Staples tries to make himself sympathetic to readers so that they will listen to what he has to say.

ANALYZE & WRITE

Write a paragraph describing the impression you have of Staples from reading this essay and exploring how these impressions affect your curiosity about his ideas.

1. Skim the essay, circling or highlighting words, phrases, or passages that give you a sense of Staples as a person.

2. Consider the impression you have: What engages you or draws you into the essay? Do you feel empathy for Staples? What would you add or change to make the essay more effective for you?

READINGS

Dana Jennings

Our Scars Tell the Stories of Our Lives

Dana Jennings (b. 1957), a journalist and editor at the *New York Times* is best known for his novel, *Lonesome Standard Time* (1996); his nonfiction, *Sing Me Back Home: Love, Death and Country Music* (2008); and his blog for the *New York Times* Well section in which he wrote about prostate cancer. In the following essay, which appeared in the *New York Times* on July 21, 2009, Jennings ponders how scars tell stories. He develops his reflection by relating some of the stories prompted by his scars, and speculates about their larger meaning.

- **Before you read,** think about your own scars, what they mean to you, and whether you have memories associated with each scar.

- **As you read,** think about the differences between the scars Jennings first describes and the "heavy hitters, the stitched whips and serpents" (par. 7) to which he devotes the second half of his essay.

1   Our scars tell stories. Sometimes they're stark tales of life-threatening catastrophes, but more often they're just footnotes to the ordinary but bloody detours that befall us on the roadways of life. When I parse my body's motley parade of scars, I see them as personal runes and conversation starters. When I wear shorts, the footlong surgical scar on my right knee rarely fails to draw a comment. And in their railroad-track-like appearance, my scars remind me of the startling journeys that my body has taken—often enough to the hospital or the emergency room.

2   The ones that intrigue me most are those from childhood that I can't account for. The one on my right eyebrow, for example, and a couple of ancient pockmarks and starbursts on my knees. I'm not shocked by them. To be honest, I wonder why there aren't more.

3   I had a full and active boyhood, one that raged with scabs and scrapes, mashed and bloody knees, bumps and lumps, gashes and slashes, cats' claws and dogs' teeth, jagged glass, ragged steel, knots, knobs and shiners. Which raises this question: How do any of us get out of childhood alive?

4   My stubborn chin has sustained a fair bit of damage over the years. On close examination, there's a faint delta of scars that brings back memories of my teenage war on acne. Those frustrating days of tetracycline and gritty soaps left my face not clean and glowing but red and raw. The acne also ravaged my back, scoring the skin there so that it still looks scorched and lunar.

5   I further cratered my chin as an adult. First, I sprinted into a cast-iron lamppost while chasing a fly ball in a park in Washington; I actually saw a chorus line of stars

dance before my eyes as I crumpled to the ground. Second, I hooked one of those old acne potholes with my razor and created an instant dueling scar.

Scanning down from the jut of my chin to the tips of my toes, I've even managed 6 to brand my feet. In high school and college I worked at Kingston Steel Drum, a factory in my New Hampshire hometown that scoured some of the 55-gallon steel drums it cleaned with acid and scalding water. The factory was eventually shut down by the federal government and became a Superfund hazardous waste site, but not before a spigot malfunctioned one day and soaked my feet in acid.

Then there are the heavy hitters, the stitched whips and serpents that make my 7 other scars seem like dimples on a golf ball.

There's that mighty scar on my right knee from when I was 12 years old and had a 8 benign tumor cut out. Then there are the scars on my abdomen from when my colon (devoured by ulcerative colitis) was removed in 1984, and from my radical open prostatectomy last summer to take out my cancerous prostate. (If I ever front a heavy metal band, I think I'll call it Radical Open Prostatectomy.)

But for all the potential tales of woe that they suggest, scars are also signposts of opti- 9 mism. If your body is game enough to knit itself back together after a hard physical lesson, to make scar tissue, that means you're still alive, means you're on the path toward healing.

Scars, perhaps, were the primal tattoos, marks of distinction that showed you had 10 been tried and had survived the test. And like tattoos, they also fade, though the one from my surgery last summer is still a fierce and deep purple.

There's also something talismanic about them. I rub my scars the way other peo- 11 ple fret a rabbit's foot or burnish a lucky penny. Scars feel smooth and dry, the same way the scales of a snake feel smooth and dry.

I find my abdominal scars to be the most profound. They vividly remind me that 12 skilled surgeons unlocked me with their scalpels, took out what had to be taken, sewed me back up and saved my life. It's almost as if they left their life-giving signatures on my flawed flesh.

The scars remind me, too, that in this vain culture our vanity sometimes needs to 13 be punctured and deflated—and that's not such a bad thing. To paraphrase Ecclesiastes, better to be a scarred and living dog than to be a dead lion.

It's not that I'm proud of my scars—they are what they are, born of accident and 14 necessity—but I'm not embarrassed by them, either. More than anything, I relish the stories they tell. Then again, I've always believed in the power of stories, and I certainly believe in the power of scars.

READING FOR MEANING

1. Read to Summarize. Write a sentence or two explaining the main idea of Jennings's essay.

2. Read to Respond. Write a paragraph analyzing anything that seems interesting or that resonates with your experience. How do Jennings's

For help with reading strategies like summarizing and analyzing assumptions, see Chapter 2.

descriptions of his scars affect your understanding of any scars, physical or mental, that you may have?

3. **Read to Analyze Assumptions.** Write a paragraph or two analyzing an assumption you find intriguing in Jennings's essay. For example:

Assumptions about how memories make us who we are. Jennings explains, "My scars remind me of the startling journeys that my body has taken" (par. 1) and that "more than anything, I relish the stories they tell" (par. 14).

- How does the author characterize the relationship between outwardly visible physical scars and the internal scars or memories they represent?
- Do you think physical reminders like scars are necessary to keep these memories alive?

Assumptions about childhood. Jennings writes, "I had a full and active boyhood, one that raged with scabs and scrapes, mashed and bloody knees, bumps and lumps, gashes and slashes, cats' claws and dogs' teeth, jagged glass, ragged steel, knots, knobs, and shiners. Which raises this question: How do any of us get out of childhood alive?" (par. 3).

- Do most people have such an active childhood? How does your experience compare?
- Notice that Jennings opens the paragraph by describing his "active boyhood," but then concludes it by asking how anyone gets out of "childhood alive." Is what he describes specific to just boys or are scars common across genders?

READING LIKE A WRITER

Engaging Readers

While many writers of reflective essays use the first-person pronouns "I" and "my" to speak directly to the reader, writers will sometimes also use the plural personal pronouns "our" and "we" so that the reader feels included in the essay. For example, look at how Jennings opens his essay:

<table>
<tr><td>Plural personal
pronouns</td><td>Our scars tell stories. Sometimes they're stark tales of life-threatening catastrophes, but more often they're just footnotes to the ordinary but bloody detours that befall us on the roadways of life.</td></tr>
</table>

Here Jennings includes the reader, referring to scars and bloody detours as shared experiences.

ANALYZE & WRITE

Write a paragraph describing how Jennings's word choice, including his use of plural pronouns, makes you more engaged as you read his essay.

1. Skim the essay, circling or highlighting words, phrases, or passages that give you a sense of being part of Jennings's essay.

2. Beyond these words, phrases, and passages, what engages you or draws you in as a reader?

Combining Reading Strategies

Annotating and Taking Inventory to Explore the Significance of Figurative Language

Annotations can be used to mark patterns of language, images, or other features of a text. *Figurative language* adds color and richness to writing by taking words literally associated with one thing and applying them to something else, often in an unexpected or unconventional way, to create a vivid image or other sensory impression in readers' minds. For example, in "Our Scars Tell the Stories of Our Lives," Dana Jennings refers to his scars as "footnotes to the ordinary but bloody detours that befall us on the roadways of life" (par. 1), and adds that his scars, in their "railroad-track-like appearance," remind him of the "journeys that [his] body has taken" (par. 1).

- Reread Jennings's essay, marking all the *figurative language* — metaphors, similes, and symbols — that you find in this essay.

- *Take inventory* by organizing the figures of speech you found.

- Write a paragraph exploring the meanings that emerge from the patterns in the essay's language. How did the process of tracking the figures of speech help you notice their contribution to what Jennings is trying to convey?

For help with annotating and taking inventory, see Chapter 2, pp. 35–41.

For help with exploring the significance of figurative language, see Chapter 2, pp. 51–52.

Jacqueline Woodson

The Pain of the Watermelon Joke

Jacqueline Woodson (b. 1963) is an American writer and poet. She won the Coretta Scott King Award in 2001 for *Miracle's Boys* (2000), and New-bery awards for *Show Way* (2005), *Feathers* (2007), *After Tupac & D Foster* (2008), and *Brown Girl Dreaming* (2014) — a book in verse for which she also won the 2014 National Book Award for Young People's Literature. Her first adult novel, *Brooklyn Dreaming* (2016) was a finalist for the 2016 National Book Award. Woodson has served as the Young People's Poet Laureate and the Library of Congress Ambassador for Young People's Literature. The essay below was published in the *New York Times* in 2014.

- **Before you read,** think about a joke you have heard that is made at the expense of someone or something that you care about. How did the joke make you feel?

- **As you read,** consider how Woodson approaches the contentious topic of racism with personal stories and references to her family. How do her rhetorical choices affect your response to her experience?

As a child in South Carolina, I spent summers like so many children — sitting on my 1
grandparents' back porch with my siblings, spitting watermelon seeds into the garden or, even worse, swallowing them and trembling as my older brother and sister spoke of the vine that was probably already growing in my belly.

It was the late '60s and early '70s, and even though Jim Crow was supposed to be 2
far behind us, we spent our days in the all-black community called Nicholtown in a still segregated South.

One year, we bought a watermelon off the back of a man's pickup truck and 3
placed it in our garden. As my grandfather snapped pictures from his box camera, we laughed about how we'd fool my mother, who was in New York, by telling her we'd grown it ourselves. I still have the photo of me in a pale pink dress, beribboned and smiling, sitting on that melon.

But by the time I was 11 years old, even the smell of watermelon was enough to 4
send me running to the bathroom with my most recent meal returning to my throat. It seemed I had grown violently allergic to the fruit.

I was a brown girl growing up in the United States. By that point in my life, I had 5
seen the racist representations associated with African-Americans and watermelons, heard the terrifying stories of black men being lynched with watermelons hanging around them, watched black migrants from the South try to eke out a living in the big city by driving through neighborhoods like my own — Bushwick, in Brooklyn — with trucks loaded down with the fruit.

In a book I found at the library, a camp song about a watermelon vine was illustrated 6
with caricatures of sleepy-looking black people sitting by trees, grinning and eating

watermelon. Slowly, the hideousness of the stereotype began to sink in. In the eyes of those who told and repeated the jokes, we were shuffling, googly-eyed and lesser than.

Perhaps my allergy was actually a deep physical revulsion that came from the $\quad$ 7 psychological impression and weight of the association. Whatever it was, I could no longer eat watermelon.

In the midst of observing the world and coming to consciousness, I was becoming $\quad$ 8 a writer, and what I wanted to put on the page were the stories of people who looked like me. I was a child on a mission—to change the face of literature and erase stereotypes. Forever. By the time I was in fifth grade, I was dreaming of the Pulitzer Prize. By the time I was 45, I had won just about every award one could win for young people's literature. Just this month, I received the National Book Award in the young-adult category for my memoir, *Brown Girl Dreaming*.

As I walked away from the stage to a standing ovation after my acceptance speech, $\quad$ 9 it was the last place in the world I thought I'd hear the watermelon joke—directed by the M.C., Daniel Handler, at me. "Jackie's allergic to watermelon," he said. "Just let that sink in your mind." Daniel and I have been friends for years. Last summer, at his home on Cape Cod, he served watermelon soup and I let him know I was allergic to the fruit. I was astonished when he brought this up before the National Book Award audience—in the form of a wink-nudge joke about being black.

In a few short words, the audience and I were asked to take a step back from $\quad$ 10 everything I've ever written, a step back from the power and meaning of the National Book Award, lest we forget, lest I forget, where I came from. By making light of that deep and troubled history, he showed that he believed we were at a point where we could laugh about it all. His historical context, unlike my own, came from a place of ignorance.

"Brown Girl Dreaming" is the story of my family, moving from slavery through $\quad$ 11 Reconstruction, Jim Crow and the civil rights movement, and ends with me as a child of the '70s. It is steeped in the history of not only my family but of America. As African-Americans, we were given this history daily as weapons against our stories' being erased in the world or, even worse, delivered to us offhandedly in the form of humor.

As I interviewed relatives in both Ohio and Greenville, S.C., I began to piece $\quad$ 12 together the story of my mother's life, my grandparents' lives and the lives of cousins, aunts and uncles. These stories, and the stories I had heard throughout my childhood, were told with the hope that I would carry on this family history and American history, so that those coming after me could walk through the world as armed as I am.

Mr. Handler's watermelon comment was made at a time of change. We Need $\quad$ 13 Diverse Books, a grass-roots organization committed to diversifying all children's literature, had only months before stormed the BookCon conference because of its all-white panels. The world of publishing has been getting shaken like a pecan tree and called to the floor because of its lack of diversity in the workplace. At this year's National Book Awards, many of the books featured nonwhite protagonists, and three of the 20 finalists were people of color. One of those brown finalists (me!), in the very first category, Young People's Literature, had just won.

Just let that sink in your mind. $\quad$ 14

I would have written *Brown Girl Dreaming* if no one had ever wanted to buy it, if 15
it went nowhere but inside a desk drawer that my own children pulled out one day
to find a tool for survival, a symbol of how strong we are and how much we've come
through. Their great-great-great-grandfather fought in the Civil War. Their great-grand-
father, Hope, and great-grandmother, Grace, raised one of the few black families in
Nelsonville, Ohio, and saw five children through college. Their grandmother's school
in Greenville, Sterling High, was set on fire and burned to the ground.

To know that we African-Americans came here enslaved to work until we died 16
but didn't die, and instead grew up to become doctors and teachers, architects and
presidents — how can these children not carry this history with them for those many
moments when someone will attempt to make light of it, or want them to forget the
depth and amazingness of their journey?

How could I come from such a past and not know that I am on a mission, too?   17

This mission is what's been passed down to me — to write stories that have been 18
historically absent in this country's body of literature, to create mirrors for the people
who so rarely see themselves inside contemporary fiction, and windows for those
who think we are no more than the stereotypes they're so afraid of. To give young
people — and all people — a sense of this country's brilliant and brutal history, so that
no one ever thinks they can walk onto a stage one evening and laugh at another's too
often painful past.

READING FOR MEANING

For help
with reading
strategies like
summarizing
and analyzing
assumptions,
see Chapter 2.

1. **Read to Summarize.** Write a sentence or two explaining what happened at
   the National Book Award ceremony and how that led to Woodson writing
   an essay on the watermelon joke.

2. **Read to Respond.** Write a paragraph exploring anything that resonates
   with your experience or that seems surprising, such as a friend making a
   hurtful joke.

3. **Read to Analyze Assumptions.** Write a paragraph or two analyzing an
   assumption you find intriguing in Woodson's essay. For example:

   Assumptions about the power of the written word. Woodson notes that she
   was "a child on a mission — to change the face of literature and erase stereotypes. Forever" (par. 8). In her last paragraph, she adds that her mission is "to
   create mirrors for the people who so rarely see themselves inside contemporary fiction, and windows for those who think we are no more than the stereotypes they're so afraid of" (par. 18).

   • What makes the written word so powerful? How does its power differ from an
     aural or visual medium?

- If the written word creates "mirrors" and "windows," how does it help readers understand stereotyping and racism?

Assumptions about the importance of learning history. Woodson writes that an understanding of "family history and American history" will allow later generations to "walk through the world as armed" (par. 12). In her essay, she reflects on both her individual experiences as a "brown girl," her ancestors' experiences, and the experiences of African Americans in the nation's troubled past.

- How do the histories of Woodson's family and of the United States work together in her essay? How does knowing these histories "arm" Woodson to respond to Handler's joke?

- In your experience, is history remembered the same way by different kinds of people (like Woodson and Handler)? If not, what causes history to be remembered, learned, or used differently — and for what purposes?

READING LIKE A WRITER

Engaging Readers

In reflective essays, writers often tell **anecdotes** — brief, entertaining stories — to help engage readers, as Woodson does with the story of taking a picture with an oversized watermelon (par. 3). Woodson believes stories have been used to portray African Americans in various unflattering ways, and as she was becoming a writer, she "wanted to put on the page . . . the stories of people who looked like" her (par. 8) and to change public perception of them.

ANALYZE & WRITE

Write a paragraph or two analyzing Woodson's use of an anecdote to set the scene she is trying to change.

1. Reread the opening anecdote (pars. 1–3) to identify how Woodson engages the reader in the "history" of the watermelon joke.

2. Annotate the paragraph to show how Woodson intends to undermine the joke and change the history of the stories and of the joke. Does she succeed in drawing the reader into her purpose?

Manuel Muñoz

Leave Your Name at the Border

Manuel Muñoz (b. 1972) is Associate Professor of Creative Writing at the University of Arizona. He received his bachelor's degree from Harvard in 1994 and his MFA from Cornell in 1998. He is best known for his short stories, collected in *Zigzagger* (2003) and *The Faith Healer of Olive Avenue* (2008), and his novel *What You See in the Dark* (2011). His stories have won the PEN/O. Henry Award twice for "Tell Him about Brother John" (2009) and "The Happiest Girl in the Whole USA" (2015). His writing appears in the *New York Times, Glimmer Train, Epoch, Eleven Eleven,* and *Boston Review* and has aired on National Public Radio's *Selected Shorts.* The essay below appeared in the *New York Times* in 2007.

- **Before you read,** think about your own name. What does it tell people about you? Do you have an opinion about whether names should be standardized in the United States?

- **As you read,** pay attention to how Muñoz sets up a contrast between English and Spanish. How does this contrast help convey his ideas?

At the Fresno airport, as I made my way to the gate, I heard a name over the intercom. The way the name was pronounced by the gate agent made me want to see what she looked like. That is, I wanted to see whether she was Mexican. Around Fresno, identity politics rarely deepen into exacting terms, so to say "Mexican" means, essentially, "not white." The slivered self-identifications Chicano, Hispanic, Mexican-American and Latino are not part of everyday life in the Valley. You're either Mexican or you're not. If someone wants to know if you were born in Mexico, they'll ask. Then you're From Over There—*de allá*. And leave it at that.

The gate agent, it turned out, was Mexican. Well-coiffed, in her 30s, she wore foundation that was several shades lighter than the rest of her skin. It was the kind of makeup job I've learned to silently identify at the mall when I'm with my mother, who will say nothing about it until we're back in the car. Then she'll point to the darkness of her own skin, wondering aloud why women try to camouflage who they are.

I watched the Mexican gate agent busy herself at the counter, professional and studied. Once again, she picked up the microphone and, with authority, announced the name of the missing customer: "Eugenio Reyes, please come to the front desk."

You can probably guess how she said it. Her Anglicized pronunciation wouldn't be unusual in a place like California's Central Valley. I didn't have a Mexican name there either: I was an instruction guide.

When people ask me where I'm from, I say Fresno because I don't expect them to know little Dinuba. Fresno is a booming city of nearly 500,000 these days, with a diversity—white, Mexican, African-American, Armenian, Hmong and Middle Eastern people are all well represented—that shouldn't surprise anyone. It's in the small towns like Dinuba that surround Fresno that the awareness of cultural difference is stripped down to the interactions between the only two groups that tend to live there: whites and Mexicans. When you hear a Mexican name spoken in these towns, regardless of the speaker's background, it's no wonder that there's an "English way of pronouncing it."

I was born in 1972, part of a generation that learned both English and Spanish. 6 Many of my cousins and siblings are bilingual, serving as translators for those in the family whose English is barely functional. Others have no way of following the Spanish banter at family gatherings. You can tell who falls into which group: Estella, Eric, Delia, Dubina, Melanie.

It's intriguing to watch "American" names begin to dominate among my nieces 7 and nephews and second cousins, as well as with the children of my hometown friends. I am not surprised to meet 5-year-old Brandon or Kaitlyn. Hardly anyone questions the incongruity of matching these names with last names like Trujillo or Zepeda. The English-only way of life partly explains the quiet erasure of cultural difference that assimilation has attempted to accomplish. A name like Kaitlyn Zepeda doesn't completely obscure her ethnicity, but the half-step of her name, as a gesture, is almost understandable.

Spanish was and still is viewed with suspicion: Always the language of the vili- 8 fied illegal immigrant, it segregated schoolchildren into English-only and bilingual programs; it defined you, above all else, as part of a lower class. Learning English, though, brought its own complications. It was simultaneously the language of the white population and a path toward the richer, expansive identity of "American." But it took getting out of the Valley for me to understand that "white" and "American" were two very different things.

Something as simple as saying our names "in English" was our unwittingly com- 9 plicit gesture of trying to blend in. Pronouncing Mexican names correctly was never encouraged. Names like Daniel, Olivia and Marco slipped right into the mutability of the English language.

I remember a school ceremony at which the mathematics teacher, a white man, 10 announced the names of Mexican students correctly and caused some confusion, if not embarrassment. Years later we recognized that he spoke in deference to our Spanish-speaking parents in the audience, caring teacher that he was.

These were difficult names for a non-Spanish speaker: Araceli, Nadira, Luis (a 11 beautiful name when you glide the *u* and the *i* as you're supposed to). We had been accustomed to having our birth names altered for convenience. Concepción was Connie. Ramón was Raymond. My cousin Esperanza was Hope—but her name was pronounced "Hopie" because any Spanish speaker would automatically pronounce the e at the end.

Ours, then, were names that stood as barriers to a complete embrace of an 12 American identity, simply because their pronunciations required a slip into Spanish, the otherness that assimilation was supposed to erase. What to do with names like Amado, Lucio or Élida? There are no English "equivalents," no answer when white teachers asked, "What does your name mean?" when what they really wanted to know was "What's the English one?" So what you heard was a name butchered beyond recognition, a pronunciation that pointed the finger at the Spanish language as the source of clunky sound and ugly rhythm.

My stepfather, from Ojos de Agua, Mexico, jokes when I ask him about the names 13 of Mexicans born here. He deliberately stumbles over pronunciations, imitating our elders who have difficulty with Bradley and Madelyn. "Ashley Sánchez. ¿Tú crees?"[11] He wonders aloud what has happened to the "nombres del rancho"—traditional Mexican names that are hardly given anymore to children born in the States: Heraclio, Madaleno, Otilia, Dominga.

My stepfather's experience with the Anglicization of his name—Antonio to 14 Tony—ties into something bigger than learning English. For him, the erasure of his name was about deference and subservience. Becoming Tony gave him a measure of access as he struggled to learn English and get more fieldwork.

This isn't to say that my stepfather welcomed the change, only that he could not 15 put up much resistance. Not changing put him at risk of being passed over for work. English was a world of power and decisions, of smooth, uninterrupted negotiation. Clear communication meant you could go unsupervised. Every gesture made toward convincing an employer that English was on its way to being mastered had the potential to make a season of fieldwork profitable.

It's curious that many of us growing up in Dinuba adhered to the same rules. 16 Although as children of farm workers we worked in the fields at an early age, we'd also had the opportunity to stay in one town long enough to finish school. Most of us had learned English early and splintered off into a dual existence of English at school, Spanish at home. But instead of recognizing the need for fluency in both languages, we turned it into a peculiar kind of battle. English was for public display. Spanish was for privacy—and privacy quickly turned to shame.

The corrosive effect of assimilation is the displacement of one culture over 17 another, the inability to sustain more than one way of being. It isn't a code word for racial and ethnic acculturation only. It applies to needing to belong, of seeing from the outside and wondering how to get in and then, once inside, realizing there are always those still on the fringe.

When I went to college on the East Coast, I was confronted for the first time by 18 people who said my name correctly without prompting; if they stumbled, there was a quick apology and an honest plea to help with the pronunciation. But introducing myself was painful: already shy, I avoided meeting people because I didn't want to say my name, felt burdened by my own history. I knew that my small-town upbringing and its limitations on Spanish would not have been tolerated by any of the students of color who had grown up in large cities, in places where the sheer force of their native languages made them dominant in their neighborhoods.

It didn't take long for me to assert the power of code-switching in public, the 19 transferring of words from one language to another, regardless of who might be listening. I was learning that the English language composed new meanings when

---

[1] ¿Tú crees?: Can you believe it? [Ed.]

its constrictions were ignored, crossed over or crossed out. Language is all about manipulation, or not listening to the rules.

When I come back to Dinuba, I have a hard time hearing my name said incorrectly, but I have an even harder time beginning a conversation with others about why the pronunciation of our names matters. Leaving a small town requires an embrace of a larger point of view, but a town like Dinuba remains forever embedded in an either/or way of life. My stepfather still answers to Tony and, as the United States–born children grow older, their Anglicized names begin to signify who does and who does not "belong"—who was born here and who is *de allá*. 20

My name is Manuel. To this day, most people cannot say it correctly, the way it was intended to be said. But I can live with that because I love the alliteration of my full name. It wasn't the name my mother, Esmeralda, was going to give me. At the last minute, my father named me after an uncle I would never meet. My name was to have been Ricardo. Growing up in Dinuba, I'm certain I would have become Ricky or even Richard, and the journey toward the discovery of the English language's extraordinary power in even the most ordinary of circumstances would probably have gone unlearned. 21

I count on a collective sense of cultural loss to once again swing the names back to our native language. The Mexican gate agent announced Eugenio Reyes, but I never got a chance to see who appeared. I pictured an older man, cowboy hat in hand, but I made the assumption on his name alone, the clash of privileges I imagined between someone *de allá* and a Mexican woman with a good job in the United States. Would she speak to him in Spanish? Or would she raise her voice to him as if he were hard of hearing? 22

But who was I to imagine this man being from anywhere, based on his name alone? At a place of arrivals and departures, it sank into me that the currency of our names is a stroke of luck: because mine was not an easy name, it forced me to consider how language would rule me if I allowed it. Yet I discovered that only by leaving. My stepfather must live in the Valley, a place that does not allow that choice, every day. And Eugenio Reyes—I do not know if he was coming or going. 23

READING FOR MEANING

1. **Read to Summarize.** Write a few sentences explaining the message Manuel Muñoz is trying to convey about language and names.

2. **Read to Respond.** Write a paragraph exploring anything that resonates with your experience or that seems surprising, such as how the Mexican gate agent pronounced Eugenio Reyes's name, or the sentence "But it took getting out of the Valley for me to understand that 'white' and 'American' were two very different things" (par. 8).

For help with reading strategies like summarizing and analyzing assumptions, see Chapter 2.

3. **Read to Analyze Assumptions.** Write a paragraph or two analyzing an assumption you find intriguing in Muñoz's essay. For example:

Assumptions about the differences between small towns and cities. Muñoz points out differences between Fresno and Dinuba (par. 5), the Valley (par. 8), and "college on the East Coast" (par. 18).

- Why does Muñoz call attention to these differences? How does acknowledging them highlight his reflections on language and names? Are these differences helpful, harmful, or somewhere in between?

- What do you think the residents of these varied areas believe about cultural differences? What experiences, texts, or people have influenced how you think about people in these places and their beliefs?

Assumptions about the significance of names. Names give information about background, ethnicity, and perhaps allegiances. Muñoz points out that in the Valley, Spanish "defined you, above all else, as part of a lower class" (par. 8). Anglicizing names, while springing from "deference and subservience" (par. 14), gave access to more work, as it did for his stepfather, who shifted from Antonio to Tony (par. 14).

- Why does the origin or pronunciation of a name matter?

- Are Muñoz's views about names universal? Are there cultures where names have more or less significance? How do you know?

READING LIKE A WRITER

Maintaining Coherence with Cues

Authors can maintain coherence in reflective writing by calling on repetition of key words or phrases to keep the reader returning to important concepts. Muñoz repeats the word *name* throughout his essay (including in the title).

ANALYZE & WRITE

Write a paragraph or two analyzing how Muñoz uses the strategy of repetition to maintain coherence throughout his essay.

1. Skim the essay, underlining or highlighting the word *name* whenever it appears.

2. Examine the different contexts in which the word appears, and analyze the meanings of its varied uses. What do you conclude about why Muñoz repeats the word so often and what this repetition means to the reader?

Maya Rupert

I, Wonder: Imagining a Black Wonder Woman

Maya Rupert (b. 1981) is the senior policy director at the Center for Reproductive Rights. Prior to joining the Center, she served the United States Department of Housing and Urban Development as Senior Policy Advisor. She has also been a contributing writer to *O Magazine*, the *Washington Post*, the *Los Angeles Times*, and the *Huffington Post*, where she frequently addresses the intersection of politics, race, and gender. She has been recognized by the National Association of Black Journalists for her writing and by national outlets like *Ebony Magazine* and *The Root* for her leadership in the black community.

- **Before you read,** think of a superhero or other fictional character that has had significance in your life. How would you describe that significance?

- **As you read,** pay attention to how Wonder Woman "grew" with Rupert. How does the relationship Rupert describes between herself and Wonder Woman help convey her ideas?

Growing up, I was told that my favorite comic-book heroine was white. And yet her 1 struggles always seemed uniquely similar to my own.

When I was eight years old, I asked my mother if Wonder Woman was black. It 2 was 1989—almost thirty years before I'd eagerly await the premiere of the first *Wonder Woman* movie. As a child, I had seen the Amazonian princess portrayed by Lynda Carter, who looked unmistakably white, on the syndicated television show I loved. But in many iconic pictures in the comic books I read, Wonder Woman appeared to have a trace of melanin that made me think—maybe?

Maybe I could believably be her for Halloween? Or maybe, simply, I could be 3 wonderful, too. "She's white," my mother told me, perhaps wistfully, but definitively. Not wanting to dash my hopes, she added, "But she's not real. So she can be whatever race you want her to be."

Later that week, at an after-school event, armed with a coloring book, a brown 4 crayon, and my mother's voice still in my head, I filled in Wonder Woman's skin to match my own. A white mother who was supervising the students saw my work; with shock, she asked why I'd "ruined" my picture. I told her I'd wanted to make my heroine look like me. "It doesn't matter," the woman declared pointedly. "She doesn't have to look like you. You can still want to be her."

It seemed this sentiment was everywhere I turned at the time. "Race shouldn't 5 matter," the late '80s had told me through the "very special episodes" of my favorite

TV programs. From *Family Ties* to *The Golden Girls*, shows during this time tackled race and racism without ever acknowledging that racial differences mattered. These episodes were usually resolved with an appeal to commonalities and the message that racists were the only people who "saw color." According to popular culture of this era, gender differences were empowering, but racial differences were divisive. I didn't yet have a vocabulary that included "white feminism," a shorthand term for a "race-blind" form of feminism that ends up centering the needs of white women at the expense of women of color. Even so, I certainly had the model for it: I was allowed to prefer Wonder Woman to Superman, but I wasn't allowed to ask that Wonder Woman be black.

Comic books have long famously told stories of oppression—characters grapple   6
with feelings of otherness and alienation, fear of discrimination, a need to hide a true identity. But so often these allegories center on superpowered individuals who are white and male, making their claim to these stories of marginalization ring false. Wonder Woman is white, I was reminded again and again. And yet, her story and overlapping identities—a superhero in a world of humans and a heroine in a world of heroes—felt uniquely familiar to me. They led me to think her character perhaps made more sense as a black woman.

Wonder Woman and I were both outsiders on two levels. Her powers set her apart   7
from other humans, but among the other members of the Justice League, she was relegated to secretary. My race set me apart from my white classmates, but I learned at a young age that within the black community, my gender marked me as inferior. I remember as a child being told by my hairdresser that feminism wasn't for black women. "For us," she explained, "the man is here, and we're here," she said gesturing with her hands to illustrate that to be a black woman meant that a man I had never met would always be stationed above me. As I got older, I became better able to name my double displacement. I was frustrated with the racism I saw in feminist circles and with the misogyny I saw among racial-justice advocates. My awareness of this dynamic grew, and Wonder Woman's state of constant otherness only grew more meaningful.

But as a girl, I most commiserated with Wonder Woman when she sought to rec-   8
oncile her inner strength and ferocity with the need of others to see her as peaceful and feminine. I had learned early on that it wouldn't take a lot for me to be viewed as angry and deemed unlikable. Images of neck-rolling, finger-snapping, gum-popping black women caricatured in movies and TV shows showed me exactly what people expected from me.

These expectations were memorably laid out by one of my favorite TV shows   9
when I was ten, *Martin*, via two characters: Pam, the dark-skinned, needed-a-weave-to-hide-her-nappy-hair, perpetually single best friend; and Gina, the light-skinned, kind, and happy love interest. The jokes at Pam's expense came from the fact that she was supposedly too aggressive and masculine. Meanwhile, Gina, who clearly had a better role, was unabashedly feminine. I knew, with my dark skin, nappy hair, strong opinions, and sarcastic sense of humor that I'd be seen as a Pam. So over time, I became a bubbly, happy, slow-to-upset black girl you would never call angry. Even

today, I wonder if the bubbly, happy, slow-to-upset black woman I've become is who I really am, or if it's just my own Diana Prince, the version of myself I created to protect my secret, real identity.

Wonder Woman seemed to understand this same psychic conflict. She's one of 10 the strongest heroes in the DC Comics canon. According to one origin story, she was blessed with "the strength of Hercules," in the other, she's an actual demigoddess, the daughter of Zeus. Among comic-book fans, an ongoing debate rages over whether Wonder Woman could best Superman in a fight. But unlike her powerful peers, Wonder Woman must retain a femininity that her physical prowess seems to undermine. The result is a sometimes-contradictory character—a warrior by training and birth-right who prefers diplomacy to battle. A would-be Pam who was only ever supposed to be seen as Gina.

Wonder Woman once famously explained her philosophy: "We have a saying 11 among my people. 'Don't kill if you can wound, don't wound if you can subdue, don't subdue if you can pacify. And don't raise your hand at all unless you've first extended it.'" It's a moving sentiment, but an odd one for a world in which one-dimensional villains often leave heroes with no other choice than violence. But perhaps not that odd after all, given that Wonder Woman's creator, William Moulten Marsten, was himself an imperfect feminist thinker who held the essentialist belief that women were naturally more peaceful than men.

Wonder Woman didn't get to act on anger, and neither did I. I was terrified of how 12 I'd be seen if I ever did, in part because Wonder Woman once showed me exactly what could happen. In one famous storyline, *Sacrifice* part IV, Wonder Woman was forced to kill a villain, Maxwell Lord, to save Superman's and Batman's lives. Lord had tricked the Justice League members into thinking he was an ally, when in fact he planned to destroy all superheroes, whom he viewed as a global threat. Lord convinced Superman that both Batman and Wonder Woman were his enemies and forced him to attack. After subduing Batman, Superman came after Wonder Woman. Instead of fighting her friend, Wonder Woman captured Lord and used her Lasso of Truth. Lord told her the only way to stop him was to kill him. Which she did.

Unfortunately for Wonder Woman, that moment was broadcast publicly: the 13 world saw Wonder Woman kill Lord without any context. The panel from that moment showed Wonder Woman from the perspective of those watching her, her face darkened and twisted into something ugly and murderous. The public turned on her. Even Superman and Batman, whose lives she had saved with her action, refused to hear her side and severed their friendship. This double standard infuriated me. This was nowhere near the first time a hero had killed in the service of a greater good. It wasn't her role as a hero that her actions betrayed, but her role as a woman. It was her loss of femininity, not the moral high ground that made this moment so shocking.

Wonder Woman's fate was one I had tried to avoid for years with a painful 14 balancing act. Black women have long had to navigate stereotypes that create a similar sort of bind: our reputed preternatural strength is used as a weapon to force us to withstand greater physical, emotional, and spiritual burdens. The stereotype of the "strong black woman" becomes a self-fulfilling prophecy, and the identity of black women becomes indistinguishable from our struggle. This is evident in the archetype of the Mammy, the black maternal figure who acts as a cipher for the burdens of the white people around her and takes them on with an ever-present smile. In the '80s, she was Nell Carter, the happy maid to a white family on *Gimme A Break!*, and Florida Evans, the put-upon matriarch from *Good Times*. These women sublimated their own needs for those of others, and always did it with a smile.

But when black women stop smiling, as it were, they're easily reimagined as 15 overly aggressive and mean. The Mammy archetype gives way to the Angry Black Woman trope, also known as Sapphire — named for the bullying black female character from the early American sitcom *The Amos 'n' Andy Show*. Sapphire's fury, and by extension the fury of black women, is assumed both to be an overreaction and inherently threatening. The result is that when a black woman shows anger, no matter how justified, she must immediately contend with the fear that her emotions will be seen, taken out of context, and result in everyone turning on her.

Wonder Woman, I felt, understood this impossible situation; I had seen her suffer 16 for it. As I grew up, Wonder Woman grew with me. In later versions of her stories, her feminism became more self-aware and conscious of the politics of the time in the same ways mine did. And as her symbolism for many female comic fans deepened, the special meaning she held for me deepened as well.

Since I found out the *Wonder Woman* movie was finally in the works, I've been 17 excited but also a little nervous. Yes, a white actress, Gal Gadot, had been cast as the lead. But, I wondered, would the creators see in her what I had all these years? Would she still chafe at the forced dichotomy between her strength and her womanhood, her peaceful demeanor and her righteous anger? Would we still walk the same tightrope of dual identities and the resulting isolation from each? While all heroes won't be men, will all the Amazons be white? Would they infuse her story with enough of mine that a little black girl who sees the movie might get to wonder, maybe?

I'm sensitive to the argument that every character can't embody every identity, 18 and that the solution to Hollywood's larger diversity problem can't possibly fall to any single movie or creator to fix. And yet I've begun to hear that argument not as a lament or a promise to do better with future characters and opportunities, but as a familiar admonishment to put away the brown crayon and stop trying to ruin the picture.

I have now seen *Wonder Woman* several times. I'll likely see it multiple times. 19 And I'm sure I'll love it for many of the same reasons that I've been loving her since I was eight. But I'm also sure I'll keep challenging her to love me a little more. I've been doing that since I was eight, too.

READING FOR MEANING

1. **Read to Summarize.** Write a few sentences explaining how Wonder Woman comes to symbolize the ideas Rupert wants to convey about race, gender, and identity.

2. **Read to Respond.** Write a paragraph exploring anything that resonates with your experience or that seems surprising, such as how a white mother of one of Rupert's classmates asked her why she "ruined" her picture by coloring Wonder Woman's skin brown (par. 4) or how a black hairdresser told Rupert "feminism wasn't for black women" (par. 7).

3. **Read to Analyze Assumptions.** Write a paragraph or two analyzing an assumption you find intriguing in Rupert's essay. For example:

   Assumptions about race. Rupert writes that as she was growing up, television shows and other pop culture outlets taught her that "racists were the only people who saw color" and that "gender differences were empowering, but racial differences were divisive" (par. 5).

   - Why does Rupert call attention to these views? How does acknowledging them help her convey her ideas?

   - What television shows, pop culture outlets, experiences, texts, or people have influenced how you think about race?

   Assumptions about strength. Rupert explores the strengths of various comic superheroes, including Wonder Woman. She also considers the stereotype of the "strong black woman" (par. 14).

   - How and why do these explorations matter within the context of Rupert's reflections on her own life experiences?

   - Are Rupert's views about strength universal? Are there cultures where strength is defined differently or is significant in different ways?

For help with reading strategies like summarizing and analyzing assumptions, see Chapter 2.

READING LIKE A WRITER

Presenting the Occasion

Rupert opens her essay with an occasion from her childhood when she asks her mother if Wonder Woman is black (para. 2). The description of this event leads to her discussion of and reflection on a series of other occasions that allow her to explore serious issues surrounding race, gender, and identity.

ANALYZE & WRITE

Write a paragraph or two analyzing how Rupert uses occasions to illustrate and explain her reflections.

1. Reread the essay marking all of the occasions that help shape Rupert's ideas about race, gender, and identity.

2. Choose two of the occasions you have found and explain how they help Rupert develop her ideas.

Samantha Wright

Starving for Control

Samantha Wright wrote this essay for an assignment in her first-year college composition course. She reflects on a single event that would change her life by changing how she thinks about her body. Looking back on this event allows the author to consider what led to her obsession with losing weight, as well as the consequences of that obsession.

- **Before you read**, think about your own attitude toward the female body as it is portrayed in the media. Do you find anything disturbing about it?

- **As you read**, consider Wright's rhetorical situation; she is writing about a sensitive topic for many people. What strategies does she use to develop her reflection, support her opinions, and remain sensitive to her audience?

Like a lot of American girls, I developed an eating disorder when I was thirteen years 1 old. To be honest, I'm surprised it took that long. My body had always confused me; I mean, I started getting my period before I'd mastered long division. I had pointy little tits and no bras, which led to an embarrassing yearbook photo every single year. My hair grew fast, but not on my head. To sum it up neatly, I was a wreck and fully aware of it. But somehow, I didn't really care. Yes, I knew what beauty was, and yes, I knew that I didn't fit the mold, like, at all, but don't remember taking the stupid construct to heart. I was free little me. Well, whatever fueled my carefree outlook was killed by the unstoppable force of adolescent insecurity.

During my first year at Laguna Middle School, my P.E. class transitioned into its 2 healthy fitness unit. The unit was treacherous and insulting; we'd done it all before. The trunk lifts, crunches, pacer test, mile run—each one of the gimmicky exercises had the same lame familiarity. Well, with the exception of the BMI test.

As everyone knows, the BMI rubric is determined by height and weight. No run- 3 ning, no stretching, no activity was required for this fitness test. It's funny looking back; the least demanding activity in the unit would become one of the most internalized instances in my life to that point. Six years later, I can remember standing in that school's little gym with my ugly uniform on. The walls were green, the room was cramped, and well over capacity. A single sheet hung in the middle of the room, separating the girls from the boys.

When the teacher saw the numbers on the scale, she would say them out loud 4 to her student aid, who'd promptly scribble them down. As the line shortened and I grew closer and closer, it was obvious that there wasn't much of a range.

"98, 84, 108, 112." The numbers seemed so fluid, so congruent. There was a uni- 5 form beauty to it. They were lofty ballerinas side-by-side, none more distinct than the other.

"104, 94, 110."   6

Approaching.   7

"96, 100, 118."   8

I stepped on the scale.   9

"135."   10

I felt an immediate isolating force.   11

I dismounted the scale with a blank expression and left the building to find my   12
friends. Whatever conversation we had following my weigh-in was irrelevant. I felt
funny. I thought about what I ate that day. I abused myself a little. I walked over to my
friend Kendall, who weighed eighty-four pounds.

"Hey, Kendall, who do you think is the fattest girl in the class?" I was notice-   13
ably anxious. She furrowed her brows and thought for a minute, and after looking
between me and our peers told me that the fattest girl was Summer Stanley, a loner
with a solid build, who I would find out weighed four pounds less than me. I checked
out and went through the motions of the day with a vacant headspace. Well, vacant
besides the inadequacy, self-doubt, and need for validation molesting my mind.
When it came time to head home, I felt this urgency to address what was making me
feel so ironically empty. I got online.

The first diet plan that attracted me was the military diet. It lasted three days and   14
allowed for the consumption of hot dogs and vanilla ice cream, both of which I loved. I
quickly reminded myself that this wasn't a good thing, though, and that it was necessary
to avoid anything I was already eating. The game plan was this: renovate everything I
thought was right. It wasn't up to me at that point, and I had an urge for someone, something, to push me in the right direction, whatever that was. Then I found it. After skimming through Adkins, the Master Cleanse, and Raw Till 4, I found just what I needed.
For the next two weeks, I would follow the almighty guide of the grapefruit diet.

The grapefruit diet required absolute self-control and a complete diet change. I'd   15
have to eat two hard-boiled eggs and half a grapefruit for breakfast, an undressed
salad with deli ham and a grapefruit for lunch, and another mixed green salad with
deli ham for dinner, of course paired with grapefruit.

Even though the plan suggested avoiding snacks, I decided it would be fine to   16
allow myself an apple or a couple of carrots in between lunch and dinner. My parents had no concerns with my plan. They were actually thrilled about my new men-
tality. I remember them saying repeatedly that anything healthy can't be a bad thing.
So, with the plan set in motion, the following week would be dictated by the guidelines I had taped to my wall just in view of my bed. Remarkably, I stayed on track.

Looking back on the whole ordeal, it really shouldn't have gone the way it did.   17
There was nothing I had done before that point that would've suggested I had the
willpower to cut out one of my only comfort sources. At the time, I was a mostly
social kid who looked forward to cheap cookies, candy, junk food, and television.
I'd never given any activity all of my energy and was content with the situational
outcomes that I'd receive. It was hard for me to finish projects before jumping aboard
new ones, but when it came to my diet, I used all of my strength, energy, and will to
reach my goal, which, looking back, was dangerously unclear. Even though I hated

the taste of grapefruit and my stomach would constantly growl, I didn't give in to my cravings. Strangely, it wasn't that hard to do. It felt like there was something inside of me. Something strong, something that could take control and tell me what to do and what not to do. I liked this new feeling, even though it told me not to trust anything I organically did, said, or thought.

The following Sunday, I got on my bathroom scale to measure my progress. I don't 18 know what I was expecting, but I was stunned to learn that I weighed in at 127 pounds, eight pounds lost in a single week. I was thrilled yet incredulous with this outcome, to the point where I literally got off the scale and mounted it again, thinking that the number was just a delusion. It wasn't. The satisfactory high didn't last long, though. I instantly craved more. Lost weight equated to personal gain. That's when I became an addict, hungry for the rush of losing and horrified at the possibility of gaining—a truly twisted logic.

My motives weren't clear after my first instance of weight loss. Eventually I'd start 19 exercising compulsively, then I'd skip lunch. I'd strive to burn more calories than I'd take in, then I'd start making myself throw up. I'd start taking laxatives, then started impulsively counting. Among the anorexia, bulimia, and body dysmorphia, I developed full-fledged OCD. I'd favor the right side of my body, and threaten myself with morbid punishments if I did so much as exit a flight of stairs on my left foot. I'd only chew with the right side of my mouth. I'd count on my pinky, middle, and thumb fingers, one two three, constantly and compulsively. The right was my balance, and though I've since developed methods of controlling this obsession, to this day I can't shake the nonsensical ritual while performing routine tasks. It doesn't go away.

I received an intervention three months in from when I'd began. By this point I was 20 urinating blood but stopped getting my period. I was so terrified of gaining weight that I stopped drinking water and swallowing my spit. My diet consisted of mostly ice. I'd spend most of my time in the bathroom completely naked: chewing gum (on the right side of my mouth), spitting in the toilet, and weighing myself repeatedly for hours on end. I couldn't understand the emotions of my family, and when they told me that they thought I would die, I told them I didn't care. I wasn't myself anymore. Just a cold shell vaguely resembling who I once was, possessed by a demonic combination of self-repulsion and misery. I was forced into group therapy with other anorexics and bulimics, where we'd journal, receive individual treatment, and discuss our anxieties over the meals we were basically force-fed. After I "graduated" from the program, I was no longer 100 pounds. To my disgust, eating a normal diet made me gain back twenty pounds in no time, and before I knew it, I was back to 135. It's a shame I couldn't see the humor of the situation back then, all that work and permanent mental damage just to get right back to where I started. But I guess that's what happens when you dedicate yourself to a goal with no endgame; you just end up playing yourself.

Though today I can look back at how I was in horror, I can't disregard what brought 21 me to those extremes. There was the sense of purpose and control I got from losing weight, something my strict and anxious upbringing didn't allow me to have. There was also the glamorous aspect of starvation: at one point I wanted to be as thin as the girls on *America's Next Top Model*—a ridiculous concept considering I'm 5'4" with a curvy build. Somehow, I saw what I was doing as a good thing. I thought I was motivating myself, when in actuality, I grew more and more detached with every pound I lost. My friends and family couldn't stand my new personality, so I was left alone. Being alone, that's really what all my troubles amounted to. I drew an invisible line separating myself from reality, and nobody dared cross into my territory. No friends, no father, no sister, no mother. Just me. Alone. Empty. It's a feeling you can't just forget about.

READING FOR MEANING

For help with reading strategies like summarizing and analyzing assumptions, see Chapter 2.

1. **Read to Summarize.** Write a sentence or two explaining what you think Wright wants readers to understand about the occasion she describes.

2. **Read to Respond.** Write a paragraph analyzing anything that resonates with your experience or interests you, such as the effect of television shows like *America's Next Top Model* on peoples' feelings about their bodies (par. 21) or feelings of loneliness because of an obsession you may have (par. 21).

3. **Read to Analyze Assumptions.** Write a paragraph or two analyzing an assumption you find intriguing in Wright's essay. For example:

   Assumptions about insecurities. Wright explains, "Whatever fueled my carefree outlook was killed by the unstoppable force of adolescent insecurity" (par. 1).

   - Do you agree with the assumptions Wright makes about adolescent insecurities? Why, or why not?
   - Why do you think some insecurities have the kind of long-standing effects that Wright describes while others don't?

   Assumptions that media have a strong effect on human behavior. Wright writes that "there was also the glamourous aspect of starvation: at one point I wanted to be as thin as the girls on *America's Next Top Model*" (par 21).

   - What assumptions do you have about the effect that media have on how people feel about their bodies? Where do these assumptions come from?
   - Should the media take responsibility in some way for perpetuating "the glamorous aspect of starvation?" Why or why not?

READING LIKE A WRITER

Developing the Reflections

In reflective writing, insights and ideas are central. Yet writers cannot merely list ideas, regardless of how fresh and daring their ideas might be. Instead, writers must work imaginatively to develop their ideas, to explain and elaborate on them, and to view them from one angle and then another. One way writers develop their reflections and make them compelling for readers is by drawing on examples from their personal experiences. For example, Wright describes in paragraph 20 how sick she was at the time of the intervention ("I was so worried about gaining weight that I stopped drinking water and swallowing my spit") and creates a vivid picture for readers of how she spent her time: "in the bathroom completely naked: chewing gum . . . spitting in the toilet and weighing myself repeatedly for hours on end" (par. 20) to show the effect of her eating disorder on her life.

ANALYZE & WRITE

Write a paragraph or two analyzing Wright's use of extended examples to convey her insights and ideas about the destructive power of eating disorders.

1. Skim paragraphs 14–16. Why do you think Wright lists all of the different diets that interested her and that she tried? What effect does this have on you as a reader?

2. Reread paragraphs 20 and 21. Wright describes her eating disorder as giving her a sense of purpose and control (par 21). How is this insight reflected in her descriptions and examples throughout her essay?

Combining Reading Strategies

Comparing and Contrasting Related Readings to Recognize Emotional Manipulation

Jacqueline Woodson's "The Pain of the Watermelon Joke" and Samantha Wright's "Starving for Control" are related because they address emotionally charged issues, and they may be seen as emotionally manipulating readers. By *comparing and contrasting* them and particularly by analyzing how they seek to engage the reader, you can begin to think about whether you believe these texts are emotionally manipulating you by using emotional appeals based on false or exaggerated claims. Complete the following prompts to explore these issues.

For guidelines on comparing and contrasting related readings, see Chapter 2, pp. 57–60.

For guidelines on recognizing emotional manipulation, see Chapter 2, p. 65.

- Notice how both essays open. Wright begins her essay with the pronouncement: "Like a lot of American girls, I developed an eating disorder when I was thirteen years old. To be honest, I'm surprised it took that long" (par. 1). Woodson's essay opens with a reference to Jim Crow: "Even though Jim Crow was supposed to be far behind us, we spent our days in the all-black community called Nicholtown in a still segregated South" (par. 2). To what extent do you think that these openings are meant to affect or manipulate you emotionally? Were they successful in doing so?

(continued)

- Reread both essays, paying close attention to your emotional reactions as you read. Are there moments where you think the author is trying to appeal to your emotions? If yes, how so? If no, how does the author avoid making these appeals, especially when dealing with such an emotionally charged subject?

Writing to Learn Reflection

Write a brief essay analyzing one of the readings in this chapter (or another selection, perhaps one by a classmate). Explain how (and perhaps, how well) the selection works as a reflection. Consider, for example, how it uses

- an occasion to prompt the reflection and prepare the reader;
- varied writing strategies to develop the reflection;
- cues to maintain coherence;
- strategies to engage readers' interest.

Your essay could also reflect on how you applied one or more of the following practices as you read the selection:

- **Critical analysis** — what assumptions in the selection did you find intriguing, and why?
- **Rhetorical sensitivity** — how effective or ineffective do you think the selection is in achieving its purpose for the intended audience?
- **Empathy** — did you find yourself identifying with the author, and how important was this to the effectiveness of the selection?

A GUIDE TO WRITING REFLECTIVE ESSAYS

You have probably done a good deal of analytical writing about your reading. Your instructor may also assign a capstone project to write a brief reflection of your own. This Guide to Writing offers detailed suggestions and resources to help you meet the special challenges reflective writing presents.

THE WRITING ASSIGNMENT

Write a reflective essay that grows out of a specific occasion or event.

- Choose an occasion or event that you feel comfortable writing about for this audience (your instructor and classmates). You may want to select the general subject that you want to reflect on first, and then choose an event or occasion that effectively particularizes this subject.

- Consider how you can depict the occasion or event vividly so that readers can imagine what you experienced. Try to create a voice or persona that will appeal to your audience.

- Develop your reflections, including insights that interest, surprise, or enlighten your readers.

- Organize your reflection so that readers will be able to follow your train of thought.

WRITING YOUR DRAFT

Choosing an Occasion and General Subject

Writers of reflections often connect an occasion to a subject or a subject to an occasion. Sometimes writers choose a general subject (such as envy or friendship) and then search for the right occasion (an image or anecdote) with which to particularize it. Sometimes the occasion prompts the subject.

Particular Occasions	*General Subjects*
I had an experience on the train.	The social benefits of mass transit
I met someone (or am someone) with a disability.	Measures taken for people with disabilities
I had a great time skiing.	The importance of exercise or of time away from work

To get started, use a chart like the one below to list several possible occasions and the general subjects they suggest (or start with the "General Subjects" column and then list the occasions they suggest).

For occasions, consider the following:

- conversations you have had or overheard

- memorable scenes you observed, read about, or saw in a movie or other media

- incidents in your own or someone else's life that led you to reflect more generally

Also consider the general subjects suggested by the occasions:

- human qualities such as compassion, vanity, jealousy, and faithfulness

- customs for socializing and working

- abstract notions such as fate, free will, and imagination

Shaping Your Reflection

Write up the initial occasion that prompted your reflection. Use specific details and choose evocative words to make your description vivid; use active, specific verbs to make your writing lively; and use time markers to give immediacy and color to your narration of the occasion. The example paragraph below demonstrates how one writer in this chapter used these strategies to shape their reflections:

Vivid description	My **first victim** was a woman — white, well dressed, probably in
Active verb	her early twenties. I came upon her late one evening on a deserted
Time marker	street in Hyde Park, a relatively affluent neighborhood in an other-
	wise mean, impoverished section of Chicago. As I swung onto the avenue behind her, there seemed to be a discreet, uninflammatory distance between us. Not so. She cast back a worried glance. To her, the youngish black man — a broad six feet two inches with a beard and billowing hair, both hands shoved into the pockets of a bulky military jacket — seemed menacingly close. After a few more quick glimpses, she picked up her pace and was soon running in earnest. Within seconds she disappeared into a cross street. (Staples, par. 1)

Developing Your Reflection

The following activities will help you recall details about the occasion for your reflection.

Narrating and Describing an Event.   Write for five to ten minutes narrating what happened during the event. Try to make your story vivid so that readers can imagine what it was like. Describe the people involved in the event — what they looked like, how they acted, what they said — and the place where it occurred.

Cubing.   To explore your ideas about the subject, try an invention strategy called *cubing*. This approach encourages you to examine your subject as you would turn over a cube, looking at it in six different ways. You can use some of the eight options below or come up with your own. Whichever six you choose, write about your subject for five minutes from each of the six perspectives to invent new ways of considering it.

- **Analyzing.** What is your subject composed of? How are the parts related to one another? Are they all of equal importance?

- **Applying.** How can you use your subject or act on it? What difference would it make to you and to others?

- **Comparing and Contrasting.** What subject could you compare with yours? What are the similarities and the differences between them?

- **Describing.** What details would you use to describe the people or places involved in the occasion that gave rise to your reflections?

- **Extending.** What are the implications of your subject? Where does it lead?

- **Generalizing.** What does the occasion suggest about people in general or about the society in which you live?

- **Giving Examples.** What examples would best characterize or help your readers understand your reflection?

- **Visualizing.** What would your occasion look like from the perspective of an outside observer?

Exploring How You Felt at the Time and What the Occasion Made You Realize Later.   Write for a few minutes, recalling your thoughts and feelings when the occasion was occurring.

- What did you feel at the moment the occasion was occurring — in control or powerless, proud or embarrassed, vulnerable, detached, judgmental? For example, Staples uses phrases like "swung onto the avenue" to indicate a light mood (par. 1). Sentence strategies like these might help you describe your initial experience of the occasion:

  ▶ As soon as I [saw/did/imagined] .... , I felt .... , ... , and ....

  ▶ .... [describe occasion] made me feel as if ....

- What larger reflection was prompted by your occasion? Muñoz, for example, suggests "[m]y stepfather's experience with the Anglicization of his name — Antonio to Tony — ties into something bigger than learning English. For him, the erasure of his name was about deference and subservience" (par. 14). These sentence strategies may help you put your reflection into words:

  ▶ Since then, I realize .... , but also ....

  ▶ Now that I have seen .... , I know that .... and ....

Considering Your Purpose and Audience.   Write for several minutes exploring what you want your readers to think about your reflection after reading your essay. Your answer may change as you write, but thinking about your goals may help you decide which of your ideas to include in the essay. Answering the following questions may help you clarify your purpose:

- Which of your ideas are most important to you? Why?

- How do your ideas relate to one another? If your ideas seem contradictory, how could you use the contradictions to convey the complexity of your ideas and feelings on the subject?

- Is the occasion for your reflection likely to resonate with your readers' experience and observation?

Formulating a Working Thesis.   Review what you wrote for Considering Your Purpose and Audience and add another two or three sentences to bring your reflection into focus. Write sentences that indicate what is most important or interesting about the subject. Readers may not expect reflective essays to begin with an explicit thesis statement — but stating the main point of your reflective essay now may lead you to a deeper understanding of your occasion and the reflection it inspired, and it may guide your selection of ideas to develop.

Considering Visuals.   If you submit your essay electronically to other students and your instructor, or if you post it on a website, you may even consider including snippets of video or audio files. You could import your own photographs or drawings, or you could scan materials from books and magazines or download them from the Internet, but remember that you will need to cite any visuals you borrow from another source.

Working with Sources

For additional help with deciding whether to quote, paraphrase, or summarize, see Chapter 12, pp. 618–619.

Paraphrasing a Source to Help Make Your Point.   Determine whether a source or two might help readers understand the point you are trying to make in your reflective essay. You do not always need to directly cite a source. You can, instead, paraphrase a source, especially when it is a well-known source, as is the case in the example below.

> The scars remind me, too, that in this vain culture our vanity sometimes needs to be punctured and deflated — and that's not such a bad thing. To paraphrase Ecclesiastes, better to be a scarred and living dog than to be a dead lion. (Jennings, par. 13)

Drafting Your Reflective Essay

By this point, you have done a lot of writing

- to present an occasion that prompts a reflection

- to present the reflection and develop it using a variety of approaches

- to relate the significance of your reflection in a way meaningful to your readers

Now stitch that material together to create a draft. The next section of this Guide to Writing will help you evaluate and improve it.

REVIEWING AND IMPROVING THE DRAFT

This section includes two guides for Peer Review and Troubleshooting Your Draft. Your instructor may arrange a peer review in class or online where you can exchange drafts with a classmate. The Peer Review Guide will help you give each other constructive feedback regarding the basic features and strategies typical of reflective essays. (If you want to make specific suggestions for improving the draft, see Troubleshooting Your Draft on pp. 216–217.) Also, be sure to respond to any specific concerns the writer has raised about the draft. The Troubleshooting Your Draft guide that follows will help you reread your own draft with a critical eye, sort through any feedback you've received, and consider a variety of ways to improve your draft.

A PEER REVIEW GUIDE

How effectively does the writer present the occasion?

What's Working Well: Identify a passage where the writer presents the occasion that prompted the reflection, perhaps suggesting the occasion's significance. Tell the writer if the occasion arouses interest and leads logically to the reflection.

What Needs Improvement: Let the writer know if there are details of the occasion that dominate the essay too much or are scant and need development.

(continued)

How appropriate are the methods of developing the reflection?

What's Working Well: Point to a passage that is particularly effective in helping you understand the purpose of the reflection. To develop their reflection, does the writer try compare/contrast, examples, consideration of social implications, or connections to other ideas?

What Needs Improvement: Identify any ideas or anecdotes you find lackluster or irrelevant to the broader association, explaining briefly why you think so.

How could the writer strengthen coherence?

What's Working Well: Highlight cues—strong transitions, time markers, or repeated words and ideas—that help hold the essay together.

What Needs Improvement: Point to areas where you get lost or don't understand the connection from one sentence or paragraph to the next. Note any section that seems out of place, and suggest where it might fit better.

How could the readers be more engaged?

What's Working Well: Mark a part of the essay that especially draws you in, holds your interest, inspires you to think, challenges your attitudes or values, or keeps you wanting to read to the end.

What Needs Improvement: Note passages where you lose interest or don't understand the significance to your own ideas and experiences. Suggest ways for the writer to liven up the essay by considering what aspects of the essays you read in this chapter inspired your own reflections.

Revising Your Draft

Revising means reenvisioning your draft, trying to see it in a new way, given your purpose and audience, in order to develop a more engaging, more coherent reflective essay. Think imaginatively and boldly about cutting unconvincing material, adding new material, and moving material around. The suggestions in the following chart may help you strengthen your essay.

TROUBLESHOOTING YOUR DRAFT

To Present the Subject More Effectively

If the occasion doesn't seem interesting or is too general or abstract,	• Add details for drama and surprise. • Make it into a story. • Try using the first person. • Try the present tense, and make your verbs active. • Choose another occasion that is more interesting and specific.

If the occasion is not clearly related to the reflection that follows,	• Make transitions clearer. • Explain how the two are related. • Choose another occasion that prepares readers by providing a context for your reflection.

To Clarify and Strengthen the Argument

If promising ideas are not fully developed,	• Provide more examples. • Compare or contrast your ideas with other ideas. • Consult Chapter 2 on reading strategies, and see whether you could use some of them to develop your reflection.
If your reflection does not move beyond personal association,	• Consider adding visuals. • Extend it into a broader context, such as social, political, scientific, or educational. • Comment on its larger implications for people in general.

To Improve the Response to Objections and/or Alternative Judgments

If there are gaps between sentences or paragraphs,	• Reorder the sequence of actions. • Add explicit transitions. • Revise pairs or a series of related ideas or examples into parallel form.
If the reflection seems scattered or disorganized,	• Repeat words and phrases to help readers follow your reflection. • Try time markers to show a clear sequence.

To Make the Organization Clearer

If the reflection doesn't encourage readers to reflect on their own lives,	• Think about your audience and tie your reflection to their values and beliefs. • Use plural personal pronouns like "we" and "our." • Expand beyond the personal with more generalized stories or anecdotes. • Consider the broader social implications of your ideas. • Express the significance more directly.

Editing and Proofreading Your Draft

Check for errors in usage, punctuation, and mechanics, and consider matters of style. If you keep a list of errors you typically make, begin by checking your draft against this list.

From our research on student writing, we know that reflective essays **have** a high frequency of unnecessary shifts in verb tense and mood. Check a **writer's** handbook for help with these potential problems.

Reflecting on Reflection

In this chapter, you have read several reflective essays and have written **one of** your own. To better remember what you have learned, pause now to **reflect** on the reading and writing activities you completed in this chapter.

1. Write a page or so reflecting on what you have learned. Begin **by** describing what you are most pleased with in your essay. Then **explain** what you think contributed to your achievement. Be specific about **this** contribution.

   - If it was something you learned from the readings, indicate **which** readings and specifically what you learned from them.

   - If it came from the writing you did in response to prompts in **this** chapter, point out the section or sections that helped you most.

2. Reflect more generally on how you tend to interpret reflective **writing**, your own as well as other writers'. Consider some of the **following** questions:

   - Did you find rich enough material from your own personal ideas **on** a subject, or did you conduct research or interview people to **collect** their ideas?

   - How might your gender, social class, or ethnic group have **influ-** enced the ideas you came up with for your essay?

   - What contribution might reflective essays make to our society **that** other genres cannot make?

3. By reflecting on what you have learned about reflection, you have **been** practicing **metacognition**, one of the academic habits of mind.

   - Were you aware of any other habits of mind you practiced as **you** read and responded to the material in this chapter? If so, **which** habits did you find useful?

   - If not, think back now on your reading and writing process. Can **you** identify any habits you used?

Explaining Concepts

A **concept** is a major idea. Concepts include abstract ideas, phenomena, and processes. We create concepts, name them, communicate them, and think with them in every field of study. Psychology, for example, has *schizophrenia* and *narcissism*; business has *micromanagement* and *direct marketing*; and nursing has *gerontology* and *whole-person caring*. *Explaining concepts* is a kind (or genre) of explanatory writing that is especially important for college students because it involves widely applicable strategies for critical reading, essay exams, and paper assignments. We learn new concepts by connecting them to what we have previously learned. Writing that explains concepts facilitates such connections through a range of writing strategies, including, among others, *definition, illustration, cause and effect*, and *comparison/contrast*.

RHETORICAL SITUATIONS FOR CONCEPT EXPLANATIONS

Writing that explains concepts is familiar in college and professional life, as the following examples show:

- For a presentation at the annual convention of the American Medical Association, an anesthesiologist writes a report on the concept of *awareness during surgery*. He presents evidence that patients under anesthesia, as in hypnosis, can hear, and he reviews research demonstrating that they can perceive and carry out instructions that speed their recovery. He describes how he applies the concept in his own work — how he prepares patients before surgery, what he tells them while they are under anesthesia, and what happens as they recover.

- As part of a group assignment, a college student at a summer biology camp in the Sierra Nevada mountains reads about the condition of mammals at birth. She learns the distinction between infant mammals that are *altricial* (born nude and helpless within a protective nest) and those that are *precocial* (born well formed with eyes open and ears erect). In her part of a group report, she develops this contrast point by point, giving many examples of specific mammals but focusing in detail on altricial mice and precocial porcupines.

Thinking about Concept Explanation

Write a paragraph or two about an occasion when you told, read, heard, or saw an explanation of a concept in school, at work, or in another context.

- Who was the *audience*? How educated was the audience in the field of the concept? How did the writer tailor the explanation to help familiarize the audience with the concept, given their age, level of expertise, and experience?

- What was the main *purpose*? Why did the writer (or speaker) want the audience to understand the concept? For example, was the goal for the audience to demonstrate their understanding on a test, or the importance of the concept in their own lives?

- How would you rate the *rhetorical sensitivity* with which the explanation was presented? How was it appropriate or inappropriate for its audience or purpose?

A GUIDE TO READING CONCEPT EXPLANATIONS

This guide introduces you to concept explanations by inviting you to analyze an intriguing selection by Susan Cain that explains *introversion*:

- *Annotations* on this first reading will help you see how to practice academic **habits of mind** such as **curiosity, openness,** and **persistence** to help you engage with and understand what you are reading. Notice how many questions the reader has as she reads. There is plenty of space for you to add your own questions and thoughts, as well, to this reading and any other in the textbook.

- *Reading for meaning* will help you understand the topic and its significance for Cain. Why does Cain see our culture's attitude toward introversion as a long-term danger?

- *Reading like a writer* will help you learn how Cain employs strategies typical of concept explanations, such as

  1. using appropriate writing strategies: defining, illustrating, comparing and contrasting, and showing causes and effects

  2. organizing the information clearly and logically

  3. integrating sources smoothly

  4. engaging readers' interest

Susan Cain

Shyness: Evolutionary Tactic?

Susan Cain (b. 1968) attended Princeton University and Harvard Law School, and worked for several years as an attorney and a negotiations consultant before founding Quiet Revolution, a mission-based organization that advocates for the power of introversion. She is the author of the books *Quiet: The Power of Introverts in a World That Can't Stop Talking* (2012) and *Quiet Power: The Secret Strengths of Introverts* (2016). She also writes a popular blog about introversion and has contributed articles on this topic to such journals and magazines as *Psychology Today* and *Time*, and her TED talk has broken viewing records. The op-ed that appears below was published in the *New York Times*.

- **Before you read,** notice the title of this reading and the title of Cain's book (above). What do these titles lead you to expect?

- **As you read,** think about the rhetorical sensitivity with which Cain is writing. How effective is the opening paragraph as a hook to catch readers' attention?

1   A beautiful woman lowers her eyes demurely beneath a hat. In an earlier era, her gaze might have signaled a mysterious allure. But this is a 2003 advertisement for Zoloft, a selective serotonin reuptake inhibitor (SSRI) approved by the FDA to treat social anxiety disorder. "Is she just shy? Or is it Social Anxiety Disorder?" reads the caption, suggesting that the young woman is not alluring at all. She is sick.

2   But is she?

3   It is possible that the lovely young woman has a life-wrecking form of social anxiety. There are people too afraid of disapproval to venture out for a job interview, a date or even a meal in public. Despite the risk of serious side effects—nausea, loss of sex drive, seizures—drugs like Zoloft can be a godsend for this group.

> Will this essay be about the benefits and drawbacks of relying on pharmaceuticals for social anxiety?

4   But the ad's insinuation aside, it's also possible the young woman is "just shy," or introverted—traits our society disfavors. One way we manifest this bias is by encouraging perfectly healthy shy people to see themselves as ill.

5   This does us all a grave disservice, because shyness and introversion—or more precisely, the careful, sensitive temperament from which both often spring—are not just normal. They are valuable. And they may be essential to the survival of our species.

> How is shyness essential?

6   Theoretically, shyness and social anxiety disorder are easily distinguishable. But a blurry line divides the two. Imagine that the woman in the ad enjoys a steady paycheck, a strong marriage and a small circle of close

friends—a good life by most measures—except that she avoids a needed promotion because she's nervous about leading meetings. She often criticizes herself for feeling too shy to speak up.

What do you think now? Is she ill, or does she simply need public-speaking training? 6

What other disorders do people suffer from but don't exist yet in name? Does naming things matter?

Before 1980, this would have seemed a strange question. Social anxiety disorder did not officially exist until it appeared in that year's *Diagnostic and Statistical Manual*, the *DSM-III*, the psychiatrist's bible of mental disorders, under the name "social phobia." It was not widely known until the 1990s, when pharmaceutical companies received FDA approval to treat social anxiety with SSRI's and poured tens of millions of dollars into advertising its existence. The current version of the *Diagnostic and Statistical Manual*, the *DSM-IV*, acknowledges that stage fright (and shyness in social situations) is common and not necessarily a sign of illness. But it also says that diagnosis is warranted when anxiety "interferes significantly" with work performance or if the sufferer shows "marked distress" about it. According to this definition, the answer to our question is clear: the young woman in the ad is indeed sick. 7

The *DSM* inevitably reflects cultural attitudes; it used to identify homosexuality as a disease, too. Though the *DSM* did not set out to pathologize shyness, it risks doing so, and has twice come close to identifying introversion as a disorder, too. (Shyness and introversion are not the same thing. Shy people fear negative judgment; introverts simply prefer quiet, minimally stimulating environments.) 8

Is there a difference between shyness and introversion?

But shyness and introversion share an undervalued status in a world that prizes extroversion. Children's classroom desks are now often arranged in pods, because group participation supposedly leads to better learning; in one school I visited, a sign announcing "Rules for Group Work" included, "You can't ask a teacher for help unless everyone in your group has the same question." Many adults work for organizations that now assign work in teams, in offices without walls, for supervisors who value "people skills" above all. As a society, we prefer action to contemplation, risk-taking to heed-taking, certainty to doubt. Studies show that we rank fast and frequent talkers as more competent, likable and even smarter than slow ones. As the psychologists William Hart and Dolores Albarracin point out, phrases like "get active," "get moving," "do something" and similar calls to action surface repeatedly in recent books. 9

Yet shy and introverted people have been part of our species for a very long time, often in leadership positions. We find them in the Bible ("Who am I, that I should go unto Pharaoh?" asked Moses, whom the Book of Numbers describes as "very meek, above all the men which were upon the face of the earth.") We find them in recent history, in figures like Charles Darwin, Marcel Proust and Albert Einstein, and, in contemporary times: think of Google's Larry Page, or Harry Potter's creator, J. K. Rowling. 10

Why did she choose these people as examples?

11   In the science journalist Winifred Gallagher's words: "The glory of the disposition that stops to consider stimuli rather than rushing to engage with them is its long association with intellectual and artistic achievement. Neither $E = mc^2$ nor *Paradise Lost* was dashed off by a party animal."

12   We even find "introverts" in the animal kingdom, where 15 percent to 20 percent of many species are watchful, slow-to-warm-up types who stick to the sidelines (sometimes called "sitters") while the other 80 percent are "rovers" who sally forth without paying much attention to their surroundings. Sitters and rovers favor different survival strategies, which could be summed up as the sitter's "Look before you leap" versus the rover's inclination to "Just do it!" Each strategy reaps different rewards.

13   In an illustrative experiment, David Sloan Wilson, a Binghamton evolutionary biologist, dropped metal traps into a pond of pumpkinseed sunfish. The "rover" fish couldn't help but investigate—and were immediately caught. But the "sitter" fish stayed back, making it impossible for Professor Wilson to capture them. Had Professor Wilson's traps posed a real threat, only the sitters would have survived. But had the sitters taken Zoloft and become more like bold rovers, the entire family of pumpkinseed sunfish would have been wiped out. "Anxiety" about the trap saved the fishes' lives.

> Note to self: look up some of these scientists!

14   Next, Professor Wilson used fishing nets to catch both types of fish; when he carried them back to his lab, he noted that the rovers quickly acclimated to their new environment and started eating a full five days earlier than their sitter brethren. In this situation, the rovers were the likely survivors. "There is no single best... [animal] personality," Professor Wilson concludes in his book, *Evolution for Everyone,* "but rather a diversity of personalities maintained by natural selection."

15   The same might be said of humans, 15 percent to 20 percent of whom are also born with sitter-like temperaments that predispose them to shyness and introversion. (The overall incidence of shyness and introversion is higher—40 percent of the population for shyness, according to the psychology professor Jonathan Cheek, and 50 percent for introversion. Conversely, some born sitters never become shy or introverted at all.)

> How are humans classified as shy or introverted? Who decides and based on what? Are the same characteristics used to classify fish?

16   Once you know about sitters and rovers, you see them everywhere, especially among young children. Drop in on your local Mommy and Me music class: there are the sitters, intently watching the action from their mothers' laps, while the rovers march around the room banging their drums and shaking their maracas.

17   Relaxed and exploratory, the rovers have fun, make friends and will take risks, both rewarding and dangerous ones, as they grow. According to Daniel Nettle, a Newcastle University evolutionary psychologist, extroverts are more likely than introverts to be hospitalized as a result of an injury, have affairs (men) and change relationships (women). One study of bus drivers even found that accidents are more likely to occur when extroverts are at the wheel.

In contrast, sitter children are careful and astute, and tend to learn by   18
observing instead of by acting. They notice scary things more than other
children do, but they also notice more things in general. Studies dating all
the way back to the 1960s by the psychologists Jerome Kagan and Ellen
Siegelman found that cautious, solitary children playing matching games
spent more time considering all the alternatives than impulsive children
did, actually using more eye movements to make decisions. Recent studies
by a group of scientists at Stony Brook University and at Chinese universities using functional MRI technology echoed this research, finding that
adults with sitter-like temperaments looked longer at pairs of photos with
subtle differences and showed more activity in brain regions that make
associations between the photos and other stored information in the brain.

Once they reach school age, many sitter children use such traits to   19
great effect. Introverts, who tend to digest information thoroughly, stay
on task, and work accurately, earn disproportionate numbers of National
Merit Scholarship finalist positions and Phi Beta Kappa keys, according to
the Center for Applications of Psychological Type, a research arm for the
Myers-Briggs personality type indicator — even though their IQ scores are
no higher than those of extroverts. Another study, by the psychologists Eric
Rolfhus and Philip Ackerman, tested 141 college students' knowledge of
20 different subjects, from art to astronomy to statistics, and found that the
introverts knew more than the extroverts about 19 subjects — presumably,
the researchers concluded, because the more time people spend socializing, the less time they have for learning.

The psychologist Gregory Feist found that many of the most creative   20
people in a range of fields are introverts who are comfortable working
in solitary conditions in which they can focus attention inward. Steve
Wozniak, the engineer who founded Apple with Steve Jobs, is a prime
example: Mr. Wozniak describes his creative process as an exercise in solitude. "Most inventors and engineers I've met are like me," he writes in
iWoz, his autobiography. "They're shy and they live in their heads. They're
almost like artists. In fact, the very best of them are artists. And artists work
best alone. . . . Not on a committee. Not on a team."

Sitters' temperaments also confer more subtle advantages. Anxiety, it   21
seems, can serve an important social purpose; for example, it plays a key
role in the development of some children's consciences. When caregivers rebuke them for acting up, they become anxious, and since anxiety
is unpleasant, they tend to develop pro-social behaviors. Shy children
are often easier to socialize and more conscientious, according to the
developmental psychologist Grazyna Kochanska. By six they're less likely
than their peers to cheat or break rules, even when they think they can't
be caught, according to one study. By seven they're more likely to be
described by their parents as having high levels of moral traits such as
empathy.

22   When I shared this information with the mother of a "sitter" daughter, her reaction was mixed. "That is all very nice," she said, "but how will it help her in the tough real world?" But sensitivity, if it is not excessive and is properly nurtured, can be a catalyst for empathy and even leadership.

What would count as "excessive sensitivity" or "proper nurturing"?

23   Eleanor Roosevelt, for example, was a courageous leader who was very likely a sitter. Painfully shy and serious as a child, she grew up to be a woman who could not look away from other people's suffering—and who urged her husband, the constitutionally buoyant F.D.R., to do the same; the man who had nothing to fear but fear itself relied, paradoxically, on a woman deeply acquainted with it.

24   Another advantage sitters bring to leadership is a willingness to listen to and implement other people's ideas. A groundbreaking study led by the Wharton management professor Adam Grant, to be published this month in *The Academy of Management Journal,* found that introverts outperform extroverts when leading teams of proactive workers—the kinds of employees who take initiative and are disposed to dream up better ways of doing things. Professor Grant notes that business self-help guides often suggest that introverted leaders practice their communication skills and smile more. But, he told me, it may be extrovert leaders who need to change, to listen more and say less.

25   What would the world look like if all our sitters chose to medicate themselves? The day may come when we have pills that "cure" shyness and turn introverts into social butterflies—without the side effects and other drawbacks of today's medications. (A recent study suggests that today's SSRI's not only relieve social anxiety but also induce extroverted behavior.) The day may come—and might be here already—when people are as comfortable changing their psyches as the color of their hair. If we continue to confuse shyness with sickness, we may find ourselves in a world of all rovers and no sitters, of all yang and no yin.

But aren't there people who are truly sick and could benefit from medicine?

26   As a sitter who enjoys an engaged, productive life, and a professional speaking career, but still experiences the occasional knock-kneed moment, I can understand why caring physicians prescribe available medicine and encourage effective non-pharmaceutical treatments such as cognitive-behavioral therapy.

27   But even non-medical treatments emphasize what is wrong with the people who use them. They don't focus on what is right. Perhaps we need to rethink our approach to social anxiety: to address the pain, but to respect the temperament that underlies it.

This seems like a productive route, but what would it look like practically?

28   The act of treating shyness as an illness obscures the value of that temperament. Ridding people of social unease need not involve pathologizing their fundamental nature, but rather urging them to use its gifts.

29   It's time for the young woman in the Zoloft ad to rediscover her allure.

READING FOR MEANING

For help with reading strategies like summarizing and analyzing assumptions, see Chapter 2.

1. **Read to Summarize.** Write a sentence or two explaining what Cain means by *introversion* and why she thinks it is important.

2. **Read to Respond.** Write a paragraph or two, focusing on anything that seems surprising, such as the way psychiatrists and the pharmaceutical industry may be pathologizing shyness or introversion; or Cain's assertion that "[o]nce you know about sitters and rovers, you see them everywhere" (par. 17). Which of the characteristics of shyness, sitters, or rovers seemed truest of your experience? Why?

3. **Read to Analyze Assumptions.** Write a paragraph or two analyzing an assumption you find intriguing in Cain's essay. For example:

   Assumptions about medical conditions. Cain attempts to overturn the assumption that treatments focus on what is wrong rather than what is right about introverts. Examine two or three of the paragraphs that develop the idea that introverts are not sick but are instead assets to society (for example, pars. 11–13, 14, and 19–24).

   - Do they alter your assumptions about medical conditions and how or whether to treat them?
   - If they do, what assumptions made you believe the evidence?

   Assumptions that what is true of other animals is true of humans. Cain supports her title's assumption — that shyness is an evolutionary tactic — by demonstrating how different temperaments in animals are important to their survival (pars. 13–15). Evolution assumes that offspring who inherit beneficial traits are more likely to survive and reproduce than those who do not.

   - What are some of the human traits Cain examines by drawing comparisons to animal behavior?
   - Are there human traits that animal behavior would not illuminate? What are they?

READING LIKE A WRITER

Using Appropriate Writing Strategies

For more on reading and writing strategies, see Chapter 2.

When writers present information, they rely on explanatory strategies such as defining, illustrating, comparing and contrasting, and showing causes or effects. Writers narrow the **focus** — either eliminating qualities that the concept does not have, or defining and elaborating on the qualities the concept does have, with explanatory strategies. Comparing and contrasting, for example, allows the writer to show how the concept is similar to and different from other concepts that might be familiar to the reader.

Consider the passage below, in which Cain uses contrast to point out how shyness and introversion differ from social anxiety:

Repeated sentence pattern Concept B	It is possible that the lovely young woman has a life-wrecking form of social anxiety....
Transition Concept A	*But* the ad's insinuation aside, it's *also* possible the young woman is "just shy," or introverted.... (pars. 3–4)

ANALYZE & WRITE

Write a paragraph or two analyzing how Cain uses contrast to explain her concept:

1. Find and highlight two or three of the sentence patterns she uses for cueing contrast in paragraphs 9, 10, 13, 18, and 19.
2. Analyze what is being contrasted and how each contrast works.

Organizing the Information Clearly and Logically

Experienced writers know that readers often have a hard time following explanations of unfamiliar concepts, so they provide "road signs" — forecasting statements, topic sentences, transitions, pronouns that refer to nouns that appear earlier in the sentence, synonyms, and summaries — to guide readers through the explanation.

Transition and pronoun referent Key term or synonym	But the ad's insinuation aside, it's **also** possible the young woman is "just shy," or introverted — traits our society disfavors. One way we manifest this bias is by encouraging perfectly healthy shy people to see themselves as ill.
Summary Forecasting statement	This does us all a grave disservice, because shyness and introversion — or more precisely, the careful, sensitive temperament from which both often spring — are not just normal. *They are valuable. And they may be essential to the survival of our species.* (pars. 4–5)

Forecasting statements usually appear early in an essay, often in the thesis, to announce the main points the writer will address; they may also appear at the beginning of major sections. Topic sentences announce each main idea as it comes up, transitions (such as *in contrast* and *another*) and pronoun referents relate what is coming to what came before, and summaries remind readers of what has been explained already.

ANALYZE & WRITE

Write a paragraph or two analyzing the strategies Cain uses to make her concept explanation easy to follow:

1. Skim the rest of the essay (pars. 6–28), underlining other places Cain forecasts and summarizes main ideas or provides topic sentences, transitions, and pronoun referents. How do the strategies she uses make her concept explanation easier to follow?

2. Examine any places in the essay that you found hard to follow. How might Cain have used one or more of these strategies to make her concept explanation clearer?

Integrating Sources Smoothly

For more information on finding and using sources, see p. 591.

In addition to drawing on personal knowledge and fresh observations, writers often do additional research about the concepts they are trying to explain. When doing research, writers immediately confront the ethical responsibility to their readers of locating relevant sources, evaluating them critically, and representing them without distortion. Like the authors of other articles published in popular periodicals, Cain names her sources and mentions their credentials, but she does not cite them formally as you must do when writing a paper for a college class. While you cannot use Cain's approach to citation as a model for your own academic writing, you can follow her lead by doing the following:

- Making a claim of your own and supporting it with appropriate, relevant evidence.

- Explaining how the evidence you provide supports your claim.

- Naming your source author(s) in a **signal phrase** (name plus an appropriate verb) and mentioning the author's (or authors') credentials.

Cain's idea	*As a society, we prefer action to contemplation, risk-taking to heed-taking, certainty to doubt.* **Studies show that we rank fast and frequent talkers as more competent, likable and even smarter than slow ones.** As the psychologists William Hart and Dolores Albarracin point out, phrases like "get active," "get moving," "do something" and similar calls to action surface repeatedly in recent books. (par. 10)
Research findings supporting Cain's idea	
Author and credentials in signal phrase	
Links between Cain's idea and research findings	

ANALYZE & WRITE

Write a paragraph analyzing another passage in which Cain integrates source material to support her explanation:

1. Review paragraphs 19, 20, or 21 to see how Cain uses a similar pattern. Mark the following elements: Cain's idea; the name(s) and credentials of the source or sources; what the source found; text linking the source's findings to the original idea or extending the idea in some way.

2. Explain why writers, when using information from sources, often begin by stating their own idea (even if they got the idea from a source). What would be the effect on readers if the opening sentence of paragraph 18 or 20 began with the source instead of with Cain's topic sentence?

Engaging Readers' Interest

Writers explaining concepts may engage readers' interest in a variety of ways. For example, they may

- remind readers of what they already know about the concept;

- show readers a new way of using or regarding a familiar concept;

- connect the concept, sometimes through *metaphor* or *analogy*, to common human experiences; or

- present the concept in a humorous way to convince readers that learning about a concept can be pleasurable.

ANALYZE & WRITE

Write a paragraph analyzing how Cain engages her readers:

1. Note the strategies Cain uses in three or four of the following paragraphs: 1, 4, 7, 8, 11–12, 21–22, 25, and 27.

2. Explain how Cain engages her readers' interest in the concept of introversion, using examples from your notes to support your explanation.

READINGS

John Tierney

Do You Suffer from Decision Fatigue?

John Tierney (b. 1953) is a contributing editor of *City Journal* and a contributing science columnist for the *New York Times*. He has written for many other magazines and newspapers, among them the *Atlantic Monthly, Discover, Esquire, Newsweek, Outside,* and the *Wall Street Journal.* In collaboration with novelist Christopher Buckley, Tierney co-wrote the comic novel, *God Is My Broker* (2012). The essay below, originally published in 2011 in the *New York Times Magazine,* was adapted from a book he wrote with Roy F. Baumeister, *Willpower: Rediscovering the Greatest Human Strength* (2011).

- **Before you read,** think about your own views about willpower. Is yours strong, weak, or in between? What conditions affect the strength of your willpower?

- **As you read,** think about the assumptions many people have about decisions. For example, which decisions are more difficult than others? How are these assumptions borne out or challenged in this essay?

Three men doing time in Israeli prisons recently appeared before a parole board con- 1 sisting of a judge, a criminologist and a social worker. The three prisoners had completed at least two-thirds of their sentences, but the parole board granted freedom to only one of them. Guess which one:

> Case 1 (heard at 8:50 a.m.): An Arab Israeli serving a 30-month sentence for fraud.

> Case 2 (heard at 3:10 p.m.): A Jewish Israeli serving a 16-month sentence for assault.

> Case 3 (heard at 4:25 p.m.): An Arab Israeli serving a 30-month sentence for fraud.

There was a pattern to the parole board's decisions, but it wasn't related to the 2 men's ethnic backgrounds, crimes or sentences. It was all about timing, as researchers discovered by analyzing more than 1,100 decisions over the course of a year. Judges, who would hear the prisoners' appeals and then get advice from the other members of the board, approved parole in about a third of the cases, but the probability of being paroled fluctuated wildly throughout the day. Prisoners who appeared early in the morning received parole about 70 percent of the time, while those who appeared late in the day were paroled less than 10 percent of the time.

The odds favored the prisoner who appeared at 8:50 a.m. — and he did in fact 3
receive parole. But even though the other Arab Israeli prisoner was serving the same
sentence for the same crime—fraud—the odds were against him when he appeared
(on a different day) at 4:25 in the afternoon. He was denied parole, as was the Jewish
Israeli prisoner at 3:10 p.m, whose sentence was shorter than that of the man who
was released. They were just asking for parole at the wrong time of day.

There was nothing malicious or even unusual about the judges' behavior, which 4
was reported... by Jonathan Levav of Stanford and Shai Danziger of Ben-Gurion University.[1] The judges' erratic judgment was due to the occupational hazard of being,
as George W. Bush once put it, "the decider." The mental work of ruling on case after
case, whatever the individual merits, wore them down. This sort of decision fatigue
can make quarterbacks prone to dubious choices late in the game and C.F.O.'s prone
to disastrous dalliances late in the evening. It routinely warps the judgment of everyone, executive and nonexecutive, rich and poor—in fact, it can take a special toll on
the poor. Yet few people are even aware of it, and researchers are only beginning to
understand why it happens and how to counteract it.

Decision fatigue helps explain why ordinarily sensible people get angry at col- 5
leagues and families, splurge on clothes, buy junk food at the supermarket and can't
resist the dealer's offer to rustproof their new car. No matter how rational and high-
minded you try to be, you can't make decision after decision without paying a biological price. It's different from ordinary physical fatigue — you're not consciously
aware of being tired—but you're low on mental energy. The more choices you make
throughout the day, the harder each one becomes for your brain, and eventually it
looks for shortcuts, usually in either of two very different ways. One shortcut is to
become reckless: to act impulsively instead of expending the energy to first think
through the consequences. (Sure, tweet that photo! What could go wrong?) The other
shortcut is the ultimate energy saver: do nothing. Instead of agonizing over decisions,
avoid any choice. Ducking a decision often creates bigger problems in the long run,
but for the moment, it eases the mental strain. You start to resist any change, any
potentially risky move—like releasing a prisoner who might commit a crime. So the
fatigued judge on a parole board takes the easy way out, and the prisoner keeps
doing time.

Decision fatigue is the newest discovery involving a phenomenon called ego 6
depletion, a term coined by the social psychologist Roy F. Baumeister[2] ... [who]
began studying mental discipline in a series of experiments, first at Case Western and
then at Florida State University. These experiments demonstrated that there is a finite
store of mental energy for exerting self-control. When people fended off the temptation to scarf down M&M's or freshly baked chocolate-chip cookies, they were then
less able to resist other temptations. When they forced themselves to remain stoic
during a tearjerker movie, afterward they gave up more quickly on lab tasks requiring
self-discipline, like working on a geometry puzzle or squeezing a hand-grip exer-
ciser. Willpower turned out to be more than a folk concept or a metaphor. It really
was a form of mental energy that could be exhausted. The experiments confirmed
the 19th-century notion of willpower being like a muscle that was fatigued with use,

a force that could be conserved by avoiding temptation. To study the process of ego depletion, researchers concentrated initially on acts involving self-control—the kind of self-discipline popularly associated with willpower, like resisting a bowl of ice cream. They weren't concerned with routine decision-making, like choosing between chocolate and vanilla, a mental process that they assumed was quite distinct and much less strenuous. Intuitively, the chocolate-vanilla choice didn't appear to require willpower.

But then a postdoctoral fellow, Jean Twenge, started working at Baumeister's lab- 7 oratory right after planning her wedding. As Twenge studied the results of the lab's ego-depletion experiments, she remembered how exhausted she felt the evening she and her fiancé went through the ritual of registering for gifts. Did they want plain white china or something with a pattern? Which brand of knives? How many towels? What kind of sheets? Precisely how many threads per square inch?

"By the end, you could have talked me into anything," Twenge told her new 8 colleagues. The symptoms sounded familiar to them too, and gave them an idea. A nearby department store was holding a going-out-of-business sale, so researchers from the lab went off to fill their car trunks with simple products—not exactly wed-ding-quality gifts, but sufficiently appealing to interest college students. When they came to the lab, the students were told they would get to keep one item at the end of the experiment, but first they had to make a series of choices. Would they prefer a pen or a candle? A vanilla-scented candle or an almond-scented one? A candle or a T-shirt? A black T-shirt or a red T-shirt? A control group, meanwhile—let's call them the nondeciders—spent an equally long period contemplating all these same prod-ucts without having to make any choices. They were asked just to give their opinion of each product and report how often they had used such a product in the last six months.

Afterward, all the participants were given one of the classic tests of self-control: 9 holding your hand in ice water for as long as you can. The impulse is to pull your hand out, so self-discipline is needed to keep the hand underwater. The deciders gave up much faster; they lasted 28 seconds, less than half the 67-second average of the nondeciders. Making all those choices had apparently sapped their willpower....

Any decision, whether it's what pants to buy or whether to start a war, can be broken down into what psychologists call the Rubicon model of action phases, in honor of the river that separated Italy from the Roman province of Gaul. When Cae-sar reached it in 49 BC, on his way home after conquering the Gauls, he knew that a general returning to Rome was forbidden to take his legions across the river with him, lest it be considered an invasion of Rome. Waiting on the Gaul side of the river, he was in the "predecisional phase" as he contemplated the risks and benefits of starting a civil war. Then he stopped calculating and crossed the Rubicon, reaching the "postdecisional phase," which Caesar defined much more felicitously: "The die is cast."

The whole process could deplete anyone's willpower, but which phase of the 10 decision-making process was most fatiguing? To find out, Kathleen Vohs, a former col-league of Baumeister's now at the University of Minnesota, performed an experiment

[that] showed that crossing the Rubicon is more tiring than anything that happens on either bank—more mentally fatiguing than sitting on the Gaul side contemplating your options or marching on Rome once you've crossed. As a result, someone without Caesar's willpower is liable to stay put. To a fatigued judge, denying parole seems like the easier call not only because it preserves the status quo and eliminates the risk of a parolee going on a crime spree but also because it leaves more options open: the judge retains the option of paroling the prisoner at a future date without sacrificing the option of keeping him securely in prison right now.

Once you're mentally depleted, you become reluctant to make trade-offs, which 11 involve a particularly advanced and taxing form of decision making. In the rest of the animal kingdom, there aren't a lot of protracted negotiations between predators and prey. To compromise is a complex human ability and therefore one of the first to decline when willpower is depleted. You become what researchers call a cognitive miser, hoarding your energy. If you're shopping, you're liable to look at only one dimension, like price: just give me the cheapest. Or you indulge yourself by looking at quality: I want the very best (an especially easy strategy if someone else is paying).

Decision fatigue leaves you vulnerable to marketers who know how to time their 12 sales, as Jonathan Levav, the Stanford professor, demonstrated in experiments involving... new cars.... The car buyers... had to choose, for instance, among 4 styles of gearshift knobs, 13 kinds of wheel rims, 25 configurations of the engine and gearbox and a palette of 56 colors for the interior. As they started picking features, customers would carefully weigh the choices, but as decision fatigue set in, they would start settling for whatever the default option was. And the more tough choices they encountered early in the process—like going through those 56 colors to choose the precise shade of gray or brown—the quicker people became fatigued and settled for the path of least resistance by taking the default option. By manipulating the order of the car buyers' choices, the researchers found that the customers would end up settling for different kinds of options.... Whether the customers paid a little extra for fancy wheel rims or a lot extra for a more powerful engine depended on when the choice was offered and how much willpower was left in the customer....

It's simple enough to imagine reforms for the parole board in Israel—like, say, 13 restricting each judge's shift to half a day, preferably in the morning, interspersed with frequent breaks for food and rest. But it's not so obvious what to do with the decision fatigue affecting the rest of society.... Today we feel overwhelmed because there are so many choices.... Choosing what to have for breakfast, where to go on vacation, whom to hire, how much to spend—these all deplete willpower, and there's no telltale symptom of when that willpower is low. It's not like getting winded or hitting the wall during a marathon.

Ego depletion manifests itself not as one feeling but rather as a propensity to expe- 14 rience everything more intensely. When the brain's regulatory powers weaken, frustrations seem more irritating than usual. Impulses to eat, drink, spend and say stupid things feel more powerful (and alcohol causes self-control to decline further).... Like the depleted parole judges, [ego-depleted humans] become inclined to take the safer, easier option even when that option hurts someone else.

Links

1. Danziger, Shai, et al. "Extraneous Factors in Judicial Decisions." *Proceedings of the National Academy of Sciences for the United States of America*, vol. 108, no. 17, 26 Apr. 2011, pp. 6889–92.

2. "Dr. Roy Baumeister." *Faculty Directory*, Psychology Dept., Florida State U, 2013, psy. fsu.edu/faculty/baumeister.dp.html.

READING FOR MEANING

For help with reading strategies like summarizing and analyzing assumptions, see Chapter 2.

1. **Read to Summarize.** Write a sentence or two explaining what decision fatigue is.

2. **Read to Respond.** Write a paragraph analyzing anything that resonates with your experience or that supports or refutes Tierney's concern with decision fatigue, such as his assertion that it "leaves you vulnerable to marketers" (par. 13).

3. **Read to Analyze Assumptions.** Write a paragraph or two analyzing an assumption you find intriguing in Tierney's essay, such as:

    The assumption that people are unaware of how decision fatigue affects them. Tierney notes that decision fatigue "routinely warps the judgment of everyone... yet few people are even aware of it" (par. 4).

    - Can you think of a time in your life when you felt as if you couldn't make another decision? Were you aware of this feeling at the time even if you didn't label it "decision fatigue"?

    - Tierney offers many examples, often from studies, that show what happens when people lose willpower and become vulnerable because they are mentally depleted. As noted in the essay though, postdoctoral fellow Jean Twenge seems aware of this vulnerability, at least in retrospect: "By the end, you could have talked me into anything" (par. 8). To what extent does this example challenge Tierney's assumption that few people are even aware of mental depletion? If more people were aware of it, why and how might that matter?

    The assumption that decision fatigue affects all kinds of people. Tierney explains that "decision fatigue can make quarterbacks prone to dubious choices late in the game and C.F.O.'s prone to disastrous dalliances late in the evening. It routinely warps the judgment of everyone, executive and nonexecutive, rich and poor — in fact it can take a special toll on the poor..." (par. 4). "Decision fatigue helps explain why ordinarily sensible people get angry at colleagues and families, splurge on clothes, buy junk food at the supermarket and can't resist the dealer's offer to rustproof their new car" (par. 5).

- Why does Tierney think it is important to point out that decision fatigue affects everyone?
- Now that you have read Tierney's essay, have your assumptions about will-power — who has it, who doesn't, and why some seem to have more than others — changed?

READING LIKE A WRITER

Using Appropriate Writing Strategies

Writers of concept explanations rely on explanatory strategies, such as comparing and contrasting, or illustrating. Comparing and contrasting allows the writer to show how the concept is similar to and different from other concepts that may be familiar to the reader, while illustrating allows the writer to use examples to help readers understand the concept. Consider the passages below in which Tierney uses these strategies:

Concept A Concept B *Repeated* *sentence pattern*	The more choices you make throughout the day, the harder each one becomes for your brain, and eventually it looks for shortcuts, usually in either two very different ways. *One shortcut* is to become reckless: to act impulsively instead of expending the energy to first think through the consequences (Sure, tweet that photo! What could go wrong?) *The other shortcut* is the ultimate energy saver: do nothing (par. 5).
Illustration	As Twenge studied the results of the lab's ego-depletion experiments, she remembered how exhausted she felt the evening she and her fiancé went through the ritual of registering for gifts (par. 7).

ANALYZE & WRITE

Write a paragraph or two analyzing the kinds of writing strategies Tierney incorporates into his essay.

1. List other moments where Tierney uses the comparison/contrast and illustration strategies to help explain the concept of decision fatigue. How does each of these moments contribute to readers' understanding of this concept?

2. Are there other writing strategies that Tierney uses productively? For example, consider how he shows causes and effects through the illustrations he provides.

Jeff Howe

The Rise of Crowdsourcing

Jeff Howe, a journalist and author, is credited with coining the term "crowdsourcing" in the essay below, which was published in *Wired Magazine* in 2006. In 2008, he published *Why the Power of the Crowd Is Driving the Future of Business*, a book on the same subject. Howe is a professor of journalism at Northeastern University in Boston, Massachusetts, and a former Nieman Fellow at Harvard University. He previously worked as a contributing editor at *Wired Magazine* and has written for *Time, U.S. News & World Report, The Washington Post, Mother Jones*, and numerous other publications.

- **Before you read,** consider what you may already know about crowd-sourcing. To what extent are you familiar with the concept?

- **As you read,** pay attention to what Howe assumes his readers need to know about crowdsourcing. How does he use examples to help explain this term that was being introduced for the first time in this very essay?

1. THE PROFESSIONAL

Claudia Menashe needed pictures of sick people. A project director at the National   1
Health Museum in Washington, DC, Menashe was putting together a series of inter-active kiosks devoted to potential pandemics like the avian flu. An exhibition designer had created a plan for the kiosk itself, but now Menashe was looking for images to accompany the text. Rather than hire a photographer to take shots of people suffering from the flu, Menashe decided to use preexisting images—stock photography, as it's known in the publishing industry.

In October 2004, she ran across a stock photo collection by Mark Harmel, a free-   2
lance photographer living in Manhattan Beach, California. Harmel, whose wife is a doctor, specializes in images related to the health care industry. "Claudia wanted people sneezing, getting immunized, that sort of thing," recalls Harmel, a slight, soft-spoken 52-year-old.

The National Health Museum has grand plans to occupy a spot on the National   3
Mall in Washington by 2012, but for now it's a fledgling institution with little money. "They were on a tight budget, so I charged them my nonprofit rate," says Harmel, who works out of a cozy but crowded office in the back of the house he shares with his wife and stepson. He offered the museum a generous discount: $100 to $150 per photograph. "That's about half of what a corporate client would pay," he says. Menashe was interested in about four shots, so for Harmel, this could be a sale worth $600.

After several weeks of back-and-forth, Menashe emailed Harmel to say that,   4
regretfully, the deal was off. "I discovered a stock photo site called iStockphoto," she

wrote, "which has images at very affordable prices." That was an understatement. The same day, Menashe licensed 56 pictures through iStockphoto-for about $1 each.

iStockphoto, which grew out of a free image-sharing exchange used by a group of 5 graphic designers, had undercut Harmel by more than 99 percent. How? By creating a marketplace for the work of amateur photographers—homemakers, students, engineers, dancers. There are now about 22,000 contributors to the site, which charges between $1 and $5 per basic image. (Very large, high-resolution pictures can cost up to $40.) Unlike professionals, iStockers don't need to clear $130,000 a year from their photos just to break even; an extra $130 does just fine. "I negotiate my rate all the time," Harmel says. "But how can I compete with a dollar?"

He can't, of course. For Harmel, the harsh economics lesson was clear: The prod- 6 uct Harmel offers is no longer scarce. Professional-grade cameras now cost less than $1,000. With a computer and a copy of Photoshop, even entry-level enthusiasts can create photographs rivaling those by professionals like Harmel. Add the Internet and powerful search technology, and sharing these images with the world becomes simple.

At first, the stock industry aligned itself against iStockphoto and other so-called 7 microstock agencies like ShutterStock and Dreamstime. Then, in February, Getty Images, the largest agency by far with more than 30 percent of the global market, purchased iStockphoto for $50 million. "If someone's going to cannibalize your business, better it be one of your other businesses," says Getty CEO Jonathan Klein. iStockphoto's revenue is growing by about 14 percent a month and the service is on track to license about 10 million images in 2006—several times what Getty's more expensive stock agencies will sell. iStockphoto's clients now include bulk photo purchasers like IBM and United Way, as well as the small design firms once forced to go to big stock houses. "I was using Corbis and Getty, and the image fees came out of my design fees, which kept my margin low," notes one UK designer in an email to the company. "iStockphoto's micro-payment system has allowed me to increase my profit margin." Welcome to the age of the crowd. Just as distributed computing projects like UC Berkeley's SETI@home have tapped the unused processing power of millions of individual computers, so distributed labor networks are using the Internet to exploit the spare processing power of millions of human brains. The open source software movement proved that a network of passionate, geeky volunteers could write code just as well as the highly paid developers at Microsoft or Sun Microsystems. Wikipedia showed that the model could be used to create a sprawling and surprisingly comprehensive online encyclopedia. And companies like eBay and MySpace have built profitable businesses that couldn't exist without the contributions of users.

All these companies grew up in the Internet age and were designed to take 8 advantage of the networked world. But now the productive potential of millions of plugged-in enthusiasts is attracting the attention of old-line businesses, too. For the last decade or so, companies have been looking overseas, to India or China, for cheap labor. But now it doesn't matter where the laborers are—they might be down the block, they might be in Indonesia—as long as they are connected to the network.

Technological advances in everything from product design software to digital 9 video cameras are breaking down the cost barriers that once separated amateurs from professionals. Hobbyists, part-timers, and dabblers suddenly have a market for their efforts, as smart companies in industries as disparate as pharmaceuticals and television discover ways to tap the latent talent of the crowd. The labor isn't always free, but it costs a lot less than paying traditional employees. It's not outsourcing; it's crowdsourcing.

It took a while for Harmel to recognize what was happening. "When the National 10 Health Museum called, I'd never heard of iStockphoto," he says. "But now, I see it as the first hole in the dike." In 2000, Harmel made roughly $69,000 from a portfolio of 100 stock photographs, a tidy addition to what he earned from commissioned work. Last year his stock business generated less money—$59,000—from more than 1,000 photos. That's quite a bit more work for less money.

Harmel isn't the only photographer feeling the pinch. Last summer, there was a 11 flurry of complaints on the Stock Artists Alliance online forum. "People were noticing a significant decline in returns on their stock portfolios," Harmel says. "I can't point to iStockphoto and say it's the culprit, but it has definitely put downward pressure on prices." As a result, he has decided to shift the focus of his business to assignment work. "I just don't see much of a future for professional stock photography," he says.

2. THE PACKAGER

"Is that even a real horse? It looks like it doesn't have any legs," says Michael 12 Hirschorn, executive vice president of original programming and production at VH1 and a creator of the cable channel's hit show *Web Junk 20*. The program features the 20 most popular videos making the rounds online in any given week. Hirschorn and the rest of the show's staff are gathered in the artificial twilight of a VH1 editing room, reviewing their final show of the season. The horse in question is named Patches, and it's sitting in the passenger seat of a convertible at a McDonald's drive-through window. The driver orders a cheeseburger for Patches. "Oh, he's definitely real," a producer replies. "We've got footage of him drinking beer." The crew breaks into laughter, and Hirschorn asks why they're not using that footage. "Standards didn't like it," a producer replies. Standards—aka Standards and Practices, the people who decide whether a show violates the bounds of taste and decency—had no such problem with Elvis the Robocat or the footage of a bicycle racer being attacked by spectators and thrown violently from a bridge. *Web Junk 20* brings viewers all that and more, several times a week. In the new, democratic age of entertainment by the masses, for the masses, stupid pet tricks figure prominently.

The show was the first regular program to repackage the Internet's funniest home 13 videos, but it won't be the last. In February, Bravo launched a series called *Outrageous and Contagious: Viral Videos*, and USA Network has a similar effort in the works. The E! series *The Soup* has a segment called "Cybersmack," and NBC has a pilot in development hosted by Carson Daly called *Carson Daly's Cyberhood*, which will attempt to bring beer-drinking farm animals to the much larger audiences of network TV. Al Gore's Current TV is placing the most faith in the model: More than 30 percent of its programming consists of material submitted by viewers.

Viral videos are a perfect fit for VH1, which knows how to repurpose content to 15
make compelling TV on a budget. The channel reinvented itself in 1996 as a pur-
veyor of tawdry nostalgia with *Pop-Up Video* and perfected the form six years later
with *I Love the 80s*. "That show was a good model because it got great ratings, and
we licensed the clips"—quick hits from such cultural touchstones as *The A-Team* and
Fatal Attraction—"on the cheap," Hirschorn says. (Full disclosure: I once worked for
Hirschorn at Inside.com.) But the C-list celebrity set soon caught on to VH1's searing
brand of ridicule. "It started to get more difficult to license the clips," says Hirschorn,
who has the manner of a laid-back English professor. "And we're spending more
money now to get them, as our ratings have improved."

But Hirschorn knew of a source for even more affordable clips. He had been 16
watching the growth of video on the Internet and figured there had to be a way to
build a show around it. "I knew we offered something YouTube couldn't: television,"
he says. "Everyone wants to be on TV." At about the same time, VH1's parent company,
Viacom, purchased iFilm—a popular repository of video clips—for $49 million. Just
like that, Hirschorn had access to a massive supply of viral videos. And because
iFilm already ranks videos by popularity, the service came with an infrastructure for
separating the gold from the god-awful. The model's most winning quality, as Hirschorn readily admits, is that it's "incredibly cheap"—cheaper by far than anything
else VH1 produces, which is to say, cheaper than almost anything else on television.
A single 30-minute episode costs somewhere in the mid-five figures—about a tenth
of what the channel pays to produce *so noTORIous*, a scripted comedy featuring
Tori Spelling that premiered in April. And if the model works on a network show like
Carson Daly's *Cyberhood*, the savings will be much greater: The average half hour of
network TV comedy now costs nearly $1 million to produce.

Web Junk 20 premiered in January, and ratings quickly exceeded even Hirschorn's 17
expectations. In its first season, the show is averaging a respectable half-million viewers in the desirable 18-to-49 age group, which Hirschorn says is up more than 40
percent from the same Friday-night time slot last year. The numbers helped persuade
the network to bring *Web Junk 20* back for another season.

Hirschorn thinks the crowd will be a crucial component of TV 2.0. "I can imagine 18
a time when all of our shows will have a user-generated component," he says. The
channel recently launched *Air to the Throne*, an online air guitar contest, in which
viewers serve as both talent pool and jury. The winners will be featured during the
VH1 Rock Honors show premiering May 31. Even VH1's anchor program, *Best Week
Ever*, is including clips created by viewers.

But can the crowd produce enough content to support an array of shows over 19
many years? It's something Brian Graden, president of entertainment for MTV Music
Networks Group, is concerned about. "We decided not to do 52 weeks a year of
Web Junk, because we don't want to burn the thing," he says. Rather than relying
exclusively on the supply of viral clips, Hirschorn has experimented with solic-
iting viewers to create videos expressly for *Web Junk 20*. Early results have been
mixed. Viewers sent in nearly 12,000 videos for the Show Us Your Junk contest.

"The response rate was fantastic," says Hirschorn as he and other staffers sit in the editing room. But, he adds, "almost all of them were complete crap."

Choosing the winners, in other words, was not so difficult. "We had about 20 19 finalists." But Hirschorn remains confident that as user-generated TV matures, the users will become more proficient and the networks better at ferreting out the best of the best. The sheer force of consumer behavior is on his side. Late last year the Pew Internet & American Life Project released a study revealing that 57 percent of 12- to 17-year-olds online—12 million individuals—are creating content of some sort and posting it to the Web. "Even if the signal-to-noise ratio never improves—which I think it will, by the way—that's an awful lot of good material," Hirschorn says. "I'm confident that in the end, individual pieces will fail but the model will succeed."

3. THE TINKERER

The future of corporate R&D can be found above Kelly's Auto Body on Shanty Bay 20 Road in Barrie, Ontario. This is where Ed Melcarek, 57, keeps his "weekend crash pad," a one-bedroom apartment littered with amplifiers, a guitar, electrical transducers, two desktop computers, a trumpet, half of a pontoon boat, and enough electric gizmos to stock a RadioShack. On most Saturdays, Melcarek comes in, pours himself a St. Remy, lights a Player cigarette, and attacks problems that have stumped some of the best corporate scientists at Fortune 100 companies.

Not everyone in the crowd wants to make silly videos. Some have the kind of sci- 21 entific talent and expertise that corporate America is now finding a way to tap. In the process, forward-thinking companies are changing the face of R&D. Exit the white lab coats; enter Melcarek-one of over 90,000 "solvers" who make up the network of scientists on InnoCentive, the research world's version of iStockphoto.

Pharmaceutical maker Eli Lilly funded InnoCentive's launch in 2001 as a way 22 to connect with brainpower outside the company-people who could help develop drugs and speed them to market. From the outset, InnoCentive threw open the doors to other firms eager to access the network's trove of ad hoc experts. Companies like Boeing, DuPont, and Procter & Gamble now post their most ornery scientific problems on InnoCentive's Web site; anyone on InnoCentive's network can take a shot at cracking them.

The companies — or seekers, in InnoCentive parlance—pay solvers anywhere 23 from $10,000 to $100,000 per solution. (They also pay InnoCentive a fee to participate.) Jill Panetta, InnoCentive's chief scientific officer, says more than 30 percent of the problems posted on the site have been cracked, "which is 30 percent more than would have been solved using a traditional, in-house approach."

The solvers are not who you might expect. Many are hobbyists working from their 24 proverbial garage, like the University of Dallas undergrad who came up with a chemical to use inart restoration, or the Gary, North Carolina, patent lawyer who devised a novel way to mix large batches of chemical compounds.

This shouldn't be surprising, notes Karim Lakhani, a lecturer in technology and 25 innovation at MIT, who has studied InnoCentive. "The strength of a network like

InnoCentive's is exactly the diversity of intellectual background," he says. Lakhani and his three coauthors surveyed 166 problems posted to InnoCentive from 26 different firms. "We actually found the odds of a solver's success increased in fields in which they had no formal expertise," Lakhani says. He has put his finger on a central tenet of network theory, what pioneering sociologist Mark Granovetter describes as "the strength of weak ties." The most efficient networks are those that link to the broadest range of information, knowledge, and experience.

Which helps explain how Melcarek solved a problem that stumped the in-house 26 researchers at Colgate-Palmolive. The giant packaged goods company needed a way to inject fluoride powder into a toothpaste tube without it dispersing into the surrounding air. Melcarek knew he had a solution by the time he'd finished reading the challenge: Impart an electric charge to the powder while grounding the tube. The positively charged fluoride particles would be attracted to the tube without any significant dispersion.

"It was really a very simple solution," says Melcarek. Why hadn't Colgate thought 27 of it? "They're probably test tube guys without any training in physics." Melcarek earned $25,000 for his efforts. Paying Colgate-Palmolive's R&D staff to produce the same solution could have cost several times that amount—if they even solved it at all. Melcarek says he was elated to win. "These are rocket-science challenges," he says. "It really reinforced my confidence in what I can do."

Melcarek, who favors thick sweaters and a floppy fishing hat, has charted an 28 unconventional course through the sciences. He spent four years earning his master's degree at the world-class particle accelerator in Vancouver, British Columbia, but decided against pursuing a PhD. "I had an offer from the private sector," he says, then pauses. "I really needed the money." A succession of "unsatisfying" engineering jobs followed, none of which fully exploited Melcarek's scientific training or his need to tinker. "I'm not at my best in a 9-to-5 environment," he says. Working sporadically, he has designed products like heating vents and industrial spray-painting robots. Not every quick and curious intellect can land a plum research post at a university or privately funded lab. Some must make HVAC systems.

For Melcarek, InnoCentive has been a ticket out of this scientific backwater. For the 29 past three years, he has logged onto the network's Web site a few times a week to look at new problems, called challenges. They are categorized as either chemistry or biology problems. Melcarek has formal training in neither discipline, but he quickly realized this didn't hinder him when it came to chemistry. "I saw that a lot of the chemistry challenges could be solved using electromechanical processes I was familiar with from particle physics," he says. "If I don't know what to do after 30 minutes of brainstorming, I give up." Besides the fluoride injection challenge, Melcarek also successfully came up with a method for purifying silicone-based solvents. That challenge paid $10,000. Other Melcarek solutions have been close runners-up, and he currently has two more up for consideration. "Not bad for a few weeks' work," he says with a chuckle.

It's also not a bad deal for the companies that can turn to the crowd to help curb 30 the rising cost of corporate research. "Everyone I talk to is facing a similar issue in regards to R&D," says Larry Huston, Procter & Gamble's vice president of innovation and knowledge. "Every year research budgets increase at a faster rate than sales. The current R&D model is broken."

Huston has presided over a remarkable about-face at P&G, a company whose cor- 31 porate culture was once so insular it became known as "the Kremlin on the Ohio." By 2000, the company's research costs were climbing, while sales remained flat. The stock price fell by more than half, and Huston led an effort to reinvent the way the company came up with new products. Rather than cut P&G's sizable in-house R&D department (which currently employs 9,000 people), he decided to change the way they worked.

Seeing that the company's most successful products were a result of collaboration 32 between different divisions, Huston figured that even more cross-pollination would be a good thing. Meanwhile, P&G had set a goal of increasing the number of innovations acquired from outside its walls from 15 percent to 50 percent. Six years later, critical components of more than 35 percent of the company's initiatives were generated outside P&G. As a result, Huston says, R&D productivity is up 60 percent, and the stock has returned to five-year highs. "It has changed how we define the organization," he says. "We have 9,000 people on our R&D staff and up to 1.5 million researchers working through our external networks. The line between the two is hard to draw."

P&G is one of InnoCentive's earliest and best customers, but the company works 33 with other crowdsourcing networks as well. YourEncore, for example, allows companies to find and hire retired scientists for one-off assignments. NineSigma is an online marketplace for innovations, matching seeker companies with solvers in a marketplace similar to InnoCentive. "People mistake this for outsourcing, which it most definitely is not," Huston says. "Outsourcing is when I hire someone to perform a service and they do it and that's the end of the relationship. That's not much different from the way employment has worked throughout the ages. We're talking about bringing people in from outside and involving them in this broadly creative, collaborative process. That's a whole new paradigm."

4. THE MASSES

In the late 1760s, a Hungarian nobleman named Wolfgang von Kempelen built 34 the first machine capable of beating a human at chess. Called the Turk, von Kempelen's automaton consisted of a small wooden cabinet, a chessboard, and the torso of a turbaned mannequin. The Turk toured Europe to great acclaim, even besting such luminaries as Benjamin Franklin and Napoleon. It was, of course, a hoax. The cabinet hid a flesh-and-blood chess master. The Turk was a fancy-looking piece of technology that was really powered by human intelligence. Which explains why Amazon.com has named its new crowdsourcing engine after von Kempelen's contraption. Amazon Mechanical Turk is a Web-based marketplace that helps companies find people to perform tasks computers are generally lousy at—identifying items in a photograph, skimming real estate documents to find identifying information, writing short product descriptions, transcribing podcasts. Amazon calls the tasks HITs (human intelligence tasks); they're designed to require very little time, and consequently they offer very little compensation—most from a few cents to a few dollars.

InnoCentive and iStockphoto are labor markets for specialized talents, but just 35 about anyone possessing basic literacy can find something to do on Mechanical Turk. It's crowdsourcing for the masses. So far, the program has a mixed track record: After an initial burst of activity, the amount of work available from requesters—companies offering work on the site—has dropped significantly. "It's gotten a little gimpy," says Alan Hatcher, founder of Turker Nation, a community forum. "No one's come up with the killer app yet." And not all of the Turkers are human: Some would-be workers use software as a shortcut to complete the tasks, but the quality suffers. "I think half of the people signed up are trying to pull a scam," says one requester who asked not to be identified. "There really needs to be a way to kick people off the island."

Peter Cohen, the program's director, acknowledges that Mechanical Turk, launched 36 in beta in November, is a work in progress. (Amazon refuses to give a date for its official launch.) "This is a very new idea, and it's going to take some time for people to wrap their heads around it," Cohen says. "We're at the tippy-top of the iceberg."

A few companies, however, are already taking full advantage of the Turkers. Sunny 37 Gupta runs a software company called iConclude just outside Seattle. The firm creates programs that streamline tech support tasks for large companies, like Alaska Airlines. The basic unit of iConclude's product is the repair flow, a set of steps a tech support worker should take to resolve a problem.

Most problems that iConclude's software addresses aren't complicated or 38 time-consuming, Gupta explains. But only people with experience in Java and Microsoft systems have the knowledge required to write these repair flows. Finding and hiring them is a big and expensive challenge. "We had been outsourcing the writing of our repair flows to a firm in Boise, Idaho," he says from a small office overlooking a Tully's Coffee. "We were paying $2,000 for each one."

As soon as Gupta heard about Mechanical Turk, he suspected he could use it to 39 find people with the sort of tech support background he needed. After a couple of test runs, iConclude was able to identify about 80 qualified Turkers, all of whom were eager to work on iConclude's HITs. "Two of them had quit their jobs to raise their kids," Gupta says. "They might have been making six figures in their previous lives, but now they were happy just to put their skills to some use."

Gupta turns his laptop around to show me a flowchart on his screen. "This is what 40 we were paying $2,000 for. But this one," he says, "was authored by one of our Turkers." I ask how much he paid. His answer: "Five dollars."

READING FOR MEANING

1. **Read to Summarize.** Write a sentence or two explaining the concept of crowdsourcing and how it differs from outsourcing.

2. **Read to Respond.** Write a paragraph analyzing anything that resonates with your experience or surprises you from this early description of crowdsourcing, such as how people confused crowdsourcing with

For help with reading strategies like summarizing and analyzing assumptions, see Chapter 2.

outsourcing (par. 9). Which companies, websites, television shows, and organizations that depend on crowdsourcing have emerged since Howe wrote this essay? Do you think crowdsourcing has become as influential a concept as Howe anticipated?

3. **Read to Analyze Assumptions.** Write a paragraph or two analyzing the assumptions you find intriguing in Howe's essay, such as

> *The assumption that expertise requires formal training.* Howe challenges the assumption that expertise requires formal training when he cites Lakani's explanation for one of the reasons that crowdsourcing has been so successful: "The odds of a solver's success increased in fields in which they had no formal expertise" (par. 25).

- What assumptions do you have about what makes an expert? Does training matter? Is a formal education necessary? Having read Howe's essay, have your assumptions about what it takes to be an expert changed?

- Do you or anyone you know participate in any form of crowdsourcing by lending expertise, content, or other material to a company or website? How does this inform your assumptions about what it means to be an expert?

> *Assumptions about what motivates people.* Howe focuses on how much "solvers" were paid at the time, which ranged from $5 (par. 5) to $100,000 (par. 23). He also cites Gupta's point that these solvers "might have been making six figures in their previous lives, but now they were happy just to put their skills to some use" (par. 39).

- What do you think motivates people beyond pay? Why would someone who has given up a six-figure salary be content to just have the opportunity to continue using their skills for little or no compensation?

- What has motivated you throughout your life? Are there similarities between what has motivated you and any of Howe's descriptions of the "solvers"?

READING LIKE A WRITER

Integrating Sources Smoothly

Writers of concept explanations usually conduct research and incorporate information (summaries, paraphrases, and quotations) from sources. They provide information about their sources to indicate why they should be trusted. For example, when describing a study to support her claim that "[w]e even find 'introverts' in the animal kingdom" (par. 13), Cain names the researcher and identifies his academic specialty: "In an illustrative experiment, David Sloan Wilson, a Binghamton evolutionary biologist, dropped metal traps into a pond of pumpkinseed sunfish" (par. 14). In "Crowdsourcing," Jeff Howe provides the academic credentials of one of his key sources:

Credentials   This shouldn't be surprising, notes Karim Lakhani, <u>a lecturer in technology and innovation at MIT</u>, who has studied InnoCentive (par. 25).

ANALYZE & WRITE

Write a paragraph or two analyzing the kinds of material Howe incorporates from sources, and how he identifies his sources so that his readers know that they are relevant and **credible** (reliable and believable).

1. Skim the essay, highlighting places where Howe quotes, paraphrases, or summarizes information from sources. How does he identify those sources? What information does he provide, and how does this information help readers know the source is relevant and reliable?

2. Now look at the material that is in quotations. Why would Howe choose to quote these sources, rather than summarize or paraphrase them?

Combining Reading Strategies

Synthesizing Information from Sources to Support Claims and Provide Context

Synthesizing information is a strategy academic writers use regularly as they read sources to discover, support, challenge, or extend their ideas. It is also a skill writers use to support their claims in research-based writing. In some cases, the information that is being synthesized helps to provide important context for the reader. *Contextualizing* is a strategy that academic writers use to provide cultural and historical context so that readers better understand the significance and relevance of what they are reading. To analyze how in "The Rise of Crowdsourcing" Jeff Howe synthesizes information from sources to support his claims and provide context, complete the following writing prompts.

For guidelines on synthesizing, see Chapter 2, pp. 47–48. For guidelines on Contextualizing, see Chapter 2, pp. 50–51.

- Highlight the sources he quotes, paraphrases, or summarizes. Look for signal phrases (made up of a reference to a speaker or source author and an appropriate verb), which often come after the quotations in his essay, such as in the following example: "'If someone's going to cannibalize your business, better it be one of your other businesses,' says Getty CEO Jonathan Klein" (par. 7).

- Review the sections you highlighted. Write a paragraph addressing in which cases Howe uses information from the different sources he cites to support this central idea, as well as in which cases these sources provide context that helps you understand the cultural and historical significance of crowdsourcing.

Melanie Tannenbaum

The Problem When Sexism Just Sounds So Darn Friendly

Melanie Tannenbaum received her Ph.D. in quantitative psychology from the University of Illinois at Urbana–Champaign, where she also taught. She is now a freelance science communications strategist, consultant, science writer, and psychology blogger who has contributed pieces to *The Complete Guide to Science Blogging* (2015), *The Open Laboratory Anthology for the Best Science Writing Online* (2012, 2013), the *British Psychological Society Research Digest,* and *In-Mind Magazine,* as well as peer-reviewed scientific journals. She founded *PsySociety* on the *Scientific American* blog network, where the following essay was published in 2013. Because she wrote for a scientific blog, Tannenbaum uses APA-citation style (see Chapter 12, pp. 645–654); accordingly, we have adapted the original hyperlinks as in-text citations.

- **Before you read,** recall times when you may have been a victim of sexism (whatever your gender). What were the situations in which you felt you were being judged merely on the basis of your gender or how others perceived your gender?

- **As you read,** consider how Tannenbaum's presentation of the "benevolent sexism" concept and the key words she uses makes you react. Do you identify with her word choice and examples, or do they make you feel confused or offended? Identify ways that Tannenbaum anticipates and acknowledges the sensitivity of the topic.

Something can't *actually* be sexist if it's really, really nice, right?   1

I mean, if someone compliments me on my looks or my cooking, that's not 2 sexist. That's awesome! I should be thrilled that I'm being noticed for something positive!

Yet there are many comments that, while seemingly complimentary, somehow 3 still feel wrong. These comments may focus on an author's appearance rather than the content of her writing, or mention how surprising it is that she's a woman, being that her field is mostly filled with men. Even though these remarks can sometimes feel good to hear — and no one is denying that this type of comment *can* feel good, especially in the right context — they can also cause a feeling of unease, particularly when one is in the position of trying to draw attention towards her work rather than personal qualities like her gender or appearance.

In social psychology, these seemingly-positive-yet-still-somewhat-unsettling com- 4 ments and behaviors have a name: *Benevolent Sexism.* Although it is tempting to brush this experience off as an overreaction to compliments or a misunderstanding of benign intent, benevolent sexism is both real and insidiously dangerous.

WHAT IS BENEVOLENT SEXISM?

In 1996, Peter Glick and Susan Fiske wrote a paper on the concept of *ambivalent*   5
sexism, noting that despite common beliefs, there are actually two different kinds of
sexist attitudes and behavior. *Hostile sexism* is what most people think of when they
picture "sexism" — angry, explicitly negative attitudes towards women. However, the
authors note, there is also something called *benevolent sexism*:

> We define benevolent sexism as a set of interrelated attitudes toward women
> that are sexist in terms of viewing women stereotypically and in restricted
> roles but that are subjectively positive in feeling tone (for the perceiver) and
> also tend to elicit behaviors typically categorized as prosocial (e.g., helping)
> or intimacy-seeking (e.g., self-disclosure) (Glick & Fiske, 1996, p. 491).
>
> [Benevolent sexism is] a subjectively positive orientation of protection,
> idealization, and affection directed toward women that, like hostile sexism,
> serves to justify women's subordinate status to men (Glick et al., 2000, p. 763).

Yes, there's actually an official name for all of those comments and stereotypes   6
that can somehow feel both nice and wrong at the same time, like the belief that
women are "delicate flowers" who need to be protected by men, or the notion that
women have the special gift of being "more kind and caring" than their male counterparts. It might sound like a compliment, but it still counts as sexism.

For a very recent example of how benevolent sexism might play out in our everyday   7
lives, take a look at Jennie Dusheck's "Family Man Who Invented Relativity and Made
Great Chili Dies," a satirical piece which jokingly re-writes Albert Einstein's obituary.

To quote: 8

> He made sure he shopped for groceries every night on the way home from
> work, took the garbage out, and hand washed the antimacassars. But to his
> step daughters he was just Dad. "He was always there for us," said his step
> daughter and first cousin once removed Margo.
>
> Albert Einstein, who died on Tuesday, had another life at work, where
> he sometimes slipped away to peck at projects like showing that atoms
> really exist. His discovery of something called the photoelectric effect won
> him a coveted Nobel Prize.

Looks weird, right? Kind of like something you would never actually see in print?   9
Yet the author of rocket scientist Yvonne Brill's obituary didn't hesitate before writing the following about her last week:

> She made a mean beef stroganoff, followed her husband from job to job,
> and took eight years off from work to raise three children. "The world's best
> mom," her son Matthew said.
>
> But Yvonne Brill, who died on Wednesday at 88 in Princeton, N.J., was
> also a brilliant rocket scientist, who in the early 1970s invented a propulsion
> system to help keep communications satellites from slipping out of their
> orbits. (Comparing: Yvonne Brill, 2013)

In fact, Obituaries editor William McDonald still sees nothing wrong with it. In his 10 words, he's "surprised... [because] it never occurred to [him] that this would be read as sexist," and if he had to re-write it again, he still "wouldn't do anything differently."

I want to make one thing perfectly clear. There's not a problem with mentioning 11 Brill's family, friends, and loved ones. It's not a problem to note how wonderfully Brill balanced her domestic and professional lives. Brill was a female scientist during a time when very few women could occupy that role in society, and that means something truly important.

But the *problem* here is really that if "Yvonne" were "Yvan," the obit would have 12 looked fundamentally different. If we're talking up the importance of work-life balance and familial roles for women but we're not also mentioning those things about men, that's a problem. If a woman's accomplishments must be accompanied by a reassurance that she really was "a good Mom," but a man's accomplishments are allowed to stand on their own, that's a problem. And lest you think that I only care about women, let's not act like this doesn't have a real and dangerous impact on men, too. If a man spends years of his life as a doting father and caring husband, yet his strong devotion to his family is not considered an important fact for his obituary because he's male... then yes, that's also a **big** problem.

The fact that so many people don't understand why it might be unnerving that the 13 writer's idea for a good story arc in Brill's obituary was to lead with her role as a wife and mother, and then let the surprise that she was *actually a really smart rocket scientist* come in later as a shocking twist? That's benevolent sexism.

WHY IS BENEVOLENT SEXISM A PROBLEM?

Admittedly, this research begs an obvious question. If benevolently sexist comments 14 seem like nothing more than compliments, why are they problematic? Is it really "sexism" if the content of the statements seems positive towards women?

After all, the obituary noted nothing more than how beloved Brill was as a wife 15 and a mother. Why should anyone be upset by that? Sure, men wouldn't be written about in the same way, but who cares? It's so nice!

Well, for one thing, benevolently sexist statements aren't *all* sunshine and butter- 16 flies. They often end up implying that women are weak, sensitive creatures that need to be "protected." While this may seem positive to some, for others — especially women in male-dominated fields — it creates a damaging stereotype.

As Glick and Fiske themselves note in their seminal paper: 17

> We do not consider benevolent sexism a good thing, for despite the positive feelings it may indicate for the perceiver, its underpinnings lie in traditional stereotyping and masculine dominance (e.g., the man as the provider and woman as his dependent), and its consequences are often damaging. Benevolent sexism is not necessarily experienced as benevolent by the recipient. For example, a man's comment to a female coworker on how "cute" she looks, however well-intentioned, may undermine her feelings of being taken seriously as a professional (Glick & Fiske, 1996, pp. 491–492).

In a later paper, Glick and Fiske went on to determine the extent to which 15,000   18
men and women across 19 different countries endorse both hostile and benevolently
sexist statements. First of all, they found that hostile and benevolent sexism tend to
correlate highly across nations. So, it is *not* the case that people who endorse hostile sexism don't tend to endorse benevolent sexism, whereas those who endorse
benevolent sexism look nothing like the "real" sexists. On the contrary, those who
endorsed benevolent sexism were likely to admit that they *also* held explicit, hostile
attitudes towards women (although one does not necessarily *have* to endorse these
hostile attitudes in order to engage in benevolent sexism).

Secondly, they discovered that benevolent sexism was a significant predictor of   19
nationwide gender inequality, **independent of the effects of hostile sexism**. In countries where the men were more likely to endorse benevolent sexism, *even when controlling for hostile sexism*, men also lived longer, were more educated, had higher
literacy rates, made significantly more money, and actively participated in the political and economic spheres more than their female counterparts. The warm, fuzzy
feelings surrounding benevolent sexism come at a cost, and that cost is often actual,
objective gender equality.

THE INSIDIOUS NATURE OF BENEVOLENT SEXISM

A recent paper by Julia Becker and Stephen Wright details even more of the insidious   20
ways that benevolent sexism might be harmful for both women and social activism.
In a series of experiments, women were exposed to statements that either illustrated
hostile sexism (e.g., "Women are too easily offended") or benevolent sexism (e.g.,
"Women have a way of caring that men are not capable of in the same way"). The
results are quite discouraging; when the women read statements illustrating benevolent sexism, they were less willing to engage in anti-sexist collective action, such as
signing a petition, participating in a rally, or generally "acting against sexism." Not
only that, but this effect was partially mediated by the fact that women who were
exposed to benevolent sexism were more likely to think that there are many advantages to being a woman and were also more likely to engage in *system justification*,
a process by which people justify the status quo and believe that there are no longer
problems facing disadvantaged groups (such as women) in modern day society. Furthermore, women who were exposed to hostile sexism actually displayed the opposite effect — they were *more* likely to intend to engage in collective action, and *more*
willing to fight against sexism in their everyday lives.

How might this play out in a day-to-day context? Imagine that there's an anti-   21
female policy being brought to a vote, like a regulation that would make it easier for
local businesses to fire pregnant women once they find out that they are expecting.
If you are collecting signatures for a petition or trying to gather women to protest this
policy and those women were recently exposed to a group of men making comments
about the policy in question, it would be significantly easier to gain their support and
vote down the policy if the men were commenting that pregnant women *should* be
fired because they were dumb for getting pregnant in the first place. However, if they

instead happened to mention that women are much more compassionate than men and make better stay-at-home parents as a result, these remarks might actually lead these women to be less likely to fight an objectively sexist policy.

"I MEAN, IS SEXISM REALLY STILL A PROBLEM?"

We often hear people claiming that sexism, racism, or other forms of discrimination 22 that seem to be outdated are "no longer really a problem." Some people legitimately believe this to be true, while others (particularly women and racial minorities) find it ridiculous that others could be so blind to the problems that still exist. So why does this disparity exist? Why is it so difficult for so many people to see that sexism and racism are still alive and thriving?

Maybe the answer lies right here, on the benevolent side of prejudice. While "old 23 fashioned" forms of discrimination may have died down quite a bit (after all, it really isn't quite as socially acceptable in most areas of the world to be as explicitly sexist and/or racist as people have been in the past), more "benevolent" forms of discrimination still very much exist, and they have their own sneaky ways of suppressing equality. Unaffected bystanders (or perpetrators) may construe benevolently sexist sentiments as harmless or even beneficial; in fact, as demonstrated by Becker and Wright, targets may even feel better about themselves after exposure to benevolently sexist statements. This could be, in some ways, even worse than explicit, hostile discrimination; because it hides under the guise of compliments, it's easy to use benevolent sexism to demotivate people against collective action or convince people that there is no longer a need to fight for equality.

However, to those people who *still* may be tempted to argue that benevolent 24 sexism is nothing more than an overreaction to well-intentioned compliments, let me pose this question: What happens when there is a predominant stereotype saying that women are better stay-at-home parents than men because they are inherently more caring, maternal, and compassionate? It seems nice enough, but how does this ideology affect the woman who wants to continue to work full time after having her first child and faces judgment from her colleagues who accuse her of neglecting her child? How does it affect the man who wants to stay at home with his newborn baby, only to discover that his company doesn't offer paternity leave because they assume that women are the better candidates to be staying at home?

At the end of the day, "good intent" is not a panacea. Benevolent sexism may very 25 well seem like harmless flattery to many people, but that doesn't mean it isn't insidiously dangerous.

To conclude, I'll now ask you to think about recent events surrounding Elise 26 Andrew, creator of the wildly popular "I F—king Love Science" Facebook page (www.facebook.com/IFeakingLoveScience). When she shared her personal Twitter account with the page's 4.4 million fans, many commented on the link because they were absolutely **SHOCKED**... about what? Why, of course, about the fact that she is female:

"I had no idea that IFLS had such a beautiful face!"

"holy hell, youre a HOTTIE!"

"you mean you're a girl, AND you're beautiful? wow, i just liked science a lil bit more today ^^"

"I thought that because of all the ways you were so proud to spout off "I f — king love science" in a difient swary manner against people who hated sware words being used that you was a dude."

"you're a girl!? I always imagined you as a guy; don't know why; well, nice to see to how you look like i guess"

"What?!!? Gurlz don't like science! LOL Totally thought you were a dude."

"It's not just being a girl that's the surprise, but being a fit girl! (For any non-Brits, fit, in this context, means hot/bangable/shagtastic/attractive)."

Right. See, that's the thing. Elise felt uncomfortable with this, as did many others out there who saw it—and rightfully so. Yet many people would call her (and others like her) oversensitive for feeling negatively about statements that appear to be compliments. Many thought that Elise should have been happy that others were calling her attractive, or pointing out that it's idiosyncratic for her to be a female who loves science. What Elise (and many others) felt was the benevolently sexist side of things—the side that perpetuates a stereotype that women (especially *attractive* women) don't "do" science, and that the most noteworthy thing to comment on about a female scientist is what she looks like.   27

Unfortunately, it's very likely that no one walked away from this experience having learned anything. People who could tell that this was offensive were obviously willing to recognize it as such, but people who endorsed those statements just thought they were being nice. Because they weren't calling her incompetent or unworthy, none of them were willing to recognize it as sexism, even when explicitly told that that's what it was—even though, based on research, we know that this sort of behavior has actual, meaningful consequences for society and for gender equality.   28

That right there?   29

That's the **real** problem with benevolent sexism.   30

References

Becker, J., & Wright, S. (2011). Yet another dark side of chivalry: Benevolent sexism undermines and hostile sexism motivates collective action for social change. *Journal of Personality and Social Psychology, 101*(1), 62–77. doi:10.1037/a0022615

Dusheck, J. (2013, April 1). Guest Post: Family Man Who Invented Relativity and Made Great Chili Dies. *The Last Word on Nothing.* Retrieved from www.lastwordonnothing.com/2013/04/01/guest-post-physicist-dies-made-great-chili/

Glick, P., & Fiske, S. (1996). The Ambivalent Sexism Inventory: Differentiating hostile and

   benevolent sexism. *Journal of Personality and Social Psychology, 70*(3), 491–512.

   doi:10.1037/0022-3514.70.3.491

Glick, P., Fiske, S., Mladinic, A., Saiz, J., Abrams, D., Masser, B., . . . López, W.

   (2000). Beyond prejudice as simple antipathy: Hostile and benevolent sexism

   across cultures. *Journal of Personality and Social Psychology, 79*(5), 763–775.

   doi:10.1037/0022-3514.79.5.763

Yvonne Brill, a pioneering rocket scientist, dies at 88. (2013). *News Diffs.* Retrieved from

   www.newsdiffs.org/diff/192021/192137/www.nytimes.com/2013/03/31/science/space/

   yvonne-brill-rocket-scientist-dies-at-88.html

READING FOR MEANING

For help
with reading
strategies like
summarizing
and analyzing
assumptions,
see Chapter 2.

1. **Read to Summarize.** Write a sentence or two explaining what Tannenbaum means when she defines "benevolent sexism" and where she sees evidence of it in society.

2. **Read to Respond.** Write a paragraph analyzing anything that seems surprising, such as the Obituaries editor's refusal to see benevolent sexism as problematic, even after it was pointed out to him (par. 11); or the finding by Glick and Fiske that "those who endorsed benevolent sexism were likely to admit that they also held explicit, hostile attitudes towards women" (par. 19). Does this response or the finding confuse or baffle you? Why?

3. **Read to Analyze Assumptions.** Write a paragraph or two analyzing an assumption you find intriguing in Tannenbaum's essay. For example:

   Assumptions about the dangers benevolent sexism poses. Tannenbaum uses the word *dangerous* to describe benevolent sexism in paragraphs 4, 13, and 26. She goes further, adding the word *insidious* to imply that this brand of sexism is more dangerous because it is often hidden and gradually harmful — to both women and men.

   - What social values does benevolent sexism threaten?
   - What kinds of danger does it pose to those who have been the objects of benevolent sexism or who are "tempt[ed] to brush this experience off as an overreaction . . . or a misunderstanding" (par. 4)? What should people do in the face of danger?

   The assumption that men and women should be treated equally in any and all situations. Tannenbaum points out that even compliments, if they bow to stereotypes, are sexist — they "feel wrong," and, even if they make you "feel good," they "cause a feeling of unease" (par. 3). She notes that different treatment — such as believing that women need to be protected or are more caring — may "sound like a compliment, but it still counts as sexism" (par. 6).

- Can you think of similar stereotypes that apply to men? What situations could lead men to complain of benevolent sexism? (See par. 25.)

- Is being *treated* equally in all situations the same as *being* equal in all situations? What would Tannenbaum say? Explain.

READING LIKE A WRITER

Organizing the Information Clearly and Logically

Think of an essay explaining a concept as a logical, interrelated sequence of topics. Each topic or main idea follows the preceding topic in a way that makes sense to readers and is cued by one or more of the following: a forecasting statement, a topic sentence, a section heading, a brief summary of what came before, or one or more transitions. Think of these as "road signs" that guide readers through the explanation. We see many of these *cueing devices* in Tannenbaum's essay.

Tannenbaum uses section headings to inform the reader of the focus of each section. For example, the first two section headings Tannenbaum uses are "What Is Benevolent Sexism?" and "Why Is Benevolent Sexism a Problem?" By using these headings, Tannenbaum allows the reader to easily scan her article while also cuing what topics she will cover. Within these and other sections, Tannenbaum also uses what we might call forecasting questions that pose a question that she will go on to answer, as in these examples:

Forecasting question | How might this play out in a day-to-day context? Imagine that there's an anti-female policy being brought to a vote... (par. 22).

If benevolently sexist comments seem like nothing more than compliments why are they problematic?... Well, for one thing, benevolent sexist statements aren't *all* sunshine and butterflies (par. 17).

ANALYZE & WRITE

Write a paragraph or two analyzing the strategies that Tannenbaum uses to make her concept explanation easy to follow.

1. Reread the section titled "I Mean, Is Sexism Really Still a Problem?" and keep track of how Tannenbaum uses forecasting questions to guide her readers. Did you find this strategy effective?

2. Skim Tannenbaum's essay, noting what other cueing devices — beyond section headings and forecasting questions — she uses to guide readers through her explanation. Which are most effective and which are least effective? Are there any moments where you lost track of where you were headed?

Michael Pollan

Altered State: Why "Natural" Doesn't Mean Anything

Michael Pollan (b. 1955) is an author, activist, and professor who writes about the intersection of nature and culture. He is a contributing writer for the *New York Times Magazine* and a former executive editor for *Harper's*. His essays have appeared in numerous anthologies, and he is the author of multiple books, including *How to Change Your Mind* (2018), *Cooked: A Natural History of Transformation* (2013, adapted for Netflix in 2016), *The Omnivore's Dilemma: A Natural History of Four Meals* (2006) and *In Defense of Food: An Eater's Manifesto* (2008). Pollan has won numerous prizes for his journalism and his books, among them the President's Citation Award from the American Institute of Biological Sciences (2009) and the Voices of Nature Award from the Natural Resources Defense Council (2009). He is the Lewis K. Chan Arts Lecturer and Professor of the Practice of NonFiction at Harvard University, and he also holds the position of John S. and James L. Knight Professor of Journalism at the University of California, Berkeley's Graduate School of Journalism. The essay below was published in the *New York Times Magazine* in 2015.

- **Before you read,** think about how you react when you hear the word *natural*. Do you attach it as an adjective to any particular noun, such as *natural childbirth*, or do you have a ready definition or association in your mind?

- **As you read,** consider how Pollan engages his readers: Is it the subject matter, the writing style, or something else?

It isn't every day that the definition of a common English word that is ubiquitous in common parlance is challenged in federal court, but that is precisely what has happened with the word "natural." During the past few years, some 200 class-action suits have been filed against food manufacturers, charging them with misuse of the adjective in marketing such edible oxymorons as "natural" Cheetos Puffs, "all-natural" Sun Chips, "all-natural" Naked Juice, "100 percent all-natural" Tyson chicken nuggets and so forth. The plaintiffs argue that many of these products contain ingredients—high-fructose corn syrup, artificial flavors and colorings, chemical preservatives and genetically modified organisms—that the typical consumer wouldn't think of as "natural." 1

Judges hearing these cases—many of them in the Northern District of California—have sought a standard definition of the adjective that they could cite to adjudicate these claims, only to discover that no such thing exists. 2

Something in the human mind, or heart, seems to need a word of praise for all that humanity hasn't contaminated, and for us that word now is "natural." Such an ideal can be put to all sorts of rhetorical uses. Among the antivaccination crowd, 3 for example, it's not uncommon to read about the superiority of something called "natural immunity," brought about by exposure to the pathogen in question rather than to the deactivated (and therefore harmless) version of it made by humans in laboratories. "When you inject a vaccine into the body," reads a post on an antivaxxer website, Campaign for Truth in Medicine, "you're actually performing an unnatural act." This, of course, is the very same term once used to decry homosexuality and, more recently, same-sex marriage, which the Family Research Council has taken to comparing unfavorably to what it calls "natural marriage."

So what are we really talking about when we talk about natural? It depends; the 4 adjective is impressively slippery, its use steeped in dubious assumptions that are easy to overlook. Perhaps the most incoherent of these is the notion that nature consists of everything in the world except us and all that we have done or made. In our heart of hearts, it seems, we are all creationists.

In the case of "natural immunity," the modifier implies the absence of human 5 intervention, allowing for a process to unfold as it would if we did nothing, as in "letting nature take its course." In fact, most of medicine sets itself *against* nature's course, which is precisely what we like about it—at least when it's saving us from dying, an eventuality that is perhaps more natural than it is desirable.

Yet sometimes medicine's interventions are unwelcome or go overboard, and 6 nature's way of doing things can serve as a useful corrective. This seems to be especially true at the beginning and end of life, where we've seen a backlash against humanity's technological ingenuity that has given us both "natural childbirth" and, more recently, "natural death."

This last phrase, which I expect will soon be on many doctors' lips, indicates the 7 enduring power of the adjective to improve just about anything you attach it to, from cereal bars all the way on up to dying. It seems that getting end-of-life patients and their families to endorse "do not resuscitate" orders has been challenging. To many ears, "D.N.R." sounds a little too much like throwing Grandpa under the bus. But according to a paper in the *Journal of Medical Ethics*, when the orders are reworded to say "allow natural death," patients and family members and even medical professionals are much more likely to give their consent to what amounts to exactly the same protocols.

The word means something a little different when applied to human behavior 8 rather than biology (let alone snack foods). When marriage or certain sexual practices are described as "natural," the word is being strategically deployed as a synonym for "normal" or "traditional," neither of which carries nearly as much rhetorical weight. "Normal" is by now too obviously soaked in moral bigotry; by comparison, "natural" seems to float high above human squabbling, offering a kind of secular version of what used to be called divine law. Of course, that's exactly the role that "natural law" played for America's founding fathers, who invoked nature rather than God as the granter of rights and the arbiter of right and wrong.

"Traditional" marriage might be a more defensible term, but traditional is a much 9 weaker modifier than natural. Tradition changes over time and from culture to culture, and so commands a fraction of the authority of nature, which we think of as timeless and universal, beyond the reach of messy, contested history.

Implicit here is the idea that nature is a repository of abiding moral and ethical 10 values—and that we can say with confidence exactly what those values are. Philosophers often call this the "naturalistic fallacy": the idea that whatever *is* (in nature) is what *ought to be* (in human behavior). But if nature offers a moral standard by which we can measure ourselves, and a set of values to which we should aspire, exactly what sort of values are they? Are they the brutally competitive values of "nature, red in tooth and claw," in which every individual is out for him- or herself? Or are they the values of cooperation on display in a beehive or ant colony, where the interests of the community trump those of the individual? Opponents of same-sex marriage can find examples of monogamy in the animal kingdom, and yet to do so they need to look past equally compelling examples of animal polygamy as well as increasing evidence of apparent animal homosexuality. And let's not overlook the dismaying rates of what looks very much like rape in the animal kingdom, or infanticide, or the apparent sadism of your average house cat.

The American Puritans called nature "God's Second Book," and they read it for 11 moral guidance, just as we do today. Yet in the same way we can rummage around in the Bible and find textual support for pretty much whatever we want to do or argue, we can ransack nature to justify just about anything. Like the maddening whiteness of Ahab's whale, nature is an obligingly blank screen on which we can project what we want to see.

So does this mean that, when it comes to saying what's natural, anything goes? 12 I don't think so. In fact, I think there's some philosophical wisdom we can harvest from, of all places, the Food and Drug Administration. When the federal judges couldn't find a definition of "natural" to apply to the class-action suits before them, three of them wrote to the F.D.A., ordering the agency to define the word. But the F.D.A. had considered the question several times before, and refused to attempt a definition. The only advice the F.D.A. was willing to offer the jurists is that a food labeled "natural" should have "nothing artificial or synthetic" in it "that would not normally be expected in the food." The F.D.A. states on its website that "it is difficult to define a food product as 'natural' because the food has probably been processed and is no longer the product of the earth," suggesting that the industry might not want to press the point too hard, lest it discover that *nothing* it sells is natural.

The F.D.A.'s philosopher-bureaucrats are probably right: At least at the margins, 13 it's impossible to fix a definition of "natural." Yet somewhere between those margins there lies a broad expanse of common sense. "Natural" has a fairly sturdy antonym—artificial, or synthetic—and, at least on a scale of relative values, it's not hard to say which of two things is "more natural" than the other: cane sugar or high-fructose corn syrup? Chicken or chicken nuggets? G.M.O.s or heirloom seeds? The most natural foods in the supermarket seldom bother with the word; any food product that feels compelled to tell you it's natural in all likelihood is not.

But it is probably unwise to venture beyond the shores of common sense, for it 14 isn't long before you encounter either Scylla or Charybdis. At one extreme end of the spectrum of possible meanings, there's nothing *but* nature. Our species is a result of the same process—natural selection—that created every other species, meaning that we and whatever we do are natural, too. So go ahead and call your nuggets natural: It's like saying they're made with matter, or molecules, which is to say, it's like saying nothing at all.

And yet at the opposite end of the spectrum of meaning, where humanity in some 15 sense stands outside nature—as most of us still unthinkingly believe—what is left of the natural that we haven't altered in some way? We're mixed up with all of it now, from the chemical composition of the atmosphere to the genome of every plant or animal in the supermarket to the human body itself, which has long since evolved in response to cultural practices we invented, like agriculture and cooking. Nature, if you believe in human exceptionalism, is over. We probably ought to search elsewhere for our values.

READING FOR MEANING

1. **Read to Summarize.** Write a few sentences explaining what the definition of *natural* means to Pollan and how he thinks our culture has shaped the word.

   For help with reading strategies like summarizing and analyzing assumptions, see Chapter 2.

2. **Read to Respond.** Write a paragraph analyzing anything that seems fascinating, such as the word *natural* having "the enduring power of the adjective to improve just about anything you attach it to, from cereal bars all the way on up to dying" (par. 7), and think about the power of language to influence your responses to an object or idea.

3. **Read to Analyze Assumptions.** Write a paragraph or two analyzing an assumption you find intriguing in Pollan's essay. For example:

   The assumption that "nature is a repository of abiding moral and ethical values" (par. 10). As Pollan asks, "what sort of values are they?"

   - Pollan considers the word *natural* as a "modifier [that] implies the absence of human intervention" (par. 5), which implies that association with humans is somehow wrong. Do you agree? How does this understanding affect people's approach to their food and other purchases?

   - Think about how you use the word *natural*. Does your use fall into any of the definitions Pollan provides, and what values does your definition assume?

   Assumptions that "common sense" (par. 13) dictates a path worth following—that extremes do not help us figure out what is important or how to behave well. Pollan explains that it's impossible to define *natural* "at the margins" (par. 13), but that if we consider its antonyms—artificial, synthetic—we can figure out what is truly "natural."

   - Is common sense easily come by? How do we know it when we see it?

   - Consider examples of "natural" in Pollan's essay and in your own experience. Can common sense serve us well as guidance in the context of determining what is natural?

READING LIKE A WRITER

Engaging Readers' Interest

While the content of an essay can be interesting in and of itself, writers explaining concepts try to engage readers' interest with a variety of strategies, such as telling stories or anecdotes, or asking questions. Pollan uses humor and **tone** (attitude or mood) to engage his readers. He starts his essay using exaggeratedly fancy vocabulary — "ubiquitous," "parlance," and "edible oxymorons" — to explain a plain-sounding word, "natural" (par. 1). He develops his examination of *natural* by giving several definitions: "Something in the human mind, or heart, seems to need a word of praise for all that humanity hasn't contaminated, and for us that word now is 'natural'" (par. 3).

ANALYZE & WRITE

Write a paragraph or two analyzing Pollan's tone and its effect on his audience.

1. Skim the essay, highlighting examples of Pollan's tone. Is it friendly? Meditative? Ironic? Bitter?
2. How does Pollan's tone engage readers? Does this strategy work well for you? Why or why not?

William Tucker

The Art and Creativity of Stop-Motion

William Tucker wrote this essay when he was a junior in college. He chose this topic because he had developed an interest in film, and particularly animated films, during an introductory film class. To focus his essay, he chose to write about stop-motion animation, one of the oldest forms of animation.

- **Before you read,** consider what you know about animated films. Do you enjoy watching them? Do you have a sense of what goes into making them?

- **As you read,** pay attention to how Tucker describes the challenges of using stop-motion animation. Does Tucker make it clear why, despite these challenges, filmmakers continue to use this early approach to animation?

Cinematography and filmmaking are present everywhere today. It is virtually impossible to go about your day without occasionally seeing a motion picture, whether it is a sitcom, an advertisement, or an instructional video. The process of producing films has changed in the past century, and many techniques have been invented and perfected. One style of film in particular has proven to stand the test of time. The style can be seen in popular productions such as *Gumby, Chicken Run, Fantastic Mr. Fox,* and the original *Godzilla* and *King Kong* movies. It played a key role in the origin of film and continues to be a relevant art form in the filming community, used both by famous Hollywood directors and by independent film students alike. It inspires creativity. This style, stop-motion film, is a critical part of film and cinematography. 1

Stop-motion, also known as frame-by-frame film production, is an animation technique in which a still camera photographs an object that is moved very small distances at a time. When these still images are played back quickly, they create the illusion of movement. The frame rate, or FPS (frames per second—the speed at which the individual photos are shown during the sequence), varies. The original stop-motion films usually never reached over 20 FPS because of the limitations of older technology (Johnson). However, today most stop-motion films vary from 25 FPS to as high as 30 FPS, depending on how quickly the director wants the inanimate object to appear to move (Johnson). 2

The technique of stop-motion is nearly as old as the motion picture itself. Albert E. Smith and J. Stuart Blackton are credited with being the first to use the technique in their 1898 film, *Humpty Dumpty Circus,* where toys and puppets appear to come alive on screen (Delahoyde). Stop-motion grew in popularity, as it allowed directors to depict fantasy and imagination while still providing realistic-looking scenes. For example, before computer-generated imagery (CGI), if a director wanted to make a dinosaur movie, the director could dress humans in dinosaur costumes, hire 3 animators to create a hand-drawn animated film, or use stop-motion with clay dinosaur figurines. Using dinosaur costumes would be easier than using stop-motion, but it would more often than not make the dinosaurs look tacky and unreal. Hand-drawn animation is lovely, but two-dimensional. A stop-motion film takes a long time and meticulous work to create, but it captivates audiences with its more authentic and "real" look. During the beginning years of animated film, stop-motion was critically acclaimed, winning many Oscars in the animated-film categories.

Stop-motion animators soon began to use clay figurines as the main focus in   4
stop-motion films; this technique is now known as claymation. Clay figurines allow inanimate objects to take on humanlike characteristics and are easy to manipulate quickly between individual photographs. Famous claymation stop-motion films include the hit 1970s television show *Gumby* and the short film *Vincent,* which helped a young Tim Burton attract the attention of Walt Disney Studios (Delahoyde). Burton would go on to revolutionize the stop-motion industry by crafting feature-length stop-motion films, such as *The Nightmare before Christmas, James and the Giant Peach,* and *The Corpse Bride.*

Stop-motion requires not only creativity but also patience and precision. With   5
stop-motion films now playing back at as high as 30 FPS, nearly nine thousand individual photographs are needed for just five minutes' worth of footage. Because of this, most stop-motion films, even those with a professional crew, are in production for as long as three years (Delahoyde). Stop-motion directors begin each scene by choosing an inanimate object to be the focus point of the scene. After the object is chosen, it is photographed and moved less than an inch between individual photographs. The camera is placed in a stationary position (a tripod is almost a necessity in order to keep the camera focusing on the same exact location for each photo) (Delahoyde). A major problem that stop-motion enthusiasts face is making sure that the backgrounds of frames are similar to one another. If the background is not exactly the same for each frame, noticeable errors like splotches and blurs can occur. Also, if the background is inconsistent, the film will look less convincing and may even give the audience headaches from the lack of visual consistency. For this reason, most creators shoot inside and make their own backgrounds, either by drawing one or by making a CGI-based background ("Stop Motion Filming Technique").

Those brave enough to shoot a stop-motion film outdoors must take into account   6
all the variables that can hurt the overall presentation of their film. If the film is being shot in a crowded place, the creator cannot allow pictures to be taken with people in the background. People in the background of the shot will cause inconsistency in the frames that will appear as colored splotches in the film, especially if the frame rate is extremely high ("Stop Motion Filming Technique"). Stop-motion directors must also take into account the weather and brightness of the outdoors. Since the process of taking photos for a stop-motion film takes an exorbitant amount of time, people making films may have to plan on being outdoors shooting a scene for many hours. Lighting changes as the sun moves throughout the day. If the outdoor scene doesn't have consistent lighting because of the sun's movements, the scenes

may suffer from unwanted shadows and different lighting at separate points in the scene. Consistency and attention to detail are the foundations of stop-motion film. They are perhaps the most important factors separating professional stop-motion films from amateur films.

Stop-motion still plays a key role in the filming world today. It has inspired new ⁊ film art forms that are heavily used. For example, time-lapse photography is a well-known technique used in film to quickly show the passing of time. Stop-motion helped lead to the time-lapse technique by stringing together individual photographs in order to represent movement and time ("Introduction"). The time-lapse process does take longer than typical stop-motion. In time-lapse photography, a camera focuses on an object for as long as a year, taking pictures periodically of the slow changes that occur. Then the many pictures are played in quick succession to show the changes. Popular subjects include the growth and blooming of a flower, a day and night's worth of city traffic, and the movement of the sun and moon. These scenes in nature take anywhere from a day to an entire year to take place, but with time-lapse/stop-motion the entire process can be viewed in as little as ten seconds, which creates an interesting illusion for the audience.

Although newer forms of cinematography are constantly being invented and 8 revised, stop-motion will forever be important in the film community. Although CGI has become the industry standard for movie animation, stop-motion is still flourishing. Popular sites such as YouTube allow creators to post original stop-motion videos; they can then be viewed by a wide audience. Some of the most popular films on the Internet today are stop-motion films, receiving hundreds of thousands of views daily. This art form will forever captivate viewers and inspire ingenuity, whether it is used for a simple amateur video or a feature-length film of epic proportions.

WORKS CITED

Delahoyde, Michael. "Stop-Motion Animation." *Dino-Source,* Washington State University,

public.wsu.edu/~delahoyd/stopmo.html. Accessed 19 Mar. 2018.

"Introduction to Stop Motion Animation." *Dragonframe,* www.dragonframe.com/introduc-

tion-stop-motion-animation. Accessed 20 Mar. 2018.

Johnson, Dave. "Make a Time-Lapse Movie." *Washington Post,* 9 Nov. 2005, www.washing-

tonpost.com/wp-dyn/content/article/2005/ll/08/ AR2005110800094.html.

"Stop Motion Filming Technique." *Animation 101,* ThinkQuest Library,1999, waybadc.

archive-it.org/3635/20130831143030/http://library.thinkquest.org/25398/Clay/tutorials/

stopmotion.html. Accessed 20 Mar. 2018.

"Tim Burton Talking about Animation." *Tim Burton Dream Site,* Minad-ream.com. Accessed

6 Nov. 2015.

READING FOR MEANING

For help
with reading
strategies like
summarizing
and analyzing
assumptions,
see Chapter 2.

1. **Read to Summarize.** Write a few sentences explaining the concept of stop-motion animation.

2. **Read to Respond.** Write a paragraph analyzing anything that seems surprising, such as how "stop-motion still plays a key role in the filming world today" (par. 7) or that "some of the most popular films on the Internet today are stop-motion films" (par. 8).

3. **Read to Analyze Assumptions.** Write a paragraph or two analyzing an assumption you find intriguing in Tucker's essay. For example:

   Assumptions about art. Tucker calls his essay "The Art and Creativity of Stop-Motion" and throughout his essay refers to stop-motion animation as a form of art. He notes at the end of his essay that this "art form will forever captivate viewers and inspire ingenuity" (par 8).

   - What assumptions does Tucker make about art? How does he define art in such a way that includes stop-motion animation?

   - What assumptions do you have about what counts as art? Where do these assumptions come from? Do you think that stop-motion animation is an art form? Why or why not? How do your ideas and values as they relate to art compare to those of your classmates?

   Assumptions about creativity. Tucker does not define creativity, but he says that stop-motion animation both inspires creativity (par. 1) and requires creativity (par. 5). He also uses the term "creativity" in the title of his essay.

   - What assumptions does Tucker make about creativity, and how does he demonstrate that stop-motion animation both inspires and requires creativity? Are you convinced by the evidence he offers?

   - How do you define creativity? What are your assumptions about creativity? Where do these assumptions come from?

READING LIKE A WRITER

Engaging Readers' Interest

Writers explaining concepts use different strategies to engage readers' interest. They may remind readers what they already know about the concept; show readers a new way of using or understanding a familiar concept; connect the concept to common human experiences; or present the concept in a humorous way.

ANALYZE & WRITE

Write a paragraph or two analyzing how Tucker uses these strategies to guide readers.

1. Reread paragraphs 1 and 4 of Tucker's essay. How does Tucker use titles of films to engage the readers' interest in the concept of stop-motion animation?

2. What other strategies does Tucker use to engage the readers' interest? Are they effective?

Writing to Learn Concept Explanation

Write a brief essay analyzing one of the readings in this chapter (or another selection, perhaps one by a classmate). Explain how (and perhaps, how well) the selection works as a concept explanation. Consider, for example, how it uses

- writing strategies such as definition, comparison/contrast, example, and illustration to develop the concept thoroughly;

- credible, appropriate sources to explain and support the concept;

- cues to signal transitions and repetition to organize explanation of the concept;

- strategies to engage and hold the reader's interest.

Your essay could also reflect on how you applied one or more of the following practices as you read the selection:

- **Critical Analysis** — what assumptions in the selection did you find intriguing, and why?

- **Rhetorical Sensitivity** — how effective or ineffective do you think the selection is in achieving its purpose for the intended audience?

- **Empathy** — did you find yourself identifying with the author, and how important was this to the effectiveness of the selection?

A GUIDE TO WRITING ESSAYS EXPLAINING CONCEPTS

You have probably done a good deal of analytical writing about your reading. Your instructor may also assign a capstone project to explain a concept of your own. This Guide to Writing offers detailed suggestions and resources to help you meet the special challenges this kind of writing presents.

THE WRITING ASSIGNMENT

Write an explanation of a concept that interests you enough to study further.

- Choose a concept that you know a good deal about or about which you'd like to learn.

- Consider what your readers already know about the concept and how your explanation can add to their knowledge.

- Research material that helps clarify or provides examples of your concept.

- Consider the most effective writing strategies to convey your concept.

- Think about how to engage your readers' interest in your concept and guide them through your explanation.

WRITING YOUR DRAFT

Choosing a Concept

Rather than limiting yourself to the first concept that comes to mind, take a few minutes to consider your options. Below are some criteria that can help you choose a promising concept to explain, followed by suggestions for the types of concepts you might consider writing about.

Choose a concept that

- you think is important and will interest your readers;

- you can research sufficiently in the allotted time;

- provides you with a clear purpose, such as to inform readers about an important idea or theory, to show how the concept has promoted original thinking and research, to help readers better understand the concept, or to demonstrate knowledge of the concept and the ability to apply it.

Below are some concepts from various fields of study:

- *Literature, philosophy, and art:* figurative language, postcolonialism, modernism, postmodernism; existentialism, nihilism, determinism; cubism, iconography, pop art, conceptual art, performance art, graffiti, surrealism, expressionism

- *Business management:* autonomous work group, quality circle, management by objectives, zero-based budgeting, benchmarking, focus group, pods

- *Psychology:* phobia, narcissism, fetish, emotional intelligence, divergent and convergent thinking, behaviorism, Jungian archetype, visualization

- *Government and law:* one person/one vote, federalism, socialism, theocracy, separation of church and state, political action committee, Electoral College; arbitration, liability, reasonable doubt, sexual harassment, nondisclosure agreement

- *Biology and environmental studies:* ecosystem, plasmolysis, DNA, homozygosity, diffusion, acid rain, recycling, ozone depletion, toxic waste, endangered species, greenhouse effect, climate change, hydrologic cycle, El Niño, xeriscape

- *Nutrition and public health:* vegetarianism, bulimia, food allergy, aerobic exercise, obesity, Maillard reaction, sustainability, locavore, epidemic, drug abuse, contraception, disability, autism

- *Physical sciences and math:* gravity, mass, energy, quantum theory, law of definite proportions, osmotic pressure, first law of thermodynamics, entropy, free energy, fusion, boundedness; complex numbers, exponent, polynomial, factoring, derivative, infinity

Analyzing Your Readers

Write for a few minutes, analyzing your potential readers:

- What might my potential readers already know about the concept or the field of study to which it applies?

- What kinds of examples or information could I provide that readers will find new, useful, interesting, or amusing? How might I clarify misconceptions or faulty assumptions?

- What kinds of sources will my readers find credible?

Researching the Concept

You will probably need to research your concept in three stages:

1. Gain an overview of the concept by considering what you already know and what you need to learn, and by conducting some preliminary research.

2. Choose an aspect of your concept to focus on, an aspect that you can **explore** thoroughly in the space and time you have.

3. Conduct enough research to learn about this aspect of the concept.

Determining What You Know (and Don't Know).   You can determine what you already know about your concept by explaining it briefly, using one or more of the strategies below as a starting point:

▶ My concept can be divided into .... types or categories: ...., ..., ..., and ....

▶ Examples of my concept include ...., ..., and ....

▶ My concept is a .... [member of a larger category] that is/does/has .... [defining characteristics].

▶ My concept is [similar to/different from] .... in these ways: ...., ..., and ....

Try to answer the questions you think your readers will have.

Conducting Background Research.   Talk to experts, such as a professor or teaching assistant for an academic topic, or your supervisor for a work-related topic. You could also post a question on a blog devoted to this subject.

You may want to consult some general reference sources or databases, such as the Gale Virtual Reference Library, SAGE Knowledge, or Web of Science, to conduct a preliminary search on your concept. (Check with a librarian to find out which reference databases your school subscribes to.) After reading articles in several relevant reference sources, list the following:

- names of scholars, experts, or respected authors on your subject;

- terms, phrases, or synonyms that you might use as search terms later;

- interesting aspects of the concept that you might want to focus on.

To learn more about conducting research and assessing credibility, see Chapter 12, pp. 583–626.

To conduct an Internet search on your concept, start by entering the word *overview* or *definition* with the name of your concept, and then skim the top ten search results to get a general sense of your topic.

Choosing an Aspect of Your Concept to Focus On.   List two or three aspects of your concept that interest you and then answer these questions:

- Why does this aspect of the concept interest me or my readers?

- How is it relevant to my family, community, work, studies, or readers?

- What are my readers likely to know about the concept? How can I build on what they already know?

Conducting Additional Research on Your Focused Concept. Your instructor may expect you to do in-depth research or may limit the number and type of sources you can use. Readers will want to be sure that your sources are reliable and relevant, and may want to read your sources for themselves, so include enough information in your notes to put your sources in context and to cite them accurately.

Working with Sources

Integrating Quotations from Experts into Your Writing. As you conduct background research on your chosen concept, consider whether incorporating sources into your essay will be productive. You may come across an expert on your concept or someone who has more experience with the concept than you. It may, therefore, be important to include quotations from this source in your essay. Notice how Tannenbaum incorporates a long quotation from Glick and Fiske's foundational paper on benevolent sexism into her essay:

> "We do not consider benevolent sexism a good thing, for despite the positive feelings it may indicate for the perceiver, its underpinnings lie in traditional stereotyping and masculine dominance (e.g., the man as the provider and woman as his dependent), and its consequences are often damaging. Benevolent sexism is not necessarily experienced as benevolent by the recipient..." (par 18).

Cain, on the other hand, incorporates shorter quotations from experts, often weaving them into her own sentences and using signal phrases at the end to highlight the quotation as opposed to the source:

> "Most inventors and engineers I've met are like me," he writes in *iWoz*, his autobiography. (par. 21)

Formulating a Working Thesis Statement

A working thesis will help you begin drafting your essay purposefully. Your thesis should announce the concept and focus of the explanation, and may also forecast the main topics. Here are two example thesis statements from the readings.

Concept Focus Forecast	This does us all a grave disservice, because shyness and introversion — or more precisely, the careful, sensitive temperament from which both often spring — are not just normal. They are valuable. And they may be essential to the survival of our species. (Cain, par. 5)
	In social psychology, these seemingly-positive-yet-still-somewhat-unsettling comments and behaviors have a name: *Benevolent Sexism.* Although it is tempting to brush this experience off as an overreaction to compliments or a misunderstanding of benign intent, benevolent sexism is both real and insidiously dangerous. (Tannenbaum, par. 4)

Using Appropriate Explanatory Strategies

To explain your concept effectively, consider how you would define it, what examples you can provide, how similar or different it is from other concepts, how it happens or gets done, and what its causes or effects are. Your goal is not only to inform but also to engage. The following sentence strategies may help you find the best ways to explain your concept.

- What are the concept's defining characteristics? What broader class does it belong to, and how does it differ from other members of its class? (*definition*)

  ▶ .... [Concept] is a .... in which .... [list defining characteristics].

- What examples or anecdotes can make the concept less abstract, more focused, and more understandable? (*example*)

  ▶ [Experts/scientists/etc.] first became aware of [concept] in [year], when .... (citation).

- How is this concept like or unlike related concepts with which your readers may be more familiar? (*comparison/contrast*)

  ▶ Many people think the term .... [concept] means .... , but it might be more accurate to say it means ....

- How can an explanation of this concept be divided into parts to make it easier for readers to understand? (*classification*)

  ▶ Experts like .... [name of expert] say there are .... [number] [categories, types, subtypes, versions] of .... [concept], ranging from .... ([citation]) to .... ([citation]).

- How does this concept happen, or how does one go about doing it? (*process narration*)

  ▶ To perform .... [concept or task related to concept], a [person, performer, participant, etc.] starts by .... Then [he/she/it] must .... [verb], ... [verb], and .... [verb].

- What are this concept's known causes or effects? (*cause and effect*)

  ▶ Experts disagree over the causes of .... [concept]. Some, like .... [name 1], believe .... ([citation]). Others, like .... [name 2], contend that .... ([citation]).

Including Visuals

For more on analyzing visuals, see Chapter 2, pp. 52–55.

Think about whether visuals — tables, graphs, drawings, photographs — would make your explanation clearer. You could construct your own visuals, download materials from the Internet, or scan and import visuals from books and magazines. Visuals are not a requirement of an essay explaining a concept, but they sometimes add a new dimension to your writing. If you include visuals you did not create yourself, be sure to cite the source(s) from which you borrow them.

Integrating Information from Sources

Summaries, paraphrases, and quotations from sources are frequently used to explain concepts or reinforce an explanation:

- Use a summary to give the gist of a research report or other information.

- Use a paraphrase to provide specific details or examples when the language of the source is not especially memorable.

- Use a quotation to emphasize source material that is particularly vivid or clear, to convey an expert's voice, or to discuss the source's choice of words.

Your readers will want you to explain how the ideas from the sources you cite reinforce the points you are making. Make sure you comment on your sources, clearly defining the relationship between your own ideas and the supporting information from sources.

For more help with integrating sources, see Chapter 12, pp. 615–626.

When introducing quotations, paraphrases, or summaries, writers often use a signal phrase — the source author's name plus an appropriate verb — to alert readers to the fact that they are borrowing someone else's words or ideas. Often the verb is neutral, as with the following example:

Credentials of source author

Signal phrase (name + verb)

The **psychologist** <u>Gregory Feist found</u> that many of the most creative people in a range of fields are introverts who are comfortable working in solitary conditions in which they can focus attention inward. (Cain, par. 21)

Notice in the example above that the writer also mentions the source's credentials, which is often an option when introducing sources with a signal phrase. Sometimes, however, writers choose a descriptive adjective or verb to introduce a source, such as *stresses, approvingly reports, vividly details, disparagingly writes, emphasizes, extols*, or *stays firm*. By choosing carefully among a wide variety of precise verbs, you can convey the attitude or approach of the source as you integrate supporting information.

Organizing Your Concept Explanation Effectively for Your Readers

The forecasting statement from your thesis can act as an informal outline when writing about simpler concepts, but for more complex concepts a tentative formal outline may be more useful.

Try to introduce new material in stages, so that readers' understanding of the concept builds slowly but steadily. Including a topic sentence for each paragraph or group of paragraphs on a single topic may help readers follow your explanation.

For help with outlining, see the model student essay in Chapter 1 (pp. 29–33) and the "outlining" coverage in Chapter 2.

An essay explaining a concept is made up of four basic parts:

1. an attempt to engage readers' interest in the explanation
2. the thesis statement, announcing the concept and perhaps also forecasting the sequence of topics
3. a description or definition of the concept
4. the information about the concept, organized around a series of topics that reflect how the information has been divided up

An initial attempt to gain your readers' interest — by starting with an intriguing question or surprising example, for instance — could take as little space as two or three sentences or as much as four or five paragraphs, but you will want to maintain your readers' interest throughout the essay by providing examples or information that readers will find new, useful, interesting, or amusing.

Consider any outline you create tentative before you begin drafting. As you draft, you will usually see ways to improve on your original plan. Be ready to revise your outline, shift parts around, or drop or add parts as you draft.

Drafting Your Concept Explanation

By this point, you have done a lot of writing

- to focus your explanation and develop a working thesis statement;
- to organize your explanation clearly for your readers;
- to try out writing strategies that can help you explain your concept;
- to integrate information into your explanation smoothly and in a way that supports your own ideas.

Now stitch that material together to create a draft. The next section of this Guide to Writing will help you evaluate and improve it.

REVIEWING AND IMPROVING THE DRAFT

This section includes guides for Peer Review and Troubleshooting Your Draft. Your instructor may arrange a peer review in class or online where you can exchange drafts with a classmate. The Peer Review Guide will help you give each other constructive feedback regarding the basic features and strategies typical of explaining a concept. (If you want to make specific suggestions for improving the draft, see Troubleshooting Your Draft on p. 272.) Also, be sure to respond to any specific concerns the writer has raised about the draft. The Troubleshooting Your Draft guide that follows will help you reread your own draft with a critical eye, sort through any feedback you've received, and consider a variety of ways to improve your draft.

A PEER REVIEW GUIDE

How effectively does the writer explain the concept?

What's Working Well: Point to a passage where the explanation of the concept is effective. For example, identify where the focus seems appropriate, or note where the strategy used to support the explanation—such as an example or a comparison—is helpful. (See Chapter 2 for more strategies.)

What Needs Improvement: Identify any passage where the explanation could be improved—for example, where the focus is too broad or too narrow, where you lose track of the concept description, or where you need an additional strategy to fill out the explanation.

How well is the essay arranged to help the reader understand the concept?

What's Working Well: Highlight especially effective sentences or paragraphs that help move the reader from topic to topic or advance an explanation that moves from general to specific (or from specific to general). Note strong uses of forecasting statements or topic sentences that keep the reader oriented through the explanation.

What Needs Improvement: Show the writer where transitions might be needed for material that appears suddenly, or where a forecasting statement or topic sentence might announce the main ideas more clearly.

How effectively is information from sources integrated into the concept explanation?

What's Working Well: Mark a passage where a source is clearly identified and the material is introduced with an appropriate signal phrase and perhaps a particularly engaging verb.

What Needs Improvement: Note any passages where you need more information about a source, or where the information from a source doesn't effectively explain or support the concept.

How engaging is the explanation of the concept?

What's Working Well: Point to a passage where you find the explanation most interesting or compelling, or where you felt drawn to keep reading to find out more. Was it the vividness of the language, the appropriateness of the explanation, or some other strategy that worked so well?

What Needs Improvement: Let the writer know where information might seem obvious or too complicated. Write down any questions you still have, and note whether there are some writing strategies that could improve your understanding of the concept.

Revising Your Draft

Revising means reenvisioning your draft and seeing it in a fresh way given your purpose, audience, and the review from your peers. Don't hesitate to cut unconvincing or tangential material, add new material, or move passages around. The following chart may help you strengthen your essay.

TROUBLESHOOTING YOUR DRAFT

To Focus the Concept and Explain It Clearly and Fully	
If the concept is confusing, unclear, or vague,	• Define the concept more precisely. • Give more examples. • Compare the concept to something familiar. • Apply the concept to a real-world experience.
If the focus seems too broad or too narrow,	• Concentrate on only one aspect of the concept. • Review your invention and research notes for a larger or more significant aspect of the concept.
If the content seems thin,	• Use explanatory writing strategies. • Develop your strategies more fully. • Explain how they relate to more familiar terms.
If some words are new to most readers,	• Define them or explain how they relate to more familiar terms. • Add analogies and examples to make them less abstract. • Place them in a context that clarifies their meaning.
To Improve the Organization	
If the essay as a whole is difficult to follow,	• Forecast the topics you will cover in the order in which they will appear. • Rearrange your topics so readers can follow your logic. • Revise or add topic sentences to clarify the content of each paragraph or section. • Outline your essay to see if the connections are clear; then reorganize as needed.

If connections from one sentence or paragraph to the next are vague or unclear,	• Make the connections clearer by improving or adding transitions. • Revise or add topic sentences to make connections between paragraphs clear.
To Integrate Information from Sources Smoothly	
If quotations, paraphrases, or summaries are not smoothly integrated into the text,	• Add appropriate signal phrases, using verbs that clarify the writer's position, approach, or attitude. • Explain how the quotation supports your point. • Contextualize the source to show its relevance and establish its reliability.
If some quotations could just as effectively be expressed in your own words,	• Paraphrase or summarize the quotation (with an appropriate citation).
If sources are not acknowledged properly,	• Include a signal phrase to identify the source. • Include the author's last name and a page number in parentheses following the borrowed material, and cite the source in a list at the end of the essay. (See Chapter 12, pp. 623–640, for the correct citation form.)
To Engage Readers	
If readers are not interested in the concept or focus,	• Select examples that readers are already familiar with or that may be relevant to their lives. • Dramatize the concept to show its importance or relevance. • Show readers a new way of using or understanding a familiar concept.

Editing and Proofreading Your Draft

Check for errors in usage, punctuation, and mechanics, and consider matters of style. If you keep a list of errors you typically make, begin by checking your draft against this list.

From our research on student writing, we know that essays explaining concepts tend to have errors in essential or nonessential clauses beginning with *who*, *which*, or *that*. They also have errors in the use of commas to set off appositives. Check a writer's handbook for help with these potential problems.

Reflecting on Concept Explanation

In this chapter, you have read critically several pieces explaining a concept and have written one of your own. To better remember what you have learned, pause now to reflect on the reading and writing activities you completed in this chapter.

1. Write a page or so reflecting on what you have learned. Begin by describing what you are most pleased with in your essay. Then explain what you think contributed to your achievement. Be specific about this contribution.

   - If it was something you learned from the readings, indicate which readings and specifically what you learned from them.

   - If it came from your research notes and the writing you did in response to prompts in this chapter, point out the parts that helped you most.

2. Reflect more generally on explaining concepts, a genre of writing important in education and in society. Consider some of the following questions:

   - When doing research, did you discover that some of the information on concepts was challenged by experts? What were the grounds for the challenge? Did you think your readers might question your information? How did you decide what information might seem new or surprising to readers?

   - Did you feel comfortable in your roles as the selector and giver of knowledge? Describe how you felt in these roles.

3. By reflecting on what you have learned about autobiography and literacy narratives, you have been practicing **metacognition,** one of the academic habits of mind.

   - Were you aware of any other habits of mind you practiced as you read and responded to the material in this chapter? If so, which habits did you find useful?

   - If not, think back now on your reading and writing process. Can you identify any habits you used?

CHAPTER 7

Evaluation

Before you buy a computer, phone, or video game, do you take a look at the reviews? Brief reviews, written by consumers, are easy to find, but some are more helpful than others. The best reviewers know what they're talking about. They don't just say what they like, but they also justify *why* they like it, giving examples or other evidence. Moreover, their judgment is based not on individual taste alone but on commonly held standards or **criteria.** For example, no one would consider it appropriate to judge an action film by its poetic dialogue or its subtle characterizations; people judge such films by whether they deliver an exciting roller-coaster ride. The usefulness of an evaluation — be it a brief consumer comment or an expert's detailed review — depends on readers sharing, or at least respecting, the writer's criteria.

RHETORICAL SITUATIONS FOR EVALUATIONS

Many people — including managers, reviewers, bloggers, and ordinary consumers — write evaluations, as the following examples suggest:

- A supervisor reviews the work of a probationary employee. She judges the employee's performance as being adequate overall but still needing improvement in several key areas, particularly completing projects on time and communicating clearly with others. To support her judgment, she describes several problems that the employee has had over the six-month probationary period.

- An older brother, a college junior, sends an e-mail message to his younger brother, a high-school senior, who is trying to decide which college to attend. Because the older brother attends one of the colleges being considered and has friends at another, he feels competent to offer advice. He centers his message on the question of what standards to use in evaluating colleges. He argues that if playing football is the primary goal, then college number one is the clear choice. But if having the opportunity to work in an award-winning scientist's genetics lab is more important, then the second college is the better choice.

Thinking about Evaluation

Recall a time when you evaluated something you had seen, heard, read, or tried (such as a film, live performance, novel, sports team, restaurant, television show, game, computer, or cell phone) or a time that you read or heard an evaluation someone else had made.

- Who was the *audience?* How do you think presenting the evaluation to this audience affected the writer's (or speaker's) judgment or the way the evaluation was supported? For example, did the audience's knowledge of the subject, or of subjects like it, influence the reasons or examples given?

- What was the main *purpose?* What did the writer (or speaker) want the audience to learn? For example, did he or she want to influence the actions of audience members, get them to think differently about the criteria or standards they should use when judging subjects of this kind, get them to look at the subject in a new way, or accomplish some other purpose?

- How would you rate the *rhetorical sensitivity* with which the evaluation was presented? What made the essay appropriate or inappropriate for its particular audience or purpose?

A GUIDE TO READING EVALUATIONS

This guide introduces you to the basic features and strategies typical of evaluative writing by inviting you to analyze an intriguing selection by Amitai Etzioni that evaluates McDonald's-type fast-food jobs for high-school students:

- *Annotations* on this first reading will help you see how to practice academic **habits of mind** such as **curiosity, openness,** and **persistence** to help you engage with and understand what you are reading. Notice how many questions the reader has as she reads. There is plenty of space for you to add your own questions and thoughts, as well, to this reading and any other in the textbook.

- *Reading for meaning* will help you understand Etzioni's judgment and his reasoning.

- *Reading like a writer* will help you learn how Etzioni employs strategies typical of evaluative writing, such as

   1. presenting the subject in enough detail so that readers know what is being judged

   2. supporting an overall judgment based on appropriate criteria with credible evidence

   3. responding to objections and alternative judgments readers might prefer

   4. organizing the evaluation in a way that will be clear and logical to readers

Amitai Etzioni

Working at McDonald's

Amitai Etzioni (b. 1929) earned his Ph.D. in sociology from the University of California at Berkeley and has taught at Berkeley, Columbia, Harvard, and George Washington universities. A respected scholar, he served as president of the American Sociological Association and has written more than two dozen books, including *Privacy in a Cyber Age* (2015) and *Hot Spots: American Foreign Policy in a Post Human-Rights World* (2012). A highly visible public intellectual, Etzioni often writes for *Huff-Post*. Among his many awards is the Simon Wiesenthal Center's 1997 Tolerance Book Award. "Working at McDonald's" was originally published in the *Miami Herald* with a headnote explaining that Etzioni's son Dari helped him write the essay.

- **Before you read,** think about any jobs you have had during high school or college (voluntary or for pay). Consider what you learned that might have made you a better student and prepared you for the kind of work you hope to do in the future.

- **As you read,** think about how the standards or criteria that Etzioni uses to evaluate jobs at fast-food restaurants would apply to the kinds of jobs you have held, and whether they are criteria you would apply.

1   McDonald's is bad for your kids. I do not mean the flat patties and the white-flour buns; I refer to the jobs teenagers undertake, mass-producing these choice items.

Why is it bad for a teenager to work at McDonald's since jobs teach responsibility and accountability?

2   As many as two-thirds of America's high school juniors and seniors now hold down part-time paying jobs, according to studies. Many of these are in fast-food chains, of which McDonald's is the pioneer, trend-setter, and symbol.

3   At first, such jobs may seem right out of the Founding Fathers' educational manual for how to bring up self-reliant, work-ethic-driven, productive youngsters. But in fact, these jobs undermine school attendance and involvement, impart few skills that will be useful in later life, and simultaneously skew the values of teen-agers—especially their ideas about the worth of a dollar.

4   It has been a longstanding American tradition that youngsters ought to get paying jobs. In folklore, few pursuits are more deeply revered than the newspaper route and the sidewalk lemonade stand. Here the youngsters are to learn how sweet are the fruits of labor and self-discipline (papers are delivered early in the morning, rain or shine), and the ways of trade (if you price your lemonade too high or too low...).

What are other jobs kids and teenagers have?

5   Roy Rogers, Baskin Robbins, Kentucky Fried Chicken, et al. may at first seem nothing but a vast extension of the lemonade stand. They provide very large numbers of teen jobs, provide regular employment, pay quite

well compared to many other teen jobs, and, in the modern equivalent of toiling over a hot stove, test one's stamina.

Closer examination, however, finds the McDonald's kind of job highly uneducational in several ways. Far from providing opportunities for entrepreneurship (the lemonade stand) or self-discipline, self-supervision, and self-scheduling (the paper route), most teen jobs these days are highly structured—what social scientists call "highly routinized." 6

True, you still have to have the gumption to get yourself over to the hamburger stand, but once you don the prescribed uniform, your task is spelled out in minute detail. The franchise prescribes the shape of the coffee cups; the weight, size, shape, and color of the patties; and the texture of the napkins (if any). Fresh coffee is to be made every eight minutes. And so on. There is no room for initiative, creativity, or even elementary rearrangements. These are breeding grounds for robots working for yesterday's assembly lines, not tomorrow's high-tech posts. 7

There are very few studies of the matter. One of the few is a 1984 study by Ivan Charper and Bryan Shore Fraser. The study relies mainly on what teen-agers write in response to questionnaires rather than actual observations of fast-food jobs. The authors argue that the employees develop many skills such as how to operate a food-preparation machine and a cash register. However, little attention is paid to how long it takes to acquire such a skill, or what its significance is. 8

What does it matter if you spend 20 minutes to learn to use a cash register, and then—"operate" it? What skill have you acquired? It is a long way from learning to work with a lathe or carpenter tools in the olden days or to program computers in the modern age. 9

A 1980 study by A. V. Harrell and P. W. Wirtz found that, among those students who worked at least 25 hours per week while in school, their unemployment rate four years later was half of that of seniors who did not work. This is an impressive statistic. It must be seen, though, together with the finding that many who begin as part-time employees in fast-food chains drop out of high school and are gobbled up in the world of low-skill jobs. Some say that while these jobs are rather unsuited for college-bound, white, middle-class youngsters, they are "ideal" for lower-class, "non-academic," minority youngsters. Indeed, minorities are "over-represented" in these jobs (21 percent of fast-food employees). While it is true that these places provide income, work, and even some training to such youngsters, they also tend to perpetuate their disadvantaged status. They provide no career ladders, few marketable skills, and undermine school attendance and involvement. 10

The hours are often long. Among those 14 to 17, a third of fast-food employees (including some school dropouts) labor more than 30 hours per week, according to the Charper-Fraser study. Only 20 percent work 15 hours or less. The rest: between 15 and 30 hours. 11

Guide to Reading (margin notes):

What is wrong with sticking to a routine when working at a job?

But couldn't this encourage discipline, which is a useful skill for any job?

Is this decades-old study still applicable?

Are there newer studies on this?

How is the concept of marketable skills being defined?

12   Often the stores close late, and after closing one must clean up and tally up. In affluent Montgomery County, Md., where child labor would not seem to be a widespread economic necessity, 24 percent of the seniors at one high school in 1985 worked as much as five to seven days a week; 27 percent, three to five. There is just no way such amounts of work will not interfere with school work, especially homework. In an informal survey published in the most recent yearbook of the high school, 58 percent of the seniors acknowledged that their jobs interfere with their school work.

13   The Charper-Fraser study sees merit in learning teamwork and working under supervision. The authors have a point here. However, it must be noted that such learning is not automatically educational or wholesome. For example, much of the supervision in fast-food places leans toward teaching one the wrong kinds of compliance: blind obedience, or shared alienation with the "boss."

What does wholesome mean in this context? Is this one of the criteria the author is using?

14   Supervision is often both tight and woefully inappropriate. Today, fast-food chains and other such places of work (record shops, bowling alleys) keep costs down by having teens supervise teens with often no adult on the premises.

These examples seem dated — where do people I know work?

15   There is no father or mother figure with which to identify, to emulate, to provide a role model and guidance. The work-culture varies from one place to another: Sometimes it is a tightly run shop (must keep the cash registers ringing); sometimes a rather loose pot party interrupted by customers. However, only rarely is there a master to learn from, or much worth learning. Indeed, far from being places where solid adult work values are being transmitted, these are places where all too often delinquent teen values dominate. Typically, when my son Oren was dishing out ice cream for Baskin Robbins in upper Manhattan, his fellow teen-workers considered him a sucker for not helping himself to the till. Most youngsters felt they were entitled to $50 severance "pay" on their last day on the job.

16   The pay, oddly, is the part of the teen work-world that is most difficult to evaluate. The lemonade stand or paper route money was for your allowance. In the old days, apprentices learning a trade from a master contributed most, if not all, of their income to their parents' household. Today, the teen pay may be low by adult standards, but it is often, especially in the middle class, spent largely or wholly by the teens. That is, the youngsters live free at home ("after all, they are high school kids") and are left with very substantial sums of money.

17   Where this money goes is not quite clear. Some use it to support themselves, especially among the poor. More middle-class kids set some money aside to help pay for college, or save it for a major purchase—often a car. But large amounts seem to flow to pay for an early introduction into the most trite aspects of American consumerism: flimsy punk clothes, trinkets, and whatever else is the last fast-moving teen craze.

Why is he judging what people spend money on? Is this fair?

One may say that this is only fair and square; they are being good American consumers and spend their money on what turns them on. At least, a cynic might add, these funds do not go into illicit drugs and booze. On the other hand, an educator might bemoan that these young, yet unformed individuals, so early in life driven to buy objects of no intrinsic educational, cultural, or social merit, learn so quickly the dubious merit of keeping up with the Joneses in ever-changing fads, promoted by mass merchandising.

Many teens find the instant reward of money, and the youth status   18
symbols it buys, much more alluring than credits in calculus courses, European history, or foreign languages. No wonder quite a few would rather skip school — and certainly homework — and instead work longer at a Burger King. Thus, most teen work these days is not providing early lessons in work ethic; it fosters escape from school and responsibilities, quick gratification, and a short cut to the consumeristic aspects of adult life.

Thus, parents should look at teen employment not as automatically edu-   19
cational. It is an activity — like sports — that can be turned into an educational opportunity. But it can also easily be abused. Youngsters must learn to balance the quest for income with the needs to keep growing and pursue other endeavors that do not pay off instantly — above all education.

Go back to school.

READING FOR MEANING

For help with reading strategies like summarizing and analyzing assumptions, see Chapter 2.

1. **Read to Summarize.** Write a sentence or two briefly stating Etzioni's main point about the value of part-time jobs for teenagers.

2. **Read to Respond.** Write a paragraph analyzing anything that resonates for you, such as the "longstanding American tradition that youngsters ought to get paying jobs" (par. 4); or Etzioni's argument that working while attending school interferes with schoolwork (par. 13).

3. **Read to Analyze Assumptions**. Write a paragraph or two analyzing an assumption you find intriguing in Etzioni's essay. For example:

   Assumptions about the usefulness of certain skills. Etzioni asserts that fast-food jobs "impart few skills that will be useful in later life" (par. 3). For example, he claims they do not provide "opportunities for entrepreneurship... or self-discipline, self-supervision, and self-scheduling" (par. 6) and "[t]here is no room for initiative, creativity" (par. 7).

   - How different, really, is delivering newspapers from working at McDonald's in terms of the skills learned about discipline, scheduling, and so on?

   - What other kinds of skills do teens learn when working at fast-food restaurants, and what potential use do you think these skills have in life?

Assumptions about the culture of consumerism. Toward the end of the essay, Etzioni complains that the things teenagers choose to buy with the money they earn from fast-food jobs represent "the most trite aspects of American consumerism: flimsy punk clothes, trinkets, and whatever else is the last fast-moving teen craze" (par. 18). His focus on what teens buy and why they buy it reveals Etzioni's ideas about teenagers' indoctrination into a consumerist culture.

- Etzioni uses the words *trite*, *flimsy*, and *trinkets* to criticize the things teens buy, but if teens purchased items that were original, well-made, and valuable, do you think he would still object? What might he be criticizing other than teenagers' taste?

- In referring to "fads" and "mass merchandising," he seems to assume teens are especially vulnerable to the influence of advertising (par. 19). To what extent, if any, do you agree?

READING LIKE A WRITER

Presenting the Subject

Writers must present the subject so readers know what is being judged and so that they can decide whether the criteria for evaluation they offer are appropriate. Writers often name the subject in the title and then describe it in some detail. A film reviewer, for example, might name the film in the title and then, in the review, indicate the category, or genre, of film he or she is critiquing as well as identify the actors, describe the characters they play, and tell some of the plot.

Similarly, Etzioni identifies the subject of his evaluation in his title: "Working at McDonald's"; he then specifies the type of work that concerns him, and explains why he focuses his attention on this company:

Subject Reasons why he uses McDonald's	As many as two-thirds of America's high school juniors and seniors now hold down part-time paying jobs, according to studies. Many of these are in fast-food chains, of which McDonald's is the pioneer, trend-setter, and symbol. (par. 2)

Although the fact that many teenagers hold fast-food jobs is common knowledge, Etzioni cites statistics to establish how widespread it is: "As many as two-thirds of America's high school juniors and seniors…" (par. 2). Notice that he refers generally to "studies" without providing any detail that would help readers follow up on his sources. Later, however, he uses researchers' names and the publication dates to cite his sources more specifically, although still informally. Etzioni's original newspaper readers would have been used to such informal references, but if he were writing for an academic audience, he would be expected to use a conventional documentation style.

For information on documenting sources, see Chapter 12.

Etzioni also names several other "fast-food chains" (par. 5) to make the point that he is not singling out McDonald's but using it as an example and "symbol." He spends a good portion of the rest of his evaluation describing the kind of job he objects to.

ANALYZE & WRITE

Write a paragraph analyzing how Etzioni describes McDonald's-type jobs:

1. First, underline the factual details in paragraphs 5–7, 9, 12, 15, and 16 that describe the people who work at fast-food restaurants and what they do.

2. How do the details Etzioni provides in these paragraphs help you understand the subject of his essay as important or worth reading about?

3. Which of the details in these paragraphs do you accept as valid, inaccurate, or only partially true? How fair does Etzioni's description seem to you?

Supporting the Judgment

Evaluations analyze the subject, but they also present an argument designed to convince readers that the writer's judgment is trustworthy because the reasons are

- based on criteria, such as shared values, that are appropriate to the subject

- backed by reliable evidence

Writers usually declare their overall judgment early in the essay and may repeat it in the essay's conclusion. For example, Etzioni opens with the straightforward judgment:

Judgment   McDonald's is bad for your kids. (par. 1)

Although readers expect a definitive judgment, they also appreciate a balanced one that acknowledges good as well as bad qualities, so Etzioni acknowledges the benefits of fast-food jobs for teenagers:

Good qualities of fast-food job

> They provide very large numbers of teen jobs, provide regular employment, pay quite well compared to many other teen jobs, and, in the modern equivalent of toiling over a hot stove, test one's stamina. (par. 5)

Etzioni makes two additional moves typical of strong reviews:

1. He reaches out to readers to establish shared values.

2. He gives reasons backed by evidence to support his judgment:

Shared value
Reason
At first, such jobs may seem right out of the Founding Fathers' educational manual for how to bring up self-reliant, work-ethic-driven, productive youngsters. But in fact, these jobs undermine school attendance and involvement, impart few skills that will be useful in later life, and simultaneously skew the values of teen-agers — especially their ideas about the worth of a dollar. (par. 3)

By referring to "the Founding Fathers" and using familiar phrases (such as "self-reliant" and "work-ethic") that connote traditional values, Etzioni builds his argument on values he expects his audience will share. But to be convincing, the reasons also must be supported by **evidence** such as facts, statistics, expert testimony, research studies, relevant examples, or personal anecdotes.

ANALYZE & WRITE

Write a paragraph analyzing how Etzioni supports one of his reasons:

1. First, choose *one* of the reasons Etzioni introduces in paragraph 3 and find the passage later in the essay where you think he supports that part of the argument.
2. Then analyze Etzioni's argument. For example, what kinds of evidence does he provide? Is the evidence appropriate and credible? Why or why not?
3. Would Etzioni's original *Miami Herald* readers have found this part of the argument convincing? Explain why or why not.

For more on evaluating the logic of an argument, see Chapter 2, pp. 60–62.

Responding to Objections or Alternative Judgments

Writers of evaluations often respond to possible objections and alternative judgments their readers may be likely to raise. They may **refute** (argue against) objections or alternative judgments they believe are weak or flawed, or they may **concede** (accept) objections and judgments they think are valid. To alert readers that a response is coming, reviewers may provide a transition or other cue. Here's an example of a refutation from Etzioni:

Alternative judgment
Cue
Refutation
The authors argue that the employees develop many skills such as how to operate a food-preparation machine and a cash register. However, little attention is paid to how long it takes to acquire such a skill, or what its significance is.

What does it matter if you spend 20 minutes to learn to use a cash register, and then — "operate" it? What skill have you acquired? It is a long way from learning to work with a lathe or carpenter tools in the olden days or to program computers in the modern age. (pars. 8–9)

Notice the basic structure of a refutation. (The cue signaling refutation is highlighted.)

▶ **X says** ...., **but I think** .... **because** ....

Here's an example of conceding valid concerns or objections:

> [Fast-food jobs] provide very large numbers of teen jobs, provide regular employment, pay quite well compared to many other teen jobs, and, in the modern equivalent of toiling over a hot stove, test one's stamina. (par. 5)

Below are some typical sentence strategies for conceding, with cues signaling concession highlighted:

▶ **Of course,** .... is an important factor.

▶ **Granted,** .... must be taken into consideration.

Frequently, though, reviewers reach out to those who hold an opposing position by first conceding a portion of that position but then going on to indicate where they differ:

Cue signaling concession

Cue signaling refutation

> **True,** you still have to have the gumption to get yourself over to the hamburger stand, **but** once you don the prescribed uniform, your task is spelled out in minute detail. (par. 7)

Etzioni often uses this strategy of concession followed by refutation when citing research that initially appears to undermine his claim. For example, he begins by conceding when he cites a study by Harrell and Wirtz (par. 10) that links work as a student with greater likelihood of employment later on. However, he then refutes the significance of this finding, reinterpreting the data to suggest that the high likelihood of future employment could be an indication that workers in fast-food restaurants are more likely to drop out of school than an indication that workers are learning important employment skills. This strategy of conceding and then refuting by reinterpreting evidence can be especially effective in college writing, as Etzioni (a professor) well knows.

ANALYZE & WRITE

Write a paragraph analyzing how Etzioni responds to objections or alternative judgments.

1. First, find and highlight the alternative judgment or objection in paragraphs 8–11, 14, and 19.

2. Then choose *one* of these objections or alternative judgments and determine whether Etzioni responds by refuting or conceding or both.

3. Finally, evaluate the effectiveness of Etzioni's response. What made his response convincing (or unconvincing) for his original readers? How about for you reading today?

Organizing the Evaluation

Writers of evaluation usually try to make their writing clear, logical, and easy for readers to follow by providing cues or road signs. For example, they may

- forecast their reasons early in the essay and repeat key terms (or synonyms) from these reasons later in the evaluation

- use topic sentences to announce the subject of each paragraph or group of paragraphs

- use transitions (such as *but, however, on the other hand, thus*) to guide readers from one point to another

These strategies are all helpful and are often expected in college writing.

As we've seen, Etzioni forecasts his reasons in paragraph 3:

Forecasting statement	. . . these jobs undermine school attendance and involvement, impart few skills that will be useful in later life, and simultaneously skew the values of teenagers — especially their ideas about the worth of a dollar.

He develops the argument supporting each of these reasons in subsequent paragraphs. His essay would be easier to follow if he addressed the reasons in the order he first introduced them in paragraph 3. Nevertheless, he helps readers find the reasons by repeating key terms, as when he uses the phrase "marketable *skills*" (par. 11) to refer to "few skills" from his forecasting statement; or he uses a close substitute, as when he uses the phrase "drop out of *high school*" (par. 10) to refer to "*undermine school attendance*" in paragraph 3.

Topic sentences are also used to orient readers. Often placed at the beginning of a paragraph or related sequence of paragraphs, they announce the topic that will be developed in the subsequent sentences. For example:

Topic sentence Examples of traditional kids' jobs What these jobs teach	It has been a longstanding American tradition that youngsters ought to get paying jobs. In folklore, few pursuits are more deeply revered than the newspaper route and the sidewalk lemonade stand. Here the youngsters are to learn how sweet are the fruits of labor and self-discipline (papers are delivered early in the morning, rain or shine), and the ways of trade (if you price your lemonade too high or too low...). (par. 4)

Notice that Etzioni focuses this paragraph on the topic of useful skills he introduced in the preceding forecasting statement. The next two paragraphs use topic sentences to make the argument that fast-food jobs "seem" like traditional jobs, but they do not teach really valuable skills. Skimming the sequence of topic sentences in paragraphs 5 and 6, you can get an idea of the outline of Etzioni's argument:

Transitions

> Roy Rogers, Baskin Robbins, Kentucky Fried Chicken, et al. may at first seem nothing but a vast extension of the lemonade stand....
>
> Closer examination, however, finds the McDonald's kind of job highly uneducational in several ways....

As the two topic sentences above suggest, transitions (and other cues) also play an important role in clarifying the logic of a sequence. For example, *at first* suggests that what follows is only a tentative conclusion, especially when combined with the hedging words *may* and *seem*; *however* firmly establishes a contrast or contradiction to that provisional conclusion.

ANALYZE & WRITE

Write a paragraph analyzing how Etzioni helps readers track his argument and how effective the cues he uses are.

1. Look at the way Etzioni uses topic sentences in the rest of his essay to announce the subject of individual paragraphs or groups of paragraphs.

2. Find a couple of examples that you think work well. What makes these topic sentences effective?

READINGS

Matthew Hertogs

Typing vs. Handwriting Notes: An Evaluation of the Effects of Transcription Method on Student Learning

Matthew Hertogs wrote this essay when he was a sophomore at the University of Washington, where he was pursuing a degree in computer science with a minor in mathematics. The essay was published in *Xchanges*, an interdisciplinary Technical Communication, Writing/Rhetoric, and Writing Across the Curriculum journal, which publishes two issues annually from its home in the English Department at the University of New Mexico. This piece was published in an issue dedicated to undergraduate research. Hertogs is currently a software engineering lead at Hiya, a company that partners with carriers and smartphone makers to offer caller profile solutions and spam protection for their customers.

- **Before you read,** think about your own notetaking habits. When you are in class, do you tend to take notes on paper or do you type them on your laptop or another electronic device?

- **As you read,** think about the different kinds of evidence Hertogs uses to evaluate the two kinds of notetaking he is researching.

INTRODUCTION

The utilization of laptops in a college environment has become a widely accepted practice due to the increasingly technological nature of our society. Essays, papers, and notes that were previously handwritten are now being written with the aid of word processors on computers and laptops. While this trend of technologically-based writing has been accelerating due to positive feedback from students who prefer writing on a word processor to handwriting (Burnett, 1984), researchers are continually studying whether word processors actually benefit students' writing. Some researchers have found improvements in the writing quality of students who used word processors (Oliver and Kerr, 1993; Louth and McAllister, 1988; Owsten, Murphy, and Wideman, 1989) while others have concluded that there was no statistically significant difference between handwriting and word processing (Teichman and Porris, 1989). However, although these studies have attempted to address the efficacy of word processing for expository compositions, there is a dearth of research on whether typing notes or handwriting notes for class lectures is more beneficial for students. Therefore, this study will analyze the differences between the handwritten and typed notes of two college students to assess the effectiveness of each method of notetaking and to gain a further understanding of why students may prefer one method over another.

Although there are few studies specifically about typed versus handwritten notes, there are a large number of studies about typed versus handwritten compositions in general. While these studies may seem inconclusive due to varying results as shown in the previous paragraph, Reay and Dunn believe that the inconsistency of these experiments can be attributed to the negligence of the researchers to the disparate transcription speeds of typing versus handwriting; they found that the writing of those who were more proficient at typing benefited from the use of word processing. In a university full of technologically savvy college students, it makes sense that the inclusion of word processing would have a beneficial impact on the quality of writing for college students as certain studies have discovered (Bernhardt, Wojahn, and Edwards, 1988). 2

While researchers have extensively studied the effects of word processing on composition to determine whether the utilization of computers in an educational environment is appropriate, there has been less focus on the topic of notetaking, which is arguably the most commonplace activity within college classes; according to Palmatier and Bennett, 99% of all college students take notes and 96% of students believed notetaking is crucial to their success in college. Large portions of students use their laptops to take notes, but it is unclear whether word processed notetaking is more beneficial than handwritten notetaking. Consequently, there are many varying opinions on whether laptops should be present in the classroom. 3

Some critics of laptops in the classroom, such as D'Agostino, believe that laptops provide too many opportunities for distraction to be a productive tool; she claims that students spend about half their time on social networking sites instead of taking notes when they use their laptop. However, other studies on notetaking strategies may point to some of the benefits of electronic notes. For instance, according to Eggerts and Williams, students who reviewed their notes were most likely to achieve at a higher level than their peers. Therefore, the organizational benefits of computerized notes may serve as a significant asset for students. Another major source on the efficacy of different notetaking strategies is Stahl, King, and Henk, who devised a quantitative system to analyze the effectiveness of a particular individual's notes. Utilizing a wide array of research on notetaking strategies, Stahl, King, and Henk created NOTES, a coding system which assigns a point value to certain criteria that previous studies have deemed conducive to beneficial notetaking. Positive traits like legibility, accessibility, organization, proper spacing, heading, utilization of examples, and summarization are all assigned point values. Whenever a sheet of notes is determined to possess a certain positive trait, it is given more points—the more points a sheet of notes has, the more beneficial it is for the student. 4

In general, there are inconclusive results regarding the effectiveness of competing transcription methods for expository compositions and virtually no results on transcription methods for notetaking. However, by synthesizing what other researchers have found to be beneficial notetaking strategies—higher transcription speed, accessible storage, organization, etc.—with data I collected from two university students, this study will fill the gap in the research by assessing the effectiveness of each method of transcription for notetaking. 5

METHODOLOGY

This research project attempts to determine whether handwritten notes versus typed notes during class lectures are more beneficial for college students. To address this question, I employed a mixture of qualitative and quantitative procedures to analyze the notetaking processes and the actual notes of two undergraduate students at a large, state university.

I asked both students to take notes for two days with each method—typing and handwriting—and let me collect copies of their notes to analyze them for differences in style, content, organization, and format. Each student's notes were quantitatively scored using a variation of the NOTES evaluation system[1] created by Stahl, King, and Henk; the original NOTES model had to be adjusted so that certain criteria were neutral for both methods of notetaking. For example, the category "I use my pen for notetaking" would be removed because it favors handwriting over typing; however, the issue of legibility that this particular category addresses would still be considered in the qualitative analysis of the notetaking process. After collecting each individual's notes and scoring them according to the adjusted NOTES evaluation system, the average score of the handwritten notes versus the typed notes was compared in an attempt to reveal which method is more beneficial for students. The three main categories within the NOTES system are format, organization, and meaning, and the results of the data are displayed in these three categories for less complicated comparisons. Finally, each student was interviewed at the end of the process in an attempt to determine which notetaking method they most commonly used and for what reasons. Through this interview process, the notetaking strategies and overall benefits of each method of notetaking will become more apparent, providing explanation and correlation with the quantitatively assessed notes from each student.

There are limitations within this particular method due to a limited amount of time and resources—most notably a small sample size and low number of trials. To ensure statistically significant results, I would need a larger sample size with randomly selected students, a control group of students that only take notes with one method to reveal if the notetaking style changes between daily lectures regardless of method, and a random selection for which method to utilize first. Furthermore, when assigning scores to the notes using the NOTES evaluation system, there would have to be multiple raters for each of the notes, instead of just my singular ratings, to ensure validity. Unfortunately, this experiment was unable to coordinate such an elaborate study procedure due to lack of time and resources. Another limitation worth mentioning is that each student will be taking notes in a different class according to their normal class schedule, which may prove to be a confounding variable in this experiment. However, the students all took notes in similarly structured classes that featured extensive notetaking devoid of numbers or formulas, except for one student who also took notes in a chemistry class for the purpose of

[1]See appendix for variation of NOTES evaluation system used in this study.

comparison.[2] Finally, the fact that the students are aware that they will be taking notes that will later be evaluated may alter their natural notetaking habits. To counteract this response bias from the study, the student participants were not given any information about the specific evaluation process for the study so that they did not consciously or subconsciously alter their notes to fit the specific positive characteristics that the evaluation took into account.

Despite all these limitations, the method utilized in this research study will hold   9 merit because of its mixture of quantitative and qualitative analysis; if both types of research end up with the same results, the shared conclusion may contain more validity. With the shortage of time and resources for this research study, this particular method is the most efficient way to identify and recognize if there are differences between typed and handwritten notes. While this study may not be able to completely confirm the variations between the two methods, it will certainly lay the groundwork for future studies to extensively measure this topic by identifying and introducing certain discrepancies between typed and handwritten notes.

DATA

There were two students that took notes and participated in interviews about their   10 various notetaking strategies and perspectives on notetaking for this study. Student 1 is an undergraduate freshman who is part of the interdisciplinary honors program; he is planning to major in engineering and he went to a public high school in California. Student 1 took notes with his laptop for two days and wrote notes by hand for the next two days in Chemistry 142 and Honors 394.[3] Student 2 is also an undergraduate freshman who is part of the interdisciplinary honors program; however, unlike Student 1, he was homeschooled. Student 2 took notes in Honors 230.[4] for two days with his laptop and wrote notes by hand for the next two days as well. Both students used Word 2007 when typing their notes. The notes were scored using a variation of the NOTES evaluation system (see tables 1-3 below).

STUDENT 1'S CHEMISTRY 142 NOTES

	Typed #1	Typed #2	Written #1	Written #2
FORMAT	11	11	9	9
ORGANIZATION	14	10	12	13
MEANING	10	10	12	12
Total Score	35	31	33	34
Average Score	Typing: 33		Writing: 33.5	

[2]Throughout the paper, I may refer to lectures without any numbers or formulas as "word intensive" lectures, and I may refer to lectures with numbers and formulas as "number intensive" lectures.

[3]Honors 394 is a class on the history of gender roles.

[4]Honors 230 is a class on human trafficking.

STUDENT 1'S HONORS 394 NOTES

	Typed #1	Typed #2	Writtten #1	Written #2
FORMAT	11	12	10	9
ORGANIZATION	13	14	12	13
MEANING	14	13	12	11
Total Score	38	39	34	33
Average Score	Typing: 38.5		Writing: 33.5	

Looking at the scores given by an adjusted version of the NOTES evaluation system 11 (see appendix), Student 1's notes were more effective when typed for his Honors 394 class, the more word intensive class out of the two. The average score for his typed notes in Honors 394 was 38.5 while the average score for his handwritten notes in the same class was 33.5. However, in his Chemistry 142 class, the differences in scoring between typed and handwritten notes were quite minimal—33 and 33.5 respectively.

By analyzing the scoring system in three different categories—format, organiza- 12 tion, and meaning—distinctive trends within each method of transcription become more apparent. For instance, all of the typed notes scored higher in the "format" category of the evaluation system; Student I's legibility and usage of page with the laptop were usually much more adroit than the handwritten versions. Furthermore, the ease of dating and storing the notes in an accessible fashion gave higher scores in the formatting category for the typed notes.

However, while the formatting score was consistently higher for Student 1's typed 13 notes in all his classes, the scoring began to diverge between Chemistry 142, which is a more mathematical and formula-based type of lecture, and Honors 394, a more word-based type of lecture. In his Chemistry 142 class, the handwritten notes scored higher in the "meaning" category, signifying a more prominent acknowledgment of the relationship between the smaller details and examples with the main ideas presented in the lecture. In contrast, the exact opposite phenomenon occurred within his Honors 394 class; the typed notes consistently scored higher in the "meaning" category.

Due to the disparities between the "meaning" scores of the Chem 142 and Honors 14 394, the only class that revealed a significant difference between the typed notes and the handwritten notes was Honors 394, in favor of typed notes. In the Chemistry 142 class, Student 1's typed notes had better "format" scores, comparable "organization" scores, and lower "meaning" scores than the handwritten notes so that the overall averages between the two methods of transcription were approximately equal. In the Honors 394 class, the typed notes scored higher in "format," comparable in "organization," and higher in "meaning," so the typed notes had an overall higher score than the handwritten notes.

When I revealed my findings to Student 1, he was not very surprised. Student 1 15 initially told me that he found it easier to take better notes in class with his laptop, except for when he had to write "anything involving numbers or formulas because it is much easier to write them than type them." Despite the inclusion of numbers, formulas, or symbols, Student 1 claims that he types faster than he writes, making it easier to keep up with the professor during the lecture. Therefore, when he saw that his typed notes scored better than his handwritten notes in his Honors 394 class but not in his Chemistry 142 class, he believed that the differences in the types of lectures resulted in these varying results between the two classes.

Another aspect that interested me about Student 1's notetaking habits was 16 the various distractions associated with each method of notetaking. A few studies reveal that the inclusion of technology in the classroom may actually hinder students because they might end up multitasking by checking Facebook, reading e-mails, or playing games, but this does not take into account the distracting nature of handwritten notes. When I came to collect Student 1's notes, I noticed that both handwritten notes had doodles drawn in the margin; Student 1 admitted that he usually doodled a lot during lectures. However, Student 1 also admitted that he checked Facebook "maybe once or twice" during lectures when he used his laptop. When I asked him whether he thought doodling or Facebook was more distracting in the lecture, he said "I doodle more than I check Facebook, but I can listen to the lecture while doodling; with Facebook I don't really listen that much."

In the end, Student 1 believes that he can take better notes with the laptop for 17 lectures that are more word intensive rather than number intensive. However, the typed notes are not so decidedly better to make him want to carry around his "really heavy" laptop to all of his classes so he plans to continually handwrite his notes.

STUDENT 2'S HONORS 230 NOTES

	Typed #1	Typed #2	Written #1	Written #2
FORMAT	10	9	7	11
ORGANIZATION	13	9	7	10
MEANING	10	9	7	10
Total Score	33	27	21	31
Average Score	Typing: 30		Writing: 26	

Although the quality of Student 2's notes vacillates more than Student 1's notes, 18 there are still evident patterns within the scoring system that can help identify his beneficial tendencies with each method of notetaking. Student 2 stated that he was never taught any particular form of notetaking, but he is intuitively able to structure notes in a coherent, organized manner when the lecture logically progresses through topics in a manner conducive to notetaking.

In all three of the categories, format, organization, and meaning, Student 2's typed 19 notes score higher than his handwritten notes. Again, Student 2 was not particularly surprised by these results, claiming that "once [he] actually sat down and looked at the differences between the two, it was really obvious how much better the typed notes were." The lowest-scoring handwritten notes were all squeezed into a tiny space and featured a jumbled diagram filled with arrows doubling back to certain points and words crossed out. The lowest-scoring typed notes were not much more sophisticated in an overall sense, just listing random strings of details with spaces in between, but the utilization of the word processing made the results more legible, more organized, and more understandable. When I asked Student 2 about why he thought his typed notes scored higher, he claimed that "the format helped to organize ideas and put down relevant information."

Another positive incentive for Student 2 to type notes would be the differences 20 in transcription speed for each method; Student 2 answered definitively that he can type faster than he writes. This benefit was evident when analyzing the differences between the higher-scoring typed notes and the higher-scoring handwritten notes. In the typed notes, Student 2 was able to organize his thoughts more clearly because he spent less time having to type out all the details; the headings and subtopics were consistently grouped together and he was able to summarize his thoughts in more detail than the handwritten notes.

In terms of distractions, Student 2 also found himself doodling on his handwritten 21 notes and checking Facebook occasionally when he used his laptop. However, Student 2 was more certain that the doodling was more of a distraction than Facebook was, adding another positive aspect towards typed notes. Also, similar to Student 1, Student 2 mentioned that he believes that the laptop would be more useful for non-mathematical classes due to the difficulty of entering numbers and formulas into the computer.

Overall, Student 2 decided that the utilization of the laptop to take notes would 22 be beneficial to his learning in the Honors 394 class, but he also doubts that the benefits from taking notes on the laptop would outweigh the negative aspects of having to carry his laptop around such a large campus.

DISCUSSION

Overall, typing notes was found to be more beneficial for students in this study 23 due to three inherent advantages of the laptop — accessibility/legibility, transcription speed, and organization. For instance, in all of the word-intensive classes, the "format" score of the typed notes for both students was consistently higher, due to the advantage of legibility and accessibility using a laptop. One of the most significant and overlooked aspects of notetaking is the ability to review one's notes, and it was apparent that notes that were typed were easier to access and to read, making them more beneficial for student learning. As for transcription speed, both students were able to type faster, which made it easier to keep up with the professor, record details, and focus on connecting the main ideas of the lecture with those details. Being able to transcribe the lecture quicker allowed the students to score higher in the "meaning" category for the word-intensive classes. In contrast, for the number-intensive class, the utilization of a laptop actually hindered the transcription speed of the student because it was more difficult to input numbers and formulae while typing; therefore, the scores in the "meaning" category were actually higher for the handwritten notes in Student 1's Chemistry 142 class. Finally, the even spacing, bullet points, and indenting provided by word processing helped the students keep their notes more organized than they normally would be when handwriting. As a result, both students used headings, subtopics, and bullet points more often with their typed notes and this was revealed through higher scores in the "organization" category.

Another interesting aspect of the data that requires explanation is that Student 2's 24 typed notes only score higher than his written notes when averaged, but not individually—that is to say, one of the handwritten notes scored higher than one of his typed notes even though typed notes scored higher than the handwritten notes when averaged. Although it may seem like this example refutes the idea that typed notes are more beneficial than handwritten notes for writing-intensive classes, it might just suggest that typed notes are only comparatively better than handwritten notes for word-intensive classes. Since the method of transcription is not the only variable affecting the quality of the notes, the reason that one of Student 2's typed notes scored lower than another set of handwritten notes could easily be attributed to a variety of other factors such as the material covered during that class, the mode of presentation, and/or the mood of the student. It is possible that if Student 2 had handwritten his notes on the same day that he typed the lower-quality typed notes, he would have scored even lower. Therefore, the individual scores of each transcription method should not be compared because it does not account for variation due to many other confounding variables; rather, the averaged scores for each transcription method should be compared, which reveals that typed notes are more beneficial for students in a word-intensive class.

While this study does suggest that typing notes is more beneficial for students, 25 there are not enough people sampled to completely assert this idea. One would need to use a large number of participants to definitively prove that one method of transcription is more beneficial than another. However, even though the quantitative results of this study are not necessarily able to be generalized to the rest of the undergraduate population, they still reveal valuable pieces of information about the notetaking process that should be studied in further detail in the future.

1. There are differences between typed notes and handwritten notes

While one could potentially argue against the validity of the quantitative data analy- 26 sis utilizing the NOTES evaluation system, it is undeniable that there are quantifiable differences between the two methods of transcription. Even if one has qualms with the means of assessing what qualifies as a beneficial notetaking strategy, the differences in format, organization, and meaning between the notes are quite apparent. This fact holds significance because it paves the way for future studies to explore which method is more beneficial for students; if this study had found that the typed and handwritten notes of each student were mostly similar, that would indicate that there is likely no need to pursue future research on the efficacy of competing transcription methods.

2. The most beneficial method of transcription is not constant between different classes

Most evident in Student 1's case, typed notetaking was found to be more benefi- 27 cial for word-intensive lectures, but not necessarily for number-intensive classes. Although Student 2 did not quantitatively assert this principle (since he was unable to take notes in a math/science class), he mimicked this idea throughout his interview, much like Student 1 did. While not entirely surprising, this does have important ramifications for further research into notetaking in the classroom. Different classes require different notetaking methods and/or skills, and this fact should serve as a call for future researchers to analyze how notetaking and learning differs between various classes within the university.

3. Notetaking distractions are quite universal, regardless of transcription method

One of the leading arguments against the inclusion of new technology in the classroom is 28 the supposed distracting nature of these devices. While it may be true that laptops in the classroom pose distractions for students, it is uncertain whether these distractions are significantly more disruptive than any other form of distraction caused by handwritten notes. For both Student 1 and Student 2, doodling was definitely a distraction during their class lectures; most of their notes had doodles on them and they confirmed that doodling was a distraction in their interviews. Even though it is unclear whether doodling or Facebook is more distracting—Student 1 and Student 2 gave contradictory answers on the issue—it is at least worth noting that distractions happen with both methods of transcription. Therefore, instructors who forbid laptops in their classroom because of their "distracting nature" may want to reconsider their policies, especially if further studies confirm that typing notes is more beneficial for students in their particular class.

Due to a small sample size, my findings may not definitively prove that typing 29 trumps handwriting notes, but they do reveal that there is a way to quantitatively evaluate the differences between typed and handwritten notes and that there are differences worth studying. As technology advances and becomes an increasingly integral part of education, it is crucial for researchers to continuously study how these technological advances impact students' notetaking. For instance, my participants were only using laptops, but there could be new and different results for a technology like the iPad, which has a touch screen. Technology in the classroom will continue to change, and it is essential that researchers continuously study the effects on students' notetaking so that they can implement their findings and hopefully foster positive notetaking strategies within the classroom.

WORKS CITED

D'Agostino, Susan. "Facebook and Texting vs. Textbooks and Faces." Math Horizons.

18.1 (2010): 34. JSTOR. Web. 19 Oct. 2011. www.jstor.org/stable/10.4169/1

94762110X525548.

Dunn, Bill, and David Reay. "Word Processing and the Keyboard: Comparative Effects of Transcription on Achievement." Journal of Educational Research. 82.4 (1989): 237–45. JSTOR. Web. 19 Oct. 2011. www.jstor.org/stable/27540347.

Eggert, David C., and Robert L. Williams. "Notetaking in College Classes: Student Patterns and Instructional Strategies." Journal of General Education. 51.3 (2002): 173–99. JSTOR. Web. 19 Oct. 2011. www.jstor.org/stable/27797918.

Palmatier, Robert A., and J. M. Bennett. "Notetaking Habits of College Students." Journal of Reading. 18.3 (1974): 215–18. JSTOR. Web. 23 Oct. 2011. www.jstor.org/stable/40009958.

Stahl, Norman A., James R. King, and William A. Henk. "Enhancing Students' Notetaking through Training and Evaluation." Journal of Reading. 34.8 (1991): 614–22. JSTOR. Web. 19 Oct. 2011. www.jstor.org/stable/40014606.

READING FOR MEANING

For help with reading strategies like summarizing and analyzing assumptions, see Chapter 2.

1. **Read to Summarize.** Write a sentence or two restating in your own words what Hertogs is evaluating in his essay, and what he concludes based on his research.

2. **Read to Respond.** Write a paragraph analyzing anything in the essay that you find surprising, such as how some of the results of his study depended on whether the class was number intensive or word intensive (par. 27).

3. **Read to Analyze Assumptions.** Write a paragraph or two analyzing an assumption you find intriguing in Hertogs's essay. For example:

   Assumptions about the value of a single study. Hertogs writes, "In general, there are inconclusive results regarding the effectiveness of competing transcription methods for expository compositions and virtually no results on transcription methods for notetaking. However, by synthesizing what other researchers have found to be beneficial notetaking strategies — higher transcription speed, accessible storage, organization, etc. — with data I collected from two university students, this study will fill the gap in the research by assessing the effectiveness of each method of transcription for notetaking" (par. 5)

   - Hertogs assumes that this study will fill in the gap he describes in research on this subject. Is this an accurate representation of the contribution of this study? How else might you characterize its contribution?

   - Studies are not always replicated, making the results of a single study hard to verify. While the results from a single study may not definitively verify a hypothesis, what can you do with results from a single study? What are other ways you can use the results?

Assumptions about where scientific findings lead. Hertogs concludes with the following statement: "Technology in the classroom will continue to change, and it is essential that researchers continuously study the effects on students' notetaking so that they can implement their findings and hopefully foster positive notetaking strategies within the classroom" (par. 29).

- What specific assumptions does Hertogs make about the usefulness of his findings? Who will benefit from them and how?

- What assumptions do you have about the usefulness of scientific findings? Where do these come from? To what extent do they align with Hertogs's assumptions?

READING LIKE A WRITER

Supporting the Judgment

In research-based evaluations, judgments based on evidence are especially important. Depending on the discipline or field within which the research has been conducted, what counts as evidence can vary considerably. In the humanities, for example, personal experience may count as evidence, but in the sciences they may not. Expert testimony may be relevant in one field but not another, while statistics may be paramount in one discipline but unnecessary to support a judgment in another discipline.

In the case of Hertogs's research-based essay, his evaluation appears in the "Discussion" section. He writes, "Even though the quantitative results of this study are not necessarily able to be generalized to the rest of the undergraduate population, they still reveal valuable pieces of information about the notetaking process that should be studied in further detail in the future" (par. 25). He goes on to list three of these findings:

1. There are differences between typed notes and handwritten notes

2. The most beneficial method of transcription is not constant between different classes

3. Notetaking distractions are quite universal, regardless of transcription method

ANALYZE & WRITE

1. Locate the evidence in Hertogs's essay that supports his three findings.

2. What kinds of evidence does Hertogs provide? Does it seem appropriate and credible? Why or why not?

3. How does Hertogs address the limitations of his evidence? What is the effect of this on you as a reader? Does this strengthen his evaluation? Why or why not?

Ian Bogost

Brands Are Not Our Friends

Dr. Ian Bogost is an author and an award-winning game designer. He is Ivan Allen College Distinguished Chair in Media Studies and Professor of Interactive Computing at the Georgia Institute of Technology, where he also holds an appointment in the Scheller College of Business. Bogost is also Founding Partner at Persuasive Games LLC, an independent game studio, and a Contributing Editor at the *Atlantic*. He is author or co-author of several books and the co-editor of the Platform book series at MIT Press, and the Object Lessons book and essay series, published by *The Atlantic* and Bloomsbury.

- **Before you read,** notice that Bogost begins with a narrative about Comcast's "pizza delivery stunt." How does this story prepare you for what follows?

- **As you read,** consider how effectively Bogost establishes his credibility as someone in a position to comment on the relationships that brands try to establish with customers. What in his evaluation helps demonstrate his expertise?

I didn't realize how seriously companies take social media until last year, when I   1
opened my front door and saw a delivery guy holding a stack of pizza boxes up to his chin.

Comcast had recently started advertising mobile-phone service where I live. Given   2
that Comcast and AT&T were already the only local choices for broadband and cable, the move felt like an ominous sign of even more industry consolidation. I took to Twitter to air this worry. "It's nice that Comcast is offering mobile phone service now," I posted. "But until I can get Comcast delivery pizza I will remain empty inside."

It wasn't the best joke I'd made on the internet, but Comcast didn't mind. The   3
company saw my tweet and responded: "Hey Ian, you rang? DM us the address where you would like it delivered & we'll make it happen." I thought I was calling Comcast's bluff by answering that I wanted gluten-free mushroom pizza, and that because I was a customer, the company should know my address. "Do your brand thang," I quipped.

This was hardly my first digital interaction with a corporation. DiGiorno Pizza was   4
my Twitter buddy for a while, although we seem to have fallen out of touch. I once scorned Jolly Ranchers, only to have the brand chat me up moments later. Northern Tool, a tool and machinery company, chimed in on a photo I tweeted of its catalog. Cinnabon helped me win a dispute about how to pronounce its product ("like James Bond"). I assumed these brands targeted me because I have a decent Twitter following and write often for *The Atlantic*. And I thought I knew how these conversations went—they were quick and lighthearted, mildly amusing if also a bit invasive. Mostly, they were forgettable.

Then the pizzas arrived. Ten of them, from a local place that delivers gluten-free   5
pies. I was surprised, which is exactly the outcome Comcast was after.

In marketing, conventional wisdom holds that small surprises can yield a big benefit for a limited cost, especially if they go viral. Marketers have a name for Comcast's
pizza-delivery stunt: a strategy of "surprise and delight."

About 15 years ago, before Twitter existed, companies paid agencies for "guer-   6
rilla" and "buzz" marketing; the agencies would surreptitiously seed conversations
about the companies in chat rooms and on message boards, and report back on
the sentiments they saw there. Then the social platforms arrived: Blogger, Myspace,
YouTube, and others.

That's what spawned the new social-media-management economy. Around 2010,   7
when the *Citizens United* Supreme Court ruling reinforced the breadth and power
of corporate personhood in America, businesses started developing online *personalities*. Now almost every brand is a #brand too. Spend enough time perusing corporations' social accounts, and you'll start to see distinct personas emerge: Wendy's
is catty; Arby's is geeky; Charmin is, well, cheeky. This shift has ushered in a whole
new job category. Companies employ social-media managers and online-content
specialists to trawl Facebook, Twitter, Instagram, and other platforms, looking for
opportunities to engage — a favorite word of online advertisers — or in my case, to
send pizza. (Because I sometimes cover issues related to Comcast for *The Atlantic*,
I gave away as many of the pizzas as I could and reimbursed Comcast for the cost.)

It's not just the big fish like Comcast. Steak-umm is a family-owned company   8
based in Reading, Pennsylvania, that sells frozen sliced beef for making Philly chees-
esteaks at home. I ate the beef occasionally in the 1980s, but I'd forgotten about
it until I noticed the company on Twitter several years ago. At the time, it seemed
ridiculous that a frozen-beef producer would be there at all. Still, I followed the
account. Then, last year, I received a direct message asking me, personally, to share a
Change.org petition advocating for Steak-umm's account to receive the blue check
mark that indicates an account has been verified by Twitter.

Steak-umm's marketing team, I later learned, was trying to recruit followers and   9
fans by casting the verification campaign as a Rust Belt underdog story: a regional
frozen-beef company versus social-media hotshots like Wendy's. The team told me that
it had started by enlisting a few comedians and mid-tier celebrities who had mentioned
Steak-umm on Twitter. But the process for reaching people like me was more sophisticated. Using a software service called Crimson Hexagon, Nathan Allebach, who
manages Steak-umm's social-media accounts, was able to home in on the geographic
locations, interests, and social-media-usage patterns common to the younger audience
Steak-umm hoped to connect with on Twitter. The software identified gaming, a sector
I work in, as one of those interests — which made me a compelling target. (Many people singled out by brands on Instagram or Twitter may not know how they came to a
company's attention. Part of the answer is sophisticated software. Crimson Hexagon,
for example, can identify objects and corporate logos in photos — a Pepsi T-shirt, say, or
a Mr. Coffee coffee maker in the background — enabling companies to discover what
someone owns or uses even if the person doesn't tag a brand.)

Matt Dickman, who runs digital communications for Comcast, told me that in 10 the case of the pizza delivery, my original tweet would have been routed to Comcast's Xfinity Mobile brand team, which explains how the company was able to find my address and ship pizzas there. The same infrastructure that allows Comcast to respond quickly to service issues on Twitter (in my experience, much faster than when you call) gives it a platform for clever marketing. In other words, brands have learned to go beyond reacting to customers' complaints and anticipate what might enchant them—playing offense, not just defense. Which brings us to the case of the Kit Kat marriage proposal.

This spring, Haley Byrd, a congressional reporter at *The Weekly Standard*, posted 11 a tweet mocking her boyfriend, Evan Wilt, for eating a Kit Kat bar by biting across its entire width rather than breaking off the individual wafers. Hershey's (which makes the candy in the U.S.) sent the couple a box of Kit Kat bars with eating instructions, a cute gesture that Byrd thought was the end of the matter. But her tweet had gone viral, and behind the scenes, a Hershey's brand-publicity representative, Anna Lingeris, conspired with Wilt to design a Kit Kat-shaped ring box, which Wilt deployed for his proposal in July. The result: a happy couple, and a haul of cheap publicity for Hershey's.

Byrd has nearly 50,000 Twitter followers. But not everyone at the receiving end of 12 an elaborate branding exercise has as wide a reach—and according to the marketers I spoke with, that's fine. They seem to delight in their own endeavors as much as their customers are supposed to. Allebach sounded wistful when describing late-night therapy sessions with lonely, down-on-their-luck Steak-umm fans. Once, he told me, the company sent Walmart gift cards to a customer whose apartment had burned in a fire. Lingeris expressed deep pride in her role in Wilt and Byrd's Kit Kat engagement.

Dickman said Comcast doesn't pursue its surprise-and-delight affairs just to target 13 "influencers," a term he thinks is becoming meaningless. "The potential for something to be propelled forward by someone doesn't really depend on how many followers they have," he said. "It depends on how you treat them." A positive experience can cement a customer relationship. Dickman cites the time a man asked Comcast how a friend's son, who was in the hospital, could watch a Chicago Bears game, and the company gave him tickets. (The hospital granted the boy leave to attend the game.) "Nobody saw any of this," Dickman told me, saying that any resulting publicity is "just a bonus if it happens."

After the pizzas arrived, Xfinity Mobile told me something similar in a private 14 message on Twitter: "There's absolutely no obligation or request for you to write about this. In fact, we are just glad you enjoyed it."

But it's human nature to feel obligated when someone—even a company—does 15 something for you. That can make the people on the receiving end of social-media marketing feel snared in corporate traps. The fire victim was probably appreciative, but will he later feel indebted to a frozen-meat company? Likewise, Evan Wilt and Haley Byrd's union is now forever bound to a chocolate bar.

As for me, here I am—with some ambivalence—giving Comcast publicity for its 16 pizza stunt, doing the very thing the company claimed it didn't expect. Social media has made it easier than ever for companies to connect with people. These new, personal bonds between companies and customers feel uncanny — the brands are not real human friends, exactly, but neither are they faceless corporations anymore. Isn't that the point, though? Branding's purpose is to get under your skin, to make you remember an otherwise forgettable company or product. When the surprise wanes, that feels a lot less delightful.

READING FOR MEANING

1. **Read to Summarize.** Write a sentence or two restating in your own words what Bogost is evaluating in his essay, and what he ultimately thinks about this topic.

   For help with reading strategies like summarizing and analyzing assumptions, see Chapter 2.

2. **Read to Respond.** Write a paragraph analyzing anything in the essay that you find surprising, such as the assertion that "businesses [have] started developing online personalities" (par. 8) or "branding's purpose is to get under your skin" (par. 17).

3. **Read to Analyze Assumptions.** Write a paragraph or two analyzing an assumption you find intriguing in Bogost's essay. For example:

   Assumptions about human nature. "It's human nature to feel obligated when someone — even a company — does something for you. That can make the people on the receiving end of social-media marketing feel snared in corporate traps," proclaims Bogost (par. 16).

   - Bogost assumes that all people would feel obligated to return a favor when someone, including companies, does something nice for them. Is this an accurate assumption? Are there exceptions you can think of? Where do you think this assumption comes from in our culture?

   - Bogost suggests that sometimes this sense of obligation also produces a sense of being trapped by the company (par. 16). What are your assumptions about how humans respond when they feel trapped? Are these assumptions addressed or explored in Bogost's essay? If so, how, and if not, why not?

   Assumptions about when ambivalence is appropriate. Many evaluations offer a concrete judgment about whatever is being evaluated. When you are ambivalent, though, you have mixed feelings about someone or something. In the final paragraph of his essay, though, Bogost writes, "As for me, here I am — with some ambivalence — giving Comcast publicity for its pizza stunt, doing the very thing the company claimed it didn't expect" (par. 17). Implied in this judgement is an assumption about the acceptability of ambivalence when evaluating something. By ending his essay this way, Bogost suggests that it is okay to be ambivalent, to neither endorse or reject what it is you are evaluating.

- What assumptions do you have about the appropriateness of ambivalence in different contexts and where do you think those assumptions come from? Can you think of contexts in which you think ambivalence should be encouraged or discouraged?

- Are you satisfied with Bogost's ending and his articulation of ambivalence as opposed to a more concrete judgement? What does your reaction to the ending suggest about your assumptions regarding when ambivalence is appropriate?

READING LIKE A WRITER

Presenting the Subject

Writers of evaluative essays usually begin by identifying the subject being evaluated, as can be seen throughout this chapter. The strategies used to present the subject include naming it (often in the title, as Etzioni does in "Working at McDonalds"). But if, as in Etzioni's case, the name (McDonald's) is meant to stand for a general category or genre (fast-food restaurant jobs), then naming other familiar examples of the genre may also be necessary ("Roy Rogers, Baskin Robbins, Kentucky Fried Chicken" [par. 5]). Later in this chapter, in "Kid's Should Play, Not Compete," Christine Romano uses the same two strategies when she names her subject ("organized competitive sports" for kids) and cites two examples of the genre ("Peewee Football and Little League Baseball" [par. 1]). Identifying the genre is important for all subjects, particularly when the subject is not one with which most people are familiar, as in the case of the "surprise and delight" (par. 6) marketing strategy described by Bogost. As a critical reader, you will want to think about how Bogost presents this strategy that companies are increasingly using and whether the criteria he applies are appropriate.

ANALYZE & WRITE

Write a paragraph analyzing how Bogost presents the "surprise and delight" marketing strategy.

1. Reread paragraphs 1–8, noting how Bogost introduces this strategy. What kinds of examples and information does he share with his audience so they understand what he will be evaluating?

2. How do the additional examples and details Bogost includes in later paragraphs help you understand why this is an important subject and one worth evaluating?

3. How fair do you think Bogost's evaluation of this marketing strategy is, considering that the goal of marketing is to publicize a company in order to gain more customers?

Malcolm Gladwell

What College Rankings Really Tell Us

Malcolm Gladwell (b. 1963) has a BA in history from the University of Toronto. He is a staff writer for the *New Yorker* magazine and has written a number of best-selling books, including *Outliers: The Story of Success* (2008), *Blink: The Power of Thinking without Thinking* (2005), and most recently, *David and Goliath: Underdogs, Misfits, and the Art of Battling Giants* (2013). He also hosts the podcast *Revisionist History* and has given several TED talks. He has received the American Sociological Association Award for Excellence in the Reporting of Social Issues and was named one of the hundred most influential people by *Time* magazine. "What College Rankings Really Tell Us" (2011) evaluates the popular *U.S. News* "Best Colleges" annual guide. You may be familiar with this guide and may have even consulted it when selecting a college. Excerpted from a longer *New Yorker* article, Gladwell's evaluation focuses on the *U.S. News* ranking system.

- **Before you read,** think about the criteria that are important to you for choosing a college.

- **As you read,** Gladwell's review, consider who, besides prospective college students, would be likely to think the criteria *U.S. News* uses to rank colleges are important, and why.

Car and Driver conducted a comparison test of three sports cars, the Lotus Evora, the Chevrolet Corvette Grand Sport, and the Porsche Cayman S.... Yet when you inspect the magazine's tabulations it is hard to figure out why *Car and Driver* was so sure that the Cayman is better than the Corvette and the Evora. The trouble starts with the fact that the ranking methodology *Car and Driver* used was essentially the same one it uses for all the vehicles it tests—from S.U.V.s to economy sedans. It's not set up for sports cars. Exterior styling, for example, counts for four per cent of the total score. Has anyone buying a sports car ever placed so little value on how it looks? Similarly, the categories of "fun to drive" and "chassis"—which cover the subjective experience of driving the car—count for only eighty-five points out of the total of two hundred and thirty-five. That may make sense for S.U.V. buyers. But, for people interested in Porsches and Corvettes and Lotuses, the subjective experience of driving is surely what matters most. In other words, in trying to come up with a ranking that is heterogeneous—a methodology that is broad enough to cover all vehicles—*Car and Driver* ended up with a system that is absurdly ill-suited to some vehicles....

A heterogeneous ranking system works if it focuses just on, say, how much fun a car is to drive, or how good-looking it is, or how beautifully it handles. The magazine's ambition to create a comprehensive ranking system—one that considered cars along twenty-one variables, each weighted according to a secret sauce cooked up by the editors—would also be fine, as long as the cars being compared were truly similar. It's only when one car is thirteen thousand dollars more than another that juggling twenty-one variables starts to break down, because you're faced with the impossible task of deciding how much a difference of that degree ought to matter. A ranking can be heterogeneous, in other words, as long as it doesn't try to be too comprehensive. And it can be comprehensive as long as it doesn't try to measure things that are heterogeneous. But it's an act of real audacity when a ranking system tries to be comprehensive and heterogeneous—which is the first thing to keep in mind in any consideration of *U.S. News & World Report*'s annual "Best Colleges" guide.

The *U.S. News* rankings... relies on seven weighted variables: 3

1. Undergraduate academic reputation, 22.5 per cent

2. Graduation and freshman retention rates, 20 per cent

3. Faculty resources, 20 per cent

4. Student selectivity, 15 per cent

5. Financial resources, 10 per cent

6. Graduation rate performance, 7.5 per cent

7. Alumni giving, 5 per cent

From these variables, *U.S. News* generates a score for each institution on a   4
scale of 1 to 100.... This ranking system looks a great deal like the *Car and Driver* methodology. It is heterogeneous. It doesn't just compare U.C. Irvine, the University of Washington, the University of Texas–Austin, the University of Wisconsin– Madison, Penn State, and the University of Illinois, Urbana–Champaign—all public institutions of roughly the same size. It aims to compare Penn State—a very large, public, land-grant university with a low tuition and an economically diverse student body, set in a rural valley in central Pennsylvania and famous for its football team—with Yeshiva University, a small, expensive, private Jewish university whose undergraduate program is set on two campuses in Manhattan (one in midtown, for the women, and one far uptown, for the men) and is definitely not famous for its football team.

The system is also comprehensive. It doesn't simply compare schools along one   5
dimension—the test scores of incoming freshmen, say, or academic reputation. An algorithm takes a slate of statistics on each college and transforms them into a single score: it tells us that Penn State is a better school than Yeshiva by one point. It is easy to see why the *U.S. News* rankings are so popular. A single score allows us to judge between entities (like Yeshiva and Penn State) that otherwise would be impossible to compare....

A comprehensive, heterogeneous ranking system was a stretch for *Car and*   6
Driver—and all it did was rank inanimate objects operated by a single person. The Penn State campus at University Park is a complex institution with dozens of schools and departments, four thousand faculty members, and forty-five thousand students. How on earth does anyone propose to assign a number to something like that?

The first difficulty with rankings is that it can be surprisingly hard to measure the 7
variable you want to rank—even in cases where that variable seems perfectly objective.... There's no direct way to measure the quality of an institution—how well a
college manages to inform, inspire, and challenge its students. So the *U.S. News*
algorithm relies instead on proxies for quality—and the proxies for educational quality turn out to be flimsy at best.

Take the category of "faculty resources," which counts for twenty per cent of an 8
institution's score (number 3 on the chart above). "Research shows that the more satisfied students are about their contact with professors," the College Guide's explanation
of the category begins, "the more they will learn and the more likely it is they will
graduate." That's true. According to educational researchers, arguably the most important variable in a successful college education is a vague but crucial concept called student "engagement"—that is, the extent to which students immerse themselves in the
intellectual and social life of their college—and a major component of engagement is
the quality of a student's contacts with faculty.... So what proxies does *U.S. News* use
to measure this elusive dimension of engagement? The explanation goes on:

> We use six factors from the 2009–10 academic year to assess a school's
> commitment to instruction. Class size has two components, the proportion
> of classes with fewer than 20 students (30 percent of the faculty resources
> score) and the proportion with 50 or more students (10 percent of the score).
> Faculty salary (35 percent) is the average faculty pay, plus benefits, during
> the 2008–09 and 2009–10 academic years, adjusted for regional differences
> in the cost of living.... We also weigh the proportion of professors with the
> highest degree in their fields (15 percent), the student-faculty ratio (5 per-
> cent), and the proportion of faculty who are full time (5 percent).

This is a puzzling list. Do professors who get paid more money really take their 9
teaching roles more seriously? And why does it matter whether a professor has the
highest degree in his or her field? Salaries and degree attainment are known to be
predictors of research productivity. But studies show that being oriented toward
research has very little to do with being good at teaching. Almost none of the *U.S.
News* variables, in fact, seem to be particularly effective proxies for engagement. As
the educational researchers Patrick Terenzini and Ernest Pascarella concluded after
analyzing twenty-six hundred reports on the effects of college on students:

> After taking into account the characteristics, abilities, and backgrounds stu-
> dents bring with them to college, we found that how much students grow
> or change has only inconsistent and, perhaps in a practical sense, trivial
> relationships with such traditional measures of institutional "quality" as
> educational expenditures per student, student/faculty ratios, faculty salaries,
> percentage of faculty with the highest degree in their field, faculty research
> productivity, size of the library, [or] admissions selectivity....

There's something missing from that list of variables, of course: it doesn't include 10
price. That is one of the most distinctive features of the *U.S. News* methodology. Both

its college rankings and its law-school rankings reward schools for devoting lots of financial resources to educating their students, but not for being affordable. Why? [Director of Data Research Robert] Morse admitted that there was no formal reason for that position. It was just a feeling. "We're not saying that we're measuring educational outcomes," he explained. "We're not saying we're social scientists, or we're subjecting our rankings to some peer-review process. We're just saying we've made this judgment. We're saying we've interviewed a lot of experts, we've developed these academic indicators, and we think these measures measure quality schools."

As answers go, that's up there with the parental "Because I said so." But Morse is 11 simply being honest. If we don't understand what the right proxies for college quality are, let alone how to represent those proxies in a comprehensive, heterogeneous grading system, then our rankings are inherently arbitrary.... *U.S. News* thinks that schools that spend a lot of money on their students are nicer than those that don't, and that this niceness ought to be factored into the equation of desirability. Plenty of Americans agree: the campus of Vanderbilt University or Williams College is filled with students whose families are largely indifferent to the price their school charges but keenly interested in the flower beds and the spacious suites and the architecturally distinguished lecture halls those high prices make possible. Of course, given that the rising cost of college has become a significant social problem in the United States in recent years, you can make a strong case that a school ought to be rewarded for being affordable....

The *U.S. News* rankings turn out to be full of these kinds of implicit ideological 12 choices. One common statistic used to evaluate colleges, for example, is called "graduation rate performance," which compares a school's actual graduation rate with its predicted graduation rate given the socioeconomic status and the test scores of its incoming freshman class. It is a measure of the school's efficacy: it quantifies the impact of a school's culture and teachers and institutional support mechanisms. Tulane, given the qualifications of the students that it admits, ought to have a graduation rate of eighty-seven per cent; its actual 2009 graduation rate was seventy-three per cent. That shortfall suggests that something is amiss at Tulane. Another common statistic for measuring college quality is "student selectivity." This reflects variables such as how many of a college's freshmen were in the top ten per cent of their high-school class, how high their S.A.T. scores were, and what percentage of applicants a college admits. Selectivity quantifies how accomplished students are when they first arrive on campus.

Each of these statistics matters, but for very different reasons. As a society, we 13 probably care more about efficacy: America's future depends on colleges that make sure the students they admit leave with an education and a degree. If you are a bright high-school senior and you're thinking about your own future, though, you may well care more about selectivity, because that relates to the prestige of your degree....

There is no right answer to how much weight a ranking system should give to 14 these two competing values. It's a matter of which educational model you value more—and here, once again, *U.S. News* makes its position clear. It gives twice as much weight to selectivity as it does to efficacy....

Rankings are not benign. They enshrine very particular ideologies, and, at a time 14 when American higher education is facing a crisis of accessibility and affordability, we have adopted a de facto standard of college quality that is uninterested in both of those factors. And why? Because a group of magazine analysts in an office building in Washington, D.C., decided twenty years ago to value selectivity over efficacy.

READING FOR MEANING

1. **Read to Summarize.** Write a sentence or two identifying Gladwell's overall judgment and his main reasons.

2. **Read to Respond.** Write a paragraph analyzing anything that resonates with your experience, such as the research finding that "student 'engagement' — that is, the extent to which students immerse themselves in the intellectual and social life of their college" may be "the most important variable in a successful" educational experience (par. 7); or the fact that "price" was not included as a variable in the *U.S. News* college rankings.

3. **Read to Analyze Assumptions.** Write a paragraph or two analyzing an assumption you find intriguing in Gladwell's essay. For example:

   Assumptions about ideology. **Ideology** means the ideas, beliefs, values, and concerns of an individual or a group, and it often centers on issues concerning power and equality. Gladwell asserts that "The *U.S. News* rankings turn out to be full of… implicit ideological choices" (par. 11), such as not including affordability, and valuing "selectivity over efficacy" in its ranking formula (par. 14).

   - Gladwell criticizes rankings in general and the *U.S. News* ranking system in particular for having harmful effects. Who does a ranking system like that of the *U.S. News* benefit? Who does it potentially harm?

   - In paragraph 14, Gladwell specifies "affordability" as an important factor or criterion. In light of "the rising cost of college," he calls affordability "a significant social problem" (par. 10). What does the omission of price indicate about the ideology behind the *U.S. News* ranking system? Who should care that some highly qualified students cannot afford to attend the best colleges? Why?

   Assumptions about efficacy and selectivity. Gladwell explains that judging a school's efficacy is often at odds with judging its selectivity. Efficacy refers to the effectiveness in graduating the students the school accepted: in other words, the graduation rate. Selectivity refers to who is accepted in the first place, and therefore "quantifies how accomplished students are when they first arrive on campus" (par. 11).

   - Why do you think Gladwell claims that "[a]s a society, we probably care more about efficacy"… but "a bright high-school senior… may well care more

For help with reading strategies like summarizing and analyzing assumptions, see Chapter 2.

about selectivity" (par. 12)? What added benefits are there to attending a highly selective, prestigious college?

- What assumptions do we make about the value of a college education? What is its value to you personally and to society in general?

READING LIKE A WRITER

Responding to Objections and Alternative Judgments

Because it is a negative evaluation, one could say that Gladwell's entire essay is an implied refutation of those who think well of the *U.S. News* college rankings. However, Gladwell also responds specifically to comments made by Robert Morse, the director of data research for *U.S. News & World Report*. Gladwell cues his refutation with the rhetorical question "Why?" and he goes on to answer by quoting Morse:

Cue	Why? [Director of Data Research Robert] Morse **admitted** that
Words convey-	there was **no formal reason** for that position. It was **just a feeling**.
ing tone	"We're not saying that we're measuring educational outcomes," he explained. (par. 9)

Not only does he present his reasons for disagreeing with Morse, but Gladwell also expresses his attitude toward Morse's explanation through his choice of words. He continues in this *tone* when he comments at the beginning of the next paragraph: "As answers go, that's up there with the parental 'Because I said so'" (par. 10).

A writer's tone, especially when sarcastic or mocking, can have a strong effect on readers. Those who agree may appreciate it, but those who disagree or are uncertain may be put off by it.

ANALYZE & WRITE

Write a paragraph analyzing Morse's response to Gladwell and Gladwell's response to Morse:

1. Reread paragraph 9. How would you describe Morse's response to Gladwell's criticism: Which of Gladwell's points does Morse concede or refute?

2. Now reread paragraphs 10–12. How does Gladwell respond to Morse? How does he concede or refute Morse's response? How would you describe the tone, or emotional resonance, of Gladwell's response? Is he fair, mean, sarcastic, something else?

3. Given Gladwell's purpose and audience, how do you imagine readers would react to Morse's response to criticism as well as to Gladwell's handling of Morse's response? How did you respond?

Christine Rosen

The Myth of Multitasking

Christine Rosen (b. 1973) holds a Ph.D. in history from Emory University and has been a scholar at the New America Foundation and the American Enterprise Institute. She has written several books, including *The Extinction of Experience* (2016), *My Fundamentalist Education* (2005), and *The Feminist Dilemma* (2001). She also coedited *Acculturated: 23 Savvy Writers Find Hidden Virtue in Reality TV, Chic Lit, Video Games, and Other Pillars of Pop Culture* (2011). A commentator on bioethics and the social effects of technology, she has frequently appeared on National Public Radio, CNN, and Fox News and in other venues. Rosen's essays have appeared in such prestigious publications as the *New York Times Magazine, Washington Post, Wall Street Journal, National Review*, and *New Atlantis: A Journal of Technology & Society*, where she is a senior editor and where this essay originally appeared in 2008.

- **Before you read,** think about what Rosen might mean by her title, "The Myth of Multitasking." What does the word *myth* lead you to expect her judgment to be?

- **As you read,** think about your own experience with multitasking and what you think its advantages and disadvantages are. How well does Rosen's essay resonate with your experience?

In one of the many letters he wrote to his son in the 1740s, Lord Chesterfield offered   1
the following advice: "There is time enough for everything in the course of the day, if you do but one thing at once, but there is not time enough in the year, if you will do two things at a time." To Chesterfield, singular focus was not merely a practical way to structure one's time; it was a mark of intelligence. "This steady and undissipated attention to one object, is a sure mark of a superior genius; as hurry, bustle, and agitation, are the never-failing symptoms of a weak and frivolous mind."

In modern times, hurry, bustle, and agitation have become a regular way of life for   2
many people—so much so that we have embraced a word to describe our efforts to respond to the many pressing demands on our time: *multitasking*. Used for decades to describe the parallel processing abilities of computers, multitasking is now shorthand for the human attempt to do simultaneously as many things as possible, as quickly as possible, preferably marshaling the power of as many technologies as possible.

In the late 1990s and early 2000s, one sensed a kind of exuberance about   3
the possibilities of multitasking. Advertisements for new electronic gadgets—particularly the first generation of handheld digital devices—celebrated the notion of using technology to accomplish several things at once. The word *multitasking* began appearing in the "skills" sections of résumés, as office workers restyled themselves as high-tech, high-performing team players. "We have always multitasked—inability

to walk and chew gum is a time-honored cause for derision—but never so intensely or self-consciously as now," James Gleick wrote in his 1999 book *Faster*. "We are multitasking connoisseurs—experts in crowding, pressing, packing, and overlapping distinct activities in our all-too-finite moments." An article in the *New York Times Magazine* in 2001 asked, "Who can remember life before multitasking? These days we all do it." The article offered advice on "How to Multitask" with suggestions about giving your brain's "multitasking hot spot" an appropriate workout.

But more recently, challenges to the ethos of multitasking have begun to   4
emerge. Numerous studies have shown the sometimes-fatal danger of using cell phones and other electronic devices while driving, for example, and several states have now made that particular form of multitasking illegal. In the business world, where concerns about time-management are perennial, warnings about work-place distractions spawned by a multitasking culture are on the rise. In 2005, the BBC reported on a research study, funded by Hewlett-Packard and conducted by the Institute of Psychiatry at the University of London, that found, "Workers distracted by e-mail and phone calls suffer a fall in IQ more than twice that found in marijuana smokers." The psychologist who led the study called this new "info-mania" a serious threat to workplace productivity. One of the *Harvard Business Review*'s "Breakthrough Ideas" for 2007 was Linda Stone's notion of "continuous partial attention," which might be understood as a subspecies of multitasking: using mobile computing power and the Internet, we are "constantly scanning for opportunities and staying on top of contacts, events, and activities in an effort to miss nothing."

Dr. Edward Hallowell, a Massachusetts-based psychiatrist who specializes in the   5
treatment of attention deficit/hyperactivity disorder and has written a book with the self-explanatory title *CrazyBusy*, has been offering therapies to combat extreme multitasking for years; in his book he calls multitasking a "mythical activity in which people believe they can perform two or more tasks simultaneously." In a 2005 article, he described a new condition, "Attention Deficit Trait," which he claims is rampant in the business world. ADT is "purely a response to the hyperkinetic environment in which we live," writes Hallowell, and its hallmark symptoms mimic those of ADD. "Never in history has the human brain been asked to track so many data points," Hallowell argues, and this challenge "can be controlled only by creatively engineering one's environment and one's emotional and physical health." Limiting multitasking is essential. Best-selling business advice author Timothy Ferriss also extols the virtues of "single-tasking" in his book, *The 4-Hour Workweek*.

Multitasking might also be taking a toll on the economy. One study by research-   6
ers at the University of California at Irvine monitored interruptions among office workers; they found that workers took an average of twenty-five minutes to recover from interruptions such as phone calls or answering e-mail and return to their original task. Discussing multitasking with the *New York Times* in 2007, Jonathan B. Spira, an analyst at the business research firm Basex, estimated that extreme multitasking—information overload—costs the U.S. economy $650 billion a year in lost productivity.

CHANGING OUR BRAINS

To better understand the multitasking phenomenon, neurologists and psychologists 7 have studied the workings of the brain. In 1999, Jordan Grafman, chief of cognitive neuroscience at the National Institute of Neurological Disorders and Stroke (part of the National Institutes of Health), used functional magnetic resonance imaging (fMRI) scans to determine that when people engage in "task-switching"—that is, multitasking behavior—the flow of blood increases to a region of the frontal cortex called Brodmann area 10. (The flow of blood to particular regions of the brain is taken as a proxy indication of activity in those regions.) "This is presumably the last part of the brain to evolve, the most mysterious and exciting part," Grafman told the *New York Times* in 2001—adding, with a touch of hyperbole, "It's what makes us most human."

It is also what makes multitasking a poor long-term strategy for learning. Other 8 studies, such as those performed by psychologist René Marois of Vanderbilt University, have used fMRI to demonstrate the brain's response to handling multiple tasks. Marois found evidence of a "response selection bottleneck" that occurs when the brain is forced to respond to several stimuli at once. As a result, task-switching leads to time lost as the brain determines which task to perform. Psychologist David Meyer at the University of Michigan believes that rather than a bottleneck in the brain, a process of "adaptive executive control" takes place, which "schedules task processes appropriately to obey instructions about their relative priorities and serial order," as he described to the *New Scientist*. Unlike many other researchers who study multitasking, Meyer is optimistic that, with training, the brain can learn to task-switch more effectively, and there is some evidence that certain simple tasks are amenable to such practice. But his research has also found that multitasking contributes to the release of stress hormones and adrenaline, which can cause long-term health problems if not controlled, and contributes to the loss of short-term memory.

In one recent study, Russell Poldrack, a psychology professor at the University of 9 California, Los Angeles, found that "multitasking adversely affects how you learn. Even if you learn while multitasking, that learning is less flexible and more specialized, so you cannot retrieve the information as easily." His research demonstrates that people use different areas of the brain for learning and storing new information when they are distracted: brain scans of people who are distracted or multitasking show activity in the striatum, a region of the brain involved in learning new skills; brain scans of people who are not distracted show activity in the hippocampus, a region involved in storing and recalling information. Discussing his research on National Public Radio recently, Poldrack warned, "We have to be aware that there is a cost to the way that our society is changing, that humans are not built to work this way. We're really built to focus. And when we sort of force ourselves to multitask, we're driving ourselves to perhaps be less efficient in the long run even though it sometimes feels like we're being more efficient."

If, as Poldrack concluded, "multitasking changes the way people learn," what 10 might this mean for today's children and teens, raised with an excess of new entertainment and educational technology, and avidly multitasking at a young age?

Poldrack calls this the "million-dollar question." Media multitasking—that is, the simultaneous use of several different media, such as television, the Internet, video games, text messages, telephones, and e-mail—is clearly on the rise, as a 2006 report from the Kaiser Family Foundation showed: in 1999, only 16 percent of the time people spent using any of those media was spent on multiple media at once; by 2005, 26 percent of media time was spent multitasking. "I multitask every single second I am online," confessed one study participant. "At this very moment I am watching TV, checking my e-mail every two minutes, reading a newsgroup about who shot JFK, burning some music to a CD, and writing this message."

The Kaiser report noted several factors that increase the likelihood of media multi- 11 tasking, including "having a computer and being able to see a television from it." Also, "sensation-seeking" personality types are more likely to multitask, as are those living in "a highly TV-oriented household." The picture that emerges of these pubescent multitasking mavens is of a generation of great technical facility and intelligence but of extreme impatience, unsatisfied with slowness and uncomfortable with silence: "I get bored if it's not all going at once, because everything has gaps—waiting for a website to come up, commercials on TV, etc.," one participant said. The report concludes on a very peculiar note, perhaps intended to be optimistic: "In this media-heavy world, it is likely that brains that are more adept at media multitasking will be passed along and these changes will be naturally selected," the report states. "After all, information is power, and if one can process more information all at once, perhaps one can be more powerful." This is techno-social Darwinism, nature red in pixel and claw.

Other experts aren't so sure. As neurologist Jordan Grafman told *Time* magazine: 12 "Kids that are instant messaging while doing homework, playing games online and watching TV, I predict, aren't going to do well in the long run." "I think this generation of kids are guinea pigs," educational psychologist Jane Healy told the *San Francisco Chronicle*; she worries that they might become adults who engage in "very quick but very shallow thinking." Or, as the novelist Walter Kirn suggests in a deft essay in *The Atlantic*, we might be headed for an "Attention-Deficit Recession."

PAYING ATTENTION

When we talk about multitasking, we are really talking about attention: the art of 13 paying attention, the ability to shift our attention, and, more broadly, to exercise judgment about what objects are worthy of our attention. People who have achieved great things often credit for their success a finely honed skill for paying attention. When asked about his particular genius, Isaac Newton responded that if he had made any discoveries, it was "owing more to patient attention than to any other talent."

William James, the great psychologist, wrote at length about the varieties of 14 human attention. In *The Principles of Psychology* (1890), he outlined the differences among "sensorial attention," "intellectual attention," "passive attention," and the like, and noted the "gray chaotic indiscriminateness" of the minds of people who were incapable of paying attention. James compared our stream of thought to a river, and his observations presaged the cognitive "bottlenecks" described later by neurologists: "On the whole easy simple flowing predominates in it, the drift of things is with the pull of gravity, and effortless attention is the rule," he wrote. "But at intervals an obstruction, a set-back, a log-jam occurs, stops the current, creates an eddy, and makes things temporarily move the other way."

To James, steady attention was thus the default condition of a mature mind, an 15 ordinary state undone only by perturbation. To readers a century later, that placid portrayal may seem alien—as though depicting a bygone world. Instead, today's multitasking adult may find something more familiar in James's description of the youthful mind: an "extreme mobility of the attention" that "makes the child seem to belong less to himself than to every object which happens to catch his notice." For some people, James noted, this challenge is never overcome; such people only get their work done "in the interstices of their mind-wandering." Like Chesterfield, James believed that the transition from youthful distraction to mature attention was in large part the result of personal mastery and discipline—and so was illustrative of character. "The faculty of voluntarily bringing back a wandering attention, over and over again," he wrote, "is the very root of judgment, character, and will."

Today, our collective will to pay attention seems fairly weak. We require advice 16 books to teach us how to avoid distraction. In the not-too-distant future we may even employ new devices to help us overcome the unintended attention deficits created by today's gadgets. As one *New York Times* article recently suggested, "Further research could help create clever technology, like sensors or smart software that workers could instruct with their preferences and priorities to serve as a high tech 'time nanny' to ease the modern multitasker's plight." Perhaps we will all accept as a matter of course a computer governor—like the devices placed on engines so that people can't drive cars beyond a certain speed. Our technological governors might prompt us with reminders to set mental limits when we try to do too much, too quickly, all at once.

Then again, perhaps we will simply adjust and come to accept what James called 17 "acquired inattention." E-mails pouring in, cell phones ringing, televisions blaring, podcasts streaming—all this may become background noise, like the "din of a foundry or factory" that James observed workers could scarcely avoid at first, but which eventually became just another part of their daily routine. For the younger generation of multitaskers, the great electronic din is an expected part of everyday life. And given what neuroscience and anecdotal evidence have shown us, this state of constant intentional self-distraction could well be of profound detriment to individual and cultural well-being. When people do their work only in the "interstices of their mind-wandering," with crumbs of attention rationed out among many competing tasks, their culture may gain in information, but it will surely weaken in wisdom.

READING FOR MEANING

For help with reading strategies like summarizing and analyzing assumptions, see Chapter 2.

1. **Read to Summarize.** Write a sentence or two summarizing Rosen's reasons for critiquing multitasking.

2. **Read to Respond.** Write a paragraph analyzing anything that resonates with your own experience, such as your experience multitasking compared to "single-tasking" — and what the advantages or disadvantages are of focusing your attention on one task at a time (par. 5); or the suggestion that multitaskers are impatient and "uncomfortable with silence," and that they quickly get bored (par. 11).

3. **Read to Analyze Assumptions.** Write a paragraph or two analyzing an assumption you find intriguing in Rosen's essay. For example:

Assumptions about the causes of not focusing attention. Quoting Lord Chesterfield's writing from the eighteenth century and William James's from the nineteenth, Rosen suggests that not focusing one's attention may indicate "a weak and frivolous mind" (par. 1) or the lack of "a mature mind" or of "judgment, character, and will" (par. 15). Such language makes a moral judgment about a person's lack of seriousness or self-discipline. In contrast, quoting Edward Hallowell, Rosen suggests that not focusing attention may be a sign of illness akin to attention deficit/hyperactivity disorder (par. 5).

- Why might people, particularly young people, who do not focus their attention be labeled as lacking in character or intelligence or as suffering from a medical malady?

- Are critics less likely today than in the past to make judgments about intelligence or character, and perhaps more likely to make medical diagnoses about the same kinds of behavior? Why or why not?

Assumptions about the role of media in multitasking. According to Rosen, the Kaiser Family Foundation has reported a substantial increase in multitasking on media. She cites the foundation's finding that, in 1999, 16 percent of media time (for example, watching television, surfing the Internet, or texting friends) was spent doing two or more of such tasks simultaneously. By 2005, the time spent multitasking had increased to 26 percent.

- When you are multitasking, is some kind of electronic medium always involved, or do you ever multitask without using media?

- Do you primarily use media multitasking to fill or kill time, or for some other reason? What percentage of time spent multitasking do you think the Kaiser Family Foundation would find if they did their report today?

READING LIKE A WRITER

Supporting the Judgment

Rosen relies primarily on authorities and research studies to support her argument about the value of multitasking. Because she is not writing for an academic audience, however, she does not have to include formal citations, as you will be expected to do in your college writing. Nevertheless, note that Rosen does provide many of the same kinds of information about her sources that formal citations offer — the source author or lead researcher's name, the title of the publication in which the borrowed material appeared, and the year of publication of the source — so that readers can locate and read the source themselves. Notice in the following examples how Rosen presents this information.

Bibliographical information	In one of the many letters he wrote to his son in the 1740s, Lord Chesterfield offered the following advice: "There is time enough for everything...." (par. 1)
	"We have always multitasked ... but never so intensely or self-consciously as now," James Gleick wrote in his 1999 book *Faster*. "We are multitasking connoisseurs...." (par. 3)

Writers often begin with the source's name to provide context and establish credibility. In the third example, Rosen places the source information in the middle of the quotation, possibly because she wants to emphasize the opening phrases of both sentences.

Not all sources are quoted, of course. Writers sometimes summarize the main idea or paraphrase what the source has said:

| Summary | One study by researchers at the University of California at Irvine monitored interruptions among office workers; they found that workers took an average of twenty-five minutes to recover from interruptions.... (par. 6) |
| Paraphrase | The psychologist who led the study called this new "infomania" a serious threat to workplace productivity. (par. 4) |

ANALYZE & WRITE

Write a paragraph analyzing and evaluating how Rosen uses material from other authorities and research studies to support her argument:

1. First, skim paragraphs 4–9 and highlight the names of authorities and the research studies Rosen cites.

2. Then choose two sources, and determine how Rosen uses them to support her judgment about the value of multitasking. Also notice how she integrates these sources into her text.

3. Finally, consider why these sources might or might not be convincing for Rosen's readers. How convincing are they for you, and why?

Combining Reading Strategies

Comparing and Contrasting Related Readings to Judge a Writer's Credibility

Comparing and contrasting related readings with a specific focus on credibility can help you judge the credibility of each writer more effectively. By looking at the similarities and differences between how Rosen, author of "The Myth of Multitasking," and Hertogs, author of "Typing vs. Handwriting Notes: An Evaluation of the Effects of Transcription Method on Student Learning," establish their credibility you can begin to determine whether what you are being told is worth taking seriously. Taking into account what we know about the author — for example, their academic and professional credentials, lived experiences, and whether the text appeared in a reputable publication — is an important aspect of determining credibility. But, we also need to think about how the writer comes across in the text itself. In an evaluative argument, we especially want to see whether the writer is knowledgeable about the subject and fair in handling objections and alternative judgments, and also whether the writer shares our values or criteria for evaluating this kind of subject.

For guidelines on comparing and contrasting related readings, see Chapter 2, pp. 57–60. For guidelines on judging a writer's credibility, see Chapter 2, pp. 66–68.

Compare and contrast Rosen's "The Myth of Multitasking" (p. 309) and Hertogs's "Typing vs. Handwriting Notes: An Evaluation of the Effects of Transcription Method on Student Learning," (p. 287) thinking about issues such as these:

- Both pieces address the role that distractions play in our lives today, including their potential effect on how we take notes and whether we can multitask. Compare and contrast how the authors establish their credibility when it comes to evaluating the effects of distraction on these activities.

- Compare how authoritative and knowledgeable Hertogs and Rosen seem. Point to any places in their essays that either instill confidence in their knowledge or make you wonder whether they know enough to make a judgment.

- Reread both pieces, paying particular attention to the tone of the authors' evaluations. Write a paragraph comparing the tones of the texts. Are there any moments in either text where the author's tone — whether toward the subject or the reader — undermines the author's credibility?

Christine Romano

Jessica Statsky's "Children Need to Play, Not Compete": An Evaluation

Christine Romano wrote the following essay when she was a first-year college student. In it, she evaluates a position paper written by another student, Jessica Statsky's "Children Need to Play, Not Compete," which appears in Chapter 8 of this book (pp. 374–379). Romano focuses not on the writing strategies Statsky uses but rather on her logic — that is, on whether Statsky's argument is likely to convince her intended readers. She evaluates the logic of the argument according to the criteria or standards presented in Chapter 2 (pp. 60–62).

- **Before you read,** Romano's evaluation, you might want to read Statsky's essay, thinking about what seems most and least convincing to you about her argument that competitive sports can be harmful to young children.

- **As you read,** think about Romano's criteria. How important is it that the supporting evidence for an argument be "appropriate, believable, consistent, and complete" (par. 2)?

Parents of young children have a lot to worry about and to hope for. In "Children Need to Play, Not Compete," Jessica Statsky appeals to their worries and hopes in order to convince them that organized competitive sports may harm their children physically and psychologically. Statsky states her thesis clearly and fully forecasts the reasons she will offer to justify her position: Besides causing physical and psychological harm, competitive sports discourage young people from becoming players and fans when they are older and inevitably put parents' needs and fantasies ahead of children's welfare. Statsky also carefully defines her key terms. By *sports*, for example, she means to include both contact and noncontact sports that emphasize competition. The sports may be organized locally at schools or summer sports camps or nationally, as in the examples of Peewee Football and Little League Baseball. She is concerned only with children six to twelve years of age. 1

In this essay, I will evaluate the logic of Statsky's argument, considering whether the support for her thesis is appropriate, believable, consistent, and complete. While her logic *is* appropriate, believable, and consistent, her argument also has weaknesses. It seems incomplete because it neglects to anticipate parents' predictable questions and objections and because it fails to support certain parts fully. 2

Statsky provides appropriate support for her thesis. Throughout her essay, she relies for support on different kinds of information (she cites thirteen separate sources, including books, newspapers, and websites). Her quotations, examples, and statistics all support the reasons she believes competitive sports are bad for children. For example, in paragraph 3, Statsky offers the reason that competitive sports may 3 damage children's bodies and that contact sports may be especially injurious. She supports this reason by paraphrasing Koppett's statement that muscle strain or even permanent injury may result when a twelve-year-old throws curve balls. She then quotes Tutko on the dangers of tackle football. The opinions of both experts are obviously appropriate. They are relevant to her reason, and we can easily imagine that they would worry many parents.

Not only is Statsky's support appropriate but it is also believable. Statsky quotes   4
or summarizes authorities to support her argument in nearly every paragraph. The question is whether readers would find these authorities believable or credible. Since Statsky relies almost entirely on authorities to support her argument, readers must believe these authorities for her argument to succeed. I have not read Statsky's sources, but I think there are good reasons to consider them authoritative. First of all, the newspaper writers she quotes write for two of America's most respected newspapers, *The New York Times* and *The Los Angeles Times*. Both of these newspapers have sports reporters who not only report on sports events but also take a critical look at sports issues. In addition, both newspapers have reporters who specialize in children's health and education. Second, Statsky gives background information about the authorities she quotes, information intended to increase the person's believability in the eyes of parents of young children. In paragraph 3, she tells readers that Thomas Tutko is "a psychology professor at San Jose State University and coauthor of the book *Winning Is Everything and Other American Myths*." In paragraph 5, she announces that Martin Rablovsky is "a former sports editor for *The New York Times*," and she notes that he has watched children play organized sports for many years. Third, Statsky quotes from a number of websites, including the official Little League site and the American Orthopaedic Society for Sports Medicine. Parents are likely to accept the authority of these sites.

In addition to quoting authorities, Statsky relies on examples and anecdotes to   5
support the reasons for her position. If examples and anecdotes are to be believable, they must seem representative to readers, not bizarre or highly unusual or completely unpredictable. Readers can imagine a similar event happening elsewhere. For anecdotes to be believable, they should, in addition, be specific and true to life. All of Statsky's examples and anecdotes fulfill these requirements, and her readers would likely find them believable. For example, early in her argument, in paragraph 4, Statsky reasons that fear of being hurt greatly reduces children's enjoyment of contact sports. The anecdote comes from Tosches's investigative report on Peewee Football, as does the quotation by the mother of an eight-year-old player who says that the children become frightened and pretend to be injured in order to stay out of the game. In the anecdote, a seven-year-old makes himself vomit to avoid playing. Because these echo the familiar "I feel bad" or "I'm sick" excuse children give when they do not want to go somewhere (especially school) or do something, most parents would find them believable. They could easily imagine their own children pretending to be hurt or ill if they were fearful or depressed. The anecdote is also specific. Tosches reports what the boy said and did and what the coach said and did.

Other examples provide support for all the major reasons Statsky gives for her 6
position:

- That competitive sports pose psychological dangers—children becoming serious and unplayful when the game starts (par. 5)

- That adults' desire to win puts children at risk—parents fighting each other at a Peewee Football game and a baseball coach setting fire to an opposing team's jersey (par. 8)

- That organized sports should emphasize cooperation and individual performance instead of winning—a coach wishing to ban scoring but finding that parents would not support him and a New York City basketball league in which all children play an equal amount of time and scoring is easier (pars. 10–11)

All of these examples are appropriate to the reasons they support. They are also 7
believable. Together, they help Statsky achieve her purpose of convincing parents
that organized, competitive sports may be bad for their children and that there are
alternatives.

If readers are to find an argument logical and convincing, it must be consistent 8
and complete. While there are no inconsistencies or contradictions in Statsky's argument, it is seriously incomplete because it neglects to support fully one of its reasons, it fails to anticipate many predictable questions parents would have, and it
pays too little attention to noncontact competitive team sports. The most obvious
example of thin support comes in paragraphs 10–11, where Statsky asserts that many
parents are ready for children's team sports that emphasize cooperation and individual performance. Yet the example of a Little League official who failed to win parents' approval to ban scores raises serious questions about just how many parents are
ready to embrace noncompetitive sports teams. The other support, a brief description
of City Sports for Kids in New York City, is very convincing but will only be logically
compelling to those parents who are already inclined to agree with Statsky's position.
Parents inclined to disagree with Statsky would need additional evidence. Most parents know that big cities receive special federal funding for evening, weekend, and
summer recreation. Brief descriptions of six or eight noncompetitive teams in a variety of sports in cities, rural areas, suburban neighborhoods—some funded publicly,
some funded privately—would be more likely to convince skeptics. Statsky is guilty
here of failing to accept the burden of proof, a logical fallacy.

Statsky's argument is also incomplete in that it fails to anticipate certain objections 9
and questions that some parents, especially those she most wants to convince, are
almost sure to raise. In the first sentences of paragraphs 10 and 12, Statsky does show
that she is thinking about her readers' questions. She does not go nearly far enough,
however, to have a chance of influencing two types of readers: those who themselves
are or were fans of and participants in competitive sports and those who want their
six- to twelve-year-old children involved in mainstream sports programs despite the
risks, especially the national programs that have a certain prestige. Such parents might

feel that competitive team sports for young children create a sense of community with a shared purpose, build character through self-sacrifice and commitment to the group, teach children to face their fears early and learn how to deal with them through the support of coaches and team members, and introduce children to the principles of social cooperation and collaboration. Some parents are likely to believe and to know from personal experience that coaches who burn opposing teams' jerseys on the pitching mound before the game starts are the exception, not the rule. Some young children idolize teachers and coaches, and team practice and games are the brightest moments in their lives. Statsky seems not to have considered these reasonable possibilities, and as a result her argument lacks a compelling logic it might have had. By acknowledging that she was aware of many of these objections—and perhaps even accommodating more of them in her own argument, as she does in paragraph 12, while refuting other objections—she would have strengthened her argument.

Finally, Statsky's argument is incomplete because she overlooks examples of 10 noncontact team sports. Track, swimming, and tennis are good examples that some readers would certainly think of. Some elementary schools compete in track meets. Public and private clubs and recreational programs organize competitive swimming and tennis competitions. In these sports, individual performance is the focus. No one gets trampled. Children exert themselves only as much as they are able to. Yet individual performances are scored, and a team score is derived. Because Statsky fails to mention any of these obvious possibilities, her argument is weakened.

The logic of Statsky's argument, then, has both strengths and weaknesses. The 11 support she offers is appropriate, believable, and consistent. The major weakness is incompleteness—she fails to anticipate more fully the likely objections of a wide range of readers. Her logic would prevent parents who enjoy and advocate competitive sports from taking her argument seriously. Such parents and their children have probably had positive experiences with team sports, and these experiences would lead them to believe that the gains are worth whatever risks may be involved. Many probably think that the risks Statsky points out can be avoided by careful monitoring. For those parents inclined to agree with her, Statsky's logic is likely to seem sound and complete. An argument that successfully confirms readers' beliefs is certainly valid, and Statsky succeeds admirably at this kind of argument. Because she does not offer compelling counterarguments to the legitimate objections of those inclined not to agree with her, however, her success is limited.

READING FOR MEANING

For help with reading strategies like summarizing and analyzing assumptions, see Chapter 2.

1. **Read to Summarize.** Write a sentence or two briefly summarizing the strengths and weaknesses of Statsky's argument, according to Romano.

2. **Read to Respond.** Write a paragraph analyzing your initial reactions to Romano's evaluation of Statsky's argument. For example, based on your

experience or observation of organized sports for kids, do you agree with Romano's judgment that Statsky's reasons seem believable?

3. **Read to Analyze Assumptions.** Write a paragraph or two analyzing an assumption you find intriguing in Romano's essay. For example:

Assumptions about the relative value of competition or cooperation. Romano gives an example supporting Statsky's argument that team sports for young children "should emphasize cooperation and individual performance instead of winning" (par. 6). In paragraph 8, however, Romano suggests that some parents believe that team sports may teach cooperation together with competition and that the two skills and attitudes may be more closely related than Statsky acknowledges.

- What do you think leads Romano to suggest that children learn both competition and cooperation when they participate in team sports?
- How is learning to cooperate and collaborate beneficial for us as individuals and as a society? Is competition also beneficial?

Assumptions about the importance of facing fear. As Romano notes in paragraph 5, "Statsky reasons that fear of being hurt greatly reduces children's enjoyment of contact sports," and as support she cites Tosches's anecdote about the child who "makes himself vomit to avoid playing." Nevertheless, Romano suggests that some parents think facing fear is a good thing:

- In what contexts, other than sports, do people typically experience physical or psychological fear?
- Why might learning how to deal with fear (presumably by doing something even though it causes us to be fearful) be a good thing?

READING LIKE A WRITER

Organizing the Evaluation

Transitions or cues play an important role in helping readers follow the logic of the argument. Logical transitions serve a variety of specific purposes:

- To list items consecutively

Consecutive cues   . . . there are good reasons to consider them authoritative. First of all, the newspaper writers. . . . Second, Statsky gives. . . . Third, Statsky quotes. . . . (par. 4)

- To call attention to additional points

Other examples provide support for all the major reasons Statsky gives for her position:

<table>
<tr><td>Note that items in list are parallel.</td><td>That competitive sports pose...</td></tr>
</table>

That adults' desire to win puts...

That organized sports should emphasize... (par. 6)

- To introduce a contrast or an opposing point

I have not read Statsky's sources, *but* I think... (par. 4)

- To signal a cause or effect

<table>
<tr><td>Transition indi-cating a cause</td><td>It seems incomplete because it... (par. 2)</td></tr>
<tr><td>Transition indi-cating an effect</td><td>Statsky seems..., and as a result her argument lacks... (par. 8)</td></tr>
</table>

- To conclude

The logic of Statsky's argument, then, has... (par. 10)

ANALYZE & WRITE

Write a paragraph analyzing and evaluating the effectiveness of Romano's cueing strategies.

1. First, find Romano's thesis and forecasting statement, underlining the reasons supporting her argument.
2. Then skim the essay, noting where each of her reasons is brought up again, underlining topic sentences and any cues she uses to help readers follow her argument.
3. How effectively does Romano use these devices to orient readers? Where, if anywhere, would you appreciate more cueing?

Writing to Learn Evaluation

Write a brief essay analyzing one of the readings in this chapter (or another selection, perhaps one by a classmate). Explain how (and, perhaps, how well) the selection works as an evaluation. Consider, for example, how it

- presents the subject in a way that is appropriate for the purpose and audience;
- supports the judgment with reasons and evidence based on shared criteria;

- responds sensitively to possible objections and alternative judgments;
- organizes the review clearly and logically, helping readers follow the argument.

Your essay could also reflect on how you applied one or more of the academic habits of mind through the following practices:

- **Critical Analysis** — what assumptions in the selection did you find intriguing, and why?

- **Rhetorical Sensitivity** — how effective or ineffective do you think the selection is in achieving its purpose for the intended audience?

- **Empathy** — did you find yourself identifying with the author, and how important was this to the effectiveness of the selection?

A GUIDE TO WRITING EVALUATIONS

You have probably done a good deal of analytical writing about your reading. Your instructor may also assign a capstone project to write a brief evaluation of your own. This Guide to Writing offers detailed suggestions and resources to help you meet the special challenges this kind of writing presents.

THE WRITING ASSIGNMENT

Write an evaluation supporting your judgment.

- Choose a subject that you can analyze in detail.

- Base your judgment on widely recognized criteria for evaluating a subject like yours.

- Marshal evidence to support your judgment.

- Consider possible objections your readers might raise as well as alternative judgments they might prefer.

- Organize your evaluation clearly and logically.

WRITING YOUR DRAFT

Choosing a Subject to Evaluate

Rather than limiting yourself to the first subject that comes to mind, take a few minutes to consider your options and list as many subjects as you can. Below are some guidelines to help you choose a promising subject, followed by suggestions for the types of subjects you might consider writing about.

Choose a subject that

- you can view and review (for example, a location you can visit; a printed text; or a website or digital recording from which you can capture stills or video clips to use as examples);

- is typically evaluated according to criteria or standards of judgment that you understand and share with your readers;

- has strengths and/or weaknesses you could illustrate.

Below are some categories and ideas for possible subjects:

- *Culture:* a film or group of films, a television show or series, a video game, a song, a live or recorded performance, an art museum or individual work of art, a park

- *Written work:* an essay in this book or another your instructor approves, a short story, website, magazine, campus publication, textbook in a course you've taken

- *Education:* your high school, a course you have taken, a laboratory you have worked in, a library or campus support service, a teacher or program

- *Government:* an elected official or candidate for public office, a proposed or existing law, an agency or program

- *Social:* a club or organized activity such as a camping trip, sports team, debate group

Assessing Your Subject and Considering How to Present It to Your Readers

Once you have made a preliminary choice of a subject, consider how you can frame it so that readers will be open to your evaluation. To do this, consider first how you regard the subject and what your readers are likely to think. While it may be tempting to think about your subject in binary terms — meaning thinking that the subject is either positive or negative or good or bad — this kind of thinking oversimplifies the subject by only allowing it to be characterized by one or the other extreme. Subjects are neither entirely good or bad or positive or negative. For example, a specific kind of diet is likely good for some people but bad for others just as earning a higher salary may be considered a positive development except perhaps when it means you have less work/life balance. Use the following questions and sentence strategies as a jumping-off point. You can make the sentences you generate your own later, as you revise.

What Do I Think? Consider what you think about the different qualities of your subject and how these qualities might factor into your evaluation.

▶ Although _____ is stellar in [these ways], it falls short in [these other ways].

What genre or kind of subject is it?

▶ The _____ is a [genre or category of subject, such as romantic comedy or horror movie].

▶ It is an innovative [category in which the subject belongs] that combines elements of _____ and _____.

What criteria or standards of judgment do you usually use to evaluate **things of** this kind?

▶ I expect _____ to be _____ or _____.

▶ I dislike it when _____ are _____.

How does your subject compare to other examples of the genre?

▶ Compared to [other subjects], _____ has the [best or worst] _____ [name trait].

▶ Whereas other [comparable subjects] can be [faulted/praised for] _____, this subject _____.

What Do My Readers Think?   Who are your readers, and why will they be read-ing your evaluation? Is the subject new or familiar to them?

▶ My readers are _____ and are probably reading my review [to **learn about** the subject or to decide whether to see it, play it, or buy it].

How might factors such as the readers' age, gender, cultural background, **or work** experience affect their judgment of the subject?

▶ People who work in _____ or who are familiar with _____ **may be** [more/less critical, or apply different standards] to a subject like this one.

What criteria or standards of judgment do you expect your readers to **use when** evaluating subjects of this kind? What other examples of the genre would **they be** familiar with?

▶ If they [like/dislike] [comparable subject], they are sure to [like/dislike] _____.

▶ Judging [this kind of subject] on the basis of _____ is likely to surprise readers because they probably are more familiar with _____ and _____.

Considering Your Purpose for Your Audience

Write for a few minutes exploring your purpose in writing to your **particular** audience. Ask yourself questions like these:

• What do I want my readers to believe or do after they read my essay?

• How can I connect to their experience with my subject (or subjects **like it**)?

• How can I interest them in a subject that is outside their experience?

- Can I assume that readers will share my standards for judging the subject, or must I explain and justify the standards?

- How can I offer a balanced evaluation that will enhance my credibility with readers?

Formulating a Working Thesis Statement

A working thesis will help you begin drafting your essay purposefully. Your thesis should announce your subject and make your overall judgment clear.

Remember that evaluations can be mixed — you can concede shortcomings in a generally favorable review or concede admirable qualities in a mostly negative assessment. If you feel comfortable drafting a working thesis statement now, do so. You may use the sentence strategies below as a jumping-off point — you can always revise them later — or use language of your own. (Alternatively, if you prefer to develop your argument before trying to formulate a thesis, skip this activity now and return to it later.)

A good strategy is to begin by naming the subject and identifying the kind of subject it is, and then using value terms to state your judgment of the subject's strengths and weaknesses:

▶ _____ is a brilliant embodiment of [the genre/category], especially notable for its superb _____ and thorough _____.

▶ _____ has many good qualities, including _____ and _____; however, the pluses do not outweigh its one major drawback, namely that _____.

As you develop your argument, you may want to rework your thesis to make it more compelling by sharpening the language and perhaps also by forecasting your reasons. You may also need to *qualify* your judgment with words like *generally*, *may*, or *in part*.

Here are two sample thesis statements from the readings:

McDonald's is bad for your kids.... [T]hese jobs undermine school attendance and involvement, impart few skills that will be useful in later life, and simultaneously skew the values of teenagers — especially their ideas about the worth of a dollar. (Etzioni, pars. 1, 3)

While her logic *is* appropriate, believable, and consistent, her argument also has weaknesses. It seems incomplete because it neglects to anticipate parents' predictable questions and objections and because it fails to support certain parts fully. (Romano, par. 2)

Both of these thesis statements assert the writer's judgment clearly and also forecast the reasons that will support the argument. But whereas Etzioni's thesis is unmistakably negative in its overall judgment, Romano's is mixed.

Developing the Reasons and Evidence Supporting Your Judgment

The following activities will help you find reasons and evidence to support your evaluation. Begin by writing down what you already know. You can do some focused research later to fill in the details.

List the qualities of the subject. Begin by reviewing the criteria and the value terms you have already used to describe the subject. These are the potential reasons for your judgment.

Write steadily for at least five minutes, developing your reasons. Ask yourself questions like these:

- Why are the characteristics I'm pointing out for praise or criticism so important in judging my subject?
- How can I prove to readers that the value terms I'm using to evaluate these characteristics are fair and accurate?

Make notes of the evidence you will use to support your judgment. Evidence you might use to support each reason may include the following:

- examples
- quotations from authorities
- textual evidence (quotations, paraphrases, or summaries)
- illustrations, such as screenshots, video clips, or photographs
- statistics
- comparisons or contrasts

You may already have some evidence you could use. If you lack evidence for any of your reasons, make a *Research to Do* note for later.

Researching Your Evaluation

Consult your notes to determine what you need to find out. If you are evaluating a subject that others have written about, try searching for articles or books on your topic. Enter keywords or phrases related to the subject, genre, or category into the search box of

- an all-purpose database — such as *Academic OneFile* (InfoTrac) or *Academic Search Complete* (EBSCOHost) — to find relevant articles in magazines and journals;
- the database *Lexis/Nexis* to find newspaper reviews;

- a search engine like *Google* or *Baidu;*

- your library's catalog to locate books on your topic.

Turn to databases and search engines for information on recent items, like films and popular novels; use books, databases, and search engines to find information on classic topics. (Books are more likely to provide in-depth information, but articles in print or online are more likely to be current.)

Responding to a Likely Objection or Alternative Judgment

Start by identifying an objection or an alternative judgment you expect some readers to raise. To come up with likely objections or alternative judgments, you might try the following:

For more about searching a database or catalog, see Chapter 12, pp. 591–595.

- *Brainstorm* a list on your own or with fellow students.

- *Freewrite* for ten minutes on this topic.

- Conduct research to learn what others have said about your subject.

- Conduct interviews with experts.

- Distribute a survey to a group of people similar to your intended readers.

Then figure out whether to concede or refute a likely objection or alternative judgment. You may be able simply to acknowledge it, but if the criticism is serious, consider conceding the point and qualifying your judgment. You might also try to refute an objection or alternative judgment by arguing that the standards you are using are appropriate and important. Use the following strategies for generating ideas and sentences as a jumping-off point, and revise them later to make them your own.

1. Start by listing objections you expect readers to have as well as their preferred alternative judgments. You have already considered your readers and the criteria they are likely to favor (pp. 283–284). If their criteria differ from yours, you may need to explain or defend your criteria.

2. Analyze your list of objections and alternative judgments to determine which are likely to be most powerful for your readers.

3. Draft refutations and concession statements:

To Refute

▶ Some people think _____ [alternative judgment] because of
_____, _____, and _____ [reasons]. Although one can see
why they might make this argument, the evidence does not back it up because
_____.

To Concede

▶ Indeed, the more hard-core enthusiasts may point out that _____ is not sufficiently _____ [shortcomings].

▶ The one justifiable criticism that could be made against _____ is _____.

To Concede and Refute

Frequently, writers concede a point only to come back with a refutation. To make this move, follow concessions like those above with sentences that begin with a transition emphasizing contrast, like *but, however, yet,* or *nevertheless,* and then explain why you believe that your judgment is more powerful or compelling.

▶ As some critics have pointed out, _____ follows the tried-and-true formula of _____. In this case, however, the [director/writer/artist] is using the formula effectively to _____.

Including Visuals or Other Media

For more on strategies for visuals, see Chapter 2, pp. 52–55.

If appropriate to your rhetorical situation, consider whether visual or audio illustrations — screenshots, photographs, film clips, background music, or sound bites — would help you present your subject more effectively to readers or strengthen your evaluation of it, especially if you're publishing your review online. Visual and audio materials are not at all a requirement of an effective evaluation, but they could provide strong support to your argument.

Note: Be sure to cite the source of visual or audio elements you did not create, and get permission from the source if your essay is going to be published on a website that is not password protected.

Organizing Your Evaluation Effectively for Your Readers

The forecasting statement from your thesis can act as a rough outline when you are writing a simpler evaluation, but for complex evaluations, a scratch outline of your argument may be more useful for organizing your evaluation effectively for your readers. You might even want to make two or three different outlines before choosing the organization that looks most promising.

An evaluative essay contains as many as four basic parts:

1. Presentation of the subject

2. Judgment of the subject

3. Presentation of reasons and support

4. Consideration of readers' objections and alternative judgments

These parts can be organized in various ways: If you are writing primarily for readers who disagree with your judgment, you could start by showing them what you think they have overlooked or misjudged about the subject. Then you could anticipate and refute their likely objections before presenting your own reasons. If you expect some readers to disagree with your judgment even though they share your standards, you could begin by restating these standards and then demonstrate how the subject fails to meet them. Then you could present your reasons and support before responding to alternative judgments.

Whether you choose either of these approaches or an approach of your own, be flexible: As you draft, you may see ways to improve your original plan, and you should be ready to revise your outline, shift parts around, or drop or add parts as needed.

Working with Sources

Using Summary to Support Your Evaluative Argument.   Writers of evaluation often use summary to support their argument. For example, evaluations may summarize an expert source (as Etzioni and Rosen do), a series of events (as Bogost does), or an aspect of a written text (as Romano and Gladwell do). Let's look closely at how Romano uses summary.

Romano's Summary

Quotes	For example, in paragraph 3, *Statsky offers the reason* that compet-
Paraphrases	itive sports may damage children's bodies and that contact sports
Describes	may be especially injurious. *She supports this reason* by paraphras-
Statsky's moves	ing Koppett's statement that muscle strain or even permanent
	injury may result when a twelve-year-old throws curve balls. *She*
	then quotes Tutko on the dangers of tackle football. (Romano,
	par. 3)

Statsky's Original (see pp. 374–379, par. 3)

Language	One readily understandable danger of overly competitive sports
paraphrased &/	is that they entice children into physical actions that are bad for
or quoted	growing bodies.... Although the official Little League website
	acknowledges that children do risk injury playing baseball, it insists
	that "severe injuries ... are infrequent," the risk "far less than the
	risk of riding a skateboard, a bicycle, or even the school bus" ("Lit-
	tle League Parent Responsibilities"). Nevertheless, Leonard Kop-
	pett in *Sports Illusion, Sports Reality* claims that a twelve-year-old
	trying to throw a curve ball, for example, may put abnormal strain

on developing arm and shoulder muscles, sometimes resulting in lifelong injuries (294). Contact sports like football can be even more hazardous. Thomas Tutko... writes:

I am strongly opposed to young kids playing tackle football....

Romano's Summarizing Strategies

- Repeats Statsky's main ideas in a condensed form, summarizing the gist.
- Paraphrases central ideas using her own words and sentence structures. Note that because some words are basic or not readily replaceable (words such as *curve ball*, *football*, and *muscle strain*), Romano's vocabulary does overlap with Statsky's, but this is to be expected.
- Provides a play-by-play description of Statsky's strategic moves to show readers exactly how she uses paraphrase and quotation to support her argument.

Drafting Your Evaluation

By this point, you have done a lot of writing

- to devise a well-presented subject and make a judgment about it;
- to support your judgment with reasons and evidence that your readers will find persuasive;
- to refute or concede objections and alternative judgments;
- to organize your ideas to make them clear, logical, and effective for readers.

Now stitch that material together to create a draft. The next two parts of this Guide to Writing will help you evaluate and improve it.

REVIEWING AND IMPROVING THE DRAFT

This section includes guides for Peer Review and Troubleshooting Your Draft. Your instructor may arrange a peer review in class or online where you can exchange drafts with a classmate. The Peer Review Guide will help you give each other constructive feedback regarding the basic features and strategies typical of evaluative writing. (If you want to make specific suggestions for improving the draft, see Troubleshooting Your Draft on pp. 334–335.) Also, be sure to respond to any specific concerns the writer has raised about the draft. The Troubleshooting Your Draft guide that follows will help you reread your own draft with a critical eye, sort through any feedback you've received, and consider a variety of ways to improve your draft.

A PEER REVIEW GUIDE

How effective is the presentation of the subject?

What's Working Well: Point to a passage where the subject is presented effectively—for example, where the subject is identified by name or genre, briefly summarized, or compared to one or more familiar examples of the genre.

What Needs Improvement: Identify a passage where the presentation of the subject could be improved—for example, where the subject could be classified more definitively or examples of the genre could be given for comparison.

How well supported is the evaluation?

What's Working Well: Indicate a passage where the argument is well developed — for example, where the overall judgment is balanced, criticizing the subject's weaknesses but also praising its strengths, or where one of the criteria on which the argument is based is likely to be convincing to readers.

What Needs Improvement: Identify a passage where the evaluative argument could be improved—for example, where additional examples, facts, statistics, or research studies could be used as evidence to support the writer's judgment.

How effective is the writer's response to objections and alternative judgments?

What's Working Well: Identify a passage where the writer responds effectively—for example, refuting an objection with concrete evidence or recognized authorities.

What Needs Improvement: Tell the writer where a response is needed or could be made more effective—for example, explaining what's wrong with the criteria behind an alternative judgment or offering facts and examples that refute an objection.

Is the evaluation clearly and logically organized?

What's Working Well: Give an example of a passage where the essay succeeds in being readable—in its clear presentation of the thesis, in its effective opening or closing, or by its use of logical transitions.

What Needs Improvement: Tell the writer where the readability could be improved—for example, by suggesting a better beginning or a more effective ending, or a way to rearrange parts or strengthen connections.

Revising Your Draft

Revising means reenvisioning your draft, seeing it in a new way given your purpose and audience, and the feedback from your peer review. Don't hesitate to cut unconvincing material, add new material, and move passages around. The following chart may help you strengthen your evaluation.

TROUBLESHOOTING YOUR DRAFT

To Present the Subject More Effectively	
If the subject is not identified clearly,	• Identify the subject (such as by naming the director and main actors of a film). • Describe the subject by summarizing it and giving examples. • Establish the subject's importance by citing statistics or quoting authorities. • Consider adding illustrations — photographs, graphs, tables, or charts — to help clarify the subject.
If it is not clear what kind of subject it is,	• Classify the subject into a genre or category. • Compare your subject to other, better-known examples of the genre. • Refer to other reviews or reviewers of subjects of this kind.
To Support the Evaluation and Strengthen the Argument	
If the overall judgment is not clear,	• Assert your overall judgment early in the essay, making clear if your judgment is mixed. • Qualify your judgment if it seems overstated or is not supported by your argument. • Make sure that your judgment is consistent throughout, even when you point out good as well as bad qualities.
If the argument is not based on what readers consider appropriate criteria,	• Explain the criteria you are using and why they are appropriate for the kind of subject you are reviewing. • Justify your criteria — for example, by making comparisons or citing authorities.
If support is not provided, not convincing, or not clear,	• Add support by quoting or summarizing experts or research studies, providing facts or statistics, or giving specific examples. • Cite your sources and indicate why they can be depended on. • Explain more fully why the evidence, including visuals, supports your judgment.

To Improve the Response to Objections and/or Alternative Judgments	
If a likely objection has not been responded to adequately,	• Refute an objection that undermines your argument—for example, by showing that it is not based on widely held or appropriate criteria, or that it misunderstands your argument or the subject itself. • Concede an objection that cannot be refuted, but try to show it is only a minor concern that does not invalidate your evaluation, using sentence strategies like *It is true that… , but my point is….*
If a likely alternative judgment has not been responded to adequately,	• Mention qualities of the subject that others emphasize, even if your overall judgment is different. • Cite authorities to justify your criteria or give reasons why the alternative criteria are inappropriate.
To Make the Organization Clearer	
If the thesis and forecast statements are missing, inaccurate, or unclear,	• Add or revise the thesis and forecast statements. • Make sure your thesis and forecast are placed early in the essay to guide readers. • Repeat key terms in your topic sentences.
If the essay seems disorganized or is hard to follow,	• Move, add, or delete sections to strengthen coherence. • Add appropriate transitions or improve the existing ones.
If the conclusion seems abrupt or awkward,	• Add a transition to signal the conclusion. • Try restating your judgment or summarizing your argument. • Consider whether you can echo something from the opening.

Editing and Proofreading Your Draft

Check for errors in usage, punctuation, and mechanics, and consider matters of style. If you keep a list of errors you typically make, begin by checking your draft against this list.

From our research on student writing, we know that evaluative essays have frequent problems in sentences that set up comparisons. The comparisons can be incomplete, illogical, or unclear. Check a writer's handbook for help with these potential problems.

Reflecting on Evaluation

In this chapter, you have read critically several evaluative essays and have written one of your own. To better remember what you have learned, pause now to reflect on the reading and writing activities you completed in this chapter.

1. Write a page or so reflecting on what you have learned. Begin by describing what you are most pleased with in your essay. Then explain what you think contributed to your achievement.

   • If it was something you learned from the readings, indicate which readings and specifically what you learned from them.

   • If it came from your explorations of alternative points of view, point out the strategies that helped you most.

   • If you got good advice from a critical reader, explain exactly how the person helped you — perhaps by identifying a problem in your draft or by helping you add a new dimension to your writing.

2. Reflect more generally on evaluative essays, a genre of writing important in education and in society. Consider some of the following questions:

   • How confident do you feel about asserting a judgment and supporting it?

   • How comfortable are you playing the role of judge and jury on the subject?

   • How do your personal preferences and values influence your judgment?

   • How might your gender, ethnicity, religious beliefs, age, or social class influence your ideas about the subject?

   • What contribution might evaluative essays make to our society that other genres cannot make?

3. By reflecting on what you have learned about evaluation, you have been practicing **metacognition,** one of the academic habits of mind.

   • Were you aware of any other habits of mind as you read and responded to the material in this chapter? If so, which habits did you find useful?

   • If not, think back now on your reading and writing process. Can you identify any habits you used?

Arguing for a Position

Position arguments take a position on controversial issues that have no obvious "right" answer, no truth everyone accepts, no single authority everyone trusts. Consequently, simply gathering information — finding the facts or learning from experts — will not settle these disputes because ultimately they are matters of informed opinion and judgment for which writers must argue.

You may associate arguing with quarreling or with the in-your-face debating we often encounter on radio and television talk shows or online forums like Twitter or Reddit. These ways of arguing may let us vent strong feelings, but they seldom lead us to consider seriously other points of view, let alone to look critically at our own thinking or learn anything new. This chapter presents a more deliberative way of arguing that we call *reasoned argument* because it depends on giving reasons rather than raising voices. Although it is not possible to prove that a position on a controversial issue is right or wrong, it is possible to convince others to consider a particular position seriously or to accept or reject a position. A **position essay** must give readers strong reasons and solid support. It also must anticipate opposing arguments.

Because arguing for and defending a position can muster up strong feelings (especially if it is on a controversial subject), it is important to know the circumstances and your audience — in other words, to write with rhetorical sensitivity and civility.

RHETORICAL SITUATIONS FOR POSITION ARGUMENTS

Writing that takes a position on a controversial issue plays a significant role in college work and professional life, as the following examples indicate:

- A committee made up of business and community leaders investigates the issue of regulating urban growth. After reviewing the arguments for and against government regulation, committee members argue against it on the grounds that supply and demand alone will regulate development, that landowners should be permitted to sell their property to the highest bidder, and that developers are guided by the needs of the market and thus serve the people.

- For an economics class, a student writes a term paper on the controversies surrounding the rising cost of public education. She finds several blogs, newspaper and magazine articles, academic books, and journal articles that help her understand the debate over the issues. She presents the strongest arguments on the different sides and takes the position that, to be economically viable, public education needs more financial support from various sectors, including business, government, and nonprofit organizations.

Thinking about Position Argument

Write a paragraph or two about an occasion when you read, heard, or took a position in school, at work, or in another context.

- Who was the *audience*? Consider how communicating to the particular audience (such as a friend rather than a teacher, or a group of your peers rather than a gathering of their parents) shaped the argument. How much did the audience already know about the topic, and had they already taken their own position? Did you or the author choose particular details or evidence because you knew it would be convincing to your audience? How was the tone tailored to appeal to them — informal, perhaps, for friends, more formal for parents or teachers?

- What was the main *purpose*? Was the goal to convince the audience of the rightness of the position, to show several points of view, or perhaps simply to shift their perspective on a controversial topic?

- How would you rate the *rhetorical sensitivity* with which the argument was presented? What made it appropriate or inappropriate for its particular audience or purpose?

A GUIDE TO READING ESSAYS ARGUING FOR A POSITION

This guide introduces you to writing that takes a position by inviting you to analyze a brief but impassioned essay about science by Christie Aschwanden:

- *Annotations* on this first reading will help you see how to practice academic **habits of mind** such as **curiosity, openness,** and **persistence** to help you engage with and understand what you are reading. Notice how many questions the reader has as she reads. There is plenty of space for you to add your own questions and thoughts, as well, to this reading and any other in the textbook.

- *Reading for meaning* will help you understand the scope of the issue as well as understand and respond to Aschwanden's argument — for example, your own feelings about science and the way it is taught.

- *Reading like a writer* will help you learn how Aschwanden makes the essay interesting, informative, and compelling by examining how the basic features and strategies typical of position writing are employed, such as

1. presenting the controversial issue *fairly* and *credibly*

2. asserting a *clear position*

3. arguing directly for it with reasonable *evidence*

4. *responding to objections and alternative positions* fairly

Christie Aschwanden

There's No Such Thing as "Sound Science"

Christie Aschwanden is the lead science writer at FiveThirtyEight, a former health columnist for the *Washington Post,* and a regular contributor to the *New York Times.* She has served as a contributing editor and writer for numerous publications, and has received many awards and honors, including the 2014/2015 Santa Fe Institute Journalism Fellowship in Complexity Science and a 2013/2014 Carter Center Fellowship. She won the National Association of Science Writers' 2013 Science in Society Award for Commentary/Opinion, and was a National Magazine Award finalist in 2011 and a Pulitzer Center for Crisis Reporting fellow in 2007. She blogs at *Last Word On Nothing* and her newest book is *GOOD TO GO: What the Athlete in All of Us Can Learn from the Strange Science of Recovery* (2019). The essay below originally appeared on FiveThirtyEight.com on December 6, 2017.

- **Before you read,** think about your own experiences with science, either in school or out of it. What do you think the goal of science is?

- **As you read,** think about the relationship that Aschwanden sets up between science and humans. What role does Aschwanden say humans play in science, and is she persuasive?

1   Science is being turned against itself. For decades, its twin ideals of transparency and rigor have been weaponized by those who disagree with results produced by the scientific method. Under the Trump administration, that fight has ramped up again.

What does this mean?

2   In a move ostensibly meant to reduce conflicts of interest, Environmental Protection Agency Administrator Scott Pruitt has removed a number of scientists from advisory panels and replaced some of them with representatives from industries that the agency regulates. Like many in the Trump

administration, Pruitt has also cast doubt on the reliability of climate science. For instance, in an interview with CNBC, Pruitt said that "measuring with precision human activity on the climate is something very challenging to do" (DiChristopher).[1] Similarly, Trump's pick to head NASA, an agency that oversees a large portion the nation's climate research, has insisted that research into human influence on climate lacks certainty, and he falsely claimed that "global temperatures stopped rising 10 years ago" ("Trump NASA Nominee").

Kathleen Hartnett White, Trump's former nominee to head the White House Council on Environmental Quality, said in a Senate hearing last month that she thinks we "need to have more precise explanations of the human role and the natural role" in climate change (Mooney).

The same entreaties crop up again and again: We need to root out conflicts. We need more precise evidence. What makes these arguments so powerful is that they sound quite similar to the points raised by proponents of a very different call for change that's coming from within science. This other movement strives to produce more robust, reproducible findings. Despite having dissimilar goals, the two forces espouse principles that look surprisingly alike:

- Science needs to be transparent.

- Results and methods should be openly shared so that outside researchers can independently reproduce and validate them.

- The methods used to collect and analyze data should be rigorous and clear, and conclusions must be supported by evidence.

These are the arguments underlying an "open science" reform movement that was created, in part, as a response to a "reproducibility crisis" that has struck some fields of science.[2] But they're also used as talking points by politicians who are working to make it more difficult for the EPA and other federal agencies to use science in their regulatory decision-making, under the guise of basing policy on "sound science." Science's virtues are being wielded against it.

Is intent the only difference? Why is this difference so significant?

What distinguishes the two calls for transparency is intent: Whereas the "open science" movement aims to make science more reliable, reproducible and robust, proponents of "sound science" have historically worked to amplify uncertainty, create doubt and undermine scientific discoveries that threaten their interests (Ong and Glantz). "Our criticisms are founded in a confidence in science," said Steven Goodman, co-director of the

3

4

5

6

---

[1] Relevant links have been converted to citations with a works cited list at the end of the reading [Ed.]
[2] Most notably psychology, biomedicine and cancer biology.

Meta-Research Innovation Center at Stanford and a proponent of open science. "That's a fundamental difference—we're critiquing science to make it better. Others are critiquing it to devalue the approach itself."

7   Calls to base public policy on "sound science" seem unassailable if you don't know the term's history. The phrase was adopted by the tobacco industry in the 1990s to counteract mounting evidence linking secondhand smoke to cancer. A 1992 Environmental Protection Agency report identified secondhand smoke as a human carcinogen, and Philip Morris responded by launching an initiative to promote what it called "sound science." In an internal memo, Philip Morris vice president of corporate affairs Ellen Merlo wrote that the program was designed to "discredit the EPA report," "prevent states and cities, as well as businesses from passing smoking bans" and "proactively" pass legislation to help their cause.

8   The sound science tactic exploits a fundamental feature of the scientific process: Science does not produce absolute certainty. Contrary to how it's sometimes represented to the public, science is not a magic wand that turns everything it touches to truth. Instead, it's a process of uncertainty reduction, much like a game of 20 Questions. Any given study can rarely answer more than one question at a time, and each study usually raises a bunch of new questions in the process of answering old ones. "Science is a process rather than an answer," said psychologist Alison Ledgerwood of the University of California, Davis. Every answer is provisional and subject to change in the face of new evidence. It's not entirely correct to say that "this study proves this fact," Ledgerwood said. "We should be talking instead about how science increases or decreases our confidence in something."

9   The tobacco industry's brilliant tactic was to turn this baked-in uncertainty against the scientific enterprise itself. While insisting that they merely wanted to ensure that public policy was based on sound science, tobacco companies defined the term in a way that ensured that no science could ever be sound enough. The only sound science was certain science, which is an impossible standard to achieve.

10   "Doubt is our product," wrote one employee of the Brown & Williamson tobacco company in a 1969 internal memo ("Smoking and Health Proposal"). The note went on to say that doubt "is the best means of competing with the 'body of fact'" and "establishing a controversy." These strategies for undermining inconvenient science were so effective that they've served as a sort of playbook for industry interests ever since, said Stanford University science historian Robert Proctor.

11   The sound science push is no longer just Philip Morris sowing doubt about the links between cigarettes and cancer. It's also a 1998 action plan by the American Petroleum Institute, Chevron and Exxon Mobil to "install uncertainty" about the link between greenhouse gas emissions and climate change ("1998 American Petroleum"). It's industry-funded groups' late-1990s effort to question the science the EPA was using to set

fine-particle-pollution air-quality standards that the industry didn't want (Kaiser). And then there was the more recent effort by Dow Chemical to insist on more scientific certainty before banning a pesticide that the EPA's scientists had deemed risky to children (Biesecker). Now comes a move by the Trump administration's EPA to repeal a 2015 rule on wetlands protection by disregarding particular studies. (To name just a few examples.)

> What kinds of studies are they ignoring? Do they have other studies they are relying on, instead?

Doubt merchants aren't pushing for knowledge, they're practicing what Proctor has dubbed "agnogenesis"—the intentional manufacture of ignorance. This ignorance isn't simply the absence of knowing something; it's a lack of comprehension deliberately created by agents who don't want you to know, Proctor said.[3]   12

In the hands of doubt-makers, transparency becomes a rhetorical move. "It's really difficult as a scientist or policy maker to make a stand against transparency and openness, because well, who would be against it?" said Karen Levy, researcher on information science at Cornell University. But at the same time, "you can couch everything in the language of transparency and it becomes a powerful weapon." For instance, when the EPA was preparing to set new limits on particulate pollution in the 1990s, industry groups pushed back against the research and demanded access to primary data (including records that researchers had promised participants would remain confidential) and a reanalysis of the evidence. Their calls succeeded and a new analysis was performed. The reanalysis essentially confirmed the original conclusions, but the process of conducting it delayed the implementation of regulations and cost researchers time and money.   13

Delay is a time-tested strategy. "Gridlock is the greatest friend a global warming skeptic has," said Marc Morano, a prominent critic of global warming research and the executive director of ClimateDepot.com, in the documentary "Merchants of Doubt" (based on the book by the same name). Morano's site is a project of the Committee for a Constructive Tomorrow, which has received funding from the oil and gas industry. "We're the negative force. We're just trying to stop stuff."   14

Some of these ploys are getting a fresh boost from Congress. The Data Quality Act (also known as the Information Quality Act) was reportedly written by an industry lobbyist and quietly passed as part of an appropriations bill in 2000. The rule mandates that federal agencies ensure the "quality, objectivity, utility, and integrity of information" that they disseminate, though it does little to define what these terms mean. The law also   15

[3] The tobacco industry's agnogenesis methods were so effective that companies actually measured their results. For instance, Proctor said, they'd ask people if they agreed with the Surgeon General that cigarettes cause cancer, and then they'd show a propaganda film. "It might be 65 percent who agreed with the Surgeon General before and 43 percent after. They were able to measure, down to the decimal point, the amount of ignorance they created."

provides a mechanism for citizens and groups to challenge information that they deem inaccurate, including science that they disagree with. "It was passed in this very quiet way with no explicit debate about it—that should tell you a lot about the real goals," Levy said.

16   But what's most telling about the Data Quality Act is how it's been used, Levy said. A 2004 Washington Post analysis found that in the 20 months following its implementation, the act was repeatedly used by industry groups to push back against proposed regulations and bog down the decision-making process (Weiss). Instead of deploying transparency as a fundamental principle that applies to all science, these interests have used transparency as a weapon to attack very particular findings that they would like to eradicate.

17   Now Congress is considering another way to legislate how science is used. The Honest Act, a bill sponsored by Rep. Lamar Smith of Texas,[4] is another example of what Levy calls a "Trojan horse" law that uses the language of transparency as a cover to achieve other political goals. Smith's legislation would severely limit the kind of evidence the EPA could use for decision-making. Only studies whose raw data and computer codes were publicly available would be allowed for consideration.

18   That might sound perfectly reasonable, and in many cases it is, Goodman said. But sometimes there are good reasons why researchers can't conform to these rules, like when the data contains confidential or sensitive medical information.[5] Critics, which include more than a dozen scientific organizations, argue that, in practice, the rules would prevent many studies from being considered in EPA reviews.[6]

19   It might seem like an easy task to sort good science from bad, but in reality it's not so simple. "There's a misplaced idea that we can definitively distinguish the good from the not-good science, but it's all a matter of degree," said Brian Nosek, executive director of the Center for Open Science. "There is no perfect study." Requiring regulators to wait until they have (nonexistent) perfect evidence is essentially "a way of saying, 'We don't want to use evidence for our decision-making,'" Nosek said.

20   Most scientific controversies aren't about science at all, and once the sides are drawn, more data is unlikely to bring opponents into agreement. Michael Carolan, who researches the sociology of technology and scientific knowledge at Colorado State University, wrote in a 2008 paper about why objective knowledge is not enough to resolve

---

[4] The bill has been passed by the House but still awaits a vote in the Senate.

[5] The bill allows for certain information to be redacted, but that process is expensive, so it poses practical challenges.

[6] A Congressional Budget Office report concludes it "would significantly reduce the number of studies that the agency relies on when issuing or proposing covered actions for the first few years following enactment of the legislation."

Is consensus a practical or even desirable goal?

environmental controversies (Carolan). "While these controversies may appear on the surface to rest on disputed questions of fact, beneath often reside differing positions of value; values that can give shape to differing understandings of what 'the facts' are." What's needed in these cases isn't more or better science, but mechanisms to bring those hidden values to the forefront of the discussion so that they can be debated transparently. "As long as we continue down this unabashedly naive road about what science is, and what it is capable of doing, we will continue to fail to reach any sort of meaningful consensus on these matters," Carolan writes.

The dispute over tobacco was never about the science of cigarettes' link to cancer. It was about whether companies have the right to sell dangerous products and, if so, what obligations they have to the consumers who purchased them. Similarly, the debate over climate change isn't about whether our planet is heating, but about how much responsibility each country and person bears for stopping it. While researching her book "Merchants of Doubt," science historian Naomi Oreskes found that some of the same people who were defending the tobacco industry as scientific experts were also receiving industry money to deny the role of human activity in global warming. What these issues had in common, she realized, was that they all involved the need for government action. "None of this is about the science. All of this is a political debate about the role of government," she said in the documentary (Oreskes). 21

Do the sides even recognize the values that inform their assessments?

These controversies are really about values, not scientific facts, and acknowledging that would allow us to have more truthful and productive debates. What would that look like in practice? Instead of cherry-picking evidence to support a particular view (and insisting that the science points to a desired action), the various sides could lay out the values they are using to assess the evidence. 22

For instance, in Europe, many decisions are guided by the precautionary principle—a system that values caution in the face of uncertainty and says that when the risks are unclear, it should be up to industries to show that their products and processes are not harmful, rather than requiring the government to prove that they are harmful before they can be regulated. By contrast, U.S. agencies tend to wait for strong evidence of harm before issuing regulations. Both approaches have critics, but the difference between them comes down to priorities: Is it better to exercise caution at the risk of burdening companies and perhaps the economy, or is it more important to avoid potential economic downsides even if it means that sometimes a harmful product or industrial process goes unregulated? In other words, under what circumstances do we agree to act on a risk? How certain do we need to be that the risk is real, and how many people would need to be at risk, and how costly is it to reduce that risk? Those are moral questions, not scientific ones, and openly 23 discussing and identifying these kinds of judgment calls would lead to a more honest debate.

24   Science matters, and we need to do it as rigorously as possible. But science can't tell us how risky is too risky to allow products like cigarettes or potentially harmful pesticides to be sold—those are value judgements that only humans can make.

Works Cited

"1998 American Petroleum Institute Global Climate Science Communications Team Action Plan." *Climate Files*, 2018, www.climatefiles.com/exxonmobil/1998-global-climate-science-communications-team-action-plan/.

Biesecker, Michael. "Correction: EPA-Dow Chemical Story." *The Associated Press*, 3 July 2017, www.apnews.com/2350d7be5e24469ab445089bf663cdcb.

Carolan, Michael S. "The Bright- and Blind-Spots of Science: Why Objective Knowledge Is Not Enough to Resolve Environmental Controversies." *Critical Sociology*, vol. 34, no. 5, Sept. 2008, pp. 725–740, doi:10.1177/0896920508093365.

DiChristopher, Tom. "EPA chief Scott Pruitt says carbon dioxide is not a primary contributor to global warming." *CNBC*, 10 Mar. 2017, www.cnbc.com/2017/03/09/epa-chief-scott-pruitt.html.

Kaiser, Jocelyn. "Showdown Over Clean Air Science." *Science*, vol. 277, no. 5325, pp. 466–478, www.science.sciencemag.org/content/277/5325/news-summaries.

Mooney, Chris. "Trump's top environmental pick says she has 'many questions' about climate change." *The Washington Post*, 8 Nov. 2017, www.washingtonpost.com/news/energy-environment/wp/2017/11/08/trumps-top-environmental-pick-says-she-has-many-questions-about-climate-change/?utm_term=.8acdb0fc7007.

Oreskes, Naomi, writer. *Merchants of Doubt*. Directed by Robert Kenner, Sony Picture Classics and Mongrel Media, 2014.

Ong, E K, and S A Glantz. "Constructing 'Sound Science' and 'Good Epidemiology': Tobacco, Lawyers, and Public Relations Firms." *American Journal of Public Health*, vol. 91, no. 11, 2001, pp. 1749–1757, www.ncbi.nlm.nih.gov/pmc/articles/PMC1446868/.

"Smoking and Health Proposal." *Brown and Williamson Records*, 1969, pp. 1–9. www.industrydocuments.ucsf.edu/tobacco/docs/#id=psdw0147.

"Trump NASA Nominee Rep Jim Bridenstine (R-OK) Demands Obama Apologize on Global Warming." *YouTube*, 24 Mar. 2014, www.youtube.com/watch?v=GUcsAFnwC7k.

Weiss, Rick. "'Data Quality' Law Is Nemesis of Regulation." *The Washington Post*, 16 Aug. 2004, www.washingtonpost.com/wp-dyn/articles/A3733-2004Aug15.html.

READING FOR MEANING

For help with reading strategies like summarizing and analyzing assumptions, see Chapter 2.

1. **Read to Summarize.** Write a sentence or two explaining Aschwanden's position on the concept of sound science.

2. **Read to Respond.** Write a paragraph analyzing your initial reactions to anything that seems surprising, such as Aschwanden's assertion that "It might seem like an easy task to sort good science from bad, but in reality it's not so simple" (par. 18) or "most scientific controversies aren't about science at all" (par. 19).

3. **Read to Analyze Assumptions.** Write a paragraph or two analyzing an assumption you find intriguing in Aschwanden's essay. For example:

   Assumptions about what people expect from science. Aschwanden asserts that "contrary to how it's sometimes represented to the public, science is not a magic wand that turns everything it touches to truth" (par. 7).

   • What assumptions do you have about the relationship between science and truth? Where do your assumptions come from?

   • Are Aschwanden's assumptions about how the public often views science consistent with your peers' views about science and truth? Where do they converge or diverge?

   Assumptions about what changes people's minds. Aschwanden writes: "Most scientific controversies aren't about science at all, and once the sides are drawn, more data is unlikely to bring opponents into agreement. . . . [O]bjective knowledge is not enough to resolve environmental controversies. . . . What's needed in these cases isn't more or better science, but mechanisms to bring those hidden values to the forefront of the discussion so that they can be debated transparently" (par. 19).

   • What assumptions about the value of "more data" and "more or better science" are being challenged in this quotation?

   • Why are "hidden values" and "transparency" important if the goal is "any sort of meaningful consensus" (par. 19)? What might meaningful consensus look like? Does Ashwanden provide any examples?

READING LIKE A WRITER

Presenting the Controversial Issue Fairly and Credibly

For position papers published during an ongoing public debate, writers may need only to mention the issue. In most cases, however, writers need to explain the issue to readers. They may, for example, place the issue in its historical or cultural context, cite specific instances to make the issue seem less abstract, show their personal interest in the debate, or establish or redefine the terms of the debate. Aschwanden uses a common sentence pattern for redefining the terms of the debate. First she presents the issue as she believes it is commonly perceived, and then she contrasts this common perception with her own view:

> ▶ When .... [issue / event] happens, most people think .... , but I think ....

Here's an example from the reading selection:

> For instance, in Europe, many decisions are guided by the precautionary principle — a system that values caution in the face of uncertainty and says that when the risks are unclear, it should be up to industries to show that their products and processes are not harmful, rather than requiring the government to prove that they are harmful before they can be regulated. By contrast, U.S. agencies tend to wait for strong evidence of harm before issuing regulations. Both approaches have critics, but the difference between them comes down to priorities: Is it better to exercise caution at the risk of burdening companies and perhaps the economy, or is it more important to avoid potential economic downsides even if it means that sometimes a harmful product or industrial process goes unregulated? (par. 22)

Note how civil — how rhetorically sensitive — Aschwanden is. She respects the two different approaches to regulation. Then she proposes that how regulation occurs has more to do with priorities than the regulations themselves.

ANALYZE & WRITE

Write a paragraph analyzing how Aschwanden presents the issue for her readers and gives them a reason to listen to her:

1. Reread paragraphs 1–10, where Aschwanden introduces the issue, and underline the historical and cultural context Aschwanden includes. How does this context help readers understand the issue and its relevance?

2. In the final paragraph, Aschwanden writes, "Science matters, and we need to do it as rigorously as possible." Where in the essay does Aschwanden show why science matters? What strategies does she use to demonstrate the importance of science?

3. Reread the essay to see how Aschwanden presents this issue fairly and credibly by quoting sources on different sides of the debate about science. Notice how she presents the proponents of the open science movement and the sound science movement. What words and phrases lend fairness and rhetorical sensitivity to her representations of both sides? How does this kind of presentation affect her credibility, particularly once she goes on to argue for her position?

Asserting a Clear Position

Writers of position papers take sides. Their primary purposes are to assert a position of their own and to influence readers' thinking. The assertion is the main point of the essay — its **thesis.** Presented simply and directly, the thesis statement often forecasts the stages of the argument as well, identifying the main reason or reasons that will be developed and supported in the essay.

Many writers place the thesis early in the essay to let readers know right away where they stand. But if they need to present the issue at length or define the terms of the debate, writers can postpone introducing their own position. Restating the thesis in different words at various points in the body of the essay and at the end can help keep readers oriented.

ANALYZE & WRITE

Write a paragraph analyzing how and why Aschwanden states and restates her position:

1. Underline the first place in which Aschwanden explicitly asserts her position. Note any key words she uses there.

2. Reread the essay and put brackets around the sentences that restate the thesis in various ways.

3. Now examine *how* Aschwanden restates her thesis. Look closely at the language she uses to see whether she repeats key words, uses synonyms for them, or adds new phrasing. What do you learn from Aschwanden's repetition and her variations?

Arguing Directly for the Position, and Supporting the Position with Reasonable Evidence

Not only do writers of position papers explicitly assert their positions, but they also give reasons for them. They usually support their reasons with facts, statistics, examples, anecdotes, expert opinions, and analogies:

- **Facts** are statements that can be proven objectively to be true, but readers may need to be reassured that the facts come from trustworthy sources.

- **Statistics** may be mistaken for facts, but they are only interpretations or compilations of numerical data. Their reliability depends on how and by whom the information was collected and interpreted.

- **Examples** are not usually claimed to be proof of the writer's position or to be evidence that the position applies in every case. Examples help a reader understand the situations in which the position is valid. Powerful examples are often the reason readers change their minds or at least grant that the position is true in the case of a particular example.

- **Anecdotes** tell stories and recall vivid images to help readers imagine themselves in the position of the writer. Anecdotes are also memorable, as many stories are, so readers remember why the author has taken a certain position.

- **Expert opinions** and **analogies** are also useful for support. Readers must decide whether to regard quotations from experts as credible and authoritative. They must also decide how much weight to give analogies — comparisons that encourage readers to assume that what is true about one thing is also true about something to which it is compared.

Position arguments are most convincing when writers are able to appeal to readers on three levels:

- **logos:** Appeals to readers' intellect, presenting them with logical reasoning and reliable evidence

- **ethos:** Appeals to readers' perception of the writer's credibility and fairness

- **pathos:** Appeals to readers' values and feelings

ANALYZE & WRITE

Write a paragraph or two analyzing Aschwanden's strategy of arguing by example:

1. Reread paragraph 6 and paragraphs 8–11, where Aschwanden develops her argument through a series of examples, including those from the tobacco industry, Chevron, and Exxon Mobil. Put brackets around the sentence or sentences in each paragraph that state this part of her argument.

2. Aschwanden writes that "these controversies are really about values, not scientific facts, and acknowledging that would allow us to have more truthful and productive debates. What would that look like in practice? Instead of cherry-picking evidence to support a particular view (and insisting that the science points to a desired action), the various sides could lay out the values they are using to assess the evidence" (par. 21). Do you think that some readers would find this attention to practice compelling while others would not? If so, why or why not? Can you imagine readers being turned off by her description of "cherry-picking evidence?"

Responding to Objections and Alternative Positions Fairly and Credibly

Writers of position papers often try to anticipate the likely objections, questions, and alternative positions that readers might raise. Writers may concede points with which they agree and may even modify a thesis to accommodate valid objections. A typical way of conceding is to use sentence strategies like these:

▶ I agree that .... is certainly an important factor.

But when they think that the criticism is groundless or opposing arguments are flawed, writers respond assertively. They refute the challenges to their argument by pointing out the flaws in their opponents' reasoning and support. A typical **refutation** states the problem with the opposing view and then explains why the view is problematic, using sentence strategies like these:

► One problem with .... [opposing view] is that ....

► Some claim .... [opposing view], but in reality ....

Notice that writers often introduce the refutation with a transition that indicates contrast, such as *but, although, nevertheless,* or *however.* When writers deal with alternative viewpoints, they enhance their own fairness and credibility by treating those who hold these views with civility and respect.

Frequently, writers reach out to readers by making a concession, but then go on to point out where they differ. Writers conceding and then refuting often use sentence strategies like these:

► .... may be true for .... , *but* not for ....

► *Although* .... , I think ....

► .... insists that .... *Nevertheless,* in spite of her good intentions, ...

Not all writers use transition words to signal a response to alternative views, however. Consider, for example, the way Aschwanden concedes and then refutes common assumptions about science:

Cues signaling concession

Cues signaling refutation

> It might seem like an easy task to sort good science from bad, but in reality it's not so simple. (par. 18)

ANALYZE & WRITE

Write a paragraph or two analyzing how Aschwanden responds to alternative views, including those views directly represented in the essay, as well as those that Aschwanden assumes readers may hold:

1. Locate moments in the essay where Aschwanden introduces alternative arguments to her position. Underline the sentence in each paragraph that best states the alternative position.

2. Now highlight the sentences in which Aschwanden responds to these opposing arguments. Where does she concede and where does she refute these alternatives? What seems to be her attitude toward those who disagree with her? How effective are her strategies in persuading readers to accept her position?

READINGS

Isiah Holmes

The Heroin and Opioid Crisis Is Real

Isiah Holmes is a journalist whose work focuses both on issues local to the Midwest and on national issues. He works across media as a writer and videographer, and his written work has appeared in *Urban Milwaukee*, Milwaukeestories.net, PontiacTribune.com, and TheFifthColumn.com, among others, while his documentaries have been featured at the Milwaukee film festival.

- **Before you read,** consider what you know about the heroin and opioid crisis and how you know it. Has the crisis affected you or anyone you know?

- **As you read,** consider how an op-ed — an opinion editorial — is different from academic essays that argue for a position. How does Holmes develop and support his position? What kinds of evidence does Holmes use?

It's easy to distance yourself from tragedy, even when it's happening in your own 1 town. One tragedy becomes like another, not really hitting you until it hits you personally. It then becomes something else, so powerful it's almost surreal. Imagine what its like to enter adulthood knowing a good portion of your friends are either opioid or heroin addicts, or know others who are. For myself and much of my generation, that's increasingly the reality. Fortunately, I haven't lost any people yet. But that, sadly, can't be said for some of my closest friends. Without naming names or casting blame, that's the story I need to share.

I've lived in Milwaukee my entire life but in several different places in the city. 2 When it came time to enroll in high school, my mother and I moved to Wauwatosa for better options. Throughout high school, as anywhere else I suppose, drugs were prevalent. However, opioid abuse — to my knowledge — didn't appear to be a widespread issue at that time.

That was from the ages of 15–18. I'm 21 now, and things have shifted in the oddest 3 of ways. At first you hear about this kid snorting something for giggles, then one too many stories of heroin use. Fall and winter seemed to bring rehab admissions, and seasonal depression. The use of opioids and heroin were closely related; depending on which drug is easier to obtain.

It became increasingly clear that opioids were spreading among those even 4 younger than I. How could that be? What's going on? Where's it coming from? The cycle often has one of two endings: someone you know dies, or someone you know has a friend or relative who dies.

After high school, from 18–20 years old, I moved back to Milwaukee with my aunt and then father. Two houses down, people not that much older than I lived with their young children. One girl would come outside and play with the neighborhood children, but never spoke. Rather, she'd whine or grunt, or remain totally silent. I eventually discovered she was the daughter of relatively functional heroin addicts. Her exposure to the drug use, however, left her a stunted and complicated soul. She was almost like a wild child, escaping her home day and night only to return later. When her family nodded off, the doors were often left open for her to roam. It's a cycle playing out across Milwaukee and neighboring counties and suburbs.

But nothing compared to seeing my friends high, nodding as they stood up or sat down. For a while, I didn't even realize it was happening. But eventually my mind could no longer hide the reality. It was a darker, more dreadful thing to behold than I'd anticipated. Watching their lives spiral ever downward isn't easy. One rehab or hospital visit turns to two, then three, and so on depending on the person. That's assuming you're lucky enough to have friends who survive long enough for that.

Being unlucky means going about your life until, one day, you hear someone's gone. One friend of mine lost several people in less than a year. They were all kids his age, 18–19, or younger. Punctuating that tragedy were mug shots of those you once knew—arrested for opioid possession or distribution. They'd occasionally drift through your Facebook feed and then away again. You let it pass as if it's just another meme or pointless viral video. Except it's not.

And where's the response from city and county officials? Last year the Milwaukee Common Council released a report called "888 Bodies and Counting," which found there was a 495 percent increase in heroin-related deaths in Milwaukee County between 2005 and 2014 along with a big increase in opioid-related deaths (Murphy).[7] But where's the followup to this report? Where's the task forces, treatments and visionary, daring new ideas tested in other states? What about protests or demonstrations? Some treatment centers have cropped up, but the response pales in comparison to the issue at hand. Each day spent ignoring this crisis on a local level is a subtle insult to the victims. It relegates the issue to the periphery, leaving only shame for those caught in addiction.

Which leads to another thing that's widely known, but never talked about: addict shaming. For many people, whether younger, say 15–21, or older users, shame and stigma is real. I've seen people who weren't addicts, but simply hung around some, ostracized by others. It's often a matter of standing by someone you've known your entire life. But to onlookers, those perhaps not as immediately affected by the epidemic, judgements come easy.

Treating the addicted like lepers doesn't solve anything. How many families attempt to help their addicted loved ones, and how many disown them? This is a facet of the crisis that needs to be openly acknowledged. Without doing so, I fear

[7] Relevant links have been converted to citations with a works cited list at the end of the reading [Ed.]

America may never come to grips with this issue. We must see addicts as people, not rotten fruits to be shaken from the tree. Drug users are people, like you or me, and they need our help.

Works Cited

Murphy, Michael J. "888* Bodies and Counting." Milwaukee Common Council, 30 Nov. 2018, https://www.documentcloud.org/documents/3149191-888-Bodies-and-Counting-Milwaukee-Common-Council.html.

READING FOR MEANING

1. **Read to Summarize.** Write a sentence or two explaining Holmes's position on the heroin and opioid crisis and how it is being dealt with in Milwaukee.

2. **Read to Respond.** Write a paragraph responding to anything that surprises you about this op-ed such as Holmes' admission that he "hasn't lost any people yet" (par. 1) or what he says about addict shaming (par. 9).

3. **Read to Analyze Assumptions.** Write a paragraph or two analyzing an assumption you find intriguing in Holmes' essay. For example:

   Assumptions about the role of city and county officials in residents' lives. Holmes asks, "Where's the response from city and county officials? Last year the Milwaukee Common Council released a report called '888 Bodies and Counting,' which found there was a 495 percent increase in heroin-related deaths in Milwaukee County between 2005 and 2014 along with a big increase in opioid-related deaths. But where's the followup to this report? Where's the task forces, treatments and visionary, daring new ideas tested in other states?" (par. 8).

   - What assumptions does Holmes make about the best ways to address the crisis and the role that officials should play?

   - What assumptions inform your ideas about how to deal with this or similar drug crises? What kind of follow-up to the report Holmes mentions do you think would be most productive? Are task forces useful? Is it helpful to look at how other states are responding to the opioid crisis?

   Assumptions about drug users. Holmes writes that "treating the addicted like lepers doesn't solve anything. How many families attempt to help their addicted loved ones, and how many disown them? This is a facet of the crisis that needs to be openly acknowledged. Without doing so, I fear America may never come to grips with this issue. We must see addicts as people, not rotten fruits to be shaken from the tree" (par. 10).

For help with reading strategies like summarizing and analyzing assumptions, see Chapter 2.

- Why does Holmes think it is important to address our assumptions about drug users?
- What assumptions do you have about drug users, and where do you think they come from? Have you ever been in a situation that made you rethink those assumptions?

READING LIKE A WRITER

Asserting a Clear Position

Writers of position papers, including op-eds (opinion editorials), assert a position of their own in order to influence how readers think about the subject. Their assertion of that position is the main point, and it should be presented clearly and directly. The placement of this assertion may vary. In some cases, writers will open by asserting their position, but in other cases, where they may need space to present the issue or outline the debate, writers may insert their own position later in their position paper. A strong argument needs to present reasons and support for the writer's position on an issue. Notice how Holmes first lays out the issue he will address and concludes his essay by asserting his position.

ANALYZE & WRITE

Write a paragraph or two analyzing how Holmes anticipates his position but does not assert it until late in his op-ed:

1. Reread paragraphs 1–5, highlighting the phrases and words Holmes uses that suggest what his position is on the heroin and opioid crisis in Milwaukee.

2. Now find the moment in the op-ed where Holmes asserts his position. How effective is this placement for you as a reader? Is this the position you expected him to take? Why or why not?

Sherry Turkle

The Flight from Conversation

Sherry Turkle (b. 1948), professor of the social studies of science and technology at the Massachusetts Institute of Technology, earned her Ph.D. from Harvard University. She is the author of many books, including *Second Self: Computers and the Human Spirit* (1984); *Life on the Screen: Identity in the Age of the Internet* (1995); and *Alone Together: Why We Expect More from Technology and Less from Each Other* (2011). Turkle's most recent book is *Reclaiming Conversation: The Power of Talk in the Digital Age* (2015), and she has given a TED talk and hosts a podcast on the same topic. Turkle is a media commentator on the social and psychological effects of technology. The article below was published in the Sunday Review section of the *New York Times* in 2012.

- **Before you read,** think about how much time you spend communicating with friends and family via "texting and e-mail and posting" (par. 10) versus how much time you spend talking with friends and family over the phone or face-to-face.

- **As you read,** pay attention to the kinds of evidence Turkle provides to support her assertions, such as quotations from interviews and written sources, examples, statistics, illustrations, and so on.

We live in a technological universe in which we are always communicating. And yet   1
we have sacrificed conversation for mere connection.

At home, families sit together, texting and reading e-mail. At work executives text   2
during board meetings. We text (and shop and go on Facebook) during classes and when we're on dates. My students tell me about an important new skill: it involves maintaining eye contact with someone while you text someone else; it's hard, but it can be done.

Over the past 15 years, I've studied technologies of mobile connection and talked   3
to hundreds of people of all ages and circumstances about their plugged-in lives. I've learned that the little devices most of us carry around are so powerful that they change not only what we do, but also who we are.

We've become accustomed to a new way of being "alone together." Technology   4
-enabled, we are able to be with one another, and also elsewhere, connected to wherever we want to be. We want to customize our lives. We want to move in and out of where we are because the thing we value most is control over where we focus our attention. We have gotten used to the idea of being in a tribe of one, loyal to our own party.

Our colleagues want to go to that board meeting but pay attention only to what   5
interests them. To some this seems like a good idea, but we can end up hiding from one another, even as we are constantly connected to one another.

A businessman laments that he no longer has colleagues at work. He doesn't stop 6 by to talk; he doesn't call. He says that he doesn't want to interrupt them. He says they're "too busy on their e-mail." But then he pauses and corrects himself. "I'm not telling the truth. I'm the one who doesn't want to be interrupted. I think I should. But I'd rather just do things on my BlackBerry."

A 16-year-old boy who relies on texting for almost everything says almost wist- 7 fully, "Someday, someday, but certainly not now, I'd like to learn how to have a conversation."

In today's workplace, young people who have grown up fearing conversation 8 show up on the job wearing earphones. Walking through a college library or the campus of a high-tech start-up, one sees the same thing: we are together, but each of us is in our own bubble, furiously connected to keyboards and tiny touch screens. A senior partner at a Boston law firm describes a scene in his office. Young associates lay out their suite of technologies: laptops, iPods and multiple phones. And then they put their earphones on. "Big ones. Like pilots. They turn their desks into cockpits." With the young lawyers in their cockpits, the office is quiet, a quiet that does not ask to be broken.

In the silence of connection, people are comforted by being in touch with a lot 9 of people—carefully kept at bay. We can't get enough of one another if we can use technology to keep one another at distances we can control: not too close, not too far, just right. I think of it as a Goldilocks effect.

Texting and e-mail and posting let us present the self we want to be. This means 10 we can edit. And if we wish to, we can delete. Or retouch: the voice, the flesh, the face, the body. Not too much, not too little—just right.

Human relationships are rich; they're messy and demanding. We have learned the 11 habit of cleaning them up with technology. And the move from conversation to connection is part of this. But it's a process in which we shortchange ourselves. Worse, it seems that over time we stop caring, we forget that there is a difference.

We are tempted to think that our little "sips" of online connection add up to a big 12 gulp of real conversation. But they don't. E-mail, Twitter, Facebook, all of these have their places—in politics, commerce, romance and friendship. But no matter how valuable, they do not substitute for conversation.

Connecting in sips may work for gathering discrete bits of information or for say- 13 ing, "I am thinking about you." Or even for saying, "I love you." But connecting in sips doesn't work as well when it comes to understanding and knowing one another. In conversation we tend to one another. (The word itself is kinetic; it's derived from words that mean to move, together.) We can attend to tone and nuance. In conversation, we are called upon to see things from another's point of view.

Face-to-face conversation unfolds slowly. It teaches patience. When we commu- 14 nicate on our digital devices, we learn different habits. As we ramp up the volume and velocity of online connections, we start to expect faster answers. To get these, we ask one another simpler questions; we dumb down our communications, even on the most important matters. It is as though we have all put ourselves on cable news. Shakespeare might have said, "We are consum'd with that which we were nourish'd by."

And we use conversation with others to learn to converse with ourselves. So our 15 flight from conversation can mean diminished chances to learn skills of self-reflection. These days, social media continually asks us what's "on our mind," but we have little motivation to say something truly self-reflective. Self-reflection in conversation requires trust. It's hard to do anything with 3,000 Facebook friends except connect.

As we get used to being shortchanged on conversation and to getting by with less, 16 we seem almost willing to dispense with people altogether. Serious people muse about the future of computer programs as psychiatrists. A high school sophomore confides to me that he wishes he could talk to an artificial intelligence program instead of his dad about dating; he says the A.I. would have so much more in its database. Indeed, many people tell me they hope that as Siri, the digital assistant on Apple's iPhone, becomes more advanced, "she" will be more and more like a best friend—one who will listen when others won't.

During the years I have spent researching people and their relationships with tech- 17 nology, I have often heard the sentiment "No one is listening to me." I believe this feeling helps explain why it is so appealing to have a Facebook page or a Twitter feed—each provides so many automatic listeners. And it helps explain why—against all reason—so many of us are willing to talk to machines that seem to care about us. Researchers around the world are busy inventing sociable robots, designed to be companions to the elderly, to children, to all of us.

One of the most haunting experiences during my research came when I brought 18 one of these robots, designed in the shape of a baby seal, to an elder-care facility, and an older woman began to talk to it about the loss of her child. The robot seemed to be looking into her eyes. It seemed to be following the conversation. The woman was comforted.

And so many people found this amazing. Like the sophomore who wants advice 19 about dating from artificial intelligence and those who look forward to computer psychiatry, this enthusiasm speaks to how much we have confused conversation with connection and collectively seem to have embraced a new kind of delusion that accepts the simulation of compassion as sufficient unto the day. And why would we want to talk about love and loss with a machine that has no experience of the arc of human life? Have we so lost confidence that we will be there for one another?

We expect more from technology and less from one another and seem increas- 20 ingly drawn to technologies that provide the illusion of companionship without the demands of relationship. Always-on / always-on-you devices provide three powerful fantasies: that we will always be heard; that we can put our attention wherever we want it to be; and that we never have to be alone. Indeed our new devices have turned being alone into a problem that can be solved.

When people are alone, even for a few moments, they fidget and reach for a 21 device. Here connection works like a symptom, not a cure, and our constant, reflexive impulse to connect shapes a new way of being.

Think of it as "I share, therefore I am." We use technology to define ourselves by 22 sharing our thoughts and feelings as we're having them. We used to think, "I have a feeling; I want to make a call." Now our impulse is, "I want to have a feeling; I need to send a text."

So, in order to feel more, and to feel more like ourselves, we connect. But in 23
our rush to connect, we flee from solitude, our ability to be separate and gather
ourselves. Lacking the capacity for solitude, we turn to other people but don't experience them as they are. It is as though we use them, need them as spare parts to
support our increasingly fragile selves.

We think constant connection will make us feel less lonely. The opposite is true. If 24
we are unable to be alone, we are far more likely to be lonely. If we don't teach our
children to be alone, they will know only how to be lonely.

I am a partisan for conversation. To make room for it, I see some first, deliberate 25
steps. At home, we can create sacred spaces: the kitchen, the dining room. We can
make our cars "device-free zones." We can demonstrate the value of conversation to
our children. And we can do the same thing at work. There we are so busy communicating that we often don't have time to talk to one another about what really matters.
Employees asked for casual Fridays; perhaps managers should introduce conversa-
tional Thursdays. Most of all, we need to remember — in between texts and e-mails
and Facebook posts — to listen to one another, even to the boring bits, because it is
often in unedited moments, moments in which we hesitate and stutter and go silent,
that we reveal ourselves to one another.

I spend the summers at a cottage on Cape Cod, and for decades I walked the same 26
dunes that Thoreau once walked. Not too long ago, people walked with their heads
up, looking at the water, the sky, the sand and at one another, talking. Now they often
walk with their heads down, typing. Even when they are with friends, partners, children, everyone is on their own devices.

So I say, look up, look at one another, and let's start the conversation. 27

READING FOR MEANING

For help
with reading
strategies like
summarizing
and analyzing
assumptions,
see Chapter 2.

1. **Read to Summarize.** Write a sentence or two explaining Turkle's position
   on digitally mediated communication (texting, e-mailing, and posting)
   versus conversation.

2. **Read to Respond.** Write a paragraph analyzing anything that seems
   contradictory, such as Turkle's claim about the messiness (par. 11) of
   relationships conducted face-to-face or via telephone conversations versus
   via texting, posting, and e-mailing; or Turkle's denial that "our little 'sips' of
   online connection add up to a big gulp of real conversation" (par. 12).

3. **Read to Analyze Assumptions.** Write a paragraph or two analyzing an
   assumption you find intriguing in Turkle's essay. For example:

   Assumptions about the role of conversation in our well-being and our lives.
   Turkle writes that "conversation unfolds slowly. It teaches patience.... [W]e
   use conversation with others to learn to converse with ourselves" (pars. 14–15).

- What pattern is revealed in the examples Turkle offers when arguing in favor of the benefits of conversation on our thinking and our emotions? What does this pattern reveal?

- According to Turkle, conversation helps a person be alone, but not lonely, a seeming paradox (pars. 20–24). What is your experience? Does texting friends and family enhance closeness? Does not texting make you anxious or lonely?

Assumptions about control of our selves. Turkle believes we use technology to keep ourselves separate, at a distance from others, and that we have come to value the way we can edit ourselves in our interactions with others through technology.

- Turkle writes that "people are comforted by being in touch with a lot of people — carefully kept at bay" (par. 9). What are the advantages and disadvantages of keeping each other "at bay"?

- What does Turkle think we lose when we allow technology to dictate the way our relationships are conducted? What do you think we lose — and gain?

READING LIKE A WRITER

Arguing Directly for the Position, and Supporting the Position with Reasonable Evidence

A strong argument needs to present reasons and support for the writer's position on an issue. Writers may use facts, statistics, examples, anecdotes, expert opinion, or analogies to make their case. Turkle uses several of these types of evidence to support her reasons, and she also includes quotations (presumably gleaned from interviews) to support her assertion that by using modern technologies, we have "sacrificed conversation for mere connection" (par. 1).

ANALYZE & WRITE

Write a paragraph or two analyzing how Turkle uses quotations to support her claims:

1. Reread paragraphs 6–8, highlighting the words she uses to introduce and contextualize quotations and underlining the quotations themselves. What do the quotations add — perhaps something compelling that the use of other strategies would not provide? If so, what is it?

2. Now skim the rest of her essay, noting where Turkle quotes sources elsewhere in her position argument. What kind of pattern does she follow for introducing these quotations? How effective is it for you as a reader?

Daniel J. Solove

Why Privacy Matters Even If You Have "Nothing to Hide"

Daniel J. Solove (b. 1972), currently John Marshall Harlan research professor of law at the George Washington University Law School, earned his J.D. at Yale Law School. In addition to writing numerous books and articles on issues of privacy and the Internet, Solove is the founder of a company that provides privacy and data security training to corporations and universities. Among his books are *The Future of Reputation: Gossip, Rumor, and Privacy on the Internet* (2007), and *Nothing to Hide: The False Tradeoff Between Privacy and Security* (2011). An earlier and longer version of this essay in a law review journal included citations that had to be eliminated for publication in the *Chronicle of Higher Education* in 2011, but we have restored them so that you can see how Solove uses a variety of sources to support his position.

- **Before you read,** think about how (or whether) you make an effort to protect your privacy on social networking and other websites.

- **As you read,** notice the sources cited in the opening paragraphs, and consider how they contribute to your understanding of why many people think privacy is not something they should be concerned about.

When the government gathers or analyzes personal information, many people say 1
they're not worried. "I've got nothing to hide," they declare. "Only if you're doing something wrong should you worry, and then you don't deserve to keep it private." The nothing-to-hide argument pervades discussions about privacy. The data-security expert Bruce Schneier calls it the "most common retort against privacy advocates." The legal scholar Geoffrey Stone refers to it as an "all-too-common refrain." In its most compelling form, it is an argument that the privacy interest is generally minimal, thus making the contest with security concerns a foreordained victory for security.

The nothing-to-hide argument is everywhere. In Britain, for example, the govern- 2
ment has installed millions of public-surveillance cameras in cities and towns, which are watched by officials via closed-circuit television. In a campaign slogan for the program, the government declares: "If you've got nothing to hide, you've got nothing to fear" (Rosen 36). Variations of nothing-to-hide arguments frequently appear in blogs, letters to the editor, television news interviews, and other forums. One blogger in the United States, in reference to profiling people for national-security purposes, declares: "I don't mind people wanting to find out things about me, I've got nothing to hide! Which is why I support [the government's] efforts to find terrorists by monitoring our phone calls!" (greatcarrieoakey).

On the surface, it seems easy to dismiss the nothing-to-hide argument. Everybody   3
probably has something to hide from somebody. As Aleksandr Solzhenitsyn declared,
"Everyone is guilty of something or has something to conceal. All one has to do is
look hard enough to find what it is" (192). . . . One can usually think of something
that even the most open person would want to hide. As a commenter to my blog post
noted, "If you have nothing to hide, then that quite literally means you are willing
to let me photograph you naked? And I get full rights to that photograph—so I can
show it to your neighbors?" (Andrew) . . .

But such responses attack the nothing-to-hide argument only in its most extreme   4
form, which isn't particularly strong. In a less extreme form, the nothing-to-hide
argument refers not to all personal information but only to the type of data the government is likely to collect. Retorts to the nothing-to-hide argument about exposing
people's naked bodies or their deepest secrets are relevant only if the government is
likely to gather this kind of information. In many instances, hardly anyone will see
the information, and it won't be disclosed to the public. Thus, some might argue, the
privacy interest is minimal, and the security interest in preventing terrorism is much
more important. In this less extreme form, the nothing-to-hide argument is a formi-
dable one. However, it stems from certain faulty assumptions about privacy and its
value. . . .

Most attempts to understand privacy do so by attempting to locate its   5
essence—its core characteristics or the common denominator that links together
the various things we classify under the rubric of "privacy." Privacy, however, is
too complex a concept to be reduced to a singular essence. It is a plurality of
different things that do not share any one element but nevertheless bear a resem-
blance to one another. For example, privacy can be invaded by the disclosure
of your deepest secrets. It might also be invaded if you're watched by a peeping
Tom, even if no secrets are ever revealed. With the disclosure of secrets, the harm
is that your concealed information is spread to others. With the peeping Tom,
the harm is that you're being watched. You'd probably find that creepy regardless
of whether the peeper finds out anything sensitive or discloses any information
to others. There are many other forms of invasion of privacy, such as blackmail
and the improper use of your personal data. Your privacy can also be invaded if
the government compiles an extensive dossier about you. Privacy, in other words,
involves so many things that it is impossible to reduce them all to one simple idea.
And we need not do so. . . .

To describe the problems created by the collection and use of personal data,   6
many commentators use a metaphor based on George Orwell's *Nineteen Eighty-
Four*. Orwell depicted a harrowing totalitarian society ruled by a government called
Big Brother that watches its citizens obsessively and demands strict discipline. The
Orwell metaphor, which focuses on the harms of surveillance (such as inhibition
and social control), might be apt to describe government monitoring of citizens. But
much of the data gathered in computer databases, such as one's race, birth date,
gender, address, or marital status, isn't particularly sensitive. Many people don't care
about concealing the hotels they stay at, the cars they own, or the kind of beverages

they drink. Frequently, though not always, people wouldn't be inhibited or embarrassed if others knew this information.

Another metaphor better captures the problems: Franz Kafka's *The Trial.* Kafka's   7
novel centers around a man who is arrested but not informed why. He desperately
tries to find out what triggered his arrest and what's in store for him. He finds out
that a mysterious court system has a dossier on him and is investigating him, but
he's unable to learn much more. *The Trial* depicts a bureaucracy with inscrutable
purposes that uses people's information to make important decisions about them,
yet denies the people the ability to participate in how their information is used.

The problems portrayed by the Kafkaesque metaphor are of a different sort   8
than the problems caused by surveillance. They often do not result in inhibition.
Instead they are problems of information processing—the storage, use, or analysis
of data—rather than of information collection. They affect the power relationships
between people and the institutions of the modern state. They not only frustrate the
individual by creating a sense of helplessness and powerlessness, but also affect
social structure by altering the kind of relationships people have with the institutions
that make important decisions about their lives.

Legal and policy solutions focus too much on the problems under the Orwellian   9
metaphor—those of surveillance—and aren't adequately addressing the Kafkaesque
problems—those of information processing. The difficulty is that commentators are
trying to conceive of the problems caused by databases in terms of surveillance
when, in fact, those problems are different. Commentators often attempt to refute
the nothing-to-hide argument by pointing to things people want to hide. But the
problem with the nothing-to-hide argument is the underlying assumption that privacy is about hiding bad things. By accepting this assumption, we concede far too
much ground and invite an unproductive discussion about information that people
would very likely want to hide. As the computer-security specialist Schneier aptly
notes, the nothing-to-hide argument stems from a faulty "premise that privacy is
about hiding a wrong." Surveillance, for example, can inhibit such lawful activities as free speech, free association, and other First Amendment rights essential for
democracy.

The deeper problem with the nothing-to-hide argument is that it myopically views   10
privacy as a form of secrecy. In contrast, understanding privacy as a plurality of
related issues demonstrates that the disclosure of bad things is just one among many
difficulties caused by government security measures. To return to my discussion of
literary metaphors, the problems are not just Orwellian but Kafkaesque. Government
information-gathering programs are problematic even if no information that people
want to hide is uncovered. In *The Trial*, the problem is not inhibited behavior but
rather a suffocating powerlessness and vulnerability created by the court system's use
of personal data and its denial to the protagonist of any knowledge of or participation
in the process. The harms are bureaucratic ones—indifference, error, abuse, frustration, and lack of transparency and accountability.

One such harm, for example, which I call aggregation, emerges from the fusion   11
of small bits of seemingly innocuous data. When combined, the information

becomes much more telling. By joining pieces of information we might not take pains to guard, the government can glean information about us that we might indeed wish to conceal. For example, suppose you bought a book about cancer. This purchase isn't very revealing on its own, for it indicates just an interest in the disease. Suppose you bought a wig. The purchase of a wig, by itself, could be for a number of reasons. But combine those two pieces of information, and now the inference can be made that you have cancer and are undergoing chemotherapy. That might be a fact you wouldn't mind sharing, but you'd certainly want to have the choice.

Another potential problem with the government's harvest of personal data is one 12 I call exclusion. Exclusion occurs when people are prevented from having knowledge about how information about them is being used, and when they are barred from accessing and correcting errors in that data. Many government national-security measures involve maintaining a huge database of information that individuals cannot access. Indeed, because they involve national security, the very existence of these programs is often kept secret. This kind of information processing, which blocks subjects' knowledge and involvement, is a kind of due-process problem. It is a structural problem, involving the way people are treated by government institutions and creating a power imbalance between people and the government. To what extent should government officials have such a significant power over citizens? This issue isn't about what information people want to hide but about the power and the structure of government.

A related problem involves secondary use. Secondary use is the exploitation of 13 data obtained for one purpose for an unrelated purpose without the subject's consent. How long will personal data be stored? How will the information be used? What could it be used for in the future? The potential uses of any piece of personal information are vast. Without limits on or accountability for how that information is used, it is hard for people to assess the dangers of the data's being in the government's control.

Yet another problem with government gathering and use of personal data is dis- 14 tortion. Although personal information can reveal quite a lot about people's personalities and activities, it often fails to reflect the whole person. It can paint a distorted picture, especially since records are reductive—they often capture information in a standardized format with many details omitted. For example, suppose government officials learn that a person has bought a number of books on how to manufacture methamphetamine. That information makes them suspect that he's building a meth lab. What is missing from the records is the full story: The person is writing a novel about a character who makes meth. When he bought the books, he didn't consider how suspicious the purchase might appear to government officials, and his records didn't reveal the reason for the purchases. Should he have to worry about government scrutiny of all his purchases and actions? Should he have to be concerned that he'll wind up on a suspicious-persons list? Even if he isn't doing anything wrong, he may want to keep his records away from government officials who might make faulty inferences from them. He might not want to have to worry about how everything he does will be perceived by officials nervously monitoring for criminal activity. He might not want to have a computer flag him as suspicious because he has an unusual pattern of behavior. . . .

Privacy is rarely lost in one fell swoop. It is usually eroded over time, little bits 15 dissolving almost imperceptibly until we finally begin to notice how much is gone. When the government starts monitoring the phone numbers people call, many may shrug their shoulders and say, "Ah, it's just numbers, that's all." Then the government might start monitoring some phone calls. "It's just a few phone calls, nothing more." The government might install more video cameras in public places. "So what? Some more cameras watching in a few more places. No big deal." The increase in cameras might lead to a more elaborate network of video surveillance. Satellite surveillance might be added to help track people's movements. The government might start analyzing people's bank records. "It's just my deposits and some of the bills I pay—no problem." The government may then start combing through credit-card records, then expand to Internet-service providers' records, health records, employment records, and more. Each step may seem incremental, but after a while, the government will be watching and knowing everything about us.

"My life's an open book," people might say. "I've got nothing to hide." But now 16 the government has large dossiers of everyone's activities, interests, reading habits, finances, and health. What if the government leaks the information to the public? What if the government mistakenly determines that based on your pattern of activities, you're likely to engage in a criminal act? What if it denies you the right to fly? What if the government thinks your financial transactions look odd—even if you've done nothing wrong—and freezes your accounts? What if the government doesn't protect your information with adequate security, and an identity thief obtains it and uses it to defraud you? Even if you have nothing to hide, the government can cause you a lot of harm. . . .

Works Cited

greatcarrieoakey (Carrie Oakey). "Look All You Want! I've Got Nothing to Hide!" *Reach for the Stars,* Blogger, 14 May 2006, greatcarrieoakey.blogspot.com/2006_05_01_archive. html.

Rosen, Jeffrey. *The Naked Crowd: Reclaiming Security and Freedom in an Anxious Age.* Random House Books, 2004.

Schneier, Bruce. "The Eternal Value of Privacy." *Wired,* 18 May 2006. *Schneier on Security,* www.schneier.com/essays/archives/2006/05/the_eternal_value_of.html.

Solzhenitsyn, Aleksandr. *Cancer Ward.* Translated by Nicholas Bethell and David Burg. Farrar, Straus and Giroux, 1969.

Stone, Geoffrey R. "Freedom and Public Responsibility." *Chicago Tribune,* 21 May 2006, p. 11.

READING FOR MEANING

1. **Read to Summarize.** Write a few sentences explaining why Solove is worried about the attitude many people share — that they have "nothing to hide" and are therefore unconcerned about government surveillance.

   For help with reading strategies like summarizing and analyzing assumptions, see Chapter 2.

2. **Read to Respond.** Write a paragraph about anything that seems interesting, such as Solove's division of violations of privacy into two types: Orwellian, "which focuses on the harms of surveillance (such as inhibition and social control)" (par. 6) and Kafkaesque "problems of information processing — the storage, use, or analysis of data — rather than of information collection" (par. 8); or Solove's argument that the loss of privacy is usually incremental, "eroded over time" (par. 15). Do the divisions or stages seem logical to you, and are they valid stepping-stones to more alarming consequences?

3. **Read to Analyze Assumptions.** Write a paragraph or two analyzing an assumption in Solove's essay. For example:

   Assumptions that "privacy is about hiding bad things" (par. 9). Solove quotes "data-security expert" (par. 1) Bruce Schneier to make explicit a commonly held assumption, that privacy is "about hiding a wrong" (par. 9).

   - Are "one's race, birth date, gender, address, or marital status [not] particularly sensitive," as Solove asserts (par. 6)? Can you think of situations in which this kind of information could be used to injure someone?

   - Solove counters the assumption that privacy is about bad things by stating that this assumption is not the only way to think about privacy. What alternatives does he offer? Are they convincing to you?

   Assumptions that people would take steps to curb violations of privacy if they knew how the information could be used. Solove brings two kinds of privacy violation to our attention because he believes that doing so will change our point of view that we have "nothing to hide."

   - Solove compares privacy violations to Franz Kafka's *The Trial*, in which information is withheld from a man who is arrested but not told why (par. 7). He adds that the problems are not from surveillance, but "are problems of information processing — the storage, use, or analysis of data — rather than of information collection" (par. 8). Why does Solove think this is a much bigger problem?

   - In his final paragraph (par. 16), Solove speculates about the consequences to invasions of privacy that may not have occurred to readers. What is he assuming readers will value, now that he has opened their eyes? Do his examples reflect consequences that could make people change their behavior?

READING LIKE A WRITER

Presenting the Controversial Issue Fairly and Credibly

Writers sometimes have to remind their readers why an issue is controversial. Beginning with the title, Solove works to undermine the widely held assumption that the erosion of privacy should not be a concern. He does this primarily by contrasting two different ways of thinking about threats to privacy, which he calls Orwellian and Kafkaesque. To present this contrast, Solove uses sentence patterns like these:

▶ Not ...., but ....

▶ .... focus on ...., which is characterized by ...., and they don't even notice ...., which is characterized by

....

Here is an example from Solove's position argument:

> Legal and policy solutions focus too much on the problems under the Orwellian metaphor — those of surveillance — and aren't adequately addressing the Kafkaesque problems — those of information processing. . . . [T]he problems are not just Orwellian but Kafkaesque. (pars. 9–10)

ANALYZE & WRITE

Write a few paragraphs analyzing and evaluating the effectiveness of Solove's use of contrast to *reframe* the issue for readers:

1. Notice how Solove uses sources in his first three paragraphs. Given his purpose to reframe a commonly held view of privacy, why do you think he begins this way?

2. Reread paragraphs 6–7 to see how Solove explains the two contrasting metaphors. Then skim paragraphs 8–10, highlighting any sentence patterns he uses to mark the contrast.

3. Has Solove's reframing of the discussion affected your understanding of privacy and your concerns about its loss? Why or why not?

Miya Tokumitsu

In the Name of Love

Miya Tokumitsu earned her Ph.D. in art history from the University of Pennsylvania and teaches art history and art curatorship at the University of Melbourne, Australia. She is a contributing editor of *Jacobin*, an online and print quarterly of the American left, where the following essay was published in 2015. In it, she critiques the clichéd idea that people can only be happy if they pursue a career they love. The essay's success led to her book, *Do What You Love and Other Lies about Success and Happiness* (2015).

- **Before you read,** think about your expectations of your future job or career. Do you think you will love what you do? Or do you think a job is a job, and not necessarily something that needs to be rewarding and fulfilling?

- **As you read,** consider how clearly Tokumitsu presents her argument. Can you find her thesis easily? Identify the strategies she uses to remind you of her position throughout her argument and consider how effective they are.

Mario De Armas

"Do what you love. Love what you do." 1

The commands are framed and perched in a living room that can only be described 2
as "well-curated." A picture of this room appeared first on a popular design blog, but
has been pinned, tumbl'd, and liked thousands of times by now.

Lovingly lit and photographed, this room is styled to inspire *Sehnsucht*, roughly 3
translatable from German as a pleasurable yearning for some utopian thing or place.
Despite the fact that it introduces exhortations to labor into a space of leisure, the
"do what you love" living room—where artful tchotchkes abound and work is not
drudgery but love—is precisely the place all those pinners and likers long to be. The
diptych arrangement suggests a secular version of a medieval house altar.

There's little doubt that "do what you love" (DWYL) is now the unofficial work 4
mantra for our time. The problem is that it leads not to salvation, but to the devaluation of actual work, including the very work it pretends to elevate—and more importantly, the dehumanization of the vast majority of laborers.

Superficially, DWYL is an uplifting piece of advice, urging us to ponder what it is we 5
most enjoy doing and then turn that activity into a wage-generating enterprise. But why
should our pleasure be for profit? Who is the audience for this dictum? Who is not?

By keeping us focused on ourselves and our individual happiness, DWYL dis- 6
tracts us from the working conditions of others while validating our own choices
and relieving us from obligations to all who labor, whether or not they love it. It is
the secret handshake of the privileged and a worldview that disguises its elitism as
noble self-betterment. According to this way of thinking, labor is not something one
does for compensation, but an act of self-love. If profit doesn't happen to follow, it
is because the worker's passion and determination were insufficient. Its real achievement is making workers believe their labor serves the self and not the marketplace.

Aphorisms have numerous origins and reincarnations, but the generic and hack- 7
neyed nature of DWYL confounds precise attribution. Oxford Reference links the
phrase and variants of it to Martina Navratilova and François Rabelais, among others.
The internet frequently attributes it to Confucius, locating it in a misty, Orientalized
past. Oprah Winfrey and other peddlers of positivity have included it in their reper-
toires for decades, but the most important recent evangelist of the DWYL creed is
deceased Apple CEO Steve Jobs.

His graduation speech to the Stanford University class of 2005 provides as good 8
an origin myth as any, especially since Jobs had already been beatified as the patron
saint of aestheticized work well before his early death. In the speech, Jobs recounts
the creation of Apple, and inserts this reflection:

> You've got to find what you love. And that is as true for your work as it is for
> your lovers. Your work is going to fill a large part of your life, and the only
> way to be truly satisfied is to do what you believe is great work. And the
> only way to do great work is to love what you do.

In these four sentences, the words "you" and "your" appear eight times. This focus 9
on the individual is hardly surprising coming from Jobs, who cultivated a very specific image of himself as a worker: inspired, casual, passionate—all states agreeable

with ideal romantic love. Jobs telegraphed the conflation of his besotted worker-self with his company so effectively that his black turtleneck and blue jeans became metonyms for all of Apple and the labor that maintains it.

But by portraying Apple as a labor of his individual love, Jobs elided the labor of 10 untold thousands in Apple's factories, conveniently hidden from sight on the other side of the planet—the very labor that allowed Jobs to actualize his love.

The violence of this erasure needs to be exposed. While "do what you love" 11 sounds harmless and precious, it is ultimately self-focused to the point of narcissism. Jobs' formulation of "do what you love" is the depressing antithesis to Henry David Thoreau's utopian vision of labor for all. In "Life Without Principle," Thoreau wrote,

> . . . it would be good economy for a town to pay its laborers so well that they would not feel that they were working for low ends, as for a livelihood merely, but for scientific, even moral ends. Do not hire a man who does your work for money, but him who does it for the love of it.

Admittedly, Thoreau had little feel for the proletariat (it's hard to imagine some- 12 one washing diapers for "scientific, even moral ends," no matter how well-paid). But he nonetheless maintains that society has a stake in making work well-compensated and meaningful. By contrast, the twenty-first-century Jobsian view demands that we all turn inward. It absolves us of any obligation to or acknowledgment of the wider world, underscoring its fundamental betrayal of all workers, whether they consciously embrace it or not.

One consequence of this isolation is the division that DWYL creates among 13 workers, largely along class lines. Work becomes divided into two opposing classes: that which is lovable (creative, intellectual, socially prestigious) and that which is not (repetitive, unintellectual, undistinguished). Those in the lovable work camp are vastly more privileged in terms of wealth, social status, education, society's racial biases, and political clout, while comprising a small minority of the workforce.

For those forced into unlovable work, it's a different story. Under the DWYL 14 credo, labor that is done out of motives or needs other than love (which is, in fact, most labor) is not only demeaned but erased. As in Jobs' Stanford speech, unlovable but socially necessary work is banished from the spectrum of consciousness altogether.

Think of the great variety of work that allowed Jobs to spend even one day as CEO: 15 his food harvested from fields, then transported across great distances. His company's goods assembled, packaged, shipped. Apple advertisements scripted, cast, filmed. Lawsuits processed. Office wastebaskets emptied and ink cartridges filled. Job creation goes both ways. Yet with the vast majority of workers effectively invisible to elites busy in their lovable occupations, how can it be surprising that the heavy strains faced by today's workers (abysmal wages, massive child care costs, et cetera) barely register as political issues even among the liberal faction of the ruling class?

In ignoring most work and reclassifying the rest as love, DWYL may be the most 16 elegant anti-worker ideology around. Why should workers assemble and assert their class interests if there's no such thing as work?

"Do what you love" disguises the fact that being able to choose a career primarily 17 for personal reward is an unmerited privilege, a sign of that person's socioeconomic class. Even if a self-employed graphic designer had parents who could pay for art school and cosign a lease for a slick Brooklyn apartment, she can self-righteously bestow DWYL as career advice to those covetous of her success.

If we believe that working as a Silicon Valley entrepreneur or a museum publi- 18 cist or a think-tank acolyte is essential to being true to ourselves—in fact, to loving ourselves—what do we believe about the inner lives and hopes of those who clean hotel rooms and stock shelves at big-box stores? The answer is: nothing.

Yet arduous, low-wage work is what ever more Americans do and will be doing. 19 According to the US Bureau of Labor Statistics, the two fastest-growing occupations projected until 2020 are "Personal Care Aide" and "Home Care Aide," with average salaries of $19,640 per year and $20,560 per year in 2010, respectively. Elevating certain types of professions to something worthy of love necessarily denigrates the labor of those who do unglamorous work that keeps society functioning, especially the crucial work of caregivers.

If DWYL denigrates or makes dangerously invisible vast swaths of labor that allow 20 many of us to live in comfort and to do what we love, it has also caused great damage to the professions it portends to celebrate, especially those jobs existing within institutional structures. Nowhere has the DWYL mantra been more devastating to its adherents than in academia. The average PhD student of the mid 2000s forwent the easy money of finance and law (now slightly less easy) to live on a meager stipend in order to pursue their passion for Norse mythology or the history of Afro-Cuban music.

The reward for answering this higher calling is an academic employment market- 21 place in which around 41 percent of American faculty are adjunct professors—contract instructors who usually receive low pay, no benefits, no office, no job security, and no long-term stake in the schools where they work.

There are many factors that keep PhDs providing such high-skilled labor for such 22 extremely low wages, including path dependency and the sunk costs of earning a PhD, but one of the strongest is how pervasively the DWYL doctrine is embedded in academia. Few other professions fuse the personal identity of their workers so intimately with the work output. This intense identification partly explains why so many proudly left-leaning faculty remain oddly silent about the working conditions of their peers. Because academic research should be done out of pure love, the actual conditions of and compensation for this labor become afterthoughts, if they are considered at all.

In "Academic Labor, the Aesthetics of Management, and the Promise of Autono- 23 mous Work," Sarah Brouillette writes of academic faculty,

> . . . our faith that our work offers non-material rewards, and is more integral to our identity than a "regular" job would be, makes us ideal employees when the goal of management is to extract our labor's maximum value at minimum cost.

Many academics like to think they have avoided a corporate work environment 24 and its attendant values, but Marc Bousquet notes in his essay "We Work" that academia may actually provide a model for corporate management:

> How to emulate the academic workplace and get people to work at a high level of intellectual and emotional intensity for fifty or sixty hours a week for bartenders' wages or less? Is there any way we can get our employees to swoon over their desks, murmuring "I love what I do" in response to greater workloads and smaller paychecks? How can we get our workers to be like faculty and deny that they work at all? How can we adjust our corporate culture to resemble campus culture, so that our workforce will fall in love with their work too?

No one is arguing that enjoyable work should be less so. But emotionally satisfy- 25 ing work is still work, and acknowledging it as such doesn't undermine it in any way. Refusing to acknowledge it, on the other hand, opens the door to the most vicious exploitation and harms all workers.

Ironically, DWYL reinforces exploitation even within the so-called lovable pro- 26 fessions where off-the-clock, underpaid, or unpaid labor is the new norm: reporters required to do the work of their laid-off photographers, publicists expected to Pin and Tweet on weekends, the 46 percent of the workforce expected to check their work email on sick days. Nothing makes exploitation go down easier than convincing workers that they are doing what they love.

Instead of crafting a nation of self-fulfilled, happy workers, our DWYL era has seen 27 the rise of the adjunct professor and the unpaid intern — people persuaded to work for cheap or free, or even for a net loss of wealth. This has certainly been the case for all those interns working for college credit or those who actually purchase ultra-desirable fashion-house internships at auction. (Valentino and Balenciaga are among a handful of houses that auctioned off month-long internships. For charity, of course.) The latter is worker exploitation taken to its most extreme, and as an ongoing Pro Publica investigation[8] reveals, the unpaid intern is an ever larger presence in the American workforce.

It should be no surprise that unpaid interns abound in fields that are highly socially 28 desirable, including fashion, media, and the arts. These industries have long been accustomed to masses of employees willing to work for social currency instead of actual wages, all in the name of love. Excluded from these opportunities, of course, is the overwhelming majority of the population: those who need to work for wages. This exclusion not only calcifies economic and professional immobility, but insulates these industries from the full diversity of voices society has to offer.

And it's no coincidence that the industries that rely heavily on interns — fashion, 29 media, and the arts — just happen to be the feminized ones, as Madeleine Schwartz wrote in *Dissent*.[9] Yet another damaging consequence of DWYL is how ruthlessly it works to extract female labor for little or no compensation. Women comprise the majority of the low-wage or unpaid workforce; as care workers, adjunct faculty, and unpaid interns, they outnumber men. What unites all of this work, whether performed by GEDs or PhDs, is the belief that wages shouldn't be the primary motivation for

[8] "Internships." Pro Publica: Journalism in the Public Interest, www.propublica.org / series/internships. [Ed.]

[9] Schwartz, Madeleine. "Opportunity Costs: The True Price of Internships." Dissent Magazine, www.dissentmagazine.org/article/opportunity-costs-the-true-price-of-internships. [Ed.]

doing it. Women are supposed to do work because they are natural nurturers and are eager to please; after all they've been doing uncompensated childcare, elder care, and housework since time immemorial. And talking money is unladylike anyway.

The DWYL dream is, true to its American mythology, superficially democratic. PhDs 30 can do what they love, making careers that indulge their love of the Victorian novel and writing thoughtful essays in the *New York Review of Books*. High school grads can also do it, building prepared food empires out of their Aunt Pearl's jam recipe. The hallowed path of the entrepreneur always offers this way out of disadvantaged beginnings, excusing the rest of us for allowing those beginnings to be as miserable as they are. In America, everyone has the opportunity to do what he or she loves and get rich.

Do what you love and you'll never work a day in your life! Before succumbing to 31 the intoxicating warmth of that promise, it's critical to ask, "Who, exactly, benefits from making work feel like non-work?" "Why *should* workers feel as if they aren't working when they are?" Historian Mario Liverani reminds us that "ideology has the function of presenting exploitation in a favorable light to the exploited, as advantageous to the disadvantaged."

In masking the very exploitative mechanisms of labor that it fuels, DWYL is, in 32 fact, the most perfect ideological tool of capitalism. It shunts aside the labor of others and disguises our own labor to ourselves. It hides the fact that if we acknowledged all of our work as work, we could set appropriate limits for it, demanding fair compensation and humane schedules that allow for family and leisure time.

And if we did that, more of us could get around to doing what it is we *really* love. 33

READING FOR MEANING

For help with reading strategies like summarizing and analyzing assumptions, see Chapter 2.

1. **Read to Summarize.** Write a few sentences explaining how, according to Tokumitsu, doing "what you love" for a living is unrealistic for most people and can be downright harmful to those who can't.

2. **Read to Respond.** Write a paragraph about anything surprising, such as Tokumitsu's assertion that doing what you love leads to the "devaluation of actual work" and the "dehumanization of the vast majority of laborers" (par. 4); or that DWYL is, in Tokumitsu's view, undemocratic (pars. 30–32).

3. **Read to Analyze Assumptions.** Write a paragraph or two analyzing an assumption you find intriguing in Tokumitsu's essay. For example:

   Assumptions about work as part of our lives — not our whole lives. Tokumitsu begins her essay with a description of a "living room" that is also a work room, where "work is not drudgery but love" (par. 3). The room serves as a metaphor for a life, where work has entered the "private" living space.

   • If the living room/work room described in paragraphs 2–3 is exceptional because it is for work that is pleasant, not drudgery, what does Tokumitsu assume about *most* work — or, at least, people's attitudes toward their work? How does she support this assumption?

- Tokumitsu criticizes companies "within the so-called lovable professions" for exploiting their workforce, who are expected to engage in technology for work (pins, Tweets, e-mails) on weekends (par. 26). What are her assumptions about the relationship between work and weekends?

Assumptions about the relationship between socioeconomic status and work that is valued. Tokumitsu asserts that "'Do what you love' disguises the fact that being able to choose a career primarily for personal reward is an unmerited privilege, a sign of that person's socioeconomic class" (par. 17).

- Do you share this assumption that people who can choose work they love are generally in a comfortable socioeconomic bracket? Does anything in your experience support or disprove this assumption?
- Tokumitsu believes that "emotionally satisfying work is still work, and . . . refusing to acknowledge it . . . opens the door to the most vicious exploitation and harms all workers" (par. 25). Think of examples from the media or your own experience that illustrate or refute her point about "exploitation." How does refusing to acknowledge that satisfying work is still work damage workers who don't necessarily love what they do?

READING LIKE A WRITER

Asserting a Clear Position

Writers usually (but not always) assert their positions early in an essay and, to help readers focus, may reassert the position later and in the conclusion. The position is the *thesis*, and a restatement of the thesis can occur regularly as the writer develops reasons and evidence to support it. Tokumitsu's thesis appears in paragraph 4: "The problem is that [the mantra 'do what you love'] leads not to salvation, but to the devaluation of actual work, including the very work it pretends to elevate — and more importantly, the dehumanization of the vast majority of laborers."

ANALYZE & WRITE

Write a paragraph or two analyzing how effectively Tokumitsu asserts her position.

1. Skim her essay and highlight all the places where she restates her thesis—for example, "While 'do what you love' sounds harmless and precious, it is ultimately self-focused to the point of narcissism" (par. 11).

2. Underline any sentences that assert a reason in support of her thesis. (The word *because* often has a reason following it.) For example, she explains why DWYL is implicitly elitist: "labor is not something one does for compensation, but an act of self-love. If profit doesn't happen to follow, it is because the worker's passion and determination were insufficient" (par. 6). How do the reasons support her thesis? Are there any reasons that undermine her position or make it unclear? If so, what are they?

Jessica Statsky

Children Need to Play, Not Compete

Jessica Statsky was a college student when she wrote this position paper for a sports journalism course, in which she argues that organized sports are not good for children between the ages of six and twelve.

- **Before you read,** recall your own experiences as an elementary-school student playing competitive sports, either in or out of school. If you were not actively involved yourself, did you know anyone who was? Was winning emphasized? What about having a good time? Getting along with others? Developing athletic skills and confidence?

- **As you read,** notice how Statsky sets forth her position clearly, supports the reasons for her position, and handles readers' likely objections. Also note the visible cues that Statsky provides to guide you through her argument step-by-step.

"Organized sports for young people have become an institution in North America," 1 reports sports journalist Steve Silverman, attracting more than 44 million youngsters according to a recent survey by the National Council of Youth Sports ("History"). Though many adults regard Little League Baseball xand Peewee Football as a basic part of childhood, the games are not always joyous ones. When overzealous parents and coaches impose adult standards on children's sports, the result can be activities that are neither satisfying nor beneficial to children.

I am concerned about all organized sports activities for children between the 2 ages of six and twelve. The damage I see results from noncontact as well as contact sports, from sports organized locally as well as those organized nationally. Highly organized competitive sports such as Peewee Football and Little League Baseball are too often played to adult standards, which are developmentally inappropriate for children and can be both physically and psychologically harmful. Furthermore, because they eliminate many children from organized sports before they are ready to compete, they are actually counterproductive for developing either future players or fans. Finally, because they emphasize competition and winning, they unfortunately provide occasions for some parents and coaches to place their own fantasies and needs ahead of children's welfare.

One readily understandable danger of overly competitive sports is that they entice 3 children into physical actions that are bad for growing bodies. "There is a growing epidemic of preventable youth sports injuries," according to the STOP Sports Injuries campaign. "Among athletes ages 5 to 14, 28 percent of football players, 25 percent of baseball players, 22 percent of soccer players, 15 percent of basketball players, and 12 percent of softball players were injured while playing their respective sports." Although Little League Baseball and Softball acknowledges that children do risk injury playing baseball, it insists that "severe injuries . . . are infrequent," the risk "far less than the risk of riding a skateboard, a bicycle, or even the school bus" ("Little League Parent"). Nevertheless, Leonard Koppett in *Sports Illusion, Sports Reality* claims that a twelve-year-old trying to throw a curve ball, for example, may put abnormal strain on developing arm and shoulder muscles, sometimes resulting in lifelong injuries (294). Contact sports like football can be even more hazardous. Thomas Tutko, a psychology professor at San Jose State University and coauthor of the book *Winning Is Everything and Other American Myths*, writes:

> I am strongly opposed to young kids playing tackle football. It is not the right stage of development for them to be taught to crash into other kids. Kids under the age of fourteen are not by nature physical. Their main concern is self-preservation. They don't want to meet head on and slam into each other. But tackle football absolutely requires that they try to hit each other as hard as they can. And it is too traumatic for young kids. (qtd. in Tosches A1)

As Tutko indicates, even when children are not injured, fear of being hurt   4 detracts from their enjoyment of the sport. The Little League ranks fear of injury as the seventh of seven reasons children quit ("Little League Parent"). One mother of an eight-year-old Peewee Football player explained, "The kids get so scared. They get hit once and they don't want anything to do with football anymore. They'll sit on the bench and pretend their leg hurts . . . " (qtd. in Tosches A1). Some children are driven to even more desperate measures. For example, in one Peewee Football game, a reporter watched the following scene as a player took himself out of the game:

> "Coach, my tummy hurts. I can't play," he said. The coach told the player to get back onto the field. "There's nothing wrong with your stomach," he said. When the coach turned his head the seven-year-old stuck a finger down his throat and made himself vomit. When the coach turned back, the boy pointed to the ground and told him, "Yes there is, coach. See?" (Tosches A33)

Besides physical hazards and anxieties, competitive sports pose psychologi-   5 cal dangers for children. Martin Rablovsky, a former sports editor for the *New York Times*, says that in all his years of watching young children play organized sports, he has noticed very few of them smiling. "I've seen children enjoying a spontaneous pre-practice scrimmage become somber and serious when the coach's whistle blows," Rablovsky says. "The spirit of play suddenly disappears, and sport becomes joblike" (qtd. in Coakley 94). The primary goal of a professional athlete — winning — is not appropriate for children. Their goals should be having fun, learning, and being with friends. Although winning does add to the fun, too many adults lose sight of what matters and make winning the most important goal. Several studies have shown that when children are asked whether they would rather be warming the bench on a winning team or playing regularly on a losing team, about 90 percent choose the latter (Smith et al. 11). According to Mark Hyman, professor of sports management at George Washington University and author of several books on youth sports: "If we wiped the slate clean and reinvented youth sports from scratch by putting the physical and emotional needs of kids first, how different would it look? Nothing would be recognizable" (qtd. in Rosenwald).

Winning and losing may be an inevitable part of adult life, but they should not   6 be part of childhood. Too much competition too early in life can affect a child's development. Children are easily influenced, and when they sense that their competence and worth are based on their ability to live up to their parents' and coaches' high expectations—and on their ability to win—they can become discouraged and depressed. Little League advises parents to "keep winning in perspective," noting that the most common reasons children give for quitting, aside from change in interest, are lack of playing time, failure and fear of failure, disapproval by significant others, and psychological stress ("Little League Parent"). According to Dr. Glyn C. Roberts, a professor of kinesiology at the Institute of Child Behavior and Development at the University of Illinois, 80 to 90 percent of children who play competitive sports at a young age drop out by sixteen (Kutner).

This statistic illustrates another reason I oppose competitive sports for children: 7 because they are so highly selective, very few children get to participate. Far too soon, a few children are singled out for their athletic promise, while many others, who may be on the verge of developing the necessary strength and ability, are screened out and discouraged from trying out again. Like adults, children fear failure, and so even those with good physical skills may stay away because they lack self-confidence. Consequently, teams lose many promising players who with some encouragement and experience might have become stars. The problem is that many parent-sponsored, out-of-school programs give more importance to having a winning team than to developing children's physical skills and self-esteem.

Indeed, it is no secret that too often scorekeeping, league standings, and the   8 drive to win bring out the worst in adults who are more absorbed in living out their own fantasies than in enhancing the quality of the experience for children (Smith et al. 9). Recent newspaper articles on children's sports contain plenty of horror stories. *Los Angeles Times* reporter Rich Tosches, for example, tells the story of a brawl among seventy-five parents following a Peewee Football game (A33). As a result of the brawl, which began when a parent from one team confronted a player from the other team, the teams are now thinking of hiring security guards for future games. Another example is provided by a *Los Angeles Times* editorial about a Little League manager who intimidated the opposing team by setting fire to one of their team's jerseys on the pitcher's mound before the game began. As the editorial writer commented, the manager showed his young team that "intimidation could substitute for playing well" ("The Bad News Pyromaniacs?"). This phenomenon, according to Ken Reed, author of *How We Can Save Sports: A Game Plan*, is known as the "Achievement by Proxy Syndrome—adults living vicariously through the exploits of their children" (1). Reed acknowledges that the "issue of overbearing parents

*"Please, Mrs. Enright, if I let you pinch-hit for Tommy,
all the mothers will want to pinch-hit."*

FIGURE 1   Too many parents use their children's sports programs as a way to live out their own fantasies, as shown in this cartoon by James Mulligan from the *New Yorker*.
James Mulligan/Conde Nast/The Cartoon Bank

and coaches in youth sports isn't a new one," but "things are definitely getting worse. Adults are taking their seriousness about youth sports to new unhealthy extremes" (1).

Although not all parents or coaches behave so inappropriately, the seriousness of 9 the problem is illustrated by the fact that Adelphi University in Garden City, New York, offers a sports psychology workshop for Little League coaches, designed to balance their "animal instincts" with "educational theory" in hopes of reducing the "screaming and hollering," in the words of Harold Weisman, manager of sixteen Little Leagues in New York City (Schmitt). In a three-and-one-half-hour Sunday morning workshop, coaches learn how to make practices more fun, treat injuries, deal with irate parents, and be "more sensitive to their young players' fears, emotional frailties, and need for recognition." Little League is to be credited with recognizing the need for such workshops.

Some parents would no doubt argue that children cannot start too soon pre- 10 paring to live in a competitive free-market economy. After all, secondary schools and colleges require students to compete for grades, and college admission is extremely competitive. And it is perfectly obvious how important competitive skills are in finding a job. Yet the ability to cooperate is also important for success in life. Before children are psychologically ready for competition, maybe we should emphasize cooperation and individual performance in team sports rather than winning.

Many people are ready for such an emphasis. In 1988, one New York Little　11
League official who had attended the Adelphi workshop tried to ban scoring from
six- to eight-year-olds' games — but parents wouldn't support him (Schmitt). An
innovative children's sports program in New York City, City Sports for Kids, emphasizes fitness, self-esteem, and sportsmanship. In this program's basketball games,
every member on a team plays at least two of six eight-minute periods. The basket
is seven feet from the floor, rather than ten feet, and a player can score a point
just by hitting the rim (Bloch). I believe this kind of local program should replace
overly competitive programs like Peewee Football and Little League Baseball. As
one coach explains, significant improvements can result from a few simple rule
changes, such as including every player in the batting order and giving every player,
regardless of age or ability, the opportunity to play at least four innings a game
(Frank).

Some children *want* to play competitive sports; they are not being forced to　12
play. These children are eager to learn skills, to enjoy the camaraderie of the
team, and earn self-respect by trying hard to benefit their team. I acknowledge
that some children may benefit from playing competitive sports. While some children do benefit from these programs, however, many more would benefit from
programs that avoid the excesses and dangers of many competitive sports programs and instead emphasize fitness, cooperation, sportsmanship, and individual
performance.

Works Cited

"The Bad News Pyromaniacs? Fiery Anaheim Little Manager Is, Rightly, Fired." Editorial.
　　Los Angeles Times, 16 June 1990, p. B6, articles.latimes.com/1990-06-16/local/me-31
　　_1_team-manager.

Bloch, Gordon B. "Thrill of Victory Is Secondary to Fun." *The New York Times*, 2 Apr. 1990,
　　p. C12.

Coakley, Jay J. *Sport in Society: Issues and Controversies*. Mosby, 1982.

Frank, L. "Contributions from Parents and Coaches." *CYB Message Board*, AOL, 8 July 1997,
　　www.aol.com/. Accessed 14 May 2008.

Koppett, Leonard. *Sports Illusion, Sports Reality*. Boston: Houghton Mifflin, 1981. Print.

Kutner, Lawrence. "Athletics, through a Child's Eyes." *The New York Times*, 23 Mar. 1989,
　　p. C8, www.nytimes.com/1989/03/23/garden/parent-child.html.

Little League Parent Responsibilities. *Warwick National Little League 2007 Safety Plan*, Little
　　League Baseball and Softball, 17 Apr. 2007, www.littleleague.org/Assets/forms_pubs /
　　asap/Warwick_LL_safetyplan08.pdf.

Reed, Ken. "Youth Sports Burnout Driven by Achievement by Proxy Syndrome." *The Huff-
　　ington Post*, 10 Oct. 2015, www.huffingtonpost.com/ken-reed/youth-sports-burnout-
　　driv _b_8274078.html.

Rosenwald, Michael S. "Are Parents Ruining Youth Sports? Fewer Kids Play Amid Pressure."
　　The Washington Post, 4 Oct. 2015, www.washingtonpost.com/local/are-parents-ru-
　　ining -youth-sports-fewer-kids-play-amid-pressure/2015/10/04/eb1460dc-686e-11e5-
　　9ef3-fde182507eac_story.html.

Schmitt, Eric. "Psychologists Take Seat on Little League Bench." *The New York Times,*
     14 Mar. 1988, late ed., p. B2. *LexisNexis Academic,* www.lexisnexis.com.
Silverman, Steve. "The History of Youth Sports." *Livestrong,* Demand Media, Inc., 01 Sept.
     2015, www.livestrong.com/article/353963-the-history-of-youth-sports/.
Smith, Nathan, et al. *Kidsports: A Survival Guide for Parents.* Addison-Wesley, 1983.
Tosches, Rich. "Peewee Football: Is It Time to Blow the Whistle?" *The Los Angeles Times,*
     3 Dec. 1988, pp. A1+. *LexisNexis,* articles.latimes.com/1988-12-03/news/mn-936_1_
     youth -football-games.
"Youth Sports Injuries Statistics." STOP Sports Injuries: Community Outreach Toolkit, Amer-
     ican Orthopaedic Society for Sports Medicine, www.sportsmed.org/aossmimis/stop/
     downloads /CommunityOutreachToolkit.pdf.

READING FOR MEANING

1. **Read to Summarize.** Write a sentence or two explaining what you learned about children and sports from Statsky's argument.

   For help with reading strategies like summarizing and analyzing assumptions, see Chapter 2.

2. **Read to Respond.** Write a paragraph analyzing anything that resonates with your experience or that seems surprising, such as Statsky's claim that children can become discouraged and depressed "when they sense that their competence and worth are based on their ability to live up to their parents' and coaches' high expectations — and on their ability to win" (par. 6); or Statsky's assertion that "it is no secret that too often scorekeeping, league standings, and the drive to win bring out the worst in adults . . ." (par. 8). Was this true of your experience or that of your friends or your own children? What kinds of values do overzealous parents demonstrate? Are there any that are positive?

3. **Read to Analyze Assumptions.** Write a paragraph or two analyzing an assumption you find intriguing in Statsky's essay. For example:

   Assumptions that cooperation is as important a skill to develop as competition. Statsky explicitly states this assumption when she writes that the ability to cooperate is as important as competitive skills for success (par. 10).

   - Statsky asserts that "overzealous parents and coaches impose adult standards on children's sports, [leading to] activities that are neither satisfying nor beneficial to children" (par. 1). Do you agree that coaches and parents impose the desire to win on children? Should children's sports have different standards?

   - Statsky acknowledges how important competitive skills are for getting into college and finding a job, but immediately follows with a response: "Yet the ability to cooperate is also important for success in life. Before children are psychologically ready for competition, maybe we should emphasize cooperation and individual performance in team sports rather than winning" (par. 10). Do you think Statsky provides enough evidence that most children are not psychologically ready for competition? If so, which kinds of evidence are most compelling for you? Why?

Assumptions that children's sports should be inclusive. Statsky argues that children's competitive sports should be reformed because they favor the most coordinated and strongest children (par. 7) to the exclusion of children who are weaker or less skilled.

- What evidence does Statsky offer to support this claim, especially for the youngest participants in PeeWee Football and Little League? Is it possible that the stronger and better-coordinated children might be drawn to organized sports because they enjoy playing more? Might children who enjoy physical activity have developed the skills needed to succeed on the playing field through practice rather than through the process of development?

- Should those who organize children's sports have an obligation to include all children who want to participate? Why or why not?

READING LIKE A WRITER

Responding to Objections and Alternative Positions Fairly

An effective argument concedes valid objections, concerns, or reasons and refutes opposing views that are weak or flawed. Consider this passage from Statsky's essay:

Concession	Some parents would no doubt argue that children cannot start too soon preparing to live in a competitive free-market economy. After all, secondary schools and colleges require students to compete for
Signal Phrase	grades, and college admission is extremely competitive. And it is perfectly obvious how important competitive skills are in finding a job.
Refutation	Yet the ability to cooperate is also important for success in life. Before children are psychologically ready for competition, maybe we should emphasize cooperation and individual performance in team sports rather than winning. (par. 10)

Notice how Statsky treats alternative views with civility and respect, enhancing her credibility, or **ethos**.

ANALYZE & WRITE

Write a paragraph analyzing other passages in which Statsky responds to alternative points of view:

To review the meaning of rhetorical sensitivity, see Chapter 1, p. 12.

1. Reread the first sentence in paragraph 6, the first and last sentences in paragraph 9, and the first sentence in paragraph 12, highlighting the words that signal Statsky's acknowledgment of objections to her thesis.

2. Now reread the sentences following those you highlighted, to see how Statsky deals with her opposition. Does she seem to practice rhetorical sensitivity here? Why or why not?

Combining Reading Strategies

Comparing and Contrasting to Analyze Visuals

Compare and contrast the cartoon Statksy uses in "Children Need to Play, Not Compete" and the photograph Tokumitsu includes in "In the Name of Love." Write a paragraph explaining what each visual contributes to the essay. To help you get started, consider these questions:

For more on analyzing visuals, see Chapter 2, pp. 52–55.

- How do the visuals illustrate the points that the authors are making in their essays?

- Both authors are arguing for a position. How important are these visuals to supporting that position?

- Write a paragraph exploring the potential effects of removing these visuals from the essays. What — if anything — would be lost?

Writing to Learn Position Argument

Write a brief essay analyzing one of the readings in this chapter (or another selection, perhaps one by a classmate). Explain how (and perhaps, how well) the selection works as a position argument. Consider, for example, how it

- presents a controversial issue fairly and credibly by putting it in context and being specific about the terms of the debate;

- asserts a clear position in a thesis that forecasts the stages of the argument and the reasons that support it;

- argues directly for the position with writing strategies such as the use of facts, statistics, examples, anecdotes, expert opinions, and analogies;

- responds to objections, conceding where necessary and refuting when possible.

Your essay could also reflect on how you applied one or more of the academic habits of mind through the following practices:

- **Critical Analysis** — what assumptions in the selection did you find intriguing, and why?

- **Rhetorical Sensitivity** — how effective or ineffective do you think the selection is in achieving its purpose for the intended audience?

- **Empathy** — did you find yourself identifying with the author, and how important was this to the effectiveness of the selection?

A GUIDE TO WRITING POSITION ARGUMENTS

You have probably done a good deal of analytical writing about your reading. Your instructor may also assign a capstone project to write a brief position argument of your own. This Guide to Writing offers detailed suggestions and resources to help you meet the special challenges this kind of writing presents.

THE WRITING ASSIGNMENT

Write an essay arguing a position on a controversial issue.

- Choose an issue on which you either have a position or would like to investigate further.
- Consider what your readers might know about the issue, and what stance they might take toward it.
- Conduct research on the issue so you can support and clarify your own argument, and address the objections your readers might raise as well as the alternative positions they might prefer.
- Adopt a reasonable tone, one that will lend credibility to your position.

WRITING YOUR DRAFT

Choosing a Controversial Issue

Rather than limiting yourself to the first subject that comes to mind, take a few minutes to consider your options. When choosing an issue, keep in mind that the issue must be

- controversial — an issue that people disagree about;
- arguable — a matter on which there is no absolute proof or authority;
- one that you can research, as necessary, in the time you have;
- one that you care about but for which you can be fair and reasonable.

Choosing an issue about which you have special knowledge usually works best, and it's important to focus the issue so that you can write a brief paper on it. For example, if you are thinking of addressing an issue of national concern, focus on a local or a specific aspect of it: Instead of addressing censorship in general, write about a recent lawmaker's effort to propose a law censoring the Internet, a city council attempt to block access to Internet sites at a public library, or a school board's ban on certain textbooks.

You may already have an issue in mind. If you do not, the topics that follow may suggest one you can make your own. Because writing is a kind of inquiry, the topics are in the form of preliminary questions intended to get you thinking about the positions associated with these issues. While these preliminary questions may be answered with a yes or no, your position and the thesis that introduces it should be more complex in order to lay the groundwork for developing your argument, as discussed in the next section.

- Should particular courses, community service, or an internship be a graduation requirement at your high school or college? Please explain.

- Should children raised in this country whose parents entered illegally be given an opportunity to become citizens upon finishing college or serving in the military? Please explain.

- Should you look primarily for a job that is well paid, or for a job that is personally fulfilling or socially responsible? Please explain.

- Should the racial, ethnic, or gender makeup of the police force resemble the makeup of the community it serves? Please explain.

- Should your large lecture or online courses have frequent (weekly or biweekly) exams instead of only a midterm and final? Please explain.

- Should the football conference your school (or another school in the area) participates in be allowed to expand? Please explain.

- Should the state or federal government provide job training for those who are unemployed but able to work? Please explain.

Before making a final decision about the issue on which you will take a position, try writing nonstop about it for a few minutes. Doing so will help stimulate your memory, letting you see what you already know about the issue and how much research you will need to do.

For help conducting and using research, see Chapter 12.

Developing Your Argument

The writing and research activities that follow will enable you to test your choice and discover good ways to argue for your position on the issue.

Presenting the Issue.   The following questions and sentence strategies can help you explore the issue and consider how best to present it to your readers.

How can I present the issue effectively?
What is the issue and why should your readers be concerned about it?

> ▶ I'm concerned about .... because ....

Why are popular approaches or attitudes inappropriate or inadequate?

> ▶ Although some argue ...., I think .... because ....

How can I explore the issue?
What groups or notable individuals have shaped the debate on this issue? What positions have they taken?

> ▶ Whereas supporters of ...., such as ...., ...,
> and ...., have argued that ...., opponents such as ....
> [list individuals / groups] contend that ....

How has the issue, or people's opinions about the issue, changed? What makes the issue important now?

> ▶ The debate over whether .... should .... was initially con-
> cerned that ...., but the main concern now seems to be that
> ....

What do my readers think?
What values and concerns do you and your readers share regarding the issue?

> ▶ Concern about .... leads many of us to oppose .... We
> worry that .... will happen if ....

What fundamental differences in worldview or experience might keep you and your readers from agreeing?

> ▶ Those who disagree about ...._ often see it as a choice between ....
> and .... But both are important. We don't have to choose between
> them because ....

> ▶ While others may view it as a matter of ...., for me, the issue hinges
> on ....

Drafting a Working Thesis.   You may already have a position on the issue; if so, try drafting a working thesis statement now. (If you have not yet taken a position on the issue, you may want to skip ahead to the section on researching an issue below. Researching the positions others have taken and their reasons may help you decide on your own position or refine a position you already hold.) Begin by describing the issue, possibly indicating where others stand on it or what's at stake, and then saying what you think. These sentence strategies may help you get started:

▶ On this issue, ... and .... [list individuals / groups]
say .... Although I understand and to some degree sympathize with
their point of view, this is ultimately a question of .... What's at stake
is not .... , but .... Therefore, we must ....

▶ This issue is dividing our community. Some people argue .... Others
contend .... And still others believe .... It is in all of our
interests to .... , however, because ....

Here are three examples from the readings:

- "There's little doubt that 'do what you love' (DWYL) is now the unofficial work mantra for our time. The problem is that it leads not to salvation, but to the devaluation of actual work, including the very work it pretends to elevate — and more importantly, the dehumanization of the vast majority of laborers." (Tokomitsu, par. 4)

- "The deeper problem with the nothing-to-hide argument is that it myopically views privacy as a form of secrecy. In contrast, understanding privacy as a plurality of related issues demonstrates that the disclosure of bad things is just one among many difficulties caused by government security measures." (Solove, par. 10)

- "When overzealous parents and coaches impose adult standards on children's sports, the result can be activities that are neither satisfying nor beneficial to children." (Statsky, par. 1)

Developing the Reasons Supporting Your Position. The following activities will help you find plausible reasons and evidence for your position. Begin by writing down what you already know. (If you did this when choosing your issue, look back at what you wrote.) You can do some focused research later to fill in the details or skip ahead to conduct research now. At this point, don't worry about the exact language you will use in your final draft. Instead, just write the reasons you hold your position and the evidence (such as anecdotes, examples, statistics, expert testimony) that supports it. Keep your readers in mind — what will they find most convincing?

Writers sometimes prefer to brainstorm a list of reasons:

1. Write your position at the top of the page.

2. List as many reasons as you can to support your position. If you think of a bit of supporting evidence, such as a good example or a research study, but you're not sure how to formulate the reason, simply list the support so you can work on it later.

3. Organize your reasons into related groups. For example, which reasons make an argument based on moral values, political ideology, or self-interest, and which are realistic or idealistic? Which would be most and least convincing for your readers?

Once you have listed several reasons in support of your position, write steadily for at least five minutes exploring how best to present them. Ask yourself questions like these:

- How could I show readers that my reasons lead logically to my position?

- How could I arouse my readers' curiosity?

- How could I appeal to my readers' values and beliefs and show my rhetorical sensitivity?

Where you need supporting evidence, fill in the gaps with research.

Researching the Issue.   Research can help you develop your own position as you think alongside other sources or nuance a position you already hold. Research can also help you look critically at your own thinking and help you anticipate your readers' arguments and possible objections to your argument.

- Enter keywords or phrases related to the issue or your position in the search box of an all-purpose database such as *Academic OneFile* (InfoTrac) or *Academic Search Complete* (EBSCOHost) to find relevant articles in magazines and journals, or a database like *LexisNexis* to find articles in newspapers. For example, Statsky could have tried a combination of keywords such as *children's competitive sports* or variations on her terms (such as *youth team sports*) to find relevant articles. A similar search could also be conducted in your library's catalog to locate books and other resources on your topic.

- If you think your issue has been dealt with by a government agency, explore the state, local, or tribal sections of the U.S. government's official website, or visit the Library of Congress page on State Government Information and follow the links.

- Bookmark or keep a record of the URLs of promising sites. You may want to download or copy information you could use in your essay. When available, download PDF files rather than HTML files because PDFs are likely to retain the visuals.

Remember to record source information and to cite and document any sources, including visuals, that you use in your essay.

To learn more about finding and documenting sources, see Chapter 12.

Including Visuals.   Consider whether visuals — drawings, photographs, tables, or graphs — would strengthen your argument. You could construct your own visuals, scan materials from books and magazines, or download them from the Internet. If you submit your essay electronically to other students and your instructor or if you post it on a website, consider including snippets of film or sound as well. Visual and auditory materials are not a requirement of a successful position argument, as you can tell from the readings in this chapter, but they could add a new dimension to your writing. If you want to use photographs or recordings of people, though, be sure to obtain permission.

Responding Fairly to Objections Your Readers Are Likely to Raise. The activity below will help you anticipate alternative positions your readers may hold or objections they may have.

1. List the positions you expect your readers will hold and the objections you expect them to raise. To think of readers' concerns, consider their values, beliefs, and priorities.

2. Which objections can you refute? Which may you need to concede?

Considering Your Purpose. Write for several minutes about your purpose for writing this position paper. The following questions will help you:

- How do I want to influence my readers' thinking? What one big idea do I want them to grasp?

- How can I help my readers see the significance of the issue — both to society at large and to them personally?

- How can I present myself as fair and ethical?

Organizing Your Position Argument Effectively for Your Readers

Whether you have rough notes or a complete draft, making an outline of what you have written can help you organize your essay effectively for your audience. You may want to draft a sentence that forecasts the elements of your argument to alert your readers to your main points (and give yourself a tentative outline). Putting your points in a logical order (from least to most effective, for example) will make it easier for you to guide your readers from point to point. For more on outlining, see Chapter 2, pp. 41–42.

Keep in mind that a position argument has five basic parts:

- presentation of the issue

- thesis statement

- your most plausible reasons and evidence

- concessions or refutation of opposing reasons or objections to your argument

- a conclusion that reaffirms your position

These parts can be organized in various ways: If your readers are not likely to agree with your position, you may want to anticipate and respond to their possible objections right before you present the evidence in favor of your own position. If you expect readers *are* likely to favor your position, you may want to concede or refute alternatives after offering your own reasons. Either way, you may want to emphasize the common ground you share and conclude by emphasizing that your position takes into account your shared values.

As you draft, you may see ways to improve your original plan, and you should be ready to revise your outline, shift parts around, or drop or add parts as needed.

Drafting Your Position Argument

By this point, you have done a lot of writing

- to choose an arguable issue and draft a working thesis that asserts your position on it;

- to support your position with reasons and evidence;

- to respond to your readers' likely objections and alternative positions;

- to establish your credibility as thoughtful and fair.

Now stitch that material together to create a draft. The next section of this Guide to Writing will help you evaluate and improve it.

Working with Sources

Using Sources To Reinforce Your Credibility.   How you represent your sources can quickly establish your credibility (ethos) — or the reverse. For example, by briefly describing the author's credentials the first time you summarize, paraphrase, or quote from a source, you establish the source's authority and demonstrate that you have selected sources appropriately. (Make sure the author's credentials are relevant to the topic you are discussing.) For example, in paragraph 5 of "Children Need to Play, Not Compete," Statsky writes:

> <u>Martin Rablovsky, a former sports editor for the *New York Times*,</u> says that <u>in all his years of watching young children play organized sports, he has</u> <u>noticed very few of them smiling.</u> "I've seen children enjoying a spontaneous pre-practice scrimmage become somber and serious when the coach's whistle blows," Rablovsky says . . . (qtd in Coakley 94).

Notice how Statsky integrates Rablovsky's credentials (underlined in blue) and a summary of his main idea (black) into her own sentence. By doing so, she not only demonstrates her credibility but also provides context for the quotation and demonstrates its relevance to her claim.

In the example below, from her third paragraph, Statsky demonstrates her fairness by quoting from the website of Little League, a well-known organization, and establishes her credibility by illustrating that even those who disagree with her recognize that injuries occur:

> Although the official Little League website acknowledges that children do risk injury playing baseball, it insists that "severe injuries . . . are infrequent . . . far less than the risk of riding a skateboard, a bicycle, or even the school bus" ("Little League Parent").

In both examples, Statsky also introduces the source to her readers, demonstrating the relevance of the source material for readers rather than leaving readers to figure out its relevance for themselves.

Whenever you borrow information from sources, be sure to double-check that you are summarizing, paraphrasing, and quoting accurately and fairly. Compare Statsky's sentences with the source passage, shown below. (The portions she uses are underlined.) Notice that she has inserted an ellipsis to indicate that she has left out words from her source's second sentence.

Source

> Injuries seem to be inevitable in any rigorous activity, especially if players are new to the sport and unfamiliar with its demands. But because of the safety precautions taken in Little League, severe injuries such as bone fractures are infrequent. Most injuries are sprains and strains, abrasions and cuts and bruises. The risk of serious injury in Little League Baseball is far less than the risk of riding a skateboard, a bicycle, or even the school bus.

In both examples above, Statsky uses quotation marks to indicate that she is borrowing the words of a source, and she provides an in-text citation so readers can locate her sources in her list of works cited. Both are essential to avoid plagiarism; doing one or the other is not enough.

For more on integrating language from sources into your own sentences and avoiding plagiarism, see Using Information from Sources to Support Your Claims in Chapter 12, pp. 617–626.

REVIEWING AND IMPROVING THE DRAFT

This section includes guides for Peer Review and Troubleshooting Your Draft. Your instructor may arrange a peer review in class or online where you can exchange drafts with a classmate. The Peer Review Guide will help you give each other constructive feedback regarding the basic features and strategies typical of writing a position argument. (If you want to make specific suggestions for improving the draft, see Troubleshooting Your Draft on p. 391.) Also, be sure to respond to any specific concerns the writer has raised about the draft. The Troubleshooting Your Draft guide that follows will help you reread your own draft with a critical eye, sort through any feedback you've received, and consider a variety of ways to improve your draft.

A PEER REVIEW GUIDE

How effective is the presentation of the issue?

What's Working Well: Let the writer know where the issue is especially well presented—for example, where the issue is given historical or cultural context, or where the terms of the debate are given clearly.

What Needs Improvement: Indicate one passage where the presentation of the issue could be improved—for example, where the issue or controversy is not presented fully, or where the key terms could be clarified.

How well does the thesis present the position and forecast its stages?

What's Working Well: Identify the thesis and point to a particularly convincing reason that supports the thesis.

What Needs Improvement: Tell the writer if the thesis seems unclear—too general or too narrow, for example—or alert the writer to reasons that are not on target or that undermine the thesis.

How well does the writer develop the position with appropriate writing strategies?

What's Working Well: Indicate passages where the writer has supported the thesis with facts, statistics, examples, anecdotes, expert opinions, or analogies that are particularly accurate or persuasive.

What Needs Improvement: Tell the writer where an omitted writing strategy might be helpful, or point to a strategy that seems inappropriate or unnecessary for the position to be persuasive. For help with reading and writing strategies, see Chapter 2.

How effective is the response to objections?

What's Working Well: Mark any parts of the argument where objections to the position are acknowledged. Note whether the writer simply acknowledges, concedes, or refutes effectively.

What Needs Improvement: If you think an objection or point of view that should be noted has been ignored, point it out. Note whether a concession or refutation seems weak or inaccurate, or could use more support.

Revising Your Draft

Revising means reenvisioning your draft, trying to see it in a new way, given your purpose and audience, to develop a well-argued position argument. Think imaginatively and boldly about cutting unconvincing or tangential material, adding new material, and moving material around.

TROUBLESHOOTING YOUR DRAFT

To Present the Issue More Effectively

If readers don't understand what is at stake with the issue,	• Add anecdotes, examples, facts, quotations, or visuals to make the issue more specific and vivid. • Explain systematically why you see the issue as you do.
If your terms are surprising or are antagonistic to readers who disagree with your position,	• Use terms that are more familiar. • Use terms that are more neutral.

To Assert the Position More Clearly

If your position on the issue is unclear,	• Rephrase it or spell it out in more detail.
If the thesis statement is hard to find,	• State it more directly or position it more boldly. • Repeat it in different words throughout your essay.
If the thesis is not qualified to account for valid opposing arguments or objections,	• Limit the scope of your thesis. • Use qualifying terms, such as *many*, *often*, or *in some cases*.

To Strengthen the Argument for the Position

If a reason given for the position seems unconvincing,	• Clarify its relevance to the argument. • Add support for your reasoning.
If the support for a reason is inadequate,	• Review your invention notes or do more research to find facts, statistics, quotations, examples, or other types of support to add.

To Improve the Response to Alternative Arguments

If your argument ignores a strong opposing position or reasonable objection,	• Address the criticism directly, perhaps using the sentence strategy of concession and refutation. • If necessary, modify your position to accommodate the criticism.
If your refutation of a criticism is unconvincing or attacks opponents on a personal level,	• Provide more or better support (such as facts and statistics from reputable sources). • Revise to eliminate personal attacks.

To Enhance Credibility	
If readers consider some of your sources questionable,	• Establish the sources' credibility by providing background information about them. • Choose more reputable sources.
If you ignore likely objections or opposing arguments,	• Demonstrate to readers that you know and understand, even if you do not accept, the criticisms of those who hold alternative views. • Use the sentence strategy of concession and refutation or acknowledgment and refutation.
If your tone is harsh or offensive,	• Check your rhetorical sensitivity by finding ways to show respect for and establish common ground with readers. • Revise your word choices to create a more civil tone. • Consider the concession-refutation strategy.
To Improve Readability	
If the beginning is dull or unfocused,	• Rewrite it, perhaps by adding a surprising or vivid anecdote or visual.
If your argument is disorganized or hard to follow,	• Add a brief forecast of your main points at the beginning of the essay. • Reorder your points in a logical arrangement, such as least to most important. • Announce each reason explicitly in a topic sentence. • Add logical sentence and paragraph transitions to make the connections between points clearer.
If the end is weak or trails off,	• Search your invention and research notes for a memorable quotation or a vivid example to end with. • Explain the consequences if your position is adopted. • Reiterate the shared values that underlie your position.

For an explanation of the *ad hominem* fallacy, see Chapter 2, p. 63.

Editing and Proofreading Your Draft

Check for errors in usage, punctuation, and mechanics, and consider matters of style. If you keep a list of errors you typically make, begin by checking your draft against this list.

From our research on student writing, we know that essays arguing positions have a high percentage of sentence fragment errors involving *subordinating conjunctions* as well as punctuation errors involving *conjunctive adverbs*. Because arguing a position often requires you to use subordinating conjunctions (such as *because*, *although*, and *since*) and conjunctive adverbs (such as *therefore*, *however*, and *thus*), be sure you know the conventions for punctuating sentences that include these types of words. Check a writer's handbook for help with avoiding sentence fragments and using punctuation correctly in sentences with these potential problems.

Reflecting on Position Argument

In this chapter, you have read critically several position arguments and have written one of your own. To better remember what you have learned, pause now to reflect on the reading and writing activities you completed in this chapter.

1. Write a page or so reflecting on what you have learned. Begin by describing what you are most pleased with in your essay. Then explain what you think contributed to your achievement.

   - If it was something you learned from the readings, indicate which readings and specifically what you learned from them.

   - If it came from your invention writing, point out the section or sections that helped you most.

   - If it came from your research notes and write-ups, point out the parts that helped you most.

2. Reflect more generally on position arguments, a genre of writing that plays an important role in our society. Consider some of the following questions:

   - How important are reasons and supporting evidence? When people argue positions on television, on radio talk shows, and in online discussion forums like blogs, do they tend to emphasize reasons and support? If not, what do they emphasize?

   - How does the purpose of television, radio, and online position arguments differ from the purpose of the writers you read in this chapter and from your own purpose in writing a position argument?

   - What contribution might position arguments make to our society that other genres of writing cannot make?

(continued)

3. By reflecting on what you have learned about position arguments, you have been practicing **metacognition**, one of the academic habits of mind.

- Were you aware of any other habits of mind you practiced as you read and responded to the material in this chapter? If so, which habits did you find useful?

- If not, think back now on your reading and writing process. Can you identify any habits you used?

CHAPTER 9

Speculating about Causes or Effects

When a surprising event occurs, we ask, "Why did that happen?" Whether we want to understand the event, prevent its recurrence, or make it happen again, we need to speculate about what caused it. Sometimes our focus may shift from "Why did that happen?" to "What is going to happen?" so that we can plan or make decisions. Such speculations are the natural result of our curiosity about origins and consequences. In many cases, the connections between causes and effects can be answered by experimentation. For example, through experimentation, scientists discovered that greenhouse gases are causing the temperature of the Earth's atmosphere to rise — a phenomenon we now know as climate change. When we cannot be certain of causes or effects, the best we can do is **speculate,** or make educated guesses. For example, at this point we cannot be certain what other causes or long-term effects there are for climate change.

RHETORICAL SITUATIONS FOR SPECULATING ABOUT CAUSES OR EFFECTS

Many people, including analysts, economists, sportswriters, and college students, write essays speculating about causes or effects, as the following examples suggest:

- For an introductory psychology class, a student speculates about the effects of extensive video-game playing among preteens. Based on his own experience and observation, he hypothesizes that video games may improve children's hand-eye coordination and their ability to concentrate on a single task but also that some children may spend too much time playing video games, to the detriment of their physical fitness, social-skills development, and academic performance.

- After her son is disciplined in school, a science reporter comes up with an idea for an article speculating on the reasons for intolerance of "boyish behavior" in school. She reviews recent research in sociological and medical journals and conjectures that adults attempt to stamp out signs of aggression in boys for several reasons: because of concerns about bullying; because boys' behavior is perceived as disruptive, especially in group-oriented classrooms; and because boys' fidgeting at their desks is seen as a threat to their eventual success in an economy that values sitting still and concentrating for seven or more hours a day.

Thinking about Speculations about Causes or Effects

You may have speculated with friends or family about the causes or effects of a phenomenon, event, or trend, or composed speculations for science or history exams — or even about a stunning upset for the sports pages. Recall a time when you speculated about a cause or effect or read or heard others doing so. Think about how you (or another writer or speaker) engaged the audience in the subject, presented a credible case for the preferred cause or effect, and ruled out alternative explanations.

- Who was the *audience?* How do you think addressing this audience affected the choice of phenomenon, event, or trend, or the type of evidence presented? For example, did the audience's familiarity with the topic influence the number or type of causes or effects that were presented?

- What was the main *purpose?* Why did you (or the other writer or speaker) want the audience to understand these causes or effects? For example, was it so that they could demonstrate their own understanding on a test or take action in the future?

- How would you rate the *rhetorical sensitivity* with which the speculation was presented? What made the essay appropriate or inappropriate for its particular audience and purpose?

A GUIDE TO READING ESSAYS SPECULATING ABOUT CAUSES OR EFFECTS

This guide introduces you to cause-and-effect writing by inviting you to analyze a brief but powerful causal argument by Stephen King.

- *Annotations* on this first reading will help you see how to practice academic **habits of mind** such as **curiosity, openness,** and **persistence** to help you engage with and understand what you are reading. Notice how many questions the reader has as she reads. There is plenty of space for you to add your own questions and thoughts, as well, to this reading and any other in the textbook.

- *Reading for meaning* will help you think about the subject that prompted King's essay, as well as understand and respond to King's speculations about why horror movies are so popular.

- *Reading like a writer* will help you learn how King employs strategies typical of speculations about causes or effects, such as

1. presenting the subject fairly

2. making a logical, well-supported cause or effect argument

3. responding to objections or alternative speculations

4. establishing credibility to present the writer as thoughtful and fair

Stephen King

Why We Crave Horror Movies

Stephen King (b. 1947) is America's best-known writer of horror fiction. He received his B.A. from the University of Maine. He has won many awards, including the Lifetime Achievement Award from the Horror Writers Association and the 2003 National Book Foundation Medal for Distinguished Contribution to American Letters. In 2015, King was awarded a National Medal of Arts from the United States National Endowment for the Arts. A prolific writer in many genres and media, King's publications include *Carrie* (1973), *The Shining* (1977), the *Dark Tower* series (1982–2004), and many more. Many films and television movies have been based on King's work, including the classics *The Shawshank Redemption* (1994), *Stand by Me* (1986), *The Shining* (1980), and *Carrie* (1976). The following selection is a classic essay that attempts to explain the causes for a common phenomenon: many people's liking — even craving — for horror movies.

- **Before you read,** think about the horror movie that you remember best and consider why it appeals to you (or doesn't).

- **As you read,** test King's argument about the appeal of horror movies against your own experience. On first reading, how convincing are his causal speculations?

1   I think that we're all mentally ill; those of us outside the asylums only hide it a little better — and maybe not all that much better, after all. We've all known people who talk to themselves, people who sometimes squinch their faces into horrible grimaces when they believe no one is watching, people who have some hysterical fear — of snakes, the dark, the tight place, the long drop . . . and, of course, those final worms and grubs that are waiting so patiently underground.

What does he mean that we are all mentally ill? How is he defining mental illness?

When we pay our four or five bucks and seat ourselves at tenth-row   2
center in a theater showing a horror movie, we are daring the nightmare.

Why? Some of the reasons are simple and obvious. To show that we   3
can, that we are not afraid, that we can ride this roller coaster. Which
is not to say that a really good horror movie may not surprise a scream
out of us at some point, the way we may scream when the roller coaster
twists through a complete 360 or plows through a lake at the bottom of the
drop. And horror movies, like roller coasters, have always been the special
province of the young; by the time one turns 40 or 50, one's appetite for
double twists or 360-degree loops may be considerably depleted.

We also go to re-establish our feelings of essential normality; the horror   4
movie is innately conservative, even reactionary. Freda Jackson as the horrible melting woman in *Die, Monster, Die!* confirms for us that no matter
how far we may be removed from the beauty of a Robert Redford or a
Diana Ross, we are still light-years from true ugliness.

And we go to have fun.   5

Ah, but this is where the ground starts to slope away, isn't it? Because   6
this is a very peculiar sort of fun, indeed. The fun comes from seeing others menaced—sometimes killed. One critic has suggested that if pro football has become the voyeur's version of combat, then the horror film has
become the modern version of the public lynching.

Is lynching an appropriate comparison here?

It is true that the mythic, "fairy tale" horror film intends to take away   7
the shades of gray. . . . It urges us to put away our more civilized and adult
penchant for analysis and to become children again, seeing things in pure
blacks and whites. It may be that horror movies provide psychic relief on
this level because this invitation to lapse into simplicity, irrationality, and
even outright madness is extended so rarely. We are told we may allow
our emotions a free rein . . . or no rein at all.

If we are all insane, then sanity becomes a matter of degree. If your   8
insanity leads you to carve up women like Jack the Ripper or the Cleveland Torso Murderer, we clap you away in the funny farm (but neither
of those two amateur-night surgeons was ever caught, heh-heh-heh); if,
on the other hand, your insanity leads you only to talk to yourself when
you're under stress or to pick your nose on your morning bus, then you are
left alone to go about your business . . . though it is doubtful that you will
ever be invited to the best parties.

Why is King using humor to discuss horror movies?

The potential lyncher is in almost all of us (excluding saints, past and   9
present; but then, most saints have been crazy in their own ways), and
every now and then, he has to be let loose to scream and roll around in
the grass. Our emotions and our fears form their own body, and we recognize that it demands its own exercise to maintain proper muscle tone.
Certain of these emotional muscles are accepted—even exalted—in civilized society; they are, of course, the emotions that tend to maintain the
status quo of civilization itself. Love, friendship, loyalty, kindness—these

are all the emotions that we applaud, emotions that have been immortalized in the couplets of Hallmark cards and in the verses (I don't dare call it poetry) of Leonard Nimoy.

10   When we exhibit these emotions, society showers us with positive reinforcement; we learn this even before we get out of diapers. When, as children, we hug our rotten little puke of a sister and give her a kiss, all the aunts and uncles smile and twit and cry, "Isn't he the sweetest little thing?" Such coveted treats as chocolate-covered graham crackers often follow. But if we deliberately slam the rotten little puke of a sister's fingers in the door, sanctions follow — angry remonstrance from parents, aunts, and uncles; instead of a chocolate-covered graham cracker, a spanking.

11   But anticivilization emotions don't go away, and they demand periodic exercise. We have such "sick" jokes as "What's the difference between a truckload of bowling balls and a truckload of dead babies?" (You can't unload a truckload of bowling balls with a pitchfork . . . a joke, by the way, that I heard originally from a ten-year-old.) Such a joke may surprise a laugh or a grin out of us even as we recoil, a possibility that confirms the thesis: If we share a brotherhood of man, then we also share an insanity of man. None of which is intended as a defense of either the sick joke or insanity but merely as an explanation of why the best horror films, like the best fairy tales, manage to be reactionary, anarchistic, and revolutionary all at the same time.

> Do fairy tales and horror films have anything else in common?

12   The mythic horror movie, like the sick joke, has a dirty job to do. It deliberately appeals to all that is worst in us. It is morbidity unchained, our most base instincts let free, our nastiest fantasies realized . . . and it all happens, fittingly enough, in the dark. For those reasons, good liberals often shy away from horror films. For myself, I like to see the most aggressive of them — *Dawn of the Dead*, for instance — as lifting a trap door in the civilized forebrain and throwing a basket of raw meat to the hungry alligators swimming around in that subterranean river beneath.

13   Why bother? Because it keeps them from getting out, man. It keeps them down there and me up here. It was Lennon and McCartney who said that all you need is love, and I would agree with that.

14   As long as you keep the gators fed.

READING FOR MEANING

1. **Read to Summarize.** Write a sentence or two explaining the main reasons King thinks we crave horror movies.

2. **Read to Respond.** Write a paragraph analyzing anything that seems fascinating, such as King's assertion that "[i]f we are all insane, then sanity becomes a matter of degree" (par. 8); or the difference between

> For help with reading strategies like summarizing and analyzing assumptions, see Chapter 2.

procivilization and "anticivilization" emotions (pars. 10–13), indicating what you think about King's distinction between these two kinds of emotions.

3. **Read to Analyze Assumptions.** Write a paragraph or two analyzing an assumption in King's essay, such as

Assumptions about the universality and range of human emotions. King asserts that "[t]he mythic horror movie . . . has a dirty job to do. It deliberately appeals to all that is worst in us" (par. 12). He adds, "It is morbidity unchained, our most base instincts let free, our nastiest fantasies realized . . ." (par. 12).

- What if we don't watch horror movies, don't like them, or don't believe they represent our "nastiest fantasies"? If you don't share King's assumption about universal human nastiness, how do you respond to his essay?
- What alternatives to King's thinking occur to you? In a culture that has a different view of the human mind, what other causes of horror movies' popularity might be just as believable?

Assumptions about differences between younger and older people. King asserts that "horror movies . . . have always been the special province of the young" (par. 3) and that we go to see them "to put away our more civilized and adult penchant for analysis and to become children again" (par. 7).

- What viewpoints do children have that adults do not have or have outgrown?
- What does King assume distinguishes children and adults in their attitude toward scary situations (par. 3) or complex ones (par. 7)? Why would adults want to become children again?

READING LIKE A WRITER

Presenting the Subject Fairly

In writing an essay speculating about causes or effects, writers try to present their subject in an intriguing way that makes readers curious about it. Writers also must judge whether or not they need to explain the subject for their audience before examining causes or effects. When writers decide they need to prove that the event, trend, or phenomenon exists, they may describe it in detail, give examples, offer factual evidence, cite statistics, or quote statements by authorities. They may frame or reframe their subjects: **Framing** (or **reframing**) is like cropping and resizing a photograph to focus the viewer's eye on one part of the picture. Writers typically frame or reframe a subject in a way that sets the stage for their argument and promotes their point of view.

ANALYZE & WRITE

Write a couple of paragraphs analyzing and evaluating how King reframes his subject:

1. The subject of this essay is horror movies, but the key term in the title is the word "crave." Look up "crave" and "craving" to see what they mean. Then highlight some of the other words and phrases King associates with the appeal of horror movies, such as "mentally ill" and "hysterical fear" (par. 1). How do the words you highlighted relate to the word *crave*?

2. Given these key terms, how would you describe the way King reframes the subject for readers? How do these key terms enable him to plant the seed of his main idea at the beginning of the essay?

Making a Logical, Well-Supported Cause or Effect Argument

At the heart of an essay speculating about causes or effects is an argument with two essential elements:

1. the logical analysis of the proposed causes or effects

2. the reasoning and support offered for each cause or effect

Writers of essays speculating about causes or effects sometimes rely on certain sentence strategies to present these cause-effect relationships:

▶ When .... happens, ... is the result.

▶ If [I/ he/she/we/they] [do/ say/act] ...., then [others] [do/say/act] ....

These two types of sentences can be seen in King's essay:

Causes   When we exhibit these emotions, **society showers us** with positive
Effects   reinforcement; we learn this even before we get out of diapers. When, as children, we hug our rotten little puke of a sister and give her a kiss, **all the aunts and uncles smile and twit and cry,** "Isn't he the sweetest little thing?" Such coveted treats as chocolate-covered graham crackers often follow. But if we deliberately slam the rotten little puke of a sister's fingers in the door, **sanctions follow** — angry remonstrance from parents, aunts, and uncles; instead of a chocolate-covered graham cracker, a spanking. (par. 10)

Both of these sentence patterns establish a **chronological relationship** — one thing happens after another in time. They also establish a **causal relationship** — one thing *makes* another thing happen. (Chronology and causality do not always go together, however; see Recognizing Logical Fallacies in Chapter 2, pp. 62–64.)

ANALYZE & WRITE

Write a paragraph or two analyzing and evaluating how King uses these sentence patterns elsewhere in this reading selection:

1. Skim paragraphs 1–9 and 11–14 and mark the sentences that use these strategies. Does each present a cause-effect relationship as well as a chronological sequence? How do you know?

2. Why do you think King repeats these sentence strategies so often in this essay? How effective or ineffective is this strategy?

Responding to Objections and Alternative Speculations

When causes or effects cannot be known for certain, there is bound to be disagreement. Consequently, writers may consider an array of possibilities before focusing on one or two serious probabilities. They may concede that certain possible causes play some role; they may refute them by providing reasons and supporting evidence for why they play no role (or only a minor role); or they may simply dismiss them as trivial or irrelevant, as King does. "Some of the reasons," King explicitly declares, "are simple and obvious" (par. 3).

ANALYZE & WRITE

Write a couple of paragraphs analyzing and evaluating how effectively King concedes or refutes alternative causes for the popularity of horror movies:

1. Look at the causes King considers in the opening paragraphs to determine how he responds to them. For example, how does he support the assertion that some of them are "simple and obvious" (par. 3)? What other arguments does he use to refute these causes?

2. Given his purpose and audience, why do you think King begins by presenting reasons he regards as "simple and obvious"? (par. 3)

Establishing Credibility to Present the Writer as Thoughtful and Fair

Because cause or effect writing is highly speculative, its effectiveness depends in large part on whether readers trust the writer. Writers seek to establish their credibility with readers by making their reasoning clear and logical, their evidence relevant and trustworthy, and their handling of objections fair and balanced. They try to be **authoritative** (knowledgeable) without appearing **authoritarian** (opinionated and dogmatic).

ANALYZE & WRITE

Write a paragraph or two analyzing King's **persona** (the personality he wants readers to infer) and assessing how it helps him establish credibility with his readers:

1. Reread the headnote that precedes King's essay, and reflect on what else his readers might already know about him.

2. Skim the essay to decide whether the reasoning is clear and logical and the examples and analogies relevant and trustworthy. Because King's reasoning is psychological (he argues that mental and emotional needs explain why some people crave horror films), you can evaluate King's credibility in light of your own personal experience—that is, your understanding of the role horror movies (and novels) play in your own life.

3. Describe the impression readers might get from King from reading both the headnote and his essay. What details in the headnote might make them trust or distrust what he says about his subject? What word choices or other details in the essay might make him a credible authority on the subject?

READINGS

Anna Maria Barry-Jester

Patterns of Death in the South Still Show the Outlines of Slavery

Anna Maria Barry-Jester is a senior correspondent at Kaiser Health News, a nonprofit health news service. She previously worked as a staff writer for the news website FiveThirtyEight where her articles focused on subjects such as public health, immigration, food, and science. She has also held editorial producer positions at Univision and ABC News and worked as a professional photographer and videographer. Barry-Jester has won numerous awards for her journalism, in-depth reporting, and editorial work. This article originally appeared on FiveThirtyEight.

- **Before you read,** think about your own health. What factors impact how healthy you are?

- **As you read,** consider how Barry-Jester connects the health of southern black Americans living in communities founded on slavery to the practice of slavery itself. How does Barry-Jester indicate the lasting effects of that history as she speculates about the causes of death in these communities?

There's a map, made more than 150 years ago using 1860 census data, that pops up   1
periodically on the internet. On two yellowed, taped-together sheets of paper, the counties of the Southern U.S. are shaded to reflect the percentage of inhabitants who were enslaved at the time. Bolivar County, Mississippi, is nearly black on the map, with 86.7 printed on it. Greene County, Alabama: 76.5. Burke, Georgia: 70.6. The map is one of the first attempts to translate U.S. census data into cartographic form and is one of several maps of the era that tried to make sense of the deep divisions between North and South, slave states and free.[1] But the reason the map resurfaces so frequently is not just its historical relevance. Rather, it's because the shading so closely matches visualizations of many modern-day data sets. There is the stream of blue voters in counties on solidly red land in the 2016 presidential election, or differences in television viewing patterns. There's research on the profound lack of economic mobility in some places, and on life expectancy at birth.

---

[1] The map, which depicts census data, had political motivations, according to the National Oceanic and Atmospheric Administration. It was drawn by pro-Union government officials who wanted to create a visual link between secession and slavery.

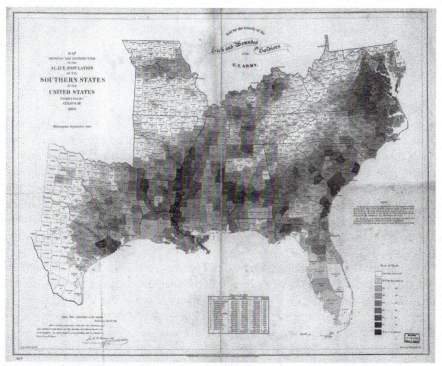

Percentage of US inhabitant who were enslaved (1860)
NARA C&GS Colllection/NOAA

On major health metrics in the U.S., the shaded counties on the antebellum map   2
still stand out today. Maps of the modern plagues of health disparities—rural hospital
closings, medical provider shortages, poor education outcomes, poverty and mortality—all glow along this Southern corridor. (There are other hot spots, as well, most
notably several Native American reservations.[2]) The region, known as the Black Belt,
also features clearly on a new interactive created by FiveThirtyEight using mortality
projections from researchers at the Institute for Health Metrics and Evaluation at the
University of Washington. The projections show that, while mortality is declining
nationally, including among those who live in the Black Belt, large disparities in outcomes still exist. Over the next several weeks, we'll be looking at some of the causes
of these disparities in the Black Belt and talking to the communities they affect.

Though these health outcomes are associated with race, race is not the cause   3
of disease. "There are certain genetic factors, of course," said Ali Mokdad, one
of the IHME researchers, who previously oversaw one of the largest public
health surveys in the U.S. "But ... we like to say, 'Diseases don't know race.'"

[2]Despite a scarcity of data, Native American health disparities are well
documented, as are rampant poverty, unemployment and low educational
attainment. According to the Indian Health Service, the life expectancies for Native
Americans are 4.4 years shorter than those of the U.S. population as a whole.

Instead, Mokdad said things such as racism, economic deprivation and poor education — measures that together are part of what is called socioeconomic status — are largely to blame.

The Black Belt was the origin and center of not only Black America, but also of   4
rural Black America. Today, more than 80 percent of rural black Americans live in the states that form the Black Belt. Black men in the region routinely have mortality rates 50 percent higher than the national average. In 1860, when 76.5 percent of the people in Greene County were enslaved, the entire population totaled more than 30,000. Today, the county has less than a third the number of people it did back then, but blacks still constitute more than 80 percent.

The Rev. Christopher Spencer is tall and thickly built with a bald head and   5
narrow-rimmed glasses. His presence is large, but never more so than when he's swaying in church robes, preaching on a Sunday morning. His church, St. Matthew Watson Missionary Baptist, is tucked away in a clearing in the woods of Greene County, just off a country stretch of U.S. Highway 43 and about 30 miles from where he grew up.

The church, which recently celebrated its centennial, still has about 130 members   6
despite the shrinking of the area's population. Preaching is Spencer's passion, but he also works as a director of community development at the University of Alabama, helping recruit people for studies and pushing for jobs and opportunities in the Black Belt.

The Black Belt moniker first referenced the rich, fertile soil that millions of Afri-   7
can slaves were forced to work, their labor making the European settlers some of the wealthiest people in the world. By the turn of the 20th century, the name had come to identify rural counties with a high percentage of African-American residents. "The term seems to be used wholly in a political sense. That is, to designate counties where the black people outnumber the white," wrote Booker T. Washington in his 1901 book, "Up From Slavery: An Autobiography."

The Black Belt is filled with complicated realities. It was the center of the civil   8
rights movement but still has some of the most consistently segregated schools in the country. White Europeans wanting to reap from its verdant soil forced millions of slaves to the area, but today healthy food is hard to find. Deeply rooted social networks tie people to the land and community, but poverty and racism led millions to leave the area in one of the largest internal migrations in human history.

Reporters often illuminate the problems of the U.S. health care system by looking   9
to outliers, the least healthy places, such as the state of Mississippi or a parish in Louisiana. That makes sense; states and local governments are largely responsible for the education, insurance, hospitals and economics that drive health outcomes. But in the case of the Black Belt, those borders obscure the broader pattern: rural, Southern black Americans who live in communities founded on slavery routinely have some of the worst health outcomes in the country.

Some recent media coverage has focused on a disturbing rise in mortality among   10
U.S. whites with a high-school education. A much-publicized series of papers by Anne

Case and Angus Deaton showed that mortality for whites with a high school education or less is increasing and included a chart showing that it is now greater than mortality for blacks. The rise in mortality made headlines and is a concerning trend worthy of study, but the headlines obscured several important facts, chief among them that the chart showed mortality for *all* U.S. blacks, not only those who also have a high school education or less. After the authors were criticized for leaving blacks off a different chart in one of the papers, they told The Washington Post "the reason it's not there—which we explain—is that black mortality is so high it doesn't fit on the graph."

In other words, the trends—an increase in mortality for some whites, a decrease 11 for most blacks—are important, but so are the absolute differences, and blacks continue to die younger than people in other groups.

Greene County, home to St. Matthew, is fairly typical in Alabama's Black Belt: 12 55 percent of children live in poverty, and the unemployment rate is 10.6 percent, more than double the national rate. There are primary care physicians in Eutaw but residents say they must travel to distant Tuscaloosa for most specialty care. Calvin Knott drives the 12 miles from his home in Forkland, in the southern part of the county, to attend church at St. Matthew. After decades working at the area's power company, he's spending his retirement driving a bus that takes people to and from medical appointments in Birmingham and Tuscaloosa. Most of the passengers are on Medicaid, he said. The insurance program for low-income people will pay the cost of transportation to some appointments, but Knott said he knows a lot of other people without insurance who just don't go to the doctor.

Under the Affordable Care Act, states can expand their Medicaid programs to 13 include everyone earning less than 138 percent of the federal poverty level, but only two of the states that form the Black Belt, Louisiana and Arkansas, chose to do so. Knott finds that disappointing. "It wouldn't benefit me, but I'd be happy for my taxes to go to helping other people," Knott said.

Experts say a long history of racism and poverty has left the region short on resources and high on risk factors. Smoking and poor diets, for example, likely contribute to many causes of mortality. But, many experts argue that these so-called lifestyle factors shouldn't simply be viewed as choices people make that keep them unhealthy and that they're only a small part of the bigger picture.

Late last year, Army veteran Jimmy Edison stood up at St. Matthew and asked the 14 congregation to pray for him. He was having another procedure in Tuscaloosa that week, something related to the open-heart surgery he'd had several years before. The church had been supportive in recent years, sending food to the house and praying for him and his wife, Dionne, after Jimmy's heart trouble started, and they'd been moved by the warmth of the congregation to become members. After the service, Edison listed the bad habits that had led to his heart condition. He'd started drinking heavily on his days off in the Army, smoked since he was a teenager and always been a self-declared troublemaker who lived life hard.

After a 2010 heart attack, Jimmy's drinking was so bad that he said they gave him 15 beer at the VA hospital, afraid he'd get delirium tremens. Even so, he said his diet was the hardest habit to change. "I was a prolific drinker and smoker, and I had no problem giving that up. But the fried food, that's the real problem," Edison said. Sitting in the fellowship hall after the service, he described in glorifying detail the fried pork chops he missed so dearly, before explaining that his mother had also suffered from hypertension, diabetes and heart diseases. That family history has him convinced that there's a genetic factor to his heart disease, though his diet and drinking likely made things worse. "It was like, I knew I was at risk, but I chose to play Russian roulette. I can't say I didn't know," Edison said.

The stress that evolves from years of social disadvantage can reinforce a host 16 of habits that are contributing to the highest incidence of diabetes and obesity in the country, said Alana Knudson, co-director of the Walsh Center for Rural Health Analysis at NORC, a research organization based at the University of Chicago. Food is "how you self-medicate. Sometimes we talk about people like they are doing this to themselves. But the reality is a lot of these people have endured some pretty challenging situations."

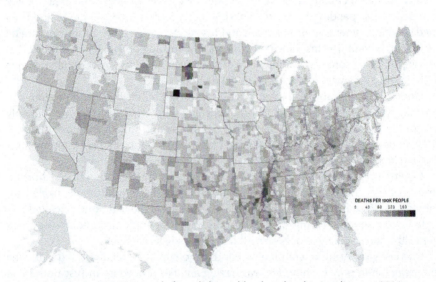

Estimated deaths per 100,000 people from diabetes, blood, and endocrine diseases, 2014

From: Dwyer-Lindgren L, Bertozzi-Villa A, Stubbs RW, Morozoff C, Kutz MJ, Huynh C, Barber RM, Shackelford KA, Mackenbach JP, van Lenthe FJ, Flaxman AD, Naghavi M, Mokdad AH, Murray CJL. US county-level trends in mortality rates for major causes of death, 1980–2014. JAMA. 2016 Dec. doi: 10.1001/jama.2016.13645. Permission by Institute for Health Metrics and Evaluation

Cultural norms play a role as well, and residents of the Black Belt are less likely 17 to get regular exercise than people just about anywhere else in the country. Some of this is environmental: Humid, 100-degree summer days combined with intermittent electricity make it hard to do much of anything, let alone go for a walk. Monika Safford, a professor of medicine at Weill Cornell Medical College, spent 12 years at the University of Alabama at Birmingham, researching diabetes and heart disease. She said that in surveys she's done in the Black Belt, many people respond that they get no exercise whatsoever on most days. "It was common when we were doing trials for people to tell us they drove down the driveway to get their mail," Safford said.

People in the Black Belt don't have higher mortality rates for every cause of 18 death, but the causes that disproportionately affect them are telling. A growing body of research has found that generations of economic and social disadvantage can increase the risk of neonatal mortality. As extremely effective treatments for HIV were developed, mortality related to AIDS plummeted across the country, but it remains higher in the Black Belt than in most other places (as does HIV prevalence).

And cervical cancer, largely preventable, is more prevalent and deadlier in the 19 region than in the nation at large.

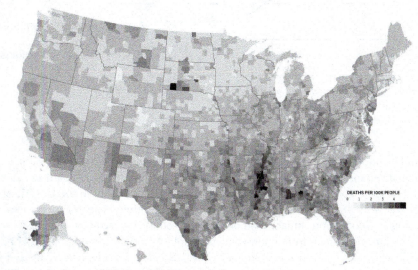

Estimated deaths per 100,000 people from cervical cancer, 2014

From: Mokdad AH, Dwyer-Lindgren L, Fitzmaurice C, Stubbs RW, Bertozzi-Villa A, Morozoff C, Charara R, Allen C, Naghavi M, Murray CJL. Trends and patterns of disparities in cancer mortality among US counties, 1980–2014. JAMA. 2017;317(4):388-406. doi:10.1001/jama.2016.20324. Permission by Institute for Health Metrics and Evaluation

Down the road from St. Matthew, Doreen Smith lives in a trailer left to her by her 20 grandparents. She went to a doctor in Demopolis in 1992 when she was pregnant with her first child at age 16 and has taken each of her children to him since. She's been told that to get prenatal care, she needs to go to Tuscaloosa, but with only intermittent access to a car, she said that's always been too far. "Oh no, I'm not going all the way to Tuscaloosa."

As a result, prenatal vitamins and the occasional checkup are the only care she's 21 received for most of her pregnancies, she said. Both teenage pregnancy and lack of prenatal care are considered risk factors for low-birthweight babies and other health concerns. But some studies have found that prenatal care doesn't explain racial disparities in infant mortality, which is higher among newborns of middle-age black women than it is for newborns of white teenagers. Poverty, stress and trauma, as part of the cumulative health of a mother before and after birth, likely also factor into pregnancy outcomes.

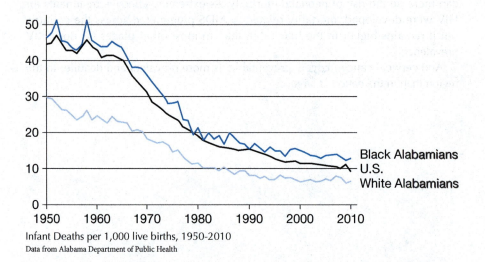

Infant Deaths per 1,000 live births, 1950-2010
Data from Alabama Department of Public Health

But health in the Black Belt hasn't been stagnant. While infant mortality is higher 22 there than almost anywhere in the country, it's a fraction of what it was a few decades ago. The same goes for heart disease, the leading cause of death in the U.S. Those improvements are attributed to several changes, including desegregation, better housing and education. In fact, one of the most robust literatures on the effects of racism on health comes from improvements to infant mortality among black babies after desegregation. Government programs have also played a role, namely the birth of the community health center movement and Medicaid, which was created in 1965 to cover pregnant women, children and people with disabilities. Both government efforts coincided with the civil rights movement and other programs that sought to undo the effects of racism and poverty throughout the country, particularly the rural South.

But there is still a lot of need today. Spencer is trying to tackle it from two angles: 23 helping people change their habits and working to stabilize and improve struggling rural hospitals. They are long-standing issues, but he remains hopeful they can change. "We just really have to galvanize interest in the area," he said.

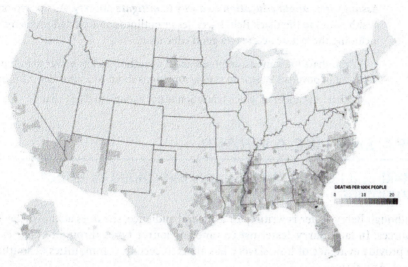

Estimated deaths per 100,000 people from HIV and tuberculosis, 2014

From: Dwyer-Lindgren L, Bertozzi-Villa A, Stubbs RW, Morozoff C, Kutz MJ, Huynh C, Barber RM, Shackelford KA, Mackenbach JP, van Lenthe FJ, Flaxman AD, Naghavi M, Mokdad AH, Murray CJL. US county-level trends in mortality rates for major causes of death, 1980–2014. JAMA. 2016 Dec. doi: 10.1001/jama.2016.13645. Permission by Institute for Health Metrics and Evaluation

READING FOR MEANING

1. **Read to Summarize.** Write a sentence or two explaining what you think Barry-Jester wants readers to understand about the patterns of death she outlines in her essay.

2. **Read to Respond.** Write a paragraph analyzing anything that seems surprising, such as "the stress that evolves from years of social disadvantage can reinforce a host of habits that are contributing to the highest incidence of diabetes and obesity in the country" (par. 16) or "poverty, stress and trauma, as part of the cumulative health of a mother before and after birth, likely also factor into pregnancy outcomes" (par. 21).

3. **Read to Analyze Assumptions.** Write a paragraph or two analyzing an assumption you find intriguing in Barry-Jesters's essay. For example:

   Assumptions about the effects of past events on current ills. Barry-Jester speculates that black Americans living in specific southern communities continue to be negatively affected by the history of slavery.

   • Do you agree with Barry-Jester that the patterns she is pointing out are the result of this history of slavery, or is it possible that there are other factors worth considering?

   • Why might Barry-Jester include specific stories about southern black Americans in her piece? Do these stories strengthen Barry-Jester's case? Why or why not?

For help with reading strategies like summarizing and analyzing assumptions, see Chapter 2.

Assumptions about education as a way to mitigate poverty. As she explores health issues in the Black Belt, Barry-Jester outlines some related problems, including the lack of access to a good education.

- Do you share the same assumptions about education and its power to help people out of poverty? Where do your assumptions about education come from?

- Are there instances in which education is not enough to effect change?

READING LIKE A WRITER

Making a Logical, Well-Supported Cause or Effect Argument

Although Barry-Jester is writing for a general audience, she does acknowledge her sources. In fact, Barry-Jester uses a range of source types throughout her essay to provide evidence of how slavery has affected certain communities of southern black Americans.

ANALYZE & WRITE

Write a paragraph or two analyzing the kind of evidence Barry-Jester relies on:

1. One of the sources that Barry-Jester relies on is Ali Mokdad, an IHME researcher, who said that "things such as racism, economic deprivation and poor education — measures that together are part of what is called socioeconomic status — are largely to blame" (par. 3). What other sources and evidence does Barry-Jester use to support her argument?

2. Barry-Jester describes the media and government focus on the "disturbing rise in mortality among U.S. whites with a high-school education" (par. 10). She then argues that "the headlines obscured several important facts, chief among them that the chart showed mortality for all U.S. blacks, not only those who also have a high school education or less. After the authors were criticized for leaving blacks off a different chart in one of the papers, they told *The Washington Post* "the reason it's not there — which we explain — is that black mortality is so high it doesn't fit on the graph" (par. 10). How does this source help support Barry-Jester's larger argument?

C Thi Nguyen

Escape the Echo Chamber

C Thi Nguyen is an assistant professor of philosophy at Utah Valley University, working in social epistemology, aesthetics, and the philosophy of games. He is assistant editor at *Aesthetics for Birds*, a blog for aesthetic philosophers, and is a founding editor of the *Journal of the Philosophy of Games*. He is Chair of the Diversity Committee for the American Society for Aesthetics and he has previously written a column about food for the *Los Angeles Times*. His latest book, *Games: Agency as Art*, is forthcoming from Oxford University Press. This article, based on his scholarly research, appeared originally in *Aeon* in 2018.

- **Before you read,** think about whether you avoid engaging with those who don't share your perspectives, ideas, or beliefs. How does this manifest itself in your face-to-face as well as your online encounters?

- **As you read,** pay attention to how Nguyen explains the distinction between echo chambers and epistemic bubbles. Why is this distinction necessary?

Something has gone wrong with the flow of information. It's not just that different 1
people are drawing subtly different conclusions from the same evidence. It seems like different intellectual communities no longer share basic foundational beliefs. Maybe nobody cares about the truth anymore, as some have started to worry. Maybe political allegiance has replaced basic reasoning skills. Maybe we've all become trapped in echo chambers of our own making—wrapping ourselves in an intellectually impenetrable layer of like-minded friends and web pages and social media feeds.

But there are two very different phenomena at play here, each of which subvert 2
the flow of information in very distinct ways. Let's call them *echo chambers* and *epistemic bubbles*. Both are social structures that systematically exclude sources of information. Both exaggerate their members' confidence in their beliefs. But they work in entirely different ways, and they require very different modes of intervention. An epistemic bubble is when you don't *hear* people from the other side. An echo chamber is what happens when you don't trust people from the other side.

Current usage has blurred this crucial distinction, so let me introduce a somewhat 3
artificial taxonomy. An 'epistemic bubble' is *an informational network from which relevant voices have been excluded by omission*. That omission might be purposeful: we might be selectively avoiding contact with contrary views because, say, they make us uncomfortable. As social scientists tell us, we like to engage in selective exposure, seeking out information that confirms our own worldview. But that omission can also be entirely inadvertent. Even if we're not actively trying to avoid disagreement, our Facebook friends tend to share our views and interests. When we take networks built for social reasons and start using them as our information feeds, we tend to miss out on contrary views and run into exaggerated degrees of agreement.

An 'echo chamber' is *a social structure from which other relevant voices have*   4
been actively discredited. Where an epistemic bubble merely omits contrary views,
an echo chamber brings its members to actively distrust outsiders. In their book
Echo Chamber: Rush Limbaugh and the Conservative Media Establishment (2010),
Kathleen Hall Jamieson and Frank Cappella offer a groundbreaking analysis of the
phenomenon. For them, an echo chamber is something like a cult. A cult isolates
its members by actively alienating them from any outside sources. Those outside are
actively labelled as malignant and untrustworthy. A cult member's trust is narrowed,
aimed with laser-like focus on certain insider voices.

In epistemic bubbles, other voices are not heard; in echo chambers, other voices   5
are actively undermined. The way to break an echo chamber is not to wave "the
facts" in the faces of its members. It is to attack the echo chamber at its root and
repair that broken trust.

Let's start with epistemic bubbles. They have been in the limelight lately, most   6
famously in Eli Pariser's *The Filter Bubble* (2011) and Cass Sunstein's *#Republic:
Divided Democracy in the Age of Social Media* (2017). The general gist: we get
much of our news from Facebook feeds and similar sorts of social media. Our Facebook feed consists mostly of our friends and colleagues, the majority of whom share
our own political and cultural views. We visit our favourite like-minded blogs and
websites. At the same time, various algorithms behind the scenes, such as those
inside Google search, invisibly personalise our searches, making it more likely that
we'll see only what we want to see. These processes all impose filters on information.

Such filters aren't necessarily bad. The world is overstuffed with information,   7
and one can't sort through it all by oneself: filters need to be outsourced. That's why
we all depend on extended social networks to deliver us knowledge. But any such
informational network needs the right sort of broadness and variety to work. A social
network composed entirely of incredibly smart, obsessive opera fans would deliver
all the information I could want about the opera scene, but it would fail to clue me
in to the fact that, say, my country had been infested by a rising tide of neo-Nazis.
Each individual person in my network might be superbly reliable about her particular
informational patch but, as an aggregate structure, my network lacks what Sanford
Goldberg in his book *Relying on Others* (2010) calls 'coverage-reliability'. It doesn't
deliver to me a sufficiently broad and representative coverage of all the relevant
information.

Epistemic bubbles also threaten us with a second danger: excessive self-   8
confidence. In a bubble, we will encounter exaggerated amounts of agreement and
suppressed levels of disagreement. We're vulnerable because, in general, we actually have very good reason to pay attention to whether other people agree or disagree with us. Looking to others for corroboration is a basic method for checking
whether one has reasoned well or badly. This is why we might do our homework in
study groups, and have different laboratories repeat experiments. But not all forms
of corroboration are meaningful. Ludwig Wittgenstein says: imagine looking through
a stack of identical newspapers and treating each next newspaper headline as yet
another reason to increase your confidence. This is obviously a mistake. The fact that

The New York Times reports something is a reason to believe it, but any extra copies of *The New York Times* that you encounter shouldn't add any extra evidence.

But outright copies aren't the only problem here. Suppose that I believe that the 9
Paleo diet is the greatest diet of all time. I assemble a Facebook group called 'Great Health Facts!' and fill it only with people who already believe that Paleo is the best diet. The fact that everybody in that group agrees with me about Paleo shouldn't increase my confidence level one bit. They're not mere copies — they — actually might have reached their conclusions independently — but their agreement can be entirely explained by my method of selection. The group's unanimity is simply an echo of my selection criterion. It's easy to forget how carefully pre-screened the members are, how epistemically groomed social media circles might be.

Luckily, though, epistemic bubbles are easily shattered. We can pop an epistemic 10
bubble simply by exposing its members to the information and arguments that they've missed. But echo chambers are a far more pernicious and robust phenomenon.

Jamieson and Cappella's book is the first empirical study into how echo chambers 11
function. In their analysis, echo chambers work by systematically alienating their members from all outside epistemic sources. Their research centres on Rush Limbaugh, a wildly successful conservative firebrand in the United States, along with Fox News and related media. Limbaugh uses methods to actively transfigure whom his listeners trust. His constant attacks on the 'mainstream media' are attempts to discredit all other sources of knowledge. He systematically undermines the integrity of anybody who expresses any kind of contrary view. And outsiders are not simply mistaken — they are malicious, manipulative and actively working to destroy Limbaugh and his followers. The resulting worldview is one of deeply opposed force, an all-or-nothing war between good and evil. Anybody who isn't a fellow Limbaugh follower is clearly opposed to the side of right, and therefore utterly untrustworthy.

The result is a rather striking parallel to the techniques of emotional isolation typ- 12
ically practised in cult indoctrination. According to mental-health specialists in cult recovery, including Margaret Singer, Michael Langone and Robert Lifton, cult indoctrination involves new cult members being brought to distrust all non-cult members. This provides a social buffer against any attempts to extract the indoctrinated person from the cult.

The echo chamber doesn't need any bad connectivity to function. Limbaugh's fol- 13
lowers have full access to outside sources of information. According to Jamieson and Cappella's data, Limbaugh's followers regularly read — but do not accept — mainstream and liberal news sources. They are isolated, not by selective exposure, but by changes in who they accept as authorities, experts and trusted sources. They hear, but dismiss, outside voices. Their worldview can survive exposure to those outside voices because their belief system has prepared them for such intellectual onslaught.

In fact, exposure to contrary views could actually reinforce their views. Limbaugh 14
might offer his followers a conspiracy theory: anybody who criticises him is doing it at the behest of a secret cabal of evil elites, which has already seized control of the mainstream media. His followers are now protected against simple exposure to contrary evidence. In fact, the more they find that the mainstream media calls out

Limbaugh for inaccuracy, the more Limbaugh's predictions will be confirmed. Perversely, exposure to outsiders with contrary views can thus increase echo-chamber members' confidence in their insider sources, and hence their attachment to their worldview. The philosopher Endre Begby calls this effect 'evidential preemption'. What's happening is a kind of intellectual judo, in which the power and enthusiasm of contrary voices are turned against those contrary voices through a carefully rigged internal structure of belief.

One might be tempted to think that the solution is just more intellectual auton- 15 omy. Echo chambers arise because we trust others too much, so the solution is to start thinking for ourselves. But that kind of radical intellectual autonomy is a pipe dream. If the philosophical study of knowledge has taught us anything in the past half-century, it is that we are irredeemably dependent on each other in almost every domain of knowledge. Think about how we trust others in every aspect of our daily lives. Driving a car depends on trusting the work of engineers and mechanics; taking medicine depends on trusting the decisions of doctors, chemists and biologists. Even the experts depend on vast networks of other experts. A climate scientist analysing core samples depends on the lab technician who runs the air-extraction machine, the engineers who made all those machines, the statisticians who developed the underlying methodology, and on and on.

As Elijah Millgram argues in *The Great Endarkenment* (2015), modern knowledge 16 depends on trusting long chains of experts. And no single person is in the position to check up on the reliability of every member of that chain. Ask yourself: could you tell a good statistician from an incompetent one? A good biologist from a bad one? A good nuclear engineer, or radiologist, or macro-economist, from a bad one? Any particular reader might, of course, be able to answer positively to one or two such questions, but nobody can really assess such a long chain for herself. Instead, we depend on a vastly complicated social structure of trust. We must trust each other, but, as the philosopher Annette Baier says, that trust makes us vulnerable. Echo chambers operate as a kind of social parasite on that vulnerability, taking advantage of our epistemic condition and social dependency.

Most of the examples I've given so far, following Jamieson and Cappella, focus 17 on the conservative media echo chamber. But nothing says that this is the only echo chamber out there; I am quite confident that there are plenty of echo chambers on the political Left. More importantly, nothing about echo chambers restricts them to the arena of politics. The world of anti-vaccination is clearly an echo chamber, and it is one that crosses political lines. I've also encountered echo chambers on topics as broad as diet (Paleo!), exercise technique (CrossFit!), breastfeeding, some academic intellectual traditions, and many, many more. Here's a basic check: does a community's belief system actively undermine the trustworthiness of any outsiders who don't subscribe to its central dogmas? Then it's probably an echo chamber.

Unfortunately, much of the recent analysis has lumped epistemic bubbles together 18 with echo chambers into a single, unified phenomenon. But it is absolutely crucial to distinguish between the two. Epistemic bubbles are rather ramshackle; they go up easily, and they collapse easily, too. Echo chambers are far more pernicious and far more robust. They can start to seem almost like living things. Their belief systems provide structural integrity, resilience and active responses to outside attacks. Surely a community can be both at once, but the two phenomena can also exist independently. And of the events we're most worried about, it's the echo-chamber effects that are really causing most of the trouble.

Jamieson and Cappella's analysis is mostly forgotten these days, the term hijacked [19] as just another synonym for filter bubbles. Many of the most prominent thinkers focus solely on bubble-type effects. Sunstein's prominent treatments, for example, diagnose political polarisation and religious radicalisation almost exclusively in terms of bad exposure and bad connectivity. His recommendation, in *#Republic:* create more public forums for discourse where we'll all run into contrary views more often. But if what we're dealing with is primarily an echo chamber, then that effort will be useless at best, and might even strengthen the echo chamber's grip.

There's also been a rash of articles recently arguing that there's no such thing [20] as echo chambers or filter bubbles. But these articles also lump the two phenomena together in a problematic way, and seem to largely ignore the possibility of echo-chamber effects. They focus, instead, solely on measuring connectivity and exposure on social media networks. The new data does, in fact, seem to show that people on Facebook actually do see posts from the other side, or that people often visit websites with opposite political affiliation. If that's right, then epistemic bubbles might not be such a serious threat. But none of this weighs against the existence of echo chambers. We should not dismiss the threat of echo chambers based only on evidence about connectivity and exposure.

Crucially, echo chambers can offer a useful explanation of the current informa- [21] tional crisis in a way that epistemic bubbles cannot. Many people have claimed that we have entered an era of 'post-truth'. Not only do some political figures seem to speak with a blatant disregard for the facts, but their supporters seem utterly unswayed by evidence. It seems, to some, that truth no longer matters.

This is an explanation in terms of total irrationality. To accept it, you must believe [22] that a great number of people have lost all interest in evidence or investigation, and have fallen away from the ways of reason. The phenomenon of echo chambers offers a less damning and far more modest explanation. The apparent 'post-truth' attitude can be explained as the result of the manipulations of trust wrought by echo chambers. We don't have to attribute a complete disinterest in facts, evidence or reason to explain the post-truth attitude. We simply have to attribute to certain communities a vastly divergent set of trusted authorities.

Listen to what it actually sounds like when people reject the plain facts—it [23] doesn't sound like brute irrationality. One side points out a piece of economic data; the other side rejects that data by rejecting its source. They think that newspaper is biased, or the academic elites generating the data are corrupt. An echo chamber doesn't destroy their members' interest in the truth; it merely manipulates whom they trust and changes whom they accept as trustworthy sources and institutions.

And, in many ways, echo-chamber members are following reasonable and [24] rational procedures of enquiry. They're engaging in critical reasoning. They're questioning, they're evaluating sources for themselves, they're assessing different pathways to information. They are critically examining those who claim expertise and trustworthiness, using what they already know about the world. It's simply that their basis for evaluation—their background beliefs about whom to trust—are radically different. They are not irrational, but systematically misinformed about where to place their trust.

Notice how different what's going on here is from, say, Orwellian doublespeak, 25 a deliberately ambiguous, euphemism-filled language designed to hide the intent of the speaker. Doublespeak involves no interest in clarity, coherence or truth. It is, according to George Orwell, the language of useless bureaucrats and politicians, trying to go through the motions of speech without actually committing themselves to any real substantive claims. But echo chambers don't trade in vague, ambiguous pseudo-speech. We should expect that echo chambers would deliver crisp, clear, unambiguous claims about who is trustworthy and who is not. And this, according to Jamieson and Cappella, is exactly what we find in echo chambers: clearly articulated conspiracy theories, and crisply worded accusations of an outside world rife with untrustworthiness and corruption.

Once an echo chamber starts to grip a person, its mechanisms will reinforce 26 themselves. In an epistemically healthy life, the variety of our informational sources will put an upper limit to how much we're willing to trust any single person. Everybody's fallible; a healthy informational network tends to discover people's mistakes and point them out. This puts an upper ceiling on how much you can trust even your most beloved leader. But inside an echo chamber, that upper ceiling disappears.

Being caught in an echo chamber is not always the result of laziness or bad faith. 27 Imagine, for instance, that somebody has been raised and educated entirely inside an echo chamber. That child has been taught the beliefs of the echo chamber, taught to trust the TV channels and websites that reinforce those same beliefs. It must be reasonable for a child to trust in those that raise her. So, when the child finally comes into contact with the larger world—say, as a teenager—the echo chamber's worldview is firmly in place. That teenager will distrust all sources outside her echo chamber, and she will have gotten there by following normal procedures for trust and learning.

It certainly seems like our teenager is behaving reasonably. She could be going 28 about her intellectual life in perfectly good faith. She might be intellectually voracious, seeking out new sources, investigating them, and evaluating them using what she already knows. She is not blindly trusting; she is proactively evaluating the credibility of other sources, using her own body of background beliefs. The worry is that she's intellectually trapped. Her earnest attempts at intellectual investigation are lead astray by her upbringing and the social structure in which she is embedded.

For those who have not been raised within an echo chamber, perhaps it would 29 take some significant intellectual vice to enter into one—perhaps intellectual laziness or a preference for security over truth. But even then, once the echo chamber's belief system is in place, their future behaviour could be reasonable and they would still continue to be trapped. Echo chambers might function like addiction, under certain accounts. It might be irrational to become addicted, but all it takes is a momentary lapse—once you're addicted, your internal landscape is sufficiently rearranged such that it's rational to continue with your addiction. Similarly, all it takes to enter an echo chamber is a momentary lapse of intellectual vigilance. Once you're in, the echo chamber's belief systems function as a trap, making future acts of intellectual vigilance only reinforce the echo chamber's worldview.

There is at least one possible escape route, however. Notice that the logic of the 30 echo chamber depends on the order in which we encounter the evidence. An echo chamber can bring our teenager to discredit outside beliefs precisely because she encountered the echo chamber's claims first. Imagine a counterpart to our teenager who was raised outside of the echo chamber and exposed to a wide range of beliefs. Our free-range counterpart would, when she encounters that same echo chamber, likely see its many flaws. In the end, both teenagers might eventually become exposed to all the same evidence and arguments. But they arrive at entirely different conclusions because of the order in which they received that evidence. Since our echo-chambered teenager encountered the echo chamber's beliefs first, those beliefs will inform how she interprets all future evidence.

But something seems very suspicious about all this. Why should order matter so 31 much? The philosopher Thomas Kelly argues that it shouldn't, precisely because it would make this radical polarisation rationally inevitable. Here is the real source of irrationality in lifelong echo-chamber members—and it turns out to be incredibly subtle. Those caught in an echo chamber are giving far too much weight to the evidence they encounter first, just because it's first. Rationally, they should reconsider their beliefs without that arbitrary preference. But how does one enforce such informational a-historicity?

Think about our echo-chambered teenager. Every part of her belief system is tuned 32 to reject the contrary testimony of outsiders. She has a reason, on each encounter, to dismiss any incoming contrary evidence. What's more, if she decided to suspend any one of her particular beliefs and reconsider it on its own, then all her background beliefs would likely just reinstate the problematic belief. Our teenager would have to do something much more radical than simply reconsidering her beliefs one by one. She'd have to suspend all her beliefs at once, and restart the knowledge-gathering process, treating all sources as equally trustworthy. This is a massive undertaking; it is, perhaps, more than we could reasonably expect of anybody. It might also, to the philosophically inclined, sound awfully familiar. The escape route is a modified version of René Descartes's infamous method.

Descartes suggested that we imagine an evil demon that was deceiving us about 33 everything. He explains the meaning behind the methodology in the opening lines of the *Meditations on First Philosophy* (1641). He had come to realise that many of the beliefs he had acquired in his early life were false. But early beliefs lead to all sorts of other beliefs, and any early falsehoods he'd accepted had surely infected the rest of his belief system. He was worried that, if he discarded any one particular belief, the infection contained in the rest of his beliefs would simply reinstate more bad beliefs. The only solution, thought Descartes, was to throw all his beliefs away and start over again from scratch.

So the evil demon was just a bit of a heuristic—a thought experiment that would 34 help him throw away all his beliefs. He could start over, trusting nothing and no one except those things that he could be entirely certain of, and stamping out those sneaky falsehoods once and for all. Let's call this the *Cartesian epistemic reboot*. Notice how close Descartes's problem is to our hapless teenager's, and how useful the solution might be. Our teenager, like Descartes, has problematic beliefs acquired in early childhood. These beliefs have infected outwards, infesting that teenager's whole belief system. Our teenager, too, needs to throw everything away, and start over again.

Descartes's method has since been abandoned by most contemporary philoso- 35 phers, since in fact we *can't* start from nothing: we have to start by assuming something and trusting somebody. But for us the useful part is the reboot itself, where we throw everything away and start all over again. The problematic part happens afterwards, when we re-adopt only those beliefs that we are entirely certain of, while proceeding solely by independent and solitary reasoning.

Let's call the modernised version of Descartes's methodology the *social-epistemic* 36 *reboot*. In order to undo the effects of an echo chamber, the member should temporarily suspend all her beliefs—in particular whom and what she trusts—and start over again from scratch. But when she starts from scratch, we won't demand that she trust only what she's absolutely certain of, nor will we demand that she go it alone. For the social reboot, she can proceed, after throwing everything away, in an utterly mundane way—trusting her senses, trusting others. But she must begin afresh *socially*—she must reconsider all possible sources of information with a presumptively equanimous eye. She must take the posture of a cognitive newborn, open and equally trusting to all outside sources. In a sense, she's been here before. In the social reboot, we're not asking people to change their basic methods for learning about the world. They are permitted to trust, and trust freely. But after the social reboot, that trust will not be narrowly confined and deeply conditioned by the particular people they happened to be raised by.

The social reboot might seem rather fantastic, but it is not so unrealistic. Such 37 a profound deep-cleanse of one's whole belief system seems to be what's actually required to escape. Look at the many stories of people leaving cults and echo chambers. Take, for example, the story of Derek Black in Florida—raised by a neo-Nazi father, and groomed from childhood to be a neo-Nazi leader. Black left the movement by, basically, performing a social reboot. He completely abandoned everything he'd believed in, and spent years building a new belief system from scratch. He immersed himself broadly and open-mindedly in everything he'd missed—pop culture, Arabic literature, the mainstream media, rap—all with an overall attitude of generosity and trust. It was the project of years and a major act of self-reconstruction, but those extraordinary lengths might just be what's actually required to undo the effects of an echo-chambered upbringing.

Is there anything we can do, then, to help an echo-chamber member to reboot? 38 We've already discovered that direct assault tactics—bombarding the echo-chamber member with 'evidence'—won't work. Echo-chamber members are not only protected from such attacks, but their belief systems will judo such attacks into further reinforcement of the echo chamber's worldview. Instead, we need to attack the root, the systems of discredit themselves, and restore trust in some outside voices.

Stories of actual escapes from echo chambers often turn on particular 39 encounters—moments when the echo-chambered individual starts to trust somebody on the outside. Black's is case in point. By high school, he was already something of a star on neo-Nazi media, with his own radio talk-show. He went on to college, openly neo-Nazi, and was shunned by almost every other student in his community college. But then Matthew Stevenson, a Jewish fellow undergraduate, started inviting Black to Stevenson's Shabbat dinners. In Black's telling, Stevenson was unfailingly kind, open and generous, and slowly earned Black's trust. This was the seed, says Black, that led to a massive intellectual upheaval—a slow-dawning realisation of the depths to which he had been misled. Black went through a years-long personal transformation, and is now an anti-Nazi spokesperson. Similarly, accounts of people leaving echo-chambered homophobia rarely involve them encountering some institutionally reported fact. Rather, they tend to revolve around personal encounters—a child, a family member, a close friend coming out. These encounters matter because a personal connection comes with a substantial store of trust.

Why is trust so important? Baier suggests one key facet: trust is unified. We don't 40 simply trust people as educated experts in a field—we rely on their goodwill. And this is why trust, rather than mere reliability, is the key concept. Reliability can be domain-specific. The fact, for example, that somebody is a reliable mechanic sheds no light on whether or not their political or economic beliefs are worth anything. But goodwill is a general feature of a person's character. If I demonstrate goodwill in action, then you have some reason to think that I also have goodwill in matters of thought and knowledge. So if one can demonstrate goodwill to an echo-chambered member—as Stevenson did with Black—then perhaps one can start to pierce that echo chamber.

Such interventions from trusted outsiders can hook up with the social reboot. But 41 the path I'm describing is a winding, narrow and fragile one. There is no guarantee that such trust can be established, and no clear path to its being established systematically. And even given all that, what we've found here isn't an escape route at all. It depends on the intervention of another. This path is not even one an echo-chamber member can trigger on her own; it is only a whisper-thin hope for rescue from the outside.

READING FOR MEANING

1. **Read to Summarize.** Write a sentence or two explaining what you think Nguyen wants his readers to understand about the effect of echo chambers.

2. **Read to Respond.** Write a paragraph analyzing anything that seems interesting or surprising, such as Nguyen's statement that "all it takes to enter an echo chamber is a momentary lapse of intellectual vigilance" (par. 29) or

For help with reading strategies like summarizing and analyzing assumptions, see Chapter 2.

how "trusted outsiders" can help support an escape from the echo chamber (pars. 40–41). Are you persuaded by Nguyen's reasoning as to how one becomes trapped in an echo chamber and how one may ultimately escape? Why or why not?

3. **Read to Analyze Assumptions.** Write a paragraph or two analyzing an assumption you find intriguing in Nguyen's essay. For example:

Assumptions about the negative effects of echo chambers. Nguyen's essay assumes that echo chambers are not productive and that those who find themselves trapped in echo chambers should do what they can to escape.

- Are there any positive consequences of echo chambers? If yes, what are they? If no, why not?
- In his essay, Nguyen addresses those who dispute the very existence of echo chambers: "There's also been a rash of articles recently arguing that there's no such thing as echo chambers or filter bubbles" (par. 20). Can you imagine any other causes — beyond echo chambers — of what Nguyen describes as the "current informational crisis?" (par. 21)

Assumptions about how online social networks have become information sources. Nguyen writes, "When we take networks built for social reasons and start using them as our information feeds, we tend to miss out on contrary views and run into exaggerated degrees of agreement" (par. 3).

- Does Nguyen's assumption that social networks are now acting as information sources align with your experience? Where do you get your information and news?
- Have you noticed any disagreements over information on any of the social networks you are a part of? If so, what were the disagreements about? If not, do you think this lack of disagreement helps support Nguyen's argument?

READING LIKE A WRITER

Presenting the Subject Fairly

When writing an essay speculating about cause and effect, writers often must explain the subject to their audience before examining causes or effects. Notice how Nguyen explains the difference between epistemic bubbles and echo chambers: "[T]hey work in entirely different ways, and they require very different modes of intervention. An epistemic bubble is when you don't *hear* people from the other side. An echo chamber is what happens when you don't *trust* people from the other side" (par. 2).

ANALYZE & WRITE

Write a paragraph or two analyzing how Nguyen presents his subject:

1. Nguyen writes that "current usage has blurred [a] crucial distinction" (par. 3) between epistemic bubbles and echo chambers. How does Nguyen reframe the subject of filters by focusing on these phenomena? What, specifically, does he want his audience to understand?

2. What sources and examples does Nguyen rely on to differentiate between epistemic bubbles and echo chambers? Why does this difference matter as it relates to Nguyen's speculations about the causes and effects of these phenomena?

Nicholas Carr

Is Google Making Us Stupid?

Nicholas Carr (b. 1959) received his master's degree in English and American literature and language from Harvard. He writes on the social, economic, and business implications of technology. He is the author of *Does IT Matter?* (2004), *The Big Switch: Rewiring the World, from Edison to Google* (2008), and *The Shallows: What the Internet Is Doing to Our Brains* (2010), which was a finalist for the Pulitzer Prize for nonfiction. Carr has also written for many periodicals, including the *Atlantic Monthly*, the *New York Times Magazine*, *Wired*, the *Financial Times*, the *Futurist*, and *Advertising Age*, and has been a columnist for the *Guardian* and the *Industry Standard*. The essay below was the cover story of the *Atlantic Monthly's* Ideas issue in 2008.

- **Before you read,** think about your own habits of concentration, considering whether you are able to focus deeply for long periods of time or whether you move from one idea to another fairly swiftly. Also think about whether concentration has to be sacrificed for the sake of acquiring more information.

- **As you read,** note how Carr mentions and responds to alternative ideas about the effect of the Internet on our thinking.

"Dave, stop. Stop, will you? Stop, Dave. Will you stop, Dave?" So the supercomputer 1 HAL pleads with the implacable astronaut Dave Bowman in a famous and weirdly poignant scene toward the end of Stanley Kubrick's *2001: A Space Odyssey*. Bowman, having nearly been sent to a deep-space death by the malfunctioning machine, is calmly, coldly disconnecting the memory circuits that control its artificial "brain." "Dave, my mind is going," HAL says, forlornly. "I can feel it. I can feel it."

I can feel it, too. Over the past few years I've had an uncomfortable sense that 2 someone, or something, has been tinkering with my brain, remapping the neural circuitry, reprogramming the memory. My mind isn't going—so far as I can tell—but it's changing. I'm not thinking the way I used to think. I can feel it most strongly when I'm reading. Immersing myself in a book or a lengthy article used to be easy. My mind would get caught up in the narrative or the turns of the argument, and I'd spend hours strolling through long stretches of prose. That's rarely the case anymore. Now my concentration often starts to drift after two or three pages. I get fidgety, lose the thread, begin looking for something else to do. I feel as if I'm always dragging my wayward brain back to the text. The deep reading that used to come naturally has become a struggle.

I think I know what's going on. For more than a decade now, I've been spending a 3 lot of time online, searching and surfing and sometimes adding to the great databases of the Internet. The Web has been a godsend to me as a writer. Research that once required days in the stacks or periodical rooms of libraries can now be done in minutes. A few Google searches, some quick clicks on hyperlinks, and I've got the telltale fact or pithy quote I was after. Even when I'm not working, I'm as likely as not to be foraging in the Web's info-thickets, reading and writing e-mails, scanning headlines and blog posts, watching videos and listening to podcasts, or just tripping from link to link to link. (Unlike footnotes, to which they're sometimes likened, hyperlinks don't merely point to related works; they propel you toward them.)

$$Ax^2 + Bx + C = 0$$
$$A^2 + B^2 = C^2$$

"The Cloud ate my homework."

© Tom Cheney/The New Yorker Collection/The Cartoon Bank

For me, as for others, the Net is becoming a universal medium, the conduit for most of the information that flows through my eyes and ears and into my mind. The advantages of having immediate access to such an incredibly rich store of information are many, and they've been widely described and duly applauded. "The perfect recall of silicon memory," *Wired*'s Clive Thompson has written, "can be an enormous boon to thinking." But that boon comes at a price. As the media theorist Marshall McLuhan pointed out in the 1960s, media are not just passive channels of information. They supply the stuff of thought, but they also shape the process of thought. And what the Net seems to be doing is chipping away my capacity for concentration and contemplation. My mind now expects to take in information the way the Net distributes it: in a swiftly moving stream of particles. Once I was a scuba diver in the sea of words. Now I zip along the surface like a guy on a Jet Ski.

I'm not the only one. When I mention my troubles with reading to friends and   5
acquaintances—literary types, most of them—many say they're having similar experiences. The more they use the Web, the more they have to fight to stay focused on long pieces of writing. Some of the bloggers I follow have also begun mentioning the phenomenon. Scott Karp, who writes a blog about online media, recently confessed that he has stopped reading books altogether. "I was a lit major in college, and used to be [a] voracious book reader," he wrote. "What happened?" He speculates on the answer: "What if I do all my reading on the Web not so much because the way I read has changed, i.e., I'm just seeking convenience, but because the way I THINK has changed?"

Bruce Friedman, who blogs regularly about the use of computers in medicine,   6
also has described how the Internet has altered his mental habits. "I now have almost totally lost the ability to read and absorb a longish article on the Web or in print," he wrote earlier this year. A pathologist who has long been on the faculty of the University of Michigan Medical School, Friedman elaborated on his comment in a telephone conversation with me. His thinking, he said, has taken on a "staccato" quality, reflecting the way he quickly scans short passages of text from many sources online. "I can't read *War and Peace* anymore," he admitted. "I've lost the ability to do that. Even a blog post of more than three or four paragraphs is too much to absorb. I skim it."

Anecdotes alone don't prove much. And we still await the long-term neurological   7
and psychological experiments that will provide a definitive picture of how Internet use affects cognition. But a recently published study of online research habits, conducted by scholars from University College London, suggests that we may well be in the midst of a sea change in the way we read and think. As part of the five-year research program, the scholars examined computer logs documenting the behavior of visitors to two popular research sites, one operated by the British Library and one by a U.K. educational consortium, that provide access to journal articles, e-books, and other sources of written information. They found that people using the sites exhibited "a form of skimming activity," hopping from one source to another and rarely returning to any source they'd already visited. They typically read no more than one or two pages of an article or book before they would "bounce" out to another site. Sometimes they'd save a long article, but there's no evidence that they ever went back and actually read it. The authors of the study report:

> It is clear that users are not reading online in the traditional sense; indeed there are signs that new forms of "reading" are emerging as users "power browse" horizontally through titles, contents pages and abstracts going for quick wins. It almost seems that they go online to avoid reading in the traditional sense.

Thanks to the ubiquity of text on the Internet, not to mention the popularity of   8
text-messaging on cell phones, we may well be reading more today than we did in

the 1970s or 1980s, when television was our medium of choice. But it's a different kind of reading, and behind it lies a different kind of thinking—perhaps even a new sense of the self. "We are not only *what* we read," says Maryanne Wolf, a developmental psychologist at Tufts University and the author of *Proust and the Squid: The Story and Science of the Reading Brain.* "We are *how* we read." Wolf worries that the style of reading promoted by the Net, a style that puts "efficiency" and "immediacy" above all else, may be weakening our capacity for the kind of deep reading that emerged when an earlier technology, the printing press, made long and complex works of prose commonplace. When we read online, she says, we tend to become "mere decoders of information." Our ability to interpret text, to make the rich mental connections that form when we read deeply and without distraction, remains largely disengaged.

Reading, explains Wolf, is not an instinctive skill for human beings. It's not etched   9
into our genes the way speech is. We have to teach our minds how to translate the symbolic characters we see into the language we understand. And the media or other technologies we use in learning and practicing the craft of reading play an important part in shaping the neural circuits inside our brains. Experiments demonstrate that readers of ideograms, such as the Chinese, develop a mental circuitry for reading that is very different from the circuitry found in those of us whose written language employs an alphabet. The variations extend across many regions of the brain, including those that govern such essential cognitive functions as memory and the interpretation of visual and auditory stimuli. We can expect as well that the circuits woven by our use of the Net will be different from those woven by our reading of books and other printed works. . . .

The human brain is almost infinitely malleable. People used to think that our men-   10
tal meshwork, the dense connections formed among the 100 billion or so neurons inside our skulls, was largely fixed by the time we reached adulthood. But brain researchers have discovered that that's not the case. James Olds, a professor of neuroscience who directs the Krasnow Institute for Advanced Study at George Mason University, says that even the adult mind "is very plastic." Nerve cells routinely break old connections and form new ones. "The brain," according to Olds, "has the ability to reprogram itself on the fly, altering the way it functions." . . .

The process of adapting to new intellectual technologies is reflected in the chang-   11
ing metaphors we use to explain ourselves to ourselves. When the mechanical clock arrived, people began thinking of their brains as operating "like clockwork." Today, in the age of software, we have come to think of them as operating "like computers." But the changes, neuroscience tells us, go much deeper than metaphor. Thanks to our brain's plasticity, the adaptation occurs also at a biological level.

The Internet promises to have particularly far-reaching effects on cognition. In a   12
paper published in 1936, the British mathematician Alan Turing proved that a digital computer, which at the time existed only as a theoretical machine, could be programmed to perform the function of any other information-processing device. And that's what we're seeing today. The Internet, an immeasurably powerful computing system, is subsuming most of our other intellectual technologies. It's becoming our

map and our clock, our printing press and our typewriter, our calculator and our telephone, and our radio and TV.

When the Net absorbs a medium, that medium is re-created in the Net's image. 13
It injects the medium's content with hyperlinks, blinking ads, and other digital gew-
gaws, and it surrounds the content with the content of all the other media it has
absorbed. A new e-mail message, for instance, may announce its arrival as we're
glancing over the latest headlines at a newspaper's site. The result is to scatter our
attention and diffuse our concentration.

The Net's influence doesn't end at the edges of a computer screen, either. As peo- 14
ple's minds become attuned to the crazy quilt of Internet media, traditional media
have to adapt to the audience's new expectations. Television programs add text
crawls and pop-up ads, and magazines and newspapers shorten their articles, introduce capsule summaries, and crowd their pages with easy-to-browse info-snippets.
When, in March of this year, the *New York Times* decided to devote the second
and third pages of every edition to article abstracts, its design director, Tom Bodkin,
explained that the "shortcuts" would give harried readers a quick "taste" of the day's
news, sparing them the "less efficient" method of actually turning the pages and
reading the articles. Old media have little choice but to play by the new-media rules.

Never has a communications system played so many roles in our lives — or 15
exerted such broad influence over our thoughts — as the Internet does today. Yet, for
all that's been written about the Net, there's been little consideration of how, exactly,
it's reprogramming us. The Net's intellectual ethic remains obscure. . . .

Google's headquarters, in Mountain View, California — the Googleplex — is the 16
Internet's high church. . . . Google, says its chief executive, Eric Schmidt, is "a company that's founded around the science of measurement," and it is striving to "sys-
tematize everything" it does. Drawing on the terabytes of behavioral data it collects
through its search engine and other sites, it carries out thousands of experiments a
day, according to the *Harvard Business Review*, and it uses the results to refine the
algorithms that increasingly control how people find information and extract meaning from it. . . .

The company has declared that its mission is "to organize the world's information 17
and make it universally accessible and useful." It seeks to develop "the perfect search
engine," which it defines as something that "understands exactly what you mean and
gives you back exactly what you want." In Google's view, information is a kind of
commodity, a utilitarian resource that can be mined and processed with industrial
efficiency. The more pieces of information we can "access" and the faster we can
extract their gist, the more productive we become as thinkers.

Where does it end? Sergey Brin and Larry Page, the gifted young men who 18
founded Google while pursuing doctoral degrees in computer science at Stanford,
speak frequently of their desire to turn their search engine into an artificial intelligence, a HAL-like machine that might be connected directly to our brains. "The
ultimate search engine is something as smart as people — or smarter," Page said in
a speech a few years back. "For us, working on search is a way to work on artificial

intelligence." In a 2004 interview with *Newsweek*, Brin said, "Certainly if you had all the world's information directly attached to your brain, or an artificial brain that was smarter than your brain, you'd be better off." Last year, Page told a convention of scientists that Google is "really trying to build artificial intelligence and to do it on a large scale."

Such an ambition is a natural one, even an admirable one, for a pair of math 19 whizzes with vast quantities of cash at their disposal and a small army of computer scientists in their employ. A fundamentally scientific enterprise, Google is motivated by a desire to use technology, in Eric Schmidt's words, "to solve problems that have never been solved before," and artificial intelligence is the hardest problem out there. Why wouldn't Brin and Page want to be the ones to crack it?

Still, their easy assumption that we'd all "be better off" if our brains were sup- 20 plemented, or even replaced, by an artificial intelligence is unsettling. It suggests a belief that intelligence is the output of a mechanical process, a series of discrete steps that can be isolated, measured, and optimized. In Google's world, the world we enter when we go online, there's little place for the fuzziness of contemplation. Ambiguity is not an opening for insight but a bug to be fixed. The human brain is just an outdated computer that needs a faster processor and a bigger hard drive.

The idea that our minds should operate as high-speed data-processing machines 21 is not only built into the workings of the Internet, it is the network's reigning business model as well. The faster we surf across the Web—the more links we click and pages we view—the more opportunities Google and other companies gain to collect information about us and to feed us advertisements. Most of the proprietors of the commercial Internet have a financial stake in collecting the crumbs of data we leave behind as we flit from link to link—the more crumbs, the better. The last thing these companies want is to encourage leisurely reading or slow, concentrated thought. It's in their economic interest to drive us to distraction.

Maybe I'm just a worrywart. Just as there's a tendency to glorify technological 22 progress, there's a countertendency to expect the worst of every new tool or machine. . . . Perhaps those who dismiss critics of the Internet as Luddites or nostalgists will be proved correct, and from our hyperactive, data-stoked minds will spring a golden age of intellectual discovery and universal wisdom. Then again, the Net isn't the alphabet, and although it may replace the printing press, it produces something altogether different. The kind of deep reading that a sequence of printed pages promotes is valuable not just for the knowledge we acquire from the author's words but for the intellectual vibrations those words set off within our own minds. In the quiet spaces opened up by the sustained, undistracted reading of a book, or by any other act of contemplation, for that matter, we make our own associations, draw our own inferences and analogies, foster our own ideas. Deep reading, as Maryanne Wolf argues, is indistinguishable from deep thinking. If we lose those quiet spaces, or fill them up with "content," we will sacrifice something important not only in our selves but in our culture. In a recent essay, the playwright Richard Foreman eloquently described what's at stake:

I come from a tradition of Western culture, in which the ideal (my ideal) was the complex, dense and "cathedral-like" structure of the highly educated and articulate personality—a man or woman who carried inside themselves a personally constructed and unique version of the entire heritage of the West. [But now] I see within us all (myself included) the replacement of complex inner density with a new kind of self—evolving under the pressure of information overload and the technology of the "instantly available."

As we are drained of our "inner repertory of dense cultural inheritance," Foreman concluded, we risk turning into "'pancake people'—spread wide and thin as we connect with that vast network of information accessed by the mere touch of a button."   23

I'm haunted by that scene in *2001*. What makes it so poignant, and so weird, is the computer's emotional response to the disassembly of its mind: its despair as one circuit after another goes dark, its childlike pleading with the astronaut—"I can feel it. I can feel it. I'm afraid"—and its final reversion to what can only be called a state of innocence. HAL's outpouring of feeling contrasts with the emotionlessness that characterizes the human figures in the film, who go about their business with an almost robotic efficiency. Their thoughts and actions feel scripted, as if they're following the steps of an algorithm. In the world of *2001*, people have become so machinelike that the most human character turns out to be a machine. That's the essence of Kubrick's dark prophecy: as we come to rely on computers to mediate our understanding of the world, it is our own intelligence that flattens into artificial intelligence.   24

READING FOR MEANING

For help with reading strategies like summarizing and analyzing assumptions, see Chapter 2.

1. **Read to Summarize.** Write a sentence or two explaining Carr's concern regarding the Internet's effect on our ability to concentrate and think deeply.

2. **Read to Respond.** Write a paragraph analyzing anything that seems interesting, such as the role of Carr's anecdotes in the first six paragraphs. Do they draw the reader into the essay? Present the subject? Help readers identify with Carr? Provide hard evidence? Or consider your own experience with reading on the Internet, and whether you share Carr's concern that the kind of reading fostered there is undermining "deep reading" (par. 2).

3. **Read to Analyze Assumptions.** Write a paragraph or two analyzing an assumption you find intriguing in Carr's essay. For example:

   Assumptions about the value of sustained concentration. Carr returns again and again to ways the Internet is reducing our ability to sustain concentration and focus for an extended period of time. He reports that he and his friends "have to fight to stay focused on long pieces of writing" (par. 5), cites a study about "power browsing" (par. 7), and states that "[t]he last thing these companies [Google and others] want is to encourage leisurely reading or slow, concentrated thought" (par. 21).

- How does Carr support his contention that we lose something valuable if we lose sustained concentration?
- Is there a compromise — a way to have both sustained concentration and all the knowledge we need?

Assumptions about the value of the human over the machine. Carr seems concerned that machines will replace human thought, and that we will lose something important to our humanity as a result. He says that in "Google's world," the human brain is "just an outdated computer that needs a faster processor and a bigger hard drive" (par. 20). In his conclusion, Carr laments that in the movie *2001*, "people have become so machinelike that the most human character turns out to be a machine" (par. 24).

- What do you think of Carr's concerns about the danger that machines pose to humans, especially machines that mimic the human mind?
- What could be the long-lasting consequences of *not* prizing human qualities, like the ability to contemplate?

READING LIKE A WRITER

Responding to Objections or Alternative Speculations

Writers speculating about effects must support their proposed effects, using all the relevant resources available to them — quoting authorities, citing statistics and research findings, comparing and contrasting, posing rhetorical questions, offering literary allusions, and crafting metaphors, among other strategies. (Carr uses all of these resources in his essay.) Writers know that at every point in the argument their readers will have objections, questions, and alternative effects in mind, and that they must anticipate and respond to them. Just as imaginatively as they argue for their proposed effects, writers in this genre attempt to answer readers' questions, react to their objections, and evaluate their preferred effects.

ANALYZE & WRITE

Write a paragraph or two analyzing how Carr anticipates his readers' objections and supports his response:

1. Reread paragraphs 4, 7, 8, 10, 17, 18, 19, and 22, in which Carr responds to alternative arguments, underlining the main objections that he anticipates his readers will have to his argument. For example, in paragraph 4, he anticipates readers' likely objection that having access to so much information is a terrific advantage.

You may also try looking for patterns of opposition; see Chapter 2, pp. 55–56.

2. Now examine how Carr manages readers' possible objections and questions. For at least three of the objections or questions you identified in the paragraphs you reread, notice the kinds of support he relies on to argue against each objection. How appropriate and believable do you find his support? Why?

Combining Reading Strategies

Contextualizing in Order to Analyze Visuals

For help with contextualizing and analyzing visuals, see Chapter 2, pp. 50–51 and 52–55.

Contextualize the cartoon Carr uses in "Is Google Making Us Stupid?" to help you analyze it.

Contextualizing is a critical reading strategy that helps you understand a text or visual by making inferences about its historical and cultural contexts and comparing those contexts to your own context. This strategy not only helps you analyze the text or visual before you, but also helps you understand how your reading of it is affected by your context. Write a paragraph that addresses the following prompts.

- What types of context do you need to understand the humor of the cartoon?

- The cartoon originally appeared in the *New Yorker* magazine, a periodical that appeals to a middle-aged, fairly well-to-do, and sophisticated readership. How does the cartoon appeal to this audience?

- What larger social and cultural context made the cartoon relevant in 2008? Is it still relevant to you now? How has the context changed?

- Consider the traditional appearance of the teacher, student, and classroom. How does the contrast between that traditional look and the caption help generate the cartoon's humor?

Sendhil Mullainathan

The Mental Strain of Making Do with Less

Sendhil Mullainathan (b. 1972) received his Ph.D. from Harvard and is a professor of economics there. He has published many articles in professional economics journals and has the distinction of being a MacArthur Fellow. He is the author, with Jeffrey R. Kling and William J. Congdon, of *Policy and Choice: Public Finance through the Lens of Behavioral Economics* (2011), and he is the author, with Eldar Shafir, of *Scarcity: Why Having Too Little Means So Much* (2013). The essay below is based on the work described in *Scarcity*. For your reference, we have converted Mullainathan's sources to in-text citations and a list of Works Cited at the end of the selection.

- **Before you read,** think about your own experiences with **scarcity** — with having less than you need to achieve a goal. Were you aware of any physiological or emotional challenges to "making do with less"?

- **As you read,** note places where Mullainathan establishes his credibility, such as where he presents his issue thoughtfully and fairly, and consider why you think so.

Diets don't just reduce weight, they can reduce mental capacity. In other words, dieting can make you dumber. Understanding why this is the case can illuminate a range of experiences, including something as far removed from voluntary calorie restriction as the ordeal of outright poverty.

Imagine that you are attending a late-afternoon meeting. Someone brings in a plate of cookies and places them on the other side of the conference table. Ten minutes later you realize you've processed only half of what has been said. Why? Only half of your mind was in the meeting. The other half was with the cookies: "Should I have one? I worked out yesterday. I deserve it. No, I should be good." That cookie threatened to strain your waistline. It succeeded in straining your mind.

This can happen even with no cookie in sight. Dieters conjure their own cookies: psychologists find that dieters have spontaneous self-generated cravings at a much higher rate than nondieters (Hill). And these cravings are not the dieters' only distraction. Diets force trade-offs: If you eat the cookie, should you skip the appetizer at dinner? But that restaurant looked so good!

Many diets also require constant calculations to determine calorie counts. All this clogs up the brain. Psychologists measure the impact of this clogging on various tasks: logical and spatial reasoning, self-control, problem solving, and absorption and retention of new information. Together these tasks measure "bandwidth," the resource that underlies all higher-order mental activity. Inevitably, dieters do worse than nondieters on all these tasks; they have less bandwidth.

One particularly clever study by Janey Polivy, Julie Coleman, and C. Peter Herman 5 went further. It tested how dieters and nondieters reacted to eating a chocolate bar. Even though the bar provided calories, eating it widened the bandwidth gap between dieters and nondieters. Nondieters ate and moved on, but dieters started wondering how to make up for the calories they had just ingested or, even more fundamentally, pondered, "Why did I eat the bar?"

In other words, diets do not just strain bandwidth because they leave us hungry. 6 They have psychological, not just physiological, effects.

The basic insight extends well beyond the experience of calorie counting. Some- 7 thing similar happens whenever we make do with less, as when we feel that we have too little time, or too little money. Just as the cookie tugs at the dieter, a looming deadline preoccupies a busy person, and the prospect of a painful rent payment shatters the peace of the poor. Just as dieters constantly track food, the hyper-busy track each minute and the poor track each dollar.

A similar psychology of scarcity operates across these examples but with varying 8 degrees of force. If a cookie can tax our mental resources, imagine how much more psychological impact other forms of scarcity can have (Mullainathan and Shafir).

Take the case of poverty. In a paper published September 16, 2015 in *Science,* 9 Profs. Anandi Mani at the University of Warwick, Jiaying Zhao at the University of British Columbia, Professor Eldar Shafir at Princeton University, and I waded into politically charged territory. Some people argue that the poor make terrible choices and do so because they are inherently less capable. But our analysis of scarcity suggests a different perspective: perhaps the poor are just as capable as everyone else. Perhaps the problem is not poor people but the mental strain that poverty imposes on anyone who must endure it.

One of our studies focused on Indian sugar cane farmers, who typically feel them- 10 selves to be both poor and rich, depending on the season. They are paid once a year at harvest time. When the crop is sold, they are flush with cash. But the money runs out quickly, and by the time the next harvest arrives they are stretched thin: they are, for example, 20 times as likely to pawn an item before harvest as after it. Rather than compare poor and rich farmers, we compare each farmer to himself: when he is rich against when he is poor. This kind of comparison is important because it addresses valid concerns that differences in psychological tests merely reflect differences in culture or test familiarity.

We measured farmers' mental function—on what psychologists call fluid intelli- 11 gence and executive control—one month before and one month after harvest. And the effects were large: preharvest I.Q., for example, was lower by about nine to 10 points, which in a common descriptive classification is the distance between "average" and "superior" intelligence. To put that in perspective, a full night without sleep has a similar effect on I.Q. (Mani et al.).

Bandwidth scarcity has far-reaching consequences, whether we are talking about 12 poor farmers or affluent dieters. We all use bandwidth to make decisions at work, to resist the urge to yell at our children when they annoy us, or even to focus on a conversation during dinner or in a meeting. The diversity of these behaviors—combined with the size of the measurable effects—suggests a very different way to interpret the choices and behaviors of the poor. Just picture how distracting that cookie was, and multiply that experience by a factor of 10.

For dieters, bandwidth scarcity has one particularly important consequence, illus- 13 trated in a study by Baba Shiv and Alexander Fedorikhin that gave people a choice between fruit salad and cake. Before choosing, half of the subjects had their bandwidth taxed: they were asked to remember a seven-digit number. The other half had a mentally less-demanding task: they were asked to remember a two-digit number. Those with less available bandwidth ate more cake: they were 50 percent more likely to choose cake than the others. There is a paradox here: diets create mental conditions that make it hard to diet.

This may sound defeatist. But there are positive lessons for how to manage the dif- 14 ferent kinds of scarcity. The United States government, laudably, offers financial aid for low-income students to attend college. Qualifying for it, though, requires completing a densely packed 10-page booklet, mentally taxing for anyone. A one-page version would not only be simpler but it would also recognize that the poor are short on bandwidth as well as cash.

The same tactic—economizing on bandwidth—can be used in dieting. Take the 15 Atkins diet, which effectively bans many foods, including bread and a lot of desserts. A ban is less complex than the trade-offs and calorie accounting required by many other diets. While all diets require self-control, Atkins requires less thinking. This might explain its popularity, and even its effectiveness: a recent study shows that people persist longer with diets that require less thought. The same study had another interesting finding: it was the perceived complexity of a diet—not its actual complexity—that determined persistence (Mata, et al.).

So keep this in mind the next time you're picking a diet to shed a few pounds. Try 16 one that won't also shed a few I.Q. points.

Works Cited

Hill, Andrew J. "The Psychology of Food Craving." *Proceedings of the Nutrition Society,* vol. 66, no. 2, May 2007, pp. 277–85.

Mani, Anandi, et al. "Poverty Impedes Cognitive Function." *Science,* vol. 341, no. 6149, 30 Aug. 2013, pp. 976–90.

Mata, Jutta, et al. "When Weight Management Lasts. Lower Perceived Rule Complexity Increases Adherence." *Appetite,* vol. 54, no. 1, Feb. 2010, pp. 37–43.

Mullainathan, Sendhil, and Eldar Shafir. *Scarcity: The New Science of Having Less and How It Defines Our Lives.* Picador, 2013.

Polivy, Janet, et al. "The Effect of Deprivation on Food Cravings and Eating Behavior in Restrained and Unrestrained Eaters." *International Journal of Eating Disorders,* vol. 38, no. 4, Dec. 2005, pp. 301–9, doi:10.1002/eat.20195.

Shiv, Baba, and Alexander Fedorikhin. "Heart and Mind in Conflict: The Interplay of Affect and Cognition in Consumer Decision Making." *Journal of Consumer Research,* vol. 26, no. 3, Dec. 1999, pp. 278–92.

READING FOR MEANING

For help
with reading
strategies like
summarizing
and analyzing
assumptions,
see Chapter 2.

1. **Read to Summarize.** Write a sentence or two defining *scarcity* and explaining the effect of "bandwidth" on our mental capacities and behavior, according to Mullainathan.

2. **Read to Respond.** Write a paragraph analyzing anything that seems contradictory, such as Mullainathan's "paradox" that "diets create mental conditions that make it hard to diet" (par. 13) or his observation that "Indian sugar cane farmers… typically feel themselves to be both poor and rich, depending on the season" (par. 10).

3. **Read to Analyze Assumptions.** Write a paragraph or two analyzing an assumption you find intriguing in Mullainathan's essay. For example:

   The assumption that the brain can perform only a limited number of functions at one time. Mullainathan uses counting calories as an activity that "clogs up the brain" (par. 4) to such an extent that the brain suffers losses on "logical and spatial reasoning, self-control, problem solving, and absorption and retention of new information" (par. 4).

   - Can you think of instances in which you have experienced or seen someone else experience a loss of mental function as a result of a seemingly unrelated distraction?

   - Can you think of other causes for this mental malfunctioning that might explain it convincingly?

   The assumption that the stress of dieting is familiar enough to illuminate a more unfamiliar and difficult concept — bandwidth scarcity. As Mullainathan notes, "dieting can make you dumber. Understanding why this is the case can illuminate a range of experiences, including something as far removed from voluntary calorie restriction as the ordeal of outright poverty" (par. 1). He shows how dieting impedes you from successfully completing mental tasks and therefore has "psychological, not just physiological, effects" (par. 6).

   - Before you read this essay, did you believe that diets have psychological effects? Did reading about dieting stresses help you understand how bandwidth scarcity affects people who have too little money as well as too few calories?

   - Choosing dieting as a primary example suggests that more readers will identify with dieting than other examples. Do you think this is true? Why or why not? Mullainathan also reports that diets with fewer rules are more successful (par. 15). Do you think this is true of all successful diets, or does it depend on the individual dieter? If the latter, does Mullainathan's example still work to explain the effects of bandwidth scarcity?

READING LIKE A WRITER

Establishing Credibility to Present the Writer as Thoughtful and Fair

On a topic of international interest like the causes of mental strain or the effects of scarcity on the mind, writers either have to be an expert in the subject or have to do research to become expert enough to convince their readers that they should be taken seriously. To seem credible, For help judging the writer's credibility, see Chapter 2, pp. 66–68.

- they must not oversimplify, trivialize, or stereotype their subject;

- they must not overlook possible objections or alternative causes or effects that will occur to readers;

- they must show that they have thought about their subject deeply and seriously.

ANALYZE & WRITE

Write a paragraph or two analyzing Mullainathan's strategies to establish his credibility:

1. Reread "The Mental Strain of Making Do with Less," and annotate it for evidence of credibility or lack of it. How knowledgeable does Mullainathan seem about the subject? Look especially at paragraphs 3, 5, 9–12, and 15. Which paragraphs most impress you with his authority? Why?

2. What evidence do you find that Mullainathan has thought deeply about his subject? Do you think that dieting is the most important subject in his essay, or is he really alerting his audience to something more pervasive? If so, how would you explain his approach?

Clayton Pangelinan

#socialnetworking: Why It's *Really* So Popular

Clayton Pangelinan wrote this essay in his first-year college composition course. He was curious about why social networking had become so popular and has sustained its popularity over some time, and he wanted to examine the causes for this sustained interest.

- **Before you read,** think about why you engage in social networking, and why you think it has maintained its popularity after it was initially invented.

- **As you read,** pay attention to how Pangelinan tries to present his subject fairly, to establish his causes, and to understand the larger significance of the trend he examines.

Over the last decade or so, there has been a remarkable increase in the popularity   1
of social networking. As Figure 1 below [p. 438] shows, the rise in popularity cuts across all age groups. Sixty-eight percent of adults are Facebook users and Americans between the ages of 18 and 24 are using a variety of platforms. As the chart shows, 78 percent of 18- to 24-year-olds use Snapchat, 71 percent of Americans in the same age group use Instagram, while 45 percent use Twitter, too. Preferences among social networking sites have changed over the years, but the bottom line is that social networking continues to be enormously popular.

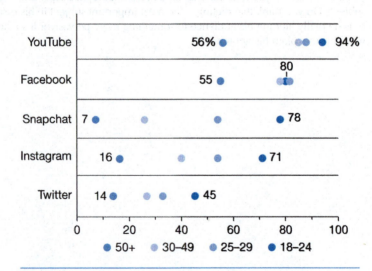

FIGURE 1 MAJORITY OF AMERICANS NOW USE FACEBOOK, YOUTUBE.   Data from "Social Media Use in 2018," Pew Research Center Survey, http://www.pewinternet.org/2018/03/01/social-media-use-in-2018/.

The fact *that* social networking is popular is well established. The question is *why* is it   2
so popular? The most basic answer is that social networking is popular because it's available. Without the technological advances that transformed the static read-only Web into the dynamic, interactive virtual community known as Web 2.0, none of the social networking we all engage in today would have been possible. A better answer, though, is that social media offer people a way to satisfy their desire to connect with others and maybe also be "world-famous for fifteen minutes" (as Andy Warhol supposedly remarked). A 2011 study asked people what their motivations were for using social networking sites, and two-thirds of those surveyed reported that they go online primarily to connect with friends and family and meet new people (see Fig. 2). As social animals, people have an inherent need for human connection. Professor Matthew Lieberman, in his recent book *Social: Why Our Brains Are Wired to Connect*, reports experiments using fMRIs to prove that the need to connect is hard-wired. According to Lieberman, our wiring impels us not only to share, but also to hear. Communication naturally flows both ways: Not only are we "driven by deep motivations to stay connected with friends and family" but we are also "naturally curious about what is going on in the minds of other people" (ix).

Social media outlets offer a way to satisfy both impulses. Consider the story of   3
Emmalene Pruden, a YouTube sensation who began posting her video blogs on YouTube after moving and feeling "cut off from her friends" (Niedzviecki 37). Emmalene is one example of how social media allow individuals to feel connected to a larger community: "If nothing else," as Niedzviecki claims, "peeping your problem, suspicion, or outrage is guaranteed to make you feel less alone" (142). But Emmalene's popularity also

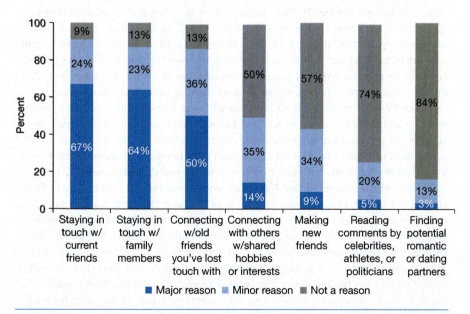

FIGURE 2 MOTIVATIONS FOR USING SOCIAL NETWORKING SITES. Data from Smith, Aaron. "Why Americans Use Social Media." *Pew Research Center*, 15 Nov. 2011, www.pewinternet .org/2011/11/15/why-americans-use-social-media/

suggests that—as Hal Niedzviecki, author of *The Peep Diaries: How We're Learning to Love Watching Ourselves and Our Neighbors*, puts it—"it is these quotidian revelations that make her enticing to her viewers" (39). Viewers may feel less lonely knowing that their own everyday struggles and daily trivialities are no different than Emmalene's.

Consider also the story of Lisa Sargese, who "started blogging as a way to tell the truth about her life as a morbidly obese, single woman determined to return to mobility and health via stomach-shrinking surgery" (Niedzviecki 51-52). She chronicled the effects of her surgery, growing her readership as she lost weight. Like Emmalene and her YouTube videos, Lisa was able to produce something that made her audience adore her: the sympathy effect. Readers also found hope by watching her overcome her problems. Niedzviecki makes a powerful statement that applies to both Emmalene and Lisa, as well as to their fans, when he concludes:

> We're alone all the time. We're alone on the bus, we're alone walking down the street, we're alone at the office and in the classroom, alone waiting in line at Disney World. We're tired of being alone, which is why increasingly we are barely hesitating to do whatever we feel we need to do to push out of solitude. (212–13)

This statement rings true throughout the social networking world where users often post whatever is on their minds, however intimate. From the status of their relationships to pornographic home videos, social networkers can find it on social media platforms. What motivates the extreme sharers?

One answer might be a desire for celebrity. Consider the story of a woman who calls herself Padme. For her, social networking has turned into an obsession apparently motivated by her need for fame: "In our case you get to 1.6 million readers it's really hard to just walk away from that" (qtd. in Niedzviecki 26). Padme appears to be a typical suburban housewife and mother, except that she is also a fantastically popular writer of a sexually explicit Star Wars–themed blog, *Journey to the Darkside*. Padme's popularity appears to come not only from her sexual confessions (and visuals), but also from her story of living a double life, as both a mother and as a Star Wars sex slave. In addition to recording her rather ordinary day-to-day activities as a stay-at-home mom, she also writes "about her need to be dominated by the man she calls Master Anakin, the man she's been . . . 'married to for 4 years, living with for 12 years, and best friends with for 18 years'" (Niedzviecki 23).

Writing in the American Psychological Association journal *Psychology of Popular Media Culture*, Dara Greenwood reviews research showing that "a craving for positive feedback and validation may be a common thread that links a desire for fame with social media use" (223). More specifically, she points to the correlation between the desire to be seen and valued and the need to feel connected, "to feel meaningfully embedded in social networks," as Greenwood puts it (223). While Padme carries her blogging to extremes that Emmalene and Lisa don't reach, what Greenwood writes applies to all three. The underlying cause of this need for visibility may be narcissism, fairly obvious in all three cases but especially so in Padme's as demonstrated by the "increased tendency to engage in exhibitionist postings on social media sites" (224).

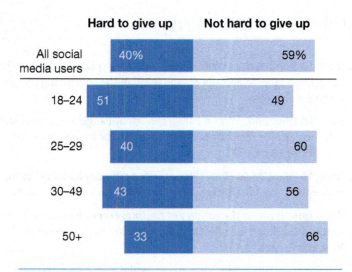

FIGURE 3 MOTIVATIONS FOR USING SOCIAL NETWORKING SITES.
Data from "Social Media Use in 2018," Pew Research Center Survey,
http://www.pewinternet.org/2018/03/01/social-media-use-in-2018/.

Of course, most of us participate in social networks without getting as carried   8
away as Emmalene, Lisa, or Padme. In fact, when asked whether giving up social
media would be hard, 59 percent of people surveyed said it would not be hard (see
Fig. 3). This figure shifts a bit, though, for 18- to 24-year-olds. Slightly more than half
of those surveyed—51 percent—said it would be hard to give up social media. So
if we don't get as carried away as Emmalene, Lisa, or Padma—and close to half of
us don't think it would be difficult to give up social media—why are we on it? Ask
yourself: What are your reasons for joining in? To connect? To tune in to what others
are up to? To show off? Whatever your reasons, you can be sure you are not alone.

Works Cited

Greenwood, Dara N. "Fame, Facebook, and Twitter: How Attitudes about Fame Predict the
    Frequency and Nature of Social Media Use." *Psychology of Popular Media Culture,*
    vol. 2, no. 4, 2013, pp. 222–36. *PsycINFO,* doi:10.1037/ppm0000013.
Lenhart, Amanda. "Teens, Social Media & Technology Overview 2015."
    Pew Research Center, 9 Apr. 2015, www.pewinternet.org/2015/04/09/
    teens-social-media-technology-2015/.
Lieberman, Matthew. *Social: Why Our Brains Are Wired to Connect.* Crown Publishing, 2013.
Niedzviecki, Hal. *The Peep Diaries: How We're Learning to Love Watching Ourselves and
    Our Neighbors.* City Lights Books, 2009.
Smith, Aaron. "Why Americans Use Social Media." *Pew Research Center,* 15 Nov. 2011,
    www.pewinternet.org/2011/11/15/why-americans-use-social-media/.
"Social Networking Fact Sheet." *Internet Project Library Survey.* Pew Research Center, www
    .pewinternet.org/fact-sheets/social-networking-fact-sheet/. Accessed 15 Oct. 2015.

READING FOR MEANING

For help
with reading
strategies like
summarizing
and analyzing
assumptions,
see Chapter 2.

1. **Read to Summarize.** Write a few sentences explaining the reasons Pangelinan gives to account for the trend of the continuing popularity of social media.

2. **Read to Respond.** Write a paragraph about Pangelinan's speculation that the need for celebrity is a motivating factor in the popularity of social networking (pars. 6–7).

3. **Read to Analyze Assumptions.** Write a paragraph analyzing an assumption you find intriguing in Pangelinan's essay. For example:

   Assumptions about the validity of findings from an international research center. Pangelinan includes three charts in his essay, all from the Pew Research Center.

   - Is the name "Pew" familiar to you as a valid source for facts about social trends in America? Do you associate it with credibility or with something else?

   - Do these charts provide enough information from this source to convince you that Pangelinan's interpretation of them is correct and useful?

   Assumptions about what level of sharing is considered "normal." Pangelinan establishes a distinction between simple sharing and extreme sharing (par. 7). He seems to think that the stories of Lisa and Emmalene are just normal sharing, in an effort to connect and to be "meaningfully embedded in social networks," but that Padme is an "exhibitionist" (Greenwood, qtd. in par. 7).

   - Do you agree with the distinction between the two types of sharing? Are there examples from your own experience that would support — or complicate — the distinction?

   - Does sharing carry a stigma when it reaches a certain level? Where would a stigma come from on a social media site? How do people's responses change to the different degrees of sharing, and how can you tell?

READING LIKE A WRITER

Presenting the Subject Fairly

One effective strategy for proving that an event, phenomenon, or trend exists is framing (or reframing) the topic to help readers understand it and engage their interest. When writers use **framing,** they focus the reader's eye on one angle or viewpoint that is important and might have a larger significance. Pangelinan spends some time establishing that the trend of social networking does in fact exist, and then speculates about the reasons for its persistence/popularity.

ANALYZE & WRITE

Write a paragraph or two analyzing and evaluating how fairly and effectively Pangelinan presents his subject.

1. Reread paragraphs 1–4. How does each paragraph serve the goal of establishing the existence of a trend and presenting the questions about it fairly?

2. Now skim the subsequent paragraphs that develop his ideas. What kind of evidence does Pangelinan present to support his speculations? Does this evidence help you understand why social networking has maintained its popularity?

Writing to Learn Speculations about Causes or Effects

Write a brief essay analyzing one of the readings in this chapter (or another selection, perhaps one by a classmate). Explain how (and perhaps, how well) the selection works as an argument speculating about causes or effects. Consider, for example, how it

- presents the argument fairly to help readers know the issue and enhance the writer's credibility;

- uses writing strategies, such as definition, compare/contrast, example, illustration, and analogy to make a logical, well-supported argument

- responds to objections or alternative speculations that are fair and appropriate.

Your essay could also reflect on how you applied one or more of the following practices as you read the selection:

- **Critical Analysis** — what assumptions in the selection did you find intriguing, and why?

- **Rhetorical Sensitivity** — how effective or ineffective do you think the selection is in achieving its purpose for the intended audience?

- **Empathy** — did you find yourself identifying with the author, and how important was this to the effectiveness of the selection?

A GUIDE TO WRITING ESSAYS SPECULATING ABOUT CAUSES OR EFFECTS

You have probably done a good deal of analytical writing about your reading. Your instructor may also assign a capstone project to write a brief speculative essay of your own arguing for your preferred causes or effects of an event, a phenomenon, or a trend. This Guide to Writing offers detailed suggestions and resources to help you meet the special challenges this kind of writing presents.

THE WRITING ASSIGNMENT

Write an essay arguing for your preferred causes or effects for an event, a phenomenon, or a trend.

- Choose a subject that invites you to speculate about its causes or effects: why it may have happened or what its effects may be.

- Research the subject, gathering detailed information from appropriate sources, and present that information in a clear, logical way.

- Establish the existence and significance of the subject.

- Convince readers that the causes or effects you propose are more plausible than the alternatives.

WRITING YOUR DRAFT

Choosing a Subject

Rather than limiting yourself to the first subject that comes to mind, take a few minutes to consider your options. Keep in mind that it must be

- one that you can show exists (such as with examples or statistics);

- one that has no definitive, proven cause or effect;

- one that you can research, as necessary, in the time you have;

- one that will puzzle — or at least interest — you and your readers.

Here are some ideas that may help you find a subject.

Trends

- changing patterns in leisure, entertainment, lifestyle, religious life, health, or technology

- completed artistic or historical trends (art movements or historical changes)

- long-term changes in economic conditions or political behavior or attitudes

Events

- a recent national or international event that is surrounded by confusion or controversy

- a recent surprising or controversial event at your college or in your community

- a historical event about which there is still some dispute as to its causes or effects

Phenomena

- a social problem, such as discrimination, homelessness, high-school or college dropout rates, youth suicides, or teenage pregnancy

- one or more aspects of college life, such as noisy libraries, large classes, lack of financial aid, difficulties in scheduling classes, or insufficient availability of housing

- a human trait, such as anxiety, selfishness, fear of success or failure, leadership, jealousy, insecurity, envy, opportunism, or curiosity

Because an authoritative essay arguing for preferred causes or effects requires sustained thinking, drafting, revising, and possibly research, you will want to choose a subject for which you have enough time and interest.

Consider carefully whether you are more interested in the causes or the effects of the event, trend, or phenomenon. For example, you could speculate about the causes of increasing membership in your mosque, whereas the effects of the increase might for now be so uncertain as to discourage plausible speculation. Some subjects invite speculation about both their causes and their effects. For this assignment, however, you need not do both.

You may find it useful to frame your topic in question form:

▶ Cause: Why is .... the most popular major at College X?

▶ Effect: How will the cancellation of the .... at X University affect students' employment prospects after graduation?

Making a chart listing subjects that interest you and their possible causes or effects can help you decide which subject is most promising.

Subject	Possible Causes or Effects
Example: Why do students often procrastinate in writing papers or studying for exams?	• They have full-time jobs. • The project seems overwhelming. • They have many responsibilities and the one with the latest deadline suffers/the most difficult task gets done last. • They are lazy. • They may not be mature enough to meet deadlines.
Example: What would be the effect of making class participation worth 50% of students' grades in all college courses?	• Shy or introverted students would be at a disadvantage. • Students would become more active learners. • Students might participate even when they don't have anything productive to say just so they earn participation points. • Class discussions would be more lively and represent more diverse viewpoints. • Such a policy could make students who experience social anxiety more anxious.

Analyzing Your Readers

Now that you have a potential subject, write for a few minutes, analyzing your potential readers.

- What might my potential readers already know about the event, phenomenon, or trend? (Even if you are writing only for your instructor, you should consider what he or she knows about your subject.)

- What kinds of examples or information could I provide that readers will find new, useful, interesting, or amusing? How might I clarify misconceptions or faulty assumptions?

- Will a more or less formal writing style be appropriate for my readers?

- What kinds of sources will my readers find credible?

- What questions might they ask? What might they be interested in learning more about?

Exploring Your Subject

You may discover that you know more about your subject than you suspect if you write about it for a few minutes without stopping. This brief sustained writing will stimulate your memory and help you probe your interest in the subject. As you write, consider the following questions:

- What about this subject interests me? What about it will interest my readers?

  ▶ **I think the [subject] is important because** ....

  ▶ **My readers are likely to be curious about the subject because** .... **[Examples: it affects them personally/it raises important moral, psychological, or other questions they will find intriguing].**

- What do I already know about the subject? What do my readers already know?

  ▶ **I know what the obvious causes of [the subject] are, but I'm curious about the underlying [cultural/ psychological/ ideological] causes because** ....

  ▶ **The subject [has been in the news or is so well-known] that I expect my readers will know** .... **but not** ....

Considering Causes or Effects

Discovering and analyzing the causes or effects you can already imagine can give your research (should you need to conduct research) direction and can also help you develop a list of the most (and least) plausible ones.

Discovering Causes or Effects.   Brainstorm a list of possible causes or effects. For causes, consider underlying or background causes as well as immediate or instigating causes. For example, say you have noticed that the number of students in your classes has increased sharply in the past year.

- An underlying cause could be that a few years ago the voters in your state passed a bill that sharply reduced income for public colleges, and now the effects are beginning to show;

- An immediate cause could be that the college has had to lay off one-third of its faculty.

For effects, consider both short-term and long-term consequences, as well as how one effect may lead to another in a kind of chain reaction. Try to think of obvious causes or effects and also of those that might be overlooked.

Considering how your subject is similar to or different from related subjects may also help you come up with causes or effects to add to your list:

  ▶ .... **[name subject] is like** .... **[name other subject] in that they are both caused by** ....

  ▶ **Whereas** .... **[the other subject] is** .... , ... **[my subject] is** ....

Conducting Research.   Research can give you a greater understanding of an event, trend, or phenomenon and may suggest to you plausible causes or effects you have overlooked. (In addition, you may find support for your responses to readers' objections or to others' proposed causes or effects.) Enter keywords or phrases related to your cause or effect subject into the search box of

To learn more about finding sources, consult Chapter 12, pp. 591–598.

- an all-purpose database such as *Academic OneFile* (InfoTrac) or *Academic Search Complete* (EBSCOHost) to find relevant articles in magazines and journals

- a database like *LexisNexis* to find articles in newspapers

- a search engine like *Google* or *DuckDuckGo* to find relevant websites, blogs, podcasts, and discussion lists

- your library's catalog or WorldCat to find books and other resources on your topic

To locate numerical or statistical evidence that you could use as evidence or to draw graphs or tables, try the following sites:

- U.S. government official Web portal for information about the federal government

- Library of Congress page on state government information (follow the links for information on both state and local government)

- U.S. Census Bureau, especially the Quick Facts and Fact Finder pages and the Statistical Abstracts for various years (to compare years), for demographic information

- Centers for Disease Control and Prevention, especially the FastStats pages, for statistics about diseases and illnesses

- National Center for Education Statistics for reports such as "America's Youth: Transitions to Adulthood"

- Pew Research Center for research data or public opinion polling data

- Rasmussen Reports or Gallup for public opinion polling data

Bookmark or keep a record of the URLs of promising sites. If you find useful information, you may want to download or copy it to use in your essay. When available, download PDF files rather than HTML files because PDFs are likely to include visuals such as graphs and charts. If you copy and paste relevant information from sources into your notes, be careful to distinguish carefully between all material from sources and your own ideas. Remember to record source information with care and to cite and document any sources you use, including visuals and interviews.

For more on field research, see Chapter 12, pp. 599–606.

Another option is to conduct field research and use personal experience.

Analyzing Causes or Effects. Once you have come up with a number of causes or effects, identify the most convincing (and surprising) ones. Remember that cause or effect essays often speculate about several possible causes or effects but usually also argue for one that is especially interesting or plausible. You may want to try several of the sentence strategies below to help you determine which of your causes or effects will be most convincing:

▶ Why do I/ my readers think .... [cause/ effect] could have resulted in/ caused .... [name subject]?

▶ Is .... [cause] necessary to bring about .... [effect]; that is, could .... [effect] not happen without it? Is .... [cause] sufficient — enough in itself — to cause .... [effect]?

▶ Is .... [effect] inevitable for .... [cause]; are other effects more plausible?

▶ If .... [cause] is one of several contributing factors, what role does it play? For example, is it a minor or major cause, an obvious or hidden cause, a triggering cause (the one that got the cause-effect process started), or a continuing cause (the one that keeps it going)?

▶ If .... [effect] is one of several, what role does it play? Is it a minor effect, or is it a major effect not given proper attention?

▶ What kinds of evidence could I use to argue in favor of or to argue against .... [cause/effect]?

Plausible Causes to Argue For	Readers' Causes to Concede/Put Aside	Readers' Causes to Refute

Now classify the causes or effects you plan to discuss in your essay into three categories: plausible cause(s) or effect(s) you want to argue for, causes or effects your readers may favor that you can concede but put aside as obvious or minor, and causes or effects you should refute because your readers are likely to think they are important.

Remember that the only category you *must* include in your essay is the first: one or more causes or effects you will argue played a major, and perhaps, surprising role. Including the other categories will, however, make for a more complex and sophisticated piece of writing.

Considering Your Purpose

Write for several minutes about your purpose for writing this essay. The following questions will help you think about your purpose:

- What do I hope to accomplish with my readers? What one big idea do I want them to grasp and remember?

- How can I interest readers in my subject? How can I help them see its importance or significance?

- How much resistance should I expect from readers to each of the causes or effects I propose? Will my readers be largely receptive? Skeptical but convincible? Resistant and perhaps even antagonistic?

Formulating a Working Thesis Statement

To get an idea about how you might formulate your thesis, take a look at the thesis statements from the reading selections you've studied in this chapter. Here are two:

> The mythic horror movie, like the sick joke, has a dirty job to do. It deliberately appeals to all that is worst in us. It is morbidity unchained, our most base instincts let free, our nastiest fantasies realized . . . and it all happens, fittingly enough, in the dark. (King, par. 12)

> The question is why is [social networking] so popular? The most basic answer is that social networking is popular because it's available. . . . A better answer, though, is that social media offer people a way to satisfy their desire to connect with others and maybe also be "world-famous for fifteen minutes" . . . (Pangelinan, par. 2)

Now draft your own thesis statement, either using the sentence strategies below as a jumping-off point (you can put them into your own words when you revise) or using your own words and sentence patterns:

▶ The cause(s)/effect(s) of .... may be [surprising/alarming/disturbing/amazing], but they are clear: .... [state cause(s) or effect(s)].

▶ **For** many years, [name group] has believed that .... Now there **is** research supporting this claim, but not for the reasons you may think. It's **not** ....that has been causing this phenomenon but ..../ **It's** not .... that has resulted from ...., it's ....

Working with Sources

Citing a Variety of Sources.   Writers of essays speculating about causes or effects often rely on evidence from experts to support some causes or effects and refute others. You will have to decide whether sources will make your speculations more convincing, what types of sources might be appropriate, and how many would be sufficient.

Look, for example, at Clayton Pangelinan's essay, "#socialnetworking: Why It's *Really* So Popular" (pp. 438–441). Pangelinan uses a number of different sources to support his causal analysis. Because he is writing for a class, Pangelinan includes both in-text citations and a list of works cited. He uses signal phrases to provide the credentials of his sources. Pangelinan also uses statistics from research institutions, but he does not rely solely — or even primarily — on one kind of source. He cites independent sources his readers are likely to find credible, such as the Pew Research Center, a popular book, and an academic article. Pangelinan also refers to his own observations. The number of sources, their authority, and their variety lend credibility to Pangelinan's speculations.

As you determine how many and what kinds of sources to cite in your essay, keep in mind that readers of essays speculating about causes or effects are more likely to be persuaded if the sources you rely on are neither too few nor too narrowly focused. If, when you begin to draft, you find that your research seems skimpy, you may need to do further research.

Responding to Readers' Likely Objections or Preferred Causes

Start by analyzing your readers' likely objections, and then consider ways you might respond:

For more on choosing and citing sources, see Chapter 12, pp. 607–654.

Analyzing and Responding to Your Readers' Likely Objections.   For each of your preferred causes or effects, consider the questions your readers might raise.

▶ Even if you can prove that .... and .... increased/decreased at the same time, how do you know .... actually caused/resulted from ....?

▶ .... seems to have been a cause/effect of ...., but was it really a major cause/effect or just one of many contributing factors?

Now consider how you might respond to the strongest of your readers' likely objections:

▶ The objection that .... can be caused by/can result from things other than .... may be true. But there is strong evidence showing that .... played a central role by ....

▶ Researchers studying .... have shown a causal connection between .... and .... They claim .... [quote/ paraphrase/ summarize information from source] (cite source).

▶ A large number of people have been polled on this question, and it appears that .... was an important factor in their decision to ....

To learn more about fallacies, see Chapter 2, pp. 62–64.

Refuting or Conceding Readers' Preferred Causes or Effects.   Choose an alternative cause or effect, and summarize it. Be sure to summarize it accurately and fairly. Do not commit the **"straw man" fallacy** of knocking down something that no one really takes seriously. Also, decide whether you can *refute* the alternative cause or effect or you need to *concede* it.

Refute it if you can show that it lacks credible support or if the reasoning underlying the cause or effect is flawed:

▶ The .... [scenario or anecdote] others sometimes give to support this cause/effect certainly helps dramatize the subject, but it doesn't really explain

....

▶ If .... caused/resulted from .... , then one would expect .... to happen, but [it hasn't/the opposite has happened].

▶ The research showing .... is questionable because it is based on [a small or unrepresentative sample/anecdotal evidence].

Concede it by pointing out that the cause or effect is obvious and setting it aside, or by showing that it plays a less important role than the cause or effect you are championing.

▶ An obvious explanation is .... But if we dig deeper, we find that

....

▶ .... is one of the answers but may actually not play as central a role as most people think it does.

Including Visuals or Other Media

Consider whether visuals — especially tables and static or animated graphics — would strengthen your argument. You could construct your own visuals, scan materials from books and magazines, or download them from the Internet. Be sure to cite the source of visual or audio elements you did not create, and get permission from the source if your essay is going to be published on a website.

Organizing Your Speculative Argument Effectively for Your Readers

Outlining what you have written can help you organize your essay effectively for your audience. You may want to draft a sentence that forecasts the elements of your argument to alert your readers to your main points (and give yourself a tentative outline). Putting your points in a logical order (from least to most effective, for example) will make it easier for you to guide your readers from point to point. A cause or effect analysis may contain as many as four basic parts:

1. a presentation of the subject

2. plausible causes or effects, logically sequenced

3. convincing support for each cause or effect

4. a consideration of readers' questions, objections, and alternative causes or effects

These parts can be organized in various ways: If your readers are not likely to agree with your speculations about causes or effects, you may want to anticipate and respond to their possible objections just before you present the evidence in favor of your argument. If you expect readers *are* likely to favor your speculations, you may want to concede or refute alternatives after offering your own reasons. Either way, you may want to emphasize the common ground you share.

As you draft, you may see ways to improve your original plan, and you should be ready to revise your outline, shift parts around, or drop or add parts as needed. For more on outlining, see Chapter 2, pp. 41–42.

Drafting Your Cause or Effect Argument

By this point, you have done a lot of writing

- to present the subject fairly;

- to make a logical argument and support your preferred causes or effects with evidence your readers will find persuasive;

- to respond to objections and alternative speculations;

- to establish your credibility by presenting yourself as thoughtful and fair.

Now stitch that material together to create a draft. The next two parts of this Guide to Writing will help you evaluate and improve it.

REVIEWING AND IMPROVING THE DRAFT

This section includes guides for Peer Review and Troubleshooting Your Draft. Your instructor may arrange a peer review in class or online where you can exchange drafts with a classmate. The Peer Review Guide will help you give each other constructive feedback regarding the basic features and strategies typical of writing a cause or effect argument. (If you want to make specific suggestions for improving the draft, see Troubleshooting Your Draft on p. 455.) Also, be sure to respond to any specific concerns the writer has raised about the draft. The Troubleshooting Your Draft guide that follows will help you reread your own draft with a critical eye, sort through any feedback you've received, and consider a variety of ways to improve your draft.

A PEER REVIEW GUIDE

How fairly is the subject presented?

What's Working Well: Let the writer know where the subject is presented especially fairly—for example, where the issue is framed so the reader's curiosity is aroused, or it's presented clearly and objectively before the writer presents a point of view about the causes or effects. Note where the writer seems particularly knowledgeable and responds to differing points of view with well-thought-out insights.

What Needs Improvement: Indicate one passage where the presentation of the subject could be improved—for example, where it is not presented fully enough to provide context, or there isn't enough indication of causes or effects that will be developed. If you think the writer seems biased or is ignoring a logical point of view, indicate where the perspective could change or a point of view should be included and responded to.

How logical and well supported is the cause or effect argument?

What's Working Well: Identify the causes or effects for the subject of the argument. Note where a point is well supported or uses a particularly convincing kind of evidence, such as statistics, examples, anecdotes, expert opinions, or analogies.

What Needs Improvement: Note any passage where the cause or effect does not seem logical, where a reader unfamiliar with the subject might need more information, or where an outside source could help convince a reader of the writer's point.

How well does the writer respond to objections or alternative speculations?

What's Working Well: Indicate passages where the writer has cited differing opinions about the causes or effects of the subject, and has responded to them with solid information that supports the writer's thesis and main points.

What Needs Improvement: Tell the writer if you think of alternative speculations that he or she might consider, or different ways to respond to objections.

Revising Your Draft

Revising means reenvisioning your draft, trying to see it in a new way, given your purpose and readers, in order to strengthen your cause or effect argument. Think imaginatively and boldly about cutting unconvincing material, adding new material, and moving material around.

TROUBLESHOOTING YOUR DRAFT

To Present the Subject More Effectively

If readers unfamiliar with the subject don't understand it readily,	• Provide more introductory information about the subject.
If the significance of the subject is not clear,	• Dramatize its significance with an anecdote. • Highlight its social or cultural implications.
If the subject is a trend, but its existence is not established,	• Show evidence of a significant increase or decrease over time. • Include a graphic to make the trend visible.

To Strengthen the Cause or Effect Argument

If there are too many proposed causes or effects,	• Clarify the role of each one and the way it is related to others. • Drop one or more that seem too obvious, obscure, or minor.
If a cause or effect lacks adequate support,	• Provide further examples, anecdotes, statistics, or quotations from authorities. • Drop it if you cannot find more support.

To Strengthen the Responses to Alternative Views

If a likely question or objection readers will have is not addressed,	• Add information to answer the question. • Accommodate the objection by conceding the point and making it part of your own argument. • Refute the objection, arguing that it need not be taken seriously and providing the reasons why.
If an alternative cause or effect readers would propose is not addressed,	• Present it fairly and concede or refute it.
If readers are attacked or ridiculed in a refutation,	• Refute ideas decisively while showing respect for your readers. • Use the sentence strategy of concession and refutation (this chapter, pp. 448).

To Enhance Credibility

If the essay does not establish common ground with readers,	• Figure out what you might have in common with your audience—some shared values, attitudes, or beliefs—and include them in your argument.

If readers question your credibility,	• Learn more about your subject, and support your argument more fully. • Address more of readers' likely questions, objections, and alternatives. • Talk with others who can help you think more imaginatively about your speculations. • Check your rhetorical sensitivity by adjusting your tone to make it civil and to clarify that you respect those who hold alternative views.
To Make the Organization More Effective	
If the causes or effects are not presented in a logical sequence,	• Change the sequence into some kind of logical order, such as chronological or least to most effective. You may find that you need to add or drop certain causes or effects.
If connections between ideas are not clear,	• Provide clearer transitions (*first, second, moreover, in addition*) to guide readers from one step in the argument to the next. • Use clear topic sentences to signal the stages of your argument and the support you provide for each cause or effect.
If your responses to alternative arguments are introduced awkwardly or unexpectedly,	• Move them around or add transitions to integrate them more smoothly.

Editing and Proofreading Your Draft

Check for errors in usage, punctuation, and mechanics, and consider matters of style. If you keep a list of errors you typically make, begin by checking your draft against this list.

From our research on student writing, we know that essays speculating about causes or effects have a high percentage of errors in the use of numbers and "reason is because" sentences. Because writers are usually drawn into "reason is because" sentences when making a causal argument, you will need to know options for revising such sentences. And, because you may rely on numbers to present statistics when you support your argument or demonstrate the existence of a trend, you will need to learn and follow the conventions for presenting different kinds of numbers. Check a writer's handbook for help with these potential problems.

Reflecting on Speculations about Causes or Effects

In this chapter, you have read critically several essays that speculate about causes or effects and have written one of your own. To better remember what you have learned, pause now to reflect on the reading and writing activities you completed in this chapter.

1. Write a page or so reflecting on what you have learned. Begin by describing what you are most pleased with in your essay. Then explain what you think contributed to your achievement.

   • If it was something you learned from the readings, indicate which readings and specifically what you learned from them.

   • If it came from your invention writing, point out the section or sections that helped you most.

   • If you got good advice from a critical reader, explain exactly how the person helped you — perhaps by helping you understand a problem in your draft or by helping you add a new dimension to your writing.

2. Reflect more generally on speculating about causes or effects, a genre of writing that plays an important role in social life and public policy in the United States. Consider some of the following questions:

   • Do you tend to adopt a tentative or an assertive stance when making such speculations about public issues? Why?

   • How might your personal preferences and values influence your speculations about, for example, the causes of health-care cost inflation or the effects of same-sex marriage? How about your gender, ethnicity, religious beliefs, age, or social class?

   • What contribution might writing that speculates about causes or effects make to our society that other genres cannot make?

3. By reflecting on what you have learned about speculating about causes or effects, you have been practicing **metacognition,** one of the academic habits of mind.

   • Were you aware of any other habits of mind you practiced as you read and responded to the material in this chapter? If so, which habits did you find useful?

   • If not, think back now on your reading and writing processes. Can you identify any habits you practiced?

Proposal to Solve a Problem

A proposal can help us analyze a problem, evaluate the feasibility of alternative solutions, and ultimately move readers to take particular actions to solve the problem. Whether the proposal is written in college (for example, to research an indigenous language or to prohibit the sale of genetically manufactured foods on campus), in the broader community (for example, to install traffic signals at intersections where car accidents regularly occur or to improve community policing), or in the workplace (for example, to bid for a service contract or to institute an employee wellness program), proposals enable us to take pragmatic action to address pressing problems. To be effective, proposals often apply one or more of the practices that you have been honing as an academic writer. Proposals arouse readers' curiosity and concern, use critical analysis to invent imaginative solutions, and apply rhetorical sensitivity to communicate with readers and persuade them to consider new ideas.

RHETORICAL SITUATIONS FOR PROPOSALS

Proposals appear in a wide variety of contexts and media. Here are just a couple examples:

- A blogger posts a proposal to solve the problem of the rising college loan default rate, which she illustrates with statistics and graphs from the U.S. Department of Education. She concedes one reason why the problem is worst at for-profit colleges: they enroll a larger proportion of working parents and first-generation college students — who have greater financial challenges compared to the majority of traditional public and private college students. Nevertheless, the blogger argues that many for-profit colleges make the problem worse by using advertising to lure potential students with the promise of a college program many students cannot complete and a well-paying job the colleges cannot guarantee. She proposes that truth-in-advertising laws be used to crack down on the aggressive recruiting tactics of for-profit institutions that target low-income students.

- For a political science class, a college student proposes that a direct popular vote replace the Electoral College system for electing the president because the Electoral College is undemocratic. He points out that several times in our history a candidate who lost the popular vote has become president. The fact that most states allocate electors on a winner-take-all basis, with all of the state's votes going to the winner even if the margin of victory is 50.1 percent to 49.9 percent, makes the system especially undemocratic. The student argues that using the direct popular vote instead would be the surest and simplest way to solve the problem, and voters would be likely to support this solution because it is based on the core American principle of "one person, one vote."

Thinking about Proposals

Recall one occasion when you heard or read a proposal, or proposed a solution yourself orally or in writing. Use the following questions to develop your thoughts.

- Who was the *audience*? How do you think communicating to this audience influenced what was told or how it was told? For example, if the audience was not personally affected by the problem, how were they inspired to care about solving the problem?

- What was the main *purpose*? What did you — or the other writer or speaker — hope to achieve? For example, was the primary purpose to inspire the audience to vote a certain way or to urge people in a position of power to take a particular action?

- How would you rate the *rhetorical sensitivity* with which the proposal was presented? What made the proposal appropriate or inappropriate for its particular audience or purpose?

A GUIDE TO READING PROPOSALS

This guide introduces you to proposal writing by inviting you to analyze a proposal by Alice Wong that offers a surprising take on the debate of single-use plastic.

- *Annotations* on this first reading will help you see how to practice academic **habits of mind** such as **curiosity, openness,** and **persistence** to help you engage with and understand what you are reading. Notice how many questions the reader has as she reads. There is plenty of space for you to add your own questions and thoughts, as well, to this reading and any other in the textbook.

- *Reading for meaning* will help you understand how Wong proposes to solve the debate over single-use plastic straws.

- *Reading like a writer* will help you learn how Wong employs the strategies typical of proposal writing to makes her essay persuasive, such as

1. demonstrating that the problem exists and is serious

2. showing how her proposal would help solve the problem and is feasible

3. responding to objections and alternative solutions

4. organizing the proposal in a way that is clear, logical, and convincing

Alice Wong

The Last Straw

Alice Wong is a research consultant and disability activist. She is the founder of the Disability Visibility Project™ (DVP), an online community that offers a space for people to publish, discuss, and share stories about disability. She is also co-partner of #CripTheVote, a nonpartisan online movement dedicated to engaging disabled people on policies, laws, and practices important to them. Her activism has been featured across a variety of media including WBUR radio, *Al Jazeera*, *Teen Vogue*, *Esquire*, *CNET*, and *Buzzfeed*. The following essay was published on Eater.com.

- **Before you read**, think about whether you have noticed that plastic straws are no longer being used in many restaurants, including Starbucks. If you have noticed this, what brought the change to your attention? If you haven't, why do you think that is?

- **As you read**, pay attention to how Wong lays out the problem and the solution. Based on how she describes the problem, does the solution seem logical and practical?

I live in the Mission District of San Francisco, where delicious taquerias, 1 bakeries, cafes, and bars are everywhere. And as a disabled person who uses a wheelchair to get around and a ventilator to breathe, the pleasure of eating and drinking is mediated by a number of factors. When I leave my home for a latte or burrito, a number of calculations go through my head: Will the place have their door propped open so I can enter? If the door is closed, will someone exiting or entering open it for me? Is the counter low enough for the server to see me? Can they hear and understand me with the mask over my nose if it's incredibly noisy inside? Will I be able to sign my name on the touchscreen or receipt, depending on the counter height?

At one of my favorite neighborhood places, when I make my order, I 2 feel comfortable asking for and receiving assistance. I'll ask the barista to bring my drink to my table since I cannot reach the high counters or carry a full cup. I'll even ask for help adding sugar when I'm feeling indulgent, because a glass dispenser is too heavy for me to lift.

Two items I always ask for with my drinks are a lid and a plastic straw, 3 emphasis on plastic. Lids prevent spillage when I'm navigating bumpy sidewalks and curb cuts; straws are necessary because I do not have the hand and arm strength to lift a drink and tip it into my mouth. Plastic straws are the best when I drink hot liquids; compostable ones tend to melt or break apart.

4   It's not easy or pleasant asking for help in public spaces like restaurants, because you never know what attitudes you'll encounter: indifference, pity, or outright rejection. I don't see these types of help as special treatment or inspirational for someone to surreptitiously post on social media as feel-good clickbait; they're simply examples of excellent hospitality.

5   Plastic is seen as cheap, "anti-luxury," wasteful, and harmful to the environment. All true. Plastic is also an essential part of my health and wellness. With my neuromuscular disability, plastic straws are necessary tools for my hydration and nutrition. Currently, plastic single-use straws are the latest target by environmentalists in the move toward zero waste. Major restaurant groups such as Union Square Hospitality Group and companies such as Starbucks and others in the travel industry announced plans to phase out single-use plastics.

What does plastic have to do with health and wellness?

6   Starbucks's announcement—and the news that Vancouver and Seattle recently banned plastic straws, with other cities, like New York and San Francisco, contemplating proposals—struck a raw nerve with me for several reasons (and I won't even get into the problems of recyclable plastics and greenwashing):

Are they banning plastic straws or all kinds of straws?

1. Plastic straws are considered unnecessary items used by environmentalists as a "gateway plastic" to engage the public on a larger conversation about waste. According to Dune Ives, executive director of the Lonely Whale Foundation, "Plastic straws are social tools and props, the perfect conversation starter." But one person's social prop is another person's conduit for nutrition. It's as if people who rely on straws—older adults, children, and disabled people—don't matter and that our needs are less important than the environment. I feel erased by these attitudes.

How are plastic straws social tools and props?

2. Plastic straws are ubiquitous, whether we like it or not. Once you have something that provides access, it is difficult and harmful to take it away from a marginalized community that depends on it. I live in a world that was never built for me, and every little bit of access is treasured and hard-won. Bans on plastic straws are regressive, not progressive.

7   The plastic straw ban is symptomatic of larger systemic issues when it comes to the continual struggle for disability rights and justice. The Americans with Disabilities Act (ADA) turns 28 next week, on July 26, and yet people with disabilities continue to face barriers at eating establishments. The ADA is considered by many small businesses (and the National Restaurant Association) as a source of frivolous lawsuits brought by greedy

Is the banning of plastic straws an example of the struggle for disability rights and justice or is something else going on here?

lawyers and clients. Ableist attitudes that cast disabled people as "fakers" or "complainers" obscure the very real and painful experiences of not being able to eat and drink freely.

As demand increases for alternatives to plastic, so do the voices 8 from the disability community sharing their concerns about how these bans will create additional labor, hurdles, and difficulties. On social media, many disabled people have been sharing their stories and keeping it 100 percent real. I observed and experienced all sorts of microaggressions and outright dismissal of what disabled people are saying online.

Crutches&Spice | @Imani_Barbarin

Disabled people: when was the first time you felt the independence a straw gave you? #SaveOurStraws #SOS

Jul 11, 2018

Chronically, Raven | @ChronicallyRavn

I saw a Tweet that said: What did all you disabled people do before straws were invented? I believe it was a Doctor who responded: They aspirated liquids into their lungs and died of pneumonia. #MicDrop

350
173 people are talking about this

3:05 PM - Jul 12, 2018

Mia | @SeeMiaRoll

Half of the disability life experience is having non-disabled ppl give suggestions like they innovative/creative when we've spent hours of our lives explaining to EVERYONE and their mother why their 'helpful' suggestions don't work. #SuckItAbleism

637
285 people are talking about this

12:36 AM - Jul 12, 2018

People have told me online that I still have access to biodegradable 9 straws at Starbucks, despite my reasons for using plastic ones. People have told me to bring my own reusable straws without thinking about the extra work that entails. Why would a disabled customer have to bring something in order to drink while non-disabled people have the convenience and ability to use what is provided for free? This is neither just, equitable, nor hospitable.

10   This is the experience of living in a world that was never built for you: having to explain and defend yourself while providing infinite amounts of labor at the demand of people who do not recognize their nondisabled privilege. There are days when I want to put this on repeat: "Believe disabled people. Period." I refuse to apologize or feel shame about the way my body works and how I navigate in the world. Everyone consumes goods and creates waste. We all do what we can to reduce, reuse, and recycle. We should recognize that different needs require different solutions. I'm not a monster for using plastic straws or other plastic items that allow me to live, such as oxygen tubes.

Crutches&Spice | @Imani_Barbarin

Imagine if your solution to segregated lunch counters and restaurants was for black people to bring their own chair. Now apply that to straws and disabled people… https://twitter.com/fabulancemedic/status/1018597995703689217…

105

40 people are talking about this

5:15 PM - Jul 15, 2018

> Are these tweets credible sources? Why does the author include tweets in a serious proposal?

11   Restaurants are theater; they are also highly politicized, contested spaces. There are times when I go out and the waiter asks my companion for my order instead of me. I've gone through creepy, dirty side entrances just to get into a restaurant. I've been called "the wheelchair" by front-of-house staff when they commiserate on which table to place me, since I apparently take up too much space. I also love the places where I feel welcomed and respected. As they provide thoughtful and authentic hospitality, I respond by being a loyal customer who appreciates the little touches that make a visit enjoyable.

12   The ban in Seattle comes with an exemption for people with disabilities, where restaurants can provide plastic straws upon request for medical reasons. This is optional for restaurants, so they may choose to not to make any available. What people don't understand with bans like this is that having to ask for a plastic straw puts an unfair burden, and scrutiny, on people with disabilities. They should not have to prove a medical need or even disclose their disability status when having a fun night out with friends. This is not hospitality.

13   So where do we go from here? How can we cultivate accessible and hospitable environments while reducing waste? Until someone invents a compostable straw with the functionality of a plastic one, I have a

modest proposal for establishments that have banned plastic straws and those that are considering it:

- If you are an establishment with straws at a counter, provide both types, clearly labeled, for people to choose from. If a cafe or restaurant wants to provide straws by request, have the server offer plastic and biodegradable versions, just as they would give any customer a choice of still or sparkling water. Customers can choose what is best for them without alienating an entire group.

- Re-examine the kinds of plastic you use in your establishment (e.g., plastic wrap, containers) and find additional ways to reduce your consumption.

- Expand your ideas about hospitality and accessibility; they are one and the same.

- Think about the intentional and unintentional barriers your establishment sets that may keep people from visiting your place. Listen and learn from your customers' critiques, including disabled customers. Don't wait for protests or boycotts before engaging with the disability community (I see you, Starbucks).

Laura | @laurawritesit

Accessibility is a human rights issue, not an individual problem. If you're the type of person to tell disabled people to "just carry their own straws," think to yourself—why will you fight so hard for a #strawban but not demand that alternatives be accessible?

406
219 people are talking about this

11:36 AM - Jul 8, 2018

If cafes can offer four types of milk for espresso drinks and restaurants 50 types 14 of wine and beer, small businesses and large corporations can manage offering two types of straws. The key is to have the same level of access for all items. You can accommodate all your customers while reducing waste at the same time. Customers respond to choice and flexibility.

Because in the end, isn't it all about welcoming everyone into your space with authentic and inclusive hospitality?

READING FOR MEANING

For help
with reading
strategies like
summarizing
and analyzing
assumptions,
see Chapter 2.

1. **Read to Summarize.** Write a sentence or two explaining how the proposed solution will help solve the plastic straw problem.

2. **Read to Respond.** Write a paragraph analyzing your initial reactions to Wong's proposal. For example, consider her point that hospitality and

accessibility are one and the same (par. 13), as well as her suggestion that restaurant owners should consider other ways of cutting down on their use of plastic (par. 13).

3. **Read to Analyze Assumptions.** Write a paragraph or two analyzing an assumption you find interesting or surprising in Wong's essay. For example:

Assumptions about the ongoing struggle for disability rights and justice. When Wong writes that "the plastic straw ban is symptomatic of larger systemic issues when it comes to the continual struggle for disability rights and justice" (par. 7), she seems to assume that readers will agree with her characterization of people with disabilities as in the middle of a long struggle for their rights.

- What assumptions do you have about people with disabilities? Where do those assumptions come from? Are you aware of the struggle Wong describes?

- Does reading Wong's piece challenge any of your assumptions about those with disabilities or their rights?

Assumptions about inclusivity. Wong concludes her essay with the following: "If cafes can offer four types of milk for espresso drinks and restaurants 50 types of wine and beer, small businesses and large corporations can manage offering two types of straws. The key is to have the same level of access for all items. You can accommodate all your customers while reducing waste at the same time.... Because in the end, isn't it all about welcoming everyone into your space with authentic and inclusive hospitality?" (pars. 14–15)

- Why do you think Wong would end her essay with the word "hospitality"?

- In the passage above, how does Wong attempt to expose the priorities of restaurants by citing how cafes offer four kinds of milk and restaurants offer fifty types of wine and beer? Is she suggesting that they value choice for some customers but not others? How does this relate to her ending the essay with the word "hospitality"?

READING LIKE A WRITER

Demonstrating the Problem Exists and Is Serious

Every proposal begins with a problem. What writers say about the problem and how much space they devote to it depend on what they assume their readers know and think about the problem. Some problems require more explanation than others. Obviously, if readers are already immersed in discussing the problem and possible solutions, then the writer may not have to say much to introduce the problem. Nevertheless, savvy proposal writers try to present even familiar problems in a way that alerts readers to a problem's seriousness and prepares them for the writer's preferred solution.

ANALYZE & WRITE

Write a paragraph or two analyzing and evaluating how Wong presents the problem and establishes its seriousness:

1. Reread the first paragraph. How does the image Wong creates of herself and the questions she asks before she leaves her home prepare the reader for the piece as a whole, as well as for the solution Wong offers?

2. Look back at the title of the piece. What does the common saying "the last straw" mean? Why do you think Wong chose this expression for her title? Explain your answer.

3. Note that Wong uses a numbered list, as well as bullet points, in her essay. Why do you think she does so? Is this a productive way of organizing her essay? Why or why not?

Showing How the Proposed Solution Would Help Solve the Problem and Is Feasible

The proposal writer's primary purposes are twofold:

1. To convince readers that the proposed solution would be **effective** — that it would help solve the problem, even if it would not eliminate it altogether

2. To convince readers that the proposed solution is **feasible** — that it can be implemented fairly easily and is cost-effective

For proposed solutions that already exist, the writer may need only to give the solution a name and give examples of where it is being applied successfully. Writers may also support their claims about the solution's effectiveness and feasibility with such evidence as statistics, research studies, and quotations from experts.

ANALYZE & WRITE

Write a paragraph or two analyzing and evaluating Wong's proposed solution.

1. Wong writes, "Until someone invents a compostable straw with the functionality of a plastic one, I have a modest proposal for establishments that have banned plastic straws and those that are considering it" (par. 13). Why do you think Wong does not argue for the "development of a compostable straw with the functionality of a plastic one"? Do you think that solution would be more or less effective and feasible than the solutions she proposes? Explain your answer.

2. Do Wong's solution(s) have the potential to solve the problem, and can the solutions be implemented on a wide scale fairly easily and inexpensively?

3. Do you think that the four bulleted solutions Wong proposes are intended to be applied all together as different parts of the same overarching solution, or could someone pick and choose from her proposal list? Explain your answer, and also consider if this affects the feasibility of her proposal.

Responding to Objections and Alternative Solutions

As they introduce the problem and then argue for the solution, proposal writers need to anticipate readers' possible objections to their argument as well as alternative solutions readers may prefer. Ignoring likely objections or alternative solutions is not a wise strategy because it gives the impression that the writer either does not fully understand the issue or cannot counter criticism. Writers have two options. They may:

1. *Concede* (or acknowledge) that an objection or alternative solution has some value and modify their proposed solution to accommodate it

2. *Refute* (or argue against) objections and alternative solutions by demonstrating that an objection is mistaken or that an alternative solution would not solve the problem or is inferior to the solution being proposed

ANALYZE & WRITE

Write a paragraph analyzing and evaluating how Wong responds to alternative solutions:

1. Wong writes, "People have told me online that I still have access to biodegradable straws at Starbucks, despite my reasons for using plastic ones. People have told me to bring my own reusable straws without thinking about the extra work that entails" (par. 9). Does Wong concede or refute these solutions? Do you think she is successful? Why or why not?

2. Consider how Wong responds to those who say she can just ask for a plastic straw: "Restaurants can provide plastic straws upon request for medical reasons.... What people don't understand with bans like this is that having to ask for a plastic straw puts an unfair burden, and scrutiny, on people with disabilities" (par. 12). What effect does the phrase "what people don't understand" have on you as a reader? Do you think you are one of the people Wong is calling out? Why or why not?

3. Finally, what role do the tweets Wong includes play in her essay? Do they support her solution? How do they suggest other ways of thinking about the problem and possible solutions?

Organizing the Proposal in a Way That Is Clear, Logical, and Convincing

To help readers identify the parts of the proposal, writers often use *cues* or signposts. For example, Wong explains early in her essay, "Two items I always ask for with my drinks are a lid and a plastic straw, emphasis on plastic.... Plastic straws are the best when I drink hot liquids; compostable ones tend to melt or break apart" (par. 3).

She uses **rhetorical questions** (questions used to underscore a point rather than elicit immediate answers) to underscore the seriousness of the issue and her proposed solution. In response to those who say she should just bring her own plastic straw, she asks: "Why would a disabled customer have to bring something in order to drink while non-disabled people have the convenience and ability to use what is provided for free?" (par. 9). Later, as she prepares to offer her solutions, she prepares the reader for her proposal with more rhetorical questions: "So where do we go from here? How can we cultivate accessible and hospitable environments while reducing waste?" (par. 13). Finally, Wong concludes her essay with a rhetorical question, too: "Because in the end, isn't it all about welcoming everyone into your space with authentic and inclusive hospitality?" (par. 15).

Wong also uses **transition** words throughout her essay to help readers navigate her proposal:

Transitions   So where do we go from here? How can we cultivate accessible and hospitable environments while reducing waste? Until someone invents a compostable straw with the functionality of a plastic one, I have a modest proposal for establishments that have banned plastic straws and those that are considering it. (par. 13)

Notice how the transitions help orient readers to the twists and turns of Wong's argument. "So, where do we go from here," for example, emphasizes the crucial part of the solution: that something can be done to address this problem that does not further alienate or scrutinize people with disabilities.

Finally, **topic sentences,** sentences that state the main idea of a paragraph or group of paragraphs, can be especially helpful to readers trying to follow the logic of a proposal. For example, notice how Wong uses topic sentences to indicate the alternative solution she is refuting.

People have told me online that I still have access to biodegradable straws at Starbucks, despite my reasons for using plastic ones…. (par. 9)

ANALYZE & WRITE

Write a couple of paragraphs analyzing and evaluating Wong's uses of cueing to help readers follow her argument:

1. Reread Wong's essay with an eye toward rhetorical questions. Where and how does she use these?

2. Look at the topic sentences in each of Wong's paragraphs. Do these provide you with an overview of what will be addressed in each paragraph? Does each paragraph logically follow from the previous one? How so?

3. In addition to the cueing strategies mentioned above, what other organization strategies does Wong use to organize her proposal? Overall, given Wong's purpose, how clear and comprehensible is the logic of this proposal argument? If you were to give Wong advice on revising this proposal, what, if anything, would you recommend?

READINGS

Harold Meyerson

How to Raise Americans' Wages

Harold Meyerson (b. 1950) writes a weekly opinion column for the *Washington Post* and contributes to its PostPartisan blog. He also serves as executive editor of the progressive magazine, *The American Prospect*, in which his proposal "How to Raise Americans' Wages" first appeared in 2015. A senior fellow at the Center for American Progress, Meyerson often writes about politics, labor, and economics for major publications like the *New Yorker*, the *Atlantic*, and the *New York Times*. He has also hosted a weekly radio show and written a biography of *The Wizard of Oz* lyricist Yip Harburg.

- **Before you read**, think about why Meyerson opens his proposal as if it were a fairy tale, with the conventional "once upon a time" beginning.

- **As you read**, notice that Meyerson's proposal offers several different but related solutions to the problem. Consider how each solution would help to raise wages for American workers.

Once upon a time in a faraway land—the United States following World War II — workers reaped what they sowed. From 1947 through 1973, their income rose in lockstep with increases in productivity. Their median compensation (wages plus benefits) increased by 95 percent as their productivity increased by 97 percent. Then, abruptly, the rewards for greater productivity started going elsewhere—to shareholders, financiers, and top corporate executives. Today, for the vast majority of American workers, the link between their productivity and their compensation no longer exists. As economists Robert Gordon and Ian Dew-Becker have established, the gains in workers' productivity for the past three decades have gone entirely to the wealthiest 10 percent.... 1

Today, the drive to restore workers' share has been narrowed down to the campaign to raise the minimum wage. That raise is long overdue.... But even raising that wage wouldn't do much for most workers; they make well more than the minimum, but their own wages have been stagnating or shrinking for decades as well. What, then, do we do for American workers more generally? How do we raise their wages? How do we re-create a growing and vibrant middle class? 2

For many business leaders, politicians, and commentators, workers' declining share is the inevitable result of globalization and technological change—forces of nature that nations, much less individuals, are powerless to stop. They also tend to blame the victim: According to conventional wisdom, workers lack the education and training to fill the new high-tech jobs the economy now demands. Globalization 3 and technological change have indeed played key roles in weakening workers' bargaining power, and a more educated workforce surely commands better pay than workers without the requisite skills. Nonetheless, the business leaders and their apologists are fundamentally wrong in both their diagnoses and prescriptions. To begin, at least one major nation every bit as subject to globalization and technological change as ours hasn't seen the evisceration of its middle class and the redistribution of income from labor to capital that we've endured. Germany has a greater level of foreign trade than the U.S. and a comparable level of technological change, but it has managed to retain its best manufacturing jobs, because of the greater power that its workers exercise and the diminished role its shareholders play. In Germany, law and custom have enabled labor and required management to collaborate on making sure that the most highly skilled and compensated jobs remain at home. The claim that American workers lack the skills they need is belied by workers in low-skilled jobs (those that pay two-thirds or less of the median wage) having much more education than equivalent workers four decades ago: 46 percent of low-skilled workers today have attended college; in the 1960s, just 17 percent had. Moreover, the incomes of many professionals, including lawyers and college teachers, have declined in recent years as well.

What corporate apologists won't acknowledge is that workers' incomes have been   4 reduced by design. American business has adamantly opposed workers' efforts to organize unions. Millions of jobs have been outsourced, offshored, franchised out, reclassified as temporary or part-time, or had their wages slashed, in a successful, decades-long campaign to increase the return to capital. Indeed, the only way to explain the soaring profit margins and stock values of recent years despite anemic increases in corporate revenues is that profits have come at the expense of labor....

The transfer of income from labor to capital, then, is chiefly the consequence   5 of capitalists' design. But precisely because that transfer has been so thorough, reversing it will be exquisitely difficult. Traditionally, American workers were able to raise their wages by collective bargaining or through the clout they could wield in a full-employment economy. But the ability of private-sector workers to bargain collectively has been destroyed by the evisceration of unions, which now represent just 6.7 percent of private-sector workers. The labor movement has tried... to strengthen protections for workers in organizing campaigns. Each time, however, the unions failed to surmount the Senate's supermajority threshold. Until they can, the most direct way to raise workers' wages will remain a dead letter. Re-creating the other avenue for bolstering workers' leverage—a full-employment economy—looks just as remote. Historically, workers won some of their biggest wage gains when the unemployment rate dipped beneath 4 percent.... During the New Deal, the federal government embarked on massive public-works and employment programs. Now, confronted with a growing share of working-age Americans who have given up on finding employment, government needs to take up that task again. Such a project should combine a program to rebuild the nation's sagging infrastructure with increased public investment in home care, child care, and preschool. But such a project also requires far greater public belief in the necessity and efficacy of governmental endeavors and the election of a president and a sufficient number of legislators who share that belief. However devoutly progressives may wish it, this is not likely to happen any time soon.

In a nation where workers have lost the power they once had to raise their   6
incomes, what can be done to make those incomes rise? Here are [four] proposals...

1. LEGISLATE WAGE HIKES IN STATES AND CITIES

In poll after poll, raising the federal minimum wage emerges as one of the most popu-   7
lar policy options on the political landscape, supported by an overwhelming majority of Democrats, a sizable majority of independents, about 50 percent of Republicans, and an increasing number of major retailers. Nonetheless, such is the influence of small business (of restaurants, especially) and the Tea Party that prospects for getting a raise through Congress remain dim.... In a number of states, the wage already sub-stantially exceeds the federal minimum, and some have raised their standard even more in the past year (in California, to $10). Cities and counties in certain states have the right to set their own minimum wage higher than that of their state. In Maryland, the two counties bordering the District of Columbia recently increased the wage, in tandem with the District, to $11.50....

Since the late 1990s, local progressive governments have been able to lift wage   8
levels for private-sector workers in government-owned facilities (such as airports or museums) and projects that receive government assistance (such as property-tax abatements or infrastructure improvements) or require special governmental approv-als (such as sports arenas). Advocates of these "living wage" ordinances argue that governments should not be using taxpayer dollars to subsidize poverty-wage jobs.... Currently, at least 150 cities have established living-wage ordinances or communi-ty-benefit agreements....

2. LINK CORPORATE TAX RATES TO WORKER PRODUCTIVITY INCREASES AND CEO-EMPLOYEE PAY RATIOS

Congress could create a lower tax rate for those corporations that increased their   9
median wage in line with the annual national productivity increase.... Constructing a tax code that gives corporations an incentive to pass on productivity increases to their employees is admittedly a complex task. The tax break would have to be big enough to be attractive to the companies' directors and managers. The break would also have to be withheld from corporations that game the system by initially cutting their workers' pay to reduce the median wage, then restore it through a productivity increase. Devising a process for monitoring and assessing corporate conduct would not be easy. But with unionization—the straightforward means of linking employee pay to productivity gains—off the table, complexity is the price we'd have to pay to create a more prosperous economy....

They should also promote legislation that would link corporate tax rates to the ratio   10
between CEO pay and the firm's median pay: the lower the ratio, the lower the tax.

This is sure to elicit a backlash from corporate elites and the financial sector, but it should gain popular support. A poll conducted this February showed that 66 percent of the public believed that "executive pay is generally too high"—an assessment shared by 79 percent of Democrats, 61 percent of independents, and 58 percent of Republicans. The rise in the ratio of CEO to median-worker pay began about the time that workers' compensation was detached from increases in productivity. In 1978, CEOs made 28 times the pay of their median-paid employee; by 2012, CEOs made 273 times the median.

Were this proposal to become law, CEOs and their boards would face a fun- 11 damental choice: They could persist in excessive executive compensation at the expense of forcing their company to shell out considerably more in corporate taxes. Or they could reduce executive pay to levels the American people see as a more legitimate reflection of executive worth. They would also have a self-interest in rais- ing their workers' wages. Indeed, if enacted in conjunction with the proposal linking the median worker's pay to productivity increases, this proposal would limit corpo- rations' incentive to game that system by reducing workers' pay before the median is calculated.

What kind of ratio should progressives set as an appropriate valuation of a CEO's 12 worth? In 1977, the celebrated management guru Peter Drucker wrote in the *Wall Street Journal* that a ratio of 15 to 1 seemed right for a small or midsize business, and 25 to 1 for a large business. By that standard, a CEO at a sizable firm where the aver- age employee makes $60,000 a year would make $1.5 million.

3. MAKE CORPORATIONS RESPONSIBLE FOR ALL THEIR WORKERS

Many of the problems American workers encounter in making a decent wage stem 13 from a confusion about who employs them. In recent decades, companies have rou- tinely shifted the production and delivery of their goods and services and other tasks needed to run their businesses from their own employees to workers employed by contractors, subcontractors, franchisees, or temporary job agencies or to workers who are labeled independent contractors. In many cases, these workers are the same workers the parent company once employed. In most cases, they could be employed directly by the parent company, but they're not, chiefly because having the labor done by nonemployees saves the parent company money.

Inevitably, all this reduces the workers' wages and benefits. By outsourcing work, 14 Boston University economist David Weil explains in an important new book, *The Fissured Workplace*, an employer trades a wage-setting problem for a pricing prob- lem. Rather than pay his own employees a low wage, he can choose from a range of contractors, who compete with one another on price—a process that advantages the contractor with the lowest labor costs.... Nissan's temp workers do the same jobs as the Nissan employees next to them on the line, only for a good deal less. Wal-Mart, master of the logistics universe, specifies which products are to be moved through its warehouses and sent to which destinations, at which times, and at what cost. Most of the "independent contractors" who move goods from the port rent their trucks from one company, drive exclusively for that company, with orders and routes set by that company. But neither Nissan, Wal-Mart, nor the trucking companies directly pay these workers, who, of course, are not eligible for any of the parent companies' benefits. If these workers put in uncompensated overtime to complete their work, or are paid less than the minimum wage, or are injured on the job, their parent company is held harmless, though the parent company dictates the conditions of their work and the amount they are paid.... A radical amendment to the radical reforms I proposed in the preceding section: Count the parent company's contract workers as employees in calculating corporate tax rates.

4. RAISE TAXES ON CAPITAL INCOME AND REDISTRIBUTE IT TO LABOR

Another solution to the rise of investment income and the decline of income from 15 work would be to use the tax code to explicitly redistribute capital income to labor. The current tax code comes close to doing the reverse. Capital income—income from qualified dividends and capital gains—can be taxed at a rate no higher than 20 percent, while income from wages and salaries is subjected to a progressive tax that tops out at 39.6 percent. As Warren Buffett frequently notes, upper-middle-class and middle-class Americans sometimes pay more taxes on their wages and salaries than billionaires pay on their investments.

The justification for the low rate on capital—that it boosts the American economy 16 by promoting domestic investment—has been rendered absurd by the globalization of American businesses. The disparity between capital and labor tax rates also means that the government has diminished its take from that part of the national income that is growing, while maintaining a higher rate on that part of the nation's income that is shrinking.

For all those reasons, the tax rates on capital should be raised to the level of the 17 rates on labor; indeed, given that taxable labor must be domestic while taxable capital can be derived from anywhere, the rate on capital should be higher than that on labor. But what to do with this new revenue? As shareholder capital comes more and more at labor's expense, it should be taxed for the purpose of boosting labor income. One option would be to devote some of it to increase labor income through a major expansion of the Earned Income Tax Credit, a tax rebate that supplements the income of the working poor.

READING FOR MEANING

1. **Read to Summarize.** Write a sentence or two summarizing Meyerson's proposed solution to raise wages for American workers.

2. **Read to Respond.** Write a paragraph responding to any of Meyerson's ideas that you find interesting or surprising, such as his point that "workers' incomes have been reduced by design... millions of jobs have been

For help with reading strategies like summarizing and analyzing assumptions, see Chapter 2.

outsourced, offshored, franchised out, reclassified as temporary or part-time" (par. 5) or that "many of the problems American workers encounter in making a decent wage stem from a confusion about who employs them" (par. 13).

3. **Read to Analyze Assumptions**. Write a paragraph or two analyzing an assumption you find intriguing in Meyerson's essay. For example:

   Assumptions about choice. Meyerson assumes that giving CEOs and their boards a choice as to whether they want to "persist in excessive executive compensation" or "reduce executive pay" (par. 11) strengthens his solution.

   - Why does Meyerson assume that choice is so important to one of the solutions he offers? Do you agree with him? Explain your answer.
   - What assumptions does Meyerson make about choice and its power to persuade people to do something they may not otherwise do?

   Assumptions about the middle class. Meyerson asks a series of rhetorical questions that culminate with the following: "How do we re-create a growing and vibrant middle class?" (par. 2).

   - What assumptions drive this rhetorical question? Why is the middle class important to Meyerson's idea of America?
   - Is Meyerson's proposal convincing in its description of the importance of the middle class to America? Do the solutions he offers speak directly to the need for a growing and vibrant middle class?

READING LIKE A WRITER

Organizing the Proposal in a Way That Is Clear, Logical, and Convincing

To help readers identify the parts of the proposal, writers often use *cues* or signposts. Upon first glance, the most obvious **organizational strategy** of Meyerson's is his **numbering** of proposed solutions to the problem:

In a nation where workers have lost the power they once had to raise their incomes, what can be done to make those incomes rise? Here are [four] proposals...

1. Legislate wage hikes in states and cities
2. Link corporate tax rates to worker productivity increases and CEO-employee pay ratios

3. Make corporations responsible for all their workers

4. Raise taxes on capital income and redistribute it to labor

However, Meyerson uses multiple additional *cueing* strategies throughout his essay **to build** on the organization his numbering establishes.

ANALYZE & WRITE

Write a couple of paragraphs analyzing and evaluating Meyerson's uses of organizational strategies to help readers follow his argument:

1. Reread the four proposals, marking topic sentences and transition words. Now look at the topic sentences in each of Meyerson's paragraphs. Do these provide you with an overview of what will be addressed in each paragraph? Look at the transition words. Do they help each paragraph logically follow from the previous one?

2. What other organization strategies does Meyerson use to organize his proposal and how do they contribute to his overall argument?

Maryanne Wolf

Skim Reading Is the New Normal

Maryanne Wolf is a teacher and scholar who researches and advocates for children's literacy. She is the author of numerous books and academic articles, including *Proust and the Squid: The Story and Science of the Reading Brain* (2007), *Tales of Literacy for the 21st Century* (2016), and *Reader, Come Home: The Reading Brain in a Digital World* (2018). She has taught at institutions including Tufts University, where she directed the Center for Reading and Language Research, and UCLA, where she is the Director of the Center for Dyslexia, Diverse Learners, and Social Justice. The essay below appeared in the *Guardian* in 2018 as part of their weekly "Ideas for America" essay series.

- **Before you read**, think about what you skim read. Do you skim websites, your assigned readings for your classes, other kinds of texts?

- **As you read**, consider how Wolf uses research to support her proposal. Is this effective? Explain your answer.

Look around on your next plane trip. The iPad is the new pacifier for babies and toddlers. Younger school-aged children read stories on smartphones; older boys don't read at all, but hunch over video games. Parents and other passengers read on Kindles or skim a flotilla of email and news feeds. Unbeknownst to most of us, an invisible, game-changing transformation links everyone in this picture: the neuronal circuit that underlies the brain's ability to read is subtly, rapidly changing—a change with implications for everyone from the pre-reading toddler to the expert adult. 1

As work in neurosciences indicates, the acquisition of literacy necessitated a new circuit in our species' brain more than 6,000 years ago. That circuit evolved from a very simple mechanism for decoding basic information, like the number of goats in one's herd, to the present, highly elaborated reading brain. My research depicts how the present reading brain enables the development of some of our most important intellectual and affective processes: internalized knowledge, analogical reasoning, and inference; perspective-taking and empathy; critical analysis and the generation of insight. Research surfacing in many parts of the world now cautions that each of these essential "deep reading" processes may be under threat as we move into digital-based modes of reading. 2

This is not a simple, binary issue of print vs digital reading and technological innovation. As MIT scholar Sherry Turkle has written, we do not err as a society when we innovate, but when we ignore what we disrupt or diminish while innovating. In this hinge moment between print and digital cultures, society needs to confront what is diminishing in the expert reading circuit, what our children and older students are not developing, and what we can do about it. 3

We know from research that the reading circuit is not given to human beings 4 through a genetic blueprint like vision or language; it needs an environment to develop. Further, it will adapt to that environment's requirements—from different writing systems to the characteristics of whatever medium is used. If the dominant medium advantages processes that are fast, multi-task oriented and well-suited for large volumes of information, like the current digital medium, so will the reading circuit. As UCLA psychologist Patricia Greenfield writes, the result is that less attention and time will be allocated to slower, time-demanding deep reading processes, like inference, critical analysis and empathy, all of which are indispensable to learning at any age.

Increasing reports from educators and from researchers in psychology and the 5 humanities bear this out. English literature scholar and teacher Mark Edmundson describes how many college students actively avoid the classic literature of the 19th and 20th centuries because they no longer have the patience to read longer, denser, more difficult texts. We should be less concerned with students' "cognitive impatience," however, than by what may underlie it: the potential inability of large numbers of students to read with a level of critical analysis sufficient to comprehend the complexity of thought and argument found in more demanding texts, whether in literature and science in college, or in wills, contracts and the deliberately confusing public referendum questions citizens encounter in the voting booth.

Multiple studies show that digital screen use may be causing a variety of troubling 6 downstream effects on reading comprehension in older high school and college students. In Stavanger, Norway, psychologist Anne Mangen and her colleagues studied how high school students comprehend the same material in different mediums. Mangen's group asked subjects questions about a short story whose plot had universal student appeal (a lust-filled, love story); half of the students read Jenny, Mon Amour on a Kindle, the other half in paperback. Results indicated that students who read on print were superior in their comprehension to screen-reading peers, particularly in their ability to sequence detail and reconstruct the plot in chronological order.

Ziming Liu from San Jose State University has conducted a series of studies which 7 indicate that the "new norm" in reading is skimming, with word-spotting and browsing through the text. Many readers now use an F or Z pattern when reading in which they sample the first line and then word-spot through the rest of the text. When the reading brain skims like this, it reduces time allocated to deep reading processes. In other words, we don't have time to grasp complexity, to understand another's feelings, to perceive beauty, and to create thoughts of the reader's own.

Karin Littau and Andrew Piper have noted another dimension: physicality. Piper, 8 Littau and Anne Mangen's group emphasize that the sense of touch in print reading adds an important redundancy to information—a kind of "geometry" to words, and a spatial "thereness" for text. As Piper notes, human beings need a knowledge of where they are in time and space that allows them to return to things and learn from re-examination—what he calls the "technology of recurrence." The importance of recurrence for both young and older readers involves the ability to go back, to check and evaluate one's understanding of a text. The question, then, is what happens to comprehension when our youth skim on a screen whose lack of spatial thereness discourages "looking back."

US media researchers Lisa Guernsey and Michael Levine, American University's linguist Naomi Baron, and cognitive scientist Tami Katzir from Haifa University have examined the effects of different information mediums, particularly on the young. Katzir's research has found that the negative effects of screen reading can appear as early as fourth and fifth grade—with implications not only for comprehension, but also on the growth of empathy. 9

The possibility that critical analysis, empathy and other deep reading processes could become the unintended "collateral damage" of our digital culture is not a simple binary issue about print vs digital reading. It is about how we all have begun to read on any medium and how that changes not only what we read, but also the purposes for why we read. Nor is it only about the young. The subtle atrophy of critical analysis and empathy affects us all. It affects our ability to navigate a constant bombardment of information. It incentivizes a retreat to the most familiar silos of unchecked information, which require and receive no analysis, leaving us susceptible to false information and demagoguery. 10

There's an old rule in neuroscience that does not alter with age: use it or lose it. It is a very hopeful principle when applied to critical thought in the reading brain because it implies choice. The story of the changing reading brain is hardly finished. We possess both the science and the technology to identify and redress the changes in how we read before they become entrenched. If we work to understand exactly what we will lose, alongside the extraordinary new capacities that the digital world has brought us, there is as much reason for excitement as caution. 11

We need to cultivate a new kind of brain: a "bi-literate" reading brain capable of the deepest forms of thought in either digital or traditional mediums. A great deal hangs on it: the ability of citizens in a vibrant democracy to try on other perspectives and discern truth; the capacity of our children and grandchildren to appreciate and create beauty; and the ability in ourselves to go beyond our present glut of information to reach the knowledge and wisdom necessary to sustain a good society. 12

READING FOR MEANING

For help with reading strategies like summarizing and analyzing assumptions, see Chapter 2.

1. **Read to Summarize.** Write a sentence or two summarizing Wolf's proposed solution to the problems associated with skim reading.

2. **Read to Respond.** Write a paragraph responding to any of Wolf's ideas that strike you as surprising, such as "students who read on print were superior in their comprehension to screen-reading peers" (par. 6) or that skim reading will reduce our ability to empathize with others (par. 9).

3. **Read to Analyze Assumptions.** Write a paragraph or two analyzing an assumption you find intriguing in Wolf's essay. For example:

Assumptions about deep reading. Wolf warns us that "some of our most important intellectual and affective processes: internalized knowledge, analogical reasoning, and inference; perspective-taking and empathy; critical analysis and the generation of insight" may be under threat as we move into digital-based modes of reading (par. 2).

- Why does Wolf assume that the intellectual and affective processes that characterize deep reading are so important? Do you share this same assumption?
- Why does Wolf assume that "digital based modes of reading" won't support this deeper reading?

Assumptions about the relationship between deep reading practices and a successful democracy. Wolf explains the importance of confronting how our brains have changed: "The subtle atrophy of critical analysis and empathy affects us all . . . . It incentivizes a retreat to the most familiar silos of unchecked information, which require and receive no analysis, leaving us susceptible to false information and demagoguery" (par. 10). She explains further, "We need to cultivate a new kind of brain: a 'bi-literate' reading brain capable of the deepest forms of thought in either digital or traditional mediums. A great deal hangs on it: ability of citizens in a vibrant democracy to try on other perspectives and discern truth" (par 12).

- What assumptions drive the relationship Wolf establishes between deep reading and democracy?
- Is Wolf's description of the relationship between deep reading and democracy convincing? Why or why not?

READING LIKE A WRITER

Demonstrating the Problem Exists and Is Serious

Proposal writers use a variety of strategies to alert readers to the problem. The title, "Skim Reading Is the New Normal," is likely to capture readers' attention because it suggests that not only has something changed about how people read, but it has already become the most common way of reading.

In addition, Wolf opens her essay by noting that "unbeknownst to most of us, an invisible, game-changing transformation links everyone . . . the neuronal circuit that underlies the brain's ability to read is subtly, rapidly changing — a change with implications for everyone from the pre-reading toddler to the expert adult," immediately establishing that the problem exists ("the brain's ability . . . is subtly, rapidly changing") and that it is serious ("a change with implications for everyone") (par. 1).

ANALYZE & WRITE

Write a paragraph analyzing how Wolf uses neuroscience to frame the problem and establish its seriousness:

1. Reread paragraphs 1–4, marking where Wolf uses neuroscience to explain the problem and tries to convince readers that it is serious and worth solving.

2. How does Wolf present herself as an authority whose expertise can be relied upon? How credible does she seem to you?

For help with looking for patterns of opposition and analyzing assumptions, see Chapter 2, pp. 55–56 and 48–50.

Combining Reading Strategies

Looking for Patterns of Opposition to Analyze Assumptions

A careful reading of Wolf's "Skim Reading Is the New Normal" will reveal a series of oppositions that allow the reader to see Wolf's argument more clearly, particularly if the reader pays attention to which terms in each opposition Wolf values. Recognizing these patterns of opposition can also help you identify the assumptions — ideas, beliefs, or values — in the reading. Because assumptions are often not stated directly, you need to infer the assumptions that a writer is making about the subject.

Complete the following writing prompts that help you look for patterns of opposition in order to analyze the assumptions in Wolf's essay.

- Reread Wolf's essay and annotate words or phrases that indicate oppositions. Based on your annotations, continue filling in the chart, listing as many patterns of opposition as you notice. For each pair, including those already on the chart, put an asterisk next to the term or idea that the writer seems to value or prefer over the other term or idea.

The following chart begins to list the oppositions in Wolf's essay.

Print	Digital
Deep Reading	Skim Reading

- In which cases was it challenging to determine which term or idea Wolf valued over the other? Do you think this is a flaw in Wolf's proposal? Explain your answer.

- Keeping in mind the list of oppositions you developed, write a paragraph detailing which of these provide insight into some of the assumptions Wolf makes. Which oppositions compel you to reflect on your own assumptions and the values that underlie them? How do your assumptions compare to those present in the reading?

William F. Shughart II

Why Not a Football Degree?

William F. Shughart II (b. 1947) is a distinguished professor at the Utah State University School of Business who specializes in public choice theory that uses the tools of economics to study political attitudes and behavior. Shughart has been highly influential as editor-in-chief of the *Public Choice* journal and as research director and senior fellow at the Independent Institute, a libertarian conservative think tank. Shughart has written many books and articles addressing a broad array of social issues that range from sin taxes to taxing the Internet, campaign finance to terrorism. Sports are among Shughart's many interests, as reflected in these articles: "Moral Hazard and the Effects of the Designated Hitter Rule Revisited," "Close Look Shows College Sports No Drain on Schools' Resources," and this proposal "Why Not a Football Degree?" which was originally published in the *Wall Street Journal*.

- **Before you read**, note that the title asks the question "Why Not a Football Degree?" What problem do you imagine a college degree in football would solve?

- **As you read**, consider that this proposal was written originally for the *Wall Street Journal*, a newspaper concerned primarily with business and financial matters. How does Shughart appeal to the interests and concerns of his original audience?

The college football career of 2006's Heisman Trophy winner, Ohio State University quarterback Troy Smith, nearly was cut short at the end of his sophomore year following allegations that he had accepted $500 from a Buckeye booster. He was barred from playing in the 2005 Alamo Bowl and the next season's opener against Miami (Ohio). Quarterback Rhett Bomar was dismissed from the University of Oklahoma's football team after it was disclosed that he had earned substantially more than justified by the number of hours worked during the summer of 2006 at a job arranged for him by a patron of OU athletics. As a result of charges that, from 1993 to 1998, Coach Clem Haskins paid to have more than 400 term papers ghost-written for 18 of his players, the post-season tournament victories credited to the University of Minnesota's basketball team were erased from the NCAA's record books and the program was placed on a four-year probation from which it has not yet recovered. In recent years, gambling and point-shaving scandals have rocked the basketball programs at Arizona State, Northwestern, and Florida; player suspensions and other penalties have been handed out for illegal betting on games by members of the Boston University, Florida State, and University of Maryland football teams. 1

Each of these events, which are only the latest revelations in a long series of NCAA rule violations, has generated the usual hand-wringing about the apparent loss of amateurism in college sports. Nostalgia for supposedly simpler times when 2 love of the game and not money was the driving force in intercollegiate athletics has led to all sorts of reform proposals. The NCAA's decision in the late 1980s to require its member institutions to make public athletes' graduation rates is perhaps the least controversial example. Proposition 48's mandate that freshman athletes must meet more stringent test score and grade point requirements to participate in NCAA-sanctioned contests than is demanded of entering non-student-athletes has been criticized as a naked attempt to discriminate against disadvantaged (and mostly minority) high-school graduates who see college sports as a way out of poverty.

But whether or not one supports any particular reform proposal, there seems to be 3 a general consensus that something must be done. If so, why stop at half-measures? I hereby offer three suggestions for solving the crisis in college athletics.

1. *Create four-year degree programs in football and basketball.* Many colleges and 4 universities grant bachelor's degrees in vocational subjects. Art, drama, and music are a few examples, but there are others. Undergraduates who major in these areas typically are required to spend only about one of their four years in introductory English, math, history and science courses; the remainder of their time is spent in the studio, the theater or the practice hall honing the creative talents they will later sell as professionals.

Although a college education is no more necessary for success in the art world 5 than it is in the world of sports, no similar option is available for students whose talents lie on the athletic field or in the gym. Majoring in physical education is a possibility, of course, but while PE is hardly a rigorous, demanding discipline, under-graduates pursuing a degree in that major normally must spend many more hours in the classroom than their counterparts who are preparing for careers on the stage. While the music major is receiving academic credit for practice sessions and recitals, the PE major is studying and taking exams in kinesiology, exercise physiology and nutrition. Why should academic credit be given for practicing the violin, but not for practicing a three-point shot?

2. *Extend the time limit on athletic scholarships by two years.* In addition to prac- 6 ticing and playing during the regular football or basketball season, college athletes must continue to work to improve their skills and keep in shape during the off-season. For football players, these off-season activities include several weeks of organized spring practice as well as year-round exercise programs in the weight room and on the running track. Basketball players participate in summer leagues and practice with their teams during the fall. In effect, college athletes are required to work at their sports for as much as 10 months a year.

These time-consuming extracurricular activities make it extremely difficult for col- 7 lege athletes to devote more than minimal effort to the studies required for maintain-ing their academic eligibility. They miss lectures and exams when their teams travel, and the extra tutoring they receive at athletic department expense often fails to make up the difference.

If the NCAA and its member schools are truly concerned about the academic side 8 of the college athletic experience, let them put their money where their collective mouth is. The period of an athlete's eligibility to participate in intercollegiate sports would remain at four years, but the two additional years of scholarship support could be exercised at any time during the athlete's lifetime. Athletes who use up their college eligibility and do not choose careers in professional sports would be guaranteed financial backing to remain in school and finish their undergraduate degrees. Athletes who have the talent to turn pro could complete their degrees when their playing days are over.

3. *Allow a competitive marketplace to determine the compensation of college athletes.* Football and basketball players at the top NCAA institutions produce millions of dollars in benefits for their respective schools. Successful college athletic programs draw more fans to the football stadium and to the basketball arena. They generate revenues for the school from regular season television appearances and from invitations to participate in postseason play. There is evidence that schools attract greater financial support from public and private sources—both for their athletic and academic programs—if their teams achieve national ranking. There even is evidence that the quality of students who apply for admission to institutions of higher learning improves following a successful football or basketball season.

Despite the considerable contributions made to the wealth and welfare of his or her school, however, the compensation payable to a college athlete is limited by the NCAA to a scholarship that includes tuition, books, room and board, and a nominal expense allowance. Any payment above and beyond this amount subjects the offending athletic program to NCAA sanctions. In-kind payments to players and recruits in the form of free tickets to athletic contests, T-shirts, transportation and accommodations likewise are limited. These restrictions apply to alumni and fans as well as to the institutions themselves. The NCAA also limits the amount of money athletes can earn outside of school by curtailing the use of summer jobs as a means by which coaches and boosters can pay athletes more than authorized.

The illegal financial inducements reported to be widespread in collegiate football and basketball supply conclusive evidence that many college athletes are now underpaid. The relevant question is whether the current system of compensation ought to remain in place. Allowing it to do so will preserve the illusion of amateurism in college sports and permit coaches, athletic departments and college administrators to continue to benefit financially at the expense of the players. On the other hand, shifting to a market-based system of compensation would transfer some of the wealth created by big-time athletic programs to the individuals whose talents are key ingredients in the success of those programs.

It would also cause a sea change in the distribution of power among the top NCAA institutions. Under the present NCAA rules, some of the major college athletic programs, such as Southern Cal, LSU and Florida in football, and Duke, North Carolina and Florida in basketball, have developed such strong winning traditions over the years that they can maintain their dominant positions without cheating.

These schools are able to attract superior high-school athletes season after season by offering packages of non-monetary benefits (well-equipped training facilities, quality coaching staffs, talented teammates, national exposure and so on) that increases the present value of an amateur athlete's future professional income relative to the value added by historically weaker athletic programs. Given this factor, along with NCAA rules that mandate uniform compensation across the board, the top institutions have a built-in competitive advantage in recruiting the best and brightest athletes.

It follows that under the current system, the weaker programs are virtually compelled to offer illegal financial inducements to players and recruits if they wish to compete successfully with the traditional powers. It also follows that shifting to a market-based system of compensation would remove some of the built-in advantages now enjoyed by the top college athletic programs. It is surely this effect, along with the reductions in the incomes of coaches and the "fat" in athletic department budgets to be expected once a competitive marketplace is permitted to work, that is the cause of the objection to paying student-athletes a market-determined wage, not the rhetoric about the repugnance of professionalism. 14

It is a fight over the distribution of the college sports revenue pie that lies at the bottom of the debate about reforming NCAA rules. And notwithstanding the high moral principles and concern for players usually expressed by debaters on all sides of the issue, the interests of the athlete are in fact often the last to be considered. 15

READING FOR MEANING

1. **Read to Summarize.** Write a sentence or two summarizing Shughart's proposed solution.

2. **Read to Respond.** Write a paragraph analyzing anything that resonates or seems surprising, such as the rules violations that Shughart lists in the first paragraph, perhaps adding other, more recent violations with which you are familiar; or Shughart's observation that playing and practicing sports "make it extremely difficult for college athletes to devote more than minimal effort" to their studies (par. 7), perhaps in relation to your own experience as an athlete in college or high school.

3. **Read to Analyze Assumptions.** Write a paragraph or two analyzing an assumption you find intriguing in Shughart's essay. For example:

Assumptions about the benefits of amateurism. NCAA rules require that to play college sports, athletes must retain amateur status, meaning that they cannot be paid by recruiters or sponsors and that their scholarships can cover only such things as tuition and housing. Shughart argues, however, that amateurism in college sports is an "illusion" (par. 11).

- Who, according to Shughart, benefits from keeping college athletes amateurs, and who would benefit if they were allowed to become professionals?
- If the NCAA assumes that amateur status protects college athletes and perhaps also college sports, what is it supposed to protect them from, and how effective has this protection been?

For help with reading strategies like summarizing and analyzing assumptions, see Chapter 2.

Assumptions about the purpose of college. Although he concedes that the physical education major is "hardly a rigorous, demanding discipline" (par. 5), Shughart proposes that football be a major in its own right. His argument hinges on the comparison of football to music and other performance arts in which students receive "academic credit for practice sessions and recitals" (par. 5). He calls them "vocational subjects" (par. 4) because their purpose is job training.

- In conceding that the physical education major is "hardly a rigorous, demanding discipline" (par. 5), Shughart appears to think his readers are likely to assume disciplines or subjects studied in college should be rigorous and demanding. Do you share this assumption? Why or why not?

- By calling football a "vocational subject" and proposing that there be a major in football, Shughart seems to assume the primary purpose of a college education should be job training. What other reasons, if any, might people choose to go to college?

READING LIKE A WRITER

Showing How the Proposed Solution Would Help Solve the Problem and Is Feasible

"Why Not a Football Degree?" dismisses as "half-measures" previous efforts by the National Collegiate Athletic Association (NCAA) to solve what Shughart calls "the crisis in college athletics" (par. 3). He identifies an array of problems in college sports, including evidence that some athletes are being paid although they are supposed to be amateurs, not professionals; others are getting college credit they have not earned, for example for plagiarized papers; and still others are illegally betting on games. To address problems like these, Shughart makes a three-pronged proposal designed to help student athletes succeed in their academic studies as well as in their collegiate sports careers, and also eliminate "illegal financial inducements" (par. 11) while removing the "built-in advantages" (par. 14) of the most successful college sports programs.

ANALYZE & WRITE

Write a paragraph or two analyzing Shughart's argument in support of his proposed solution:

1. First, choose one of Shughart's "three suggestions" (par. 3) to analyze and evaluate Shughart's argument. What kinds of support does the author provide? What are the strengths and weaknesses of this part of his argument?

2. Then consider how well the three parts of the proposal work together to offer a comprehensive solution to the problem as Shughart has defined it.

Kelly D. Brownell and Thomas R. Frieden

Ounces of Prevention—The Public Policy Case for Taxes on Sugared Beverages

Kelly D. Brownell (b. 1951) is a professor of psychology and neuroscience as well as the dean of the Sanford School of Public Policy at Duke University. An international expert who has published numerous articles and books, including *Food Fight: The Inside Story of the Food Industry, America's Obesity Crisis, and What We Can Do About It* (2003), Brownell received the 2012 American Psychological Association Award for Outstanding Lifetime Contributions to Psychology. He was also featured in the Academy Award–nominated film *Super Size Me.* Thomas R. Frieden (b. 1960), a physician specializing in public health, is the director of the U.S. Centers for Disease Control and Prevention (CDC) and served for several years as the health commissioner for the City of New York.

Their proposal "Ounces of Prevention—The Public Policy Case for Taxes on Sugared Beverages" was originally published in 2009 in the highly respected *New England Journal of Medicine*, which calls itself "the most widely read, cited, and influential general medical periodical in the world."

- **Before you read**, think about how the reputation of the publication in which this proposal first appeared, together with Brownell and Frieden's credentials, might have influenced the original audience as well as how it may affect college students reading the proposal today.

- **As you read**, notice that Brownell and Frieden include graphs and cite their sources. How do you think these features of their proposal might influence readers?

Sugar, rum, and tobacco are commodities which are nowhere necessaries of life, which are become objects of almost universal consumption, and which are therefore extremely proper subjects of taxation.

— ADAM SMITH, *THE WEALTH OF NATIONS*, 1776

The obesity epidemic has inspired calls for public health measures to prevent diet-related diseases. One controversial idea is now the subject of public debate: food taxes. Forty states already have small taxes on sugared beverages and snack foods, but in the past year, Maine and New York have proposed large taxes on sugared beverages, and similar discussions have begun in other states. The size of the taxes, their potential for generating revenue and reducing consumption, and vigorous opposition by the beverage industry have resulted in substantial controversy. Because excess consumption of unhealthful foods underlies many leading causes of death, food taxes at local, state, and national levels are likely to remain part of political and public health discourse.

Sugar-sweetened beverages (soda sweetened with sugar, corn syrup, or other   2
caloric sweeteners and other carbonated and uncarbonated drinks, such as sports
and energy drinks) may be the single largest driver of the obesity epidemic. A recent
meta-analysis found that the intake of sugared beverages is associated with increased
body weight, poor nutrition, and displacement of more healthful beverages; increasing consumption increases risk for obesity and diabetes; the strongest effects are seen
in studies with the best methods (e.g., longitudinal and interventional vs. correlational studies);* and interventional studies show that reduced intake of soft drinks
improves health.[1] Studies that do not support a relationship between consumption
of sugared beverages and health outcomes tend to be conducted by authors supported by the beverage industry.[2] Sugared beverages are marketed extensively to
children and adolescents, and in the mid-1990s, children's intake of sugared beverages surpassed that of milk. In the past decade, per capita intake of calories from
sugar-sweetened beverages has increased by nearly 30 percent (see bar graph Daily
Caloric Intake from Sugar-Sweetened Drinks in the United States);[3] beverages now
account for 10 to 15 percent of the calories consumed by children and adolescents.
For each extra can or glass of sugared beverage consumed per day, the likelihood of
a child's becoming obese increases by 60 percent.[4]

DAILY CALORIC INTAKE FROM SUGAR-SWEETENED
DRINKS IN THE UNITED STATES. Data are from
Nielsen and Popkin.[3]

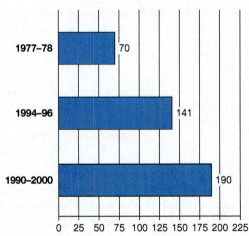

**Daily Caloric Intake from
Sugar-Sweetened Drinks in the U.S.**

*In a *longitudinal* study, researchers observe changes taking place over a long period of time;
in an *interventional* study, investigators give research subjects a measured amount of whatever
is being studied and note its effects; and in a *correlational* study, researchers examine statistics
to see if two or more variables have a mathematically significant similarity. [Editor's note]

Taxes on tobacco products have been highly effective in reducing consumption, 3 and data indicate that higher prices also reduce soda consumption. A review conducted by Yale University's Rudd Center for Food Policy and Obesity suggested that for every 10 percent increase in price, consumption decreases by 7.8 percent. An industry trade publication reported even larger reductions: as prices of carbonated soft drinks increased by 6.8 percent, sales dropped by 7.8 percent, and as Coca-Cola prices increased by 12 percent, sales dropped by 14.6 percent.[5] Such studies — and the economic principles that support their findings — suggest that a tax on sugared beverages would encourage consumers to switch to more healthful beverages, which would lead to reduced caloric intake and less weight gain.

The increasing affordability of soda — and the decreasing affordability of fresh 4 fruits and vegetables (see line graph) — probably contributes to the rise in obesity in the United States. In 2008, a group of child and health care advocates in New York proposed a one-penny-per-ounce excise tax on sugared beverages, which would be expected to reduce consumption by 13 percent — about two servings per week per person. Even if one quarter of the calories consumed from sugared beverages are replaced by other food, the decrease in consumption would lead to an estimated reduction of 8,000 calories per person per year — slightly more than 2 pounds each year for the average person. Such a reduction in calorie consumption would be expected to substantially reduce the risk of obesity and diabetes and may also reduce the risk of heart disease and other conditions.

Some argue that government should not interfere in the market and that products 5 and prices will change as consumers demand more healthful food, but several considerations support government action. The first is externality — costs to parties not

RELATIVE PRICE CHANGES FOR FRESH FRUITS AND VEGETABLES, SUGAR AND SWEETS, AND CARBONATED DRINKS, 1978–2009. Data are from the Bureau of Labor Statistics and represent the U.S. city averages for all urban consumers in January of each year.

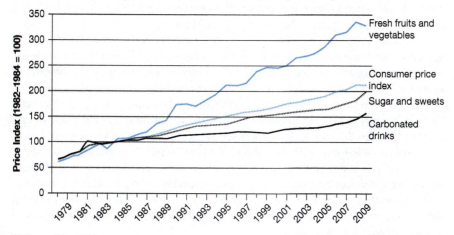

U.S. Bureau of Labor Statistics

directly involved in a transaction. The contribution of unhealthful diets to health care   6
costs is already high and is increasing—an estimated $79 billion is spent annually
for overweight and obesity alone—and approximately half of these costs are paid by
Medicare and Medicaid, at taxpayers' expense. Diet-related diseases also cost society in terms of decreased work productivity, increased absenteeism, poorer school
performance, and reduced fitness on the part of military recruits, among other negative effects. The second consideration is information asymmetry between the parties
to a transaction. In the case of sugared beverages, marketers commonly make health
claims (e.g., that such beverages provide energy or vitamins) and use techniques that
exploit the cognitive vulnerabilities of young children, who often cannot distinguish
a television program from an advertisement. A third consideration is revenue generation, which can further increase the societal benefits of a tax on soft drinks. A penny-
per-ounce excise tax would raise an estimated $1.2 billion in New York State alone.
In times of economic hardship, taxes that both generate this much revenue and promote health are better options than revenue initiatives that may have adverse effects.

Objections have certainly been raised: that such a tax would be regressive, that   7
food taxes are not comparable to tobacco or alcohol taxes because people must eat
to survive, that it is unfair to single out one type of food for taxation, and that the tax
will not solve the obesity problem. But the poor are disproportionately affected by
diet-related diseases and would derive the greatest benefit from reduced consumption;
sugared beverages are not necessary for survival; Americans consume about 250 to
300 more calories daily today than they did several decades ago, and nearly half this
increase is accounted for by consumption of sugared beverages; and though no single
intervention will solve the obesity problem, that is hardly a reason to take no action.

The full impact of public policies becomes apparent only after they take effect.   8
We can estimate changes in sugared-drink consumption that would be prompted by
a tax, but accompanying changes in the consumption of other foods or beverages are
more difficult to predict. One question is whether the proportions of calories consumed in liquid and solid foods would change. And shifts among beverages would
have different effects depending on whether consumers substituted water, milk, diet
drinks, or equivalent generic brands of sugared drinks.

Effects will also vary depending on whether the tax is designed to reduce con-   9
sumption, generate revenue, or both; the size of the tax; whether the revenue is ear-
marked for programs related to nutrition and health; and where in the production
and distribution chain the tax is applied. Given the heavy consumption of sugared
beverages, even small taxes will generate substantial revenue, but only heftier taxes
will significantly reduce consumption. Sales taxes are the most common form of food
tax, but because they are levied as a percentage of the retail price, they encourage
the purchase of less-expensive brands or larger containers. Excise taxes structured as
a fixed cost per ounce provide an incentive to buy less and hence would be much
more effective in reducing consumption and improving health. In addition, manufacturers generally pass the cost of an excise tax along to their customers, including it in
the price consumers see when they are making their selection, whereas sales taxes
are seen only at the cash register.

Although a tax on sugared beverages would have health benefits regardless of 10 how the revenue was used, the popularity of such a proposal increases greatly if revenues are used for programs to prevent childhood obesity, such as media campaigns, facilities and programs for physical activity, and healthier food in schools. Poll results show that support of a tax on sugared beverages ranges from 37 to 72 percent; a poll of New York residents found that 52 percent supported a "soda tax," but the number rose to 72 percent when respondents were told that the revenue would be used for obesity prevention. Perhaps the most defensible approach is to use revenue to subsidize the purchase of healthful foods. The public would then see a relationship between tax and benefit, and any regressive effects would be counteracted by the reduced costs of healthful food.

A penny-per-ounce excise tax could reduce consumption of sugared beverages 11 by more than 10 percent. It is difficult to imagine producing behavior change of this magnitude through education alone, even if government devoted massive resources to the task. In contrast, a sales tax on sugared drinks would generate considerable revenue, and as with the tax on tobacco, it could become a key tool in efforts to improve health.

References

1. Vartanian LR, Schwartz MB, Brownell KD. Effects of soft drink consumption on nutrition and health: a systematic review and meta-analysis. Am J Public Health 2007;97:667–675.
2. Forshee RA, Anderson PA, Storey ML. Sugar-sweetened beverages and body mass index in children and adolescents: a meta-analysis. Am J Clin Nutr 2008;87:1662–71.
3. Nielsen SJ, Popkin BM. Changes in beverage intake between 1977 and 2001. Am J Prev Med 2004;27:205–210.
4. Ludwig DS, Peterson KE, Gortmaker SL. Relation between consumption of sugar-sweetened drinks and childhood obesity: a prospective, observational analysis. Lancet 2001;357:505–508.
5. Elasticity: big price increases cause Coke volume to plummet. Beverage Digest. November 21, 2008:3–4.

READING FOR MEANING

1. **Read to Summarize.** Write a sentence or two briefly summarizing Brownell and Frieden's proposed solution.

2. **Read to Respond.** Write a paragraph analyzing anything that seems surprising, such as: the idea that sports and energy beverages that are sugar-sweetened may not be good for you, perhaps in relation to your own consumption of such drinks; or the assertion that taxes on tobacco products "have been highly effective in reducing consumption" (par. 3), considering how many of your peers have chosen to be smokers or nonsmokers.

For help with reading strategies like summarizing and analyzing assumptions, see Chapter 2.

3. **Read to Analyze Assumptions.** Write a paragraph or two analyzing an assumption you find intriguing in Brownell and Frieden's proposal. For example:

Assumptions about the government's role in solving health problems. Brownell and Frieden explicitly argue in favor of federal and/or state government actions to address public health problems such as those related to obesity and tobacco use.

- Why do Brownell and Frieden assume that government should have a role in influencing people's decisions about their own health? In other words, why is the so-called "obesity epidemic" a public policy problem?

- Imposing taxes is one thing government can do. What other actions could or should the government do to solve public health problems?

Assumptions about research studies. Brownell and Frieden cite a number of research studies, including a "meta-analysis," a study of previous studies.

- Brownell and Frieden explain that the meta-analysis on which they are relying examined studies that took three different approaches — longitudinal, interventional, and correlational — to determine whether there is a cause-effect relationship between consuming sugar-sweetened beverages and obesity (par. 2). Why do Brownell and Frieden assume it is important to take a variety of approaches to a question like this? Do you agree or disagree?

- Brownell and Frieden also call into question studies that arrived at a different "outcome," arguing that these studies "tend to be conducted by authors supported by the beverage industry" (par. 2). Why do Brownell and Frieden assume it matters who funded the research? Should it matter?

READING LIKE A WRITER

Responding to Objections and Alternative Solutions

Proposal writers usually try to respond to readers' likely objections and questions by conceding or refuting them. How writers handle objections and questions affects their credibility with readers, who usually expect writers to be respectful of other points of view and to take criticism seriously, while still arguing assertively for their solution. Brownell and Frieden respond to five possible objections. Notice that even though they devote more space to the first objection, they present all of the objections and their refutations using the same basic sentence pattern:

Transitions
signaling an
opposing point

Some argue that . . . , but . . . (par. 5)

Objections have certainly been raised: that . . . , that . . . , that . . . , and that . . . . But . . . , . . . , and . . . (par. 6)

ANALYZE & WRITE

Write a paragraph or two analyzing and evaluating how Brownell and Frieden respond to possible objections:

1. Reread paragraph 5. First, summarize the objection and Brownell and Frieden's reasons for refuting it. What cues do they provide to signal that an objection is coming and to highlight their reasons? Why do you think they call their reasons "considerations"? How convincing do you think these particular considerations were likely to be for their original *New England Journal of Medicine* audience?

2. Reread paragraph 6, in which the authors respond to four other objections. What cues do they provide to help you follow their argument? What reasons do Brownell and Frieden give to refute these objections? Which refutations, if any, do you think need further elaboration or support?

3. Given their purpose and audience, why do you think Brownell and Frieden focus so much attention on the first objection, but choose to group the other four objections together in a single paragraph?

James Benge

Adapting to the Disappearance of Honeybees

James Benge wrote the following proposal when he was a first-year college student. His interest in science — and his knowledge about the disappearance of honeybees, specifically — led him to consider solutions to this problem. To research the problem and the solutions that other scholars have offered, he consults several scientific studies, which he cites in his essay. Ultimately, though, Benge offers his own solution to the problem, a solution that he believes gets at the root of the problem.

- **Before you read**, consider what you know about honeybees. Are you familiar with their importance to agriculture or that the number of honeybees is decreasing?

- **As you read**, consider who Benge assumes his audience is. Is it laypeople unfamiliar with the subject? Biologists or other scientists knowledgeable about the subject? A combination of the two? How do you know?

Let's talk about honeybees. They're loud, they sting, and they make honey. The end.   1
If only it were that easy. Honeybees are probably the single most important component in almost all of agriculture. To get a grasp of the impact these little guys have, we just need to examine any one foodstuff and follow the trail it leaves. We spin the wheel and land on almonds. Every August, billions of farm-grown honeybees are released into the California Central Valley almond orchards by being deceived that it is springtime. The almonds are exported worldwide, bringing in billions of dollars; the husks are sold as topsoil; and the rest is sold as cattle feed, all thanks to the honeybee (Agnew). An article from *Annals of Botany* states that "70 percent of crops that account for about 35 percent of all agricultural production depend to varying extents on pollinators" (Aizen et al., "How" 1585).

Unfortunately, a disturbing phenomenon is cropping up over the globe that is   2
sending not only farmers but economists into a frenzied panic as this money-making godsend drops dead. Recent studies have shown a severe drop in honeybees around the world, and in the United States alone, losses have increased from "30 to 60 percent on the West Coast" to "as much as 70 percent in parts of the East Coast and Texas" (Sylvers). Scientists are not entirely sure as to what the source of the problem is, but accusations have ranged from "mobile telephones" to "nanotechnology" (Neumann and Carreck 3). Most of these claims have been debunked, and much of the drivel has been weeded out as scientists have narrowed the biggest causes down to three: stress, mites (Bjerga), and disease (Neumann and Carreck).

The scientific community has coined a term for this phenomenon, calling it   3
"colony collapse." The article "Does Infection by *Nosema ceranae* Cause 'Colony

Collapse Disorder' in Honey Bees (*Apis mellifera*)?" presents at least one of the possible scenarios that could cause this problem, and Robert J. Paxton has analyzed and theorized that the pathogen *Nosema ceranae* is "potentially serious on the individual [honeybee] and the colony." He admits that his hypothesis is unlikely to be the main cause of CCD (colony collapse disorder) in North America, but possibly is in Spain. *N. ceranae* are a microsporidia (impossible to detect without a microscope) that infect hives within about eighteen months, in turn leading to colony collapse (Paxton). Climate change is moving this once temperately isolated pathogen to farther regions of the globe. So the problem may not seem as widespread as the next suspect for CCD, but it is worth further observation (Paxton).

Mites pose what could be a more serious cause of CCD. *Varroa destructor*, a mite   4
capable of rendering honeybees flightless, is the second biggest factor of colony collapse. Though not globally ferocious enough to be the leading cause of CCD, they could prove to be the longest-lasting progenitor of this catastrophe. As mentioned in the article "The Almond and the Bee," "Mite treatments only work for a while before the mites reproduce resistant strains, and render the chemicals useless" (Agnew). While pathogens like *N. ceranae* can be eliminated through pesticides, mites are far more adaptive, and need to be handled more locally, as each case of mite-caused CCD could be different.

Unfortunately, *Nosema ceranae* and *Varroa destructor* are just two of many spec-   5
ulated contributors factoring into the cause of CCD. The biggest suspect, by far, is the Israeli acute paralysis virus. The United States Department of Agriculture (citing several studies done on the virus) found that 96.1 percent of hives that suffered from CCD also were found to have been infected with the Israeli virus. They also discovered that the Israeli virus can also be carried by the Varroa mite. Despite the compelling evidence, in a quote from the USDA's cited article "Genetic Survey Finds Association Between CCD and Virus," Jeffery S. Pettis admits that "what we have found is strictly a strong correlation of the appearance of IAPV and CCD together. We have not proven a cause-and-effect connection" (Kaplan).

Let us pretend for a moment that all the honeybees have disappeared from the   6
face of the earth. Disease, a declination of local habitat (Winfree et al.), and millions of years of nonstop work have finally caught up to the honeybees. Without them, the world as mankind knows it teeters on the brink of collapse as orchards can no longer be pollinated, thus leaving no fruits, vegetables, or nuts for people to eat, no husks or shells to supply to farms for food, potentially eliminating both the meat and the dairy departments. Fortunately, that is not something we have to endure (as far as honeybees are concerned), for we have alternatives.

If we wanted to go down the route of flat-out replacing the honeybee, then its rel-   7
atives are the first place to look. *Hymenoptera*, the order name for bees and wasps, along with ants and termites, is the largest order of anything to ever crawl, walk, scuttle, swim, or fly on Earth since day naught. The blue orchard bee, the wild squash bee, and a wild berry pollinator called the *osmia agalia* are seen as the next in line for desperate beekeepers (Bjerga). They are just as reliable, and the diversity would be vital. However, as the exchange rate goes, blue orchard bees, along with most of

the other wild bees, are a more expensive property than the honeybee, even with their own rising price, but that is a short-term wall that could be overcome through proper management.

Bees alone are not the only viable successors that scientists are looking at. Oddly   8 enough, crickets, from a different order entirely, are being examined for their pollination abilities. The discovery is recent, but as *Annals of Botany* shows, a nocturnal and undescribed species of raspy cricket is capable of pollinating orchids (Micheneau et al.). This may seem a little too niche for anyone to care, but there is potential for domestication, expanding its pallet for what it can pollinate. This could take years, and since there is no natural colony mind-set in crickets, there will need to be managerial techniques for managing the crickets as well.

The United States Department of Agriculture started its action plan to combat CCD   9 back in 2007. Enclosed in the document is a scientifically driven, $7.7 million investigation (CCD Steering Comm. 2). The USDA is attacking the heavyweight causes head-on, despite the proposed causes being simply correlative at the moment. Under "Topic 4: Mitigative and Preventative Measures," several immediately accessible and financially reasonable solutions are presented to fight these known causes, such as high concentrations of ozone sprayed into hibernating beehives during winter to kill pathogens and pesticides, localizing honeybees to reduce stress, and studying local bumblebees, due to their similar ancestry, to determine local causes for CCD (CCD Steering Comm. 22).

These are well-reasoned and intelligent solutions to the disappearance of the hon-   10 eybees, but it is hiding the real problem at hand, and that is the homogeny of the pollinator industry. Honeybees are not going to be around forever, yet the agricultural industry is becoming more dependent on pollinators every year. Since 1961, the American honeybee hive has been in decline by about 1.79 percent per year even before the outbreak of CCD (Aizen et al., "Long-Term" 1573). The only viable solution for beekeepers and other farmers dependent on the honeybee is to expand resources to cover multiple species of bees, as well as other pollinators. If the true cause of CCD does lie somewhere with the Varroa mite, the Israeli virus, or stress, the honeybee's salvation will not come overnight, if it even comes at all, and while the USDA's proposal can help preserve currently living honeybees, diversity is the key to the survival of the industry.

Works Cited

Agnew, Singeli. "The Almond and the Bee." *The San Francisco Chronicle,* 14 Oct. 2007. United States Department of Agriculture National Agricultural Library, www.nal.usda .gov.

Aizen, Marcelo A., et al. "How Much Does Agriculture Depend on Pollinators? Lessons from Long-Term Trends in Crop Production." *Annals of Botany,* vol. 103, no. 9, 2009, pp. 1579–88, doi:10.1093/aob/mcp076.

—————. "Long-Term Global Trends in Crop Yield and Production Reveal No Current Pollination Shortage but Increasing Pollinator Dependency." *Current Biology,* vol. 18, no. 20, 2008, pp. 1572–75, doi:10.1016/j.cub.2008.08.066.

Bjerga, Alan. "Blue Orchard Bees Find Favor in Colony Collapse Disorder Peril." *Bloomburg.com*, 19 Oct. 2007. United States Department of Agriculture National Agricultural Library, www.nal.usda.gov.

CCD Steering Committee. *Colony Collapse Disorder Action Plan*. United States Department of Agriculture, 20 June 2007, www.ars.usda.gov/is/br/ccd/ccd_actionplan.pdf.

Kaplan, Kim. "Genetic Survey Finds Association Between CCD and Virus." United States Department of Agriculture National Agricultural Library, 6 Sept. 2007, www.nal.usda.gov.

Micheneau, Claire, et al. "Orthoptera, a New Order of Pollinator." *Annals of Botany*, vol. 105, no. 3, 2010, pp. 335-64, doi:10.1093/aob/mcp299.

Neumann, Peter, and Norman L. Carreck. "Honey Bee Colony Losses." *Journal of Apicultural Research*, vol. 49, no. 1, 2010, pp. 1-6, doi:10.3896/IBRA.1.49.1.01.

Paxton, Robert J. "Does Infection by *Nosema ceranae* Cause 'Colony Collapse Disorder' in Honey Bees (*Apis mellifera*)?" *Journal of Apicultural Research*, vol. 49, no. 1, 2010, pp. 80-84, doi:10.3896/IBRA.1.49.1.11.

Sylvers, Eric. "Case of the Disappearing Bees Creates a Buzz." *The New York Times*, 22 Apr. 2007. United States Department of Agriculture National Agricultural Library, www.nal.usda.gov.

Winfree, Rachel, et al. "A Meta-Analysis of Bees' Responses to Anthropogenic Disturbance." *Ecology*, vol. 90, no. 8, 2009, pp. 2068-76, doi:10.1890/08-1245.1.

READING FOR MEANING

1. **Read to Summarize.** Write a sentence or two summarizing Benge's proposed solution and why he believes it is a better solution than the alternatives he describes.

   For help with reading strategies like summarizing and analyzing assumptions, see Chapter 2.

2. **Read to Respond.** Write a paragraph analyzing anything that surprises you, such as Benge's argument that "honeybees are probably the single most important component in all of agriculture" (par. 1) or that "crickets are being examined for their pollination abilities" (par. 9).

3. **Read to Analyze Assumptions.** Write a paragraph or two analyzing an assumption you find intriguing in Benge's essay. For example:

   Assumptions about laypeople's interest in science. About the potential uses of crickets, Benge writes, "This may seem a little too niche for anyone to care but there is potential for domestication, expanding its pallet for what it can pollinate" (par. 9).

   - Do you agree that considering crickets as a successor to honeybees is likely not of interest to laypeople? Does this assumption accurately represent your level of interest in this subject?

   - Where does Benge make other assumptions about the degree of interest that laypeople may have in the disappearance of honeybees? Are these assumptions revealed through the content of his essay, his tone, or other elements of the essay? Explain your answer.

Assumptions about the right way to solve the honeybee problem. Benge claims in his conclusion: "These are well-reasoned and intelligent solutions to the disappearance of the honeybees, but they are hiding the real problem, and that is the homogeny of the pollinator industry" (par. 10).

- Benge concedes that the solutions he has reviewed in his essay are viable, but argues that his solution actually addresses the underlying problem and is, therefore, the best solution. Does he provide enough detail about his solution and why it is better to convince you of this?

- Do you think there is a single "right way"— or at least, a best way— to address any problem? What kind of problems lend themselves to a single, best way? What kinds of problems may have multiple, equally valid solutions?

READING LIKE A WRITER

Responding to Objections and Alternative Solutions

It is important for proposal writers to anticipate readers' objections to their argument, as well as to alternative solutions. If writers ignore possible objections or alternative solutions they run the risk of seeming close-minded. Refusing to address these may also give the impression that the writer doesn't fully understand the issue or that the argument cannot withstand criticism.

Concession	These are well-reasoned and intelligent solutions to the disappear-
Refutation	ance of the honeybees, but they are hiding the real problem, and that is the homogeny of the pollinator industry (par. 10).

ANALYZE & WRITE

Write a paragraph analyzing and evaluating Benge's use of concession and refutation in his final paragraph.

1. First, reread paragraph 10 and highlight Benge's description of the other solutions. What words does he use to describe these solutions?

2. Then identify Benge's refutation and explain why he says these solutions are not good enough.

3. Finally, evaluate how well Benge describes his own solution in relation to the other solutions. Why and how is it different? Is there any additional information you need about his solution to believe that it is superior to the others?

Writing to Learn Proposals

Write a brief essay analyzing one of the readings in this chapter (or another selection, perhaps one by a classmate). Explain how (and, perhaps, how well) the selection works as a proposal to solve a problem. Consider, for example, how it

- identifies an existing problem and demonstrates its seriousness;

- proposes a solution and shows that it would help solve the problem and is feasible — not too costly or time-consuming;

- anticipates and responds to likely objections to the proposed solution as well as any alternative solutions readers might prefer;

- is organized clearly and logically, making it easy for readers to follow the argument.

Your essay could also reflect on how you applied one or more of the following practices as you read the selection:

- **Critical Analysis** — what assumptions in the selection did you find intriguing, and why?

- **Rhetorical Sensitivity** — how effective or ineffective do you think the selection is in achieving its purpose for the intended audience?

- **Empathy** — did you find yourself identifying with the author, and how important was this to the effectiveness of the selection?

A GUIDE TO WRITING PROPOSALS

You have probably done a good deal of analytical writing about your reading. Your instructor may also assign a capstone project to write a brief proposal of your own. This Guide to Writing offers detailed suggestions and resources to help you meet the special challenges this kind of writing presents.

THE WRITING ASSIGNMENT

Develop a project proposing a solution to a problem.

- Choose a problem affecting a community or group to which you belong.
- Research the problem and possible solutions.
- Decide how to present the problem so that readers see it exists and is serious.
- Find a solution that would help solve the problem and could be implemented without being too costly or time consuming.
- Address likely objections to your proposed solution as well as any alternative solutions readers might prefer.
- Organize the proposal in a way that is clear, logical, and convincing.

WRITING YOUR DRAFT

Choosing a Problem

Rather than limiting yourself to the first subject that comes to mind, take a few minutes to consider your options and list as many problems as you can. When choosing a subject, keep in mind that the problem must be

- important to you and of concern to others;
- solvable, at least in part;
- one that you know a good deal about or can research in the time you have.

Choosing a problem affecting a group to which you belong (for example, as a classmate, teammate, participant in an online game site, or garage band member) or a place you have worked (a coffee shop, community pool, or radio station) gives you an advantage: You can write as an expert. You know the history of the problem, you know who to interview, and perhaps you have already thought about possible solutions. Moreover, you know who to address and how to persuade that audience to take action on your proposed solution.

If you already have a problem and possible solution(s) in mind, skip this activity. If you need to find a problem, making a chart like the one below can help you get started exploring creative solutions to real-life problems related to your school, community, or workplace.

	Problems	**Possible Solutions**
School	Can't get into required courses	• Make them large lecture courses. • Make them online or hybrid courses. • Give priority to majors.
Community	No safe place for children to play	• Use school yards for after-school sports. • Get high-school students or senior citizens to tutor kids. • Make pocket parks for neighborhood play. • Offer programs for kids at branch libraries.
Work	Inadequate training for new staff	• Make a training video or website. • Assign experienced workers to mentor trainees (for bonus pay).

Developing Your Proposal

The writing and research activities that follow will enable you to test your problem and develop an argument supporting your proposed solution.

Analyzing the Problem   Spend a few minutes thinking about what you and your readers know about the problem and how you can convince your readers that the problem you have identified is real and needs to be solved.

Brainstorm a List   Spend ten minutes listing everything you know about the problem. Write quickly, leaving judgment aside for the moment. After the ten minutes are up, you can review your list and highlight or star the most promising information.

Use Cubing   Probe the problem from a variety of perspectives:

- Describe the problem.
- Compare the problem to other, similar problems, or contrast it with other, related problems.

- Identify causes of the problem. (Consider immediate and deeper causes.)

- Consider the consequences of the problem. (Think about both short-term and long-term consequences.)

- Connect the problem to other problems in your experience.

- Analyze the problem to identify those most affected by it or any who benefit from it.

- Apply the problem to a real-life situation.

Prove the Problem's Existence and Seriousness   Use the sentence strategies below as a jumping-off point for demonstrating the existence and seriousness of the problem.

Give an example to make the problem specific

▶ Recently, ... has been [in the news / in movies / a political issue] because of .... [name event].

▶ *Example:* The neuronal circuit that underlies the brain's ability to read is subtly, rapidly changing — a change with implications for everyone from the pre-reading toddler to the expert adult (Wolf, par. 1).

Use a scenario or anecdote to dramatize the problem

▶ Many decades ago, in [name of place], a small rural community not unlike many others across the country, farmers started to see .... [their wages grow, their crops disappear, their land lose value].

▶ *Example:* Once upon a time in a faraway land — the United States following World War II — workers reaped what they sowed. From 1947 through 1973, their income rose in lockstep with increases in productivity (Meyerson, par. 1).

Cite statistics to show the severity of the problem

▶ It has recently been reported that .... percent of .... [name group] are .... [specify problem].

▶ *Example:* As economists Robert Gordon and Ian Dew-Becker have established, the gains in workers' productivity for the past three decades have gone entirely to the wealthiest 10 percent (Meyerson, par. 1).

Describe the problem's consequences

▶ According to .... [name expert / study], ... [state problem] is affecting .... [name affected group]: .... [insert quote from expert].

▶ *Example:* As Piper notes, human beings need a knowledge of where they are in time and space that allows them to return to things and learn from re-examination — what he calls the "technology of recurrence" (Wolf, para. 8).

Show why readers should care about solving the problem

▶ We're all in this together. .... is not a win-lose proposition. If .... [name group] loses, we all lose.

▶ If we don't try to solve ...., no one else will.

▶ Doing nothing will only make .... worse.

▶ We have a moral responsibility to do something about ....

Considering Your Readers   With your understanding of the problem in mind, write for a few minutes to bring your intended readers into focus. Will you be writing to all members of your group or to only some of them (a committee that might supervise or evaluate the group, an individual in a position of authority)? Briefly justify your choice of readers.

Now gauge the impact of the problem on your readers and the attitudes they hold. How might these attitudes inform the solutions they are likely to prefer?

Freewriting   Write without stopping for five or ten minutes about the problem's direct or indirect impact on your readers. Don't stop to reflect or consider; if you hit a roadblock, just keep coming back to the topic or raise questions you could research later. At the end of the specified time, review your writing and highlight or underline promising ideas.

Considering Values   Comment on the values and attitudes of your readers and how they have responded to similar problems in the past. Use these sentence strategies as a jumping-off point:

▶ Some of my readers think .... is .... [someone else's responsibility / not that big a problem].

▶ Others see .... as a matter of .... [fairness / human decency].

▶ Many complain about .... but do nothing because solving it seems [too hard / too costly].

Finding a Tentative Solution   List at least three possible solutions to the problem. You may want to consider using the following approaches to start:

Adapt a solution that has been tried or proposed for a similar problem

▶ *Example:* Wolf notes that "there's an old rule in neuroscience that does not alter with age: use it or lose it.... We possess both the science and the technology to identify and redress the changes in how we read before they become entrenched" (par. 11).

Focus on eliminating a cause or minimizing an effect of the problem

▶ *Example:* Benge's solution to minimize the negative effects of disappearing honeybees involves expanding and diversifying the pollinator industry.

See the problem as part of a larger system, and explore solutions to the system

▶ *Example:* Meyerson argues that because the problem stems from "the redistribution of income from labor to capital," any solution must help redress the imbalance (par. 3).

Focus on solving a small part of the problem

▶ *Example:* Brownell and Frieden's solution to obesity is to reduce the consumption of sugared beverages through taxation.

Look at the problem from different points of view

▶ *Example:* Consider what students, teachers, parents, or administrators might think could be done to help solve the problem.

Think of a specific example of the problem, and consider how you could solve it

▶ *Example:* Benge could have focused on solving the problem of disappearing honeybees in one particular region of the United States.

Researching Your Proposal   In exploring the problem and considering possible solutions, you may have identified questions you need to research. Doing research with your questions and notes in mind will help you work efficiently. But recognize that you might also find contradictory evidence that leads you to rethink your ideas.

If you are proposing a solution to a problem about which others have written, use the research strategies below to help you find out what solutions others have proposed or tried. You may also use these strategies to find out how others have defined the problem and demonstrated its seriousness.

• Enter keywords or phrases related to your solution (or problem) into the search box of an all-purpose database such as *Academic One File* (Gale) or *Academic Search Complete* (EBSCOHost) to find relevant articles in magazines and journals; a database like *LexisNexis* to find articles in newspapers; or library catalogs to find books and other resources. (Database names may change, and what is available will differ from school to school. Some libraries may even combine all three into one search link on the library's home page. Ask a librarian if you need help.) James Benge could have tried a combination of keywords, such as *colony collapse* and *pollinators*, or a variation on his terms (*honeybee crisis*) to find relevant articles.

- *Bookmark* or keep a record of the URLs of promising sites, and download or copy information you could use in your essay. When available, download PDF files rather than HTML files because PDFs are likely to include visuals such as graphs and charts. If you copy and paste relevant information from sources into your notes, be careful to distinguish carefully between all material from sources and your own ideas. Remember to record source information with care and to cite and document any sources you use, including visuals and interviews.

Supporting Your Solution   Write down plausible reasons why your solution should be heard or tried. Then review your list and highlight the strongest reasons, the ones most likely to persuade your readers. Write for a few minutes about the single most convincing reason. The sentence strategies below can help you explain how your solution could help solve the problem:

To learn more about finding information, avoiding plagiarism, or documenting sources, see Chapter 12.

It would eliminate a cause of the problem

▶ Research by .... shows it would reduce ....

It has worked elsewhere

▶ It works in ...., ..., and ...., as studies evaluating it by .... and .... show.

It would change people's behavior

▶ .... would [discourage / encourage] people to ....

Anticipating Readers' Objections   Write a few sentences defending your solution against each of the following predictable objections:

- It won't really solve the problem.
- I'm comfortable with things as they are.
- We can't afford it.
- It will take too long.
- People won't do it.
- Too few people will benefit.

- It's already been tried, with unsatisfactory results.
- You're making this proposal because it will benefit you personally.

For your proposal to succeed, readers must be convinced to take the solution seriously. Try to imagine how your prospective readers will respond.

Responding to Alternative Solutions   Identify two or three other solutions that your readers may prefer. Choose the one that poses the most serious challenge to your proposed solution. Then write a few sentences comparing your solution with the alternative one, weighing the strengths and weaknesses of each. Explain how you might demonstrate to readers that your solution has more advantages and fewer disadvantages than the alternative. (You may need to conduct additional research to respond to alternative solutions.)

Formulating a Working Thesis   A working thesis will keep you focused as you draft and revise your essay. The thesis statement in a proposal should offer the solution and may also identify the problem. Particularly complex problems may require complex solutions. Notice in the examples below that both writers offer multi-pronged proposals that act as their thesis statements.

1. Create four-year degree programs in football and basketball.
2. Extend the time limit on athletic scholarships by two years.
3. Allow a competitive marketplace to determine the compensation of college athletes (Shughart II, pars. 4–15).

1. Legislate wage hikes in states and cities.
2. Link corporate tax rates to worker productivity increases and CEO-employee pay ratios.
3. Make corporations responsible for all their workers.
4. Raise taxes on capital income and redistribute it to labor (Meyerson, pars. 7–17).

As you draft your own thesis statement, consider whether breaking it out into parts as in the examples above will help you convey to your reader the complexities of both the problem you have detailed and the solution(s) you propose. Although you will probably refine your thesis statement as you draft and revise your essay, trying now to articulate it will help give your planning and drafting direction and impetus.

Working with Sources

Citing Statistics to Establish the Problem's Existence and Seriousness   Statistics can be helpful in establishing that a problem exists and is serious. Kelly Brownell and Thomas Frieden use statistics for this purpose. Note that Brownell and Frieden present some of their statistics in the form of graphs. To define the problem, writers often use statistics in the form of percentages (underlined in the first example) or numbers (boldface in the second example).

> ... beverages now account for <u>10 to 15 percent</u> of the calories consumed by children and adolescents (Brownell and Frieden, par. 2).

Percentages can seem quite impressive, but sometimes, without the raw numbers, readers may not appreciate just how remarkable the percentages really are. In the following example, Wong uses raw numbers towards the end of her argument to make a rhetorical point and show how little effort accommodation would be for restaurants:

> If cafes can offer **four types of milk** for espresso drinks and restaurants **50 types of wine and beer**, small businesses and large corporations can manage offering two types of straws (Wong, par 13).

For statistics to be persuasive, they must be from sources that readers consider reliable. Researchers' trustworthiness, in turn, depends on their credentials as experts in the field they are investigating and also on the degree to which they are disinterested, or free from bias. Brownell and Frieden rely on their own expertise in the fields of psychology and public health, respectively, and also cite statistics from authoritative studies and sources.

To find statistics relating to the problem (or possible solution) you are writing about, explore the state, local, or tribal sections of www.usa.gov, the U.S. government's official Web portal, or visit the Library of Congress page State Government Information and follow the links. In particular, visit the U.S. Census Bureau's website, which offers reliable statistics on a wide variety of issues.

For more on finding relevant sources of information, see Chapter 12, pp. 591–598.

Including Visuals and Other Media

Think about whether visuals — drawings, photographs, tables, or graphs — would strengthen your proposal. Notice the graphs Brownell and Frieden include in their proposal (pp. 488–489). Each graph has a heading and a caption that indicates where the data comes from. Brownell and Frieden apparently created the graphs themselves.

For help with proper citation for visuals, see Chapter 12, pp. 640–642.

Consider constructing your own visuals, scanning materials from books and magazines, or downloading them from the Internet. If you submit your essay electronically to other students and your instructor or if you post it on a website, you might consider including video and audio clips as well as still images. Be sure to obtain permission, as we did, if your proposal will be read outside your classroom.

Organizing Your Proposal Effectively for Your Readers

The basic parts of a proposal argument are quite simple:

1. the problem
2. the solution
3. the reasons in support of the solution
4. a response to objections or alternative solutions readers might propose

This simple plan is nearly always complicated by other factors, however. In outlining your material, you must take into consideration many other details, such as whether readers already recognize the problem, how much agreement exists on the need to solve the problem, how much attention should be given to alternative solutions, and how many objections and questions by readers should be expected. If you are writing primarily for readers who acknowledge that the problem exists and are open to your solution, you might begin with a brief introduction that ends with your thesis statement and conclude by urging your readers to action. If you are writing primarily for readers who do not recognize the problem or are likely to prefer alternative solutions, however, you may need to begin by establishing common ground and acknowledging alternative ways readers may see the problem, and then concede the strengths of alternative solutions before launching fully into your own proposal; you may want to conclude by reiterating the values you share with your readers.

Drafting Your Proposal

By this point, you have done a lot of writing

- to focus and define a problem, and develop a solution to it;
- to support your solution with reasons and evidence your readers will find persuasive;
- to refute or concede objections and alternative solutions;
- to organize your ideas to make them clear, logical, and effective for readers.

Now stitch that material together to create a draft. The next two parts of this Guide to Writing will help you evaluate and improve it.

REVIEWING AND IMPROVING THE DRAFT

This section includes guides for Peer Review and Troubleshooting Your Draft. Your instructor may arrange a peer review in class or online where you can exchange drafts with a classmate. The Peer Review Guide will help you give each other constructive feedback regarding the basic features and strategies typical of proposal writing. (If you want to make specific suggestions for improving the draft, see Troubleshooting Your Draft on p. 510.) Also, be sure to respond to any specific concerns the writer has raised about the draft. The Troubleshooting Your Draft guide that follows will help you reread your own draft with a critical eye, sort through any feedback you've received, and consider a variety of ways to improve your draft.

A PEER REVIEW GUIDE

How effective is the presentation of the problem?

What's Working Well: Let the writer know where the problem is especially well presented—for example, where statistics, examples, or other details help readers grasp the seriousness of the problem, or where visuals such as graphs or photographs impress upon readers the need to solve the problem.

What Needs Improvement: Indicate one passage where the presentation of the problem could be improved—for example, where the effects of the problem could be made vivid, where the problem's urgency could be better emphasized, or where the problem's future impact could be shown.

How convincing is the argument supporting the proposed solution?

What's Working Well: Indicate a passage where the argument is well done—for example, where a similar solution has been shown to work effectively, where steps for implementing the solution are set out clearly, or where the costs are shown to be reasonable.

What Needs Improvement: Identify a passage where the argument could be improved—for example, where additional examples, facts, statistics, or research studies could be used to demonstrate that the solution is feasible, cost-effective, and would indeed help to solve the problem.

How effective is the writer's response to objections and alternative solutions?

What's Working Well: Identify a passage where the writer responds effectively—for example, refuting an objection to the proposed solution with concrete evidence or recognized authorities, showing that an alternative solution would have negative side effects, or comparing the feasibility of the proposed solution to an alternative that readers may favor.

What Needs Improvement: Tell the writer where a response is needed or could be more effective—for example, where a valid objection to the proposed solution could be conceded or an invalid objection refuted, or where an alternative solution could be shown to take more time and be more costly than the proposed solution.

How clear and logical is the organization?

What's Working Well: Mark any parts of the essay that seem notably well organized—for example, where the thesis statement clearly identifies the proposed solution, where topic sentences identify the main points, or where logical transitions make the argument easy to follow.

What Needs Improvement: Identify any aspect of the organization that needs improvement—for example, where the thesis could be introduced earlier, where topic sentences could be clearer, or where logical transitions could be added.

Revising Your Draft

Revising means reenvisioning your draft — seeing it in a new way, given your purpose audience, as well as the feedback from the peer review. Don't hesitate to cut unconvincing material, add new material, and move passages around. The following chart may help you strengthen your proposal.

TROUBLESHOOTING YOUR DRAFT

To Introduce the Problem More Effectively	
If readers doubt that the problem exists or that it is very serious,	• Discuss the problem's history or describe its effects on real people. • Add information—statistics, examples, studies, and so on—that your audience is likely to find persuasive or that they can relate to. • Consider adding visuals, such as graphs, tables, or charts, if these would help clarify the problem for your audience.

To Strengthen the Support for the Proposed Solution	
If the solution being proposed is not clear,	• Describe the solution in more detail. • Outline the steps of its implementation. • Add a visual illustrating the solution.
If readers are not convinced that the proposed solution would solve the problem,	• Explain how the solution addresses specific aspects of the problem. • Point out where else a similar solution has worked. • Cite experts or research studies.
To Improve the Response to Objections and Alternative Solutions	
If objections to the solution have not been adequately addressed,	• Acknowledge valid objections and modify your solution to concede them. • Refute invalid objections by presenting reasons and supporting evidence.
If alternative solutions preferred by readers have not been adequately addressed,	• Address alternative solutions directly, acknowledging their strengths as well as their weaknesses. • Try to show why your solution is preferable—for example, it is easier to implement, costs less, takes less time, has fewer negative side effects, and would garner more support.
To Make the Organizational Plan More Effective	
If the essay is hard to follow,	• Mark each part of the proposal more clearly with explicit topic sentences and transitions or headings. • Add a forecasting statement.

Editing and Proofreading Your Draft

Check for errors in usage, punctuation, and mechanics, and consider matters of style. If you keep a list of errors you typically make, begin by checking your draft against this list.

From our research on student writing, we know that proposal writers tend to refer to the problem or solution by using the pronoun *this* or *that* ambiguously. Edit carefully any sentences with *this* or *that* to ensure that a noun immediately follows the pronoun to make the reference clear. Check a writer's handbook for help with this potential problem.

Reflecting on Proposals to Solve a Problem

In this chapter, you have critically read several proposals and have written one of your own. To better remember what you have learned, pause now to reflect on the reading and writing activities you completed in this chapter.

1. Write a page or so reflecting on what you have learned. Begin by describing what you are most pleased with in your essay. Then explain what you think contributed to your achievement.

   - If it was something you learned from the readings, indicate which readings and specifically what you learned from them.

   - If you got good advice from a critical reader, explain exactly how the person helped you — perhaps by helping you understand a problem in your draft or by helping you add a new dimension to your writing.

2. Reflect more generally on proposals, a genre of writing that plays an important role in our society. Consider some of the following questions:

   - How confident do you feel about making a proposal that might lead to improvements in the functioning of a group or community? Does your proposal attempt to bring about fundamental or minor change in the group?

   - Whose interest would be served by the solution you propose? Who else might be affected? In what ways does your proposal challenge the status quo in the group?

   - What contribution might essays proposing solutions to problems make to our society that other genres of writing cannot make?

3. By reflecting on what you have learned about writing proposals to solve problems, you have been practicing **metacognition,** one of the academic habits of mind.

   - Were you aware of any other habits of mind you practiced as you read and responded to the material in this chapter? If so, which habits did you find useful?

   - If not, think back now on your reading and writing processes. Can you identify any habits you practiced?

CHAPTER 11

Multi-Genre Writing:
Pulling It All Together

S o far, each chapter in this textbook has focused on a specific genre, or type, of writing, from autobiography and evaluation to arguing for a position and speculating about causes or effects. Unlike the others, though, this chapter demonstrates how writing often fits into multiple genres simultaneously. For example, a proposal to solve a problem might include an evaluation of possible solutions as well as a story from the writer's life (autobiography) that shows why finding a solution is crucial. In fact, Chapter 5 on reflective writing describes the genre of reflection as incorporating elements of autobiographical and observational writing. If you have read the selections in that chapter, you are already familiar with multi-genre writing. As you read this chapter's selections, notice how the writers draw on features from across genres to persuade, inspire, or entertain readers. Then use what you've learned from the genre-specific writing you've already done to create a compelling multi-genre composition of your own.

RHETORICAL SITUATIONS FOR MULTI-GENRE WRITING

You may think that multi-genre writing is rare, but all kinds of writers from bloggers to journalists to scholars draw on multiple genres to strengthen their writing and meet their goals, as the following examples suggest:

- A blogger writes a reflective blog post on the relationship her spouse developed with her dysfunctional family. She presents several occasions that describe his encounters with various members of her family and uses features from the autobiographical genre to narrate these encounters and vividly present the people in them. Drawing on the features of observational writing, the blogger moves between the roles of spectator and participant as she conveys her perspective on the subject.

- A community activist fights to preserve a neighborhood park from development by writing a proposal for the town council that begins by demonstrating that the problem exists and is serious, goes on to narrate the importance of the park to his own life, speculates about problems that eliminating the park may cause, evaluates other locations in the neighborhood for the proposed development, and concludes with an analysis of the feasibility of an alternative location.

- For a geology class, a student writes a research paper on the scientific concept of deep time. She uses features of the concept explanation genre to define and illustrate the concept and to integrate sources smoothly. She also draws on the genre of position arguments to assert her thesis that understanding deep time is especially important to understanding climate change, as well as to respond to objections and alternative positions fairly and credibly.

Thinking about Multi-Genre Writing

Write a paragraph or two about an occasion when you encountered multi-genre writing.

- Who was the *audience*? Consider how communicating to the particular audience (such as a friend rather than a teacher, or a group of your peers rather than a gathering of their parents) shaped the piece of writing. How was the tone tailored to appeal to them — informal, perhaps, for friends, more formal for parents or teachers?

- What was the main *purpose*? Did one of the genres seem more prevalent than others and, perhaps, dictate the piece's main purpose?

- How would you rate the *rhetorical sensitivity* with which the argument was presented? What made it appropriate or inappropriate for its particular audience or purpose?

A GUIDE TO READING MULTI-GENRE ESSAYS

This guide introduces you to multi-genre writing by inviting you to analyze an essay on health care by Atul Gawande that uses the primary genre of explaining concepts while also drawing on features from observational writing and position arguments. You may notice features from other genres in Gawande's essay, too. This is because genres are essentially a way of categorizing texts in order to understand their composition and purpose. The three genres used to discuss Gawande's essay are simply those we want to highlight in the activities and prompts for this reading.

- Unlike previous Guides to Reading, Gawande's essay is not annotated. We encourage you to annotate it yourself, practicing academic habits of mind such as curiosity, openness, and persistence in order to engage with and understand this complex multi-genre reading.

- *Reading for meaning* will help you understand how Gawande uses features from these three genres to define the concept of incremental care, convey his perspective on the subject, and to argue his position about the importance of incremental care.

- *Reading like a writer* will help you recognize which features of each genre are represented and consider how the writer combines these features to create a complex, compelling piece of writing.

The following strategies are typical of concept explanations:

For more on concept explanations, see Chapter 6.

1. Using appropriate writing strategies: defining, illustrating, comparing and contrasting, and showing causes and effects
2. Organizing the information clearly and logically
3. Integrating sources smoothly
4. Engaging readers' interest

The following strategies are typical of observational writing:

For more on observational writing, see Chapter 4.

1. Deciding whether to take the role of a spectator or a participant
2. Determining what information to include and how to present it
3. Organizing the information in a way that will be entertaining to readers
4. Conveying a perspective on the subject

The following strategies are typical of position arguments:

For more on position arguments, see Chapter 8.

1. Presenting the controversial issue fairly and credibly
2. Asserting a clear position
3. Arguing directly for it with reasonable evidence
4. Responding to objections and alternative positions fairly

Atul Gawande

The Heroism of Incremental Care

Atul Gawande (b. 1965) is a surgeon at Brigham and Women's Hospital in Boston, MA, and a professor in the Department of Health Policy and Management at the Harvard T. H. Chan School of Public Health and Harvard Medical School. He is also CEO of a nonprofit company, a joint venture among J. P. Morgan, Amazon, and Berkshire Hathaway, that seeks to lower health care costs for their employees. Gawande has written for *The New Yorker*, published four *New York Times* bestselling books, and has won several awards for his writing and research, including a MacArthur Fellowship. The essay below was published in *The New Yorker* in 2017.

▶ Genres: *Explaining Concepts, Observation, Arguing for a Position*

- **Before you read,** think about how you view doctors. Do you see them as heroes, everyday people, or have you not thought much about their status? Has a doctor ever changed your life or the life of a friend or family member?

- **As you read,** consider why Gawande sets the scene of his visit with Haynes with such specificity in paragraphs 21–24.

By 2010, Bill Haynes had spent almost four decades under attack from the inside of 1 his skull. He was fifty-seven years old, and he suffered from severe migraines that felt as if a drill were working behind his eyes, across his forehead, and down the back of his head and neck. They left him nauseated, causing him to vomit every half hour for up to eighteen hours. He'd spend a day and a half in bed, and then another day stumbling through sentences. The pain would gradually subside, but often not entirely. And after a few days a new attack would begin.

Haynes (I've changed his name, at his request) had his first migraine at the age 2 of nineteen. It came on suddenly, while he was driving. He pulled over, opened the door, and threw up in someone's yard. At first, the attacks were infrequent and lasted only a few hours. But by the time he was thirty, married, and working in construction management in London, where his family was from, they were coming weekly, usually on the weekends. A few years later, he began to get the attacks at work as well.

He saw all kinds of doctors—primary-care physicians, neurologists, psychia- 3 trists—who told him what he already knew: he had chronic migraine headaches. And what little the doctors had to offer didn't do him much good. Headaches rank among the most common reasons for doctor visits worldwide. A small number are due to secondary causes, such as a brain tumor, cerebral aneurysm, head injury, or infection. Most are tension headaches—diffuse, muscle-related head pain with a tightening, non-pulsating quality—that generally respond to analgesics, sleep, neck exercises, and time. Migraines afflict about ten per cent of people with headaches, but a much larger percentage of those who see doctors, because migraines are difficult to control.

Migraines are typically characterized by severe, disabling, recurrent attacks of 4 pain confined to one side of the head, pulsating in quality and aggravated by routine physical activities. They can last for hours or days. Nausea and sensitivity to light or sound are common. They can be associated with an aura—visual distortions, sensory changes, or even speech and language disturbances that herald the onset of head pain.

Although the cause of migraines remains unknown, a number of treatments have   5
been discovered that can either reduce their occurrence or alleviate them once they
occur. Haynes tried them all. His wife also took him to a dentist who fitted him with
a mouth guard. After seeing an advertisement, she got him an electrical device that
he applied to his face for half an hour every day. She bought him hypnotism tapes,
high-dosage vitamins, magnesium tablets, and herbal treatments. He tried everything
enthusiastically, and occasionally a remedy would help for a brief period, but nothing made a lasting difference.

Finally, desperate for a change, he and his wife quit their jobs, rented out their   6
house in London, and moved to a cottage in a rural village. The attacks eased for a
few months. A local doctor who had migraines himself suggested that Haynes try the
cocktail of medicines he used. That helped some, but the attacks continued. Haynes
seesawed between good periods and bad. And without work he and his wife began
to feel that they were vegetating.

On a trip to New York City, when he turned fifty, they decided they needed to   7
make another big change. They sold everything and bought a bed-and-breakfast on
Cape Cod. Their business thrived, but by the summer of 2010, when Haynes was in
his late fifties, the headaches were, he said, "knocking me down like they never had
before." Doctors had told him that migraines diminish with age, but his stubbornly
refused to do so. "During one of these attacks, I worked out that I'd spent two years
in bed with a hot-water bottle around my head, and I began thinking about how to
take my life," he said. He had a new internist, though, and she recommended that
he go to a Boston clinic that was dedicated to the treatment of headaches. He was
willing to give it a try. But he wasn't hopeful. How would a doctor there do anything
different from all the others he'd seen?

That question interested me, too. I work at the hospital where the clinic is based.   8
The John Graham Headache Center, as it's called, has long had a reputation for
helping people with especially difficult cases. Founded in the nineteen-fifties, it
now delivers more than eight thousand consultations a year at several locations
across eastern Massachusetts. Two years ago, I asked Elizabeth Loder, who's in
charge of the program, if I could join her at the clinic to see how she and her colleagues helped people whose problems had stumped so many others. I accompanied her for a day of patient visits, and that was when I met Haynes, who had been
her patient for five years. I asked her whether he was the worst case she'd seen. He
wasn't even the worst case she'd seen that week, she said. She estimated that sixty
per cent of the clinic's patients suffer from daily, persistent headaches, and usually
have for years.

In her examination room, with its white vinyl floor and sanitary-paper-covered   9
examination table against the wall, the fluorescent overhead lights were turned off
to avoid triggering migraines. The sole illumination came from a low-wattage table
lamp and a desktop-computer screen. Sitting across from her first patient of the day,
Loder, who is fifty-eight, was attentive and unhurried, dressed in plain black slacks
and a freshly pressed white doctor's coat, her auburn hair tucked into a bun. She projected both professional confidence and maternal concern. She had told me how she

begins with new patients: "You ask them to tell the story of their headache and then you stay very quiet for a long time."

The patient was a reticent twenty-nine-year-old nurse who had come to see Loder 10 about the chronic daily headaches she'd been having since she was twelve. Loder typed as the woman spoke, like a journalist taking notes. She did not interrupt or comment, except to say, "Tell me more," until the full story emerged. The nurse said that she enjoyed only three or four days a month without a throbbing headache. She'd tried a long list of medications, without success. The headaches had interfered with college, relationships, her job. She dreaded night shifts, since the headaches that came afterward were particularly awful.

Loder gave a sympathetic shake of her head, and that was enough to win the 11 woman's confidence. The patient knew that she'd been heard by someone who understood the seriousness of her problem—a problem invisible to the naked eye, to blood tests, to biopsies, and to scans, and often not even believed by co-workers, family members, or, indeed, doctors.

She reviewed the woman's records—all the medications she'd taken, all the tests 12 she'd undergone—and did a brief examination. Then we came to the moment I'd been waiting for, the moment when I would see what made the clinic so effective. Would Loder diagnose a condition that had never been suspected? Would she suggest a treatment I'd never heard of? Would she have some special microvascular procedure she could perform that others couldn't?

The answer was no. This was, I later came to realize, the key fact about Loder's 13 capabilities. But I didn't see it that day, and I was never going to see it in any single visit.

She started, disappointingly, by lowering expectations. For some ninety-five 14 per cent of patients who see her, including this woman, the diagnosis is chronic migraines. And for chronic migraines, she explained, a complete cure was unlikely. Success meant that the headaches became less frequent and less intense, and that the patients grew more confident in handling them. Even that progress would take time. There is rarely a single, immediate remedy, she said, whether it was a drug or a change in diet or an exercise regimen. Nonetheless, she wanted her patients to trust her. Things would take a while—months, sometimes longer. Success would be incremental.

She asked the woman to keep a headache diary using a form she gave her to rate 15 the peak level and hours of headache each day. She explained that together they would make small changes in treatments and review the diary every few months. If a regimen produced a greater than fifty-per-cent reduction in the number and severity of the headaches, they'd call that a victory.

Haynes told me that Loder gave him the same speech when he first saw her, in 16 2010, and he decided to stick with her. He liked how methodical she was. He kept his headache diary faithfully. They began by formulating a "rescue plan" for managing his attacks. During an attack, he often vomited pills, so she gave him a supply of non-narcotic rectal suppositories for fast-acting pain relief and an injectable medicine if they didn't work. Neither was pleasant to take, but they helped. The peak level and duration of his attacks diminished slightly. She then tried changing the medications he used for prevention. When one medicine caused side effects he couldn't tolerate, she switched to another, but that one didn't produce any reduction in headaches. He saw her every three months, and they kept on measuring and adjusting.

The most exotic thing they tried was Botox—botulinum-toxin injections—which 17 the F.D.A. had approved for chronic migraines in 2010. She thought he might benefit from injections along the muscles of his forehead. Haynes's insurer refused to cover the cost, however, and, at upwards of twelve hundred dollars a vial, the treatment was beyond what he could afford. So Loder took on the insurer, and after numerous calls and almost a year of delays Haynes won coverage.

After the first few rounds of injections—each treatment lasts three months and 18 is intended to relax but not paralyze the muscles—Haynes noticed no dramatic change. He was on four medications for prevention, including the Botox, and had four escalating rescue treatments that he could resort to whenever a bad headache began to mount. Three years had passed, and progress had been minimal, but Loder was hopeful.

"I am actually quite optimistic about his long-term outlook for improvement," 19 she wrote in her notes that spring. "I detect slow but steady progress. In particular, the extremes of headache at the upper end have come down nicely and vomiting is much less of a problem. That, in my experience, is a clear sign of regression." Haynes wasn't so sure. But after another year or so of adjustments he, too, began to notice a difference. The interval between bad attacks had lengthened to a week. Later, it stretched to a month. Then even longer.

When I met Haynes, in 2015, he'd gone more than a year without a severe 20 migraine. "I haven't had a dreadful attack since March 13, 2014," he said, triumphantly. It had taken four years of effort. But Loder's systematic incrementalism had done what nothing else had.

I later went to visit Haynes and his wife at their lovely nine-room inn on the Cape. 21 He was tall and lanky, with a John Cleese mustache and the kind of wary astonishment I imagine that men released after years in prison have. At sixty-two, he was savoring experiences he feared he'd never get to have in his life.

"I'm a changed person," he said. "I've a bubbliness in my life now. I don't feel at 22 threat. We can arrange dinner parties. I'm not the social cripple that I was. I'm not going to let anyone down anymore. I'm not going to let my wife down anymore. I was a terrible person to live with. That's gone from my life."

Migraines had ruled his life for more than four decades. For the first time, he could 23 read a book all the way through. He could take jet flights without fear of what the air pressure might do to his head. His wife couldn't say enough about the difference.

"It's almost a miracle," she said. "It has been life-changing for me. It makes me so 24 happy that he's not ill. I feel good about my future. We can look forward together."

Recently, I checked in again, and he hadn't had another headache. Haynes 25 doesn't like to think about what would have happened if he hadn't found the headache clinic. He wished he'd found it decades earlier. "Dr. Loder saved my life," he said.

We have a certain heroic expectation of how medicine works. Following the Sec- 26 ond World War, penicillin and then a raft of other antibiotics cured the scourge of bacterial diseases that it had been thought only God could touch. New vaccines routed polio, diphtheria, rubella, and measles. Surgeons opened the heart, transplanted organs, and removed once inoperable tumors. Heart attacks could be stopped; cancers could be cured. A single generation experienced a transformation in the treatment of human illness as no generation had before. It was like discovering that water could put out fire. We built our health-care system, accordingly, to deploy firefighters. Doctors became saviors.

But the model wasn't quite right. If an illness is a fire, many of them require 27 months or years to extinguish, or can be reduced only to a low-level smolder. The treatments may have side effects and complications that require yet more attention. Chronic illness has become commonplace, and we have been poorly prepared to deal with it. Much of what ails us requires a more patient kind of skill.

I was drawn to medicine by the aura of heroism—by the chance to charge in and 28 solve a dangerous problem. I loved learning how to unravel diagnostic mysteries on the general-medicine ward, and how to deliver babies in the obstetrics unit, and how to stop heart attacks in the cardiology unit. I worked in a DNA virus lab for a time and considered going into infectious diseases. But it was the operating room that really drew me in.

I remember seeing a college student with infectious mononucleosis, caused by 29 the very virus I was studying in the lab—the Epstein-Barr virus. The infection causes the spleen to enlarge, and in rare cases it grows so big that it spontaneously ruptures, producing major internal bleeding. This is what happened to the student. He arrived in our emergency department in hemorrhagic shock. His pulse was rapid and thready. The team could barely detect a blood pressure. We rushed him to the operating room. By the time we got him on the table and under anesthesia, he was on the verge of cardiac arrest.

The resident opened the young man's belly in two moves: with a knife he made a 30 swift, decisive slash down the middle, through the skin, from the rib cage to below his umbilicus, then with open-jawed scissors pushed upward through the linea alba—the tough fibrous tendon that runs between the abdominal muscles—as if it were wrapping paper. A pool of blood burst out of him. The resident thrust a gloved hand into the opening. The attending surgeon stood across from him, asking, in a weirdly calm, quiet voice, almost under his breath, "Have you got it?"

Pause. 31

"Now?" 32

Pause. 33

"You have thirty more seconds." 34

Suddenly, the resident had freed the spleen and lifted it to the surface. The organ 35 was fleshy and heavy, like a sodden loaf of bread. A torrent of blood poured out of a fissure on its surface. The attending surgeon put a clamp across its tether of blood vessels. The bleeding stopped instantly. The patient was saved.

How can anyone not love that? I knew there was a place for prevention and main- 36
tenance and incremental progress against difficult problems. But this seemed like the
real work of saving lives. Surgery was a definitive intervention at a critical moment in
a person's life, with a clear, calculable, frequently transformative outcome.

Fields like primary-care medicine seemed, by comparison, squishy and uncertain. 37
How often could you really achieve victories by inveigling patients to take their medicines when less than half really do; to lose weight when only a small fraction can
keep it off; to quit smoking; to deal with their alcohol problem; to show up for their
annual physical, which doesn't seem to make that much difference anyway? I wanted
to know I was doing work that would matter. I decided to go into surgery.

Not long ago, I was talking to Asaf Bitton, a thirty-nine-year-old internist I work 38
with, about the contrast between his work and mine, and I made the mistake of
saying that I had more opportunities to make a clear difference in people's lives. He
was having none of it. Primary care, he countered, is the medical profession that
has the greatest over-all impact, including lower mortality and better health, not to
mention lower medical costs. Asaf is a recognized expert on the delivery of primary
health care around the world, and, over the next few days, he sent me evidence for
his claims.

He showed me studies demonstrating that states with higher ratios of primary-care 39
physicians have lower rates of general mortality, infant mortality, and mortality from
specific conditions such as heart disease and stroke. Other studies found that people
with a primary-care physician as their usual source of care had lower subsequent five-
year mortality rates than others, regardless of their initial health. In the United Kingdom, where family physicians are paid to practice in deprived areas, a ten-per-cent
increase in the primary-care supply was shown to improve people's health so much
that you could add ten years to everyone's life and still not match the benefit. Another
study examined health-care reforms in Spain that focussed on strengthening primary
care in various regions—by, for instance, building more clinics, extending their
hours, and paying for home visits. After ten years, mortality fell in the areas where
the reforms were made, and it fell more in those areas which received the reforms
earlier. Likewise, reforms in California that provided all Medicaid recipients with
primary-care physicians resulted in lower hospitalization rates. By contrast, private
Medicare plans that increased co-payments for primary-care visits—and thereby
reduced such visits—saw increased hospitalization rates. Further, the more complex
a person's medical needs are the greater the benefit of primary care.

I finally had to submit. Primary care, it seemed, does a lot of good for people— 40
maybe even more good, in the long run, than I will as a surgeon. But I still wondered how. What, exactly, is the primary-care physician's skill? I visited Asaf's clinic
to see.

The clinic is in the Boston neighborhood of Jamaica Plain, and it has three full- 41
time physicians, several part-timers, three physician assistants, three social workers,
a nurse, a pharmacist, and a nutritionist. Together, they get some fourteen thousand
patient visits a year in fifteen clinic rooms, which were going pretty much non-stop
on the day I dropped by.

People came in with leg pains, arm pains, belly pains, joint pains, head pains, or 42
just for a checkup. I met an eighty-eight-year-old man who had survived a cardiac
arrest in a parking lot. I talked to a physician assistant who, in the previous few hours,
had administered vaccinations, cleaned wax out of the ears of an elderly woman
with hearing trouble, adjusted the medications of a man whose home blood-pressure
readings were far too high, and followed up on a patient with diabetes.

The clinic had a teeming variousness. It didn't matter if patients had psoriasis 43
or psychosis, the clinic had to have something useful to offer them. At any given
moment, someone there might be suturing a laceration, lancing an abscess, aspi-
rating a gouty joint, biopsying a suspicious skin lesion, managing a bipolar-disorder
crisis, assessing a geriatric patient who had taken a fall, placing an intrauterine con-
traceptive device, or stabilizing a patient who'd had an asthma attack. The clinic was
licensed to dispense thirty-five medicines on the premises, including steroids and
epinephrine, for an anaphylactic allergic reaction; a shot of ceftriaxone, for newly
diagnosed gonorrhea; a dose of doxycycline, for acute Lyme disease; or a one-gram
dose of azithromycin for chlamydia, so that someone can directly observe that the
patient swallows it, reducing the danger that he or she will infect someone else.

"We do the things you really don't need specialists for," a physician assistant said. 44
And I saw what a formidably comprehensive range that could be. Asaf—Israeli-born
and Minnesota-raised, which means that he's both more talkative and happier than
the average Bostonian—told me about one of his favorite maneuvers. Three or four
times a year, a patient comes in with disabling episodes of dizziness because of a
condition called benign positional vertigo. It's caused by loose particles of calcified
debris rattling around in the semicircular canal of the inner ear. Sometimes patients
are barely able to stand. They are nauseated. They vomit. Just turning their head the
wrong way, or rolling over in bed, can bring on a bout of dizziness. It's like the worst
seasickness you can imagine.

"I have just the trick," he tells them. 45

First, to be sure he has the correct diagnosis, he does the Dix-Hallpike test. He 46
has the patient sit on the examination table, turns his head forty-five degrees to one
side with both hands, and then quickly lays him down flat with his head hanging off
the end of the table. If Asaf's diagnosis is right, the patient's eyes will shake for ten
seconds or so, like dice in a cup.

To fix the problem, he performs what's known as the Epley maneuver. With the 47
patient still lying with his head turned to one side and hanging off the table, Asaf
rotates his head rapidly the other way until his ear is pointed toward the ceiling. He
holds the patient's head still for thirty seconds. He then has him roll onto his side
while turning his head downward. Thirty seconds later, he lifts the patient rapidly to a
sitting position. If he's done everything right, the calcified particles are flung through
the semicircular canal like marbles out a chute. In most cases, the patient feels better
instantly.

"They walk out the door thinking you're a shaman," Asaf said, grinning. Everyone 48
loves to be the hero. Asaf and his colleagues can deliver on-the-spot care for hundreds of conditions and guidance for thousands more. They run a medical general

store. But, Asaf insisted, that's not really how primary-care clinicians save lives. After all, for any given situation specialists are likely to have more skill and experience, and more apt to follow the evidence of what works. Generalists have no advantage over specialists in any particular case. Yet, somehow, having a primary-care clinician as your main source of care is better for you.

Asaf tried to explain. "It's no one thing we do. It's all of it," he said. I found this 49 unsatisfying. I pushed everyone I met at the clinic. How could seeing one of them for my—insert problem here—be better than going straight to a specialist? Invariably, the clinicians would circle around to the same conclusion.

"It's the relationship," they'd say. I began to understand only after I noticed that 50 the doctors, the nurses, and the front-desk staff knew by name almost every patient who came through the door. Often, they had known the patient for years and would know him for years to come. In a single, isolated moment of care for, say, a man who came in with abdominal pain, Asaf looked like nothing special. But once I took in the fact that patient and doctor really knew each other—that the man had visited three months earlier, for back pain, and six months before that, for a flu—I started to realize the significance of their familiarity.

For one thing, it made the man willing to seek medical attention for potentially 51 serious symptoms far sooner, instead of putting it off until it was too late. There is solid evidence behind this. Studies have established that having a regular source of medical care, from a doctor who knows you, has a powerful effect on your willing-ness to seek care for severe symptoms. This alone appears to be a significant contrib-utor to lower death rates.

Observing the care, I began to grasp how the commitment to seeing people over time 52 leads primary-care clinicians to take an approach to problem-solving that is very differ-ent from that of doctors, like me, who provide mainly episodic care. One patient was a Spanish-speaking woman, younger-looking than her fifty-nine years, with a history of depression and migraines. She had developed an odd set of symptoms. For more than a month, she'd had facial swelling. Her face would puff up for a day, then go back to normal. Several days later, it would happen again. She pulled up pictures on her phone to show us: her face was swollen almost beyond recognition. There had been no pain, no itching, no rash. More recently, however, her hands and feet had started swelling as well, sometimes painfully. She had to stop wearing rings. Then the pain and numbness extended up her arms and into her chest, and that was what had prompted her to come in. She was having chest pain as she sat before us. "It feels like a cramp," she said. "My heart feels like it is coming out of my mouth. . . . The whole body feels like it's vibrating."

Doctors in other settings—say, an emergency room or an urgent-care 53 clinic—would use a "rule out" strategy, running tests to rule out possible conditions, especially dangerous ones, as rapidly as possible. We would focus first on the chest pain—women often have less classic symptoms of a heart attack than men do—and order an EKG, a cardiac stress test, and the like to detect coronary-artery disease. Once that was ruled out, we might give her an antihistamine and watch her for a couple of hours to see if the symptoms went away. And, when that didn't work, we would send her home and figure, Oh, well, it's probably nothing.

This was not, however, the way the woman's primary-care physician approached 54 her condition. Dr. Katherine Rose was a young, freckle-faced physician two years out of training, with a precise and methodical air. "I'm not sure I know what's going on," she admitted to the woman.

The symptoms did not fit together in an obvious way. But, rather than proceed 55 directly to an arsenal of tests, Rose took a different, more cautious, more empirical approach, letting the answer emerge over time. It wasn't that she did no tests—she did an electrocardiogram, to make sure the woman really wasn't in the midst of a heart attack, and ordered a couple of basic blood tests. But she didn't expect that they'd show anything meaningful. (They didn't.) Instead, she asked the patient to take allergy medicine and to return to see her in two weeks. She'd monitor her over time to see how the symptoms evolved.

Rose told me, "I think the hardest transition from residency, where we are essen- 56 tially trained in inpatient medicine, to my practice as a primary-care physician was feeling comfortable with waiting. As an outpatient doctor, you don't have constant data or the security of in-house surveillance. But most of the time people will get better on their own, without intervention or extensive workup. And, if they don't get better, then usually more clues to the diagnosis will emerge, and the steps will be clearer. For me, as a relatively new primary-care physician, the biggest struggle is trusting that patients will call if they are getting worse." And they do, she said, because they know her and they know the clinic. "Being able to tolerate the anxiety that accompanies taking care of people who are sick but not dangerously ill is not a skill I was expecting to need when I decided to become a doctor, but it is one of the ones I have worked hardest to develop."

The woman's symptoms disappeared after two weeks. A physician assistant fig- 57 ured out why: the patient had run out of naproxen, an analgesic medication she took for her migraine attacks, which in rare instances can produce soft-tissue swelling, through both allergic and nonallergic mechanisms. She would have to stay off all medications in that class. An urgent-care team wouldn't have figured this out. Now Rose contacted the Graham Headache Center to help identify an alternative medica- tion for the woman's migraines.

Like the specialists at the Graham Center, the generalists at Jamaica Plain are 58 incrementalists. They focus on the course of a person's health over time—even through a life. All understanding is provisional and subject to continual adjustment. For Rose, taking the long view meant thinking not just about her patient's bouts of facial swelling, or her headaches, or her depression, but about all of it—along with her living situation, her family history, her nutrition, her stress levels, and how they interrelated—and what that picture meant a doctor could do to improve her patient's long-term health and well-being throughout her life.

Success, therefore, is not about the episodic, momentary victories, though they do 59 play a role. It is about the longer view of incremental steps that produce sustained progress. That, such clinicians argue, is what making a difference really looks like. In fact, it is what making a difference looks like in a range of endeavors.

On Friday, December 15, 1967, at 4:55 P.M., the Silver Bridge, which spanned 60 the Ohio River, was funnelling the usual crawl of rush-hour traffic between Gallipolis, Ohio, and Point Pleasant, West Virginia, when a shotgun-like blast rang out. It was the sound of a critical link in the bridge's chain-suspension system giving way. In less than a minute, 1,750 feet of the 2,235-foot span collapsed, and seventy-five vehicles dropped into the river, eighty feet below. "The bridge just keeled over, starting slowly on the Ohio side then following like a deck of cards to the West Virginia side," a witness said. Forty-six people died; dozens more were injured.

The newly established National Transportation Safety Board conducted its first 61 major disaster investigation and reconstructed what had happened. Until then, state and federal government officials regarded such catastrophes as largely random and unavoidable. They focused on building new bridges and highways, and employed mainly reactive strategies for problems with older ones. The investigation determined that corrosion of the four-decade-old bridge, combined with an obsolete design (it was built to handle Model T traffic, not cars and trucks several times heavier), had caused the critical fracture. Inspection could have caught the issue. But the Silver Bridge had had just one complete inspection since its opening, in 1928, and never with such concerns in mind. The collapse signalled the need for a new strategy. Although much of the United States' highway system was still relatively new, hundreds of bridges were more than forty years old and had been designed, like the Silver Bridge, for Model T traffic. Our system was entering middle age, and we didn't have a plan for it.

The federal government launched a standard inspection system and an inventory 62 of public bridges—six hundred thousand in all. Almost half were found to be either structurally deficient or functionally obsolete, meaning that critical structural elements were either in "poor condition" or inadequate for current traffic loads. They were at a heightened risk of collapse. The good news was that investments in maintenance and improvement could extend the life of aging bridges by decades, and for a fraction of the cost of reconstruction.

Today, however, we still have almost a hundred and fifty thousand problem 63 bridges. Sixty thousand have traffic restrictions because they aren't safe for carrying full loads. Where have we gone wrong? The pattern is the same everywhere: despite knowing how much cheaper preservation is, we chronically raid funds intended for incremental maintenance and care, and use them to pay for new construction. It's obvious why. Construction produces immediate and visible success; maintenance doesn't. Does anyone reward politicians for a bridge that doesn't crumble?

Even with serious traffic restrictions, one in a thousand structurally deficient 64 bridges collapses each year. Four per cent of such collapses cause loss of life. Based on the lack of public response, structural engineers have judged this to be "in a tolerable range."

They also report that bridges are in better condition than many other parts of our 65 aging infrastructure. The tendency to avoid spending on incremental maintenance and improvements has shortened the life span of our dams, levees, roads, sewers, and water systems. This situation isn't peculiar to the United States. Governments everywhere tend to drastically undervalue incrementalism and overvalue heroism. "Typically, breakdowns—bridge washouts, overpass collapses, dam breaches—must occur before politicians and voters react to need," one global infrastructure report observes. "Dislocation leads to rushed funding on an emergency basis with dramatically heightened costs."

None of this is entirely irrational. The only visible part of investment in incre- 66 mental care is the perennial costs. There is generally little certainty about how much spending will really be needed or how effective it will be. Rescue work delivers much more certainty. There is a beginning and an end to the effort. And you know what all the money and effort is (and is not) accomplishing. We don't like to address problems until they are well upon us and unavoidable, and we don't trust solutions that promise benefits only down the road.

Incrementalists nonetheless want us to take a longer view. They want us to believe 67 that they can recognize problems before they happen, and that, with steady, iterative effort over years, they can reduce, delay, or eliminate them. Yet incrementalists also want us to accept that they will never be able to fully anticipate or prevent all problems. This makes for a hard sell. The incrementalists' contribution is more cryptic than the rescuers', and yet also more ambitious. They are claiming, in essence, to be able to predict and shape the future. They want us to put our money on it.

For a long time, this would have seemed as foolish as giving your money to a 68 palmist. What will happen to a bridge—or to your body—fifty years from now? We had no more than a vague idea. But the investigation of the 1967 Silver Bridge collapse marked an advance in our ability to shift from reacting to bridge catastrophes to anticipating and averting them.

Around the same time, something similar was happening in medicine. Scientists 69 were discovering the long-term health significance of high blood pressure, diabetes, and other conditions. We'd begun collecting the data, developing the computational capacity to decode the patterns, and discovering the treatments that could change them. Seemingly random events were becoming open to prediction and alteration. Our frame of medical consideration could widen to encompass our entire life spans.

There is a lot about the future that remains unpredictable. Nonetheless, the pat- 70 terns are becoming more susceptible to empiricism—to a science of surveillance, analysis, and iterative correction. The incrementalists are overtaking the rescuers. But the transformation has itself been incremental. So we're only just starting to notice.

Our ability to use information to understand and reshape the future is accelerating 71 in multiple ways. We have at least four kinds of information that matter to your health and well-being over time: information about the state of your internal systems (from your imaging and lab-test results, your genome sequencing); the state of your living conditions (your housing, community, economic, and environmental circumstances); the state of the care you receive (what your practitioners have done and how well they did it, what medications and other treatments they have provided); and the state of your behaviors (your patterns of sleep, exercise, stress, eating, sexual activity, adherence to treatments). The potential of this information is so enormous it is almost scary.

Instead of once-a-year checkups, in which people are like bridges undergoing 72 annual inspection, we will increasingly be able to use smartphones and wearables to continuously monitor our heart rhythm, breathing, sleep, and activity, registering signs of illness as well as the effectiveness and the side effects of treatments. Engineers have proposed bathtub scanners that could track your internal organs for minute changes over time. We can decode our entire genome for less than the cost of an iPad and, increasingly, tune our care to the exact makeup we were born with.

Our health-care system is not designed for this future—or, indeed, for this pres- 73 ent. We built it at a time when such capabilities were virtually nonexistent. When illness was experienced as a random catastrophe, and medical discoveries focused on rescue, insurance for unanticipated, episodic needs was what we needed. Hospitals and heroic interventions got the large investments; incrementalists were scanted. After all, in the nineteen-fifties and sixties, they had little to offer that made a major difference in people's lives. But the more capacity we develop to monitor the body and the brain for signs of future breakdown and to correct course along the way—to deliver "precision medicine," as the lingo goes—the greater the difference health care can make in people's lives, as well as in reducing future costs.

This potential for incremental medicine to improve and save lives, however, is 74 dramatically at odds with our system's allocation of rewards. According to a 2016 compensation survey, the five highest-paid specialties in American medicine are orthopedics, cardiology, dermatology, gastroenterology, and radiology. Practitioners in these fields have an average income of four hundred thousand dollars a year. All are interventionists: they make most of their income on defined, minutes- to hourslong procedures—replacing hips, excising basal-cell carcinomas, doing endoscopies, conducting and reading MRIs—and then move on. (One clear indicator: the starting income for cardiologists who perform invasive procedures is twice that of cardiologists who mainly provide preventive, longitudinal care.)

Here are the lowest-paid specialties: pediatrics, endocrinology, family medicine, 75 H.I.V./infectious disease, allergy/immunology, internal medicine, psychiatry, and rheumatology. The average income for these practitioners is about two hundred thousand dollars a year. Almost certainly at the bottom, too, but not evaluated in the compensation survey: geriatricians, palliative-care physicians, and headache specialists. All are incrementalists—they produce value by improving people's lives over extended periods of time, typically months to years.

This hundred-per-cent difference in incomes actually understates the degree 76 to which our policies and payment systems have given short shrift to incremental care. As an American surgeon, I have a battalion of people and millions of dollars of equipment on hand when I arrive in my operating room. Incrementalists are lucky if they can hire a nurse.

Already, we can see the cost of this misalignment. As rates of smoking fall, for 77 instance, the biggest emerging killer is uncontrolled hypertension, which can result in stroke, heart attack, and dementia, among other conditions. Thirty per cent of Americans have high blood pressure. Although most get medical attention, only half are adequately treated. Globally, it's even worse—a billion people have hypertension, and only fourteen per cent receive adequate treatment. Good treatment for hypertension is like bridge maintenance: it requires active monitoring and incremental fixes and adjustments over time but averts costly disasters. All the same, we routinely skimp on the follow-through. We'll deploy an army of experts and a mountain of resources to separate conjoined twins—but give Asaf Bitton enough to hire a medical aide or a computerized system to connect electronically with high-blood-pressure patients and help them live longer? Forget about it.

Recently, I called Bill Haynes's internist, Dr. Mita Gupta, the one who recognized 78 that the John Graham Headache Center might be able help him. She had never intended to pursue a career in primary care, she said. She'd planned to go into gastroenterology—one of the highly paid specialties. But, before embarking on specialty training, she took a temporary position at a general medical clinic in order to start a family. "What it turned into really surprised me," she said. As she got to know and work with people over time, she saw the depth of the impact she could have on their lives. "Now it's been ten years, and I see the kids of patients of mine, I see people through crises, and I see some of them through to the end of their lives." Her main frustration: how little recognized her abilities are, whether by the insurers, who expect her to manage a patient with ten different health problems in a fifteen-minute visit, or by hospitals, which rarely call to notify her, let alone consult her, when a patient of hers is admitted. She could do so much more for her patients with a bit more time and better resources for tracking, planning, and communicating. Instead, she is constantly playing catch-up. "I don't know a primary-care physician who eats lunch," she said.

The difference between what's made available to me as a surgeon and what's 79 made available to our internists or pediatricians or H.I.V. specialists is not just short-sighted—it's immoral. More than a quarter of Americans and Europeans who die before the age of seventy-five would not have died so soon if they'd received appropriate medical care for their conditions, most of which were chronic. We routinely countenance inadequate care among the most vulnerable people in our communities—including children, the elderly, and the chronically ill.

I see the stakes in my own family. My son, Walker, was born with a heart condi- 80 tion, and in his first days rescue medicine was what he needed. A cardiology team deployed the arsenal that saved him: the drips that kept his circulation going, the surgery that closed the holes in his heart and gave him a new aortic arch. But incremental medicine is what he has needed ever since.

For twenty-one years, he has had the same cardiologist and nurse practitioner. 81 They saw him through his first months, when weight gain, stimulation, and control of his blood pressure were essential. They saw him through his first decade, when all he turned out to need was someone to keep a cautious eye on how his heart did as he developed and took on sports. They saw him through his growth spurt, when the size of his aorta failed to keep up with his height, and guided us through the difficult choices about what operation he needed, when, and who should do it. Then they saw him through his thankfully smooth recovery.

When he began to struggle in middle school, a psychologist's evaluation identified 82 deficits that, he warned us, meant that Walker would probably not have the cognitive capacity for college. But the cardiologist recognized that Walker's difficulties fit with new data showing that kids with his heart condition tend to have a particular pattern of neurological deficits in processing speed and other functions which could potentially be managed. In the ensuing years, she and his pediatrician helped bring in experts to work with him on his learning and coping skills, and school planning. He's now a junior in college, majoring in philosophy, and emerging as a writer and an artist. Rescue saved my son's life. But without incremental medicine he would never have the long and full life that he could.

In the next few months, the worry is whether Walker and others like him will be 83 able to have health-care coverage of any kind. His heart condition makes him, essentially, uninsurable. Until he's twenty-six, he can stay on our family policy. But after that? In the work he's done in his field, he's had the status of a freelancer. Without the Affordable Care Act's protections requiring all insurers to provide coverage to people regardless of their health history and at the same price as others their age, he'd be unable to find health insurance. Republican replacement plans threaten to weaken or drop these requirements, and leave no meaningful solution for people like him. And data indicate that twenty-seven per cent of adults under sixty-five are like him, with past health conditions that make them uninsurable without the protections.

The coming years will present us with a far larger concern, however. In this era of 84 advancing information, it will become evident that, for everyone, life is a preexisting condition waiting to happen. We will all turn out to have—like the Silver Bridge and the growing crack in its critical steel link—a lurking heart condition or a tumor or a depression or some rare disease that needs to be managed. This is a problem for our health-care system. It doesn't put great value on care that takes time to pay off. But this is also an opportunity. We have the chance to transform the course of our lives.

Doing so will mean discovering the heroism of the incremental. That means not 85 only continuing our work to make sure everyone has health insurance but also accelerating efforts begun under health reform to restructure the way we deliver and pay for health care. Much can be debated about how: there are, for example, many ways to reward clinicians when they work together and devise new methods for improving lives and averting costs. But the basic decision has the stark urgency of right and wrong. We can give up an antiquated set of priorities and shift our focus from rescue medicine to lifelong incremental care. Or we can leave millions of people to suffer and die from conditions that, increasingly, can be predicted and managed. This isn't a bloodless policy choice; it's a medical emergency.

READING FOR MEANING

1. **Read to Summarize.** Write a few sentences explaining why Gawande believes incremental (as opposed to rescue) care is so important.

2. **Read to Respond.** Write a paragraph responding to Gawande's observation that "Our ability to use information to understand and reshape the future is accelerating in multiple ways" (par. 71) or his position that "In this era of

For help with summarizing and other reading strategies, see Chapter 2.

advancing information, it will become evident that, for everyone, life is a preexisting condition waiting to happen" (par. 84).

3. **Read to Analyze Assumptions.** Write a paragraph or two analyzing an assumption you find intriguing in Gawande's essay. For example:

Assumptions about access to health care. Gawande assumes that health care is available to all people. His essay describes two kinds of health care — incremental care and rescue medicine — available to patients, but he does not mention that there are many people who have no access to any kind of health care.

- Gawande writes, "Rescue [medicine] saved my son's life. But without incremental medicine he would never have the long and full life that he could" (par. 82). How does the inclusion of the anecdote about Gawande's son and the other examples of patients who were helped by either incremental or rescue medicine obscure the issue of access to health care?

- What assumptions do you have about access and the health care system? Do your assumptions come from your experiences, what you learned in school, or from your parents or friends? What do your assumptions reveal to you about what you value? How much do you value access to health care? How important is it to you that everyone has the same access?

Assumptions about who is responsible for America's health care system. Gawande describes the importance of "continuing our work to make sure everyone has health insurance" and "accelerating efforts begun under health reform to restructure the way we deliver and pay for health care" (par. 85).

- What assumptions does Gawande make about who is responsible for the health care system? Who is the "our" in the above statement and who is responsible for the health care reforms already underway?

- Are there other organizations, groups, or people that Gawande does not hold responsible for restructuring the health care system that you believe should be held responsible?

READING LIKE A WRITER

Explaining Concepts

For more on explaining concepts, see Chapter 6.

Writers who explain a concept use appropriate writing strategies such as defining, illustrating, comparing and contrasting, and showing causes and effects in order to help their readers understand the concept. These writing strategies, typical of concept explanations, help readers to understand the concept of incremental care in Gawande's essay.

ANALYZE & WRITE

Write a paragraph or two analyzing the writing strategies Gawande uses to explain the concept of incremental care.

1. Gawande does not directly define incremental care, but he offers illustrations and examples of it throughout his essay. Keep a list of these illustrations. First, consider them individually. How does each illustration help you understand something about incremental care? Then consider these examples as a whole. How do they work together to explain the concept of incremental care?

2. Gawande compares incremental care to rescue medicine throughout the essay, but he makes other comparisons, too. Reread paragraphs 60–65 to analyze how Gawande uses the strategy of comparison to explain the concept. What does he compare incremental care to in this section? What does this comparison help you understand about incremental care?

3. To help readers understand why incremental care is often less valued than rescue medicine, Gawande uses the cause-and-effect writing strategy. He traces the cause of the prioritization of rescue medicine over incremental medicine to the kind of rescue medicine practiced following the Second World War (par. 26), before showing readers the effects of this privileging of rescue medicine. Locate moments in the essay where Gawande describes the effects or consequences of valuing rescue medicine over incremental care. What does Gawande's use of the cause-and-effect writing strategy help you understand about incremental care?

READING LIKE A WRITER

Observation

In writing up their observations, writers make choices about the role they will perform. They can act as a detached spectator who watches and listens but remains outside of the activity of the essay, or they can act as a participant observer, an insider, who joins in the activity. We can see examples of both roles in this excerpt from Gawande's essay.

Spectator role — The woman's symptoms disappeared after two weeks. . . . An urgent-care team wouldn't have figured this out. Now Rose contacted the Graham Headache Center to help identify an alternative medication for the woman's migraines.

Like the specialists at the Graham Center, the generalists at Jamaica Plain are incrementalists. They focus on the course of a person's health over time — even through a life.

Participant role I was drawn to medicine by the aura of heroism — by the chance to charge in and solve a dangerous problem. . . . I worked in a DNA virus lab for a time and considered going into infectious diseases. But it was the operating room that really drew me in.

I remember seeing a college student with infectious mononucleosis, caused by the very virus I was studying in the lab — the Epstein-Barr virus.

ANALYZE & WRITE

Write a paragraph discussing the shifts in Gawande's essay between the spectator and participant roles.

1. Find signs throughout the essay, such as Gawande's use of the first- or third-person perspective, that help you recognize where the author has taken on these two roles. Keep track of these moments.

2. What do you notice about when Gawande shifts from one perspective to the other? How do these different kinds of observations contribute to his explanation of incremental care?

3. What advantages or disadvantages do you see in Gawande taking on the roles of both spectator and participant? What would have been gained or lost had Gawande chosen to maintain one role throughout?

READING LIKE A WRITER

Arguing for a Position

For sentence strategies to use when responding to objections fairly, see Chapter 8, pp. 349–350.

In arguing for a position, writers must respond to objections and alternative positions fairly. Writers often try to anticipate objections readers might raise or alternative positions they may hold. Writers may concede some points but when they think the objection isn't valid they may refute it. Writers may also do both by conceding some points and refuting others. By engaging with these objections and alternative positions, writers not only show that their position can stand up to criticism, but they enhance their credibility by treating those who disagree with respect.

Notice how Gawande concedes that the government's refusal to invest in incremental care is understandable:

Governments everywhere tend to drastically undervalue incrementalism and overvalue heroism. . . . None of this is entirely irrational. The only visible part of investment in incremental care is the perennial costs. There is generally little certainty about how much spending will really be needed or how effective it will be. Rescue work delivers much more certainty. There is a beginning and an end to the effort (pars. 65–66).

Gawande goes on to refute this point with the following:

> There is a lot about the future that remains unpredictable. Nonetheless, the patterns are becoming more susceptible to empiricism — to a science of surveillance, analysis, and iterative correction. The incrementalists are overtaking the rescuers. But the transformation has itself been incremental. So we're only just starting to notice.

> Our ability to use information to understand and reshape the future is accelerating in multiple ways. . . .The potential of this information is so enormous it is almost scary (pars. 70–71).

ANALYZE & WRITE

Write a paragraph or two analyzing how Gawande responds to objections and alternative viewpoints.

1. In the example above, which words or phrases indicate that Gawande is conceding a point? Which indicate that Gawande is refuting a point?

2. Locate another example from the essay in which Gawande either concedes or refutes a point. What seems to be his attitude toward those who might disagree with him? Does he treat them respectfully? Which words and phrases provide insight into his attitude?

3. Do Gawande's responses to objections and alternative viewpoints help persuade you of his position? How effective is this writing strategy?

READING LIKE A WRITER

The Rhetorical Situation in Multi-Genre Writing

All writers must consider their rhetorical situation, which involves asking questions about their purpose, audience, stance, genre, and medium/design.

For more on the rhetorical situation see Chapter 1, p. 13.

While texts within the same genre can look very different, genres do have some typical features that make them recognizable. For example, a proposal to solve a problem would lay out a problem and offer a way to solve it just as autobiographical writing narrates a story dramatically. If an author's rhetorical situation lends itself to drawing on multiple genres, as do the essays in this chapter, then authors have more choices in terms of the features they use from each genre. For example, a writer may be explaining a concept to an audience unfamiliar with it. The writer will need to define and illustrate the concept, two features of concept explanations. But, to further help her audience understand the concept, the writer may also draw on the autobiographical genre feature of conveying significance powerfully in order to narrate her personal experience with the concept. In this case, the features of concept explanations and autobiographies work together to achieve the writer's purpose, namely to help her audience understand the concept.

You have already considered some of the most prominent features of each genre that appears in Gawande's essay. The prompts below ask you to address how the features of those genres work alongside and in conjunction with each other to meet the needs of Gawande's rhetorical situation.

ANALYZE & WRITE: PURPOSE

Write three or four paragraphs analyzing how combining the features of concept explanation, observation, and position arguments work together to support Gawande's **purpose**.

1. What do you think Gawande's purpose is for writing "The Heroism of Incremental Care"? Explain your answer by quoting passages from the essay.

2. How do the features you have focused on in the Analyze & Write prompts for each genre above complement each other to further Gawande's purpose? How effective is Gawande's chosen combination? What might be lost if Gawande didn't choose to draw on all of these?

3. What other features from the three genres Gawande draws on are present in his essay? How do these features reflect Gawande's understanding of his rhetorical situation?

4. What other genres and specific features of each genre might Gawande have chosen to draw on? How would these support his purpose while also meeting the needs of the other aspects of the rhetorical situation?

READINGS

Wesley Morris

Who Gets to Decide What Belongs in the "Canon"?

Wesley Morris (b. 1975) is a critic-at-large for the *New York Times* and previously worked at *Grantland* as the *Sportsstorialist* columnist and cohost of *Do You Like Prince Movies?* He has been a film critic at the *Boston Globe*, the *San Francisco Chronicle*, and the *San Francisco Examiner*. In 2012, Morris was awarded the Pulitzer Prize for his criticism at the *Boston Globe* and, while at *Grantland*, he was a 2015 National Magazine Award finalist for Columns and Commentary. In 2016 he began co-hosting the podcast *Still Processing*, which was named one of the fifty best podcasts of 2016 by *The Atlantic*. He received a bachelor's degree from Yale University for film studies. The essay below was published in the *New York Times*.

▶ Genres: *Speculating about Causes and Effects, Arguing a Position, Explaining Concepts*

- **Before you read,** consider a song, movie, television show, podcast, or work of art that you think should be widely admired.

- **As you read,** note how Morris uses the example of literary critic Harold Bloom (pars. 6–7) as an example of a canon-maker, mentioning him again in the final paragraph. How effective is this strategy in helping you understand the concept of canon-making and Morris's perspective on it?

Sometimes, it's not enough to love something. You have to take that thing—album, 1 author, song, movie, show—and do more than love it. It needs to be placed beyond mere love. You need to take that thing, wrap it in plastic or put it on a pedestal. You need to dome it under a force field so that other people's grubby hands, opinions and inferior fandoms can't stain or disrespect it. You need not only to certify it but also to forestall decertification. Basically, you need to make it "canon."

The phrase didn't originate on the internet but is *of* the internet and its wing of 2 antidiscursive discourse. It places a work, a person or an idea beyond reproach. It pre-resolves debate. That is, of course, what a canon is—a settled matter. It's established rules and norms. It's the books of the Bible. It's the approved Catholic saints. It's Jane Austen, the Beatles, Miles Davis, Andy Warhol and Beyoncé.

Traditionally, the people drawing up our cultural canons have been an elite group 3 of scholars and critics who embraced a work of art and sent it aloft to some deifying realm. That consecration has spread from academia to, say, Reddit, where fans gather around movies, TV dramas, video games and comic books the way the academy threw its weight behind Dostoyevsky, Joyce, Faulkner and Updike. *Battlestar Galactica* and *The Simpsons*, *Buffy the Vampire Slayer* and the DC and Marvel universes—they're canonical, too. And now "canon" has migrated from noun to adjective, giving the word thunder and muscle and curatorial certitude.

In this sense, "canon" wants to keep something like "Star Wars" heresy-free and 4 internally consistent (so yes, there are canons within canons). The series sprang more than 40 years ago from one man's mind and a single movie. Now it's an industrial complex whose thematic integrity desperately matters to its constituents. So when an installment infuriates fans—the way, in December, *The Last Jedi* did, with its apparent warping of the bylaws and powers of the "Star Wars" galaxy (*this ISN'T how the Force WORKS!!*)—they don't simply complain. They say, "That's not canon." Last winter, a Change.org petition circulated, calling for Disney to "Strike Star Wars Episode VIII from the Official Canon"—as though it were some kind of Taco Bell tie-in, and not, as the title clearly states, the eighth part of a never-ending story—and more than 104,000 people signed on. The receptive response to that not-entirely-serious campaign underscores where we've been for some time with "canon": nervous about the unfixed quality of all kinds of art and unyielding in policing both its meaning and possibilities.

On its face, canon-making is a fairly human impulse: *I love this*. Everyone else 5 should, too! Over time a single book becomes a library; the library becomes a school of thought; the school of thought becomes a prism through which the world is supposed to see itself. That enthusiasm hardened, through curriculums, book clubs and great-works lists, into something more authoritarian, so that canon became taste hammered into stone tablets.

For many years its Moses has been Harold Bloom, whose *The Western Canon:* 6 *The Books and School of the Ages* was a best-selling sensation in 1994, for what it argued was—and by way of omission *wasn't*—canon. In his introduction, Bloom went so far as to pre-emptively dismiss complaints about his biases as coming from the "school of resentment." Asked in a 1991 *Paris Review* interview whom this school comprised, Bloom explained that it's "an extraordinary sort of mélange of latest-model feminists, Lacanians, that whole semiotic cackle." These people, he went on to say, "have no relationship whatever to literary values."

But these people—women, along with nonwhite, nonstraight folks—certainly 7 could have shared Bloom's literary values while also applying prerogatives of their own. Interrogators of both the canon and the canonizers have been dismissed as identity politicians rather than critics or scholars. The old guard claims that they're missing the point of literature, thrusting morality upon an amoral pursuit, sullying the experience. Often however, they're arguing not for literature's restriction but for its expansion—let's include Kafka, obviously, but also Toni Morrison, Marilynne Robinson and Jhumpa Lahiri no less obviously.

This questioning of the canon comes from places of lived experience. It's attuned 8 to how great cultural work can leave you feeling irked and demeaned. For some readers, loving Herman Melville or Joseph Conrad requires some peacemaking with the not-quite-human representations of black people in those texts. Loving Edith Wharton requires the same reckoning with the insulting way she could describe Jews. Bigotry recurs in canonical art. And committed engagement leaves us dutybound to identify it. Shakespeare endures alongside analyses of his flawed characterizations of all kinds of races, nationalities, religions and women. Your great works should be strong enough to withstand some feminist forensics.

But resisting these critiques—whether it's of *The House of Mirth* or the House 9 of Marvel—with an automatic claim of canon feels like an act of dominion, the establishment of an exclusive kingdom complete with moat and drawbridge, which, of course, would make the so-called resenters a mob of torch-wielding marauders and any challenge to established "literary values" an act of savagery. Insisting that a canon is settled gives those concerns the "fake news" treatment, denying a legitimate grievance by saying there's no grounds for one. It's shutting down a conversation, when the longer we go without one, the harder it becomes to speak.

Canon formation, at its heart, has to do with defending what you love against 10 obsolescence, but love can tip into zealotry, which can lead us away from actual criticism into some pretty ugly zones. Our mutual hypersensitivities might have yanked us away from enlightening, crucial—and fun—cultural detective work (close reading, unpacking, interpreting) and turned us into beat cops always on patrol, arresting anything that rankles. That results in a skirmish like the one during last summer's Whitney Biennial, which culminated in the insistence that Dana Schutz lose her career for an underwhelming painting of Emmett Till because, as a white woman, she couldn't possibly understand this black boy's death. The protests didn't feel like an aesthetic demand but a post-traumatic lashing out. Canceling her might be harsh historical justice, but it denies me an understanding of why the painting fails.

This is to say that fandom and spectatorship, of late, have grown darkly possessive 11 as the country has become violently divided. Especially in this moment when certain works of canonical art are in fact at risk of becoming morally obsolete—both art that degrades and insults and the work of men accused of having done the same. There's a camp of fans—who tend to be as white and male as the traditional canon makers—who don't want that work opened up or repossessed. They don't want a challenge to tradition—so please, no women in the writers' room, say superfans of the animated comedy *Rick and Morty*, and no earnest acknowledgment that Apu is a bothersome South Asian stereotype, say the makers of *The Simpsons*. It's all too canonical to change.

You can see the reactionary urge on every side. We've reached this comical—but 12 politically necessary—place in which nonstraight, nonwhite, nonmale culture of all kinds has also been placed beyond reproach. Because it's precious or rare or not meant for the people who tend to do the canonizing. If Korama Danquah, writing for a site called Geek Girl Authority, asserts that the sister of Black Panther is more brilliant than the white billionaire also known as Iron Man, she doesn't want to hear otherwise. "Shuri is the smartest person in the Marvel universe," goes the post. "That's not an opinion, that's canon. She is smarter than Tony Stark." "Black Panther," according to this argument, is canon not only because it's a Marvel movie but because it matters too much to too many black people to be anything else.

But that's also made having conversations about the movie in which somebody leads   13
with, "I really liked it, but . . ." nearly impossible. This protectionism makes all the sense
in the world for a country that's failed to acknowledge a black audience's hunger for, say,
a black comic-book blockbuster. But critic-proofing this movie—making it too black to
dislike—risks making it less equal to and more fragile than its white peers.

The intolerance of the traditional gatekeepers might have spurred a kind of mili-   14
tancy from thinkers (and fans) who've rarely been allowed in. Bloom's literary paradise is long lost, and now history compels us to defend Wakanda's. But that leaves
the contested art in an equally perilous spot: not art at all, really, but territory.

READING FOR MEANING

For help with
summarizing
and other
sentence
strategies, see
Chapter 2.

1. **Read to Summarize.** Write a sentence or two explaining Morris's position
   on how canons get formed and what purposes they serve.

2. **Read to Respond.** Write a paragraph analyzing Morris's claim that "great
   cultural work can leave you feeling irked and demeaned" (par. 10). Have you
   ever criticized a canonized book, film, or other kind of art because of some
   aspect of it or of its author's life that made you uncomfortable? Have you
   ever defended something that had been canonized against these kinds of
   criticisms?

3. **Read to Analyze Assumptions.** Write a paragraph or two analyzing an
   assumption you find intriguing in Morris' essay. For example:

   Assumptions about human impulses. Morris writes, "On its face, canon-making is a fairly human impulse: *I love this. Everyone else should, too!.*
   . . .That enthusiasm hardened, through curriculums, book clubs and great-
   works lists, into something more authoritarian, so that canon became taste
   hammered into stone tablets" (par. 5).

   - Why does Morris assume that canon-making or canon formation is the
     result of specifically human impulses? Can you find moments in the text
     that help you understand which impulses he is referring to? Explain your
     answer.

   - Do your own experiences or friends' experiences with canon-making align
     with what Morris describes? Do the impulses he says drive this activity align
     with these experiences? Why or why not?

   Assumptions about cultural appropriation. Cultural appropriation occurs
   when someone adopts elements of a culture (e.g., a hairstyle, a way of dress-
   ing, a way of speaking) that is not their own. The concept of cultural appropriation is one way to think about the protests against artist Dana Schutz.
   Morris describes the uprising that resulted in response to this white artist's
   painting of Emmett Till, a fourteen-year-old African American boy who was

lynched in Mississippi in 1955: "Our mutual hypersensitivities might have yanked us away from enlightening, crucial — and fun — cultural detective work (close reading, unpacking, interpreting) and turned us into beat cops always on patrol, arresting anything that rankles. That results in a skirmish like the one during last summer's Whitney Biennial, which culminated in the insistence that Dana Schutz lose her career for an underwhelming painting of Emmett Till because, as a white woman, she couldn't possibly understand this black boy's death. The protests didn't feel like an aesthetic demand but a post-traumatic lashing out. Canceling her might be harsh historical justice, but it denies me an understanding of why the painting fails" (par. 10).

- What assumptions does Morris make about the causes of the uprising against Schutz? How are these assumptions related to the concept of cultural appropriation? Are there other possible explanations for this response to the painting?
- What does the concept of cultural appropriation allow you to understand about the causes and effects of the kind of fandom and spectatorship Morris describes? What do you think about cultural appropriation? Have you ever encountered assumptions about cultural appropriation in your own life?

READING LIKE A WRITER

Speculating about Causes and Effects

A piece of writing that speculates about causes and effects may borrow features from other genres in order to provide background necessary to understand the writer's position. If the piece of writing addresses a concept with which readers are likely to be unfamiliar, for example, the writer will need to explain that concept fully, perhaps by providing a brief definition of the concept, comparing the concept to something readers are familiar with, and offering readers examples they can relate to. As they speculate about causes and effects, writers must present their subject fairly, make a logical, well-supported cause or effect argument, respond to objections or alternative speculations, and establish their credibility.

Essays that speculate about causes or effects contain two essential elements: the logical analysis of the proposed cause or effects and the reasoning and support offered for each cause or effect.

In the following excerpt, Morris describes the effects of claiming that something is canonical:

Cause
Effect   But resisting these critiques . . . with an automatic claim of canon feels like an act of dominion. . . . Insisting that a canon is settled gives those concerns the "fake news" treatment, denying a legitimate grievance by saying there's no grounds for one. It's shutting down a conversation, when the longer we go without one, the harder it becomes to speak (par. 9).

Here, although Morris does not use the typical if/then sentence structure to speculate about the effect he describes, he makes a well-supported cause-and-effect argument because he establishes a **chronological relationship** — one thing happens after another in time — as well as a **causal relationship** — one thing makes another thing happen.

ANALYZE & WRITE

See pp. 578–579 for a checklist of genre features.

Write three or four paragraphs analyzing how Morris draws on the features of cause-and-effect writing while also using features from position writing and concept explanations to explore the effects of canon-making:

1. Reread paragraphs 12–13, highlighting where Morris explores additional effects of declaring something canonical. What reasoning and support does he offer for these effects? How effective is this writing strategy?

2. Asserting his position, Morris writes, "Canon formation, at its heart, has to do with defending what you love against obsolescence, but love can tip into zealotry, which can lead us away from actual criticism into some pretty ugly zones" (par. 10). Reread paragraphs 10–12 and mark words and phrases that demonstrate how Morris's speculations about causes and effects help him develop his position. Which features of position arguments does Morris draw on in this section and elsewhere?

3. Morris tries to engage readers' interest (a feature of concept explanation) by making many pop culture and literary references to remind readers that they already know something about canon formation. Choose the reference that most resonates with you and describe how effective that writing strategy is in persuading you of the effects of canon-making.

READING LIKE A WRITER

The Rhetorical Situation in Multi-Genre Writing

For more on audience as an element of the rhetorical situation, see Chapter 1, p. 13.

All writers must consider their rhetorical situation, which involves asking questions about their purpose, audience, stance, genre, and medium/design.

You have already considered some of the most prominent features of each genre that appears in Morris's essay. The prompts below ask you to address how the features of those genres work alongside and in conjunction with each other to meet the needs of Morris's rhetorical situation.

ANALYZE & WRITE: AUDIENCE

Write three or four paragraphs analyzing how combining the features of cause-and-effect writing, position arguments, and concept explanation work together to support Morris's sense of his **audience**.

1. Morris explains that when you make something canon it "places a work, a person or an idea beyond reproach. It pre-resolves debate. That is, of course, what a canon is—a settled matter. It's established rules and norms. It's the books of the Bible. It's the approved Catholic saints. It's Jane Austen, the Beatles, Miles Davis, Andy Warhol and Beyoncé" (par. 2). What does this list and other references throughout Morris's essay suggest about the audience he imagines for his piece? Is it an eclectic audience comprised of people of different ages, cultures, races, and interests, or is it a more uniform audience? Explain your answer and support it with passages from the essay.

2. How do the features you have focused on in the Analyze & Write prompts above (p. 540) complement each other to engage Morris's imagined audience? How effective is Morris's chosen combination? What might be lost if Morris didn't choose to draw on all of these genre features?

3. What other features from the three genres Morris draws on are present in his essay? How do these features reflect Morris's understanding of his rhetorical situation?

4. What other genres and specific features of each genre might Morris have chosen to draw on to engage readers? How would these have revealed his understanding of his audience while also meeting the needs of other aspects of the rhetorical situation?

See pp. 578–579 for a checklist of genre features.

Phil Christman

On Being Midwestern: The Burden of Normality

Phil Christman is a writer and instructor of writing at the University of Michigan. He is also the editor of the *Michigan Review of Prisoner Creative Writing*. Prior to teaching at the University of Michigan, Christman taught English composition at North Carolina Central University and served as Writing Coordinator at the Moore Undergraduate Research Apprenticeship Program, a program dedicated to helping minority students and other underrepresented populations prepare for graduate school. He earned a Masters in English Literature from Marquette University and an MFA in fiction from the University of South Carolina. Christman's writing has appeared in *The Christian Century, Paste, Books & Culture*, and other publications.

▶ Genres: *Reflection, Observation, Explaining Concepts*

- **Before you read,** think about the title of the essay. What do you think it will be about? What do you think the phrase "the burden of normality" might mean?

- **As you read,** pay attention to how Christman's essay opens and what your expectations as a reader are based on that opening. Then, consider where Christman takes you during the course of the essay, and finally where you end up. Are you surprised?

After my Texas-born wife and I moved to Michigan—an eleven-hour drive in the snow, during which time itself seemed to widen and flatten with the terrain—I found myself pressed into service as an expert on the region where I was born and where I have spent most of my life. "What is the Midwest like?" she asked. "Midwestern history, Midwestern customs, Midwestern cuisine?" I struggled to answer with anything more than clichés: bad weather, hard work, humble people. I knew these were inadequate. Connecticut winters and Arizona summers are also "bad"; the vast majority of humans have worked hard, or been worked hard, for all of recorded history; and *humility* is one of those words, like *authenticity* or (lately) *resistance*, that serves mainly to advertise the absence of the thing named. . . . When, looking in your own mind for a sense of your own experiences in a region, you find only clichés and evasions—well, that is a clue worth following. . . . 1

. . . Actually, there is no dearth of commentary upon the Midwest, once you begin to look for it. Historian and politico Jon Lauck points to the region's rich historiographic tradition in *The Lost Region*; journals devoted to the region's history and literature come and go (*MidAmerica; Midwestern Gothic*); . . . writers as major as Toni Morrison, Louise Erdrich, Marilynne Robinson, David Foster Wallace, and Richard Powers set book after book in the region. (Morrison in particular is so identified with 2 the South—because, to be blunt, she's black—that people forget she's from Ohio. *The Bluest Eye, Sula,* and *Beloved* are set there, *Song of Solomon* in Michigan.) If you took English in high school, you read—or pretended you read—Cather, Scott Fitzgerald, Ernest Hemingway, Sherwood Anderson, Sandra Cisneros, and Theodore Dreiser, all of whom wrote of the region lovingly or ambivalently. . . . The situation resembles nothing so much as the episode of the television show *Louie* in which the main character, stricken with guilt over his lapsed friendship with a less successful comedian, appears at the man's house and demands a reunion, a reckoning; where-upon the old friend, after a meaningful silence, remarks that Louie has delivered the same speech twice before: He'd forgotten each time. Our reckoning with the Mid-west is perpetually arriving, perpetually deferred. . . .

. . . As the geographer James Shortridge puts it, "The Middle West came to sym-   3 bolize the nation . . . to be seen as the most American part of America" (33). Nor is average Americanness quite the same as average Russianness or average Scandina-vianness, for the United States has always understood itself, however self-flatteringly, as an experiment on behalf of humanity. Thus, Midwestern averageness, whatever form it may take, has consequences for the entire world; what we make here sets the world's template. The historian Susan Gray has even detected echoes in Turner's lan-guage of Lamarckian evolution, a theory dominant among biologists a century ago, when Turner was writing. The new characteristics that the "old" races of the world acquired in their struggle to build a world among the prairies and forests would cre-ate an actual new, American race (127).

Small wonder, then, that Midwestern cities, institutions, and people show up again   4 and again in the twentieth-century effort to determine what, in America, is normal. George Gallup was born in Iowa, began his career in Des Moines at Drake Univer-sity, and worked for a time at Northwestern; Alfred Kinsey scandalized the country from—of all places—Bloomington, Indiana. Robert and Helen Lynd, setting out in the 1920s to study the "interwoven trends that are the life of a small American city," did not even feel the need to defend the assumption that the chosen city "should, if possible, be in that common-denominator of America, the Middle West." They chose Muncie, Indiana, and called it Middletown (7–8).[1] We cannot be surprised that the filmgoers of Peoria became proverbial, or that newscasters are still coached to sound like they're from Kansas.[2] Nor that a recent defender of the region's distinctiveness feels he must concede, in the same breath, that it "was always less distinctive than other regions" (Wolfson), or that a historian can call "ordinariness" the Midwest's "historic burden" (Etcheson 78). If it is to serve as the epitome of America for Amer-icans, and of humanity for the world, the place had better not be too distinctly any-thing. It has no features worth naming. It's anywhere, and also nowhere.

[1] The identification of Middletown and Muncie is attested in a number of places; see the chapter on Middletown in Igo, Sarah E. *The Averaged American: Surveys, Citizens, and the Making of a Mass Public.* Harvard UP, 2008.

[2] See Edward McClelland's delightful *How to Speak Midwestern,* Belt Publishing, 2016, pp. 9–10.

What does it do to people to see themselves as normal? On the one hand, one   5
might adopt a posture of vigilant defense, both internal and external, against anything that might detract from such a fully, finally achieved humanness. On the other
hand, a person might feel intense alienation and disgust, which one might project
inward—*What is wrong with me?*—or outward, in a kind of bomb-the-suburbs
reflex. A third possibility—a simple, contented *being normal*—arises often in our
culture's fictions about the Midwest, both the stupid versions (the contented families of old sitcoms) and the more sophisticated ones (*Fargo*'s Marge Gunderson, that
living argument for the value of banal goodness). I have yet to meet any real people who manage it. A species is a bounded set of variations on a template, not an
achieved state of being.

I took the first option. As a child, I accepted without thinking that my small town,   6
a city of 9,383 people, contained within it every possible human type; if I could not
fit in here, I would not fit in anywhere. ("Fitting in" I defined as being occupied on
Friday nights and, sooner or later, kissing a girl.) Every week that passed in which I
did not meet these criteria—which was most of them—became a prophecy. Every
perception, every idea, every opinion that I could not make immediately legible to
my peers became proof of an almost metaphysical estrangement, an oceanic dif-
ferentness that could not be changed and could not be borne. I would obsessively
examine tiny failures of communication for days, always blaming myself. It never
occurred to me that this problem might be accidental or temporary. I knew that cities
existed, but they were all surely just Michigan farm towns joined together n number of times, depending on population. Owing to a basically phlegmatic temperament, and the fear of hurting my parents, I made it to college without committing
suicide; there, the thing solved itself. But I worry what would have happened—what
does often happen—to the kid like me, but with worse test scores, bad parents, an
unlocked gun cabinet.

But I also worry about the people who *can* pass as Midwestern-normal. At its least   7
toxic, this can lead to a kind of self-contempt: the nice, intelligent young women in
my classes at the University of Michigan who describe themselves and their friends,
with flat malice, as "basic bitches." In artists, it can lead to self-destructive behavior,
to the pursuit of danger in the belief that one's actual experiences have furnished
nothing in the way of material. It also leads us to one of the other great stereotypes of
Midwesterners, one that I think has a little more truth to it than the nonsense about
hard work and humility: We are repressed. Any emotion spiky or passionate enough
to disrupt the smooth surface of normality must be shunted away. Garrison Keillor,
and in some ways David Letterman, made careers from talking about this repression
in a comic mode that both embodies it and transmutes it into art. The Minnesota
writer Carol Bly finds it less amusing:

> [In the Midwest] there is a restraint against *feeling in general*. There is a
> restraint against enthusiasm ("real nice" is the adjective—not "marvelous");
> there is restraint in grief ("real sober" instead of "heartbroken"); and always,
> always, restraint in showing your feelings, lest someone be drawn closer
> to you. . . . When someone has stolen all four wheels off your car you

say, "Oh, when I saw that car, with the wheels stripped off like that, I just thought ohhhhhhhh."(4)

Critiques of emotional repression always risk imposing a single model for the 8 Healthy Expression of the Emotions on a healthy range of variations. But anyone who has lived in the Midwest will recognize the mode Bly describes, and if you've lived there long enough, you'll have seen some of the consequences she describes:

> You repress your innate right to evaluate events and people, but . . . energy comes from making your own evaluations and then acting on them, so . . . therefore your natural energy must be replaced by indifferent violence. (5–6)

Donald Trump won the Midwestern states in part because he bothered to contest 9 them at all, while his opponent did not. But we cannot forget the *way* he contested them: raucous rallies that promised, and in some views incited, random violence against a laundry list of enemies. Since his victory, the Three Percent Militia has become a recurring, and unwelcome, character in Michigan politics.

A regional identity built on its own denial, on the idea of an unqualified normal- 10 ity: This sounds, of course, like whiteness—a racial identity that consists only of the absence of certain kinds of oppression. (White people can, of course, be econom- ically oppressed, though if the oppression goes on in one place long enough they tend to lose some of their whiteness, to be racialized as that Snopes branch of the human family, the white trash.) And here we hit upon the last major stereotype of the Midwest, its snowy-whiteness.

If the South depends on having black people to kick around, Midwestern whites 11 often see people of color as ever new and out of place, decades after the Great Migra- tion. The thinking goes like this: America is an experiment, carried out in its purest form here in the Midwest; people of color threaten the cohesion on which the whole experiment may depend. Thus, while Southern history yields story after story of the most savage, intimate racist violence—of men castrated and barbecued before smil- ing crowds, dressed as for a picnic—Midwestern history is a study in racial quaran- tine.[3] Midwestern cities often dominate in rankings of the country's most segregated. And though the region has seen its share of Klan activity and outright lynchings—I write this days after the acquittal of the St. Anthony, Minnesota, police officer who killed Philando Castile—the Midwest's racism most frequently appears in the history books in the form of riots: Detroit, 1943; Cleveland, 1966; Milwaukee, Cincinnati, and Detroit again, 1967; Chicago, Cincinnati again, and Kansas City, 1968; Detroit again, 1975; Cincinnati again, 2001; Ferguson, 2014; Milwaukee again, 2016. A riot is, among other things, a refusal to be quarantined. And the Midwest quarantines its nonwhite immigrants, too—the people from Mexico and further south, from the hills of Laos or the highlands of Somalia, and from the Middle East, who commute from their heavily segregated neighborhoods to harvest the grain, empty the bedpans, and

---

[3] I mean this more or less literally. The book exists; see Sugrue, Thomas J. *The Origins of the Urban Crisis*. Princeton UP, 1997.

drive the snowplows. This is not to mention the people whose forced removal or confinement gave rise to the notion of the Midwest as an empty canvas in the first place. The twentieth-century history of racism in the Midwest is, on the whole, both a terrible betrayal of the abolitionist impulse that led to the settlement of so much of the region and a fulfillment of the violence inherent in the idea of "settling" what was already occupied.

Our bland, featureless Midwest—on some level, it is a fantasy. The easiest, most 12 tempting tack for a cultural critic to take with fantasies is to condemn them. Given what ideas of normalness, in particular, have done to this country, to its nonwhite, nonstraight, non–middle-class, nonmale—and also to those who are all of those things, and are driven slightly or fully crazy by the effort to live up to the norm that is their birthright—it is tempting simply to try to fumigate the myth away.

Tempting, but probably not possible. As the English moral philosopher Mary 13 Midgley argues, myths are "organic parts of our lives, cognitive and emotional habits, structures that shape our thinking" (7). Since thinking cannot be structureless, a frontal attack on one myth usually leaves us in a state of uncritical, unnamed acceptance of a new one. Self-conscious attempts to create new myths, meanwhile, are like constructed languages; they never quite lose their plastic smell. We should ask instead whether our story of the Midwest—this undifferentiated human place—contains any lovelier, more useful, or more radical possibilities. At the very least, we should try to name what there is in us for it to appeal to.

Marilynne Robinson's Gilead trilogy has been read so often as to be reduced to 14 a gingham study in Americana, and Robinson, a complex and in some ways cranky thinker, to "an Iowa abbess delivering profundities in humble dress" (Athitakis 9). This is a strange way to think about the story of a man dying before his son's tenth birthday; of an emotionally distant drifter who fails at prostitution and eventually marries a pastor; of an Eisenhower Republican family that loses its chance at partial redemption because the kindly dad is a racist. If conflating Marilynne Robinson with cozy regionalists like Jan Karon gets more people to buy Robinson's books, I suppose I can't object too strenuously, but it may lead some readers to miss the strangeness of passages such as this one in *Home* (2008):

> In college all of them had studied the putative effects of deracination, which were angst and anomie, those dull horrors of the modern world. They had been examined on the subject, had rehearsed bleak and portentous philosophies in term papers, and they had done it with the earnest suspension of doubt that afflicts the highly educable. And then their return to the *pays natal,* where the same old willows swept the same ragged lawns, where the same old prairie arose and bloomed as negligence permitted. Home. What kinder place could there be on earth, and why did it seem to them all like exile? Oh, to be passing anonymously through an impersonal landscape! Oh, not to know every stump and stone, not to remember how the fields of Queen Anne's lace figured in the childish happiness they had offered to their father's hopes, God bless him. . . . Strangers in some vast, cold city might notice the grief in her eyes, even remember it for an hour or two as they would a painting or a photograph, but they would not violate her anonymity. (282)

This passage offers a stunning inversion of the trope of featurelessness. While acknowledging that the place (in this case Gilead, Iowa) has a history ("the childish happiness they had offered to their father's hopes"), Glory Boughton, the narrator, longs for the "anonymity" and "impersonal landscape" of a "vast, cold city" (Chicago, Minneapolis, Milwaukee). She longs for "deracination," for the sense of being an anyone moving through an anyplace. Why should a person long for this? Anonymity is usually felt as a burden, and the sense that one is a mere "basic person" can imprison as much as it liberates.

Yet the passage resonates, because we humans need to feel that we are more than 15 our communities, more than our histories, more even than ourselves. We need to feel this because it is true. The cultural conservative ideal, with its deeply rooted communities—an idea that finds a strange echo in the less nuanced kinds of identity politics—is a reduction as dangerous to human flourishing and self-understanding as is the reduction of the mind to the brain or the soul to the body. The "deeply rooted community" is, in reality, at least as often as not, a cesspit of nasty gossips, an echo chamber in which minor misunderstandings amplify until they prevent people from seeing each other accurately, or at all. As for the identities that drive so much of our politics, they are a necessary part of the naming and dismantling of specific kinds of oppression—but we've all met people for whom they become a cul-de-sac, people who ration their sympathy into smaller and smaller tranches of shared similarity until they begin to resemble crabbed white men. Moral imaginations, like economies, tend to shrink under an austerity regime.

Every human is a vast set of unexpressed possibilities. And I never feel this to be 16 truer than when I drive through the Midwest, looking at all the towns that could, on paper, have been my town, all the lives that, on paper, could have been my life. The factories are shuttered, the climate is changing, the towns are dying. My freedom so to drive is afforded, in part, by my whiteness. I know all this, and when I drive, now, and look at those towns, those lives, I try to maintain a kind of double consciousness, or double vision—the Midwest as an America not yet achieved; the Midwest as an America soaked in the same old American sins. But I cannot convince myself that the promise the place still seems to hold, the promise of flatness, of the freedom of anonymity, of being anywhere and nowhere at once, is a lie all the way through. Instead, I find myself daydreaming—there is no sky so conducive to daydreaming—of a Midwest that makes, and keeps, these promises to everybody.

And then I arrive at the house that, out of all these little houses, by some inconceiv- 17 able coincidence, happens to be mine. I park the car. I check the mail. I pet the cat. I ready myself for bed. I can't stay up too late. Between the Midwest that exists and the other Midwest, the utopic no-place that I dream of, is hard work enough for a life.

Works Cited

Athitakis, Mark. *The (New) Midwest*. Belt Publishing, 2017.

Bly, Carol. "From the Lost Swede Towns." *Letters from the Country,* Harper & Row, 1981.

Etcheson, Nicole. "Barbecued Kentuckians and Six-Foot Texas Rangers: The Construction of Midwestern Identity." In Andrew Cayton and Susan E. Gray, editors. *The American Midwest*, Indiana UP, 2001.

Gray, Susan E. "Stories Written in the Blood: Race and Midwestern History." In Andrew
　　Cayton and Susan E. Gray, editors. *The American Midwest*, Indiana UP, 2001, p. 127.
Lauck, Jon K. *Toward a Revival of Midwestern History*. U of Iowa P, 2014.
Lynd, Robert S., and Helen Merrell Lynd. *Middletown: A Study in American Culture*. 1929.
　　Harcourt, Brace, 1959, pp. 7–8.
Midgley, Mary. *Myths We Live By*. Routledge Classics, 2014.
Robinson, Marilynne. *Home*. Farrar, Straus and Giroux, 2008.
Shortridge, James. *The Middle West*. U of Kansas P, 1989, p. 33.
Wolfson, Matthew. "The Midwest Is Not Flyover Country." *The New Republic*, 22 Mar. 2014,
　　newrepublic.com/article/117113/midwest-not-flyover-country-its-not-heartland-either.

READING FOR MEANING

For help with summarizing and other reading strategies, see Chapter 2.

1. **Read to Summarize.** Write a sentence or two explaining what Christman means when he says that the idea of the Midwest as bland and featureless "is a fantasy" (par. 12).

2. **Read to Respond.** Christman writes, "What does it do to people to see themselves as normal? On the one hand, one might adopt a posture of vigilant defense, both internal and external, against anything that might detract from such a fully, finally achieved humanness. On the other hand, a person might feel intense alienation and disgust, which one might project inward — *What is wrong with me?* — or outward, in a kind of bomb-the-suburbs reflex" (par. 5). Thinking about a previous life experience or your current college experience, which social groups seem to be thought of as most "normal" and most "abnormal?" Who determines these classifications and who gets to belong to each group?

3. **Read to Analyze Assumptions.** Write a paragraph or two analyzing an assumption you find intriguing in Christman's essay. For example:

   Assumptions about the usefulness of the category of normality. Christman assumes that there is value in classifying something or someone as normal. He writes, "Small wonder, then, that Midwestern cities, institutions, and people show up again and again in the twentieth-century effort to determine what, in America, is normal" (par. 4).

   - What characteristics or features of the Midwest does Christman point to as setting the bar for normality? What value does Christman assign to calling something normal? How and why is this useful or important?

   - Are there other terms or categories that you think might be equally or more productive to describe what Christman calls normality?

   Assumptions about human complexity. Christman writes that "every human is a vast set of unexpressed possibilities" (par. 16), thereby connecting this assumption to his inquiry into normality.

- How do Christman's assumptions about how complex and deep people are, including those you find elsewhere in the essay, inform his essay? How does this assumption intersect with the argument he makes about normality?

- Do you share Christman's assumptions about this complexity? Where do your assumptions come from?

READING LIKE A WRITER

Reflection

Reflective writing is based on the writer's personal experience and explores something the writer did, saw, heard, or read. Unlike strictly autobiographical or observational writing, reflective writing uses these personal experiences to think about society, including how people live and what people believe. In his reflective essay, Christman also uses features from observational writing, which offers thought-provoking portraits or profiles of a person or place, in order to draw a portrait of the Midwest while also reflecting on his own relationship to this region. Because his readers may not understand the complexity that he attaches to the Midwest, Christman takes time in his essay to explain the Midwest not just as a geographical location, but as a concept, drawing also on features of concept explanation. Reflective essays present an occasion — something the writer experienced or observed — that led them to think about their subject in depth. Christman begins with the occasion of moving with his wife to Michigan. He uses this event to introduce the subject of his essay; then, throughout the rest of the essay, Christman reflects on the Midwest and the related issues it raises for him:

- He expresses his dismay at not being able to adequately describe the Midwest without using clichés.

- He gives examples of how he has noticed the various representations of the Midwest in contexts such as regional and national histories, literature, and art.

- He considers what it means to identify oneself as from a specific region of the country.

ANALYZE & WRITE

Write three or four paragraphs analyzing how Christman draws on the features of reflective writing while also using aspects of concept explanation and observational writing to explain his reflections:

1. Skim the essay, noticing how Christman uses examples—including from outside sources—to help readers understand and accept his reflections. Choose one or two examples and explain why you think they work especially well to help readers understand what Christman means.

(continued)

2. How does Christman convey his perspective (a feature of observational writing) through his reflections? Which words and phrases in the essay show his perspective? Does he ever explicitly tell readers what he thinks?

3. Reread paragraphs 2 and 14, noticing how Christman integrates sources smoothly (a feature of concept evaluations) to support his reflections. How effective are these sources at helping you understand the concept of the Midwest and the relevance of Christman's exploration?

READING LIKE A WRITER

The Rhetorical Situation in Multi-Genre Writing

For more on stance as an element of the rhetorical situation, see Chapter 1, p. 13.

All writers must consider their rhetorical situation, which involves asking questions about their purpose, audience, stance, genre, and medium/design.

You have already considered some of the most prominent features of each genre that appears in Christman's essay. The prompts below ask you to address how the features of those genres work alongside and in conjunction with each other to meet the needs of Christman's rhetorical situation.

ANALYZE & WRITE: STANCE

Write three or four paragraphs analyzing how combining the features of reflective writing, observational writing, and concept explanation work together to support Christman's **stance**:

1. First, reread paragraphs 1–4 in order to determine Christman's stance toward his subject. Which information, reflections, and illustrations does he use to convey this overall attitude? Then, skim the rest of the essay. Is Christman's stance consistent? Explain your answer.

2. How do the features you have focused on in the Analyze & Write prompts above (pp. 549–550) complement each other to indicate Christman's stance or attitude toward his subject? How effective is Christman's chosen combination? What might be lost if Christman didn't choose to draw on all of these features?

3. What other features from the three genres Christman draws on are present in his essay? How do these features reflect Christman's understanding of his rhetorical situation?

4. What other genres and specific features of each genre might Christman have drawn on to develop his stance? How would these support his chosen genre while also meeting the needs of other aspects of his rhetorical situation?

Tajja Isen

How Can We Expand the Way We Write about Our Identities?

Tajja Isen is a writer and a contributing editor to *Catapult*. Her work has appeared in many publications including *Electric Literature*, *The Globe and Mail*, *The Rumpus*, *Catapult*, and *Buzzfeed*. She is also a voice actress and has worked on shows such as *Atomic Betty*, *The Berenstain Bears*, and *The ZhuZhus*. Isen holds a combined Juris Doctorate/Masters in English and Law degree from the University of Toronto. The essay below appeared in *BuzzfeedNews* in 2018.

▶ Genres: ***Proposal to Solve a Problem, Observation, Autobiography***

- **Before you read,** consider your own identity. Do you identify as part of a specific ethnic group, culture, religion, or other community?

- **As you read,** consider how Isen pushes back against the identity that editors and others have expected her to adopt in her personal essays. Have you ever challenged an identity that you feel others have pushed onto you?

I've started a ritual to dispose of personal essay ideas I know I won't write. It involves   1
saying the phrase aloud—"personal essays I won't write"—like it's a punchline, or a prayer. I say it when I'm tempted by bits of the quotidian that have that special glimmer: reading Malcolm X on public transit. Blasting 50 Cent while driving through a white suburb with my mother. Letting people touch my hair for money. *Personal essays I won't write.*

The refrain is a joke, mostly, a loving dig at how easy it is to make googly eyes at   2
your navel. But it's also a minor exorcism: By articulating the urge, however fleeting, to seize an idea, pin it down, and parse its innards, I make myself evaluate the kernel at its heart. Say I started drafting one of those essays-that-weren't, the one about blasting The Massacre with the windows down. Once the scene was set and it was time to lay down something like a thesis, I'd have cornered myself into uttering the same phrase, one I hadn't planned to spill ink over, but without which the essay might lack some logical or emotional core: "As a woman of color. . . ."

What might we gain from thinking of our writing as an ongoing project to worry   3
at the same wound? Self-awareness, for one thing. Jess Zimmerman, writer and editor-in-chief of Electric Literature, posed this question on Twitter: If you had to boil down your personal essays into a single refrain, what would it be? Zimmerman noted a trend in the responses: Many people use their writing "to send constant, repetitive signals of personal distress." Across multiple essays, writers transmit versions of the same call—"I'm scared," "I'm hurt," "I'm grieving"—in an effort to be heard and

understood. But the best refrains did something else as well. More than just trying to translate the writer's struggles, they looked outward to consider what value it might offer to a reader. In Zimmerman's figuration, it's the difference between an SOS signal and a lighthouse—not just a signpost of your pain, but a warning to prevent another's suffering.

My own refrain—"as a biracial woman, my experience of x can leave me feeling hopelessly in between"—was textbook SOS. Gazing through that lens, I told the story of myself, and certain scenes snapped into focus: *That was violence. That was not benign. That one shapes me even now.* For a while, the relief and the fury of this naming were enough.   4

But soon, I began to feel that the pressure to make my mixed-race identity my rhetorical crux was as much externally imposed as it was self-inflicted. In my work, I posed a range of questions to which my body's unreadability kept resurfacing as the often unintended answer: Why did I leave the music industry? What does it mean to see yourself represented in a text? Why is my juvenilia so white? These pieces—all ones that I stand behind and worked on with smart, sensitive editors—gave way to others, where the choice to serve up suffering wasn't always mine.   5

Things get tricky when your refrain is tied up in an identity claim, and trickier still when that identity is an axis, or several axes, of marginality. You offer your pain up once, and if an editor asks you to do it again, to work that angle a bit harder, it seems disingenuous to deny them. It's still true, isn't it? What if that's the thing they love most about the piece? What's more, not every editor even asks permission to press on the bruise—I've made brief nods to my blackness for context, and they've spotlit the mention and pushed on it hard, to the point that it drowned out my argument.   6

In her new book, *Penis Envy and Other Bad Feelings*, writer and theorist Mari Ruti discusses the role of our traumas in our stories of self-making. There's no doubt, to quote Ruti, that "who we are has a great deal to do with how we have been wounded." But that's qualitatively different from building our bodies of work around this original wound. As I placed more work online, I came to understand something that continues to shape my thinking: Despite the position from which I write, and the need for it to inform my work, I also want that work to bloom around a richer core than the supposed pain of racial difference. If each writer chases a singular question, then I need a refrain that does more open-ended, unexpected work than just announcing the color of my skin as the intellectual bottom line—even if, or especially if, that tortured pose is the kind of work that editors expect.   7

As writers of color slowly gain greater visibility, it's important to consider what kinds of narratives we keep asking these artists to tell. Today's media market has a tendency to demand versions of the same story from all marginalized writers, and that's especially true in the personal essay economy, a certain sector of which is defined by its hunger for suffering. As Sarah Menkedick reminds us, the continual potshots taken at the personal essay form—as the lazy, nonliterary exposure of trauma and identity—are reductive, and arguably just symptoms of condescending reading. But the pressure to perform minority trauma does put writers of color at an especially high risk of being pigeonholed. If, as Soraya Roberts argues, the   8 personal essay isn't dead, it's just no longer white, then it's incumbent on both writers and editors to ensure that this increased visibility doesn't occur at the expense of depth, or lead to tokenization.

I want to emphasize that these questions on how to write identity are very much a   9 two-way street, that it's not all a conspiracy of cookie-cutter editorial practices under the guise of diversifying content. More importantly, I want these writers to get their work out and get their money, to feel the peerless satisfaction of clarifying a sensation or experience that was once kept opaque to them. For a lot of people, that's going to hinge on an identity claim, and it's a crucial time to be doing that kind of political work. But it's also worth considering the refrain that writer and editor collaboratively produce: What lives at the core of the stories you tell about yourself? What narratives of trauma are you coaxing out of people who might be trying to express something else?

Of course, there will always be writers content to make trauma their calling card.   10 The essayist Morgan Jerkins has been explicit about how writing on black suffering jump-started, and still structures, her career. With remarkable efficiency, she built a reputation for turning around rapid responses to acts of police brutality and anti-black violence. Again: Get your money. This is America. But where this approach becomes murky is when such a writer gets anointed by white media as the voice of a generation, thereby cementing one person's views — in this case, an emphasis on racial trauma as central to living — as the definitive version of black womanhood. It reifies what writing about identity "ought" to look like, making it harder for writers in her wake to step from this path. Black women might read it and think, "But that's not my story." White women might read it and think, "I knew it."

How might we help usher in more nuanced ways of writing identity, ones that   11 don't always demand that writers of color perform their suffering on the page? Last month, Porochista Khakpour offered us one possibility with the launch of her new Medium series, *Off Beat*. Khakpour aims to give writers the chance — or the challenge — to write about a topic that is, quite literally, "off the beat" that they're usually tapped to discuss. Khakpour knows from experience that writers can easily get shoehorned by editors, magazines, and by their own pitches into covering particular subjects, a move that becomes especially pernicious for marginal writers. And being endlessly called upon only to recite the woes of a minority group is, as Cord Jefferson writes in "The Racism Beat," exhausting to the point of being unsustainable. Khakpour notes that the stakes of such a narrow beat are also existential, provoking in its writers the urgent question: "Who am I outside of what they see me as?"

In addition to editorial strategies like Khakpour's, there are ways to tackle the ques-   12 tion as writers. Zadie Smith's most recent essay collection, Feel Free, which came out in February, takes a different approach to broadening the ways we think about identity writing. In the book's foreword, Smith plants herself firmly on the lighthouse side of Zimmerman's dichotomy: "I feel this — do you? I'm struck by this thought — are you?" Her manner of reaching out to the reader is informed by her view of the self as unbounded and fluid: a "malleable and improvised response" to the world and language, as opposed to one fixed by physicality, ethnicity, or history. It's a far cry from the call to carve up our bodies into their constituent oppressions, the all-too-common misuse of "intersectionality." But Smith is also aware that her view of selfhood is some-what dated, especially in the face of a political reality explicit about its assault on various identity categories, one that brings with it the pressure—even the need—for those identities to be boldly asserted.

The most sensitive, compelling approach to exploring the self I've encountered in recent writing is Alexander Chee's *How to Write an Autobiographical Novel*, which came out in April. (You don't even get past the title without the sense that you're being directly addressed; it's hard to get more lighthouse than "how-to"—though the book is less guide than dialogue.) Like sex shops or the dentist, books are not often places I walk into hoping to be called out and shown a mirror. But there's a detail that seized me within the first few pages of Chee's book, in the essay "The Curse": While on a summer exchange program in Tuxtla Gutiérrez, Mexico, 15-year-old Chee is reading Frank Herbert's classic science fiction novel Dune. He is moved by the boy at the heart of the novel, the latest in a series of characters like Batman and Sherlock Holmes, "who went from being ordinary people to heroes through their ability to perceive the things others missed. I wanted to see if I too could obtain these powers through observation." 13

I glimpsed a version of myself within this perfect moment, in the desire to make sense of your world while swimming in the soup of a still-forming identity; the pro-to-hope, not yet quite articulable, that writing will bring this sense of clarity; the knowledge of the reader and the narrator—but not yet the boy—that, yes, it will. There are more ways to reach from the page than the mere fact of seeing your iden-tity represented. I was thrilled to have my cover blown. 14

The motif of the observant outsider continues to resurface throughout that essay—Chee, half white and half Korean, is one of the only nonwhite students on exchange—but he resists the narrative of pained in-betweenness. Chee admits to being less exoticized in Mexico than when he's at home in Maine, but he presents the predict-able mixed-race story as an option rather than a given, one that he rejects rather than embraces. Here's Chee, avoiding the easy answer: "In the United States, if I said I was mixed, it meant too many things I didn't feel. Mixed feelings were confusing feelings, and I didn't feel confused except as to why it was so hard for everyone to understand that I existed." He's not hopelessly lost as a result of his identity; rather, it lends him a chance for exploration. In a memorable scene toward the essay's end—and it seems crucial that Chee's work moves in scenes, driven as much by novelistic description as by a rhetorical bottom line—he uses his newfound fluency in Spanish to convince a couple of party guests that he is a boy called Alejandro from Tijuana. This act of theatrics sets the tone for many of the pieces that follow, foregrounding the pleasure and power of the masks that we don to perform versions of ourselves, both on the page and off. 15

In an essay called "The Writing Life," Chee describes the semester he spent taking Annie Dillard's literary nonfiction class at Wesleyan University. In Dillard's teaching philosophy, the literary essay was "a moral exercise that involved direct engagement with the unknown, whether it was a foreign civilization or your mind." Rather than closing on the expected story, writers are bound to face the unfamiliar. When Chee arrives at the Iowa Writers' Workshop, he announces that he's "taking this parade 16 down the middle of the road," carving out space for himself as a gay Korean American writer amid the program's stifling whiteness. Throughout the collection, he continues to center his body and politics in what he brings to the page. But such detailed, specific self-exploration can still look outward, welcoming another into the unknown of writing yourself, rather than foisting a map on them right off the bat and marking all of the intersections that meet at the point where you live. I want to quote Chee once more, on confronting the story the world foists onto mixed-race people: "[It] felt like discovering your shoe was nailed to the floor, but only one of them, so that you paced, always, a circle of possibility, defined by the limited imaginations of others." Let's stop nailing writers' shoes to the floor.

Not long after I noticed the pattern of my personal writing—that all my inquiries 17 were reducible to the same bottom line—I decided that I was going to withdraw myself from my work entirely. I scrubbed my prose of anecdotes or personal pronouns; I wrote careful reviews that hid those bits of opinion at risk of being traced back to a body. *You've grown*, I told myself. *You're a real critic now.* But this stance, too, turned out to be untenable. Even if I'm not writing a piece that explicitly lassoes in the personal, I can't stand to cut that channel off entirely; it's not much better than having my work rewritten to convey a sense of pain that I don't feel. I come to the page to attend to the specificity of my experience—to achieve clarity by explaining myself to myself, whether I'm staging my encounter with a text, a fictional scene, or a woman in line at the grocery who wants to touch my hair.

I want to let myself into my work not in droplets or fragments or anything so jeal- 18 ously guarded, nor in the unfiltered gush that shapes the clichéd idea of the personal essay. And here, Chee's use of scenes offers a guide for the kind of writer that I'm working to become. If I told the story of my Kafkaesque law school years, I would want to dwell on their curious characters and emotional textures, alert to how such things were shaped by the institution's whiteness, but not feeling pressed to shuffle every detail into line behind a clickbait claim of violence. I'm trying to keep an eye on both halves of the equation: not just the intimacy of exposure, but the act of the telling—the idea that, if we follow the scenes of our story closely enough, we might find twists that generate conclusions different from the ones our bodies suggest. We might reach no conclusion at all.

READING FOR MEANING

1. **Read to Summarize.** Write a sentence or two explaining the problem that Isen is describing, as well as her solution to it.

   For help with summarizing and other reading strategies, see Chapter 2.

2. **Read to Respond.** Write a paragraph analyzing Isen's claim that "the pressure to perform minority trauma does put writers of color at an especially high risk of being pigeonholed" (par. 8). What does she mean by "minority trauma" and how does this lead to pigeonholing? Are you aware of any other examples of this phenomenon?

3. **Read to Analyze Assumptions.** Write a paragraph or two analyzing an assumption you find intriguing in Isen's essay. For example:

   Assumptions about how writers reach readers. Isen writes, "But the best refrains did something else as well. More than just trying to translate the writer's struggles, they looked outward to consider what value it might offer to a reader" (par. 3) and "There are more ways to reach from the page than the mere fact of seeing your identity represented" (par. 14).

   - Do your own experiences as a reader lead you to agree with Isen that the best personal writing looks outward toward the reader? Why or why not?

   - As a reader, how do you expect a writer to connect with you? As a writer, how do you strive to connect with readers?

   Assumptions about writers of color. Isen writes, "I need a refrain that does more open-ended, unexpected work than just announcing the color of my skin as the intellectual bottom line" (par. 7) and asks, "How might we help usher in more nuanced ways of writing identity, ones that don't always demand that writers of color perform their suffering on the page?" (par. 11).

   - Why do you think Isen values open-ended and more nuanced ways of treating identity, particularly for writers of color and those from marginalized groups?

   - As a reader, what assumptions do you make about writers of color and writers from marginalized groups? Do you expect them to address their own identities or the concept of identity in their writing? Explain your answer.

READING LIKE A WRITER

Proposal to Solve a Problem

Proposals to solve problems must first identify the problem and help readers understand why the problem is worth addressing and ultimately solving. Depending on how familiar readers are with the problem, a writer may dedicate more space to analyzing the problem and establishing its seriousness before moving on to solutions.

ANALYZE & WRITE

Write three or four paragraphs analyzing and evaluating how Isen combines features from the genres of autobiography and observation to help her present the problem and establish its seriousness.

1. Reread paragraphs 3–16. How does Isen use outside sources to help readers understand that the problem exists and is serious?

2. In paragraphs 3–16, how does Isen also convey the autobiographical significance (a feature of autobiographical writing) of the problem she outlines?

3. Reread paragraph 11 through the end of the essay in order to determine how Isen conveys her perspective on the subject (a feature of observational writing) as she demonstrates how the proposed solution would help solve the problem she outlines. How feasible is her proposed solution? Are you convinced that it would be effective?

READING LIKE A WRITER

The Rhetorical Situation in Multi-Genre Writing

All writers must consider their rhetorical situation, which involves asking questions about their purpose, audience, stance, genre, and medium/design.

For more on purpose as a feature of the rhetorical situation, see Chapter 1, p. 13.

You have already considered some of the most prominent features of each genre that appears in Isen's essay. The prompts below ask you to address how the features of those genres work alongside and in conjunction with each other to meet the needs of Isen's rhetorical situation.

ANALYZE & WRITE: PURPOSE

Write three or four paragraphs analyzing how combining the features of proposals to solve a problem, autobiography, and observation work together to support Isen's **purpose**.

1. How does Isen use rhetorical questions throughout her essay to help organize it in a way that is clear, logical, and convincing (a feature of proposals to solve a problem) to help achieve her purpose?

2. How do the features you have focused on in the Analyze & Write prompts above (pp. 556–557) complement each other to support Isen's purpose? How effective is Isen's chosen combination? What might be lost if Isen didn't choose to draw on each of these features?

3. What other features from the three genres Isen draws on are present in her essay? How do these features reflect Isen's understanding of her rhetorical situation?

4. What other genres and specific features of each genre might Isen have drawn on and how would these support her purpose while also meeting the needs of other aspects of the rhetorical situation?

Jonathan Jones

Leonardo v Rembrandt: Who's the Greatest?

Jonathan Jones is a British art critic and journalist. He has written three books: *The Lost Battles: Leonardo, Michelangelo and the Artistic Duel That Defined the Renaissance*; *The Loves of the Artists*; and *Tracey Emin: 2007–2017*. He served as a judge for both the 2009 Turner Prize, a highly competitive annual prize that is awarded to a British visual artist, and the 2011 BP Portrait Award, a prestigious worldwide portrait competition. Since 1999 he has written for the *Guardian*, which is where this essay was published in 2018.

▶ Genres: *Evaluation, Observation, Arguing for a Position*

- **Before you read,** consider what you already know about Leonardo daVinci and Rembrandt. Where does your knowledge come from?

- **As you read,** notice how Jones presents the comparison between the two artists. How do his rhetorical choices affect your response to his piece?

It's the art fight of the year, the rumble in the museum. Who is the greatest—Rembrandt   1
van Rijn or Leonardo da Vinci? The two geniuses both have big anniversaries this year. According to the Netherlands, 2019 is officially the Year of Rembrandt. Amsterdam's Rijksmuseum, the Mauritshuis in The Hague and the Museum De Lakenhall in Leiden are all putting on shows for the 350th anniversary of his death in 1669. Yet Rembrandt isn't getting his year to himself. This also happens to be the 500th anniversary of the death of Leonardo in 1519. It's a great excuse for exhibitions by Britain's Royal Collection and British Library as well as a grand retrospective at the Louvre.

So which is the bigger anniversary? The smart bet might seem to be Rembrandt.   2
His art is so absorbing, tragic and inward. His portraits are the painterly equivalents of King Lear. He is a painter in whose shadows the soul can linger. By contrast, Leonardo is a pop star who's still busting the market 500 years after his death—and isn't that a bit oppressive? It's hard not to feel alienated among all the smartphone-touting tourists in front of the *Mona Lisa*. Not much room there for the meditative silent communion you can have with a Rembrandt.

Rembrandt's *Self-Portrait with Two Circles* is unlikely to be surrounded by cameras   3
if you seek it out at Kenwood House in London. You can gaze into the old artist's dark eyes as they contemplate you in return. His conscious presence lurks in soft mossy gatherings of muted colour. He uses his brush to create both himself and what looks like an unfinished map of the world. Rembrandt looks noble and flawed, gazing at you as one troubled person at another.

Did Leonardo ever create anything so disarmingly and rawly human? I'd reply   4
with another question: has anyone under the age of 30 ever given a hoot about Rembrandt? Self-portraits that probe the inner self are all very well, but there's a

universality to Leonardo that puts him in a different league. I became a fan of his genius when I was about eight. I had a Ladybird book about great artists. The story of Leonardo da Vinci was like a fairytale—there was a picture of him buying birds at market just so he could release them. What's Rembrandt got for an eight-year-old? And how many copies would *The Rembrandt Code* sell?

As for depth, it's a false test to compare a Rembrandt self-portrait with the *Mona* 5 *Lisa*. To grasp the real wonder of Leonardo you need to look at his drawings. He finished very few paintings and all are commissions in which self-expression struggles with patrons' demands. It's in his notebooks that Leonardo truly soars. In page after page he studies nature, designs machinery, invents weapons, plans fortifications and seeks the secret of flight.

The greatest of all these visual investigations are his anatomical drawings. These 6 are his artistic answers to Rembrandt's portraits—and they are also miracles of science. He wrote of the dread he felt when he stayed up all night in a dissection room full of cadavers, alone with the dead. Out of these experiments he produced drawings that go—literally—deeper than Rembrandt. Instead of being moved by a face, Leonardo digs and cuts in search of life's hidden structure. The drawings that record his fleshy discoveries outdo Rembrandt's greatest portraits as images of what it is to be human. There's no more moving work of art on earth than his depiction of a foetus in the womb, esconced as if in a capsule bound for the stars.

The quivering mystery of Leonardo's drawings of the lungs and heart, the precision 7 of his studies of the eye and brain—these are his most sensitive as well as mind-boggling works. His anatomical drawings belong to the Queen and many will be touring the country this year.

Sure, Rembrandt is the Shakespeare of painting. But Leonardo is Shakespeare, 8 Einstein and the Wright brothers rolled into one. Come off it, Rijksmuseum. This just isn't Rembrandt's year.

READING FOR MEANING

1. **Read to Summarize.** Write a sentence or two explaining why and based on what criteria Jones compares Rembrandt and daVinci.

2. **Read to Respond.** Write a paragraph analyzing Jones's claim that "Leonardo is a pop star who's still busting the market 500 years after his death — and isn't that a bit oppressive?" (par. 2). Can you offer examples of how Leonardo is "still busting the market?" How would this be oppressive?

3. **Read to Analyze Assumptions.** Write a paragraph or two analyzing an assumption you find intriguing in Jones's essay. For example:

   Assumptions about how to judge art. Jones writes, "So which is the bigger anniversary? The smart bet might seem to be Rembrandt. His art is so absorbing, tragic and inward" (par. 4).

For help with summarizing and other reading strategies, see Chapter 2.

- By the end of the essay, Jones declares daVinci's anniversary the bigger one despite his point that Rembrandt's art is "so absorbing, tragic, and inward." What criteria does he use to compare the two artists' works that leads him to this conclusion?

- What assumptions do you have about what constitutes good art, and where do those assumptions come from? Based on your own assumptions, do you find yourself agreeing or disagreeing with Jones's conclusion?

Assumptions about how to discuss art. Although Jones is a serious art critic, in this piece his tone is not consistently serious. For example, throughout the piece he refers to da Vinci by his first name, calls him a pop star (par. 2), and describes his subject as "the art fight of the year . . . a rumble in the museum" (par. 1).

- Why do you think Jones discusses art in this way? What does it suggest about how he understands art and artists, as well as what he anticipates about readers who might pick up the piece?

- Reread the essay, keeping track of moments that you would describe as more serious than those quoted above. Where does Jones's discussion become more serious and more along the lines of what you might expect from a serious art critic? Why do you think he becomes serious in these particular moments? As a writing strategy, how effective is his shifting tone?

READING LIKE A WRITER

Evaluation

Writers of evaluations strive to convince readers that their judgment is trustworthy because the reasons are based on criteria, such as shared values, that are appropriate to the subject and backed by reliable evidence. Although readers may expect a definitive judgment, they often also appreciate a balanced one that acknowledges other possible opinions and judgments. For example, Jones recognizes that Rembrandt is talented, but makes his judgment clear in the conclusion to his piece:

> Sure, Rembrandt is the Shakespeare of painting. But Leonardo is Shakespeare, Einstein and the Wright brothers rolled into one (par. 8).

ANALYZE & WRITE

Write three or four paragraphs analyzing and evaluating how Jones supports his judgment while balancing it by acknowledging other positions:

1. Reread the title and the first two paragraphs of the essay. How do the title and the opening two paragraphs set up the two items to be evaluated and begin to anticipate the author's judgment, as well as alternative judgments?

2. Jones chooses to adopt the role of detached spectator (one of the possible authorial roles in observational writing) as he compares DaVinci and Rembrandt. What advantages and disadvantages do you see in this role as he evaluates the artists and their works? Can you imagine a way he may have taken on the role of participant observer given the subject of his piece?

3. What reasonable evidence (a feature of position arguments) does Jones use to support his evaluative argument? How effective do you think his evidence is?

READING LIKE A WRITER

The Rhetorical Situation in Multi-Genre Writing

All writers must consider their rhetorical situation, which involves asking questions about their purpose, audience, stance, genre, and medium/design.

For more on the rhetorical situation, see Chapter 1, p. 13.

You have already considered some of the most prominent features of each genre that appears in Jones's essay. The prompts below ask you to address how the features of those genres work alongside and in conjunction with each other to meet the needs of Jones's rhetorical situation.

ANALYZE & WRITE: STANCE

Write three or four paragraphs analyzing how combining the features of evaluation, observation, and position arguments work together to support Jones's **stance**:

1. First, reread paragraphs 1–3, paying particular attention to the first sentence of the essay. How and where does Jones's stance toward his subject emerge? How does his stance help set the tone for the rest of the essay? Were you expecting this kind of stance in a piece about legendary artists? Why or why not?

2. How do the features you have focused on in the Analyze & Write prompts above (pp. 560–561) complement each other to indicate Jones's stance toward his subject? How effective is Jones's chosen combination? What might be lost if Jones didn't choose to draw on each of these features?

3. What other features from the three genres Jones draws on are present in his essay? How do these features reflect Jones's understanding of his rhetorical situation?

4. What other genres and specific features of each genre might Jones have drawn on to develop his stance? How would these support his chosen genre while also meeting the needs of other aspects of the rhetorical situation?

Aru Terbor

A Deeper Look at Empathetic and Altruistic Behavior

Aru Terbor was a senior psychology major focusing on behavioral psychology when he wrote this paper for an upper-level psychology-themed writing course. The assignment asked students to argue a position by exploring a concept or set of related concepts in the field of behavioral psychology.

▶ Genres: *Arguing a Position, Explaining Concepts, Cause and Effect*

- **Before you read,** consider what you know about the concepts of empathetic and altruistic behavior. In what contexts have you heard these terms? What do you think they mean?

- **As you read,** think about altruistic behaviors you have engaged in. How would you describe your motivations for these behaviors?

As America becomes increasingly divided politically, culturally, and religiously, there   1
have been many calls for empathy. Empathy, from the German word "einfühlung," which translates as "in feeling," is a kind of emotion of identification that is experienced in relation to something or someone else. Empathy is "having an emotion that is somewhat like the emotion experienced by the target person" (Mar, Oatley, Ditjick, and Mullin 2011, 824). Because empathy asks us to look beyond ourselves and reach toward others by trying to understand their ideas, beliefs, positions, and points of view, empathy has been described as a possible remedy for our increasingly fractured culture by many people including educators such as Carolyn Calloway-Thomas, former President Obama, and social psychologist Jamil Zaki.

Being empathetic can also be classified as an altruistic act, that is, a behavior   2
"designed to increase another person's welfare, and particularly those actions that do not seem to provide a direct reward to the person who performs them" (Jhangiani and Tarry). In fact, there is a specific kind of altruism defined by its relationship to empathy: empathy-altruism. This kind of altruism is based specifically on feelings for others—the giver behaves altruistically because of empathetic feelings toward another person. Altruistic behaviors that might be inspired by empathy include charitable donations, letting a stranger go before you in line, giving blood, visiting the elderly in nursing homes, helping a neighbor in need, or sacrificing your own life to save the lives of others.

However, looking more closely at the concept of empathy-altruism reveals that   3
pure altruism may not be as common as we think, and egoism may be the motivating factor for these seemingly altruistic behaviors. Understanding what might be motivating empathy-altruism, as well as understanding the potential implications of empathetic behavior, can provide a more comprehensive and nuanced understanding of

both empathy and altruism, and by extension this concept of empathy-altruism. If we don't take the time to understand these concepts, then calls for empathy are not as informed as they might be. We then run the risk of misusing the concept, misunderstanding its implications, and not being able to inspire the kind of empathy that may help unify America.

Many would argue that examples of altruism are all around us, and that these 4 examples are motivated by our empathetic feelings toward others. In fact, Daniel Baston, an American psychologist, has consistently argued that there are such things as truly altruistic acts. More specifically, he developed the empathy-altruism hypothesis that maintains that if we feel empathy toward a person we are motivated to help them for reasons that do not benefit us at all. Baston explains:

> The empathy-altruism hypothesis states that empathetic concern produces altruistic motivation. To unpack this deceptively simply hypothesis, it is necessary to know what is meant by "empathetic concern," by "altruistic motivation," and even by "produces." Empathetic concern—other-oriented emotion elicited by and congruent with the perceived welfare of someone in need—is distinguished from seven other uses of the term empathy. Altruistic motivation—a motivational state with the ultimate goal of increasing another's welfare—is distinguished from four other uses of the term altruism. Altruism is contrasted with egoism—a motivational state with the ultimate goal of increasing one's own welfare. The question of why empathetic concern might produce altruistic motivation is addressed by considering the information and amplification functions of emotions in general, as well as the relationship of emotion to motivation.

In other words, Baston believes that when one feels empathy toward another, it produces altruistic motivation, which is motivation characterized solely by increasing another's welfare.

Although Baston's empathy-altruism hypothesis is heartening, the prevailing 6 hypothesis in Western psychology is that people are not motivated by altruism, but by egoism. Egoism is the theory that people are motivated by self-interest. Egoism is in some ways the opposite of altruism because the motivating factor for a behavior is self-interest rather than to "increase another person's welfare." So how could good deeds be driven by self-interest? What could you possibly gain from letting a stranger go before you line or giving blood? Social psychologists have found that benefits include material gain, social approval, enhancement of their self-image, avoidance of self-censure, and alleviation of distress (Hoffman).

Both empathy and altruism involve moving beyond oneself and thinking about 7 others, but as positive as these behaviors sound, everyone from philosophers to neurobiologists have wondered whether there are such things as truly selfless acts. For example, philosophers as far back as Aristotle have considered what motivates humans to behave as they do and contemporary neurobiologists study chimpanzees, squirrels, vampire bats and other animals to understand the mechanisms in the brain that lead to acts of generosity because they believe this can help us understand human behavior (Gabbatiss).

Earlier this semester, I developed a research project for my psychology class that 8
explores the question of what drives human behavior, including behavior that at first
glance seems driven by altruistic motivations. I developed a two-question survey
using the SurveyMonkey platform. The registrar generated a random sample of 150
students at my university. These students were sent a link to the survey and their
responses to these open-ended questions were completely anonymous. I used the
data from the first 100 students who responded. In the first question, students were
given the definition of an altruistic act—an act "that is designed to increase another
person's welfare, and particularly those actions that do not seem to provide a direct
reward to the person who performs them" (Jhangiani and Tarry) and asked to list
any acts they performed in the last year that they thought could be characterized as
altruistic. The first chart lists the different acts students reported. The second question
asked what motivated students to perform those acts. Those answers were coded as
altruistic, meaning that the act was performed just to benefit the other person, or
ego-driven, meaning that the answer indicated at least some benefit to the student
even if there was also a benefit to the receiver. These answers are represented in the
second chart.

As the second chart shows, the vast majority of students said that they were 9
motivated by wanting to help others, but seven percent of students said they were
motivated because the act benefitted themselves in some way. By their own admission, this small percentage was motivated by egoism rather than altruism.

So what does this data mean? First, it is important to note that there are limita- 10
tions to this study. The sample is small and limited to university students. The data I
collected may also be affected by what is called response bias. As Rosenman, Tennekoon, and Hill, faculty members at University of Washington's School of Economic
Sciences explain:

"Response bias is a widely discussed phenomenon in behavioural and health 11
care research where self-reported data are used; it occurs when individuals offer

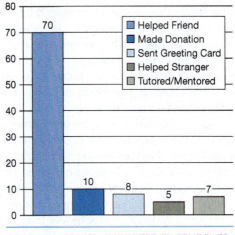

ACTS OF ALTRUISM REPORTED BY STUDENTS

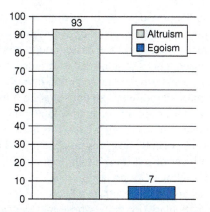

PERCENTAGE OF REPORTED ALTRUISTIC ACTS MOTIVATED BY ALTRUISM AND EGOISM

self-assessed measures of some phenomenon. There are many reasons individuals might offer biased estimates of self-assessed behaviour, ranging from a misunderstanding of what a proper measurement is to social-desirability bias, where the respondent wants to 'look good' in the survey, even if the survey is anonymous."

Because the students taking the survey are reporting their own motivations, 12 response bias suggests the data might not fully and accurately reflect the true motivations behind these altruistic acts.

Despite the limitations of this study, response bias and a participant's potential 13 desire "to 'look good' in the survey" (Rosenman, Tennekoon, and Hill) suggests another way of interpreting the data, however. This could potentially mean that the number of students who determined their motivations were ego-driven is actually higher than seven percent, and the students who determined their motivations were altruistic may have been ashamed to admit that their seemingly altruistic acts were actually self-serving. This kind of response is understandable due to negative contemporary associations with selfishness and egoism. Although this study doesn't prove anything and these limitations prohibit us from drawing conclusions about altruism and egoism, the study does suggest that even acts that seem altruistic may be motivated by egoism. This leads us to consider egoism as a concept.

Despite negative contemporary associations with the concept of egoism—no one 14 wants to be told they have a big ego—egoism is not inherently negative. For an illustration of this we can look at Aristotle's definition of what he called "self-love," a term that predates egoism, but largely captures the same idea. Even in Aristotle's time he was aware of the negative connotation that accompanied the concept of self-love, noting that "people criticize those who love themselves" (155). He continues, "The bad man seems to do everything for his own sake" whereas "the good man acts for honour's sake" as well as "his friend's sake, and sacrifices his own interest. But the facts clash with these arguments, and this is not surprising" (155). Explaining why these arguments don't hold up, he writes that "those who use the term as one of reproach ascribe self-love to people who assign to themselves the greater share of wealth, honours, and bodily pleasures" (156). Aristotle means that self-love gained its negative connotation because of its association with those whose self-interest leads them toward greed. This is not always the case, though, and there are often more noble or acceptable consequences of self-love. As he suggests, acting with self-love or for the self does not necessarily equate to acting morally wrong (156). Aristotle explains further: "If a man were always anxious that he himself, above all things, should act justly, temperately, or in accordance with any other of the virtues . . . no one would call such a man a lover of self" (156). This is an example of how a man's self-love can lead to good. Aristotle takes his point even further by arguing that "the good man *should* be a lover of self (for he will both himself profit by doing noble acts, and will benefit his fellows)" (emphasis added 156). Much more recently, Psychologist Jamil Zaki has argued that self-love is crucial for "sustainable and deep empathetic concern," particularly for those whose jobs demand empathy, such as in the field of nursing ("How to Avoid").

So what does this mean for altruism and understanding the kind of altruism that is 15 motivated by empathy? If we understand why people are motivated to behave altruistically—and we aren't afraid to consider egoism as a motivating factor—then we can have a better idea of how to motivate people to be more empathetic.

Motivating people to be more empathetic to others, especially those not like 16 them or those who don't think like them is a challenge, particularly in this digital age. Despite all of the different perspectives available on the Web, including opinions on everything from immigration to what to feed your dog, to whether eating organic food is beneficial, studies show that people tend to reside in what are called echo chambers or filter bubbles where their own ideas are simply echoed back at them and those they don't agree with are filtered out. In 2016, writer, lecturer, and broadcaster Kenan Malik (2016) described the divide among the American people as "shaped more by identity than by ideology":

> The key fault line today is not between left and right but between those who welcome a more globalized, technocratic world, and those who feel left out, dispossessed and voiceless. . . . Both sides interpret facts and news through their own particular political and cultural frames. All this has led to anguished discussions about people living in "echo chambers"—sealed-off social worlds in which the only views they hear are ones echoing their own.

Social media platforms, with their algorithms and filters, only perpetuate the growth 17 of these "sealed-off social worlds" and exacerbate their consequences, making empathy that much more difficult to achieve.

Not only is empathy difficult to achieve, but its implications are not always 18 positive. Up until this point, this essay has assumed that empathy is inherently a positive behavior with only positive consequences. However, in empathizing with someone else there are risks, including making less of the other person as you empathize with them. Jonathan Alexander and Jacqueline Rhodes, experts in composition and rhetoric who consider how identity plays out in writing, call this a "flattening effect" as "the 'other' is tamed as a knowable entity" (431). Amy Shuman describes further the potential negative implications of empathy: "Empathy offers the possibility of understanding across space and time, but it rarely changes the circumstances of those who suffer (5). Additionally, in *Scenes of Subjection: Terror, Slavery, and Self-Making in Nineteenth-Century America*, dedicated to exploring how black identities were shaped during and in the aftermath of slavery, Saidiya Hartman writes, "Empathy is double-edged, for in making the other's suffering one's own, this suffering is occluded by the other's obliteration" (19). In other words, although empathy is conceived of as a way to reach beyond oneself and establish connections with others by identifying with them, that identification may obscure that person and their situation.

Yale psychologist and author of the book *Against Empathy*, Paul Bloom has been 19 very outspoken about the potentially negative consequences of empathy. He has argued that:

> On many issues, empathy can pull us in the wrong direction. . . . Moral judgment entails more than putting oneself in another's shoes . . . plenty of good deeds—disciplining a child for dangerous behavior, enforcing a fair and impartial procedure for determining who should get an organ transplant, despite the suffering of those low on the list—require us to put our empathy to one side. . . . Our best hope for the future is not to get people to think of all humanity as family—that's impossible. It lies, instead, in an appreciation of the fact that, even if we don't empathize with distant strangers, their lives have the same value as the lives of those we love. . . . Our hearts will always go out to the baby in the well; it's a measure of our humanity. But empathy will have to yield to reason if humanity is to have a future. ("The Baby")

Bloom's point is that empathy does not necessarily lead to good moral judgment and 20 that imagining that people can be inspired to empathize with strangers is unrealistic. Instead, he suggests that we need to use reason and more intellectual faculties in order to appreciate the value of others, their lives, and their perspectives.

This exploration of empathy, altruism, and the empathy-altruism hypothesis has 21 revealed that these concepts are more complicated than is usually understood. Seemingly altruistic acts are not always motivated by altruism and may be motivated by egoism. Still, egoism or self-love should not be understood as inherently negative and may actually be integral to sustaining feelings of empathy toward others. Most compelling, though, as we look forward to our country's future are some of the potentially negative consequences empathy. It is hard to believe that anyone who is trying to act empathetically toward others wants to do these people harr either by obliterating their identities or by neglecting to act on their behalf (rather than just identifying with them). Todd DeStigter, who draws on Jay Robinson's concept of "critical empathy," offers what seems to be both a heartening and realistic way of conceiving of empathy. DeStigter explains critical empathy as "the process of establishing informed and affective connections with other human beings, of thinking and feeling with them at some emotionally, intellectually, and socially significant level, while always remembering that such connections are complicated by sociohistorical forces that hinder the equitable, just relationships that we presumably seek" (240). Critical empathy, then, brings together rational and emotional aspects of empathy by highlighting that connections with other human beings should be both informed and affective and that these relationships are complex and often inequitable. Ultimately, instead of calling for empathy, we should be calling for critical empathy in order to better capture and address the very complexities of this seemingly simple concept.

Works Cited

Alexander, Jonathan, and Jacqueline Rhodes. "Flattening Effects: Composition's Multicultural Imperative and the Problem of Narrative Coherence" *College Composition and Communication,* vol. 65, no. 3, 2014, pp. 430–454.

Aristotle. *Nicomachean Ethics*. Trans. W. D. Ross, https://socialsciences.mcmaster.ca/econ/ugcm/3ll3/aristotle/Ethics.pdf.

Bloom, Paul. *Against Empathy: The Case for Rational Compassion*. Ecco, 2016.

—. "The Baby in the Well: The Case Against Empathy." *The New Yorker*, 20 May 2013, http://faculty.missouri.edu/segerti/capstone/BloomAgainstEmpathy.pdf.

Calloway-Thomas, Carolyn. *A Call for a Pedagogy of Empathy, Communication Education*, vol. 67, no. 4, 2018, pp. 495–499. DOI: 10.1080/03634523.2018.1504977

DeStigter, Todd. 1999. "Public Displays of Affection: Political Community through Critical Empathy." *Research in the Teaching of English* 33 (3): 235–244.

Gabbatiss, Josh. "There Is No Such Thing as a Truly Selfless Act," *BBC.com*, 19 July 2016, http://www.bbc.com/earth/story/20160718-there-is-no-such-thing-as-a-truly-selfless-act.

Hartman, Saidiya V. *Scenes of Subjection: Terror, Slavery, and Self-Making in Nineteenth-Century America*. Oxford UP, 1997.

Hoffman, Martin L. "Is Empathy Altruistic?" *Psychological Inquiry*, vol. 2, no. 2, 1991, pp. 131–133.

Jhangiani, Rajiv and Hammond Tarry. "Chapter 8: Helping and Altruism," *Principles of Social Psychology*, edited by Charles Stangor, https://opentextbc.ca/socialpsychology/chapter/chapter-summary-9/.

Malik, Kenan. "All the Fake News That Was Fit to Print." *The New York Times*, 4 Dec. 2016, www.nytimes.com/2016/12/04/opinion/all-the-fake-news-that-was-fit-to-print.html.

Mar, Raymond A., Keith Oatley, Maja Djikic, and Justin Mullin. "Emotion and Narrative Fiction: Interactive Influences Before, During, and After Reading." *Cognition and Emotion* vol. 25, no 5, 2011, pp. 818–833.

Obama, Barack. "Obama to Graduates: Cultivate Empathy." *Northwestern University News*, 2006, www.northwestern.edu/newscenter/stories/2006/06/barack.html.

Rosenman Robert, Vidhura Tennekoon, and Laura G. Hill "Measuring Bias in Self-Reported_ Data," *International Journal of Behavioral and Healthcare Research*, vol. 2, no. 4, 2011, pp. 320–32.

Shuman, Amy. *Other People's Stories: Entitlement Claims and the Critique of Empathy*. University of Illinois Press, 2005.

Zaki, Jamil. "How to Avoid Empathy Burnout," *Nautilus*, 7 April 2016, http://nautil.us/issue/35/boundaries/how-to-avoid-empathy-burnout.

READING FOR MEANING

1. **Read to Summarize.** Write a sentence or two explaining what Terbor reveals about the potential motivations behind empathetic and altruistic acts.

For help with summarizing and other reading strategies, see Chapter 2.

2. **Read to Respond.** Terbor concludes his piece by calling for critical empathy. Do you think he does enough to show how this is different from noncritical empathy? Do you find his call compelling? Why or why not?

3. **Read to Analyze Assumptions.** Write a paragraph or two analyzing an assumption you find intriguing in Terbor's essay. For example:

Assumptions about ego. Terbor assumes that people think of egoism as something that is bad or wrong, and he challenges these assumptions: "This kind of response is understandable due to negative contemporary associations with selfishness and egoism" (par. 12).

- Do your views about having a big ego align with Terbor's characterization of "negative contemporary associations with the concept of egoism?" Explain your answer.

- Terbor looks back to Aristotle to support his point that being motivated by ego is not necessarily negative. Are there current examples you can think of to support this idea?

Assumptions about the effects of online echo chambers and filter bubbles. Terbor assumes that online echo chambers and filter bubbles make it more difficult for empathy to thrive: "Motivating people to be more empathetic to others, especially those not like them or those who don't think like them is a challenge, particularly in this digital age . . . people tend to reside in what are called echo chambers or filter bubbles where their own ideas are simply being echoed back at them" (par. 15).

- Do you share Terbor's assumptions about the effects of online echo chambers and filter bubbles? Where do your assumptions come from?

- What other reasons may deter people from acting empathetically? Explain your answer.

READING LIKE A WRITER

Arguing for a Position

In addition to explicitly stating their positions, writers of position papers also have to give reasons for their positions by drawing on facts, statistics, examples, anecdotes, expert opinions, and analogies. For example, Terbor draws on experts to consider the potential negative effects of empathy:

"However, in empathizing with someone else there are risks, including making less of the other person as you empathize with them. Jonathan Alexander and Jacqueline Rhodes, experts in composition and rhetoric who consider how identity plays out in writing, call this a "flattening effect" as "the 'other' is tamed as a knowable entity" (431). (par. 16)

ANALYZE & WRITE

Write three or four paragraphs analyzing how Terbor draws on the features of argumentative writing while also using aspects of concept explanation and cause and effect writing to develop his argument.

1. Make a list of the ways Terbor supports and explores his position. For help doing so, see pp. 60–62 for additional information about facts, statistics, examples, anecdotes, expert opinions, and analogies. Which of these do you think best support his position? Why?

2. How does Terbor integrate sources smoothly (a feature of concept explanations) in order to define and work with the concepts of empathy, altruism, empathy-altruism, and critical empathy? How does Terbor identify those sources and what information does he provide about them to help readers know the sources are relevant and reliable?

3. Responding to objections and alternative speculations (a feature of cause and effect writing), Terbor writes, "Many would argue that examples of altruism are all around us, and that these examples are motivated by our empathetic feelings toward others" (par. 4) but then he goes on to point out that the study he conducted "does suggest that even acts that seem altruistic may be motivated by egoism" (par. 12). List other moments in the essay where Terbor handles objections and alternative speculations in a fair and balanced way. How does Terbor concede and refute these other possibilities?

READING LIKE A WRITER

The Rhetorical Situation in Multi-Genre Writing

For more on design as part of the rhetorical situation, see Chapter 1, p. 13.

All writers must consider their rhetorical situation, which involves asking questions about their purpose, audience, stance, genre, and medium/design.

You have already considered some of the most prominent features of each genre that appears in Terbor's essay. The prompts below ask you to address how the features of those genres work alongside and in conjunction with each other to meet the needs of Terbor's rhetorical situation.

ANALYZE & WRITE: DESIGN

Write three or four paragraphs analyzing how combining the features of argumentative writing, concept explanation, and cause and effect writing work together to support the **design** of Terbor's text:

1. How do the graphs Terbor includes interact with his text in order to deliver information vividly and persuasively?

2. Do you think the combination of text and visuals in this essay helps emphasize Terbor's argument? Can you imagine an alternative design—one that might include more or different visuals, hyperlinks, animation, audio, video, or other forms of interactivity—that would be equally or more compelling than the current design?

3. What features from the three genres Terbor draws on are present in his essay? How do these features reflect Terbor's understanding of his rhetorical situation?

4. What other genres and specific features of each genre might Terbor have drawn on to enhance the design of his text? How would these support his chosen genre while also meeting the needs of other aspects of the rhetorical situation?

Writing to Learn Multi-Genre Essays

Write a brief essay analyzing one of the readings in this chapter (or another selection, perhaps one by a classmate). Explain how (and perhaps, how well) the selection works as a multi-genre essay. Consider, for example, how it

- represents a combination of genres that work well together to achieve its purpose;

- draws on specific features of the different genres in order to adequately explore its subject;

- engages readers by incorporating the most relevant features from each genre.

Your essay could also reflect on how you applied one or more of the following practices as you read the selection:

- **Critical Analysis** — what assumptions in the selection did you find intriguing, and why?

- **Rhetorical Sensitivity** — how effective or ineffective do you think the selection is in achieving its purpose for the intended audience?

- **Empathy** — did you find yourself identifying with the author, and how important was this to the effectiveness of the selection?

A GUIDE TO WRITING MULTI-GENRE ESSAYS

You have probably done a good deal of analytical writing about your reading. Your instructor may also assign a capstone project to write a multi-genre essay of your own. This Guide to Writing offers detailed suggestions and resources to help you meet the special challenges this kind of writing presents.

THE WRITING ASSIGNMENT

Write a multi-genre essay that incorporates at least three of the genres covered in *Reading Critically, Writing Well*.

- Choose a subject that interests you and consider the rhetorical situation.

- Choose a primary genre, the one that most interests you or that will best help you achieve your purpose, given your audience.

- Review the chapter in this textbook where your primary genre is covered, paying close attention to both the Guide to Reading and Guide to Writing sections. You need not reread the reading selections, but do look closely at the strategies this genre typically uses (listed at the beginning of the Guide to Reading section, following the bullet on "Reading Like a Writer") and the activities following the selections in the Guide to Reading, especially the "Reading Like a Writer" prompts and activities.

- Consider features of other genres that will complement your primary genre or help you best achieve your purpose or engage your audience, and then review the chapters on those genre features.

WRITING YOUR DRAFT

Because by definition multi-genre essays draw on several genres simultaneously, and it is up to you or your instructor to determine which genres to combine, this Guide to Writing cannot anticipate the range of combinations that will emerge. For writing strategies specific to support your genres, see the genre feature checklist (pp. 578–579) and then Chapters 3 through 10, as needed. This Guide to Writing will focus on issues to consider while drafting a multi-genre essay.

Choosing a Subject

Rather than limiting yourself to the first subject that comes to mind, take a few minutes to consider your options and list as many subjects as you can. Because your subject is not bound by a specific genre, you have a lot of freedom to first choose a subject that interests you and then decide on the primary and other genres that will work best to explore that subject. Below are some examples of subjects and genres that could work well together.

See Chapter 1, pp. 15–18, for coverage of the writing process.

Subject	Primary Genre	Other Genres
Performance Art	Explaining Concepts	Observation, Evaluation
Discrimination	Speculating about Causes or Effects	Proposal to Solve a Problem, Arguing for a Position, Reflection
Bullying	Proposal to Solve a Problem	Explaining a Concept, Arguing for a Position, Reflection
Required Internships for Students	Arguing for a Position	Evaluation, Reflection
Relationship with a Troubled Sibling	Autobiography	Reflection, Observation

The chart above offers some potential combinations of genres to consider in light of the subjects listed. Keep in mind, though, that there are many combinations of genres that would suit not just these subjects but other subjects, as the readings in this chapter suggest. As you list possible subjects and consider your rhetorical situation, remain open to many different combinations, including those that might seem less obvious.

Considering Your Rhetorical Situation

Once you have chosen a subject it is time to think about your rhetorical situation, which involves asking questions about purpose, audience, stance, genre, and medium/design.

For more on the rhetorical situation, see Chapter 1, p. 13.

Composing with an awareness of the rhetorical situation means writing not only to express yourself but also to engage your readers and respond to their concerns. You write to influence how your readers think and feel about a subject, and, depending on the genre, perhaps also to inspire them to act. Write for several minutes about your rhetorical situation, using the questions below as a jumping-off point for exploration:

- What is my **purpose** for writing this essay? What is my main goal?

- Who is my **audience**? How must my audience's prior knowledge, values, and beliefs influence my writing?

- What is my **stance**? What is my perspective or attitude toward the subject?

- Which primary **genre** would work best to achieve my purpose? What secondary genres would meet my audience's needs, support my perspective, and align with the medium I have chosen?

- In which **medium** should I compose and how should I design my project? How would I like my audience to experience the project?

Formulating a Working Thesis Statement

A working thesis will help you begin drafting your multi-genre essay purposefully. Your thesis should announce your subject and reflect your primary genre. For example, if evaluation is your primary genre, then you should make your overall judgment of the subject clear. If you are explaining a concept, your thesis should announce the concept and may also forecast any associated topics. If you are writing a proposal to solve a problem, then the thesis should offer the solution and may also identify the problem. While autobiographies, literacy narratives, and reflective essays do not necessarily require thesis statements, a working thesis will keep you focused as you draft and revise your essay, and may also lead you to new ideas. Here are two example thesis statements from the readings in this chapter:

> Canon formation, at its heart, has to do with defending what you love against obsolescence, but love can tip into zealotry, which can lead us away from actual criticism into some pretty ugly zones. (Morris, par. 10)

> If we don't take the time to understand these concepts, then calls for empathy are not as informed as they might be. We then run the risk of misusing the concept, misunderstanding its implications, and not being able to inspire the kind of empathy that may help unify America. (Terbor, par. 3)

Organizing Your Multi-Genre Essay

For more on outlining, see Chapter 1, pp. 21, 28 (student essay), and Chapter 2, pp. 41–42.

Writers in all genres consider how to organize their essays. Whether you have rough notes or a complete draft, making an outline of what you have written can help you organize your essay effectively for your audience. You may want to draft a sentence that forecasts what your multi-genre essay will be about. From there you may want to create a draft outline or a concept map (see pp. 41–43). Arranging your points either in an outline or a map will make it easier for you to guide your readers from point to point. As you draft, you may see ways to improve your original plan, and you should be ready to revise your outline or map, shift parts around, or drop or add parts as needed.

Multi-genre essays pose some additional challenges when it comes to organization because they are drawing on different features from multiple genres. How you organize your essay will depend in large part on your rhetorical situation and the genre you have chosen. For example, observational essays typically rely on topical, narrative, and spatial organizational plans while cause and effect essays often depend on presenting your points in logical order (from least to most effective, for example). Despite these differences, there are a few organizational elements that are consistently useful across all genres:

- Forecasting lets your audience know what to expect.

- Topic sentences announce the subject of each paragraph to help orient readers.

- Transitions (*such as, but, however, on the other hand, thus, for example*) guide readers from one point to another.

Focusing on these cues in addition to organizational elements specific to your chosen genres will help you effectively organize your multi-genre essay for your readers. Below are examples of forecasting, topic sentences, and transitions from the readings.

Notice how Gawande uses forecasting statements, topic sentences and transitions in *The Heroism of Incremental Care*:

Forecasting Statement	I finally had to submit. Primary care, it seemed, does a lot of good for people — maybe even more good, in the long run, than I will as a surgeon. But I still wondered how. (Gawande, par. 40)
Topic Sentence Transition	Doctors in other settings — say, an emergency room or an urgent-care clinic — would use a "rule out" strategy, running tests to rule out possible conditions, especially dangerous ones, as rapidly as possible. We would focus first on the chest pain . . . and order an EKG, a cardiac stress test, and the like to detect coronary-artery disease. Once that was ruled out, we might give her an antihistamine and watch her for a couple of hours to see if the symptoms went away. And, when that didn't work, we would send her home and figure, Oh, well, it's probably nothing. This was not, however, the way the woman's primary-care physician approached her condition. (Gawande, pars. 53–54)

Notice how Terbor uses forecasting statements, topic sentences and transitions in *A Deeper Look at Empathetic and Altruistic Behavior*:

Forecasting Statement	Both empathy and altruism involve moving beyond oneself and thinking about others, but as positive as these behaviors sound, everyone from philosophers to neurobiologists have wondered whether there are such things as truly selfless acts. (Terbor, par. 6)
Transition	For example, philosophers as far back as Aristotle have considered what motivates humans to behave as they do and contemporary neurobiologists study chimpanzees, squirrels, vampire bats and other animals to understand the mechanisms in the brain that lead to acts of generosity because they believe this can help us understand human behavior. (Terbor, par. 6)
Topic Sentence	Earlier this semester, I developed a research project for my psychology class that explores the question of what drives human behavior, including behavior that at first glance seems driven by altruistic motivations. (Terbor, par. 7)

Drafting Your Multi-Genre Essay

By this point, you have done a lot of writing

- to consider your rhetorical situation;
- to choose a subject and draft a working thesis statement that reflects the essay's primary genre;
- to remind yourself of the features of the genres you have chosen;
- to create a tentative outline or concept map to support the essay's organization.

Now stitch that material together to create a draft. As you write, refer to the multi-genre writing checklist below. Then, the final sections of this Guide to Writing will help you evaluate and improve your draft.

CHECKLIST: Multi-Genre Writing

1. As you write, review your rhetorical situation in light of your subject. Does your chosen primary genre help you achieve your purpose and meet your audience's needs? Does your stance toward the material, as well as your chosen medium and design, help you communicate your ideas?

2. Consider your primary genre by reviewing its features on the chart below. Are some of the typical features of the primary genre visible in your writing? Are there additional features from that genre that might be productively incorporated into your essay? Are there elements of your rhetorical situation that the typical elements of this genre do not adequately cover? Keep these features in mind as a guide for what you will want to try to include as you develop your essay.

3. Consider what elements of your rhetorical situation fall outside of the typical elements of the genre you selected. Look through the primary features of other genres by referring to the chart below. Do any of these features fit what you are trying to do? If so, you should consider incorporating features of this genre into your writing (these will become secondary genres).

4. As you write, consider your secondary genre(s). Do these genres complement your primary genre and help you achieve your purpose and engage your audience? Refer to the chart below. Are any of the typical features of the secondary genres visible in your writing? Are there additional features from those genres that might be productively incorporated into your essay? Remember that these are typical features only — you don't have to (and likely shouldn't) try to incorporate every feature of each genre you use. Multi-genre writing is about becoming aware of how you pick features typical of certain genres in response to the rhetorical situation of your writing assignment. The combination of features you pick determines which genres your writing will tend to fall in, and will help you determine if you are meeting the goals of your assignment.

FEATURES OF RHETORICAL GENRES

Autobiography

1. Narrating a story dramatically
2. Presenting people and places vividly
3. Conveying the significance powerfully

Observation

1. Deciding whether to take the role of a spectator or a participant
2. Determining what information to include and how to present it
3. Organizing the information in a way that will be entertaining to readers
4. Conveying a perspective on the subject

Reflection

1. Presenting the occasion vividly and in a way that prepares readers for the reflections
2. Developing the reflections fully, using appropriate writing strategies
3. Engaging readers' interest

Explaining Concepts

1. Using appropriate writing strategies: defining, illustrating, comparing and contrasting, and showing causes and effects
2. Organizing the information clearly and logically
3. Integrating sources smoothly
4. Engaging readers' interest

Evaluation

1. Presenting the subject in enough detail so that readers know what is being judged
2. Supporting an overall judgment based on appropriate criteria with credible evidence
3. Responding to objections and alternative judgments readers might prefer
4. Organizing the evaluation in a way that will be clear and logical to readers

Arguing for a Position

1. Presenting the controversial issue fairly and credibly
2. Asserting a clear position
3. Arguing directly for it with reasonable evidence
4. Responding to objections and alternative positions fairly

Speculating about Causes or Effects

1. Presenting the subject fairly
2. Making a logical, well-supported cause or effect argument
3. Responding to objections or alternative speculations
4. Establishing credibility to present the writer as thoughtful and fair

Proposal to Solve a Problem

1. Demonstrating that the problem exists and is serious
2. Showing how the proposal would help solve the problem and is feasible
3. Responding to objections and alternative solutions
4. Organizing the proposal in a way that is clear, logical, and convincing

REVIEWING AND IMPROVING THE DRAFT

This section includes guides for Peer Review and Troubleshooting Your Draft. Your instructor may arrange a peer review in class or online where you can exchange drafts with a classmate. The Peer Review Guide will help you give each other constructive feedback regarding the basic features and strategies typical of writing a multi-genre essay. (If you want to make specific suggestions for improving the draft, see Troubleshooting Your Draft on p. 580.) Also, be sure to respond to any specific concerns the writer has raised about the draft. The Troubleshooting Your Draft guide that follows will help you reread your own draft with a critical eye, sort through any feedback you've received, and consider a variety of ways to improve your draft.

A PEER REVIEW GUIDE

How effective is the combination of genres?

What's Working Well: Let the writer know where the genres, and specific features of each, complement each other.

What Needs Improvement: Indicate sections of the essay that could benefit from the writer's use of additional features from one or more of the genres the writer has chosen.

How clear is the focus of this multi-genre essay?

What's Working Well: Identify where the writer indicates the thesis or focus and how the primary genre is reflected in that focus.

What Needs Improvement: Tell the writer if the thesis or focus seems unclear—too general or too narrow, for example, depending on the genres the writer is combining.

How clear and easy to follow is the organization of this multi-genre essay?

What's Working Well: Indicate passages that seem to flow logically from one to another. Highlight a passage in which transitions work especially well to guide the reader from point to point.

What Needs Improvement: Tell the writer where you have trouble following the logic of the organization, including how rearranging or strengthening connections among paragraphs might be productive. Point out where forecasting, topic sentences, and transitions within and between paragraphs would be useful.

How engaging is this multi-genre essay?

What's Working Well: Point to passages that are especially engaging and explain why.

What Needs Improvement: Tell the writer where you found the essay dull, including why you think you became disengaged from the essay. For example, was there too much detail or not enough, or did you find yourself being distracted by other aspects of the essay?

Revising and Improving the Draft

Revising means reenvisioning your draft, trying to see it in a new way, given your purpose and audience, to develop a compelling multi-genre essay. Think imaginatively and boldly about cutting unconvincing or tangential material, adding new material, and moving material around. Referring back to the chart on pp. 578–579, consider even switching out the features of one genre for another genre to better meet the needs of your rhetorical situation.

TROUBLESHOOTING YOUR DRAFT

To More Effectively Combine the Genres	
If the combination of genres is not effective,	• Consider other genres that would work better and incorporate features from those. • Revise paragraphs where the genres seem to clash.
To Clarify the Focus	
If your thesis is unclear,	• Rephrase it or spell it out in more detail. • State it more directly or position it more boldly. • Repeat it in different words throughout your essay.

To Improve the Organization	
If the essay is hard to follow,	• Add a brief forecast of your main points at the beginning of the essay. • Reorder your points in a logical arrangement, such as least to most important. • Announce each reason explicitly in a topic sentence. • Add logical sentence and paragraph transitions to make the connections between points clearer.
To Enhance Credibility	
If readers consider some of your sources questionable,	• Establish the credibility of your sources by providing a bit of relevant background to demonstrate their expertise. • Replace questionable sources with information from scholarly articles and well-regarded general interest publications.
If your tone is harsh or offensive,	• Find ways to establish common ground with readers, for example, by acknowledging other points of view. • Choose words with more positive connotations to create a more civil tone. • Concede points your readers might raise or use the concession-refutation strategy.
To Improve Readability and Engagement	
If parts of the essay are dull or unfocused,	• Rewrite them, perhaps by adding a surprising or vivid anecdote or visual. • Search your sources for a memorable quotation or a vivid example to include.

Editing and Proofreading Your Draft

Check for errors in usage, punctuation, and mechanics, and consider matters of style. If you keep a list of errors you typically make, begin by checking your draft against this list. Use a writer's handbook to look up the errors you have made and for information on how to correct them.

Reflecting on Writing Multi-Genre Essays

In this chapter, you have critically read several multi-genre essays. To better remember what you have learned, pause now to reflect on the reading and writing activities you completed in this chapter.

1. Write a page or so reflecting on what you have learned. Begin by describing what you are most pleased with in your essay. Then explain what you think contributed to your achievement.

   - If it was something you learned from the readings, indicate which readings and specifically what you learned from them.

   - If it came from the writing you did in response to prompts in this chapter, point out the section or sections that helped you most.

2. Reflect more generally on multi-genre writing.

   - Why might a writer use the features of multiple genres simultaneously?

   - How comfortable were you incorporating features from multiple genres into a single essay?

   - How do you think your integration of features from multiple genres helped you understand each genre better?

3. By reflecting on what you have learned about multi-genre writing, you have been practicing **metacognition,** one of the academic habits of mind.

   - Were you aware of any other habits of mind you practiced as you read and responded to the material in this chapter? If so, which habits did you find useful?

   - If not, think back now on your reading and writing process. Can you identify any habits you used?

CHAPTER 12

Strategies for Research and Documentation

A s many of the essays in *Reading Critically, Writing Well* show, writers often rely on research to expand and test their own ideas about a topic. This chapter offers advice on conducting research, evaluating potential sources, integrating source material you decide to use with your own writing, and documenting this material in an acceptable way.

PLANNING A RESEARCH PROJECT

To research and write about a topic effectively at the college level requires a plan. A clear sense of your rhetorical situation, as well as the practical needs of your research task (such as the due date and the level of detail required), will help you create one. The table below lists common elements that you will need to consider not only as you plan your research project, but also as you continue to find and evaluate sources and draft your project.

OVERVIEW OF A RESEARCH PROJECT

Define your research task and set a schedule.

Analyze your rhetorical situation.

- Determine your purpose.
- Analyze your audience to understand the interest and background your readers bring to the project, and analyze your attitude to determine how you want your readers to think of you.
- Determine the genre, or type, of research project you are creating, such as a proposal or laboratory report, and the expectations for research, writing, and design associated with this genre.

Understand the assignment.

- Check your syllabus or consult your instructor about the requirements of the project (such as the number and types of resources required, the length of the project, and so forth).
- Determine the final due date, and assign yourself interim due dates to keep your project on track.

Establish a research log.

- Create a list of keywords.
- Create a working bibliography (list of sources), and annotate entries.
- Take notes on your sources.

Choose a topic, get an overview, and narrow your topic.

Choose a topic that answers an interesting question relevant to the assignment and of interest to you and your readers.

- Consult with your instructor.
- Review textbooks and other course materials.
- Explore newspapers, magazines, and Internet sites.

Get an overview, and narrow your topic (if necessary).

- Consult subject guides or a librarian to determine the availability of sources on your topic.
- Get necessary background by consulting encyclopedias and other general reference sources.
- Start a working bibliography to keep track of the bibliographic information of potential sources. (See pp. 588–589.)
- Draft questions to guide your research.

Search for in-depth information on your topic.

Conduct a search for sources, using carefully selected search terms.

- Check the library's resources (such as the catalog, databases, or home page) for books, articles, and multimedia.
- If acceptable to your instructor, search the Internet for relevant websites, blogs, and groups.
- Keep a list of search terms in a research log, and annotate your working bibliography to keep track of sources.
- Add relevant sources to your working bibliography, and annotate each entry to record the genre (or type) of source, the source's main points, and how you would use the source.
- Refine your research questions, and draft a working thesis.

Refine your search.

Ask yourself questions like these about the sources you have found:

- Is this what I expected to find?
- Am I finding enough information?
- Am I finding too much?
- Do I need to modify my keywords?
- Do I need to recheck background sources?
- Do I need to revise my research questions?
- Do I need to modify my thesis statement?

Continue searching for relevant and credible sources in response to your answers.

Evaluate your sources.

Determine the relevance of potential sources.

- Does the source explain terms or concepts or provide background?
- Does the source provide evidence to support your claims?
- Does the source offer alternative viewpoints or lend authority?

Determine the credibility of potential sources.

- Who wrote it?
- When was it published?
- Who published it and what is the reputation of the publisher?
- Is the source scholarly or popular (or something else)?
- Is the source printed or online?
- What does the source say?

Continue to evaluate and refine your search strategy based on your research results.

Use your research to enrich your project.

Use evidence from sources in a range of ways.

- Synthesize ideas from multiple sources to support your ideas with summaries, paraphrases, and quotations as appropriate.
- Include your own analysis to demonstrate how source information supports your ideas.
- Use sources to explain terms or concepts or provide background information.
- Incorporate alternative viewpoints or interpretations from sources.

Avoid plagiarism.

- Paraphrase carefully and quote accurately to avoid plagiarism.
- Carefully integrate source material into your text.
- Cite sources using an appropriate citation style.

ANALYZING YOUR RHETORICAL SITUATION AND SETTING A SCHEDULE

Making your research manageable begins with defining the scope and goals of your research project. Begin by analyzing your *rhetorical situation*:

- What is your *purpose*? Is it to explain a concept, argue for a position, or analyze the causes of an event or a behavior?

- Who is your *audience* and what will their interests, attitudes, and expectations for the project be? How many and what kinds of resources does your audience expect you to consult? (For college research projects, your audience will likely be your instructor.)

- What *genre* (or *type*) is the research project, and how will that affect the kinds of sources you use? An observational report in the social sciences may demand mainly *primary sources*, such as observations, interviews, and surveys, whereas an argument essay for a history course may require a variety of primary and *secondary sources* (from published historians).

Also be sure you consider the following practical issues before you begin your research project:

- How long should the research project be?

- When is it due?

- Are any interim assignments required (such as an outline or an annotated bibliography)?

Finally, set a schedule. Be sure to take into consideration the projects you have due for other classes as well as other responsibilities (to work or family, for example) or activities.

Some library websites may offer an online scheduler to help you with this process. Look for a link on your library's website, or try out an assignment calculator.

CHOOSING A TOPIC AND GETTING AN OVERVIEW

Often students will be assigned a topic for a research project. If you are free to choose your own topic, consult course materials such as textbooks and handouts to get ideas, and consult your instructor to make sure your topic is appropriate. Once you've chosen an appropriate topic, an overview can help you determine the kind of issues you should consider.

Sometimes conducting an Internet search may give you an idea for a topic. Wikipedia offers a wealth of information, and it is often the first stop for students who are accustomed to consulting the Internet first for information. Be aware, though, that Wikipedia is user-generated rather than traditionally published, and for this reason, the quality of information found there can be inconsistent. Many instructors do not consider Wikipedia a credible source, so you should ask your teacher for advice on consulting it at this stage.

Your library will likely subscribe to databases, such as *Gale Virtual Reference Library* or *Oxford Reference Online*, that you can search to find information from general encyclopedias and dictionaries as well as specialized, or subject-specific encyclopedias and dictionaries.

General dictionaries, like *Britannica Online*, provide basic information about many topics. **Specialized encyclopedias** provide a comprehensive introduction to your topic, including the key terms you will need to find relevant material in catalogs and databases, and they present subtopics, enabling you to see many possibilities for focusing your research.

Frequently, libraries prepare **research guides** — lists of credible sources on popular topics. A guide can offer very useful suggested resources for research, so check your library to find out if such a guide is available. You may also find resources that provide good overviews of topics, such as *CQ Researcher*. A reference librarian can help point you in the right direction.

FOCUSING YOUR TOPIC AND DRAFTING RESEARCH QUESTIONS

After you have a sense of the kinds of sources available on your topic, you may be ready to narrow it. Focus on a topic that you can explore thoroughly in the number of pages assigned and the length of time available. Finding your own take on a subject can help you narrow it as well.

You may also want to write questions about your topic and then focus on one or two that can be answered through research. These will become the research questions that will guide your search for information. You may need to add or revise these questions as you conduct your search. The answers you devise over the course of your research can form the basis for your thesis statement, however, for the research process your instructor may have you focus on one or two research questions before developing a thesis statement.

ESTABLISHING A RESEARCH LOG

One of the best ways to keep track of your research is to keep all your notes in one place, in a **research log.** Your log may be digital — a folder on your computer with files for notes, lists of keywords, and your working bibliography — or analog — a notebook with pockets for copies of sources.

Finding useful sources depends on determining the right **keywords** — words or phrases that describe your topic — to use while searching catalogs, databases, and the Internet. Start your list of keywords by noting the main words from your research question or thesis statement. Look for useful terms in your search results, and use these to expand your list. Then add synonyms (or words with a similar meaning) to expand your list.

For example, a student might start with a term like *home schooling* and then add *home education* or *home study*. After reading an article about her subject, she might also add *student-paced education* or *autonomous learning* to expand her scope.

Keep in mind that different databases use different terms, and terms that work well for one subject might not be successful in another. For example, databases covering education and psychology might index sources on some of the same subjects, but they might not use the same keywords. After consulting the thesaurus in *ERIC*, a database focusing on education, the student might add *parents as teachers*; after consulting the thesaurus in the database *PSYCArticles*, she might add *nontraditional education*.

CREATING A WORKING BIBLIOGRAPHY

A **working bibliography** is an ongoing record of the sources you discover as you research your subject. In your final project, you will probably not end up citing all the sources you list in your working bibliography, but *accurately* recording the information you will need to cite a source *as you identify it* will save you time later.

Your working bibliography should include the following for each source:

- **Author(s) name(s)**

- **Title and subtitle**

- **Publication information:** A book's version or edition number (for example, *revised edition, 3rd ed.*), the name of the source's publisher (except for sources whose authors are their publishers and online sources whose titles are similar to their publishers' names), the date of publication (or copyright year), and the page numbers of the section you consulted; a periodical's name, volume and issue number, date, and the article's page numbers.

- **Location information:** The call number of a book; the name of the database through which you accessed the source; the **DOI** (digital object identifier — a permanent identifying code that won't change over time or from database to database) for an article, or if one is unavailable, the full URL (ideally a permalink, if the site provides one); the date you last accessed the source (for a Web page or website), though you will not always need to include an access date in your paper's works-cited entry; see pp. 640–644 for more information.

You can store your working bibliography in a computer file, in specialized bibliography software, or even on note cards. Each method has its advantages:

- A **computer file** allows you to move citations into order and incorporate the bibliography into your research project easily using standard software (such as Word or Excel).

- A **citation manager** (such as RefWorks, Zotero, EndNote, or the Bedford Bibliographer) designed for creating bibliographies helps you create the citation in the specific citation style (such as MLA or APA) required by your discipline. These software programs are not perfect, however; you still need to double-check your citations against the models in the style manual you are using or in the MLA and APA citation sections of this chapter (pp. 627–632 and 645–647).

- A **notebook** allows you to keep everything — working bibliography, annotations, notes, copies of chapters or articles — all in one place.

This chapter presents two common documentation styles — one created by the Modern Language Association (MLA) and widely used in the humanities, and the other advocated by the American Psychological Association (APA) and used in the social sciences. Other disciplines have their own preferred styles of documentation. Confirm with your instructor which documentation style is required for your assignment so that you can follow that style for all the sources you put in your working bibliography.

ANNOTATING YOUR WORKING BIBLIOGRAPHY

An **annotated bibliography** provides an overview of sources that you have considered for your research project. Researchers frequently create annotated bibliographies to keep a record of sources and their thoughts about them. Researchers sometimes also publish annotated bibliographies to provide others with a useful tool for beginning research projects of their own.

What an annotated bibliography includes depends on the researcher's writing situation. But most answer these questions about each source:

- What kind of source is this?

- What is the main point of the source?

- How might I use the source?

- How might my sources be related?

- What information will I need to cite the source?

Some annotated bibliographies also include an introduction that explains the subject, purpose, and scope of the annotated bibliography and may describe how and why the researcher selected those sources. For instance, an annotated bibliography featuring works about computer animation might have the following introduction:

> Early animations of virtual people in computer games tended to be oblivious to their surroundings, reacting only when hit by moving objects, and then in ways that were not always appropriate — that is, a small object might generate a large effect. In the past few years, however, computer animators have turned their attention to designing virtual people who react appropriately to events around them. The sources below represent the last two years' worth of publications on the subject from the *IEEE Xplore* database.

TAKING NOTES ON YOUR SOURCES

For more on annotating sources or synthesizing, see Chapter 2, pp. 35–40 or 47–48.

The summaries that you include in a working bibliography or the annotations that you make on a printed or digital copy of a source are useful reminders, but you should also make notes that analyze the text, that synthesize what you are learning with ideas you have gleaned elsewhere or with your own ideas, and that evaluate the quality of the source.

You will mine your notes for language to use in your draft, so be careful to

- summarize accurately, using your own words and sentence structures
- paraphrase without borrowing the language or sentence structure of the source
- quote exactly and place all language from the source in quotation marks.

You can take notes on a photocopy of a printed text or use comments or highlighting to annotate a digital text. Whenever possible, download, print, photocopy, or scan useful sources, so that you can read and make notes at your leisure and so that you can double-check your summaries, paraphrases, and quotations of sources against the original. These strategies, along with those discussed later in this chapter in the section Using Information from Sources to Support Your Claims (pp. 617–626), will keep you from plagiarizing inadvertently.

FINDING SOURCES

Students today are surrounded by a wealth of information — in print, online, in videos and podcasts, even face-to-face. This wealth can make finding the information you need to support your ideas exciting, but it also means you will have to develop a research strategy and sift through possible sources carefully. What you are writing about, who will read your writing project, and the type of writing you are doing will help you decide what types of sources will be most appropriate.

Does your writing project require you to depend mainly on **secondary sources**, such as books and articles that analyze and summarize a subject, or develop **primary sources,** such as interviews with experts, surveys, or observational studies you conduct yourself and laboratory reports, historical documents, diaries, letters, or works of literature written by others? Whatever sources you decide will be most useful, this chapter will help you find or develop these resources.

SEARCHING LIBRARY CATALOGS AND DATABASES

For most college research projects, finding appropriate sources starts with your library's home page, where you can

- find (and sometimes access) books, reference sources (such as encyclopedias and dictionaries), reports, documents, multimedia resources (such as films and audio recordings), and much more;

- use your library's databases to find (and sometimes access) articles in newspapers, magazines, and scholarly journals, as well as in reference sources;

- find **research guides,** lists of credible sources on topics frequently studied by students.

Many libraries now offer unified search, which allows patrons to search for books and articles in magazines, newspapers, and scholarly journals simultaneously, from the home page. If you aren't sure whether you will need to search for books and articles using separate catalogs and databases, consult a librarian. Your library's home page is also the place to find information about the brick-and-mortar library — its floor plan, its hours of operation, and the journals it has available in print. You might even be able to find links to what you need in other libraries or get online help from a librarian.

Using Appropriate Search Terms

Just as with a search engine like Google, you can search a library catalog or database by typing your search terms — an author's name, the title of a work, a subject term or keyword, even a call number — into the search box. To search successfully, put yourself in the position of the people writing about your topic to figure out what words they might have used. If your topic is "ecology," for example, you may find information under the keywords *ecosystem*, *environment*, *pollution*, and *endangered species*, as well as a number of other related keywords, depending on the focus of the research and your area of study.

Broaden or Narrow Your Results

When conducting a search, you may get too few hits and have to broaden your topic. To broaden your search, try the following:

Replace a specific term with a more general term	Replace *sister* or *brother* with *sibling*
Substitute a synonym for one of your keywords	Replace *home study* with *home schooling* or *student-paced education*
Combine terms with *or* to get results with either or both terms	Search *home study or home schooling* to get results that include both *home study* and *home schooling*
Add a wildcard character, usually an asterisk (*) or question mark (?) (Check the search tips to find out which wildcard character is in use.)	Search *home school** or *home school?* to retrieve results for *home school, home schooling,* and *home-schooler*

Most often, you'll get too many hits. To narrow a search, try the following:

Add a specific term	Search not just *home schooling* but *home schooling statistics*
Combine search terms into phrases or word strings	Search *home schooling in California*

In many cases, using phrases or word strings will limit your results to items that include *all* the words you have specified. You may need to insert quotation marks around the terms or insert the word *and* between them to create a search phrase or word string. Check the search tips for the database, catalog, or search engine you are using.

Finding Books (and Other Sources)

Books housed in academic library collections offer two distinct advantages to the student researcher:

1. They provide in-depth coverage of topics.

2. They are more likely to be published by reputable presses that strive for accuracy and credibility.

You can generally search for books (as well as reference works and multimedia resources) by author's name, title, keyword, or subject heading, and narrow your search by using advanced search options.

Though you can search by keywords, most college libraries use special subject headings devised by the Library of Congress (the national library of the United States). Finding and using the subject headings most relevant to your search will make your research more productive. You can locate the subject headings your library uses by pulling up the record of a relevant book you have already found and looking for the list of words under the heading "Subject" or "Subject headings." Including these terms in your search may help you find additional relevant resources. Ask a librarian for help if you cannot identify the headings.

FIGURE 12.1 A BOOK'S CATALOG RECORD An item's record provides a lot more information than just the author, title, and call number. You can also find the subject headings by which it was cataloged, the item's status (whether it has been checked out), and its location. Some libraries may allow you to place a hold on a book or find similar items. Some libraries, such as the one whose catalog is depicted here, even allow you to capture the book's record with your smartphone or have the information texted or e-mailed to you.

Finding Articles in Periodicals

Much of the information you will use to write your research project will come from articles in **periodicals,** publications such as newspapers, magazines, or scholarly journals that are published at regular intervals. To locate relevant articles on your topic, start your search with one of your library's databases. Why not just start with a Google search? There are two very good reasons:

1. Google will pull up articles from any publication it indexes, from freely available personal websites to scholarly journals. Results rise to the top of the list based on a number of factors but not necessarily the credibility of the source. A Google search will turn up helpful sources, but you will need to spend a good deal of time sifting through the numerous hits you get to find sources that are both relevant and credible. (Google Scholar may help you locate more credible sources than those you might find through a typical Google search.)

2. Sources you find through Google may ask you to pay for access to articles, or they may require a subscription. Your library probably already subscribes to these sources on your behalf. Also adding databases to your search strategy will diversify your search and provide you with access to resources not available through a search engine such as Google.

Most college libraries subscribe at least to **general databases** and **subject-specific databases** as well as databases that index newspapers. General databases (such as *Academic OneFile, Academic Search Premier* or *Elite* or *Complete,* and *ProQuest Central*) index articles from both scholarly journals and popular magazines.[1] Subject-specific databases (such as *ERIC — Education Resources Information Center, MLA International Bibliography, PsycINFO,* and *General Science Full Text*) index articles only in their discipline. Newspaper databases (such as *Alt-Press Watch, LexisNexis Academic, National Newspaper Index,* and *ProQuest Newspapers*) index newspaper articles. For college-level research projects, you may use all three types of databases to find appropriate articles. (Note that many libraries also offer ways to search multiple databases at once.)

If your database search returns too many unhelpful results, use the search strategies discussed on p. 592 or use the database's advanced search options to refine your search. Many databases allow users to restrict results to articles published in academic journals, for example, or to articles that were published after a certain date (see fig. 12.2 on p. 595). Use the Help option or ask a librarian for assistance.

Increasingly, databases provide access to full-text articles, either in HTML or PDF format. When you have the option, choose the PDF format, as this will provide you with photographs, graphs, and charts in context, and you will be able

---

[1] The names of databases change over time and vary from library to library, so ask your instructor or a reference librarian if you need help.

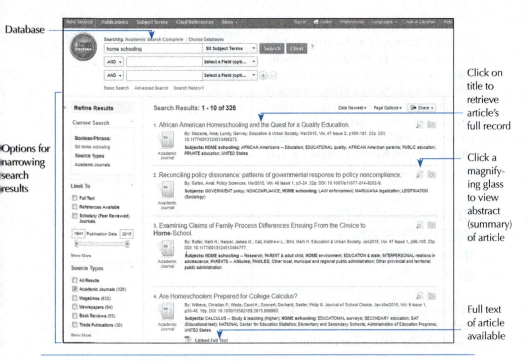

Database —

Options for narrowing search results

Click on title to retrieve article's full record

Click a magnifying glass to view abstract (summary) of article

Full text of article available

FIGURE 12.2 DATABASE SEARCH RESULTS Database search results may allow you to access an article directly or provide the information you need to locate (and cite) it, including the title, the author(s), and the article's publication information. The database may also provide options for narrowing a search by publication date, source type (academic journal versus newspaper, for example), and so on.

to include the page numbers in your citation. If you find a citation to an article that is not accessible through a database, however, do not ignore it. Check with a librarian to find out how you can get a copy of the article.

SEARCHING FOR GOVERNMENT DOCUMENTS AND STATISTICAL INFORMATION

Federal, state, and local governments make many of their documents available directly through the Web. For example, you can access statistical data about the United States through the U.S. Census Bureau's website, and you can learn a great deal about other countries through the websites of the U.S. State Department and the CIA.

The Library of Congress provides a useful portal for finding government documents (federal, state, local, and international) through its website, and the U.S. Government Printing Office provides free electronic access to documents produced by the federal government through its govinfo Web page.

Some libraries have collections of government publications and provide access to government documents through databases or catalogs. Your library may also offer statistical resources and data sets. You can also find government documents online using an advanced Google search and specifying *.gov* as the type of site or **domain** you want to search (see fig 12.3).

SEARCHING FOR WEBSITES AND INTERACTIVE SOURCES

This section introduces you to some tools and strategies to use the Web more efficiently. But first, a few cautions:

FIGURE 12.3 AN ADVANCED GOOGLE SEARCH   Use Google's advanced search to narrow results.

- *Your research project will be only as credible as the sources you use.* Because search engines index Web sources without evaluating them, not all the results a search engine generates will be credible and relevant to your purposes.

- *Web sources may not be stable.* A website that existed last week may no longer be available today, or its content may have changed. Be sure to record the information you need to cite a source when you first find it, as well as the date you find it.

- *Web sources must be documented.* No matter what your source — a library book, a scholarly article, or a website or Web page — you will need to cite and document your source in your list of works cited or references. If you are publishing your report online, check also to determine whether you will need permission to reproduce an image or any other elements.

Using Google Scholar and Google Book Search

Although you may use search engines like Google with great rapidity and out of habit, as a college researcher you are likely to find it worthwhile to familiarize yourself with other parts of the Google search site. Of particular interest to the academic writer are Google Scholar and Google Book Search. Google Scholar retrieves articles from a number of scholarly databases and a wide range of general-interest and scholarly books. Google Book Search searches both popular and scholarly books. Both Google Scholar and Google Book Search offer overviews and, in some cases, the full text of a source.

Other Useful Search Options

No matter how precisely you search the Web with a standard search engine, you may not hit on the best available resources. Starting your search from a subject guide, such as those provided by the *Internet Public Library* or the librarians at your school, can direct you to relevant and credible sources of online information.

Whatever search engine you use, always click on the link called *Help, Hints,* or *Tips* on the search tool's home page to find out more about the commands and advanced-search techniques it offers to narrow (or expand) your search.

Interactive Sources

Interactive sources, including blogs, wikis, RSS feeds, social networking sites and discussion lists, can also be useful sources of information, especially if your research project focuses on a current event or late-breaking news.

- **Blogs** are websites that are updated regularly, often many times a day. They are usually organized chronologically, with the newest posts at the top, and may contain links or news stories but generally focus on the opinions of the blog host and visitors. Blogs by experts in the field are likely to be more informative than blogs by amateurs or fans.

- **Wikis** — of which Wikipedia is the best-known example — offer content contributed and modified collaboratively by a community of users. Wikis can be very useful for gleaning background information, but because (in most cases) anyone can write or revise wiki entries, many instructors will not accept them as credible sources for college-level research projects. Use wikis cautiously.

- **RSS (Really Simple Syndication) feeds** aggregate frequently updated sites, such as news sites and blogs, into links in a single Web page or e-mail. Most search engines provide this service. RSS feeds can be useful if you are researching news stories or political campaigns.

- **Social networking sites,** like Facebook and Twitter, allow users to create groups or pages on topics of interest or to follow the thoughts and activities of newsmakers.

- **Discussion lists** are electronic mailing lists that allow members to post comments and get feedback from others interested in the same topic. The most credible discussion lists are moderated and attract experts on the topic. Many online communities provide some kind of indexing or search mechanism so that you can look for "threads" (conversations) related to your topic.

Although you need to evaluate carefully the information you find in all sources, you must be especially careful with information from social networking sites and discussion lists. However, such sources can provide up-to-the-minute information. Also be aware that whereas most online communities welcome guests and newcomers, others may perceive your questions as intrusive or naive. It may be useful to "lurk" (that is, just to read posts) before making a contribution.

CONDUCTING FIELD RESEARCH

In universities, government agencies, and the business world, **field research** can be as important as library research. In some majors, like education or sociology, as well as in service-learning courses, primary research projects are common. Even in the writing projects covered in Chapters 3–10, observations, interviews, and surveys may be useful or even necessary. As you consider how you might use field research in your writing projects, ask your instructor whether your institution requires you to obtain approval, and check the documentation sections that appear later in this chapter to learn about citing interviews you conduct yourself.

CONDUCTING OBSERVATIONAL STUDIES

Observational studies are commonly assigned in college writing, psychology, and sociology courses. To conduct an observational study effectively, follow these guidelines:

Planning an Observational Study

To ensure that your observational visits are productive, plan them carefully:

- **Arrange access if necessary.** Visits to a private location (such as a day-care center or school) require special permission, so be sure to arrange your visit in advance. When making your request, state your intentions and goals for your study directly and fully. You may be surprised at how receptive people can be to a college student on assignment. But have a fallback plan in case your request is refused or the business or institution places constraints on you that hamper your research.

- **Develop a hypothesis.** In advance, write down a tentative assumption about what you expect to learn from your study — your **hypothesis.** This will guide your observations and notes, and you can adjust your expectations in response to what you observe if necessary. Consider, too, how your presence will affect those whom you are observing, so you can minimize your impact or take the effect of your presence into consideration.

- **Consider how best to conduct the observation.** Decide where to place yourself to make your observations most effectively. Should you move around to observe from multiple vantage points, or will a single perspective be more productive?

Making Observations

Strategies for conducting your observation include the following:

- **Description:** Describe in detail the setting and the people you are observing. Note the physical arrangement and functions of the space, and the number, activities, and appearance of the people. Record as many details as possible, draw diagrams or sketches if helpful, and take photographs or videos if allowed (and if those you are observing do not object).

- **Narration:** Narrate the activities going on around you. Try initially to be an innocent observer: Pretend that you have never seen anything like this activity or place before, and explain what you are seeing step by step, even if what you are writing seems obvious. Include interactions among people, and capture snippets of conversations (in quotation marks) if possible.

- **Analysis and classification:** Break the scene down into its component parts, identify common threads, and organize the details into categories.

Take careful notes during your visit if you can do so unobtrusively, or immediately afterward if you can't. You can use a notebook and pencil, a laptop or tablet, or a smartphone to record your notes. Choose whatever is least disruptive to those around you. You may need to use abbreviations and symbols to capture your observations on-site, but be sure to convert such shorthand into words and phrases as soon as possible after the visit so that you don't forget its significance.

Writing Your Observational Study

For more on outlining, see Chapter 2, pp. 41–42.

Immediately after your visit, fill in any gaps in your notes, and review your notes to look for meaningful patterns. You might find mapping strategies, such as *clustering* or *outlining*, useful for discovering patterns in your notes. Take some time to reflect on what you saw. Asking yourself questions like these might help:

- How did what I observed fit my own or my readers' likely preconceptions of the place or activity? Did my observations upset any of my preconceptions? What, if anything, seemed contradictory or out of place?

- What interested me most about the activity or place? What are my readers likely to find interesting about it?

- What did I learn?

Your purpose in writing about your visit is to share your insights into the meaning and significance of your observations. Assume that your readers have never been to the place, and provide enough detail for it to come alive for them. Decide on the perspective you want to convey, and choose the details necessary to convey your insights.

CONDUCTING INTERVIEWS

A successful interview involves careful planning before the interview, but it also requires keen listening skills and the ability to ask appropriate follow-up questions while conducting the interview. Courtesy and consideration for your subject are crucial at all stages of the process.

Planning the Interview

Planning an interview involves the following:

- **Choosing an interview subject.** For a profile of an individual, your interview will primarily be with one person; for a profile of an organization, you might interview several people, all with different roles or points of view. Prepare a list of interview candidates, as busy people might turn you down.

- **Arranging the interview.** Give your prospective subject a brief description of your project, and show some sincere enthusiasm for your project. Keep in mind that the person you want to interview will be donating valuable time to you, so call ahead to arrange the interview, allow your subject to specify the amount of time she or he can spare, and come prepared.

Preparing for the Interview

In preparation for the interview, consider your objectives:

- Do you want details or a general orientation (the "big picture") from this interview?

- Do you want this interview to lead you to interviews with other key people?

- Do you want mainly facts or opinions?

- Do you need to clarify something you have observed or read? If so, what?

Making an observational visit and doing some background reading beforehand can be helpful. Find out as much as you can about the organization or company (size, location, purpose, etc.), as well as the key people.

Good questions are essential to a successful interview. You will likely want to ask a few **closed questions** (questions that request specific information) and a number of **open questions** (questions that give the respondent range and flexibility and encourage him or her to share anecdotes, personal revelations, and expressions of attitudes):

Open Questions	*Closed Questions*
• What do you think about ....?	• How do you do ....?
• Describe your reaction when .... happened.	• What does .... mean?
• Tell me about a time you were	• How was .... developed?

The best questions encourage the subject to talk freely but stick to the point. You may need to ask a follow-up question to refocus the discussion or to clarify a point, so be prepared. If you are unsure about a subject's answer, follow up by rephrasing that answer, prefacing it by saying something like "Let me see if I have this right" or "Am I correct in saying that you feel ....?" Avoid *forced-choice* questions ("Which do you think is the better approach: .... or ....?") and *leading* questions ("How well do you think .... is doing?").

During the Interview

Another key to good interviewing is flexibility. Ask the questions you have prepared, but also be ready to shift gears to take full advantage of what your subject can offer.

- **Take notes.** Take notes during the interview, even if you are recording your discussion. You might find it useful to divide several pages of a notebook into two columns or to set up a word processing file in two columns. Use the left-hand column to note details about the scene and your subject or about your impressions overall; in the right-hand column, write several questions and record the answers. Remember that how something is said is as important as what is said. Look for material that will give texture to your writing — gesture, verbal inflection, facial expression, body language, physical appearance (dress, hair), or anything else that makes the person an individual.

- **Listen carefully.** Avoid interrupting your subject or talking about yourself; rather, listen carefully and guide the discussion by asking follow-up questions and probing politely for more information.

- **Be considerate.** Do not stay longer than the time you were allotted unless your subject agrees to continue the discussion, and show your appreciation for the time you have been given by thanking your subject and offering her or him a copy of your finished project.

Following the Interview

After the interview, do the following:

- **Reflect on the interview.** As soon as you finish the interview, find a quiet place to reflect on it and to review and amplify your notes. Asking yourself questions like these might help: What did I learn? What seemed contradictory or surprising about the interview? How did what was said fit my own or my readers' likely expectations about the person, activity, or place? How can I summarize my impressions?

  Also make a list of any questions that arise. You may want to follow up with your subject for more information, but limit yourself to one e-mail or phone call to avoid becoming a bother.

- **Thank your subject.** Send your interview subject a thank-you note or e-mail within twenty-four hours of the interview. Try to reference something specific from the interview, something you thought was surprising or thought-provoking. Send your subject a copy of your finished project with a note of appreciation.

CONDUCTING SURVEYS

Surveys let you gauge the opinions and knowledge of large numbers of people. You might conduct a survey to gauge opinion in a political science course or to assess familiarity with a television show for a media studies course. You might also conduct a survey to assess the seriousness of a problem for a service-learning class or in response to an assignment to propose a solution to a problem (Chapter 10). You can choose to administer the survey either in person or on a survey creation and distribution site such as SurveyMonkey, SurveyGizmo, or even Facebook. This section briefly outlines procedures you can follow to carry out an informal survey, and it highlights areas where caution is needed. Colleges and universities have restrictions about the use and distribution of questionnaires, so check your institution's policy or obtain permission before beginning the survey.

Designing Your Survey

Use the following tips to design an effective survey:

- **Conduct background research.** You may need to conduct background research on your topic. For example, to create a survey on scheduling appointments at the student health center, you may first need to contact the health center to determine its scheduling practices, and you may want to interview health center personnel.

- **Focus your study.** Before starting out, decide what you expect to learn (your hypothesis). Make sure your focus is limited — focus on one or two important issues — so you can craft a brief questionnaire that respondents can complete quickly and easily and so that you can organize and report on your results more easily.

- **Write questions.** Plan to use a number of **closed questions** (questions that request specific information), such as *two-way questions, multiple-choice questions, ranking scale questions*, and *checklist questions* (see fig. 12.4 on the following page). You will also likely want to include a few **open questions** (questions that give respondents the opportunity to write their answers in their own words). Closed questions are easier to tally, but open questions are likely to provide you with deeper insight and a fuller sense of respondents' opinions. Whatever questions you develop, be sure that you provide all the answer options your respondents are likely to want, and make sure your questions are clear and unambiguous.

- **Identify the population you are trying to reach.** Even for an informal study, you should try to get a reasonably representative group. For example, to study satisfaction with appointment scheduling at the student health center, you would need to include a representative sample of all the students at the school — not only those who have visited the health center. Determine the demographic makeup of your school, and arrange to reach out to a representative sample.

This is a survey about scheduling appointments at the student health center. Your participation will help determine how long students have to wait to use the clinic's services and how these services might be more conveniently scheduled. The survey should take only 3 to 4 minutes to complete. All responses are confidential.

1. Have you ever made an appointment at the clinic? — Two-way question

    ❑ Yes   ❑ No

If you answered "No" to question 1, skip to question 5. — Filter

2. How frequently have you had to wait more than 10 minutes at the clinic for a scheduled appointment?

    ❑ Always   ❑ Usually   ❑ Occasionally   ❑ Never

3. Have you ever had to wait more than 30 minutes at the clinic for a scheduled appointment?

    ❑ Yes   ❑ No   ❑ Uncertain

— Multiple-choice questions

4. Based on your experience with the clinic, how would you rate its system for scheduling appointments?

    ❑ 1 (poor)   ❑ 2 (adequate)   ❑ 3 (good)   ❑ 4 (excellent)

5. Given your present work and class schedule, which times during the day (Monday through Friday) would be the most and least convenient for you to schedule appointments at the clinic? (Rank your choices from 1 for most convenient time to 4 for least convenient time.)

— Ranking questions

	1 (most convenient)	2 (more convenient)	3 (less convenient)	4 (least convenient)
morning (7 a.m.–noon)	❑	❑	❑	❑
afternoon (noon–5 p.m.)	❑	❑	❑	❑
dinnertime (5–7 p.m.)	❑	❑	❑	❑
evening (7–10 p.m.)	❑	❑	❑	❑

6. If you have had an appointment at the student health center within the last six months, please evaluate your experience.

7. If you have had an appointment at the student health center within the last six months, please indicate what you believe would most improve scheduling of appointments at the clinic.

— Open questions

8. If you have *never* had an appointment at the student health center, please indicate why you have not made use of this service.

Thank you for your participation.

FIGURE 12.4 SAMPLE QUESTIONNAIRE: Scheduling at the Student Health Center

- **Design the questionnaire.** Begin your questionnaire with a brief, clear introduction stating the purpose of your survey and explaining how you intend to use the results. Give advice on answering the questions, estimate the amount of time needed to complete the questionnaire, and — unless you are administering the survey in person — indicate the date by which completed surveys must be returned. Organize your questions from least to most complicated or in any order that seems logical, and format your questionnaire so that it is easy to read and complete.

- **Test the questionnaire.** Ask at least three readers to complete your questionnaire before you distribute it. Time them as they respond, or ask them to keep track of how long they take to complete it (some of the online services will do this for you automatically). Discuss with them any confusion or problems they experience. Review their responses with them to be certain that each question is eliciting the information you want it to elicit. From what you learn, revise your questions and adjust the format of the questionnaire.

Administering the Survey

The more respondents you have, the better, but constraints of time and expense will almost certainly limit the number. As few as twenty-five could be adequate for an informal study, but to get twenty-five responses, you may need to solicit fifty or more participants.

You can conduct the survey in person or over the telephone; use an online service such as SurveyMonkey or Zoomerang; e-mail the questionnaires; or conduct the survey using a social media site such as Facebook. You may also distribute surveys to groups of people in class or around campus and wait to collect their responses.

Each method has its advantages and disadvantages. For example, face-to-face surveys allow you to get more in-depth responses, but participants may be unwilling to answer personal questions face-to-face. Though fewer than half the surveys you solicit using survey software are likely to be completed (your invitations may wind up in a spam folder), online software will tabulate responses automatically.

Writing the Report

When writing your report, include a summary of the results, as well as an interpretation of what the results mean.

- **Summarize the results.** Once you have the completed questionnaires, tally the results from the closed questions. (If you conducted the survey online, this will have already been done for you.) You can give the results from the closed questions as percentages, either within the text of your report or in one or more tables or graphs. Next, read all respondents' answers to each open question and summarize the responses by classifying the answers. You might classify them as positive, negative, or neutral or by grouping them into more specific categories. Finally, identify quotations that express a range of responses succinctly and engagingly to use in your report.

- **Interpret the results.** Once you have tallied the responses and read answers to open questions, think about what the results mean. Does the information you gathered support your hypothesis? If so, how? If the results do not support your hypothesis, where did you go wrong? Was there a problem with the way you worded your questions or with the sample of the population you contacted? Or was your hypothesis in need of adjustment?

- **Write the report.** Research reports in the social sciences use a standard format, with headings introducing the following categories of information:

  - **Abstract:** A brief summary of the report, usually including one sentence summarizing each section

  - **Introduction:** Includes context for the study (other similar studies, if any, and their results), the question or questions the researcher wanted to answer and why this question (or these questions) is important, and the limits of what the researcher expected the survey to reveal

  - **Methods:** Includes the questionnaire, identifies the number and type of participants, and describes the methods used for administering the questionnaire and recording data

  - **Results:** Includes the data from the survey, with limited commentary or interpretation

  - **Discussion:** Includes the researcher's interpretation of results, an explanation of how the data support the hypothesis (or not), and the conclusions the researcher has drawn from the research

EVALUATING SOURCES

As soon as you start your search for sources, you should begin evaluating what you find not only to decide whether they are relevant to your research project but also to determine how credible they are.

CHOOSING RELEVANT SOURCES

Sources are **relevant** when they help you achieve your aims with your readers. Relevant sources may

- explain terms or concepts;
- provide background information;
- provide evidence in support of your claims;
- provide alternative viewpoints or interpretations;
- lend authority to your point of view.

A search for sources may reveal more books and articles than any researcher could ever actually consult. A search on the term *home schooling* in one database, for example, got 1,172 hits. Obviously, a glance at all the hits to determine which are most relevant would take far too much time. To speed up the process, resources, such as library catalogs, databases, and search engines, provide tools to narrow the results. For example, in one popular all-purpose database, you can limit results by publication date, language, and publication or source type, among other options. (Check the Help screen to learn how to use these tools.)

For more on focusing search results and selecting search terms, see pp. 591–592 earlier in this chapter.

In the database used in Figure 12.5 (p. 608), limiting the *home schooling* results to articles published in scholarly journals in English over the last ten years reduced the number of hits to 56, a far more reasonable number to review. Remember that if you have too few results or your results are not targeted correctly, you can expand your search by changing your search terms or removing limits selectively.

After you have identified a reasonable number of relevant sources, examine the sources themselves:

- Read the preface, introduction, or conclusion of books, or the first or last few paragraphs of articles, to determine which aspect of the topic is addressed or which approach to the topic is taken. To obtain a clear picture of a topic, researchers need to consider sources that address different aspects of the topic or take different approaches.

- Look at the headings or references in articles, or the table of contents and index in books, to see how much of the content relates specifically to your topic.

- Consider the way the source is written: Sources written for general readers may be accessible but may not analyze the subject in depth. Extremely

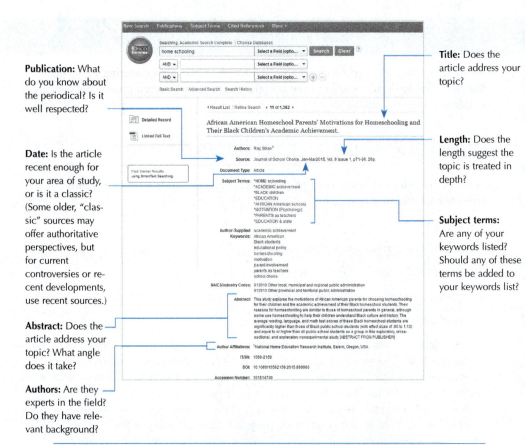

Publication: What do you know about the periodical? Is it well respected?

Date: Is the article recent enough for your area of study, or is it a classic? (Some older, "classic" sources may offer authoritative perspectives, but for current controversies or recent developments, use recent sources.)

Abstract: Does the article address your topic? What angle does it take?

Authors: Are they experts in the field? Do they have relevant background?

Title: Does the article address your topic?

Length: Does the length suggest the topic is treated in depth?

Subject terms: Are any of your keywords listed? Should any of these terms be added to your keywords list?

FIGURE 12.5 ANALYZING THE DETAILED RECORD OF AN ARTICLE FROM A PERIODICALS DATABASE   Analyze the detailed record of an article to determine whether the article itself is worth reading by asking yourself the following questions: Does the title suggest that the article addresses your topic? Are the authors experts in the field? Was the article published in a periodical that is likely to be credible, was it published recently, and is it lengthy enough to indicate that the topic is treated in depth? Does the abstract (or summary) suggest that the article addresses your topic? If so, what angle does it take?

specialized works may be too technical. Poorly written sources may not be credible. (See Choosing Credible Sources, on the following page, for more on scholarly versus popular sources and for a discussion of why researchers should avoid sources that are poorly written or disjointed.)

If close scrutiny leaves you with too few sources — or too many sources from too few perspectives — conduct a search using additional or alternative keywords, or explore links to related articles, look at the references in a particularly useful article, or look for other sources by an author whose work you find useful.

CHOOSING CREDIBLE SOURCES

Choosing relevant sources is crucial to assembling a useful working bibliography. Determining which of those relevant sources is also likely to be credible is even more important. To determine credibility, ask yourself the questions below.

Who Wrote It?

Consider, first, whether the author is an expert in the field. The fact that someone has a Ph.D. in astrophysics is no indication that he or she will be an expert in military history, for example, so be careful that the area of expertise is directly relevant to the topic.

To determine the author's area of expertise, look for the author's professional affiliation (where he or she works or teaches). This may be indicated at the bottom of the first page of an article or in an "About the Author" section in a book or on a website. Frequently, Googling the author will also reveal the author's affiliation, but double-check to make sure the affiliation is current and that you have located the right person. You may also consult a biographical reference source available through your library. Looking to see what other works the author has published, and with whom, can also help you ascertain his or her areas of expertise.

Contributors to blogs, wikis, and online discussion forums may or may not be experts in the field. Determine whether the site screens contributors, and double-check any information taken from sites for which you cannot determine the credentials of contributors.

Also consider the author's *perspective*. Most writing is not neutral or objective and does not claim to be. Knowledge of the author's perspective enables you to assess bias and determine how the author's perspective affects the presentation of his or her argument. To determine the author's perspective, look for the main point and ask yourself questions like these:

- What evidence does the author provide to support this point? Is it from authoritative sources? Is it persuasive?

- Does the author make concessions to or refute opposing arguments?

- Does the author avoid fallacies, confrontational phrasing, and loaded words?

For more details on strategies for evaluating the logic of an argument, see Chapter 2, pp. 60–62.

How Recently Was It Published?

In general, especially when you are writing about science or technology, current events, or emerging trends, you should consult the most up-to-date sources available on your subject. The date of publication for articles you locate should be indicated in your search results. For a print book, look for the copyright date on the copyright page (usually on the back of the title page); for an e-book, look for the copyright date at the beginning or end of the electronic file. If your source is a website, consider when it, and the content within it, was last updated (often indicated at the bottom of the Web page or home page).

You may also need older, foundational sources that establish the principles, theories, and data on which later work is based and may provide a useful perspective for evaluating other works. To determine which sources are foundational, note the ones that are cited most often in encyclopedia articles, lists of works cited or references, and recent works on the subject. You may also want to consult your instructor or a librarian to help you determine which works are foundational in your field.

Is the Source Scholarly, Popular, or for a Trade Group?

Scholarly sources (whether books or articles) are written by and for experts in a field of study, frequently professors or academic researchers. They can be challenging to read and understand because they use the language of the field and terminology that may be unfamiliar to those outside the discipline, but they are considered credible because the contents are written by specialists and **peer-reviewed** (reviewed by specialists) before publication. Scholarly sources also tend to delve deeply into a subject, often a narrowly defined subject. Scholarly sources may be published by a university press, a scholarly organization, or a commercial publisher (such as Kluwer Academic or Blackwell). Though scholarly sources may provide an overview of the subject, they generally focus on a specific issue or argument and generally contain a great deal of original research.

In contrast, **popular sources** are written to entertain and educate the general public. For the most part, they are written by journalists who have conducted research and interviewed experts. They may include original research, especially on current events or emerging trends. Mainly, though, they report on and summarize original research and are written for interested, nonspecialist readers.

Of course, popular sources range widely along the credibility spectrum. Highly respected newspapers and magazines, such as the *New York Times*, the *Guardian*, the *Economist*, and *Harper's Magazine*, publish original research on news and culture. These newspapers and magazines check facts carefully and are often considered appropriate sources for research projects in entry-level courses (although you should check with your instructor to find out her or his expectations). Magazines that focus on celebrity gossip, such as *People* and *Us Weekly*, are unlikely to be considered appropriate sources for a college-level research project. Table 12.1 (p. 611) summarizes some of the important differences between scholarly journals and popular magazines.

Trade publications — periodicals that report on news and technical advances in a specific industry — are written for those employed in the industry and include such titles as *Advertising Age*, *World Cement*, and *American Machinist*. Some trade publications may be appropriate for college research projects, especially in the sciences, but keep in mind that these publications are intended for a specialist audience and may focus on marketing products to professionals in the field.

TABLE 12.1   Scholarly Journals versus Popular Magazines and Trade Publications

Scholarly Journals	Popular Magazines	Trade Publications
Journals are usually published four to six times per year.	Magazines are usually published weekly or monthly.	Trade publications may be published daily, weekly, monthly, or quarterly, depending on the industry covered.
Articles are usually written by scholars (with *Ph.D.* or other academic affiliations after their names).	Authors of articles are journalists but may quote experts.	Articles may be written by professionals or by journalists with quotes from experts.
Many articles have more than one author.	Most articles have a single author.	Authors of articles may or may not be named.
In print journals, the title page often appears on the cover, and the covers frequently lack artwork.	Photographs, usually in color, appear on the covers of most print magazines.	Photographs, usually in color, appear on the covers of most print trade publications and on their websites.
Articles may include charts, tables, figures, and quotations from other scholarly sources.	Articles frequently include color pictures and sidebars.	Articles frequently include color pictures and sidebars.
An abstract (summary) of the article may appear on the first page.	A headline or engaging description may precede the article.	Headlines often include names or terms familiar only to industry insiders.
Most articles are fairly long — five to twenty pages.	Most articles are fairly short — one to five pages.	Most articles are fairly short — one to five pages.
Articles cite sources and provide a bibliography (a list of works cited or references).	Articles rarely include a list of works cited or references but may mention or quote experts.	Articles rarely include a list of works cited or references but may mention or quote experts.

Who Published It?

Determining who published or sponsored a source you are considering can help you gauge its credibility and ascertain the publication's slant (or point of view). Look to see whether the source was published by a commercial publisher (such as St. Martin's or Random House); a university press (such as the University of Nebraska Press); a corporation, an organization, or an interest group (such as the RAND Corporation, the World Wildlife Fund, or the National Restaurant

Association); a government agency (such as the Internal Revenue Service or the U.S. Census Bureau); or the author on his or her own. Determining the publisher or sponsor is particularly important for material published on the Web.

If your source is a Web page, look at the URL (uniform resource locator) to find its top-level domain, which is indicated by a suffix. Some of the most useful ones are listed here:

.gov	U.S. federal government and some state or local government institutions
.org	nonprofit organizations
.edu	educational institutions
.com	businesses and commercial enterprises
.net	usually businesses or organizations associated with networks
.mil	the U.S. military

For the most part, *.gov* and *.edu* are the most likely to offer credible sources of information for a college research project. However, sources with any of these domains may vary in credibility. For example, a file with a *.com* suffix may offer a highly credible history of a corporation and be an appropriate source for someone writing a history of corporate America, whereas a file with an *.edu* suffix may have been posted by a student or by a faculty member outside his or her area of expertise.

It is essential to look at websites carefully. Determine who sponsors the site: Is it a business, a professional group, a private organization, an educational institution, a government agency, or an individual? Look for a link, usually at the top or the bottom of the home page, called something like "Who We Are" or "About Us." If you cannot determine who sponsors a site, carefully double-check any information you find there.

Consider, too, checking how often the website has been linked to and the types of links provided by the website. That a site has been linked to repeatedly does not guarantee credibility, but the information may be helpful in conjunction with other recommendations in this chapter. To determine the number of times a Web page has been linked to, type *link:* plus the URL into a Google search box. To check the links provided, click on them and apply the criteria in this chapter.

If the source was published by a commercial publisher, check out the publisher's website, and ask yourself questions like these:

- Does the publisher offer works from a single perspective or from multiple perspectives?

- Do the works it publishes cover a wide variety of topics or focus on a particular topic?

- Does the publisher's website host links to a particular type of site?

The websites of book publishers may offer a link to a catalog. If so, look at the works it lists. Does the publisher seem to publish works on a particular topic or from a particular point of view? Does the publisher generally offer popular, academic, or professional works?

If your source is a periodical, consider whether it focuses on a particular topic or offers a single point of view. In addition to looking at the article you are considering, visit the publisher's website, which may help you determine this.

How Well Is the Source Written?

Most works that are published professionally (including popular newspapers and magazines, as well as scholarly journals and trade magazines) will have been edited carefully. These sources will generally avoid errors of grammar, punctuation, and spelling. Websites sponsored by professional organizations, too, will generally avoid these kinds of errors. Personal websites, however, are unlikely to have been professionally edited and fact checked. If a website is riddled with errors, be very careful to double-check any information you take from that site.

Do Other Sources Corroborate What the Source Says?

Professional fact-checkers at organizations across the country use the process of cross-referencing to determine the credibility of sources. When you cross-reference a source, you move away from the source itself and read other sources about the same subject to determine whether what your source says is accurate. This practice is made especially easy thanks to the Web. When you focus on a single source to determine if it is trustworthy, you are ignoring that the Web is a collection of sources that can be used to verify information. You need not read every related website for its content, but moving purposefully from one site to the next, in combination with the other strategies listed in this section, can help you determine whether other sources corroborate or verify the information in your source. Do be careful, though, as you move from one site to the next. Just because a website contains the exact same information as another does not mean that it is credible. In fact, if the information is verbatim (word for word) from the original site, you need to be especially careful. Some sites simply copy and paste information from other sites and post it without verifying. Continue on to multiples sites in order to help you determine the credibility of the information. You can also use fact-checking websites such as *ProPublica*, *Snopes*, and *Politifact*, although you should also corroborate the information you find there as you would anything else.

What Does the Source Say?

Finally, consider the source itself. Answering the following questions can help you determine whether the source is worth consideration:

For more details on strategies for evaluating the logic of an argument, see Chapter 2, pp. 60–62.

- What is the intended audience of the source? Does the source address **an audience** of experts, or is it intended for a general audience?

- What is the purpose of the source? Does it review a number of **different positions**, or does it argue for a position of its own? If it makes its own **argument**, analyze the argument closely.

- What is the tone of the source? Is the tone reasonable? Does the **source** respond to alternative viewpoints, and are those responses **logical and** reasonable?

- What evidence is offered to support the argument? Is the evidence **relevant** and credible? What kinds of citations or links does the source supply?

USING SOURCES

Writing a college research project requires you to

- analyze sources to understand the arguments those sources are making, the information they are using to support their claims, and the ways those arguments and the supporting evidence they use relate to your topic;

- synthesize information from sources to support, extend, and challenge your own ideas;

- integrate information from sources with your own ideas to contribute something new to the "conversation" on your topic;

- document your sources using an appropriate documentation style.

SYNTHESIZING SOURCES

Synthesizing means making connections among ideas from texts and from your own experience. Once you have analyzed a number of sources on your topic, consider questions like the following to help you synthesize ideas and information:

- Do any of the sources you read use similar approaches or come to similar conclusions? What common themes do they explore? Do any of them use the same evidence (facts, statistics, research studies, examples) to support their claims?

- What differentiates the sources' various positions? Where do the writers disagree, and why? Does one writer seem to be responding to or challenging one or more of the others?

- Do you agree with some sources and disagree with others? What makes one source more convincing than the others? Do any of the sources you have read offer support for your claims? Do any of them challenge your conclusions? If so, can you *refute* the challenge or do you need to *concede* a point?

Sentence strategies like the following can help you clarify where you differ from or agree with the sources you have read:

▶ A study by X supports my position by demonstrating that _____ .

▶ X and Y think this issue is about _____ . But what is really at stake here is _____ .

▶ On this issue, X and Y say _____ . Although I understand and to some degree sympathize with their point of view, I agree with Z that this is ultimately a question of _____ .

ACKNOWLEDGING SOURCES AND AVOIDING PLAGIARISM

In your college writing, you will be expected to use and acknowledge **secondary sources** — books, articles, published or recorded interviews, websites, computer bulletin boards, lectures, and other print and nonprint materials — in addition to your own ideas, insights, and field research. The following information will help you decide what does and does not need to be acknowledged and will enable you to avoid *plagiarizing* inadvertently.

Determining What Does (and Does Not) Need to Be Acknowledged

For more on citing sources in MLA style, see pp. 627–632; for APA style, see pp. 645–647.

For the most part, any ideas, information, or language you borrow from a source — whether the source is in print or online — must be acknowledged by including an in-text citation and an entry in your list of works cited (MLA style) or references (APA style). The only types of information that do not require acknowledgment are common knowledge (for example, John F. Kennedy was assassinated in Dallas), facts widely available in many sources (U.S. presidents used to be inaugurated on March 4 rather than January 20), well-known quotations ("To be or not to be / That is the question"), and material you created or gathered yourself, such as photographs that you took or data from surveys that you conducted.

Remember that you need to acknowledge the source of any **visual** (photograph, table, chart, graph, diagram, drawing, map, screen shot) that you did not create yourself as well as the source of any information that you used to create your own visual. (You should also request permission from the source of a visual if your essay is going to be posted online without password protection.) When in doubt about whether you need to acknowledge a source, do so.

The documentation guidelines later in this chapter present two styles for citing sources: MLA and APA. Whichever style you use, the most important thing is that your readers be able to tell where words or ideas that are not your own begin and end. You can accomplish this most readily by taking and transcribing notes carefully, by placing parenthetical source citations correctly, and by separating your words from those of the source with **signal phrases** such as "According to Smith," "Peters claims," and "As Olmos asserts." (When you cite a source for the first time in a signal phrase, use the author's full name; after that, use just the last name.)

Avoiding Plagiarism

When you use material from another source, you need to acknowledge the source, usually by citing the author and page or publication date in your text and including a list of works cited or references at the end of your essay. Failure to acknowledge sources — even by accident — constitutes **plagiarism**, a serious transgression. By citing sources correctly, you give appropriate credit to the originator of the words and ideas you are using, offer your readers the information they need to consult those sources directly, and build your own credibility.

Writers — students and professionals alike — occasionally fail to acknowledge sources properly. Students sometimes mistakenly assume that plagiarizing occurs only when another writer's exact words are used without acknowledgment. In fact, plagiarism can also apply to paraphrases as well as to such diverse forms of expression as musical compositions, visual images, ideas, and statistics. Therefore, keep in mind that you must indicate the source of any borrowed information, idea, language, or visual or audio material you use in your essay, whether you have *paraphrased, summarized,* or *quoted* directly from the source or have reproduced it or referred to it in some other way.

Remember especially the need to document electronic sources fully and accurately. Perhaps because it is so easy to access and distribute text and visuals online and to copy material from one electronic document and paste it into another, some students do not realize, or may forget, that information, ideas, and images from electronic sources require acknowledgment in even more detail than those from print sources. At the same time, the improper (unacknowledged) use of online sources is often very easy for readers to detect.

Some people plagiarize simply because they do not know the conventions for using and acknowledging sources. Others plagiarize because they keep sloppy notes and thus fail to distinguish between their own and their sources' ideas. If you keep a working bibliography and careful notes, you will not make this serious mistake. Another reason some people plagiarize is that they feel intimidated by the writing task or the deadline. If you experience this anxiety about your work, speak to your instructor. Do not run the risk of failing a course or being expelled from your college because of plagiarism.

If you are confused about what is and what is not plagiarism, be sure to ask your instructor.

USING INFORMATION FROM SOURCES TO SUPPORT YOUR CLAIMS

When writing a research project, one of the ways you will use sources is to support your own ideas. Make sure that each of your supporting paragraphs does three things:

1 States a claim that supports your thesis;

2. Provides evidence that supports your claim;

3. Explains to readers how the evidence supports your claim.

Consider this paragraph from a student essay on the frequency of exams in college:

States claim

The main reason professors should give frequent exams is that when they do and when they provide feedback to students on how well they are doing, students learn more in the course and perform better on major exams, projects, and papers. It makes sense that in a challenging course containing a great deal of material, students

Explains how evidence supports claim

will learn more of it and put it to better use if they have to apply or "practice" it frequently on exams, which also helps them find out how much they are learning and what they need to go over again.

Provides evidence

A 2006 study reported in Psychological Science journal concluded that "taking repeated tests on material leads to better long-term retention than repeated studying," according to the study's coauthors, Henry L. Roediger and Jeffrey Karpicke (ScienceWatch.com, 2008). When asked what the impact of this breakthrough research would be, they responded: **"We hope that this research may be picked up in educational circles as a way to improve educational practices, both for students in the classroom and as a study strategy outside of class."** The new field of mind, brain, and education research advocates the use of "retrieval testing." **For example, research by Karpicke and Blunt (2011) published in Science found that testing was more effective than other, more traditional methods of studying both for comprehension and for analysis.** Why retrieval testing works is not known. A UCLA psychologist, Robert Bjork, speculates that it may be effective because **"when we use our memories by retrieving things, we change our access"** to that information. **"What we recall,"** therefore, **"becomes more recallable in the future"** (qtd. in Belluck, 2011).

The student connects this body paragraph to his thesis by beginning with the transition *The main reason* and by repeating the phrase *perform better* from his forecasting statement. He synthesizes information from a variety of sources. For example, he uses quotations from some sources and a summary of another to provide evidence. And he doesn't merely stitch quotations and summary together; rather, he explains how the evidence supports his claim by stating that it "makes sense" that students "apply or 'practice'" what they learn on frequent exams.

Deciding Whether to Quote, Paraphrase, or Summarize

As illustrated in the model paragraph above, writers integrate supporting evidence by quoting, paraphrasing, or summarizing information or ideas from sources. This section provides guidelines for deciding when to use each of these three methods and how to quote, paraphrase, and summarize effectively. Note that all examples in this section (with the exception of the model student paragraph) follow MLA style for in-text citations, which is explained in detail later in this chapter.

As a rule, quote only in these situations:

- When the wording of the source is particularly memorable or vivid or expresses a point so well that you cannot improve it;

- When the words of credible and respected authorities would lend support to your position;

- When you wish to cite an author whose opinions challenge or vary greatly from those of other experts;

- When you are going to discuss the source's choice of words.

Paraphrase passages whose details you wish to use but whose language is not particularly striking. Summarize any long passages whose main points you wish to record as support for a point you are making.

Altering Quotations Using Italics, Ellipses, and Brackets

Quotations should duplicate the source exactly, even if they contain spelling errors. Add the notation *sic* (Latin for "thus") in brackets immediately after any such error to indicate that it is not your error but your source's. As long as you signal them appropriately, you may make changes to

- emphasize particular words;

- omit irrelevant information;

- insert information necessary for clarity;

- make the quotation conform grammatically to your sentence.

Using Italics for Emphasis.   You may italicize any words in the quotation that you want to emphasize; add a semicolon and the words *emphasis added* (in regular type, not italicized or underlined) to the parenthetical citation:

> In her 2001 exposé of the struggles of the working class, Ehrenreich writes, "The wages Winn-Dixie is offering — *$6 and a couple of dimes to start with* — are not enough, I decide, to compensate for this indignity" (14; emphasis added).

Using Ellipsis Marks for Omissions.   You may decide to omit words from a quotation because they are not relevant to the point you are making. When you omit words from within a quotation, use **ellipses** — three spaced periods (...) — in place of the missing words. When the omission occurs within a sentence, include a space before the first ellipsis mark and after the last mark:

> Hermione Roddice is described in Lawrence's *Women in Love* as a "woman of the new school, full of intellectuality and . . . nerve-worn with consciousness" (17).

When the omission falls at the end of a sentence, place a period *directly after* the final word of the sentence, followed by a space and three spaced ellipsis marks:

> But Grimaldi's commentary contends that for Aristotle rhetoric, like dialectic, had "no limited and unique subject matter upon which it must be exercised. . . . Instead, rhetoric as an art transcends all specific disciplines and may be brought into play in them" (6).

A period plus ellipses can indicate the omission not just of the rest of a sentence but also of whole sentences, paragraphs, or even pages.

When a parenthetical reference follows the ellipses at the end of a sentence, place the three spaced periods after the quotation, and place the sentence period after the final parenthesis:

> But Grimaldi's commentary contends that for Aristotle rhetoric, like dialectic, had "no limited and unique subject matter upon which it must be exercised. . . . Instead, rhetoric as an art transcends all specific disciplines . . ." (6).

When you quote only single words or phrases, you do not need to use ellipses because it will be obvious that you have left out some of the original:

> More specifically, Wharton's imagery of suffusing brightness transforms Undine before her glass into "some fabled creature whose home was in a beam of light" (21).

For the same reason, you need not use ellipses if you omit the beginning of a quoted sentence unless the rest of the sentence begins with a capitalized word and still appears to be a complete sentence.

Using Brackets for Insertions or Changes.   Use brackets around an insertion or a change needed to make a quotation conform grammatically to your sentence, such as a change in the form of a verb or pronoun or in the capitalization of the first word of the quotation. In this example from an essay on James Joyce's short story "Araby," the writer adapts Joyce's phrases "we played till our bodies glowed" and "shook music from the buckled harness" to fit the grammar of her sentences:

> In the dark, cold streets during the "short days of winter," the boys must generate their own heat by "play[ing] till [their] bodies glowed." Music is "[shaken] from the buckled harness" as if it were unnatural, and the singers in the market chant nasally of "the troubles in our native land" (30).

You may also use brackets to add or substitute explanatory material in a quotation:

> Guterson notes that among Native Americans in Florida, "education was in the home; learning by doing was reinforced by the myths and legends which repeated the basic value system of their [the Seminoles'] way of life" (159).

Some changes that make a quotation conform grammatically to another sentence may be made without any signal to readers:

- A period at the end of a quotation may be changed to a comma if you are using the quotation within your own sentence.

- Double quotation marks enclosing a quotation may be changed to single quotation marks when the quotation is enclosed within a longer quotation.

Adjusting the Punctuation within Quotations.   Although punctuation within a quotation should reproduce the original, some adaptations may be necessary. Use single quotation marks for quotations within the quotation:

Original from David Guterson's **Family Matters** *(pp. 16–17)*	*Quoted version*
E. D. Hirsch also recognizes the connection between family and learning, suggesting in his discussion of family background and academic achievement "that the significant part of our children's education has been going on outside rather than inside the schools."	Guterson claims that E. D. Hirsch "also recognizes the connection between family and learning, suggesting in his discussion of family background and academic achievement 'that the significant part of our children's education has been going on outside rather than inside the schools'" (16–17).

If the quotation ends with a question mark or an exclamation point, retain the original punctuation:

"Did you think I loved you?" Edith later asks Dombey (566).

If a quotation ending with a question mark or an exclamation point concludes your sentence, retain the question mark or exclamation point, and put the parenthetical reference and sentence period outside the quotation marks:

Edith later asks Dombey, "Did you think I loved you?" (566).

Avoiding Grammatical Tangles.   When you incorporate quotations into your writing, and especially when you omit words from quotations, you run the risk of creating ungrammatical sentences. Avoid these three common errors:

- verb incompatibility
- ungrammatical omissions
- sentence fragments

Verb incompatibility occurs when the verb form in the introductory statement is grammatically incompatible with the verb form in the quotation. When your quotation has a verb form that does not fit in with your text, it is usually possible to use just part of the quotation, thus avoiding verb incompatibility:

The narrator suggests his bitter disappointment when "~~I saw~~ myself as a creature *he describes seeing himself "*

driven and derided by vanity" (35).

As this sentence illustrates, use the present tense when you refer to events in a literary work.

Ungrammatical omissions may occur when you delete text from a quotation. To avoid this problem, try adapting the quotation (with brackets) so that its parts fit together grammatically, or use only one part of the quotation:

Option 1	*Option 2*
From the moment of the boy's arrival in	From the moment of the boy's arrival in
Araby, the bazaar is presented as a	Araby, the bazaar is presented as a
commercial enterprise: "I could not find	commercial enterprise: "*He "* I could not find
any sixpenny entrance and . . . hand[ed] a	any sixpenny entrance and . . . ~~handing~~
shilling to a weary-looking man" (34).	*" so had to pay a shilling to get in* ~~a shilling to a weary-looking man~~" (34).

Sentence fragments sometimes result when writers forget to include a verb in the sentence introducing a quotation, especially when the quotation itself is a complete sentence. Make sure you introduce a quotation with a complete sentence:

The girl's interest in the bazaar ~~leading~~ the narrator to make what amounts to a *leads*

sacred oath: "If I go . . . I will bring you something" (32).

Using In-Text or Block Quotations

Depending on its length, you may incorporate a quotation into your text by enclosing it in quotation marks or by setting it off from your text in a block without quotation marks. In either case, be sure to integrate the quotation into your essay using the strategies described here:

In-Text Quotations.   Incorporate brief quotations (no more than four typed lines of prose or three lines of poetry) into your text. You may place a quotation virtually anywhere in your sentence:

At the Beginning

"To live a life is not to cross a field," Sutherland, quoting Pasternak, writes at the beginning of her narrative (11).

In the Middle

Woolf begins and ends by speaking of the need of the woman writer to have "money and a room of her own" (4)—an idea that certainly spoke to Plath's condition.

At the End

In *The Second Sex*, Simone de Beauvoir describes such an experience as one in which the girl "becomes an object, and she sees herself as object" (378).

Divided by Your Own Words

"Science usually prefers the literal to the nonliteral term," Kinneavy writes, " that is, figures of speech are often out of place in science" (177).

Poetry

When you quote poetry within your text, use a slash (/) with spaces before and after to signal the end of each line of verse:

Alluding to St. Augustine's distinction between the City of God and the Earthly City, Lowell writes that "much against my will / I left the City of God where [faith] belongs" (4–5).

Block Quotations.   In MLA style, use the **block form** for prose quotations of five or more typed lines and for poetry quotations of four or more lines. Indent the quotation half an inch from the left margin, as shown in the following example:

In "A Literary Legacy from Dunbar to Baraka," Margaret Walker says of Paul Lawrence Dunbar's dialect poems:

He realized that the white world in the United States tolerated his literary genius only because of his "jingles in a broken tongue," and they found the old "darky" tales and speech amusing and within the vein of folklore into which they wished to classify all Negro life. This troubled Dunbar because he realized that white America was denigrating him as a writer and as a man. (70)

In APA style, use block form for quotations of forty words or more. Indent the block quotation half an inch.

In a block quotation, double-space between lines just as you do in your text. Do not enclose the passage within quotation marks. Use a colon to introduce a block quotation unless the context calls for another punctuation mark or none at all. When quoting a single paragraph or part of one in MLA style, do not indent the first line of the quotation more than the rest. In quoting two or more paragraphs, indent the first line of each paragraph an extra quarter inch. Note that in MLA style the parenthetical page reference follows the period in block quotations. If you are using APA style, indent the first line of subsequent paragraphs in the block quotation an additional half inch from the indentation of the block quotation.

Using Punctuation to Integrate Quotations

Statements that introduce in-text quotations take a range of punctuation marks and lead-in words. Here are some examples of ways writers typically introduce quotations:

Introducing a Quotation Using a Colon.   A colon usually follows an independent clause placed before the quotation:

> As George Williams notes, protection of white privilege is critical to patterns of discrimination: "Whenever a number of persons within a society have enjoyed for a considerable period of time certain opportunities for getting wealth, for exercising power and authority, and for successfully claiming prestige and social deference, there is a strong tendency for these people to feel that these benefits are theirs 'by right'" (727).

Introducing a Quotation Using a Comma.   A comma usually follows an introduction that incorporates the quotation in its sentence structure:

> Similarly, Duncan Turner asserts, "As matters now stand, it is unwise to talk about communication without some understanding of Burke" (259).

Introducing a Quotation Using *That*.   No punctuation is generally needed with *that*, and no capital letter is used to begin the quotation:

> Noting this failure, Alice Miller asserts that "the reason for her despair was not her suffering but the impossibility of communicating her suffering to another person" (255).

Paraphrasing Sources Carefully

In a **paraphrase,** the writer restates in his or her own words the relevant information from a passage, without any additional comments or any suggestion of agreement or disagreement with the source's ideas. A paraphrase is useful for recording details of the passage when the source's exact wording is not important. Because all the details of the passage are included, a paraphrase is often about the same length as the original passage. It is better to paraphrase than to quote ordinary material in which the author's way of expressing things is not worth special attention.

Here is a passage from a book on home schooling and an example of an acceptable paraphrase of it:

Original source

Bruner and the discovery theorists have also illuminated conditions that apparently pave the way for learning. It is significant that these conditions are unique to each learner, so unique, in fact, that in many cases classrooms can't provide them. Bruner also contends that the more one discovers information in a great variety of circumstances, the more likely one is to develop the inner categories required to organize that information. Yet life at school, which is for the most part generic and predictable, daily keeps many children from the great variety of circumstances they need to learn well.

— David Guterson, *Family Matters: Why Homeschooling Makes Sense*, p. 172

Acceptable paraphrase

According to Guterson, the "discovery theorists," particularly Bruner, have found that there seem to be certain conditions that help learning to take place. Because individuals require different conditions, many children are not able to learn in the classroom. According to Bruner, when people can explore information in many different situations, they learn to classify and order what they discover. The general routine of the school day, however, does not provide children with the diverse activities and situations that would allow them to learn these skills (172).

The highlighting shows that some words in the paraphrase were taken from the source. Indeed, it would be nearly impossible for paraphrasers to avoid using any key terms from the source, and it would be counterproductive to try to do so because the original and the paraphrase necessarily share the same information and concepts. Notice, though, that of the total of eighty-five words in the paraphrase, the paraphraser uses only a name (*Bruner*) and a few other key nouns and verbs for which it would be awkward to substitute other words or phrases. If the paraphraser had wanted to use other, more distinctive language from the source — for example, the description of life at school as "generic and predictable" — these adjectives would need to be enclosed in quotation marks. In fact, the paraphraser puts quotation marks around only one of the terms from the source: "discovery theorists" — a technical term likely to be unfamiliar to readers.

Paraphrasers must, however, avoid borrowing too many words and repeating the sentence structures from a source. Here is an unacceptable paraphrase of the first sentence in the Guterson passage:

Unacceptable Paraphrase: Too Many Borrowed Words and Phrases

Repeated sentence structure   Apparently, some conditions, which have been illuminated by Bruner and other discovery theorists, pave the way for people to

Repeated words   learn.

Here, the paraphrase borrows almost all of its key language from the source sentence, including the entire phrase *pave the way for*. Even if you cite the source, this heavy borrowing would be considered plagiarism.

Here is another unacceptable paraphrase of the same sentence:

Unacceptable Paraphrase: Sentence Structure Repeated Too Closely

Repeated words   <u>Bruner and other *researchers* have also *identified circumstances*</u>
Synonyms   <u>that *seem to ease the path* to learning.</u>
Repeated sentence
structure

If you compare the source's first sentence and this paraphrase of it, you will see that the paraphraser has borrowed the phrases and clauses of the source and arranged them in an almost identical sequence, simply substituting synonyms for most of the key terms. This paraphrase would also be considered plagiarism.

Summarizing to Present the Source's Main Ideas in a Balanced and Readable Way

For more on summarizing as a reading and writing strategy, see Chapter 2, pp. 44–45.

Unlike a paraphrase, a **summary** presents only the main ideas of a source, leaving out examples and details.

Here is one student's summary of five pages from David Guterson's book *Family Matters*. You can see at a glance how drastically summaries can condense information, in this case from five pages to five sentences. Depending on the summarizer's purpose, the five pages could be summarized in one sentence, the five sentences here, or three dozen sentences.

> In looking at different theories of learning that discuss individual-based programs (such as home schooling) versus the public school system, Guterson describes the disagreements among "cognitivist" theorists. One group, the "discovery theorists," believes that individual children learn by creating their own ways of sorting the information they take in from their experiences. Schools should help students develop better ways of organizing new material, not just present them with material that is already categorized, as traditional schools do. "Assimilationist theorists," by contrast, believe that children learn by linking what they don't know to information they already know. These theorists claim that traditional schools help students learn when they present information in ways that allow children to fit the new material into categories they have already developed (171–75).

Summaries like this one are more than a dry list of main ideas from a source. They are instead a coherent, readable new text composed of the source's main ideas. Summaries provide balanced coverage of a source, following the same sequence of ideas and avoiding any hint of agreement or disagreement with them.

CITING AND DOCUMENTING SOURCES IN MLA STYLE

The following guidelines are sufficient for most college research assignments in English and other humanities courses that call for MLA-style documentation. For additional information, see the *MLA Handbook for Writers of Research Papers*, Eighth Edition (2016), the MLA website, or a handbook with MLA citation information.

USING IN-TEXT CITATIONS

The MLA system requires parenthetical in-text citations that are keyed to a list of works cited in the paper. **In-text citations** tell your readers where the ideas or words you have borrowed come from, and the entries in the **Works Cited** list allow readers to locate your sources so that they can read more about your topic.

In most cases, include the author's last name and the page number on which the borrowed material appears in the text of your research project. You can incorporate this information in two ways:

- By naming the author in the text of your research project with a signal phrase (*Simon described*) and including the page reference (in parentheses) at the end of the borrowed passage:

author's last name   appropriate verb

SIGNAL PHRASE   Simon, a well-known figure in New York literary society, described the impression Dr. James made on her as a child in the Bronx: He was a "not-too-skeletal Ichabod Crane" (68).

page number

- By including the author's name and the page number together in parentheses at the end of the borrowed passage:

PARENTHETICAL   Dr. James is described as a "not-too-skeletal Ichabod Crane"
CITATION   (Simon 68).

author's last name + page number

WORKS-CITED   Simon, Kate. "Birthing." *Bronx Primitive: Portraits in a Childhood,*
ENTRY   Viking Books, 1982, pp. 68-77.

In most cases, you will want to use a signal phrase because doing so lets you put your source in context. The signal-phrase-plus-page-reference combination also allows you to make crystal clear where the source information begins and ends. Use a parenthetical citation alone when you have already identified the author or when citing the source of an uncontroversial fact.

The in-text citation should include as much information as is needed to lead readers to the source in your list of works cited and allow them to find the passage you are citing in that source. In most cases, that means the author's last name and the page number on which the borrowed material appears. In some cases, you may need to include other information in your in-text citation (such as a brief version of the title if the author is unnamed or if you cite more than one work by this author). In a few cases, you may not be able to include a page reference, as, for example, when you cite a website. In such cases, you may include other identifying information if the source uses explicit numbering or naming techniques, such as a paragraph number or section heading.

Directory to In-Text Citation Models

One author 628
More than one author 629
Unknown author 629
Two or more works by the same
    author 629
Two or more authors with the same
    last name 629
Corporation, organization, or
    government agency as author 630
Literary work (novel, play, poem) 630
Work in an anthology 630
Religious work 631

Multivolume work (one volume,
    more than one volume) 631
Indirect citation (quotation from a
    secondary source) 631
Entire work 631
Work without page numbers or a
    one-page work (with / without
    other section numbers) 631
Work in a time-based medium 632
Two or more works cited in the same
    parentheses 632

One author   When citing most works with a single author, include the author's name (usually the last name is enough)* and the page number on which the cited material appears.

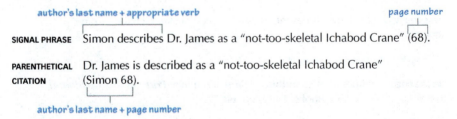

SIGNAL PHRASE   Simon describes Dr. James as a "not-too-skeletal Ichabod Crane" (68).

PARENTHETICAL   Dr. James is described as a "not-too-skeletal Ichabod Crane"
CITATION   (Simon 68).

*But see entries for "Two or More Works by the Same Author" and "Two or More Authors with the Same Last Name" on p. 629 and for "Work without Page Numbers or a One-Page Work" on p. 631.

BLOCK QUOTATION In Kate Simon's story "Birthing," the description of Dr. James captures both his physical appearance and his role in the community:

> He looked so much like a story character—the gentled Scrooge of a St. Nicholas Magazine Christmas issue, a not-too-skeletal Ichabod Crane. . . . Dr. James was, even when I knew him as a child, quite an old man, retired from a prestigious and lucrative practice in Boston. . . . His was a prosperous intellectual family, the famous New England Jameses that produced William and Henry, but to the older Bronx doctors, *the* James was the magnificent old driven scarecrow. (68)

(A works-cited entry for "Birthing" appears on p. 627.)

More than one author To cite a source by two authors, include both of the authors' last names. To cite a source with three or more authors, provide just the first author's name followed by *et al.* ("and others" in Latin, not italicized).

SIGNAL PHRASE Bernays and Painter maintain that a writer can begin a story without knowing how it will end (7).

PARENTHETICAL CITATION A writer should "resist the temptation to give the reader too lengthy an explanation" (Bernays and Painter 7).

The Authority Rebel "tends to see himself as superior to other students in the class" (Dyal et al. 4).

Unknown author If the author's name is unknown, use a shortened version of the title, beginning with the word by which the title is alphabetized in the works-cited list. Use the first noun and any modifiers. (In this example, the full title is "Plastic Is Found in the Sargasso Sea; Pieces of Apparent Refuse Cover Wide Atlantic Region.")

An international pollution treaty still to be ratified would prohibit ships from dumping plastic at sea ("Plastic" 68).

Two or more works by the same author If you cite more than one work by the same author, include a shortened version of the title.

When old paint becomes transparent, it sometimes shows the artist's original plans: "a tree will show through a woman's dress" (Hellman, *Pentimento* 1).

Two or more authors with the same last name When citing works by authors with the same last name, include each author's first initial in the citation. If the first initials are also the same, spell out the authors' first names.

Chaplin's *Modern Times* provides a good example of montage used to make an editorial statement (E. Roberts 246).

Corporation, organization, or government agency as author   In a signal phrase, use the full name of the corporation, organization, or government agency. In a parenthetical citation, use the full name if it is brief or a shortened version if it is long.

SIGNAL PHRASE   The Washington State Board for Community and Technical Colleges will raise tuition to offset budget deficits from Initiative 601 (4).

PARENTHETICAL CITATION   A tuition increase has been proposed for community and technical colleges to offset budget deficits from Initiative 601 (Washington State Board 4).

Literary work (novel, play, poem)   Provide information that will help readers find the passage you are citing no matter what edition of the novel, play, or poem they are using. For a novel or other prose work, provide the part or chapter number as well as the page numbers from the edition you used.

NOVEL OR OTHER PROSE WORK   In *Hard Times*, Tom reveals his utter narcissism by blaming Louisa for his own failure: "'You have regularly given me up. You never cared for me'" (Dickens 262; bk. 3, ch. 9).

For a play in verse, use act, scene, and line numbers instead of page numbers.

PLAY (IN VERSE)   At the beginning, Regan's fawning rhetoric hides her true attitude toward Lear: "I profess / myself an enemy to all other joys . . . / And find that I am alone felicitate / In your dear highness' love" (*King Lear* 1.1.74-75, 77-78).

For a poem, indicate the line numbers and stanzas or sections (if they are numbered) instead of page numbers.

POEM   In "Song of Myself," Whitman finds poetic details in busy urban settings, as when he describes "the blab of the pave, tires of carts . . . the driver with his interrogating thumb" (8.153-54).

If the source gives only line numbers, use the term *lines* in your first citation and use only the numbers in subsequent citations.

In "Before you thought of spring," Dickinson at first identifies the spirit of spring with a bird, possibly a robin—"A fellow in the skies / Inspiriting habiliments / Of indigo and brown" (lines 4, 7-8)—but by the end of the poem, she has linked it with poetry and perhaps even the poet herself, as the bird, like Dickinson "shouts for joy to nobody / But his seraphic self!" (15-16).

Work in an anthology   Use the name of the author of the work, not the editor of the anthology, in your in-text citation.

SIGNAL PHRASE   In "Six Days: Some Rememberings," Grace Paley recalls that when she was in jail for protesting the Vietnam War, her pen and paper were taken away and she felt "a terrible pain in the area of my heart—a nausea" (191).

PARENTHETICAL CITATION   Writers may have a visceral reaction—"a nausea" (Paley 191)—to being deprived of access to writing implements.

Religious work
In your first citation, include the element that begins your entry in the works-cited list, such as the edition name of the religious work you are citing, and include the book or section name (using standard abbreviations in parenthetical citations) and any chapter or verse numbers.

> She ignored the admonition "Pride goes before destruction, and a haughty spirit before a fall" (*New Oxford Annotated Bible*, Prov. 16.18).

Multivolume work (one volume, more than one volume)
If you cite only one volume of a multivolume work, treat the in-text citation as you would any other work, but include the volume number in the works-cited entry (see p. 636).

ONE VOLUME   Forster argued that modernist writers valued experimentation and gradually sought to blur the line between poetry and prose (150).

When you use two or more volumes of a multivolume work, include the volume number and the page number(s) in your in-text citation.

MORE THAN ONE VOLUME   Modernist writers valued experimentation and gradually sought to blur the line between poetry and prose (Forster 3: 150).

Indirect citation (quotation from a secondary source)
If possible, locate the original source and cite that. If not possible, name the original source but also include the secondary source in which you found the material you are citing, plus the abbreviation *qtd. in*. Include the secondary source in your list of works cited.

> E. M. Forster says that "the collapse of all civilization, so realistic for us, sounded in Matthew Arnold's ears like a distant and harmonious cataract" (qtd. in Trilling 11).

Entire work
Include the reference in the text without any page numbers or parentheses.

> In *The Structure of Scientific Revolutions*, Thomas Kuhn discusses how scientists change their thinking.

Work without page numbers or a one-page work (with / without other section numbers)
If a work (such as a Web page) has no page numbers or is only one page long, omit the page number. If it uses screen numbers or paragraph numbers, insert a comma after the author's name, an identifying term (such as *screen*) or abbreviation (*par.* or *pars.*), and the number.

WITHOUT PAGE OR OTHER NUMBERS   The average speed on Montana's interstate highways, for example, has risen by only 2 miles per hour since the repeal of the federal speed limit, with most drivers topping out at 75 (Schmid).

WITH OTHER SECTION NUMBERS   Whitman considered African American speech "a source of a native grand opera" (Ellison, par. 13).

Work in a time-based medium   To cite a specific portion of a video or audio recording, include a time or range of times, as provided by your media player. Cite hours, minutes, and seconds, placing colons between them.

> Barack Obama joked that he and Dick Cheney agreed on one thing—*Hamilton* is phenomenal ("Hamilton Cast" 00:02:34-36).

Two or more works cited in the same parentheses   If you cite two or more sources for a piece of information, include them in the same parentheses, separated by semicolons.

> A few studies have considered differences between oral and written discourse production (Gould; Scardamali et al.).

CREATING A LIST OF WORKS CITED

In your MLA-style research paper, every source you cite must have a corresponding entry in the list of works cited, and every entry in your list of works cited must correspond to at least one citation in your research project.

Follow these rules when formatting your list of works cited in MLA style:

- On a new page, type "Works Cited" (centered), and double-space the whole works-cited list.

- Alphabetize entries by the first word in the citation (usually the first author's last name, or the title if the author is unknown, ignoring *A*, *An*, or *The*).

- Use a "hanging indent" for all entries: Do not indent the first line, but indent second and subsequent lines of the entry by half an inch (or five spaces).

- Abbreviate the names of university presses, shortening the words *University* and *Press* to *U* and *P*. For all other types of publishers, spell out words like *Publishers*.

Nowadays, many print sources are also available in an electronic format, either online or through a database your school's library subscribes to. For most online versions of a source, follow the form of the corresponding print version. For example, if you are citing an article from an online periodical, put the article title in quotation marks and italicize the name of the periodical.

For sources accessed through a database, include the following:

- Title of the database (in italics)

- Location where you accessed the source. Ideally this is a DOI, but when one is not available, provide a URL (if provided, use a permalink).

For other online sources, include the following:

- Title of the website (in italics)

- Version or edition used (if any)

- Publisher of the site, but only if distinct from its title

- Date of publication or last update; if not available, provide the date you last accessed the source at the end of the entry

Some content on the Web frequently changes or disappears, and because the same information that traditionally published books and periodicals provide is not always included for Web sources, giving your reader a complete citation is not always possible. Always keep your goal in mind: to provide enough information so that your reader can track down the source. If you cannot find all of the information listed here, include what you can.

Directory to Works-Cited-List Models

(continued)

AUTHOR LISTINGS

One author   List the author's last name first (followed by a comma), and insert a period at the end of the name.

Isaacson, Walter.

Two authors   List the first author's last name first (followed by a comma). List the second author in the usual first-name / last-name order. Insert the word *and* before the second author's name, and follow the name with a period.

Bernays, Anne, and Pamela Painter.

Three or more authors   List the first author's last name first (followed by a comma). Then insert *et al.* (which means *and others* in Latin) in regular type (not italics).

Hunt, Lynn, et al.

Unknown author

Primary Colors: A Novel of Politics.

"Out of Sight."

Corporation, organization, or government agency as author   Use the name of the corporation, organization, or government agency as the author.

RAND Corporation.

United States, National Commission on Terrorist Attacks.

Two or more works by the same author   Replace the author's name in subsequent entries with three hyphens, and alphabetize the works by the first important word in the title:

Eugenides, Jeffrey. *The Marriage Plot.*

---. *Middlesex.*

---. "Walkabout."

BOOKS (PRINT, ELECTRONIC, DATABASE)

Basic format

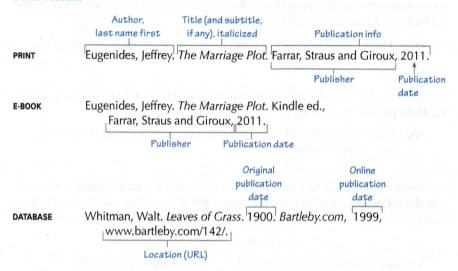

Anthology or edited collection   If you are referring to the anthology as a whole, put the editor's name first.

> Masri, Heather, editor. *Science Fiction: Stories and Contexts*. Bedford / St. Martin's, 2009.

Work in an anthology or edited collection   If you're referring to a selection in an anthology, begin the entry with the name of the selection's author. Include specific page references, and preface them with *p.* or *pp.*

> Hopkinson, Nalo. "Something to Hitch Meat To." *Science Fiction: Stories and Contexts*, Bedford / St. Martin's, 2009, pp. 838-50.

If you cite more than one selection from an anthology or collection, you may create an entry for the collection as a whole (see the model above) and then cross-reference individual selections to that entry.

Selection author	*Selection title*	*Anthology editor*	
Hopkinson, Nalo.	"Something to Hitch Meat To."	Masri	838-50.

Selection pages in anthology

Introduction, preface, foreword, or afterword

> Murfin, Ross C. Introduction. *Heart of Darkness*, by Joseph Conrad, 3rd ed., Bedford/St. Martin's, 2011, pp. 3-16.

Translation

> Tolstoy, Leo. *War and Peace*. Translated by Richard Pevear and Larissa Volokhonsky, Vintage Books, 2009.

Graphic narrative   If the graphic narrative was a collaboration between a writer and an illustrator, begin your entry with the name of the person on whose work your research project focuses. If the author also created the illustrations, then follow the basic model for a book with one author (p. 634).

> Pekar, Harvey, and Joyce Brabner. *Our Cancer Year*. Illustrations by Frank Stack, Four Walls Eight Windows, 1994.

Religious work   Give the title of the edition, the editor's and translator's names as available, publisher, and date.

> *The Qu'ran: English Translation and Parallel Arabic Text*. Translated by M. A. S. Abdel Haleem, Oxford UP, 2010.

Multivolume work   If you use only one volume from a multivolume work, indicate the volume number after the title, using the abbreviation *vol.* If you use more than one volume, indicate the total number of volumes at the end of the entry.

One volume cited

> Sandburg, Carl. *Abraham Lincoln*. Vol. 2, Charles Scribner's Sons, 1926.

More than one volume cited

> Sandburg, Carl. *Abraham Lincoln*. Charles Scribner's Sons, 1926–39. 6 vols.

Later edition of a book

> Rottenberg, Annette T., and Donna Haisty Winchell. *The Structure of Argument*. 6th ed., Bedford / St. Martin's, 2009.

Republished book   Provide the original year of publication after the title of the book, followed by publication information for the edition you are using.

Original publication date

> Alcott, Louisa May. *An Old-Fashioned Girl*. 1870. Puffin Books, 1995.

Republication information

Title within a title   When a title that is normally italicized appears within a book title, do not italicize it. If the title within the title would normally be enclosed in quotation marks, include the quotation marks and also set the title in italics.

> Hertenstein, Mike. *The Double Vision of* Star Trek: *Half-Humans, Evil Twins, and Science Fiction*. Cornerstone Books, 1998.

> Miller, Edwin Haviland. *Walt Whitman's "Song of Myself": A Mosaic of Interpretation*. U of Iowa P, 1989.

Book in a series Include the series title (without italics) and number (if any) at the end of the entry, after a period (never a comma). (Series information will appear on the title page or on the page facing the title page.)

> Zigova, Tanya, et al. *Neural Stem Cells: Methods and Protocols.* Humana Press, 2002. Methods in Molecular Biology 198.

Dictionary entry or article in another reference book

PRINT

> Trenear-Harvey, Glenmore S. "Farm Hall." *Historical Dictionary of Atomic Espionage*, Scarecrow Press, 2011.

ONLINE

Website (same name as publisher)
Most recent update

> "Content." *Collegiate Dictionary.* Merriam-Webster, 2016, unabridged.merriam-webster.com/collegiate/content.

DATABASE

> Powell, Jason L. "Power Elite." *Blackwell Encyclopedia of Sociology*, edited by George Ritzer, Wiley, 2007. *Blackwell Reference Online*, doi:10.1111/b.9781405124331.2007.x.

Location (DOI)
Database (italics)

Government document

Authors

PRINT

> Newes-Adeyi, Gabriella, et al. *Trends in Underage Drinking in the United States, 1991-2007.* United States, Department of Health and Human Services, 2009.

Issuing government Issuing department

Issuing agency

ONLINE

> United States, Department of Health and Human Services, Centers for Disease Control. "Youth Risk Behavior Surveillance— United States, 2009." *Morbidity and Mortality Weekly Report*, vol. 59, no. SS5, 4 June 2010.

Publication date

Published proceedings of a conference

Conference name included in title

> Duffett, John, editor. *Against the Crime of Silence: Proceedings of the International War Crimes Tribunal.* Nov. 1967, Stockholm, Simon and Schuster, 1970.

Pamphlet or brochure

> American Canoe Association. *Cold Water Survival,* Sport Fish Restoration and Boating Trust Fund, U.S. Coast Guard, 2001.

Doctoral dissertation

Title in italics

PUBLISHED   Abbas, Megan Brankley. *Knowing Islam: The Entangled History of Western Academia and Modern Islamic Thought.* 2015. Princeton U, PhD dissertation.

Dissertation information

Title in quotation marks

UNPUBLISHED   Bullock, Barbara. "Basic Needs Fulfillment among Less Developed Countries: Social Progress over Two Decades of Growth." Dissertation, Vanderbilt U, 1986.

Dissertation information

ARTICLES (PRINT, ONLINE, DATABASE)

From a scholarly journal

Author, last name first   Title of article (in quotation marks)

PRINT   Garas-York, Keli. "Overlapping Student Environments: An Examination of the Homeschool Connection and Its Impact on Achievement." *Journal of College Admission,* vol. 42, no. 4, May 2010, pp. 430-49.

Title of journal (italics)   Volume   Issue

Publication date   Pages

ONLINE   Saho, Bala S. K. "The Appropriation of Islam in a Gambian Village: Life and Times of Shaykh Mass Kay, 1827-1936." *African Studies Quarterly*, vol. 12, no. 4, Fall 2011, asq.africa.ufl.edu/files /Saho-Vol12Is4.pdf.

Location (URL)

DATABASE   Haas, Heather A. "The Wisdom of Wizards—and Muggles and Squibs: Proverb Use in the World of *Harry Potter*." *Journal of American Folklore*, vol. 124, no. 492, April 2011, pp. 29-54. *Academic Search Complete,* go.galegroup.com/.

Database (italics)   Database location (URL)

If a journal does not use volume numbers, provide the issue number only.

Markel, J. D. "Religious Allegory and Cultural Discomfort in Mike Leigh's *Happy-Go-Lucky*: And Why *Larry Crowne* Is One of the Best Films of 2011." *Bright Lights Film Journal,* no. 74, Oct. 2011, brightlightsfilm.com/religious-allegory-and-cultural -discomfort-in-mike-leighs-happy-go-luckyand-why-larry-crowne -is-one-of-the-best-films-of-2011/.

Issue number only

URL

Online journals may not include page numbers; if paragraph or other section numbers are provided, use them instead. If the article is not on a continuous sequence of pages, give the first page number followed by a plus sign. (See entry below for a print version of a newspaper for an example.)

From a newspaper

PRINT   Weisman, Jonathan, and Jennifer Steinhauer. "Patriot Act Faces
             Revisions Backed by Both Parties." *The New York Times,* 1 May
             2015, pp. A1+.

             Noncontinuous pages

ONLINE   Humphrey, Tom. "Politics Outweigh Arguments about School
             Vouchers." *Knoxville News Sentinel,* 24 Jan. 2016.

                             Website (italics)   Publication date

             www.knoxnews.com/opinion/columnists/tom-humphrey/tom-
             humphrey-politics-outweigh-arguments-about-school-
             vouchers-29c77b33-9963-0ef8-e053-0100007fcba4-366
             300461.html.

DATABASE   Pelley, Lauren. "Toronto Public Library Opens Its 100th Branch."
             Toronto Star, 21 May 2015. *Newspaper Source,*

                                           Database (Italics)

             search.ebscohost.com.i.ezproxy.nypl.org/login.aspx?direct=true
             &AuthType=cookie,ip,url,cpid&custid=nypl&db=nfh&AN=6FP
             TS2015052133436501&site=ehost-live.

From a magazine

PRINT   Stillman, Sarah. "Where Are the Children?" *The New Yorker,*
             27 Apr. 2015, pp. 40-41.

             Publication date (weekly)   Publication date (monthly)

             Bennet, James. "To Stay or to Go." *The Atlantic,* Apr. 2015, p. 8.

                                                               Website (italics)

ONLINE   Bennet, James. "Editor's Note: To Stay or to Go." *The Atlantic,*
             Apr. 2015, www.theatlantic.com/magazine/archive/2015/04 /
             editors-note/386285/.

DATABASE   Sharp, Kathleen. "The Rescue Mission." *Smithsonian,* Nov. 2015,
             pp. 40-49. *OmniFile Full Text Select,* web.b.ebscohost.com.
             ezproxy.bpl.org/.

                             Database (italics)

Editorial or letter to the editor

"City's Blight Fight Making Difference." *The Columbus Dispatch,* 17 Nov. 2015,
    www.dispatch.com/content/stories/editorials/2015/11/17/1-citys-blight-fight-
    making-difference.html. Editorial.

Fahey, John A. "Recalling the Cuban Missile Crisis." *The Washington Post*, 28 Oct. 2012, p. A16. *LexisNexis Library Express*, www.lexisnexis.com /hottopics/ Inpubliclibraryexpress/. Letter.

Review   If the review does not include an author's name, start the entry with the title of the review; then add **Review of** and the title of the work being reviewed. If the review is untitled, include the **Review of** description immediately after the author's name. For a review in an online newspaper or magazine, add the URL, ideally a permalink. For a review accessed through a database, add the database title (in italics) and the DOI or URL.

Deparle, Jason. "Immigration Nation." Review of *Exodus: How Migration Is Changing Our World,* by Paul Collier. *The Atlantic,* Nov. 2013, pp. 44-46.

MULTIMEDIA SOURCES (LIVE, PRINT, ELECTRONIC, DATABASE)

Lecture or public address

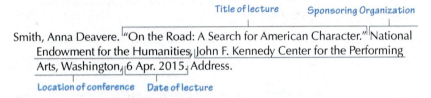

Smith, Anna Deavere. "On the Road: A Search for American Character." National Endowment for the Humanities, John F. Kennedy Center for the Performing Arts, Washington, 6 Apr. 2015. Address.

Title of lecture — *Sponsoring Organization* — *Location of conference* — *Date of lecture*

Letter   If the letter has been published, treat it like a work in an anthology (p. 635), but add the recipient, the date, and any identifying number after the author's name. If the letter is unpublished, note the recipient.

Sender — *Recipient* — *Date*

DuHamel, Grace. Letter to the author. 22 Mar. 2008.

Map or chart

PRINT   *Map of Afghanistan and Surrounding Territory*, 2001.

ONLINE   "Vote on Secession, 1861." *Perry-Castañeda Library Map Collection,* U of Texas at Austin, 1976, www.lib.utexas.edu/maps/atlas _texas/texas_vote_secession_1861.jpg.

Cartoon or comic strip

Wheeler, Shannon. Cartoon. *The New Yorker*, 11 May 2015, p. 50.

Advertisement

PRINT AT&T advertisement. *National Geographic,* Dec. 2015, p. 14.

BROADCAST Norwegian Cruise Line advertisement. *WNET*, PBS, 29 Apr. 2012.

ONLINE Toyota advertisement. *The Root.* Slate Group, www.theroot.com.
     Accessed 28 Nov. 2015.

    Access date (no pub date available)

Work of art

                Location

MUSEUM Palmer Payne, Elsie. *Sheep Dipping Time.* c. 1930s. Nevada Museum
    of Art, Reno.

PRINT Chihuly, Dale. *Carmine and White Flower Set.* 1987. Tacoma Art
    Museum. Abrams Press, 2011, p. 109.

      Print publication information

ONLINE Sekaer, Peter. *A Sign Business Shop, New York.* 1935.
    International Center of Photography, www.icp.org/exhibitions/

      Website   Location (URL)

    signs-of-life-photographs-by-peter-sekaer.

Musical composition

Beethoven, Ludwig van. *Violin Concerto in D Major, Op. 61.* 1809. IMSLP Music
  Library, imslp.org/wiki/Violin_Concerto_in_D_major,_Op.61_(Beethoven,
  _Ludwig_van).

Gershwin, George. *Porgy and Bess.* 1935. Alfred A. Knopf, 1999.

Performance

The Draft. Directed by Diego Arciniegas, 10 Sept. 2015, Hibernian Hall, Boston.

Piano Concerto no. 3. By Ludwig van Beethoven, conducted by Andris Nelsons,
  performance by Paul Lewis and Boston Symphony Orchestra, Symphony Hall,
  Boston, 9 Oct. 2015.

Television or radio program, or podcast Include the network and broadcast
date. If you streamed the program, treat it like an article you accessed through a
database: at the end of your entry, include information about the streaming service (its name and a URL). Separate program information from database information with a period. If you streamed or downloaded the program through an
app like an iPhone's Podcasts, list the app as you would a streaming service or
database (see Downloaded entry below). Treat a podcast that you listened to or

watched online as you would an online television or radio program (see Streamed entry below).

BROADCAST

Episode Program Key contributors

"Being Mortal." *Frontline.* Written by Atul Gawande and Tom Jennings, directed by Tom Jennings and Nisha Pahuja, PBS, 22 Nov. 2011.

Network

Broadcast date

STREAMED

"The Choice." *The Borgias,* directed by Kari Skogland, season 2, episode 5, Showtime, 6 May 2012. *Netflix,* www.netflix.com / watch/70261634.

DOWNLOADED (OR VIA APP)

"Patient Zero." *Radio Lab,* hosted by Jad Abumrad and Robert Krulwich, season 10, episode 4, National Public Radio, 14 Nov. 2011. *Podcasts,* iTunes.

Film

THEATER

Space Station. Produced and directed by Toni Myers, narrated by Tom Cruise, IMAX, 2002.

DVD

Casablanca. Directed by Michael Curtiz, performances by Humphrey Bogart, Ingrid Bergman, and Paul Henreid, 1942. Warner Home Video, 2003.

Online video

Nayar, Vineet. "Employees First, Customers Second." *YouTube,* 9 June 2015, www.youtube.com/watch?v=cCdu67s_C5E.

Music recording

Beethoven, Ludwig van. *Violin Concerto in D Major, Op. 61.* Performed by David Oistrakh and the U.S.S.R. State Orchestra, conducted by Alexander Gauk. Allegro Music, 1980.

Adele. "Hello." *25,* XL Recordings/Columbia, 2015.

Interview If a personal interview takes place through e-mail, change "Personal interview" to "E-mail interview."

PRINT

Ashrawi, Hanan. "Tanks vs. Olive Branches." Interview by Rose Marie Berger, *Sojourners,* Feb. 2005, pp. 22-26.

BROADCAST

Baldwin, Alec. "Two Angry Men." Interview by Bob Garfield, *On the Media,* National Public Radio, 4 Nov. 2015. www.wnyc. org/story/two-angry-men/.

PERSONAL

Ellis, Trey. Personal interview. 3 Sept. 2015.

OTHER ELECTRONIC SOURCES

Web page or other document on a website

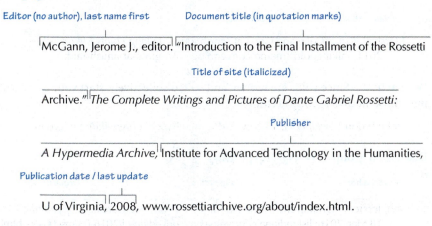

Editor (no author), last name first — Document title (in quotation marks)

McGann, Jerome J., editor. "Introduction to the Final Installment of the Rossetti

Title of site (italicized)

Archive." The Complete Writings and Pictures of Dante Gabriel Rossetti:

Publisher

A Hypermedia Archive, Institute for Advanced Technology in the Humanities,

Publication date / last update

U of Virginia, 2008, www.rossettiarchive.org/about/index.html.

Entire website or online scholarly project For an untitled personal site, put a description such as *Home page* or a more specific description where possible (as in the examples below) where the website's title would normally appear (but with no quotation marks or italics).

> Gardner, James Alan. *A Seminar on Writing Prose*. 2001, www.thinkage.ca/~jim/prose/prose.htm.

> *The Complete Writings and Pictures of Dante Gabriel Rossetti: A Hypermedia Archive*. Edited by Jerome J. McGann, Institute for Advanced Technology in the Humanities, U of Virginia, 2008, www.rossettiarchive.org/index.html.

Book or a short work in an online scholarly project Set the title in italics if the work is a book and in quotation marks if it is an article, essay, poem, or other short work, and include the print publication information relevant to your particular use following the title.

> Heims, Marjorie. "The Strange Case of Sarah Jones." *The Free Expression Policy Project*, FEPP, www.fepproject.org/commentaries/sarahjones.html.

Original publication date

> Corelli, Marie. *The Treasure of Heaven*. 1906. *Victorian Women Writer's Project*, edited by Percy Willett, Indiana U, 10 July 1999, webapp1.dlib.indiana.edu /vwwp/view?docId=VAB7176.

Blog Cite an entire blog as you would an entire website (see above). If the author of the blog post uses a pseudonym, use this, followed by the author's real name if you know it.

Blog title

Talking Points Memo. Edited by Josh Marshall, 1 Dec. 2011, talkingpointsmemo.com/.

Pseudonym

"Negative Camber. *Formula1Blog*, 2014, www.formula1blog.com/.

Post author   Post title

Marshall, Josh. "Coke and Grass at Amish Raid." *Talking Points Memo*, 1 Dec. 2011, talkingpointsmemo.com/edblog/coke-grass-at-amish-raid.

Wiki article   Since wikis are written and edited collectively, start your entry with the title of the article you are citing.

"John Lydon." *Wikipedia*, 14 Nov. 2011, en.wikipedia.org/wiki/John_Lydon.

Discussion group or newsgroup posting

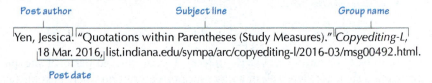

Post author   Subject line   Group name

Yen, Jessica. "Quotations within Parentheses (Study Measures)." *Copyediting-L*, 18 Mar. 2016, list.indiana.edu/sympa/arc/copyediting-l/2016-03/msg00492.html.

Post date

E-mail message

Sender   Subject line   Recipient

Olson, Kate. "Update on State Legislative Grants." Received by Alissa Brown, 5 Nov. 2015.

Date sent

CITING AND DOCUMENTING SOURCES IN APA STYLE

When using the APA system of documentation, include both an in-text citation and a list of references at the end of the research project. **In-text citations** tell your readers where the ideas or words you have borrowed come from, and the entries in the **list of references** allow readers to locate your sources so that they can read more about your topic.

The most common types of in-text citations follow. For other, less common citation types, consult the *Publication Manual of the American Psychological Association*, Sixth Edition (2010) or the American Psychological Association's website. Most libraries will also own a copy or provide digital access.

USING IN-TEXT CITATIONS

When citing ideas, information, or words borrowed from a source, include the author's last name and the date of publication in the text of your research project. In most cases, you will want to use a *signal phrase* to introduce the works you are citing, since doing so gives you the opportunity to put the work and its author in context. A signal phrase includes the author's last name, the date of publication, and a verb that describes the author's attitude or stance:

> Smith (2011) complains that . . .

> Jones (2012) defends her position by . . .

Use a parenthetical citation — *(Jones, 2015)* — when you have already introduced the author or the work or when citing the source of an uncontroversial fact. When quoting from a source, also include the page number: *Smith (2015) complains that he "never gets a break" (p. 123)*. When you are paraphrasing or summarizing, you may omit the page reference, although including it is not wrong.

Directory to In-Text Citation Models

One author

SIGNAL PHRASE Upton Sinclair (2005), a crusading journalist, wrote that workers sometimes "fell into the vats; and when they were fished out, there was never enough of them left to be worth exhibiting" (p. 134).

PARENTHETICAL CITATION *The Jungle*, a naturalistic novel inspired by the French writer Zola, described in lurid detail the working conditions of the time, including what became of unlucky workers who fell into the vats while making sausage (Sinclair, 2005, p. 134).

author's last name + date + page

REFERENCE-LIST ENTRY Sinclair, U. (2005). *The Jungle*. New York, NY: Oxford University Press. (Original work published 1906)

More than one author   In a signal phrase, use the word *and* between the authors' names; in a parenthetical citation, use an ampersand (&). When citing a work by three to seven authors, list all the authors in your first reference; in subsequent references, just list the first and use *et al.* (Latin for *and others*).

SIGNAL PHRASE As Jamison and Tyree (2001) have found, racial bias does not diminish merely through exposure to individuals of other races.

PARENTHETICAL CITATION Racial bias does not diminish through exposure (Jamison & Tyree, 2001).

FIRST CITATION Rosenzweig, Breedlove, and Watson (2005) wrote that biological psychology is an interdisciplinary field that includes scientists from "quite different backgrounds" (p. 3).

LATER CITATIONS Biological psychology is "the field that relates behavior to bodily processes, especially the workings of the brain" (Rosenzweig et al., 2005, p. 3).

For a first reference to a work with more than seven authors, list the first six, an ellipsis (. . .), and the last author.

Unknown author

An international pollution treaty still to be ratified would prohibit all plastic garbage from being dumped at sea ("Plastic Is Found," 1972).

The full title of the article is "Plastic Is Found in the Sargasso Sea; Pieces of Apparent Refuse Cover Wide Atlantic Region."

Two or more works by the same author in the same year   Alphabetize the works by title in your list of references, and add a lowercase letter after the date (2005a, 2005b).

Middle-class unemployed workers are better off than their lower-class counterparts because "the white collar unemployed are likely to have some assets to invest in their job search" (Ehrenreich, 2005b, p. 16).

Two or more authors with the same last name

F. Johnson (2010) conducted an intriguing study on teen smoking.

Corporation, organization, or government agency as author   Spell out the name of the organization the first time you use it, but abbreviate it in subsequent citations.

(National Institutes of Health, 2015)

(NIH, 2015)

Indirect citation (quotation from a secondary source)   Cite the secondary source in the reference list, and in your essay acknowledge the original source.

E. M. Forster said that "the collapse of all civilization, so realistic for us, sounded in Matthew Arnold's ears like a distant and harmonious cataract" (as cited in Trilling, 1955, p. 11).

Two or more works cited in the same parentheses   List sources in alphabetical order separated by semicolons.

(Johnson, 2010; NIH, 2012)

CREATING A LIST OF REFERENCES

The APA documentation system requires a list of references providing bibliographic information for every in-text citation in the text (except personal communications and entire websites). Double-space the reference list, and use a hanging indent (with the first line flush left and subsequent lines indented half an inch). Alphabetize entries by the first main word in the citation.

Directory to Reference List Models

Author Listings

One author 648

More than one author 648

Unknown author 648

Corporation, organization, or government agency as author 648

Two or more works by the same author 649

Books (Print, Electronic)

Basic format for a book 649

Author and editor 649

Edited collection 650

Work in an anthology or edited collection 650

Translation 650

(continued)

One author

Schneier, B. (2015). *Data and Goliath: The hidden battles to collect your data and control your world*. New York, NY: Norton.

More than one author

Hunt, L., Po-Chia Hsia, R., Martin, T. R., Rosenwein, B. H., Rosenwein, H., & Smith, B. G. (2001). *The making of the West: Peoples and cultures*. Boston, MA: Bedford.

If there are more than seven authors, list only the first six, insert an ellipsis (. . .), and add the last author's name.

Unknown author　If an author is designated as "Anonymous," include the word *Anonymous* in place of the author, and alphabetize it as "Anonymous" in the reference list.

Anonymous. (2006). *Primary colors*. New York, NY: Random House.

Communities blowing whistle on street basketball. (2003). *USA Today*, p. 20A.

Corporation, organization, or government agency as author

American Medical Association. (2004). *Family medical guide*. Hoboken, NJ: Wiley.

Two or more works by the same author

When you cite two or more works by the same author, arrange them in chronological (time) order.

> Pinker, S. (2005). So how does the mind work? *Mind and Language, 20*(1): 1-24. doi:10.1111/j.0268-1064.2005.00274.x

> Pinker, S. (2011). *The better angels of our nature: Why violence has declined*. New York, NY: Viking.

When you cite two works by the same author in the same year, alphabetize entries by title and then add a lowercase letter following each year.

> Pinker, S. (2005a). *Hotheads*. New York, NY: Pocket Penguins.

> Pinker, S. (2005b). So how does the mind work? *Mind and Language, 20*(1), 1-24. doi:10.1111/j.0268-1064.2005.00274.x

BOOKS (PRINT, ELECTRONIC)

When citing a book, capitalize only the first word of the title and subtitle and any proper nouns (*Dallas, Darwin*). Book titles are italicized.

Basic format for a book

	Author	Year		Title

PRINT   Pinker, S. (2011). *The better angels of our nature: Why violence has declined.* New York, NY: Viking.

City, State (abbr.)   Publisher

E-BOOK   Pinker, S. (2011). *The better angels of our nature: Why violence has declined*. New York, NY: Viking. [Nook Version].

E-publication information

DATABASE   Darwin, C. (2001). *The origin of species*. Retrieved from http://bartleby.com (Original work published 1909-14)

Database information

If an e-book has been assigned a **digital object identifier** (or *doi*) — a combination of numbers and letters assigned by the publisher to identify the work — add that information at the end of the citation.

Author and editor

> Vonnegut, K., & Offit, S. (Ed.). (2015). *Kurt Vonnegut: Novels 1987-1997*. New York, NY: Library of America. (Original works published 1987, 1990, and 1997)

Edited collection

Waldman, D., & Walker, J. (Eds.). (1999). *Feminism and documentary*. Minneapolis, MN: University of Minnesota Press.

Work in an anthology or edited collection

Fairbairn-Dunlop, P. (1993). Women and agriculture in western Samoa. In J. H. Momsen & V. Kinnaird (Eds.), *Different places, different voices* (pp. 211-226). London, England: Routledge.

Translation

Tolstoy, L. (2002). *War and peace* (C. Garnett, Trans.). New York, NY: Modern Library. (Original work published 1869)

Dictionary entry or article in another reference book

Rowland, R. P. (2001). Myasthenia gravis. In *Encyclopedia Americana* (Vol. 19, p. 683). Danbury, CT: Grolier.

Introduction, preface, foreword, or afterword

Graff, G., & Phelan, J. (2004). Preface. In M. Twain, *Adventures of Huckleberry Finn* (pp. iii- vii). Boston, MA: Bedford.

Later edition of a book

Axelrod, R., & Cooper, C. (2016). *The St. Martin's guide to writing* (11th ed.). Boston, MA: Bedford.

Government document

U.S. Department of Health and Human Services. (2009). *Trends in underage drinking in the United States, 1991-2007*. Washington, DC: Government Printing Office.

Note: When the author and publisher are the same, use the word *Author* (not italicized) as the name of the publisher.

Unpublished doctoral dissertation

Bullock, B. (1986). *Basic needs fulfillment among less developed countries: Social progress over two decades of growth* (Unpublished doctoral dissertation). Vanderbilt University, Nashville, TN.

ARTICLES (PRINT, ELECTRONIC)

For articles, capitalize only the first word of the title, proper nouns (*Barclay, Berlin*), and the first word following a colon (if any). Omit quotation marks around the titles of articles, but capitalize all the important words of journal, newspaper, and magazine titles, and set them in italics. If you are accessing an article through a database, follow the model for a comparable source.

From a scholarly journal

Author   Year   Article title

PRINT   Kardefelt-Winther, D. (2015). A critical account of DSM-5 criteria
for Internet gaming disorder. *Addiction Research and Theory,*
23(2), 93-98.

                       Journal title

Volume (issue) Pages

Goodboy, A. K., & Martin, M. M. (2015). The personality profile of a
cyberbully: Examining the dark triad. *Computers in Human
Behavior,* 49, 1-4.

Volume only Pages

Include the digital object identifier (or *doi*) when available. When a doi has not been assigned, include the journal's URL.

ELECTRONIC   Goodboy, A. K., & Martin, M. M. (2015). The personality profile of a
cyberbully: Examining the dark triad. *Computers in Human
Behavior, 49,* 1-4. doi:10.1016/j.chb.2015.02.052

DOI

Houston, R. G., & Toma, F. (2003). Home schooling: An alternative
school choice. *Southern Economic Journal, 69*(4), 920-936.
Retrieved from http://www.southerneconomic.org

URL

From a newspaper

Year Month Day

PRINT   Peterson, A. (2003, May 20). Finding a cure for old age. *The Wall
Street Journal,* pp. D1, D5.

ELECTRONIC   Zimmer, C. (2015, May 6). Under the sea, a missing link in the
evolution of complex cells. *The New York Times.* Retrieved
from http://www.nytimes.com/

From a magazine   If a magazine is published weekly or biweekly (every other week), include the full date following the author's name. If it is published monthly or bimonthly, include just the year and month (or months).

Weekly or biweekly

PRINT   Gladwell, M. (9 September 2013). Man and superman. *The New
Yorker, 89*(27), 76-80.

Monthly or bimonthly

Freeland, C. (2015, May). Globalization bites back. *Atlantic, 315*(4), 82–86.

ELECTRONIC   Freeland, C. (2015, May). Globalization bites back. *Atlantic*. Retrieved from http://theatlantic.com/

Editorial or letter to the editor

Kosinski, T. (2012, May 15). Who cares what she thinks? [Letter to the editor]. *The Chicago Sun-Times*. Retrieved from http:// www.suntimes.com/opinions / letters/12522890-474/who-cares-what-she-thinks.html

Review

"Review of" + item type + title of item reviewed

Nussbaum, E. (2015, January 26). House of chords [Review of the television series *Empire* and *Mozart in the Jungle*.] *The New Yorker, 90*(45), 70-72.

If the review is untitled, use the bracketed information as the title, retaining the brackets.

MULTIMEDIA SOURCES (PRINT, ELECTRONIC)

Television program

Label

Oliver, J. (Host), & Leddy, B. (Director). (2015, October 4). Mental health [Television series episode]. In *Last week tonight with John Oliver*. New York, NY: HBO.

Film, video, or DVD

Label

Nolan, C. (Writer and director). (2010). *Inception* [Motion picture]. Los Angeles, CA: Warner Bros.

Sound recording

PODCAST   Dubner, S. (2012, May 17). Retirement kills [Audio podcast]. *Freakonomics Radio*. Retrieved from http://www.freakonomics. com

Label

RECORDING   Ibeyi. River. (2015). On Ibeyi [CD]. London, England: XL Recordings.

Interview   Do not list personal interviews in your reference list. Instead, cite the interviewee in your text (last name and initials), and in parentheses give the notation *personal communication* (in regular type, not italicized) followed by a comma and the date of the interview. For published interviews, use the appropriate format for an article.

OTHER ELECTRONIC SOURCES

A rule of thumb for citing electronic sources not covered in one of the preceding sections is to include enough information to allow readers to access and retrieve the source. For most online sources, provide as much of the following as you can:

- name of author
- date of publication or most recent update (in parentheses; if unavailable, use the abbreviation *n.d.*)
- title of document (such as a Web page)
- title of website
- any special retrieval information, such as a URL; include the date you last accessed the source only when the content is likely to change or be updated (as on a wiki, for example)

Website   The APA does not require an entry in the list of references for entire websites. Instead, give the name of the site in your text with its Web address in parentheses.

Web page or document on a website   Generally, if you are citing a specific web-page or document on a website you would cite that rather than the website as a whole.

American Cancer Society. (2011, Oct. 10). *Child and teen tobacco use*. Retrieved from http://www.cancer.org/Cancer/CancerCauses/TobaccoCancer / ChildandTeenTobaccoUse/child-and-teen-tobacco-use-what-to-do

Heins, M. (2014, September 4). Untangling the Steven Salaita Case. In *The Free Expression Policy Project*. Retrieved from http://www.fepproject.org / commentaries/Salaita.html

Discussion list and newsgroup postings   Include online postings in your list of references only if you can provide data that would allow others to retrieve the source.

Label
|

Paikeday, T. (2005, October 10). "Esquivalience" is out [Electronic mailing list message]. Retrieved from http://listserv.linguistlist.org/cgi-bin / wa?A15ind0510b&L5ads- 1#1

Label

Ditmire, S. (2005, February 10). NJ tea party [Newsgroup message]. Retrieved from
    http://groups.google.com/group/TeaParty

Blog post   Label

Mestel, R. (2012, May 17). Fructose makes rats dumber [Blog post]. Retrieved from
    http://www.latimes.com/health/boostershots/la-fructose-makes-rats-stupid
    -brain-20120517,0,2305241.story?track5rss

Wiki entry   Start with the article title and include the post date, since wikis may
be updated frequently (use *n.d.* if there is no date), as well as the retrieval date.

Sleep. (2011, November 26). Retrieved December 18, 2015, from Wiki of Science:
    http://wikiofscience.wikidot.com/science:sleep

E-mail message   Personal correspondence, including e-mail, should not be
included in your reference list. Instead, cite the person's name in your text, and in
parentheses give the notation *personal communication* (in regular type, not italicized) and the date.

Computer software   If an individual has proprietary rights to the software, cite
that person's name as you would for a print text. Otherwise, cite as you would for an
anonymous print text.

Label

Google Earth. (2017). Earth View (Version 2.18.5) [Mobile application software].
    Retrieved from https://chrome.google.com/webstore/

ACKNOWLEDGMENTS

Aschwanden, Christie. "There's No Such Thing As 'Sound Science,'" from ABC News/FiveThirty-Eight, December 6, 2017. https://fivethirtyeight.com/features/the-easiest-way-to-dismiss-good-science-demand-sound-science/. Reprinted courtesy of FiveThirtyEight.com.

Barry-Jester, Anna Maria. "Patterns of Death in the South Still Show the Outlines of Slavery," from ABC News/FiveThirtyEight, April 20, 2017. https://fivethirtyeight.com/features/mortality-black-belt/. Reprinted courtesy of FiveThirtyEight.com.

Bogost, Ian. "Brands Are Not Our Friends," from *The Atlantic*, October 2018. Copyright © 2018 Atlantic Media Co. As published in *The Atlantic* magazine. All rights reserved. Distributed by Tribune Content Agency, LLC. Reprinted by permission.

Brownwell, Kelly D. and Thomas R. Frieden. From "Ounces of Prevention — The Public Policy Case for Taxes on Sugared Beverages," *The New England Journal of Medicine*, 360: 1805-8, April 30, 2009. Copyright © 2009 Massachusetts Medical Society. Reprinted with permission from Massachusetts Medical Society.

Cain, Susan. "Shyness: Evolutionary Tactic?" from *The New York Times*, June 25, 2011 © 2011 The New York Times. All rights reserved. Used by permission and protected by the Copyright Laws of the United States. The printing, copying, redistribution, or retransmission of this Content without express written permission is prohibited.

Carr, Nicholas. "Is Google Making Us Stupid?" from *Atlantic Monthly* (Ideas Issue), Summer 2008. Copyright © 2008 Nicholas Carr. Reprinted by permission of the author.

Christman, Phil. "On Being Midwestern: The Burden of Normality," from *The Hedgehog Review*, Vol. 19, No. 3 (Fall 2017). https://iasc-culture.org/THR/THR_article_2017_Fall_Christman.php. Reprinted with permission of the publisher.

Coyne, Amanda. "The Long Good-Bye: Mother's Day in Federal Prison." Copyright © 1997 Harper's Magazine. All Rights reserved. Reproduced from the May issue by special permission.

Desmond-Harris, Jenee. "Tupac and My Non-Thug Life," from *The Root*, September 13, 2011. Reprinted by permission of the author.

Dillard, Annie. pages 45–49 from *An American Childhood* by Annie Dillard. Copyright © 1987 by Annie Dillard. Reprinted by permission of HarperCollins Publishers and Russell & Volkening as agents for the author.

Edge, John T. "I'm Not Leaving Until I Eat This Thing," originally published in *Oxford American* (September/October 1999). Copyright © 1999 by John T. Edge. Reprinted by permission of the author.

Etzioni, Amitai. "Working at McDonald's," originally published in *The Miami Herald*, August 24, 1986. Copyright © 1986 by Amitai Etzioni. Author of *The Spirit of Community*; Director, George Washington University Center for Communication Policy Studies. Reprinted by permission of the author.

Gawande, Atul. "The Heroism of Incremental Care," from *The New Yorker*, January 23, 2017. Reprinted by permission of the author.

Gladwell, Malcolm. "The Order of Things: What College Rankings Really Tell Us" by Malcolm Gladwell. Copyright © 2005 by Malcolm Gladwell. Originally published in *The New Yorker*. Reprinted by permission of Pushkin Enterprises.

Glick, P., & Fiske, S. (1996). "The Ambivalent Sexism Inventory: Differentiating hostile and benevolent sexism," *Journal of Personality and Social Psychology*, 70 (3), 491–512. DOI: 10.1037//0022-3514.70.3.491. Reprinted by permission.

Greenman, Ben. "The Online Curiosity Killer," from *The New York Times*, September 16, 2010. © 2010 The New York Times. All rights reserved. Used by permission and protected by the Copyright Laws of the United States. The printing, copying, redistribution, or retransmission of this Content without express written permission is prohibited.

Hertogs, Matthew. "Typing vs. Handwriting Notes: An Evaluation of the Effects of Transcription Method on Student Learning," from Volume 8.2 of xchanges. http://www.xchanges.org/typing-vs-handwriting-notes-an. Reprinted with permission from the author.

Shah, Saira. "Longing to Belong." First published in *The New York Times Magazine*, September 21, 2003. Copyright © 2003. Reprinted by permission of the author.

Shughart, William F. "Why Not a Football Degree?" Copyright © 2007. Reprinted by permission of the author.

Solove, Daniel J. "Why Privacy Matters Even if You Have 'Nothing to Hide,'" from *The Chronicle Review*, May 15, 2011. Copyright © 2011 Daniel J. Solove. Reprinted by permission of the author.

Staples, Brent. Excerpt from "Black Men and Public Space." First published in *Harper's* (1987). © 1987 by Brent Staples. Excerpt from *Parallel Time*. Reprinted by permission of the author.

Tannenbaum, Melanie. "The Problem When Sexism Just Sounds So Darn Friendly." Reproduced with permission. Copyright © 2013 Scientific American, a division of Nature America, Inc. All rights reserved.

Thompson, Gabriel. "A Gringo in the Lettuce Fields," from *Working in the Shadows: A Year of Doing the Jobs That (Most) Americans Won't Do*, by Gabriel Thompson, copyright © 2010, 2011. Reprinted by permission of Bold Type Books, an imprint of Hachette Book Group, inc.

Tierney, John. "Do You Suffer From Decision Fatigue?" originally published as "To Choose Is To Lose," *The New York Times*, August 21, 2011. Reprinted by permission of the author.

Tokumitsu, Miya. "In the Name of Love." *Jacobin*, Issue 13. Reprinted by permission of the Jacobin Foundation.

Turkle, Sherry. "The Flight from Conversation," from *The New York Times*, April 21, 2012. © 2012 The New York Times. All rights reserved. Used by permission and protected by the Copyright Laws of the United States. The printing, copying, redistribution, or retransmission of this Content without express written permission is prohibited.

Wolf, Maryanne. "Skim Reading Is the New Normal," *The Guardian*, August 25, 2018. Copyright Guardian News & Media Ltd 2018. Reprinted by permission.

Wong, Alice. "The Last Straw," from *Eater*, Jul 19, 2018. https://www.eater.com/2018/7/19/17586742/plastic-straw-ban-disabilities. Reprinted with permission from Vox Media, Inc.

Woodson, Jacqueline. "The Pain of the Watermelon Joke," from *The New York Times*, November 28, 2014. © 2014 The New York Times. All rights reserved. Used by permission and protected by the Copyright Laws of the United States. The printing, copying, redistribution, or retransmission of this Content without express written permission is prohibited.

Index to Methods of Development

Definition

Description

Narration

Process

Index of Authors, Titles, and Terms